# Configuring SAP® ERP Financials and Controlling

# Configuring SAP® ERP Financials and Controlling

**Peter Jones**
**John Burger**

WILEY

Wiley Publishing, Inc.

Acquisitions Editor: Agatha Kim
Development Editor: Kim Wimpsett
Technical Editor: Charles Soper
Production Editor: Elizabeth Campbell
Copy Editors: Judy Flynn, Candace English, Liz Welch
Production Manager: Tim Tate
Vice President and Executive Group Publisher: Richard Swadley
Vice President and Publisher: Neil Edde
Book Designer and Compositor: Maureen Forys, Happenstance Type-O-Rama
Proofreader: Amy Morales
Indexer: Nancy Guenther
Project Coordinator, Cover: Lynsey Stanford
Cover Designer: Ryan Sneed
Cover Image: iStockPhoto

**Library of Congress Cataloging-in-Publication Data**

Jones, Peter, 1953 October 9–
  Configuring SAP ERP financials and controlling / Peter Jones, John Burger.—1st ed.
     p. cm.
  ISBN 978-0-470-42328-8 (cloth)
  1. SAP ERP. 2. Accounting—Computer programs. 3. Accounting—Data processing. 4. Investments. I. Burger, John, 1970- II. Title.
  HF5679.J635 2009
  657.0285'53--dc22

Dear Reader,

Thank you for choosing *Configuring SAP ERP Financials and Controlling*. This book is part of a family of premium-quality Sybex books, all of which are written by outstanding authors who combine practical experience with a gift for teaching.

Sybex was founded in 1976. More than thirty years later, we're still committed to producing consistently exceptional books. With each of our titles we're working hard to set a new standard for the industry. From the paper we print on, to the authors we work with, our goal is to bring you the best books available.

I hope you see all that reflected in these pages. I'd be very interested to hear your comments and get your feedback on how we're doing. Feel free to let me know what you think about this or any other Sybex book by sending me an email at nedde@wiley.com, or if you think you've found a technical error in this book, please visit http://sybex.custhelp.com. Customer feedback is critical to our efforts at Sybex.

Best regards,

Neil Edde
Vice President and Publisher
Sybex, an Imprint of Wiley

*I would like to dedicate this effort to my wife,*
*Lisa, for her unwavering support and help.*
*Without her sacrifice of the time it took to complete*
*this process, I would not have been able to focus on*
*rewriting this book and getting the best possible result.*
*—Peter Jones*


*To my wife, Christine, who has supported me and has*
*never questioned why I felt it necessary to write*
*at the strange hours that I do. Thank you.*
*—John Burger*

# ACKNOWLEDGMENTS

would like to acknowledge the help and support of SAP during the writing of the second edition of this book. Without the ability to use my experience and knowledge in the FI and CO areas that I developed over the time that I've been with SAP, I would not have been able to complete this book. Nor would I have been able to offer appropriate views of the current system for FI and CO. I would also like to acknowledge Frank Weiss, who was instrumental in my introduction to SAP and the areas of FI and CO.

—Peter Jones

I would like to acknowledge a few of the mentors who I have been fortunate enough to have over the years, without whom I would not have had the experiences that would have permitted me to write this book. They are Richard Groenewald at SafMarine in Cape Town, Robert Schmidt and Michael Spandau at Deloitte Consulting in Southern California, and Alix Zirbel at McKesson in San Francisco.

Lastly, I would like to thank Agatha Kim, the acquisitions editor, who supported me through this interesting and challenging process.

—John Burger

# ABOUT THE AUTHORS

**Peter Jones** is a principal/platinum business applications consultant with SAP Professional Services Consulting specializing in Controlling (CO), Enterprise Controlling (EC), Auditing, Business Intelligence (BI), Strategic Enterprise Management (SEM) and Corporate Performance Management (CPM), Enterprise Information Architecture, and Enterprise Data Warehouses. He has more than 10 years of consulting and educational experience in a variety of strategic and leadership roles, focused on Controlling, Profitability Analysis, Strategic Enterprise Management, Corporate Governance, Data Warehousing, Business Intelligence, and Business Analytics. Peter's diverse professional background includes not only consulting experience but also participation in the academic areas of Finance, Controlling, Data Warehousing, Enterprise Management, and Corporate Governance. He is serving as an SAP principal/platinum business consultant for areas including CO/BW/SEM. He has been involved with numerous implementations for BI and ECC, from the Blueprint phase to the Go-Live Process. His responsibilities include being a subject-matter expert in all the areas listed earlier; an active presenter at conferences including ASUG, BI conferences, and Shappire; and editor/writer for *FICO Expert* and *BI Expert*. Along with consulting, he has been involved with the academic world in developing and presenting numerous topics for the University Alliance, which included topics in the areas of CO, BI, Auditing, and SEM. He has a master's degree from Drexel University in finance and is SAP certified in the areas of FI, CO, BW, and SEM. Prior to SAP, he owned his own business for 15 years working in the area of accounting and finance.

**John Burger** has a dual finance and law degree from Rhodes University. He has more than 20 years experience in finance and SAP consulting. John's career has spanned the ship fleet and cargo freight management, high-tech, management consulting, and pharmaceutical industries. John has 10 years of experience as a SAP consultant.

As a consultant, John has serviced several Fortune 100 companies and led successful initiatives encompassing major SAP implementations, business process reengineering, and mergers and acquisitions of multibillion dollar companies. The projects resulted in him working in seven countries, across four continents, implementing solutions in all of the modules within FI/CO, including ABC and COPA.

He now works at McKesson, a Fortune 18 company.

# CONTENTS AT A GLANCE

# CONTENTS

## Chapter  13    Profit Center Accounting    749

# INTRODUCTION

. . . . . . . . . . . . . . . . .

T he purpose of this book is to serve as an introduction to configuring (a form of customizing functionality) the Financials and Controlling modules within SAP. The FI (Financials) and CO (Controlling) modules are the backbone of most, if not all, SAP implementations. The reason is that most business events culminate in a financial impact. One of SAP's biggest selling points is its integration capabilities. *Integration*, in this context, means that for any business event SAP automatically updates the related metrics, be they financial or management accounting metrics. Not only will you learn the foundational configuration elements involved in implementing the core of FI/CO functionality, but you will also learn configuration principals that can be utilized throughout SAP.

Another of SAP's strengths is its incredible breadth of functionality that it offers, both in terms of functions covered (business processes) and in terms of industries catered to. It is for these reasons that it is practically impossible to cover all the functionality or all the configuration options within the FI/CO modules. Instead, we illustrate the configuration theories and steps through the use of a hypothetical business scenario. We use Extreme Sports Inc. to define the business requirements that are configured and presented throughout the book. The "Case Company Background" section later in this introduction explains Extreme Sports's business and organizational structure.

As the configuration takes place, keep in mind that the screen shots and menu paths that are presented are based on version 6.0. It is important to note that the functionality covered in this book is generally transferable across SAP versions. The reason is that a lot of the functionality covered is typical to most companies and has been offered through many releases of SAP (a.k.a. the core functionality). In addition, this book focuses on the configuration principals that enable you to understand the logic behind them, regardless of SAP version.

## Is This Book for You?

This book is for anyone who wants to understand how to implement FI/CO, a central module to SAP's Enterprise Central Component (ECC), formerly known as SAP R/3. The primary audience to benefit from this book are project implementation team members, developers, and SAP support organizations. We also encourage people who have expertise in other SAP modules to read this book, because it will help tremendously in terms of the understanding integration points. In addition, this book makes an excellent textbook companion for those colleges and universities whose curricula covers SAP design and development. It will take you from the basic concepts all the way through to advanced configuration topics and techniques.

# How This Book Is Organized

This book begins with an explanation of the FI module and its configuration. The similar but different CO module is covered in the same fashion. Each chapter is about a specific submodule within FI/CO.

The chapters have been logically ordered so that prerequisite configuration has occurred before you begin configuring a new submodule. If you are new to configuration, it is a good idea to begin with Chapter 1 and proceed through the rest of the chapters in order. If you already have configuration experience, you can use the table of contents and chapter headings to skip to the appropriate subject matter.

# Conventions Used in This Book

Throughout this book, we have used some basic conventions to help you understand our instructions. The menu path for configuration steps is included in the text of each chapter. In the appendix, you'll find all the configuration transaction codes relevant to the topics discussed in book. We have based our project on one business model, Extreme Sports, for ease and continuity.

Reference is made to standard SAP commands and button bars (green arrow, Save, Create, and so on). In each case, when we refer to a button, we'll provide a screen shot that shows the button in question. The SAP course material is an excellent source for more information on the standard SAP nomenclature.

# Case Company Background

One of SAP's biggest selling points is the software's flexibility in handling multiple industries and organizations regardless of the complexity of the business solutions.

To accommodate this flexibility, it must allow for numerous solutions using the standard platform of tables and structures. And by introducing unique configuration settings for each implementing company, it addresses the need for complex solutions.

It would be an impossible task to document the necessary configuration settings for every industry and every business solution. However, it is not inconceivable to provide insight into how to interpret the options available to you when configuring the various modules in FI and CO.

To assist in this endeavor, we will describe the configuration for a fictitious company, Extreme Sports, as you progress through the book. Although the company's configuration will be documented, the discussion will not be limited to that specific solution. We'll discuss many options and field settings. When configuration must occur in a specific order, we'll provide the proper sequence.

We will now give you some background information about Extreme Sports and an example of its hierarchy solution. Extreme Sports is a U.S.-based manufacturer of sporting equipment and apparel. Founded in 1999, the company has seen its business grow 60 percent a year over the past three years. The revenues for 2008 were $1 billion.

Extreme Sports's sales organization consists of six regionally based offices located in New York, Chicago, Los Angeles, Atlanta, Seattle, and Kansas City. The sales organization employs approximately 250 sales representatives who sell six distinct product lines: ski equipment, ski apparel, mountaineering/hiking equipment, surfing equipment, surfing apparel, and custom boats.

To compensate for the extraordinary growth it has enjoyed, Extreme Sports has expanded its manufacturing base from four to six plants. The last two plants have both been constructed in Mexico, and the company is considering building a third next year.

Extreme Sports has made the decision to convert to SAP because of the fragmented nature of its current financial, profitability, and manufacturing systems. The corporation consists of four legal entities: ES Ski & Surf, Inc.; ES Mountaineering, Inc.; ES Custom Boats, Inc.; and ES Mexico, S.A. In addition, Extreme Sports has decided to create a shared services organization to support the accounting, human resources, purchasing, accounts payable, and IS functions. The vehicle for this organization will be a fifth company called ES Services, Inc.

The corporation has moved all its legal entities to a calendar fiscal year, removing the 4-5-4 calendar previously held by ES Custom Boats, Inc. Here's an illustration of the corporation as it was developed in SAP.

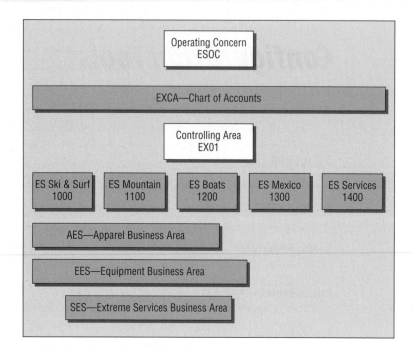

Throughout the book, we will be providing you with the configuration settings to support Extreme Sports's organization.

# Configuration Tools

**FEATURING:**

▶ INTRODUCTION TO SAP

▶ A NEW APPROACH TO SYSTEM CUSTOMIZATION

▶ THE IMPLEMENTATION GUIDE (IMG)

▶ THE SERVICE MARKET PLACE

**B**efore you undertake your first SAP configuration project, it is important to understand the concepts behind table-driven customization as well as some of the tools, tips, and tricks that can be used. The purpose of this chapter is to provide the foundation for successfully carrying out SAP Finance and Controlling (FI/CO) configuration. We'll give you an overview of SAP, talk about the new approach to system configuration, discuss how to use the implementation guide, and introduce you to the Service Market Place.

Although this chapter is a must-read for people new to configuration, configuration "old-timers" can also pick up a trick or two from reading it.

**NOTE** The terms *customization* and *configuration* are used interchangeably throughout this book.

# Introduction to SAP

SAP stands for Systems, Applications, and Products in Data Processing. Founded by five German engineers in 1972, SAP is the world's leading provider of business software, offering applications and services to companies of all sizes across more than 25 industries. SAP offers an integrated system, which means that all SAP modules are designed to share information and automatically create transactions based on various business processes.

## SAP Products

SAP has slowly evolved in terms of its product offerings. You will still come across SAP consultants who refer to the SAP system as SAP R/3, but as SAP's product offerings have broadened, the reference to R/3 has been dropped. R/3 initially referred to SAP's only product, the Enterprise Resource Planning (ERP) system, but today SAP offers a host of products of which SAP ERP Central Component is the heart (often referred to as SAP ECC). The SAP ERP Central Component is where the original ERP (R/3) functionality is housed, and it is where all the data processing/business process transacting takes place. This book is focused on the Financial (FI) and Controlling (CO) modules found in SAP ECC version 6.0.

The goal of this book is not to teach you how to implement one specific solution but to teach you how to configure the SAP system. Attempting to cover every possible configuration scenario you might encounter would be an impossible task, but after reading the book, you will be able to apply what you have learned and configure your system based on your business requirements.

SAP has now introduced many areas of functionality from its data warehouse— often referred to as its *business warehouse* (BW) or, now more correctly, *business intelligence* (BI)—which includes a host of reporting tools and functionality, not limited to business objects.

SAP also offers the following software suites:

▶ Supplier Relationship Management (SRM)

▶ Strategic Enterprise Management (SEM)

▶ Catalog Content Management

▶ Compliance Management for SOA

▶ Supply Chain Management (SCM)

▶ Product Lifecycle Management

▶ Customer Relationship Management (CRM)

## SAP Terms

Now that you understand how the different SAP products break down, you'll need to become familiar with some common terms that explain different parts of the SAP system; you will see the following terms used throughout the book:

**ABAP (ABAP/4)**   ABAP/4 stands for Advanced Business Application Programming/4th Generation Language. SAP is coded in ABAP. ABAP is also used for extensions and extra programs that are written for SAP. ABAP is similar to other fourth-generation languages and is a first cousin of COBOL, without the JCL.

**Basis**   Generally, SAP projects, and the folks who work on them, are lumped into two groups—technical and functional. The technical system includes ABAP, database administration, transport management, security, authorizations, and so on. Basis is a subset of the technical group and consists of the folks who take care of all technical components of the system except for ABAP. The Basis group, in more common terms, consists of your project database administrators (DBAs) plus more.

**Variant**    A variant is a specific setting that is saved when a program is executed. Some data input screens allow you to save and execute variants. Variants can also be created in the program maintenance screen of the program. Using variants is a good way to save time because they allow you to execute a routine transaction without having to enter all of the parameters needed by the program every time.

Menu pathSAP, like most client/server applications, utilizes menus to allow a user to navigate through the system. When we refer to or list menu paths in the book, we are starting from the root menu and progressing down through each menu hierarchy to reach the needed transaction. When we refer to only the menu path, we are talking about the Implementation Guide (IMG) menu path. SAP application menu paths are explicitly noted.

**Transaction code**    A transaction code (tcode) is generally a four-character code (later versions of SAP have introduced longer tcodes) that is entered in the command field on the toolbar. Transaction codes are not case sensitive. SAP provides two ways of executing a transaction, via a menu path and a transaction code.

**NOTE**    Although it may be tempting for you to use tcodes to get to a specific screen/transaction, it is useful to use the menu paths. The benefit is that you can get a better grasp of how SAP has logically laid out the options in configuration and the functionality in the functional menu paths. SAP has developed a large array of options to cater to almost any imaginable business scenario, and using the menu paths will allow you to see these options, which results in a broader set of options.

It is important to note that, unless you are at the main SAP menu or the main menu of a submodule such as G/L, it is necessary to include /N or /O before the transaction code in order to execute a transaction in a different module. For example, if you are currently in the Cost Center accounting module in the screen used to create cost centers and you want to enter a G/L document (transaction code FB01), you must enter /NFB01 or /OFB01 to execute the transaction. /N takes you back to the root menu and then executes the transaction code. /O opens up a new session and then executes the transaction code. Remember, you can have only six open sessions of SAP at once.

**TIP**    As stated earlier, unless you are at the main SAP menu, or a submodule main menu, it is necessary to include /N or /O before a transaction code in order to execute a transaction in a different module.

**Parameter ID**   A parameter ID is a special identifier given to some fields in SAP. It can be stored in your user profile with its default values. For example, the parameter ID for company code is BUK. A user who is responsible only for entering documents in company code 1000 would set up the BUK parameter ID with a default of 1000 in their user profile. By specifying this parameter ID, the user will never have to enter the company code in a transaction; the company code will automatically default to 1000. Parameter IDs are stored in the Technical Information field box. An explanation of how to display the Technical Information box is included in "Finding the Table to Configure" later in this chapter.

**Batch input session**   A batch input session stores values to be entered during a normal system transaction. Some transactions automatically create batch input sessions because of the heavy processing required. To complete the transaction, you must select the batch input session and then run the batch input session manager. Most data transfer programs are executed via batch input sessions. A good way to think of a batch input session is to think of it as a macro. A macro uses standard functioning to input data that is stored to automate a repeated task. You can use transaction code SM35 to run and manage batch input sessions.

**Jobs**   A job is similar to a batch input session in that it executes a standard SAP transaction in the background, usually at night. Jobs are set up and scheduled for processor-intensive transactions and reports. If you do not correctly specify the print parameters on a print request, your print request will be stored as a job. This means that when you start a print transaction from within SAP and you do not check the Print Immediately box the print request is stored in the print spool as a job and has to be manually released through the job manager to print. Your company's Basis group usually manages jobs.

**User menus**   You can create your own user menu with your most commonly used transactions. Then you can assign this personalized menu to your user ID in your user preferences. If you are developing a system to be used by a client site, user menus can also be set up for a group of users with limited access to the system. This includes users who might not use the system often enough to remember the menu paths they need to use to execute a transaction.

**Distributed systems (ALE)**   Some SAP installations have more than one productive instance of SAP running at any one time. SAP provides a tool called Application Link Enabling (ALE) to allow two different SAP systems to share data with each other.

**TIP** SAP is an integrated system, which means configuration choices and decisions made by people configuring other models in the system can have an impact on FI/CO. Any business transaction that has a financial impact will have an integration point with FI/CO; therefore, the FI/CO team is often central to all design reviews.

# A New Approach to System Customization

For many years, organizations struggled with extremely long project timelines in order to develop information systems that met their specific requirements. Most IT projects used structured development methodologies that were very unforgiving in terms of missed or changing business requirements. The development of custom code was a tedious process requiring armies of programmers as well as significant end-user involvement.

The project timeline was also extended because often business owners didn't know what they wanted until they saw it, which led to what is commonly referred to in the IT industry as *analysis paralysis* in projects. Upon project completion, large IT staffs needed to be retained to maintain the custom programming and to update the programs with requirements that may have changed during the long development cycle. Numerous companies also had departmentalized systems, which oftentimes did not share information. These numerous departmental systems became "information silos" within the organization. Separate systems per function and/or department can lead to inconsistent results.

These disparate and numerous systems also created the need for many distinct interfaces between systems that were not designed to talk with each other. Despite the interfaces, the systems would never be integrated. Worst of all, accounting systems were updated with financial data by means of batch programs. Batch programs are run on a fixed schedule, generally daily, weekly, or monthly, which means that the data is never current.

To fulfill the new requirements of information systems, a new breed of software systems, now called *Enterprise Resource Planning (ERP)* systems, was created. ERP systems provide a single source of data with designed integration between different functional modules (for example, Accounting, Sales and Distribution, Materials Management, Production Planning, and so on) to take full advantage of an enterprise's stored information. A common set of source code was needed for these packages so that changes in technology could be rapidly introduced via upgrades to the programs. To facilitate these requirements, a new way of customizing systems was needed. This new way of customizing systems is known as *table-driven customization*, or *configuration*. By configuring the system via tables rather than changing source code, you now have a very clear logical approach to managing your system.

Table-driven customization allows for rapid changes in business requirements with a common set of source code or programs. The common programs are coded to focus on settings in specific tables to make the programs react in various ways to fit different business needs. This is what makes ERP systems, and SAP in particular, so flexible—there are more than 10,000 tables in the SAP database structure! Because table settings instead of old-fashioned hard-coded program logic are what drive program functionality, new and changed business requirements can be rapidly implemented and tested in the system. Table-driven configuration (customization) is at the heart of what the functional SAP consultant delivers.

So that you can benefit from the power of SAP, a careful analysis of your company's current business processes is in order. SAP has industry-specific best business processes to take full advantage of the most efficient business and technological processes.

When using SAP ECC, you can use two menu paths: the user menu and the Implementation Guide (IMG). When you log on to SAP, the first screen and menu path you are presented with is the user menu. The user menu is where end users will be spending all of their time. This is where you would use SAP's functionality, such as creating a vendor invoice or journal entry.

The IMG menu is specifically for configuring the system so that an organization can tailor it to address the needs unique to its business.

**TIP**  You can find the configuration menu by using the following menu path or transaction code: Tools ➤ Customizing ➤ IMG ➤ SPRO – Execute Project. The command window in the upper-left side of the SAP screen will allow you to simply enter the transaction code—SPRO—to get you directly to the configuration menu.

Many companies use the implementation of SAP as an opportunity to reengineer their entire business and develop the most efficient processes available. SAP has invested a great deal of time and money into delivering the best business practices for almost all sectors of the economy. It has industry solutions for the following:

- ▶ Banking

- ▶ Defense and security

- ▶ Healthcare

- ▶ Higher education and research

- ▶ Insurance

- ▶ Public sector

- ▶ Manufacturing

  - ▶ Aerospace and defense

  - ▶ Automotive

  - ▶ Consumer products

- ▶ Service

  - ▶ Media

  - ▶ Professional services

For small companies that have neither the time nor the resources to undertake a full business process reengineering project, SAP has a very well-researched and well-designed implementation methodology that will help with business process optimization efforts. This, along with the Industry Solutions (ISs), will allow for you to utilize the software to ensure a more effective and efficient company.

For smaller companies, there are preconfigured clients with many templates and industry-standard reports.

## SAP System Environment

It is very important for everyone on the implementation project team to understand the SAP system environment used on the project. A system environment is referred to by some as an *instance*. Others will sometimes refer to a client as an instance. In this book, both *environment* and *instance* are used interchangeably to refer to different systems, such as development, quality assurance/testing environment, and production. In some cases, an SAP term may have, or may seem to have, more than one meaning, depending on which part of the system you are working in. One such term is *client*. As defined in the enterprise structure, it means the organization for which SAP is being configured (for example, the XYZ Corporation, or the example corporation used throughout this book, Extreme Sports). When defined in Basis terms (the SAP technical system), *client* means the different installations of SAP used for a specified purpose. Really, these are the same things, but it is difficult to understand the client concept in this light when you are just starting out in SAP. In the standard project setting, there will be three environments: the development environment, the quality assurance/testing environment (QA), and the production environment. Within each environment there are different clients that are used for specified purposes.

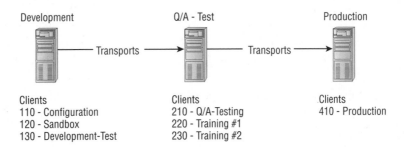

| Development | Q/A - Test | Production |
| --- | --- | --- |
| Clients | Clients | Clients |
| 110 - Configuration | 210 - Q/A-Testing | 410 - Production |
| 120 - Sandbox | 220 - Training #1 | |
| 130 - Development-Test | 230 - Training #2 | |

The development environment is where the majority of implementation work takes place. It should have a minimum of three clients: sandbox, configuration, and development testing. The sandbox client is used to test configuration ideas and theories at any time. It is also where all system design work should take place. Once you are comfortable with your configuration solution in the sandbox client, you can re-create your solution in the configuration client. The configuration client is also called the *transport client*. This is where all final configuration that needs to be moved through the testing cycle, and finally into production, takes place. The configuration client has automatic transport recording turned on (covered in the next section, "Transports"). Ideally, the configuration client should also be your "golden" client; that is, no transactions or testing should take place in this client. Once a transport has been created, it should be moved to the development-testing client. Once the configuration is in the development-testing client, the transport should be thoroughly unit-tested. Usually, only unit testing is conducted in the development system; some projects may conduct integration (string) testing in this client as well. Once the transport has been successfully tested, it is ready to move into the QA environment. Normally, all transports for particular projects or rollout phases are moved into QA at one time.

The QA environment is where all final testing is conducted prior to moving transports to the production environment. Normally, this is where integration (end-to-end business process) testing and user acceptance testing (UAT) is conducted. There is a minimum of one QA client that is used to conduct testing. There may be additional clients you can use in the QA environment to test different transactions for training, data conversion, and user sandboxes. Once the entire project solution has been tested successfully in QA, it is ready to move to production.

The production environment is where all day-to-day business activities occur. This is the client that all end users use to perform their daily job functions. There is usually only one production client per SAP installation. It is very important to move into production only transports that have passed all testing cycles. Inadequately tested or understood changes to the system can lead to production system issues. These production issues generally occur if you, as the configurator, do not fully understand the integration points between the module effecting the change and (generally) FI/CO. Production issues can be as catastrophic as the company's inability to ship goods or post cash.

## Transports

*Transports* are the vehicles by which your configuration settings are moved from client to client and environment to environment. Normally, your configuration client should be the only client that creates transports. Transports in the configuration client are created anytime you make a change to a configuration table or program. This is known as *automatic recording* of transports. The setting to allow for automatic recording of transports is made at the client level in table T000. Although you can make customizing settings in the sandbox, client transports are not automatically created. The sandbox and configuration clients are the only clients in which changes to configuration tables or programs should be allowed.

Without ensuring this level of discipline within the system, several issues with the integrity of the production system can occur. The following are some examples:

- ▶ Redundant versions of a program
- ▶ Incorrect values for a table
- ▶ Incorrect settings for a configuration table

These inconstancies can result in disruptions to the business and lengthy, often complex recollections between the systems to determine what needs to be backed out. This does not include the corrections to the business results that may be required.

**NOTE**  Your Basis group should be responsible for maintaining and moving transports from client to client. In some small implementation projects, individual consultants are responsible for moving their transports from the configuration client to the development-testing client.

**NOTE**  Most transports record only the changes to the table. However, some transports created by a small number of tables copy the entire table, not just the changes. It is very important that these whole table transports are watched and managed carefully so that only the latest changes are reflected in the target clients. This is especially important once a project is "live" and in maintenance mode. When dealing with whole table transports, you always run the risk of moving into other environments' configuration that shouldn't be moved. You can also very easily "leapfrog" transports moved by other developers and overwrite new configuration with old configuration. To avoid the leapfrogging of values in a table, the configuration team should be organized in a way that one person owns a specific area of functionality or business process. This structure should include the review of transports to ensure that common tables are being carefully monitored.

You can use the change request query screen to create a transport automatically in a configuration client. A transport number is assigned automatically, but you are free to add the description yourself.

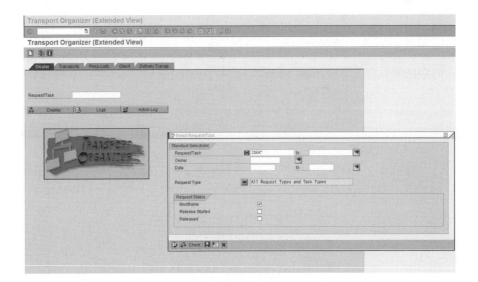

There are two types of transports: *client dependent* and *client independent*. When an environment such as the development environment is created with multiple clients, most objects are copied one for one to be used for each individual client. For example, table T030 contains the settings for automatic account assignment. In the development environment, the sandbox, configuration, and development-testing clients each have its own copy of table T030. Any change to table T030 results in a client-dependent transport—all the T030 tables in the various places reflect the change only after it is transported.

All programs and a small amount of tables are shared among the clients within an environment. These are known as client-independent objects. For example, table (view) V_T021S is client independent, meaning that, when this table is changed in the configuration client, the setting automatically takes effect in all clients in that environment because there is only one V_T021S that is used by all clients in that environment. A change to a client-independent table should be made only in the configuration client; the Basis group controls this setting when it sets up the client. The option to allow client-independent changes is set at the client level in table T000. Sometimes, when testing new design and development in the sandbox, you are required to make a change in the configuration client. It is fine to design in the configuration client as long as you are making only client-independent changes.

Each consultant/developer is responsible for keeping track of their individual transports. Transaction code SE10 allows you to view and manage all transports you have created. You can also view transports created by other developers. This transaction allows viewing of only modifiable (unreleased), only released, or both released and unreleased transports. The default is set to modifiable (unreleased) transports. Figure 1.1 shows the initial Transport Organizer screen.

**FIGURE 1.1**    You can use transaction code SE10 to view and manage transports on the Transport Organizer screen.

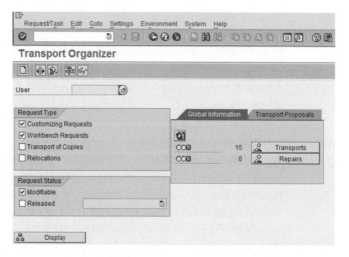

Once you are ready to unit-test your configuration, the related transports must be released so that the changes can move from the configuration client to the development-testing client. It is normally the responsibility of the consultant/developer to release their own transports and let the Basis group know that they are ready to move via the procedures set forth in their project. This is an implementation activity, and this transport movement can happen once the system is in production. Remember that it is only necessary to release and move client-dependent transports to the development-testing client. Client-independent transports are already reflected in all clients in the environment. Client-independent transports need to be released and moved only when sending changes from environment to environment. Figure 1.2 shows the listing of transports created by an individual consultant or developer. This screen is obtained by proceeding through the screen displayed by transaction code SE10 shown earlier in Figure 1.1.

**FIGURE 1.2**   The transports "owned" by John Burger

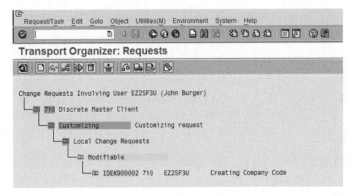

Each transport in the list (as shown in Figure 1.2) can be expanded to show the tasks included in it. Each transport has at least one related task assigned to it. The tasks actually contain the table changes. The upper-level transport acts only as a container for these tasks. When you release transports for the Basis group, you must release the individual tasks related to the transport before releasing the upper-level transport. It is important to note that each task always has objects attached to it. It is not necessary to release objects to the Basis group, only the tasks themselves. This is because the tasks carry the objects with them. When you release a task, a snapshot is taken of the key that is contained in the task. The configuration that resides in the snapshot is what is written to the operating system to be transported. It is very important to understand this timing and how it affects your transports if other consultants are configuring the same key. For example, consultant X makes a change to object key 123 on May 1st; on May 30th, consultant Y makes a change to the same object key 123. When consultant X releases his task on June 1st, it contains the changes that consultant Y made on May 30th, not the changes that consultant X made on May 1st. As you can see, communication is a key success factor on any SAP project. Transports are released using the same screen that is generated by following transaction code SE10, selecting the task, and clicking the Release Directly button, as seen Figure 1.3. When you release a task, it is released (copied) to its corresponding transport request. The transport request is then released for export. The transport request is what is actually moved between clients and environments.

**FIGURE 1.3**     Releasing a transport

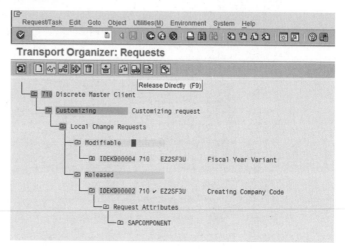

# The Implementation Guide (IMG)

The Implementation Guide (IMG) provides step-by-step details on the configuration settings that need to take place in each module of the SAP system. The IMG is grouped by functional modules and the business processes that occur in each module, as shown in Figure 1.4. It provides the front end to the customizing tables as well as explanations of the functionality affected by each table. In the design and development phase of a project, consultants and developers spend a majority of their time in the IMG.

The IMG can be displayed in three different views: the SAP Reference IMG, the Enterprise IMG, and the Project IMG. The SAP Reference IMG comes with your installation of SAP. It contains all components for all modules of SAP. The Enterprise IMG is generated from the SAP Reference IMG. The Enterprise IMG normally contains all modules and their related business processes for your specific instance of SAP and the countries being implemented. It is usually a safe bet that everything from the SAP Reference IMG has been copied to the Enterprise IMG.

**FIGURE 1.4**    The Implementation Guide (IMG) main screen

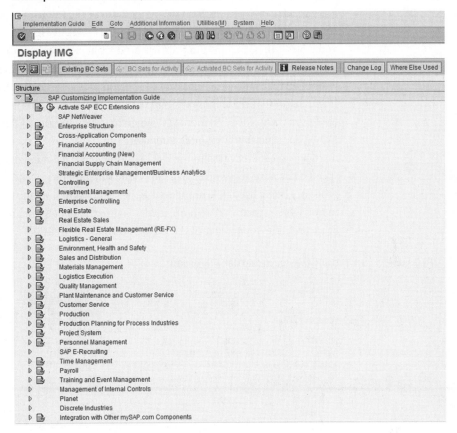

The Project IMG is created by the project team manager or by module team leaders. It contains only those modules and business processes that the creator of the Project IMG (generally a single person or the project manager) deems necessary. It is very important to carefully select what is needed and to not forget anything when generating the Project IMG. The Project IMG can also serve as a valuable project management and documentation tool. The status of project tasks can be viewed and exported to Microsoft Project for detailed project tracking. Using the IMG, you can store configuration documentation with related steps and tables.

**WARNING**   You and your customer will be happier and more productive in the long run if you keep detailed documentation on the configuration settings that are made in the system. It is not necessary to use the IMG as the documentation tool, but it is necessary to document your entire configuration. The only thing worse than trying to figure out someone else's configuration settings is going back and trying to figure out your own!

If your project doesn't use the Project IMG for documentation and status tracking, it is a good idea to use the SAP Reference IMG or the Enterprise IMG to find your configuration steps. You can expect with some certainty that all steps, processes, and tables will be included in the final product. It is not easy to discover what SAP functionality is needed if you do not have access to all of it. SAP has provided an easy view of virtually all configuration tasks, if you include all of the tasks in the IMG. If you forget to include those tasks in the IMG, you'll find that it is difficult to try to configure the needed functionality. When in doubt, use the SAP Reference IMG. The IMG can display both optional and mandatory activities, as shown in Figure 1.5. By no means must every task in the IMG be completed; the number of tasks and how specific tasks are customized depend on the functionality needed by the business processes being used. It is useful to use the search functionality included in the IMG to find where specific settings are made. To use the search function, click the binoculars icon in the top toolbar of the IMG (shown in Figure 1.5).

**FIGURE 1.5**     Using the search functionality in IMG

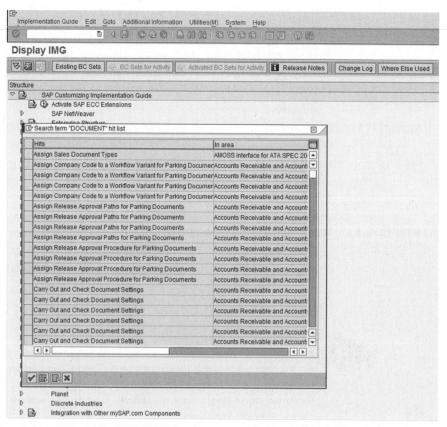

An explanation of the specific tasks can be viewed by clicking the note folder to the left of the configuration step, as shown below. The level of detail provided in the documentation can be very useful in determining which steps, or tasks, are suitable for your project.

# Other Methods of Table Maintenance and Customizing

It is sometimes difficult to find the table you need to customize in the IMG. SAP provides two transaction codes that can be used when you know the name of the table you need to customize and you're not sure where it is in the IMG. Transaction code SM30 is used to access the screen for maintaining tables or table views, shown in Figure 1.6. Although it is more common to refer to customizing objects as tables, most customizing objects are actually *views* of tables. To customize an object, you must create a maintenance interface for it. SAP very rarely creates maintenance interfaces on tables themselves. Most of the time, maintenance interfaces are created for table views by SAP for R/3 as delivered. Do not try to create maintenance interfaces for SAP-delivered tables! Transaction code SM30 is used to maintain custom-created (user-defined) tables.

**FIGURE 1.6**      Transaction code SM30 is for maintaining tables or table views.

In those instances when you know the table name and not the customizing view name, the transaction code SM31 (Extended Table Maintenance) can be used to access the table maintenance screen. Simply enter the table name into the SM31 screen's Table/View field, and click the Customizing button. The first time you use this button, you will be asked for a project number, however this is not a required field and you can hit enter to continue. Once you do that you will be presented with the screen that is displayed in Figure 1.7.

**FIGURE 1.7**    A list of configuration steps that update table T001

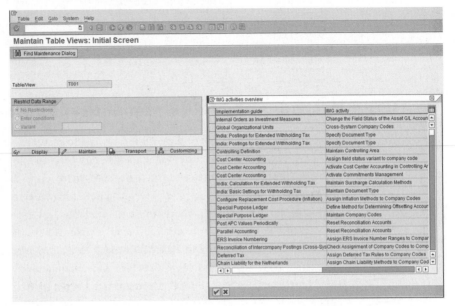

This will give you a listing of the views of maintenance interfaces for that table. Then you can click the name of the appropriate view, and SAP will take you to the proper configuration screen. Note how many configuration steps can update T001 – company codes.

## Finding the Table to Configure

Often it may be necessary to find a customizing setting when you're processing a business transaction in the system. The easiest way to accomplish this task is to select on the business transaction the field that contains the setting you want to customize.

In this example, say you want to configure a company code. You can use any transaction that references a company code; in this example, we're using the transaction used to display G/L line items—FBL3N. Figure 1.8 shows the appropriate screen.

**FIGURE 1.8**     Displaying/changing line items—FBL3N

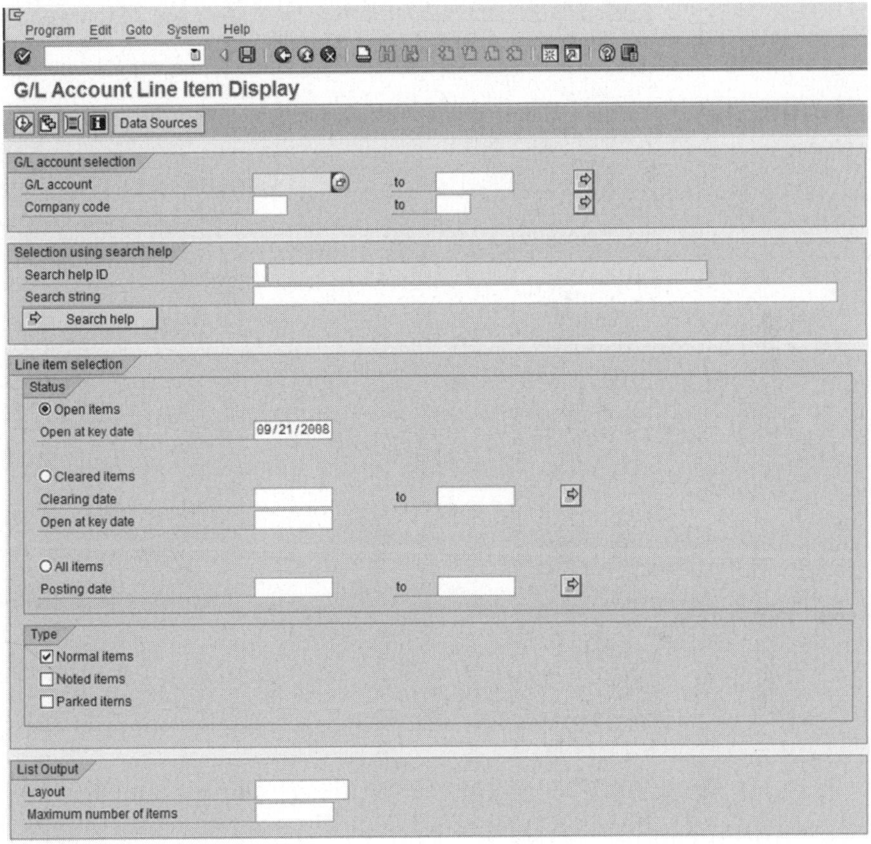

Once the field is selected, press the F1 key or select the SAP help icon. This displays general information about the selected field, as shown in Figure 1.9. You can then select the technical information box (the icon with the hammer and spanner).

**FIGURE 1.9**    The help screen that SAP refers to as a Performance Assistant, which you can open by pressing F1 or clicking the help icon, can give you general information about selected fields.

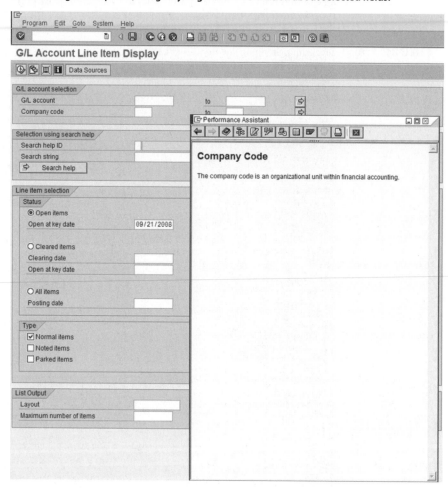

The Technical Information box lists the field name and tables of the selected setting (table SKB1, field name BUKRS), as shown in Figure 1.10. Armed with this information, you are now ready to go to the configuration table and make the desired changes.

**FIGURE 1.10**    The table and field names can be discovered by clicking the technical information box.

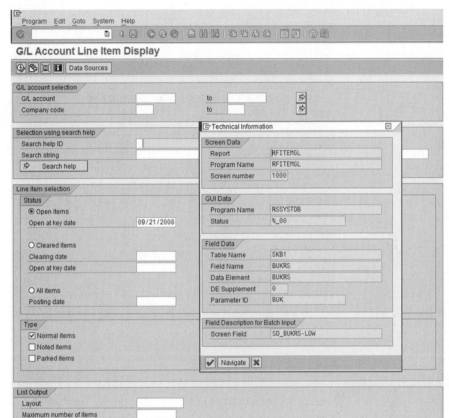

The Dictionary Display is an invaluable tool for viewing table structures as well as finding configuration tables and other pertinent system information. You can use the Dictionary Display to return to the customizing (configuration) table. Then use transaction code SE12 to display the table you found named in the help screen (the data Dictionary Display). After you click the Display button, SE12 lists all fields that are included in the table. Locate the field name found on the help screen, BUKRS (Figure 1.11).

**TIP**    You can also double-click the field or table name on the Technical Information screen and it will take you into the Dictionary Display transaction for the particular table.

**FIGURE 1.11**    The table SKB1 is displayed using transaction code SE12.

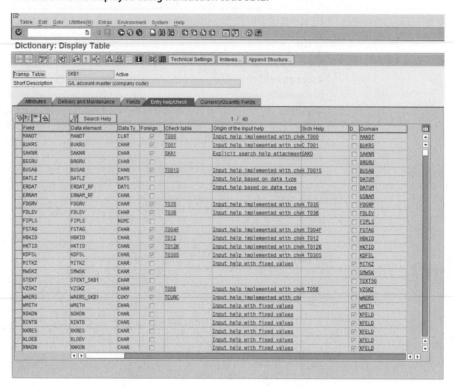

By viewing the structure of table SKB1, you can see that the field name BUKRS has a check table of T001. This is the table you need to configure in this scenario. You know you need to configure table T001 because this is where the primary key for company code (field name BUKRS) resides. In SAP, check tables always refer to the primary table that the field belongs in. If there is no check table next to the field name, you know that this instance of the field is the primary key and not included in the table via a foreign key relationship. In relational database terms, the field BUKRS in table T001 is the foreign key for table SKB1. Because it is the foreign key, you know that table T001 is the table in which BUKRS (a key field) is created and maintained. To find the configuration view you need to access, use transaction SM31 (discussed in the preceding section). Once you have entered T001 in the table name field and clicked the Find Maintenance Dialog button (shown earlier in Figure 1.6), a list of configuration views is returned.

**TIP**   In relational databases, a *key* field is a unique identifier for a table. This field is used as a reference to the same data in other tables. For example, your employer uses your Social Security number as a unique identifier for information about you. Rather than listing all the relevant statistics about you in every table, a relational database connects the various kinds of information through a single key field that represents "you." A *foreign* field is another sort of key field, but it's the key field for a "foreign" table. For example, say your employer needs a table containing names and addresses. In this table, the key field might be the last name of the employee. The last name would certainly also be referenced in a table containing Social Security numbers, but it would be a foreign key there—used only to verify that two people with the same last name stay unique as entities in the various tables.

## The Data Browser and Common Tables to Display

The Data Browser is a useful tool for displaying data table contents. Transaction SE12 is used to display the structure of a table, and the Data Browser, which is run via transaction code SE16, displays the contents of a table. Figure 1.12 shows the configuration screen for creating a company code. The same detail can be viewed through SE16 by using table T001. The difference between these two options will be how SAP presents the data in a configuration screen, often linking more than one table to the screen presented.

**FIGURE 1.12**    Creating a new company code configuration screen

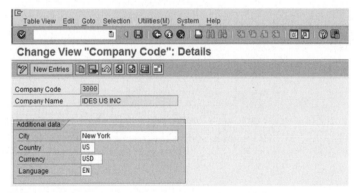

Figure 1.13 shows the results of running transaction code SE16 and entering BSEG as the table name. You can choose from the listing of options for narrowing the results that you would like returned to you.

**FIGURE 1.13**     The options for narrowing the results of transaction code SE16

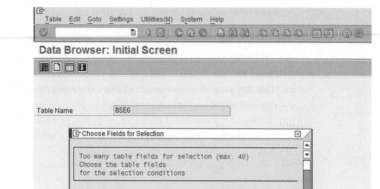

The fields that are automatically displayed for selection criteria aren't the only fields that can be used. By following the menu path Settings ➢ Fields for Selection, you can choose additional fields to select. Remember that SAP will generally include the key fields as selection fields. If you are adding in selection fields and you decide to use this new field, you will be faced with some very noticeable increase in run times because tables are indexed by the key fields. You can check to see whether a field is an indexed field by using SE12. They are usually the top 2 to 10 fields and have a check mark under the column key. Be careful, because SAP defaults so that only 500 entries are returned. If you require more than 500 entries, you can change this option via the field at the bottom of the selection screen.

Please remember that the fields being displayed are also defaulted and can be modified by using the menu path Settings ➢ Format List ➢ Choose Fields. If there are a lot of entries within your selection parameters, it may be easier to analyze your results in Excel. You can easily achieve this by following the menu path System ➢ List ➢ Save ➢ Local File.

You can save it to your hard drive, and then it is a very easy task of importing it into Excel and converting the file.

You can use the Data Browser to display data from all different types of tables, including summary and line item detail. This is very useful because reports using the Report Painter or Report Writer can be written only against summary-level tables. The Report Painter and Report Writer tools allow you to create customized reports based on users' needs. Most modules in the system can utilize Report Painter and Report Writer to create reports. Report Painter and Report Writer are especially useful for creating FI/CO custom reports. The table that is most commonly displayed by FI/CO team members is BSEG. This table contains all the segment (line item) detail behind every financial transaction in FI. You need to be very careful when displaying BSEG, or any segment-level table, because you can cripple performance on your system if you do not narrow your selection criteria enough. Running wide-ended table displays or queries is also a good way to get locked out of transactions by your friendly neighborhood Basis group, and a good way to feel the wrath of your project team.

# The Service Market Place

The Service Market Place (`https://websmp201.sap-ag.de/notes`), formerly known as Online Support System (OSS), is a web-based tool provided to you by SAP to help solve application problems. All configurators and developers should have access to this valuable database and customer service center. You can log functionality or code issues with SAP on this website. Because of the vast install base that SAP has, there are normally several other customers who have encountered your issue and therefore SAP usually has already posted a solution. These solutions are known as SAP Notes.

SAP Notes usually supply additional code to fix program bugs. They may also be "consulting" notes explaining workarounds in the system for certain functionality. Whichever the case, the information provided in the Service Market Place is invaluable. If you can't find a needed piece of functionality in the system, always make sure you check Service Market Place to see if it already exists. To find SAP Notes, one would have to first log on to the Service Market Place. Please remember you will need an OSS logon ID—that is, a user account for the Service Market Place—which you can get by going to the SAP Support Portal. If you want to search directly for SAP Notes, there is a link just below the SAP Notes Search portal heading. This will take you to your typical search parameters. Just fill in the criteria you're looking for (the release of SAP you are working with and the application area), and the applicable SAP Notes will be returned to your screen. If you find a note that applies to the problem at hand, download a copy to your hard drive for yourself, then let one of your Basis teammates know which note you would like applied. Unless you are very experienced, don't try to apply SAP Notes yourself. SAP Notes often deal with changing and adding to core SAP source code. Changing SAP programs is strongly advised against and can impact the support SAP provides to you. We will explore this in greater detail in the next section, "Modifications to SAP Source Code and User Exits."

In addition to SAP Notes (bug fixes, workarounds, and minor functionality enhancements), the Service Market Place has other purposes. As mentioned, you can log questions to SAP. Other uses include checking SAP training class schedules, reviewing new information and releases from SAP, and looking up information about Hot Packs.

> **N O T E**   In simple terms, *Hot Packs* are groups of SAP Notes that SAP recommends you should apply based on bugs in the system or on additional functionality provided by the notes. Instead of applying individual notes one by one, you can use Hot Packs to apply a group of SAP Notes.

## Modifications to SAP Source Code and User Exits

The golden rule of packaged software and of SAP in particular is this:

Do *Not* Modify The Source Code!

Always try to live by the golden rule; a modification to SAP source code is a *bad* idea, to say the least. Once you modify the source code of a program, SAP generally will not support the program and related business processes and may not support your entire installation. Source code modifications also make for a nightmare when you're applying Hot Packs and are even more of a problem when you're trying to do upgrades. Some SAP clients have made modifications to source code and have paid the price: they are now trying to remove the modifications to get back to "core" code in order to regain support from SAP.

If standard SAP functionality just doesn't work for your business, there are other options. SAP has developed specific Industry Solutions (ISs). There are prefabricated ISs for certain industries, such as IS-Aerospace & Defense, IS-Oil, IS-Retail, and many more. One of the existing ISs may work for your business. If not, work with SAP regarding your business needs; SAP may make—or allow you to make—SAP-supported modifications to your system.

SAP also provides what are called *user exits* in some standard programs. User exits allow developers to create their own code that is called by a standard SAP program. Once the custom code has finished, control returns to the standard SAP program for further processing. Contrary to programming modifications, home-brewed user exits are a good idea. SAP is providing increasing numbers of user exits in upgrades and new releases. To see if a program already has a user exit, while displaying the program source code, search for the string *customer exit*. If this string is found, the program already has a user exit. The transaction code CMOD also contains the customization projects for activating all user exits. You can search through these projects to see if the functionality you need is included.

# Summary

In this chapter, you were introduced to the basic concepts you'll need to understand to get the most out of the rest of this book. You reviewed the basic configuration of a three-tiered database and learned about a table-driven approach to designing your own system. You also learned about transports and who has control over the various aspects of preparing and implementing a transport. We walked you through the IMG screens and a few tables that will be useful in configuration and customization. And you're now more familiar with the sorts of changes that you shouldn't make and how to find out about problems and solutions using the Service Market Place.

In the next chapter, we'll cover the Organizational Structure of the FI Enterprise system and begin to configure the system for our project company, Extreme Sports.

# *Financial Accounting Enterprise Structure*

**FEATURING:**

▶ **CHART OF ACCOUNTS**

▶ **FISCAL YEAR VARIANT**

▶ **COMPANY CODE CONFIGURATION**

▶ **BUSINESS AREAS**

▶ **FUNCTIONAL AREAS**

▶ **ADVANCED VALIDATION AND SUBSTITUTION**

▶ **SALES AND USE TAX**

The Financial Accounting (FI) Enterprise Structure is the key building block to your entire organization. Most other modules in the system build upon the FI Organization Elements that you create in the Enterprise Structure. The configuration that will occur in the rest of the book will all be built upon the base elements that you will configure in this chapter.

It is very important to carefully analyze your organization before setting up the FI Enterprise Structure. It is important to have a good picture of how your organization currently looks, and it is equally important to have an idea of what your organization may look like in the future.

# Chart of Accounts

Before configuring any part of the FI Enterprise Structure, it is vital to draw out and agree upon what your structure will look like. From a purely technical point of view, the order in which you configure the chart of accounts, fiscal year variant, and company codes doesn't matter. For ease of illustration and continuity, we will cover the chart of accounts and fiscal year variant before demonstrating company code configuration.

Settling on a chart of accounts with the users in your client sites is one of the first big hurdles to overcome in a project. Before beginning design sessions on the chart, it is essential that both you and the client personnel responsible for design decisions have a clear understanding of the differences between FI and CO in SAP. The main reporting purpose of FI is external legal reporting to outside authorities (Securities and Exchange Commission, Internal Revenue Service, and so on). The main reporting purpose of CO is internal managerial reporting. This is often a very difficult subtlety for users to grasp. The conceptual differences between FI and CO is hard for many people new to SAP to understand because older systems tend to include both needs in one ledger/chart of accounts. It is common for a chart of accounts to include general ledger accounts, geographic regions, department codes, and so on. In this chapter, we will teach you how to segregate these reporting needs into the various modules and ledgers that SAP provides you as the configurator.

**NOTE**   The main reporting purpose of FI is external legal reporting to outside authorities (SEC, IRS, and so on). The main reporting purpose of CO is internal managerial reporting.

With SAP, you don't need thousands of accounts or any logic other than grouping logic (for example, all assets are in the 100000 to 199999 range) built into the G/L account number. Once you have completed your review of the existing chart for deletions, you are ready to configure in SAP. The easiest way to configure a chart of accounts is to copy an existing one. With the default system, SAP delivers the chart of accounts for the United States, known as CAUS.

You'll be following two steps to setting up your new chart of accounts:

1. **Copying the master data from an existing chart of accounts.**

   General ledger master data in SAP has two dimensions. The data that is created at the chart of accounts level, which is universal, or independent data that will be applicable to all company codes referencing this chart of accounts.

2. **Creating master data at the company code level.**

   This data is the second dimension of master data for the GL and is specific to a country/company code; this is to be covered in full in Chapter 3.

Let's look at how to copy the SAP-delivered chart of accounts, CAUS, to create the Extreme Sports chart of accounts, EXCA. You can copy CAUS by following the menu path Financial Accounting ➤ General Ledger Accounting ➤ G/L Accounts ➤ Master Data ➤ G/L Account Creation and Processing ➤ Alternative Methods ➤ Copy G/L Accounts ➤ Copy Chart of Accounts. The transaction codes are OBY7 and OB_GLACC01.

To give you a better feel of how to maneuver around in the Implementation Guide (IMG), Figure 2.1 shows the IMG path for this first piece of the configuration.

Now, you'll copy CAUS to EXCA, which includes copying the actual general ledger master data and supporting account determination settings.

Click the green check mark (shown in Figure 2.2) to copy all selected automatic account determinations from the reference chart of accounts. *Account determinations* (or automatic account assignments) are an important part of the integrated SAP system.

FI and CO are modules that have a lot of integration points. These integration points arise whenever any of the other modules complete business transactions or events that have a financial impact. Examples are when goods are shipped to a customer, moved from one warehouse to another, and so on. When you want the GL (or CO) to be automatically updated (integration point), you have to ensure that the account determinations (automatic account assignments) are correctly set up.

**FIGURE 2.1**     The IMG path to creating or copying a chart of accounts

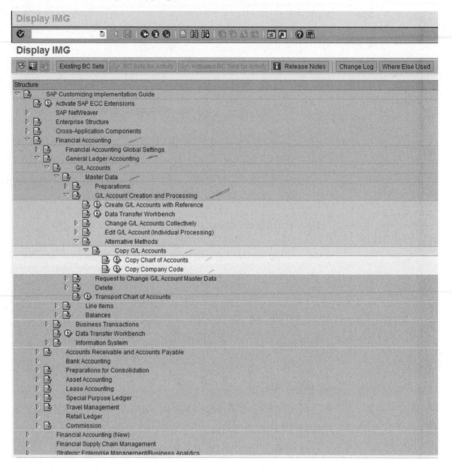

When you select the option to copy the template's account assignments, you will have to be very careful before deleting any accounts in your new chart. Deleting an account that is mapped in automatic account assignments can result in preventing business processes from functioning; for example, you wouldn't be able to produce customer invoices when shipping goods. (Automatic account assignments will be covered in Chapter 3.)

The system will confirm that the account determination and financial statement version were copied over correctly.

**FIGURE 2.2**    This dialog box allows you to customize the aspects of copying your new chart of accounts.

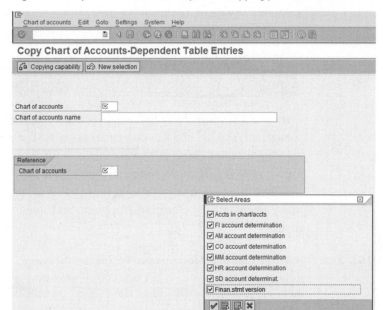

The configuration screen for copying an existing chart of accounts will contain the following fields that you will need to fill before competing this step:

**Chart of Accounts**    Enter the four-character alphanumeric value of the chart of accounts you wish to create. There is no right or wrong way to come up with a chart of account value, but usually the entry is all characters.

**Chart of Accounts Name**    Enter the description for your chart of accounts. The field is alphanumeric and can contain up to 50 characters.

**Financial Stmt Vers.**    Enter the four-character alphanumeric value of the financial statement version you want to create. The financial statement version is used by SAP to form your company's standard balance and profit and loss statements. We will cover the configuration of the financial statement version in detail in Chapter 3. For now, you only need to enter a placeholder to be used later.

**Fin. Stmt Version Name**    Enter a descriptive name for your financial statement version. The entry is alphanumeric and can contain up to 50 characters.

**Chart of Accounts**     Enter the four character alphanumeric value of the chart of accounts you wish to copy from. A listing of all available charts can be seen from the drop-down box on this field. To display the drop-down box, single-click on the field.

**Financial Stmt Vers.**     Enter the four-character alphanumeric value of the financial statement version you wish to copy from. A listing of all available financial statement versions can be seen from the drop-down box on this field.

Once you have made all of your entries, click the Copying Capability button near the top of the screen. You will then be presented with a screen detailing what is going to be copied. To actually create the chart, click the copy icon (two overlapping pages). Your new chart of accounts now exists. The newly created chart is ready to use and will now appear on the drop-down box of all available charts. The screen shown in Figure 2.3 confirms what accounts and account determination will be copied.

**FIGURE 2.3**     This screen details the actual proposed accounts to be copied.

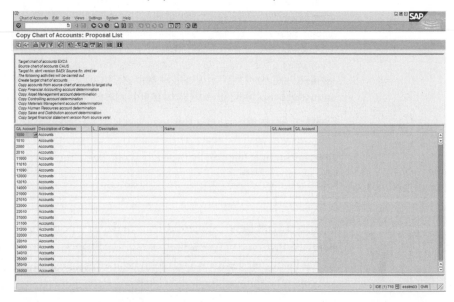

Figure 2.4 shows the actual log what the system successfully copied, including the various account determination options.

**FIGURE 2.4**    The SAP system will summarize the actual elements to be created.

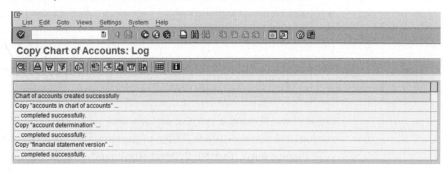

## EXTREME SPORTS CONFIGURATION ANALYSIS: CHART OF ACCOUNTS

Extreme Sports will utilize a single chart of accounts to be used by all of its company codes. The Mexican subsidiary company (company code 1300) will utilize a country chart of accounts in addition to the standard chart of accounts. The country chart of accounts configuration will be explained in "Company Code Configuration" later in this chapter. Because Extreme Sports is a U.S.-based company, the sample U.S. chart of accounts (CAUS), delivered by SAP, was used to create the Extreme Sports chart of accounts (EXCA). The sample financial statement version (BAUS) that comes with CAUS was used to create the Extreme Sports financial statement version (EX01).

The copy method is not the only method you can use to create a chart of accounts. You are also free to create your own chart of accounts in the system (by hand) or to import a chart of accounts from another system. Copying is far and away the easiest method of creating a chart of accounts (or any other configuration for that matter). By copying the chart of accounts, you are also able to copy the automatic account assignments. As discussed earlier, automatic account assignments are vital to the integration of SAP. Let the system do your configuration work for you whenever possible. We will cover the remainder of the chart of accounts configuration in Chapter 3.

# Fiscal Year Variant

The *fiscal year variant* determines the posting periods to be used by your client's company. As the name implies, it should be configured to match your client's fiscal year. The fiscal year variant is very flexible and can be configured to match any organization's fiscal calendar.

SAP allows a maximum of 16 posting periods each fiscal year. The 16 periods normally comprise 12 regular posting periods and four special posting periods, which can be used for such things as posting audit or tax adjustments to a closed fiscal year. Having four special posting periods gives you a lot of flexibility; you may want to use one special period for each quarterly and year-end audit and/or tax adjustment. When you close a period or year in SAP, you define which regular and which special periods are allowed for posting. Because the default period for each posting is one of the 12 regular posting periods, you can be safe leaving open one or more special periods for postings. To get to the fiscal year variant screen, follow the menu path Financial Accounting ➢ Financial Accounting Global Settings ➢ Fiscal Year ➢ Maintain Fiscal Year Variant (Maintain Shortened Fisc Year).

Using the screen presented in Figure 2.5, you can configure your fiscal year variant. As always, it is easier to copy an existing entry than to create one from scratch.

**FIGURE 2.5** The fiscal year variant configuration screen

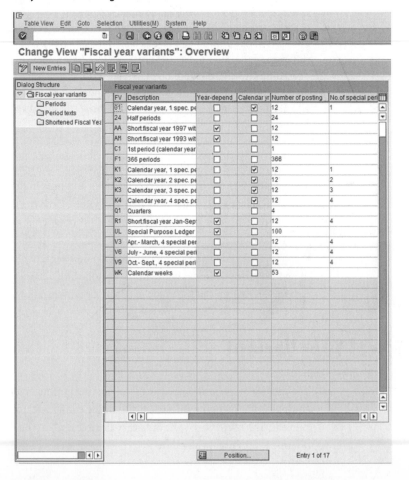

With this in mind, select the variant you want to copy (the option called V3 on the screen) and then carry out the copy command. The copy command can be executed by clicking the copy icon. The dialog box presented by executing the copy command is shown in Figure 2.6. Click the Copy All button. This will allow all three dimensions of a fiscal year variant to be copied:

► Posting periods

► Period texts

► Shortened fiscal year (in our example not applicable)

**FIGURE 2.6**     The Specify Object to Be Copied dialog box

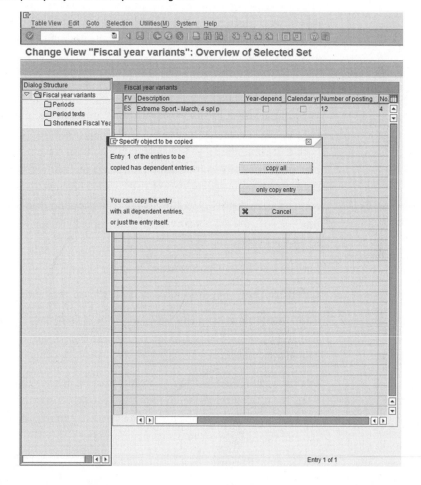

Let's look at how to enter data in the fields by using this list of entry fields:

**Fi. Year Variant**    Enter the two-character alphanumeric value of your fiscal year variant. SAP-delivered fiscal year variants normally begin with a *K* or a *V*, so avoid using these letters in your variant.

**Description**    Enter a description of your fiscal year variant. The field is alphanumeric and can contain up to 30 characters.

## EXTREME SPORTS FISCAL YEAR VARIANT CONFIGURATION ANALYSIS

**Extreme Sports operates on an April-to-March calendar month fiscal year. For this reason, we decided to copy an already existing fiscal year variant that uses an April-to-March fiscal calendar based on calendar months with 12 regular posting periods and 4 special posting periods.**

We will now cover the fiscal year variant configuration in more detail. After choosing the check mark and transacting the changes shown in Figure 2.6, you are taken back to the main fiscal year variant configuration screen. If you select the newly created fiscal year variant ES and then select one of the three folders on the left (by double clicking): Periods, Period Texts and Shortened Fiscal Years, one can see the configuration detail. By looking at the configuration, you will be able to figure out how to configure fiscal year variants manually (without copying) should you need to for your project.

*[handwritten margin note: how fiscal year variants are done manually]*

Let's look at the data entry fields:

**Calendar Year**    Set this indicator if your fiscal year is also the calendar year.

**Year-Dependent**    Set this indicator if the closing day of your fiscal year varies from year to year. You would set this indicator if you are using a 4-5-4 accounting calendar, for instance.

**Periods**    Enter the number of normal posting periods that are used for each fiscal year. The maximum number of normal posting periods in one year is 12. The standard general ledger can accommodate up to 16 periods. Most companies choose to have 12 regular periods and 4 special periods.

**No. Special Periods**    Enter the number of special posting periods that are used for each fiscal year. Four is the recommended maximum number of special posting periods. The standard general ledger can accommodate up to 16 periods. Most companies choose to have 12 regular periods and 4 special periods.

Select the Periods folder, shown earlier in Figure 2.6, and you are taken to the fiscal year variant configuration periods screen, shown in Figure 2.7. This screen is used to map calendar months to fiscal months for the variant. If you selected the Year-Dependent field, you will be prompted for a year to maintain. It is necessary to maintain the periods screen for each individual year if your variant is year dependent.

**FIGURE 2.7**       **The periods screen**

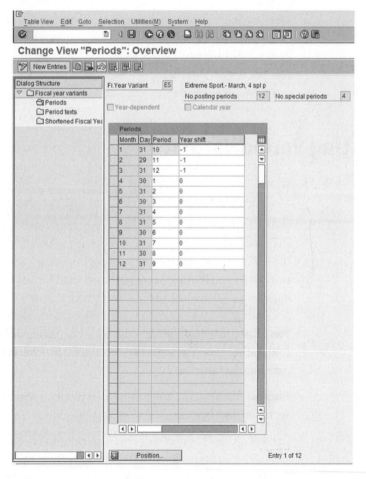

There are four entries on the periods screen:

**Month**   This entry represents the calendar month for the record being configured.

**Day**   This entry represents the last calendar day of the accounting period being configured.

**Period**   This column represents the fiscal posting period that relates to the calendar month and calendar day of the record. Because we are using an April-to-March fiscal year, the first calendar month, January, is posting period 10 of the fiscal year.

**Year Shift**   For fiscal years that do not correspond to calendar years, this entry is used to offset the calendar year to the correct fiscal year, by entering either a –1 or a +1. Using our Extreme Sports example, the first fiscal period (01) for fiscal year 1999 is April (calendar period 04). When we go into a new calendar year in January 2000, we are in posting period 10 of fiscal year 1999. Because of this, all the 1999 fiscal year posting periods that occur in calendar year 2000 require an annual displacement of –1 in order to specify the correct fiscal year.

# Posting Period Variant

The *posting period variant* controls which posting periods, both normal and special, are open for each company code. It is possible to have a different posting period variant for each company code in your organization. The posting period variant is independent of the fiscal year variant, which means a grouping of company codes with different fiscal year variants can occur, thereby centralizing month-end close activities. The number of posting period variants is determined by the closing schedules of each of your company codes. Follow the menu path Financial Accounting ➢ Financial Accounting Global Settings ➢ Document ➢ Posting Periods ➢ Define Variants for Open Posting Periods. Figure 2.8 lists all the available posting period variants. It is from here that one would create new posting period variants.

Clicking the New Entries button allows you to configure your posting period variants. Here they are:

**Variant**   Enter the four character alphanumeric value for your posting period variant. If you are using separate posting period variants for each company code, it is a good idea to name the variants the same as your company codes.

**Name**   Enter a descriptive name for your posting period variant. The field is alphanumeric and can contain up to 35 characters.

**FIGURE 2.8**    The posting period variant configuration screen

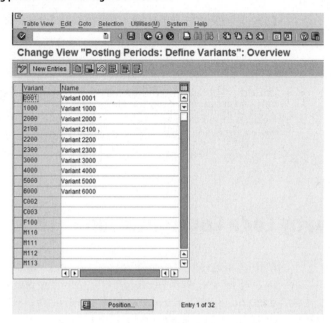

The next screen, shown in Figure 2.9, is where you create your posting period variant.

**FIGURE 2.9**    Here's how we configured the Extreme Sports posting periods.

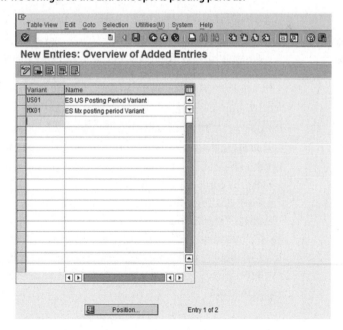

**EXTREME SPORTS MULTICOUNTRY POSTING PERIOD VARIANT CONFIGURATION**

With the implementation of SAP, Extreme Sports has decided to streamline its back-office functions. Before the SAP implementation, each company within Extreme Sports operated its own accounting department independently. Using SAP, there will be only two accounting departments: one for the U.S.-based companies and one for the Mexican-based company. Because of this change, only two posting period variants, US01 and MX01, used for U.S.- and Mexican-based companies, respectively.

# Company Code Configuration

In SAP, a *company code* is representative of a stand-alone legal entity that requires its own set of accounting records for reporting purposes. It is very important to understand this concept. There are substructures within the system to account for divisions within a company, which we will cover later in this book. We will now set up the company codes for Extreme Sports. An explanation of Extreme Sports and its organizational setup was described in the introduction in the section titled "Case Company Background."

We will begin by configuring Extreme Sports's first company, company code 1100 ES Ski & Surf. Follow the menu path Enterprise Structure ➤ Definition ➤ Financial Accounting ➤ Edit, Copy, Delete, Check Company Code.

You will have to select the Edit Company Code Data option, which will take you to a list of the company codes you already have in the system. Click the New Entries button on this screen to add the first company to the system.

The fields to be completed on this screen are self-explanatory. The one field that needs to be discussed is the currency field. The currency has to be the currency in which this company code will perform legal statutory reporting. It also will be critical when dealing with foreign currency translations and how your balance sheet is valued. Later in this chapter we will explore the concepts of parallel currencies, local currencies, and group currencies. Figure 2.10 shows your first choice in selecting to either create a company code or copy/delete/check a company code. For this example, we're going to select the former—edit company code—to create our first company code.

**FIGURE 2.10**     The Choose Activity box

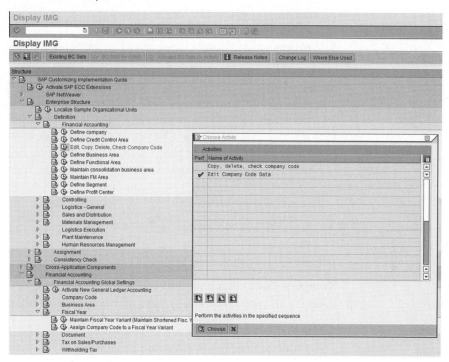

After selecting the edit company code action, you will be presented with the screen shown in Figure 2.11, which allows you to either edit an existing company code or create a new company code.

**FIGURE 2.11**     The initial screen for defining company codes

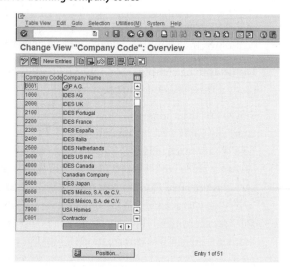

Select the New Entries button and you will be presented with the screen shown in Figure 2.12.

**FIGURE 2.12**     You can enter your own specific company code options by using the New Entries button.

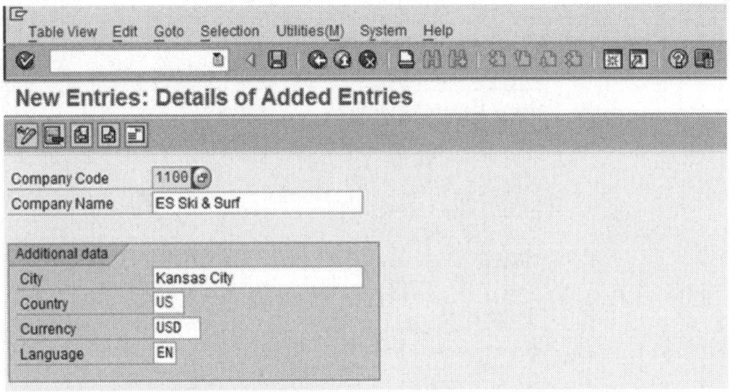

Let's look at this list of data entry fields:

**Company Code**     Enter the four-character alphanumeric value of your company code. It is usually a good idea to make the company code numeric (1100).

**Company Name**     Enter a descriptive name for your company code. This field is alphanumeric and can contain up to 25 characters.

**City**     Enter the name of the city in which your company is located or headquartered. This field is alphanumeric and can contain up to 25 characters.

**Country**     Enter the name of the country in which your company is located. This field must contain one of the two-character SAP country values.

**Currency**     Enter the currency that your company code will operate with and will report in from a tax and statutory accounting perspective. Make sure to use the pull-down menu on this field to make an entry that is acceptable to the SAP system.

**Language**     Enter the one-character language ID for the default SAP language display for this company code.

Once you click the save icon, you will be taken to the general address data of the company code, as shown in Figure 2.13. For U.S.-based companies, the Postal Code field is a required field. It is important to note that all address information in the system is stored in table SADR. Much of the required information on the address screen is repeated from the previous screen, the new entries screen. Unfortunately, it is very easy to get address information wrong when transporting data. For this reason, we recommend that you do not transport any address information but rather maintain the address information by hand in your production client.

**NOTE**   All address information in the system is stored in table SADR.

**FIGURE 2.13**   The Address screen for your company information

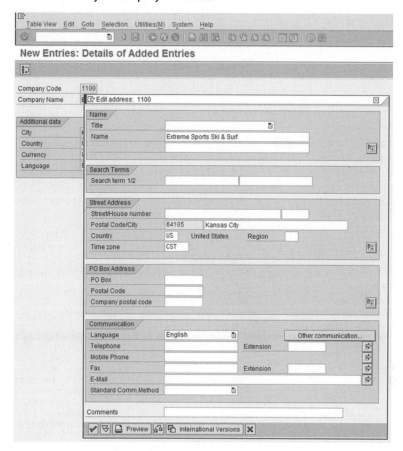

## EXTREME SPORTS COMPANY CODE CONFIGURATION ANALYSIS: PART 1

Extreme Sports has decided to use all numeric values for their company codes. There are three U.S.-based companies who all use dollars (USD) as their base currency and English (E) for the SAP default logon language. We will cover the configuration of the Mexican-based company code in a later section of this chapter.

You will now enter the *global parameters* for your company code. The configuration screen for global parameters is where we link company code to the chart of accounts, the fiscal year variant, and the posting period variants, among other settings. You can get to this screen by following the menu path Financial Accounting ➢ Financial Accounting Global Settings ➢ Company Code ➢ Enter Global Parameters.

The first screen for configuring global parameters contains a listing of all company codes configured in the system. Double-click the company code you want to configure (1100 for Extreme Sports), and you will be taken to the configuration screen shown in Figure 2.14.

**FIGURE 2.14**  The global parameters configuration screen for Extreme Sports

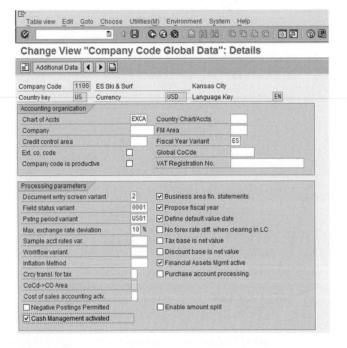

Let's look at this list of data entry fields:

**Chart of Accts**   Enter the four-character value of the chart of accounts that you wish to use for this company code. We've already set this up in the section "Chart of Accounts" earlier in this chapter. It's called EXCA for Extreme Sports.

**Country Chart/Accts**   If the company code you're configuring has a special country or statutory chart of accounts, enter the four character value for that chart here.

We will make use of this field with our Mexican company code in a later section of this chapter.

**Company**    A company is generally used in the Legal Consolidation module to roll up financial statements of several company codes. A company can consist of one or more company codes. It is important to make the distinction and remember that a company is not the same thing as a company code. If you are going to use SAP's consolidation functionality for your organization, enter the six-character alphanumeric company value that relates to this company code.

**FM Area**    *FM Area* is short for Financial Management area. Financial Management areas are used for advanced functions of the Treasury module, more specifically, for funds management. Funds Management functionality allows your client's organization to budget commitments and financial resources. If you are using Funds Management, enter the four-character alphanumeric value of the Financial Management area. FM areas can contain more than one company code. If you are using Investment Management along with Funds Management, your FM areas must be assigned to the proper controlling areas (the controlling areas that are assigned to your company codes). This is covered in more detail in the chapter on controlling, Chapter 8, "Controlling Enterprise Structure."

**Credit Control Area**    The credit control area controls the credit limits (tolerances) for your customers. Enter the four-character alphanumeric value of the credit control area for your company code. A credit control area can be linked to many company codes, but a company code can be linked to only one credit control area. We will configure the credit control area in Chapter 6.

**Fiscal Year Variant**    Enter the two-character alphanumeric value of your fiscal year variant. Fiscal year variants were configured and discussed in detail earlier in this chapter.

**Ext. Co. Code**    This setting is relevant only if you are using ALE. If you are using ALE, check this field; if not, leave it blank.

**Global CoCde**    If you checked the Ext. Co. Code indicator, you must enter the corresponding external company code ID (the one that resides in the external system) of this company code ID. For example, company code 1100 might have a corresponding external company code ID of EXSP10 that relates to company code ID 1100 in the other ALE system. Once again, this setting is relevant only if you are using ALE.

**Company Code Is Productive**    Only make this setting in your production client. Once you set your company code to productive, it is impossible to delete transactional data from your system. It is very handy to be able to wipe out transactional data in your development system, and it is equally important to make sure this indicator is set in your production client so that your business data is not wiped out!

**VAT Registration No.**   If your company code is subject to European Union (EU) regulations, enter your Value Added Tax (VAT) registration number here.

**Document Entry Screen Variant**   This setting controls country-specific onscreen fields for accounting documents. The most common U.S. setting is 2; this setting is for countries with withholding tax, like the U.S.

**Business Area Fin. Statements**   Set this indicator if you want to use business areas for your organization. We will cover business area configuration in detail later in this chapter.

**Field Status Variant**   The field status variant groups together several field status groups. Field status groups specify which fields are required, optional, or suppressed when processing transactions. Field status groups will be covered in detail in Chapter 3.

**Propose Fiscal Year**   Setting this field in effect makes the fiscal year part of the concatenated key field for looking up document numbers in either display or change mode. It is usually a good idea to set this indicator so you can cycle through document numbers from year to year. Number ranges will be explained in more detail in Chapter 3. Regardless of document number strategy, it is also a good idea to use this field because the more detailed the primary key is, the faster the search will be.

**Pstng Period Variant**   The posting period variant controls the opening and closing of posting periods for each company code. The posting period variant was discussed in detail earlier in this chapter.

**Define Default Value Date**   Set this indicator if you want the system to make the current date the default date for the value date. Value dating is used for A/P, A/R, and Treasury transactions. In A/P and A/R, the value date is also referred to as the baseline date.

**Max. Exchange Rate Deviation**   If you are working with more than one currency in your organization, enter the maximum percentage rate in which a foreign currency transaction can deviate from the rates entered in the exchange rate tables. An exchange rate can deviate because SAP gives you the option of specifying an exchange rate when entering a document in a foreign currency. If the exchange rate entered manually on the document deviates from the exchange rate specified in the exchange rate table by more than the percentage specified in this field, a warning message is displayed. The exchange rate tables will be covered in Chapter 6.

**No Forex Rate Diff. When Clearing in LC**    When this indicator is set, documents posted in foreign currency (such as pesos) that are cleared in local currency (dollars) will use the local currency value at the time the document is posted in order to determine exchange rate gains or losses. If this indicator is not set, the clearing will use the exchange rate at the date of clearing. In the following example, *open item clearing* refers to receiving a payment for an invoice created or paying a vendor for a product received. The payment offsets the invoice amount and "clears" both items. For example, company code 1000, whose local currency is U.S. dollars, bills a customer in the foreign currency of pesos—500 pesos. At the time the billing document is posted, the exchange rate is .25, thus giving the item a local currency amount of $125. The customer decides to pay the invoice using dollars, in the amount of $125. At the time the payment is received, the exchange rate is .20, giving the local currency value of the open item $100. If, at the time of posting, this indicator is set, no exchange rate gain or loss will be recognized because the payment amount ($125) matches the local currency amount of the document ($125) at the document posting date. If, at the time of posting, this indicator is not set, the system will recognize an exchange rate gain of $25 because the system recalculates the local currency amount of the open item at the time of payment (the new exchange rate of .20).

**Sample Acct Rules Var.**    This variant determines which field settings are carried over from a sample account to a newly created G/L account. Sample accounts will be discussed in more detail in Chapter 3.

**Tax Base Is Net Value**    The cash discount is deducted from the total invoice amount to calculate the tax base by means of this setting. Whether this field can be used is based upon the laws of the country where the company conducts business. For example, let's say an invoice has a total amount of $100 but offers a cash discount of $2 for payment within 10 days. If this indicator is set, the tax base is $98—the total invoice amount ($100) less the cash discount amount ($2). The tax calculation carried out by the system will then be $98 times the applicable tax rate. If this indicator were not set, the tax base would be $100—the total invoice amount. For countries that use tax jurisdictions for their taxing procedure, such as the U.S., any entry in this field is ignored. For these countries, the tax base is configured on the tax jurisdiction code. Taxes will be covered in more detail later in this chapter.

**Workflow Variant**   If workflow is active in your system, enter the appropriate four-character alphanumeric value of the workflow variant. Workflow allows for documents to be routed to other users and processes in the system for approval or further processing.

**Discount Base Is Net Value**   If this indicator is set, the sales and use taxes are not included in the base-amount calculation for cash discounts. For example, an invoice is received in the amount of $225 and offers a cash discount of 2% if paid within 10 days. Of the total amount of the invoice, $200 relates to materials and $25 relates to sales taxes. If this indicator is set in this example, the cash discount base will be $200, the amount of the materials only, relating to a total payment of $221, that is, $200* (1.00 – .02) plus the $25 tax amount. In the same example, if the indicator is not set, the total payment would be $220.50, $225* (1.00 – .02). For countries that use tax jurisdictions for their taxing procedure, any entry in this field is ignored. The discount base is configured on the tax jurisdiction code for countries utilizing the tax jurisdiction taxing procedure.

**Inflation Method**   This field is required if you are activating inflation accounting functionality. SAP has inflation indexes that are predelivered. They are specific to a country. This would be a good starting point for creating your specific inflation index if the standard index does not support your industry.

**Financial Assets Mgmt Active**   This field is an integration point with the Treasury Model functionality. The system will link automatic payments due on loans (for assets) to the reporting repository.

**Crcy Transl. for Tax**   If you do not want tax amounts to be translated using the exchange rate defined by the tax base amount, you can use this field to override the tax base setting. This allows you to use an exchange rate for tax amounts that is different than the one used for other amounts on the document. The possible entries are as follows:

> ▶ Blank: Exchange Rate According to Document Header: This is the default handling of translation of currencies, by the document header data

> ▶ Code 1: Manual Exchange Rate Entry Possible: This option allows you to manually enter a separate exchange rate to be used for taxes.

> ▶ Code 2: Exchange Rate Determined Using Posting Date: This option uses the exchange rate that is valid on the posting date when the document is cleared.

> ▶ Code 3: Exchange Rate Determined Using Document Date: This option uses the exchange rate that is valid on the document date of the affected transaction.

> ▶ Code 4: Exch. Rate Determ. Acc. to Pstg Date with Distr. of Diffs: This setting allows one to have different accounts to be used based on posting date.

**Purchase Account Processing**    Set this indicator if you wish to utilize purchase accounting. Purchase accounting segments the cost of externally related materials. For example, you would want to utilize purchase account processing if you do not want freight values for moving average-priced materials to be included in your inventory balance.

**CoCd->CO Area**    This indicator is defaulted from the configuration of the controlling area to which this company code is assigned. This setting will be explained in more detail in Chapter 7. The possible entries are as follows:

**Code 1**    If the controlling area contains only one company code (no cross-company accounting in controlling)

**Code 2**    If the controlling area contains more than one company code (cross-company accounting is active in controlling)

**Cost of Sales Accounting Actv.**    This field is set active if you would like to use functional areas in your master data, thereby creating an additional dimension for categorizing costs. So not only can you group financial activity by company code, business area, and account, you can group it by function too.

**Cash Management Activated**    Set this indicator if you are going to use the cash management positions and liquidity forecast functionality within the Treasury module. The cash management position and liquidity forecast will be explained in Chapter 6.

**Negative Postings Permitted**    This is a setting that allows the reversing document to be presented as the same as the original document, just as a negative. This is a departure from conventional accounting methodology where the originating entry, for example, may be a debit entry and the reversal would therefore be a credit entry. This setting would present the reversal as a negative debit entry.

**Enable Amount Split**    You would select this functionality if you would like to split an amount while document processing, for example, a vendor invoice where different taxes apply.

## EXTREME SPORTS COMPANY CODE CONFIGURATION ANALYSIS: PART 2

As you can see from Figure 2.14, we were able to make use of the chart of accounts (EXCA), fiscal year variant (ES), and posting period variant (US01) that were configured earlier. Currently, legal consolidation funds management and fixed assets are beyond the scope of the Extreme Sports project (and the book). The credit control area for Extreme Sports will be configured in Chapter 6. At that time, we will come back and enter in the values.

Extreme Sports has used document entry screen variant 2 because the company identified with company code 1100 is a U.S.-based company that utilizes withholding taxes. Extreme Sports will also use business areas, which will be discussed in greater detail later in this chapter.

The CFO of Extreme Sports has determined that a 10% exchange rate deviation is acceptable. Extreme Sports will also utilize the standard field status variant 0001, with custom field status groups added to the variant. Field status groups will be covered in detail in Chapter 3. In addition, Extreme Sports wants the system to use the fiscal year as part of the key field for looking up documents because document numbers can be used over from fiscal year to fiscal year if desired. Document number configuration will be explained in Chapter 3. Finally, Extreme Sports wants the system to default to the current date for the baseline date and value date in accounting transactions.

By clicking the Additional Data button, shown in Figure 2.14, you are able to enter the tax identification number of your company code. The completed screen is shown in Figure 2.15.

**FIGURE 2.15**  The tax identification number code is filled in using the Additional Details button of the global parameters configuration screen.

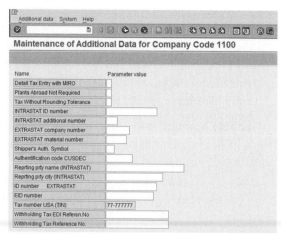

# Creating New Companies by Copying Existing Company Code

In the preceding section, we configured company code 1100, ES Ski & Surf. We now need to configure company codes 1110, 1120, and 1140, the U.S. subsidiaries of Extreme Sports. We cover configuration of our Mexican company code 1300 in a later section of this chapter. Fortunately, we did most of the hard work in the preceding section; we now need only to copy our sample company code 1100 to create 1110, 1120, and 1140. You will use the configuration command you learned earlier by again following the menu path Enterprise Structure ➢ Definition ➢ Financial Accounting ➢ Edit, Copy, Delete, Check Company Code.

The Choose Activity dialog box that you saw in Figure 2.10 appears. This time, after following the menu path, we will select the Copy, Delete, Check Company Code option. The next configuration screen, shown in Figure 2.16, appears.

**FIGURE 2.16**    The Organizational Object Company Code screen

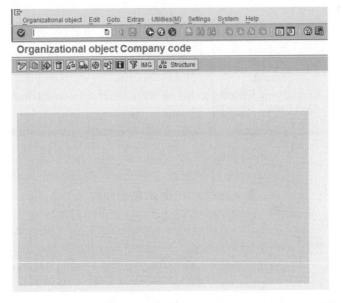

From this screen, follow the menu path Organizational Object ➢ Copy Org.obj. The resulting screen is displayed in Figure 2.17.

**FIGURE 2.17**    The Copy pop-up box

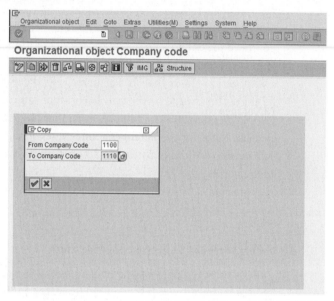

In the Copy pop-up box, fill in the From Company Code and the To Company Code fields. We have filled in the from box with company code 1100 (the company code that was configured earlier in the chapter) and the to box with company code 1110 (the company code that we want to create). We will then repeat the process for the remaining U.S. subsidiaries using company code 1100 as the from company code.

The copy transaction copies all of the general and global parameter settings that we entered by hand for company code 1100. The only remaining step is to add the company name and address information. This is done the same way it was done for company code 1100—by using the same transaction code that we just executed—but this time, select the Define Company Code option (remember that the transaction code for defining is OX02). You will then double-click each of the new company codes, which will take you to their respective configuration screens (the configuration screens were explained earlier in this chapter). You can refer to Figure 2.12 to refresh your memory.

## Configuring International Companies

In this section, we will configure company code 1300 ES Mexico S.A. The goal in this section is not to present the legal requirements needed to actually configure a Mexican company code, but rather to show the configuration settings you need when dealing with international company codes.

The configuration to set up the Mexican company code is very similar to the configuration for U.S.-based companies. We will need to change and add only a few additional entries to accomplish the company code assignment.

The first step is to define our company code. The same configuration paths and screens used in the U.S. company code configuration are used here. The only changes we will make are to set the country code to MX (Mexico) and the currency code to MXN (pesos).

Because Mexico has different government reporting requirements than the U.S., we will need to create a country chart of accounts to be used by ES Mexico in addition to the normal chart of accounts, EXCA. First, follow the configuration procedures documented in "Chart of Accounts" at the beginning of this chapter. The only difference is that we will copy the SAP-delivered Mexican chart of accounts to our new chart of accounts, EXMX. The chart of accounts EXMX will be used as our country chart of accounts in company code 1300.

You are now ready to enter global parameters for company code 1300. You will use the following configuration screens and paths, which were already demonstrated in "Company Code Configuration" earlier in this chapter. Follow the menu path Financial Accounting ➢ Financial Accounting Global Settings ➢ Company Code ➢ Enter Global Parameters. Figure 2.18 shows the configuration screen where you will enter all the settings for your company code that will have a universal effect on all business transactions that have a financial impact.

**FIGURE 2.18**    The configuration for company code 1300

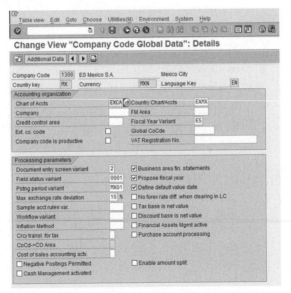

## EXTREME SPORTS INTERNATIONAL COMPANY CODE CONFIGURATION ANALYSIS: PART 1

The country chart of accounts was set to EXMX for company code 1300. This will allow Extreme Sports to comply with external reporting obligations to the Mexican government. The link between the regular chart of accounts and the country chart of accounts appears in the alternate account number field of the G/L master record. This will be explained in more detail in Chapter 3.

Because company code 1300 has a different accounting staff than the rest of the company codes, we assigned posting period variant MX01. You will recall from the case company background in the introduction that company code 1400, Extreme Sports Shared Services, provides all of the back-office and administrative functions for all U.S.-based subsidiaries of Extreme Sports. This will allow company code 1300 to close its books at a different time than the U.S.-based companies to facilitate Mexican reporting requirements.

**NOTE** Sharing services or not is ultimately a business decision. We decided to do this as part of the case company code in order to show the reengineering that occurs in the project and to be able to better demonstrate how to use more than one posting period variant, among other things.

SAP caters to the tracking of multiple currencies. As a minimum, SAP tracks three currencies. The following are a few examples of the types of currencies that can be tracked:

► Company code currency: The currency of the legal entity; dictated by legal/statutory requirements where the company is registered

► Transaction currency: The currency of the original document/business event (can be the same as the company code currency)

► Group currency: The common currency in which all companies belonging to a group report

► Hard currency: An additional currency for the system to track and that is generally linked to a more stable currency, in this case the U.S. dollar

To set the parallel currencies, follow the menu path Financial Accounting ➤ Financial Accounting Global Settings ➤ Company Code ➤ Parallel Currencies ➤ Define Additional Local Currencies.

Click the New Entries button to create a new record for your configuration settings. In Figure 2.19, you can see how the system is designed to be able to track three currencies in parallel.

**FIGURE 2.19**     The new entries screen for configuring alternate local currencies

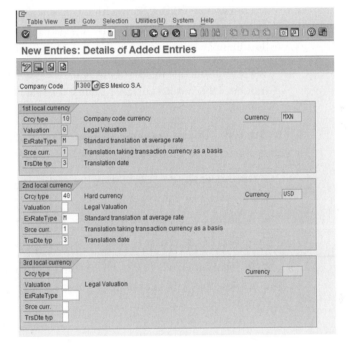

Let's look at this list of data entry fields:

**Company Code**     Enter the four character value of the company code that you wish to configure.

**1st Local Currency**     These fields will fill in automatically with default information based on the currency defined in the company code definition.

**2nd and 3rd Local Currency**     As explained earlier, each company code can have two additional parallel currencies that can be used in conjunction with local currency defined for the company code.

**Crcy Type**    The currency type field specifies which type of parallel currency you want to configure.

**ExRate Type**    The exchange rate type determines how foreign currencies are revalued at the time of foreign currency revaluation and translation. The number of possible entries is too numerous to list here.

**Srce Curr.**    Enter the source currency against which the foreign currency is to be translated. The possible entries are as follows:

**1: Translation Taking Transaction Currency as Basis**    This option always tries to translate the parallel currency against the transaction currency of the document.

**2: Translation Taking First Local Currency as Basis**    This option always translates the parallel currency against the first local currency (company code currency).

**TrsDte Typ**    This setting is used to determine which date is used for foreign currency translations. The available options are as follows:

**1: Document Date**    Select this option if you want the translation calculation to use the exchange rate that was in effect on the day the document was dated.

**2: Posting Date**    Select this option if you want the translation calculation to use the exchange rate that was in effect on the posting date in the document.

**3: Translation Date**    Select this option if you want the translation calculation to use the exchange rate that is in effect on the date of the foreign currency translation.

## EXTREME SPORTS INTERNATIONAL COMPANY CODE CONFIGURATION ANALYSIS: PART 2

Extreme Sports has decided to use a hard currency to help offset the inflationary pressures of its Mexican-based company code. U.S. dollars are used as the hard currency. The peso is the company code currency for the Mexican division. Extreme Sports has decided to use the transaction currency as the base currency for translation and to use the translation date to determine the proper exchange rate. Because we have company codes with different currencies using the same controlling area, we also configured a group currency of U.S. dollars for all company codes. The group currency will allow us to make cross-company code postings in the Controlling module. We will also need to make entries for all of the U.S. company codes to add the group currency to their records.

# Business Areas

The function of *business areas* is to create balance sheets and profit and loss statements below the company code level. Some common uses of business areas are to produce divisional financial statements or SEC segment-level reporting. It is important to note that business area functionality can be duplicated using Profit Center Accounting. The decision to use or not to use business areas should be made early on in the design phase of your project. Many new projects are leaning away from business areas and toward profit centers, but ultimately, the decision is an individual project decision based on what fits in to the overall system design of the project implementation. Some of the deciding factors are the need to report on business lines across company codes, the need for full balance sheets at the divisional or business line level, and the cost and benefits of business areas versus profit centers. Profit Center Accounting will be explained in Chapter 13.

**NOTE**   Business area functionality can be duplicated using Profit Center Accounting. Getting a full balance sheet in Profit Center Accounting is tricky but not impossible.

Business areas are independent of any other FI Enterprise Structure. Therefore, business areas are designed to cut across company codes. (For example, company code 1100 and company code 1110 are both allowed to post transactions to business area AES as is shown in the graphic explaining Extreme Sports in the case company background in this book's introduction.) A common mistake that some companies make is to try to force a one-to-one relationship between the business area and the company code. Having a one-to-one relationship defeats the entire purpose of business areas. The purpose of business areas is to be able to report on similar activities that occur across company codes. There is no residual benefit to configuring business areas in that manner. As a matter of fact, it often causes a lot of reconciliation problems because business areas are not linked to company codes in standard configuration. In the Extreme Sports example, more than one company code produces apparel. To report balance sheet and income statement information on the apparel business line, a business area for apparel will be configured (AES). Let's set up the business areas. First, follow the menu path Enterprise Structure ➤ Maintain Structure ➤ Financial Accounting ➤ Define Business Area to get to the screen you'll need.

## EXTREME SPORTS BUSINESS AREA CONFIGURATION ANALYSIS

Extreme Sports has decided to use three business areas. The CFO has determined that he would like a cross-company balance sheet for both the apparel and equipment industries in which Extreme Sports conducts business activity. In order to better track non-value-added administrative assets and expenses, the services business area was created. The new shared services department that provides centralized administration functions for the organization is being implemented as part of the business process reengineering effort portion of the SAP project implementation. It is important to remember that the idea is for all company codes to share all the business areas. The one exception is that the accounting department wants to ensure that postings from company code 1120 (ES Boats) are only posted to the equipment business area (EES) because this company code produces equipment and not apparel. We will fulfill this business requirement through a validation of company codes, which will be the subject of the next section.

As you recall from the section "Company Code Configuration" earlier in this chapter, we enabled business area balance sheets as part of our company code configuration. These are the only settings that we need to make to utilize business areas. In Chapter 3, we'll cover how to set up field status variants to allow the Business Area field on document entry of business transactions in the system. Although business areas are not linked to any other FI Enterprise Structures, they can be linked to other organizational elements in the system, such as, for example, the following:

**Plant/Valuation Area & Division**    It is very useful to link a business area to a plant/valuation area and division because single plants usually produce products for only one business area (for example, a ball manufacturer would not be likely to also manufacture rock-climbing shoes). This ensures that postings are made to the correct business area.

**Plant & Division**    This setting is almost identical to the Plant/Valuation Area & Division setting. The decision to use valuation areas is made by your Materials Management (MM) team. You will use this setting when your MM team does not utilize valuation areas.

**Sales Area** If your sales organizations are designed to sell a single grouping of products, it may make sense to link business areas to sales areas to ensure that your revenue postings are made to the correct business area.

**Cost Centers** Depending on the design of the CO module, it may make sense to map business areas to cost centers. Cost centers are explained in detail in Chapter 10.

**Assets** The Fixed Asset module captures fixed asset information. Once you enable the Business Area Balance Sheet indicator in the company code, Business Area becomes a required field in the Fixed Asset module regardless of how you configure the screen layout for asset classes.

**Consolidation Business Areas** If you are utilizing the consolidation functionality of SAP, you can make several business areas into one consolidation business area for reporting purposes.

# FI Validations

*Validations* are used to check settings and return a message if the prerequisite check condition is met. You can use validations to supplement existing SAP logic to fit your business needs. A validation is a valuable tool that can be used in many of the Financial and Controlling modules. In this section, we will configure an FI validation to fulfill our requirement of allowing postings from company code 1120 to be posted to only business area EES. To maintain the validation, follow the menu path Financial Accounting ≻ Special Purpose Ledger ≻ Tools ≻ Maintain Validation/Substitution/Rules ≻ Maintain Validation.

The first validation configuration screen, shown in Figure 2.20, presents the configurator with options to create a validation in various functional areas within SAP. You have to select from the menu on the sidebar that aligns to the business event for which you would like to create a validation.

To create a new validation, select the appropriate validation point from the menu on the side; in this example it is the menu option called Financial Accounting. After selecting Financial Accounting, you will be required to select the Document Header option. It is here that you can click the Validation button on the upper-right side of the screen. This will bring you to the screen shown in Figure 2.21.

**FIGURE 2.20**    The first validation configuration screen

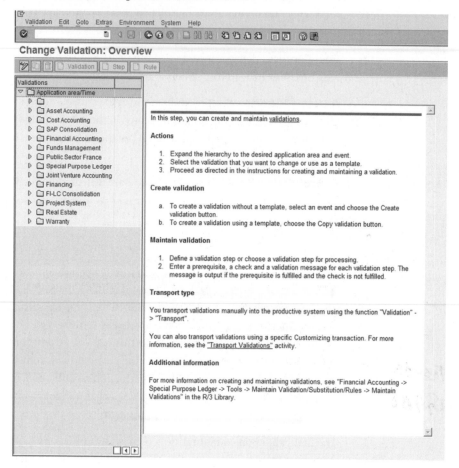

Let's look at the data entry fields on the Create Validation screen:

**Validation Name**    Enter the name of the validation you wish to create. The entry can be up to seven characters in length and is alphanumeric.

**Applicatn Area**    The application area is the module or submodule for which you wish to create the validation. The available options are as follows:

- ► Asset Accounting

- ► Cost Accounting

- ► SAP Consolidation

- ► Financial Accounting

- Funds Management

- Public Sector Finance

- Special Purpose Ledger

- Joint Venture Accounting

- Financing

- FI - LC Consolidation

- Project System

- Real Estate

- Warranty

**FIGURE 2.21**    The Create Validation screen is used to create a validation configuration for business areas.

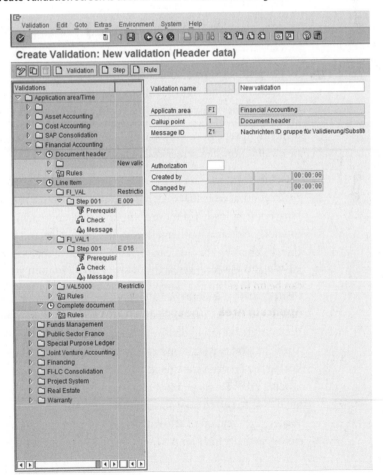

**Callup Point**   Callup points determine when the validation is run. The callup points that are available are dependent upon the application area that is selected. For the FI application area, the following callup points are available:

**0001 Document Header**   Use this callup point to validate entries at the document header level. The entries that are usually available for validation at this point are stored in the BKPF table.

**0002 Line Item**   Use this callup point to check line item entries within a document. The entries that are usually available for validation at this point are stored in the BSEG table.

**0003 Complete Document**   This is also known as a matrix validation. This callup point checks settings for the document as a whole.

**0005 Cost of Sales Accounting**   Validation will take place based on the functional area.

**0006 Cost of Sales Accounting (New)**   This is an option available in the New GL.

To get to the next page (and step), you need to use the insert step icon at the top of validation page (as shown earlier in Figure 2.21). On this screen, you will enter a description of your validation and define the steps that are to be carried out.

Validation steps store the logic and message that the validation will carry out. The new validation step screen is displayed in Figure 2.22.

It is important to enter a description for each step next to the step number. The really good news is that SAP has moved away from a more technical look and feel of pure Boolean logic to a more point-and-click approach. The configurator is now able to select fields and mathematical values from a list and then double-click the value, thereby creating the Boolean formula. These are the major sections of the validation steps and their descriptions:

**Prerequisite**   Before the validation step is executed, the *prerequisite* must be met. Prerequisites use Boolean logic to verify that a condition exists. Click the Prerequisite button to display and select the available fields to be used in your logic. The valid Boolean logic operators are =, >, <, and <>. The entry immediately following the Boolean statement must be put in single quotation marks (") unless a set is being used. Sets group together a number of entries. When you use sets, the system needs to match only one of the entries in the set. Sets are defined using Report Writer. The creation of sets will be covered later in this chapter. To link multiple logic steps together, either an AND or an OR is required at the end of each statement line.

**FIGURE 2.22** Entering a validation step into the business area description

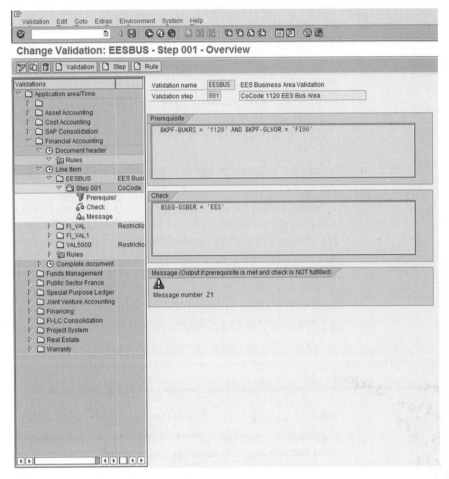

**Check** If the prerequisite is met, the *check* is carried out. The check also uses Boolean logic to check whether a particular system setting is made.

**Message** A message is displayed if the prerequisite is met and the check is not fulfilled. A message can be defined as an error (E), warning (W), cancel (A), or information (I). You must also select the message to be displayed. You can also create a custom message. If a variable such as & or $ is used, you can specify the field contents to display for it. The variable number is determined by the order in which it appears in the message. Select the table name and field name for each variable you would like to populate.

Once you have completed your validation step configuration, make sure you run the check syntax function to see if your Boolean logic has any errors. The check syntax icon is the one that looks like a hanging scale with two monitors on it. You can also execute the validation check of the actual step, by selecting the check icon on the left-hand side of the menu bar. Once you have checked your validation step and there are no errors, click the green arrow to move back a screen to the validation description screen. Click the save icon to generate the ABAP code that runs your validation.

## EXTREME SPORTS FI VALIDATION CONFIGURATION ANALYSIS

As stated earlier, the accounting department of Extreme Sports has requested that company code 1120 (ES Boats) be allowed to post only the equipment business area (EES) because ES Boats is not involved in creating any apparel merchandise. We configured the prerequisite of the validation to see if the line item is for company code 1120 and if the activity that created the line item is from FI. The check section of our validation verifies that the posting is made to business area EES if the prerequisite is fulfilled. If the check is not true, then a message number is displayed as an error that will stop the processing of the transaction.

Activate
Validation-step
OB28
GGB4.

Now that you have defined and generated the ABAP code for validation, you must activate the validation. Let's walk through the configuration steps to activate our newly created validation. Get to the appropriate screen by following the menu path Financial Accounting ➢ Financial Accounting Global Settings ➢ Document ➢ Line Item ➢ Define Validations for Posting. Or you can use transaction code OB28 or GGB4.

As is the case with most configuration screens, there are many different ways to get there. The IMG path and transaction code (OB28) take you specifically to the FI validation application area. Using transaction code GGB4, you can manage the activation of all validations in the system for any application area or callup point. Our configuration example will use the FI validation application area screen shown in Figure 2.23.

**FIGURE 2.23**    The activate FI validation screen

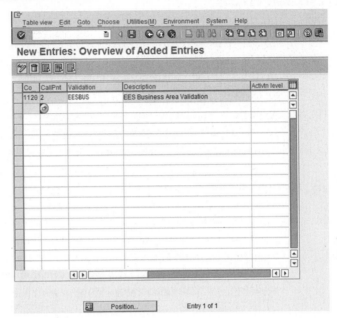

To set the validation for your application, enter values in the following fields:

**CoCd**    Enter the four-character value company code you want to activate your validation with. Only one validation can be active per company code per callup point. You can add additional steps to your validation in order to carry out more validations.

**CallPnt**    Enter the callup point you want your validation to be executed with. Callup points were explained in detail earlier in this section.

**Validation**    Enter the value of the validation you wish to activate.

**Description**    The Description field fills in automatically based on the validation you choose.

**Activtn Level**    Enter the activation level for the validation:

- ▶ 0: Not Active (validation will not execute)
- ▶ 1: Activated at all levels throughout the system
- ▶ 2: Activated at all levels throughout the system except for batch input

# Functional Areas

*Functional areas* within the FI Enterprise Structure are used to organize your business for Cost of Sales (COS) accounting. Functional areas allow you to segregate and classify different types of costs within one expense account. This makes it possible, for example, to use a single labor account to determine what amount of labor is spent directly on production as opposed to sales or administration. It is possible to report on functional areas from both FI and Profit Center Accounting (functional area information is available in both FI and Profit Center Accounting).

## Functional Area Organizational Elements

Let's set up the functional area organizational elements. As always, it is important to have clearly defined your requirements and thought of any existing or future requirements. To get to the maintenance screen for functional areas, follow the menu path Enterprise Structure ➤ Maintain Structure ➤ Definition ➤ Financial Accounting ➤ Maintain Functional Areas. This menu path will take you to the screen, shown in Figure 2.24, where you can create your functional areas.

The fields on this screen are as follows:

**Functional Area**    Enter the four-character alphanumeric value for your functional area.

**Name**    Enter a descriptive name for your functional area. This entry is alphanumeric and can be up to 25 characters long.

---

### EXTREME SPORTS FUNCTIONAL AREA CONFIGURATION ANALYSIS: PART 1

Extreme Sports has determined that it requires five functional areas to classify Cost of Sales accounting. The functional areas are Administration, Sales, Production, Research & Development, and Marketing. By using these functional areas, Extreme Sports will be able to report on an individual expense account using these five categories. Our next piece of configuration will be to enable SAP to populate our postings with functional areas.

**FIGURE 2.24**    The configuration screen for the functional areas

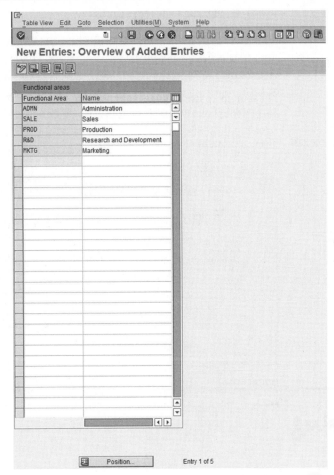

## Functional Area Substitution

In order to populate your postings with functional areas, you must set up a *substitution*. Substitutions are similar to validations, which were discussed in the section "FI Validations" earlier in this chapter. Unlike validations that create onscreen messages to the user, substitutions actually replace and fill in field values behind the scenes without the user's knowledge. Similar to validations, substitutions can be set up for a number of different application areas and callup points. Substitutions are activated on the company code level, so it is important to ensure that you have followed all steps for each company code.

Let's set up a functional area substitution. The menu path and transaction codes are very similar to those used for validations. Follow the menu path Financial Accounting ➤ Special Purpose Ledger ➤ Tools ➤ Maintain Validation/ Substitution/Rules ➤ Maintain Substitution. The screen is similar to that of the validation creation screen. Figure 2.25 shows the presentation for substitutions.

**FIGURE 2.25**    The first substitution configuration screen

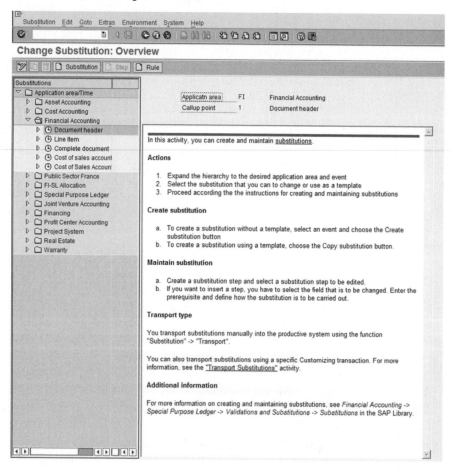

From here, select a function module in which to create the substitution. In this case it will be Financial Accounting. Execute the menu path Substitution ➤ Create. You'll be taken to the screen shown in Figure 2.26.

**FIGURE 2.26** The Create Substitution screen

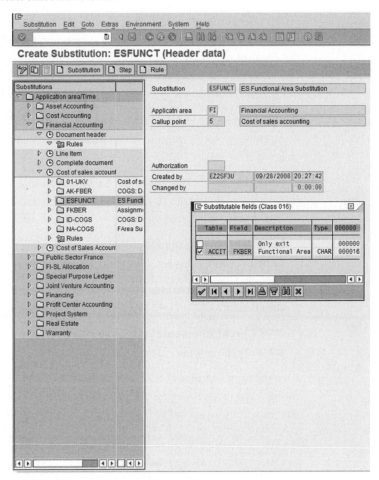

Here are the fields on the Create Substitution screen:

**Substitution**     Enter the seven-character alphanumeric value for your substitution. The value can be any alphanumeric value you like.

**Applicatn Area**     This field is defaulted in, based on the substitutions application area that you chose in the previous step.

**Callup Point**     Enter the appropriate callup point. Callup points determine when the substitution is run. The available callup points are dependent upon the application area that is selected. For the FI application area, the following callup points are available:

**0001 Document Header**     Use this callup point to substitute entries at the document header level. The entries that are usually available for substitution at this point are stored in the BKPF table.

**0002 Line Item**     Use this callup point to substitute line item entries within a document. The entries that are usually available for substitution at this point are stored in the BSEG table.

**0003 Complete Document**     This callup point substitutes settings for the document as a whole. This activity is also known as a matrix substitution.

**0005 Cost of Sales Accounting**     This callup point is used for functional area substitutions.

**0006 Cost of Sale Accounting (New)**     This callup point is available only if you are using the new GL.

After pressing Enter (or clicking the green check mark), you are taken to the next configuration screen (Figure 2.27). On this screen, you will enter a description of your substitution and define the steps that are to be carried out.

**FIGURE 2.27**    The blank substitution description screen

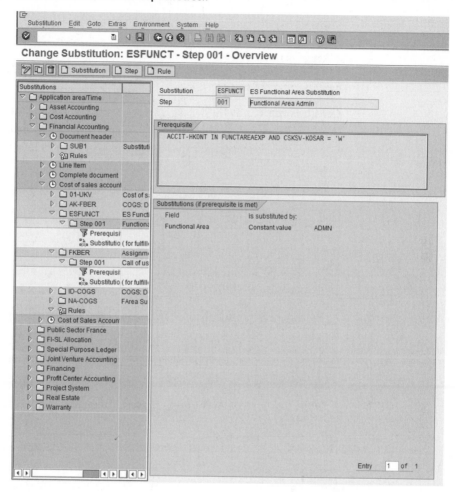

After entering the description of your substitution, click the Step button to add a step to your substitution. Substitution steps store the logic and field contents that the substitution will use. When you click the Prerequisite menu option on the left, the dialog box shown in Figure 2.28 appears.

**FIGURE 2.28**   The Fields for Substitution dialog box

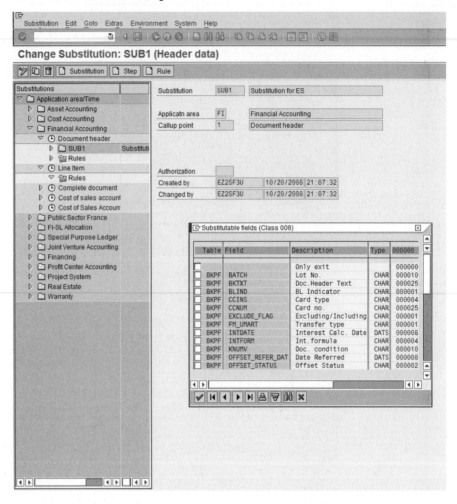

In the Fields for Substitution dialog box, either select the field you wish to substitute or specify that you are going to carry out a user exit. In this example, we are going to substitute the field ACCIT-FKBER (functional area). Once you have selected this option, you are presented with the substitution prerequisite configuration screen, shown in Figure 2.29.

**FIGURE 2.29**    The substitution prerequisite configuration screen

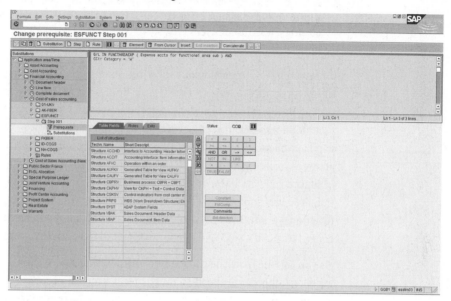

It is important to enter a description for your step next to the step number. The major sections of the substitution steps are as follows:

**Prerequisite**    The prerequisite uses Boolean logic to determine if a condition is true. If the condition is true, the substitution is carried out. If it the condition is not true, no further processing occurs. Double-click the list of structures on the left to display and select the available fields to use in your logic. The valid Boolean logic operators are =, >,<, and <>. The entry immediately following the Boolean statement must be put in singe quotation marks (") unless a set is being used. Sets group together of a number of entries. When you use sets, the system needs to match only one of the entries in the set for the prerequisite to be true. Sets are defined using Report Writer. The creation of sets will be covered later in this section. To link multiple logic steps together, either an AND or an OR is required at the end of each statement line.

**Substitutions**    The Substitutions section is where you tell the system what values to replace. You have the option of either using constant values or using a user-exit to specify values or carry out other logic statements. As you can see from the screen in Figure 2.29, your substituted field is automatically displayed.

**NOTE** Within validations and substitutions, some of the logic is case sensitive. Be sure to type in your logic using ALL CAPS. The syntax check will not tell you that you have an error if it's in lowercase.

Once you have completed your substitution step configuration, make sure you run the check syntax function to see if your Boolean logic has any errors. The check syntax button is the one at the top of the screen that looks like a hanging scale with two monitors on it. You can also follow the menu path Edit ➤ Syntax Check. Once you have checked your substitution step and there are no errors, click the green arrow to move back a screen to the substitution description screen, shown earlier in Figure 2.27. Click the save icon to generate the ABAP code to run your substitution. You will soon create additional entries from this screen to populate your other functional areas. The only differences in the new steps will be the cost center category (<CSKSV> $KOSAR) that is mapped to the remaining functional areas.

As you can see from the completed configuration screen shown in Figure 2.27, we used a *set* in order to specify a range of G/L account numbers. Sets simply hold a number of values for a characteristic (field). Sets are used in the same way that arrays are used in standard programming. Although there are several types of sets, we will cover only the simplest, the basic set. A basic set contains several values for a single characteristic (field). To create a set, follow the menu path (of your application, not the IMG) Information Systems ➤ Ad Hoc Reports ➤ Report Painter ➤ Report Writer ➤ Set ➤ Create.

The screen shown in Figure 2.30 is your first exposure to the Report Writer tool, which can be used for writing basic reports and, in this case, creating a set.

Follow these steps to create a set:

1. Enter the 12-character alphanumeric value of your set in the Set Name box. This is the set name that you will refer to when using the set.

2. Enter the name of the table that contains the field you want to create the set for in the Table box. This field and others like it appear in many different tables. It is important to know which table is being used at the time you are using the set. For example, we are creating a set for the field HKONT (G/L account number). HKONT appears in BSEG, COBL, ACCIT, and many other tables. As you already know from selecting the field to substitute earlier, table ACCIT is being read in our substitution, and we will use this table to create our set.

**FIGURE 2.30**    The Report Writer tool for creating a set

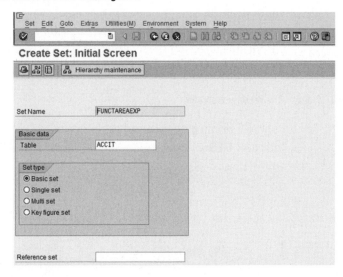

Once you press Enter or click the green check mark, you are presented with the pop-up box shown in Figure 2.31, which guides you through selecting the appropriate field for the set. You can use the drop-down menu  and select from the existing tables, or if you know the field name, you can type it in.

**FIGURE 2.31**    Naming the set field

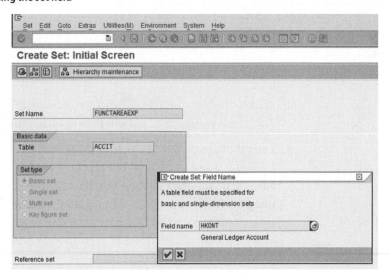

Enter a name in the description field to identify your set. Once you have entered the description, hit Enter to select the values you wish to include in your set. You are taken to the configuration screen that allows you to set the field's parameters, as shown in Figure 2.32. The screen in Figure 2.32 has already been filled in with the values we would like included in our set.

**FIGURE 2.32** The set values screen

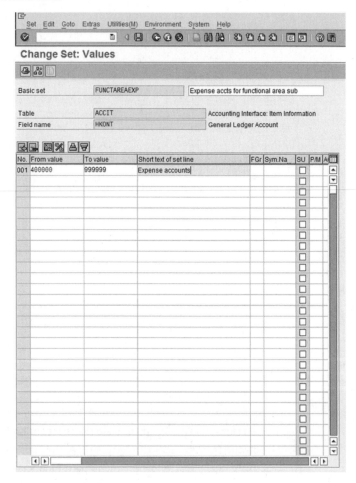

## EXTREME SPORTS FUNCTIONAL AREA CONFIGURATION ANALYSIS: PART 2

Extreme Sports has decided to use five different functional areas to analyze individual expense accounts:

▶ Administration

▶ Sales

▶ Production

▶ Research & Development

▶ Marketing

Extreme Sports will be utilizing cost centers to capture all of its expenses. Because it is using cost centers, we will use an attribute of cost center (cost center type) to populate our functional area on postings. You can use other fields in your substitution, but cost center type makes the most sense for Extreme Sports. A detailed explanation of cost centers will be given in Chapter 9. In the configured substitution, we created and used a set of all expense G/L accounts and the cost center type field (CSKSV-KOSAR). Although only one substitution step was shown, a separate step for each functional area was configured. A mapping of cost center type to functional location follows:

| Cost Center Type | Functional Areas |
| --- | --- |
| W: Administration | ADMN |
| M: Marketing | MKTG |
| F: Production | PROD |
| R: R&D | R&D |
| V: Sales | SALE |

Although you have created your substitution and generated the code for your substitution steps, you must still activate the substitution for your company codes. We will activate the same substitution for all of the Extreme Sports company codes. To activate the codes, follow the menu path Financial Accounting ➢ Financial Accounting Global Settings ➢ Company Code ➢ Cost of Sales Accounting ➢ Activate Cost of Sale Accounting for Preparation.

As is the case with most configuration screens, there are many different ways to get there. The IMG path and transaction code (OBBZ) take you specifically to the FI substitution application area for the Cost of Sales accounting callup point. Using transaction code GGB4, you can manage the activation of all substitutions in the system for any application area or callup point. The following configuration example, shown in Figure 2.33, will use the IMG path (transaction code OBBZ).

**FIGURE 2.33**  The configuration screen for the substitution activation

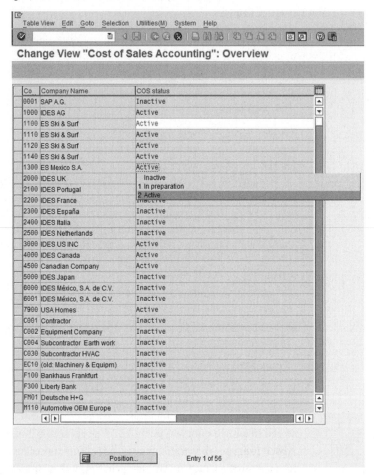

# Advanced Validation and Substitution Configuration

In the previous two sections, we configured an example of both a validation and a substitution. In the following sections, you will build upon that knowledge to learn about advanced topics in the configuration of validations and substitutions.

# Validations

The basics of validation were explained earlier in the chapter. You will now learn more about the specific method of adding a message class to your validations.

## Message Classes

When you set up your first validation in the system, you will be prompted to provide a message class to be used by all validations. A custom message class should be used. That is, you should create a new message class with a prefix of *Z* to denote a customer-maintained class. To create a new message class, click the Message menu on the left, shown earlier in Figure 2.22. You are then taken to the screen where messages can be selected. From this screen, select the pencil icon to enter a new digit value for your new message class. When new system objects are created, usually only the *Z* and *Y* prefixes are available; all other prefixes are reserved by SAP. If you need to change message classes in the future, from the first validation configuration screen (Figure 2.22), follow the menu path Environment ➤ Maintain messages. Remember, only one message class can be used by all validations in the system.

# Substitutions

The basics of substitutions were explained earlier in the chapter. You will now learn more about setting the user-exit program feature of substitutions.

# Setting the User-Exit Program

In addition to substituting fixed values, a substitution can call a user-exit to substitute the field or carry out another piece of logic. The substitution user-exits are stored in a form pool (a type of ABAP program). All substitutions use the same ABAP program to store their user-exits. SAP comes delivered with a form pool to be used for the substitution user-exit. You will need to copy this program and give it a name beginning with a *Z* or a *Y* to denote a customer-maintained object. A single user-exit can be called in more than one substitution or substitution step. To get to configuration screen for linking programs to substitutions that you need for this activity, follow the menu path Financial Accounting ➤ Special Purpose Ledger ➤ Basic Settings ➤ User Exits ➤ Maintain Client-Specific User Exits.

The configuration screen for linking programs to substitutions is presented in Figure 2.34.

**FIGURE 2.34** The substitution linking screen

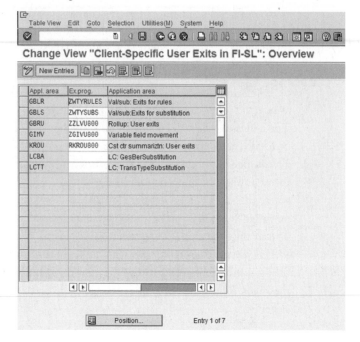

As you can see, application area GBLS is used for our validation and substitution user exits. When your system is delivered, the exit program provided is named RG******. Do not modify this program or use it for your user-exit. Make a copy of it and put it in the customer name range (Z*******). You will probably need to enlist the help of one of your ABAP teammates in order to copy the program. The ABAPer is also usually responsible for coding the exits that are placed in the program.

## Validations and Substitutions

The advanced features that relate to both validations and substitutions will be explained in the following sections.

### Adding or Deleting Fields to the Boolean Class and Substituted Field List

As you use validations and substitutions, you may find that you want to add a field to be used in Boolean logic or substitution, or you may want to prevent a field from being used. Table GB01 contains a listing of all fields that are currently allowed or disallowed in validations and substitutions. Use the Data Browser (transaction code

SE16) to display the contents of table GB01. The contents of table GB01 are shown in Figure 2.35.

**FIGURE 2.35**    The validation and substitution field availability listing

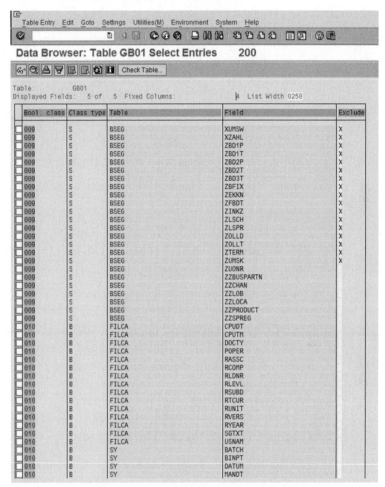

An explanation of the fields in table GB01 and their contents follows:

**Bool. Class**    The Boolean class specifies where the field is being used or is excluded. Boolean classes map roughly to the combination of application area and callup point. Here is a partial listing of Boolean classes:

   **1: Coding Block**    Used for CO line items

   **8: Document Header**    Used for FI items

**9: Document Header and Line Item**   Used for FI items

**16: Cost of Sales Accounting**   Used for functional areas

**100: Document Header**   Used for CO items

**Class Type**   A class type refers to whether a field is used in Boolean statements, substitution fields, or both. Here's a listing of them:

**B**   Used for fields that are to be used in Boolean statements

**S**   Used for fields that are to be used for substitution

**A**   Used for fields that can be used in both Boolean statements and for substitution

**Table**   The name of the table in which the field you wish to use or exclude resides.

**Field**   The name of the field you wish to use or exclude.

**Exclude**   If this field is checked, the field is excluded for use for the class type specified in the record. If this indicator is set, you cannot change it, and you cannot add the field in the configuration table that adds or excludes fields.

If the field you wish to add is not excluded in GB01, you can add it to the available fields for substitutions. You can maintain view V_GB01C using the table maintenance transaction SM30. You add fields using view V_GB01C. You can only add fields if they are already defined in table GB01 for the Boolean class into which you wish to add the field. The fields in V_GB01C are exactly the same as the fields in table GB01. The only trick is to remember to click the New Entries button. You must click the New Entries button because the entry for the field to be added does not exist in view V_GB01C until you create it.

## Testing the Validation or Substitution

SAP provides two special functions to test your validation or substitution. The first function is the Simulate action. To simulate the validation or substitution, you will need to go to the change validation or the change substitution screen (transaction codes GGB0 and GGB1, respectively). From either screen, follow the appropriate menu path, either Validation ➤ Simulate or Substitution ➤ Simulate.

You are then presented with an entry screen for all possible fields that your substitution or validation can use. Enter the data you wish to test. Once all the data is entered, click the Execute button. You will then be presented with analysis of how your validation or substitution would act during an actual transaction. The fields that will be displayed will correspond to the substitution or validation based on the application area of the substitution or validation. For example, a substitution that is created for FI line items will display all the fields that are normally available when FI transactions are entered as long as they are available to the substitution. The screen shown in Figure 2.36 is a very useful tool that allows the user to simulate how the system will respond to the substitution with a combination of values for the fields in the substitution.

**FIGURE 2.36**    The simulation screen

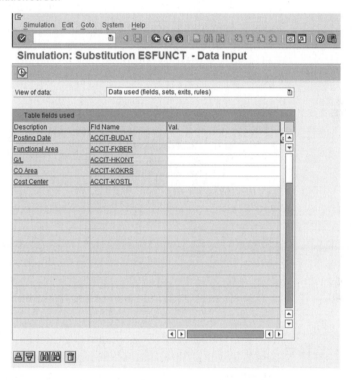

The second function that can be used to test your validation or substitution is the trace function. Tracing shows the results of your substitution or validation as you are entering actual transactions in the system. This function should only be used in the development environment. To invoke this function, go to the first substitution configuration screen or the first validation configuration screen (transaction codes GGB1 and GGB0, respectively). Select the name of your substitution or validation and press Enter. You are then taken to the configuration screen where you add new steps or change existing steps in your substitution or validation. From this screen, follow the menu path Extras ➤ Activate trace. Once you have tested your validation or substitutions, go back to the configuration screen and follow the menu path Extras ➤ Deactivate total trace.

## Transporting Validations and Substitutions

Even when automatic recording of transports is turned on, a transport request for validations and substitutions is not created automatically. You must create the transport by hand. To create the transport, you need to go to the first validation configuration screen or the first substitution configuration screen (transaction codes GGB0 and GGB1, respectively) From this screen, select the name of the validation or substitution that you wish to transport and then follow the appropriate menu path, either Validation ➤ Transport or Substitution ➤ Transport. You are then presented with the transport screen for substitutions and validations, shown in Figure 2.37.

**FIGURE 2.37**   The transport screen for validations and substitutions

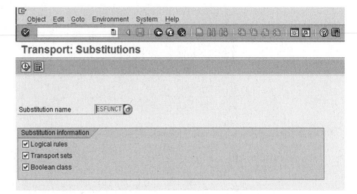

Make sure you select all three options: Logical Rules, Transport Sets, and Boolean Class. Selecting all three options ensures that your entire substitution or validation will be transported. If you don't select all three options, you are in peril of not transporting all of the logic, sets, or Boolean fields that are used in your validation or substitution. Without all three of these elements, your validation or substitution won't work properly. Once you have selected the three options, click the Execute button. You will then be presented with the normal transport screen.

Once you have transported your substitution or validation to the target client, you must run a special program in that client to generate the ABAP code and activate the sets. The name of the program is RGUGBR00; it is also affectionately known as the RugBurner program. You will run the program using transaction code SA38. After you click the execute icon in SA38, you are presented with the program settings screen for RGUGBR00 (Figure 2.38). The screen shown in Figure 2.38 has already been filled in with the appropriate settings. Once you have made all the settings, click the execute icon to generate the ABAP code that runs your substitution or validation and to create the sets used by your substitution.

**FIGURE 2.38**    The RGUGBR00 program settings

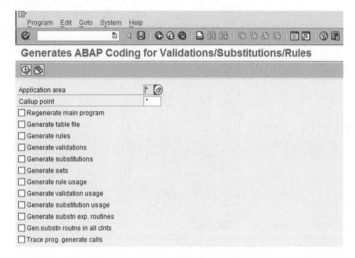

# Sales and Use Tax

Settings for *sales* and *use taxes* are made at the country level in SAP. There are standard taxing procedures defined in the R/3 System for many countries. You can also create your own taxing procedure if you want, although this is not recommended. In this section, you will concentrate on U.S. sales and use tax procedures and settings. There are two basic U.S. tax procedures: TAXUSJ and TAXUSX. In TAXUSJ, you create and maintain the tax percentage rates for each taxing jurisdiction by hand. Procedure TAXUSX utilizes a third-party tax system to maintain tax rates in the system. We will cover the basic configuration of TAXUSJ in this section.

The first setting you need to make is assigning a tax procedure to your company's country. In the example that follows, we have already assigned the procedure TAXUSJ to country US. Assign the country by following the menu path Financial

Accounting ➤ Financial Accounting Global Settings ➤ Tax on Sales/Purchases ➤ Basic Settings ➤ Assign Country to Calculation Procedure.

The configuration screen shown in Figure 2.39 is where you assign the calculation procedure to the country code.

**FIGURE 2.39**   The assign country to calculation procedure configuration screen

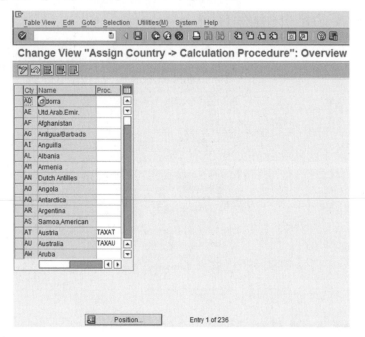

The next step is to set up the structure for the tax jurisdiction codes. The tax jurisdiction codes represent the different taxing authorities to which you submit payments. You can have up to four levels representing State, County, City, and Other in your tax jurisdiction structure. Normally, the tax jurisdiction structure is set up with three levels (Other is for special circumstances). We will now set up our tax jurisdiction structure. First, follow the menu path Financial Accounting ➤ Financial Accounting Global Settings ➤ Tax on Sales/Purchases ➤ Basic Settings ➤ Specify Structure for Tax Jurisdiction Code.

Figure 2.40 illustrates the multiple levels of logic available to the user to cater to various taxation requirements.

**FIGURE 2.40**    The tax jurisdiction structure

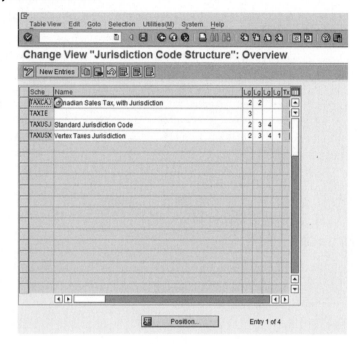

Here's what each of the fields represents:

**Schema**    Enter the name of the tax procedure for which you want to configure a tax jurisdiction code structure.

**Name**    Enter a description of the procedure for which you are configuring a tax jurisdiction code structure.

**LG**    Enter the character length of the first level of hierarchy within your tax jurisdiction code structure.

**LG**    Enter the character length of the second level of hierarchy within your tax jurisdiction code structure.

**LG**    Enter the character length of the third level of hierarchy within your tax jurisdiction code structure.

**LG**    Enter the character length of the fourth level of hierarchy within your tax jurisdiction code structure.

**TX**    Set this indicator if you want the system to determine taxes on a line-by-line basis instead of determining them on a cumulative basis per tax jurisdiction code.

## EXTREME SPORTS SALES/USE TAX CONFIGURATION ANALYSIS

Extreme Sports has decided not to use a third-party tax software program at this point (your company will probably want to use an external system). For this reason, Extreme Sports has opted to use tax procedure TAXUSJ, which uses tax jurisdictions and has rates entered manually. Extreme Sports's tax jurisdiction code structure uses three levels: the first level contains two characters (state), the second level contains three characters (county), and the third level contains four characters (city).

The next step is to configure our tax jurisdiction codes. As stated earlier, the tax jurisdiction codes represent taxing authorities. Using the structure that we configured earlier, we'll use the first two characters to represent state, the next three characters to represent county, and the next four characters to represent city. To set the definition, follow the menu path Financial Accounting ➢ Financial Accounting Global Settings ➢ Tax on Sales/Purchases ➢ Basic Settings ➢ Define Tax Jurisdiction Code.

**N O T E**   Every nation has a different tax structure. We used the example we knew best, the U.S. You should be able to extrapolate your country's structure according to your country's requirements from this example.

An example of a configured screen appears in Figure 2.41. Before entering the screen, you are prompted to enter the tax procedure that you are setting up tax jurisdictions for. Then as normal, click the New Entries button to configure your settings.

The fields have the following uses:

**Tax Jur.**   Enter the tax jurisdiction code you wish to configure based on the settings you made when you defined the jurisdiction code structure. As you can see from our example, we use KS for all of our Kansas jurisdiction codes. KS0000000 represents the base-level jurisdiction for all of Kansas. KS0001000 represents the base-level jurisdiction for all of Riley County in Kansas. KS00010001 represents our lowest level of jurisdiction, which is the city of Manhattan in the county of Riley and in the state of Kansas.

**FIGURE 2.41**    The configured tax jurisdiction codes

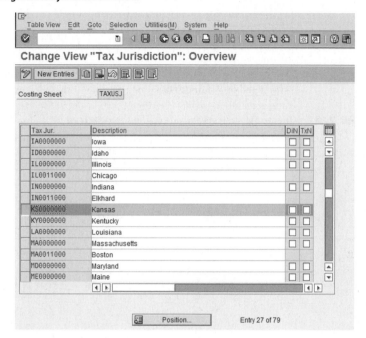

**Description**    Enter a descriptive name for your tax jurisdiction code. This entry is alphanumeric and can contain up to 50 characters.

**DiN**    Set this indicator if you do not want tax amounts included in the base amount used for calculating cash discounts.

**TxN**    Set this indicator if you want the cash discount amount deducted from the base amount that is used to calculate taxes.

Now that you have determined your tax determination procedure, tax jurisdiction code structure, and tax jurisdiction codes, you need to understand the function of tax codes in the system. Tax codes represent different tax types, such as sales tax charged by the company, sales tax charged to the company, and use tax accrued by the company. The most commonly used tax codes in the system are O1 (output tax charged by the company), O0 (output tax exempt), I1 (input tax charged to the company), I0 (input tax exempt), U1 (use tax accrued by the company), and U0 (use tax exempt). Now that you have an understanding of tax codes, you are ready to enter tax rates in the system. First, follow the menu path Financial Accounting ➢ Financial Accounting Global Settings ➢ Taxes on Sales/Purchases ➢ Calculation ➢ Define Tax Codes for Sales and Purchases.

When first entering this transaction, you are presented with a pop-up screen asking for the country that you are configuring. Once you have entered the country, the configuration screen shown in Figure 2.42 appears. As you can see, we are getting ready to enter the tax rate of tax type O1 (Sales Tax). Page down the configuration screen to find the appropriate account keys to configure. Account keys will be covered in detail in Chapter 3.

**FIGURE 2.42**    The taxable percentage rate configuration screen

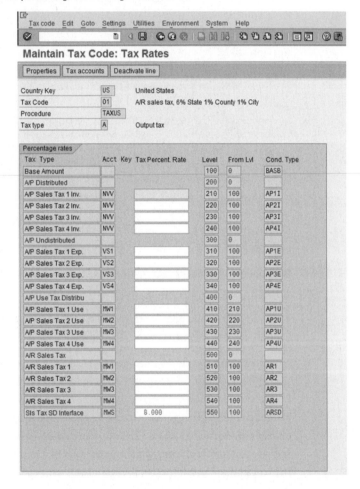

Transporting tax rates can be a very tricky process. Tax rate changes are not automatically recorded in a change request. You have to manually create the transport. It is best to create your transport after all tax rates for all tax codes have been maintained because tax rate transports are very complicated and do not always work as planned. By having a single transport, you minimize the risk of incorrect data getting into the target clients. To create your transport, follow the menu path Tax Code ➢ Transport ➢ Transport ➢ Export. You will be presented with a warning message. Be sure to display the long text of this message; it thoroughly explains the next steps that are needed once the transport reaches the target client. After processing through the warning message, you are allowed to pick which tax codes and jurisdiction codes you wish to transport. As was stated earlier, it is best to transport all of the codes. Once you have moved into a production environment, it is best to have your Basis group make the configuration of tax codes a current setting (a setting that doesn't require configuration access) that can be done directly in the production client. Once your transport has been moved to the production client, you must execute a special program that will create a batch input session to set up your tax codes.

**N O T E**   Even though you send the tax rate configuration to target clients in a transport, in order to execute the batch input session, the client you're in must be opened up for configuration. Because of this, it is best to create as few tax rate transports as possible. This way, you preserve the integrity of the data as well as lessen the risk of other customizing taking place while you are creating the tax rates

The screen in Figure 2.43 allows you to import tax codes from different clients.

**FIGURE 2.43**   The Import Tax Codes After Transport screen

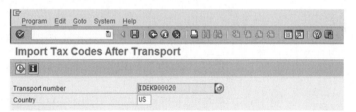

Enter your transport number in the Transport Number field and your two-digit country value in the Country field (US in our example). After you fill in these fields and execute the program, the program will create a batch input session. To execute the batch input session, execute transaction code SM35.

The next step is to assign tax codes to nontaxable transactions. SAP carries out some system movements that are not tax related but that affect tax-related accounts. To allow proper processing of these movements, we need to assign nontaxable tax codes to each company code. The default nontaxable tax codes are I0 and O0. These codes are maintained at a 0 rate in the system. A 0 rate ensures that no taxes will be calculated ($100 \times 0 = 0$). To set the nontaxable tax codes, follow the menu path Financial Accounting ➢ Financial Accounting Global Settings ➢ Taxes on Sales/ Purchases ➢ Posting ➢ Assign Tax Codes for Non-Taxable Transactions.

The fully configured screen appears in Figure 2.44. You almost always want to use I0 and O0 as the settings in this table because this is the intended use of these tax codes (they are nontaxable by definition).

**FIGURE 2.44** The configuration of Extreme Sports's nontaxable codes

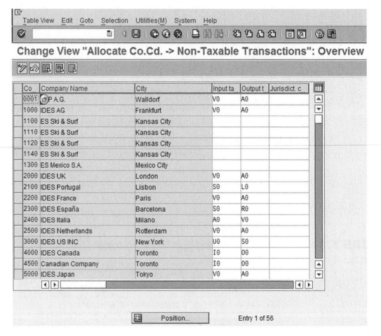

| Co | Company Name | City | Input ta | Output t | Jurisdict. c |
|----|-------------|------|----------|----------|--------------|
| 0001 | P A.G. | Walldorf | V0 | A0 | |
| 1000 | IDES AG | Frankfurt | V0 | A0 | |
| 1100 | ES Ski & Surf | Kansas City | | | |
| 1110 | ES Ski & Surf | Kansas City | | | |
| 1120 | ES Ski & Surf | Kansas City | | | |
| 1140 | ES Ski & Surf | Kansas City | | | |
| 1300 | ES Mexico S.A. | Mexico City | | | |
| 2000 | IDES UK | London | V0 | A0 | |
| 2100 | IDES Portugal | Lisbon | S0 | L0 | |
| 2200 | IDES France | Paris | V0 | A0 | |
| 2300 | IDES España | Barcelona | S0 | R0 | |
| 2400 | IDES Italia | Milano | A0 | V0 | |
| 2500 | IDES Netherlands | Rotterdam | V0 | A0 | |
| 3000 | IDES US INC | New York | U0 | S0 | |
| 4000 | IDES Canada | Toronto | I0 | O0 | |
| 4500 | Canadian Company | Toronto | I0 | O0 | |
| 5000 | IDES Japan | Tokyo | V0 | A0 | |

The only remaining task is to assign G/L accounts for taxes using automatic account assignment. Automatic account assignment will be covered in detail in Chapter 3.

# Summary

This chapter covered the most important information about the Financial Accounting Enterprise Structure. All of the remaining chapters on FI will build upon the elements that were configured in this chapter. A lot of ground was covered, so it may be necessary to revisit some of the sections several times.

# General Ledger

## FEATURING:

▶ CONTINUING WITH THE CHART OF ACCOUNTS

▶ FIELD STATUS GROUPS

▶ POSTING KEYS

▶ AUTOMATIC ACCOUNT DETERMINATION

n this chapter, we'll build upon the base chart of accounts configuration that we started as part of the FI Enterprise Structure in Chapter 2. We'll cover a combination of configuration and master data maintenance. It is important that you understand the master data maintenance explanation because configuration settings affect the available master data options as well as the overall processing of the general ledger (G/L) accounts in the system.

# Continuing with the Chart of Accounts

The base configuration for chart of accounts EXCA was done in Chapter 2. We'll now complete the chart of account configuration to make it functional for the production system. As explained in Chapter 2, it is necessary to go through your existing chart of accounts and reduce the number of accounts to only those that are essential. There is no need to build logic into the account numbers other than to group similar types of accounts by account group. Remember, the G/L is no longer your sole reporting system. We will show you how to utilize the CO module to achieve your controlling/managerial reporting needs. For accounts that require a detailed reconciliation, there are other dimensions such as the allocation field that allow for further categorization of transactions.

## Account Groups

The next step in our chart of accounts configuration is to set up account groups. Account groups determine which fields you can configure on the G/L master record. At the minimum, it is necessary to have at least two account groups, one for balance sheet accounts and one for income statement (Profit and Loss, or P&L) accounts. It is best to have a lot of account groups; of course, the exact number will depend on your business and the overall system design of your project.

Following the menu path Financial Accounting ➤ General Ledger Accounting ➤ G/L Accounts ➤ Master Data ➤ Preparations ➤ Define Account Group, you can define the screen's appearance for account groups. Figure 3.1 shows the account groups that have been configured for chart of accounts EXCA. As you will recall from Chapter 2, when we created the chart, we chose the option to copy the account groups and all automatic account assignments from SAP-delivered examples for the United States. Extreme Sports has added to and changed some of the standard groupings to fit with its implementation. If you want to create new account groups, simply click the New Entries button (shown in the toolbar at the top of Figure 3.1), create an account group identifier, specify the range of accounts that make up the group, and enter a description of the account group.

**FIGURE 3.1**    The account groups for EXCA

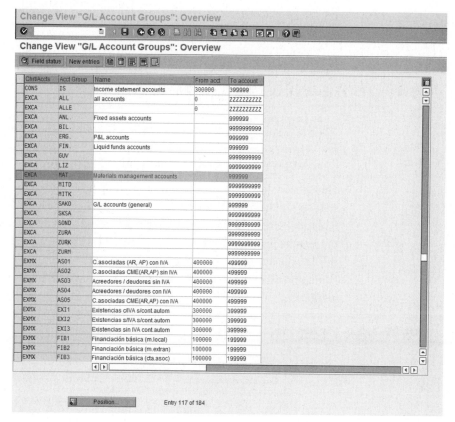

By double-clicking any of the entries in the account group listing, you can configure the field status for the account group. It is important to note that field statuses appear at four different levels in the system:

- ▶ The account group: This will dictate how master data is created.

- ▶ The G/L account: This will dictate what kind of data is required while processing transactions in the general ledger against this account.

- ▶ The posting key: This has an impact on how entries are processed from a debit versus a credit perspective.

- ▶ The activity: Here the system controls what fields are required when using different transactions/activities in the system.

The field status is maintained in different tables and different configuration steps for each of the levels.

This is a very exciting part of FICO configuration because here you can truly see how the system behaves differently, based on the configuration choices we make. Generally, there are four options when dealing with field status:

▶ Required: The system will not permit the transaction/business event to be complete until there is a valid entry in this field.

▶ Optional: An entry is permitted.

▶ Display (not always a status in all four levels): This field can be seen, but no editing is allowed.

▶ Suppressed: The field is not even visible to the end user.

This section deals only with the account group field status; the other types of field statuses will be covered in later sections of this chapter. Figure 3.2 displays the configuration screen for the account group field status. The field status is maintained independently for all account groups. The field status for account groups controls the fields that can be configured in the company code setup of G/L accounts. The configuration of the actual G/L accounts will be covered in greater detail in the next section.

**FIGURE 3.2**     The configuration screen for the account group field status

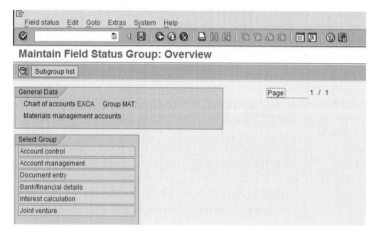

The various fields that can be maintained are grouped into different categories, as you can see in Figure 3.2. The default for all options within the categories is to make the field optional. SAP also provides the ability to make the fields required or suppressed. When dealing with field statuses, the safest thing to do is to keep all fields optional if at all possible; this rule is more important for field statuses at the other levels (the G/L account, the posting key, and the activity). Figure 3.3 displays the Account Control category for the account group Fixed Assets. Because Extreme Sports is not utilizing Application Link Enabling (ALE), it would be safe to suppress the Account Managed in Ext. System field.

**FIGURE 3.3**    The field status screen

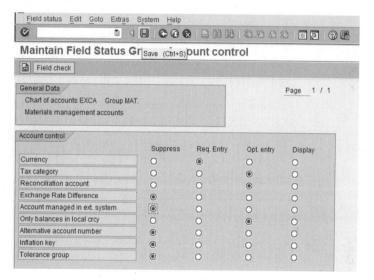

## EXTREME SPORTS ACCOUNT GROUP CONFIGURATION ANALYSIS

Extreme Sports decided to add to and modify the account groups that were copied from the standard chart of accounts (CAUS) when creating the Extreme Sports chart of accounts (EXCA). The account groups will control which fields can be configured for various types of accounts when the company code portion of the G/L accounts is set up. The chart of accounts configuration screen for G/L accounts cannot be modified. The account groups will also be used in the standard G/L reporting delivered with SAP.

# Configuring G/L Account Master Records

Configuring G/L accounts is more like maintenance of master records than true configuration. G/L master data requires you to understand the configuration behind the chart of accounts as well as the system flow of accounting transactions in SAP. You've already taken the necessary configuration steps that allow you to set up a G/L account (in Chapter 2). Setting up the G/L accounts will determine how the G/L accounts act, are reconciled, are reported on, and indirectly how they post in the G/L.

You can set up a G/L account in the system in several ways. You can initially set up a G/L account in the chart of accounts or in the company code. If you initially set up the G/L account in the company code, it is also set up in the chart of accounts automatically. If you initially set up your G/L account in the chart of accounts, it is available only to the chart. A company code will not be able to post to the account until the account is created (extended) in that company code.

As you will recall from Chapter 2, when we created the Extreme Sports chart of accounts (EXCA), we copied it from the SAP-delivered chart of accounts (CAUS). Because EXCA was created by copying, all of the accounts that exist in CAUS are already set up at the chart of accounts level in EXCA. Before creating the G/L accounts, let's view a G/L account at the chart of accounts level in order to better understand the configuration that has occurred up to this point.

You can get to the display screen of the chart of accounts by using the application menu path (not IMG) Accounting ➢ Financial Accounting ➢ General Ledger ➢ Master Records ➢ G/L Accounts ➢ Individual Processing ➢ In Chart of Accounts ➢ Display or by using transaction code FSP0. Follow the menu to get to the display screen for the chart of accounts, shown in Figure 3.4. In this screen, enter the G/L account (790000). The chart of accounts (EXCA) defaults into the transaction based on the company code.

After entering the G/L account to be analyzed, you are presented with the screen that shows the effect of the relationship you just created.

As you can see, the chart of accounts determines a lot of the overriding information for the account. Specifically, this screen is where you give the G/L account a textual name, define whether it is a balance sheet or an income statement account, assign the account group that it belongs to, select the sample account (an optional entry), and enter consolidation information if you are using SAP consolidation functions.

**FIGURE 3.4**     The chart of accounts display screen

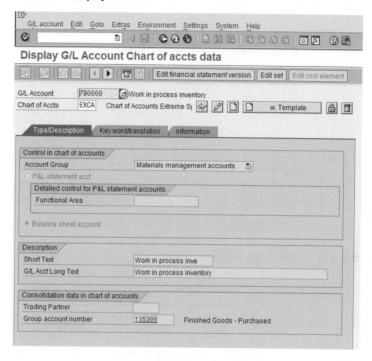

When you set an account as an income statement account, you must choose a variant that determines the retained earnings account that it rolls to. The configuration of the retained earnings account will be shown in the next configuration step. Note the account group that is displayed in Figure 3.4 (Materials Management accounts). This account group has several of its fields set to suppressed. This means that when the account is set up at the company code level, those fields will be unavailable for entry. In this example Trading Partner is an optional entry. SAP has new functionality that allows you to use a previously created account to act as a template. All you have to do is use the w. Template button at the top of the page and all the data will automatically be copied in.

## Retained Earnings

SAP gives you the flexibility to utilize multiple retained earnings accounts (each P&L G/L account will be assigned to only one retained earnings account). Because of this, you are required to enter a variant specifying which retained earnings account to use when you specify an account as an income statement account. Let's try it.

You can use the following method path to get to the define retained earnings account screen: Financial Accounting ➢ General Ledger Accounting ➢ G/L Accounts ➢ Master Data ➢ Preparations ➢ Define Retained Earnings Account. Or you can use transaction code OB53.

This configuration screen is relatively simple. All you have to do is create a variant ID and specify which account belongs to the variant. As you can see in Figure 3.5, this screen utilizes a process key of BIL (Balance Carried Forward). Any account configuration screen that utilizes processes is really a case of automatic account assignment. If you press the F1 key while you're in the account field and then click the Technical Information icon, SAP will tell you that it is Table T030 (not displayed in Figure 3.5), which is a giveaway that what we are dealing with automatic account assignment. Automatic account assignment will be covered in detail in the later section "Automatic Account Determination."

**FIGURE 3.5**    The retained earnings configuration screen

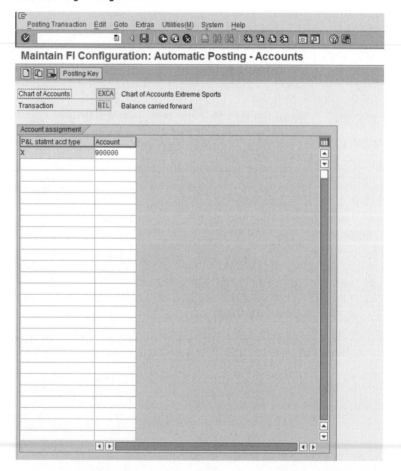

**EXTREME SPORTS RETAINED EARNINGS CONFIGURATION ANALYSIS**

Extreme Sports requires a retained earnings account for financial reporting purposes. Because of this requirement, P&L accounts will point to account 900000. When you create an income statement (P&L) account, you are effectively summarizing all of these entries to the G/L account 900000.

## Creating G/L Accounts

Now that the entire prerequisite configuration has been completed, you are ready to create the G/L accounts for your company codes. In this example, an account that already exists in the chart will be created for the company code; therefore, only the company code configuration screen will be displayed, as you can see in Figure 3.6. The chart of accounts configuration screen was presented earlier (in Chapter 2). If you create in the company code an account that doesn't exist in the chart of accounts, you will be presented with the chart of accounts screen before being allowed to configure the company code screen. The entry point for both configuration screens is the G/L account master records creation screen.

**FIGURE 3.6**     The edit G/L account company code data

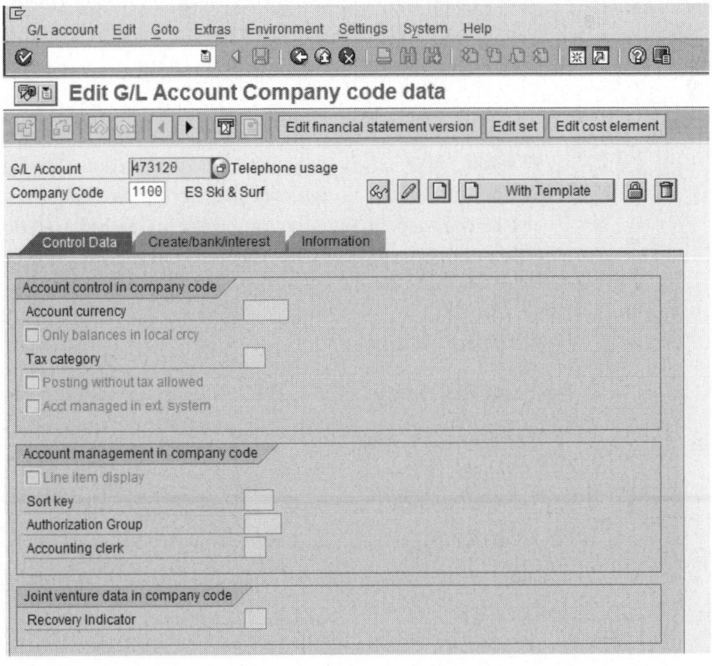

You can use the following menu path to get to the G/L account master records creation screen: Application Menu Path (not IMG): Accounting ➤ Financial Accounting ➤ General Ledger ➤ Master Records ➤ G/L Accounts ➤ Individual Processing ➤ In Company Code. You can also use the transaction code FSS0.

SAP defaults to the edit screen in Figure 3.6, with the assumption that the account already exists. This is one of the few transaction codes where the user can create, change, and display the master record/data. To create a new G/L account, you have to click the create icon on the upper-right side of the screen. On the G/L account master records creation screen, enter G/L account 473120 and company code 1100 in the appropriate fields to proceed through our example (G/L account 473120 is delivered with CAUS, and company code 1100 relates to Extreme Sports).

If the G/L account you are creating already exists in another company code, you can reference that G/L account and company code in the fields in the reference section of the screen and all the settings will be copied from the reference account. After entering the account number and company code and pressing Enter, you are presented with the G/L company code configuration screen, shown in Figure 3.7 (the screen has been configured for Extreme Sports). It is important to note that the chart of accounts G/L configuration screen (not shown) is valid for all company codes that use that account in the chart. If this screen is changed, the chart of accounts configuration is changed for all company codes. If someone creating the G/L account does not understand this concept, it can lead to problems, such as a company code changing the description of the account for all other company codes. The G/L company code configuration screen can be different for each company code that is using the same chart of accounts.

**WARNING**   If you change the chart of accounts configuration when you're configuring the G/L account's company code, all company codes that use the chart of accounts will also be changed, further illustrating the hierarchical relationship of the chart of accounts data and how it controls what is possible at the company code level.

Here are the options:

**Account Currency**   Enter the currency in which the account should be managed. You should almost always use the company code currency. By doing so, you can post entries in any currency in the account. If you use anything other than the company code currency, you can only post in the currency that is specified in your entry. Make sure you have all the requirements for the account before setting up this entry because it is difficult to change this setting after the account has been posted to the general ledger.

**FIGURE 3.7**     Create G/L account company code—Control Data

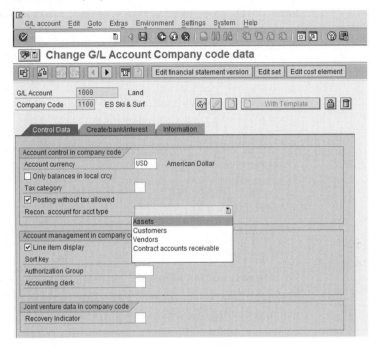

**Only Balances in Local Crcy**   Set this indicator only if you want the balances in the account to be updated in the local currency. This indicator affects how clearing will work in this account if it is to be managed on an open item basis. *Open item basis* means that you want to view all individual line items that make up the balance of the account and clear individual line items with offsetting line items so that you can view both open and cleared line items. Open item management is a further reconciliation function. This indicator should usually be set for clearing accounts. If the account is not managed on the open item basis, this indicator is not needed. You must activate this indicator on your GR/IR account in order to allow Goods Receipts transactions to post correctly.

**Exchange Rate Difference Key (suppressed in Figure 3.7)**   This key determines which account valuation gains or losses are posted to for the account you are configuring. This indicator is typically set only for accounts that are not managed on an open item basis and are kept in a foreign currency instead of the local currency. The exchange rate difference key is configured in table T030S.

**Tax Category**    This indicator controls what types of taxes can be posted to with this account. The possible entries based on the standard tax categories in the system are as follows:

-    -    Indicates that only input tax postings are allowed with this account. Input taxes are sales and use taxes paid by the company.

-    +    Denotes that only output tax postings are allowed with this account. Output taxes are sales taxes charged by the company to its customers.

-    *    Specifies that both input and output tax postings are allowed with this account.

-    <    Signifies input taxes on a tax account. This symbol should be used only for tax accounts.

-    >    Signifies output taxes on a tax account. This symbol should be used only for tax accounts.

**Posting without Tax Allowed**    Set this indicator to allow both taxable and non-taxable postings to this account. If you specify a tax category in the earlier field without selecting this indicator, you will not be able to post nontaxable items (without a nontaxable tax category indicator) to this account. Refer back to "Sales and Use Tax" in Chapter 2 for more details.

**Recon. Acct for Acct Type**    This field denotes that the G/L account being created is a reconciliation account for one of the subledgers. The available selections for this field are listed here:

**Assets**    Select this indicator if you are setting up a reconciliation account for the Fixed Assets subledger.

**Customers**    Select this indicator if you are setting up a reconciliation account for the Customer subledger.

**Vendors**    Select this indicator if you are setting up a reconciliation account for the Vendor sub ledger.

**Contract accounts receivable**    This is a reconciliation ledger used for large transaction volumes in both vendor or customer transactions.

**Alternative Account No. (suppressed in Figure 3.7)**    The alternative account number is used when you are using a country chart of accounts for the company code in addition to the regular chart. Enter the account number of the G/L account in the country chart of accounts.

**Acct Managed In Ext. System (suppressed in Figure 3.7)**   Select this indicator if you are utilizing ALE on your project and want the account managed in one of the other instances.

**Open Item Management (suppressed in Figure 3.7)**   Select this box if you want to manage the account with open item management. Open item basis means that you want to view all individual line items that make up the balance of the account and clear individual line items with offsetting line items so that you can view both open and cleared line items. Open item management is a further reconciliation function. Open item management allows you to display the open and cleared items and amounts in an account. Open item management should be used if an offsetting entry is made for every line item posted in the account (the account is reconciled and cleared against another account). A good example for the use of open item management is for clearing accounts such as the GR/IR account. It is generally used in balance sheet accounts.

**Line Item Display**   Select this box if you want to be able to see account balances by individual postings to the account. Be careful not to set this indicator on accounts with a very large number of postings. If you selected the Open Item Management indicator, this indicator should also be set. However, setting this indicator does not require that you also make the account open item managed.

Remember, if you do *not* select this, you will *not* be able to perform any drill-down analysis of the actual financial postings/documents that make up the balance in an account.

**Sort Key**   The sort key determines what is populated in the Allocation field of the G/L line item posting for the account. The system uses the Allocation field to sort postings when displaying the line items of the account. The Allocation field is populated automatically by the system with information from either the document header or line item, or it can be populated manually by the user at the time of document entry. The Allocation field can also be used as a tool to help in the reconciliation process.

**Authorization Group**   If you want to limit who can make master data changes to this account, populate this field with the authorization group that is needed to change the account. The authorization group is tied to authorization objects, which are tied to user profiles in the system. You should work closely with your Basis team in setting up authorization groups and profiles.

**Accounting Clerk**   In this field, you can enter the identifier to assign the accounting clerk who will reconcile this account. For example, this might be used to report who is to reconcile certain accounts.

As you can see in Figure 3.8 on tab Create/bank/interest, field status group G001 General (with text, allocation) is being displayed. Here's a quick explanation of the fields that appear on the G/L company code configuration screen:

**Field Status Group**   As you can see from the screen, the field status group G001 has defaulted. The field status group controls the account assignments that are made to the account. Specifically, the field status group controls whether postings to cost centers, internal orders, profitability segments, and so on are required, not allowed (suppressed), or optional. The configuration of field status groups will be covered later in this chapter.

**Post Automatically Only**   Select this indicator if you do not want users posting manually to this account. When the indicator is selected, only the system can post to this account based on configuration in the account assignment tables. This indicator is normally set on inventory accounts, material variance accounts, and such. Once it is set and postings have been made to the account, be careful about deselecting this indicator. If you deselect it on your inventory accounts, it could cause your G/L account to become out of balance with the material ledger.

**Supplement auto. postings**   With this indicator selected, you can manually update the account assignments (cost centers, internal orders, and so on) for line items that are generated automatically by the system. The field status group on the account will determine what account assignments can be updated manually.

**Rec. Acct. Ready for Input (suppressed in Figure 3.8)**   This field indicates that the reconciliation account is ready for posting when you're creating a document. This indicator is used primarily for Fixed Asset reconciliation accounts.

Figure 3.8 displays the rest of the G/L company code configuration screen. The fields are used mostly for G/L cash accounts. Let's take a look at the fields on this screen.

**Planning Level**   The Planning Level indicator is used in displaying the cash management position in the Treasury submodule. Planning levels denote such things as outgoing payments, incoming payments, and outgoing wires. Planning levels will be covered in more detail in Chapter 6, "Financial Supply Chain Management."

**Relevant to Cash Flow (suppressed in Figure 3.8)**   This indicator tells the system that the account affects cash flow (receives incoming payments or sends outgoing payments, for example).

**House Bank (suppressed in Figure 3.8)**   If you are creating G/L accounts for a bank account, select the house bank that the G/L account belongs to in this field. House banks will be covered in more detail in Chapter 4, "Accounts Payable."

**FIGURE 3.8**    Account creation—Create/Bank/Interest tab

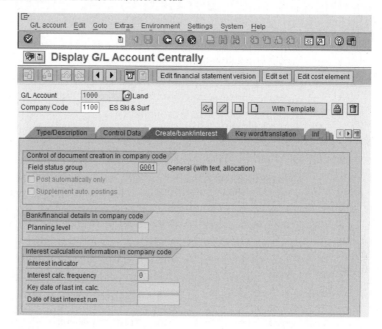

**Bank Account (suppressed in Figure 3.8)**    If you selected a house bank in the preceding field, select the account ID for the house bank that this G/L account belongs to.

**Interest indicator**    If you want to calculate interest on the G/L account (on bank accounts, for instance), select the indicator ID for the interest calculation procedure you want to use.

## EXTREME SPORTS G/L COMPANY CODE CONFIGURATION ANALYSIS

Because G/L account 1000 is a Fixed Assets account, it is not applicable for taxes. That's why the Posting without Tax Allowed indicator has been set. This setting is for a kind of safety measure because this account may not be exclusively posted to with an A/P transaction. The accounting clerk in charge of this account needs to see all of the individual line items that make up this account. Because the number of postings should not be large, the Line Item Display indicator was chosen. The account will be using the posting date as the sort key to aid transaction analysis.

# Copying and Transporting G/L Accounts

As you read in the preceding section, G/L accounts are set up at the chart and company code level. If your company uses a central account management with a single chart of accounts, it is easy to copy and "sync" up G/L accounts across company codes.

Before trying to transport G/L accounts across clients, you must first transport the chart of accounts. The chart of accounts does not automatically record a transport. To transport the chart of accounts, follow the menu path Financial Accounting ➤ General Ledger Accounting ➤ G/L Accounts ➤ Master Data ➤ Transport Chart of Accounts.

When you're creating an account in the company code, it is also possible to reference another account in another company code. Refer to the discussion about Figure 3.8 for more information. If you enter a reference to a G/L account number but you enter a company code that is different than the company code for which the G/L account was created, all entries are copied over to the new company code.

The easiest and quickest way to transfer G/L accounts is to do so while creating your initial company code. When creating your first company code, copy the SAP-delivered company code for the country in which your company is located. You are then given the option to copy all G/L accounts and automatic account assignments. This will give you a good head start. From here you can modify the accounts to meet your needs. After modifying all of the accounts, create the rest of your company codes by copying your first company code. You can copy the company code by following the menu path Financial Accounting ➤ General Ledger Accounting ➤ G/L Accounts ➤ Master Data ➤ G/L Account Creation and Processing ➤ Alternative Methods ➤ Copy G/L Accounts ➤ Copy Company Code. This configuration path can also be used after your company code has been created (if it did not reference another company code) to copy G/L accounts from one company code to another.

SAP delivers two standard programs (RFBISA10 and RFBISA20) for copying G/L accounts between company codes and to "sync" up G/L accounts among clients. A lot of projects allow G/L accounts to be set up directly in production because G/L accounts are master data and not configuration data. If your project does this, be very careful; it is easy to miss settings that differ from client to client. Alternatively, you can set up all G/L accounts in your configuration client and use standard SAP programs to copy the G/L accounts across clients and environments.

The programs RFBISA10 and RFBISA20 appear in the application menu path. The programs can be accessed in the user (application) menu via the following path: Accounting ➤ Financial Accounting ➤ General Ledger ➤ Master Records ➤ G/L Accounts ➤ Compare Company Code ➤ Send (RFBISA10) or Receive (RFBISA20). You can also execute the programs via transaction code SE38 or SA38. The transaction codes SE38 and SA38 allow you to execute ABAP programs. Transaction code SE38 allows you to display the items such as source code, documentation, and variants as well as execute the program. Transaction code SA38 only allows you to execute a program. The example screens in this section will utilize transaction code SA38. Figure 3.9 shows you the program RFBISA10 entered in the program field in transaction code SA38.

**FIGURE 3.9**    Transaction code SA38 allows you to execute a program by entering a program name in the available field.

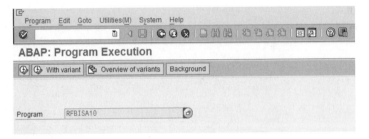

Program RFBISA10 allows you to copy G/L accounts from one company code to another within a client or to create a sequential file that can be uploaded into other clients via the program RFBISA20.

After entering RFBISA10 (to copy a G/L account) in the input box and clicking the execute icon, you are presented with the data entry screen.

The data entry screen gives you many options. You must first decide the range of G/L accounts that you want to transfer as well as the company code in which those G/L accounts reside. You have the option to transfer master data, block indicators, delete flags, or any combination of these. The program does not automatically transfer the data; it creates a batch input session that must be processed. The default for the batch session name is RFBISA10. You can change the name of the session if you so desire as long as it fits in the field length. Then you must decide if you want to transfer the data to company codes within your client or if you want to transfer the data to other clients. To transfer the data to other company codes in the same client, enter the target company codes in the Transfer Data Directly section. To transfer the data to other clients, enter the filename of the sequential file for the program to write to and make sure there is no data in the Transfer Data Directly section. Figure 3.10 displays the screen and shows the parameters needed to transfer data within the client. After the program runs, you must process the batch input session via transaction code SM35.

**FIGURE 3.10**    The transfer information has been set using the RFBISA10 program.

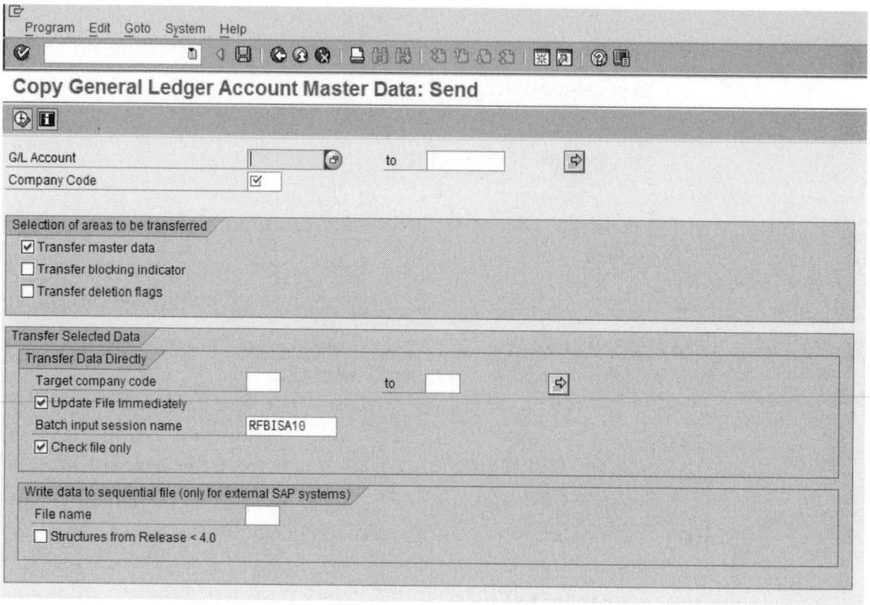

The sequential file is written to the application server of the client. When you want to send the G/L accounts to clients in other environments, someone on your Basis team must transfer the file to the proper path on the application server for that environment.

After creating the file, you must run program RFBISA20 in the client into which you are transferring the G/L accounts. The screen in Figure 3.11 illustrates what the entry fields look like for program RFBISA20, executed via using transaction code SA38.

On the RFBISA20 input screen, enter the name of the file that you created when you ran program RFBISA10 in the source client. The next step is to enter the company codes that you would like to update in the target client. You must deselect the Check File Only box in order for the program to update. Much like program RFBISA10, program RFBISA20 does not directly update the records but instead creates a batch input session that must be processed using transaction code SM35.

**FIGURE 3.11**    The input screen for RFBISA20

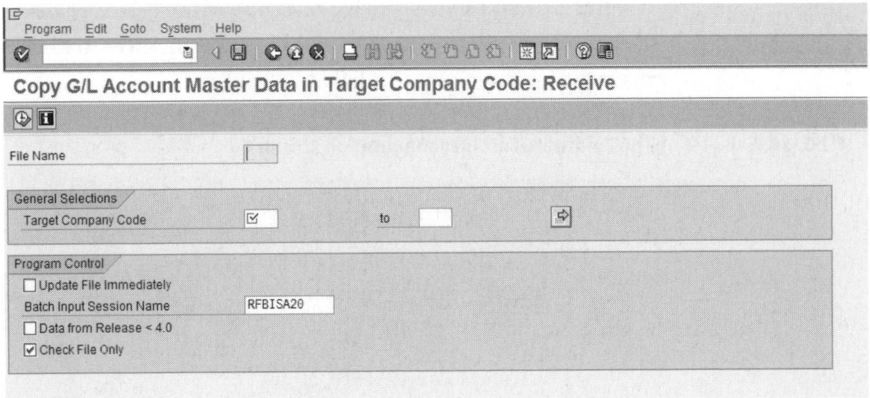

# Field Status Groups

*Field status groups* control the additional account assignments and other fields that can be posted at the line item level for a G/L account. It is important to remember that the field status of your account must mesh with the field status group of the posting key and/or Materials Management (MM) movement types. A common posting error occurs when a field in the G/L field status group is required and the same field in the MM movement type field status group is suppressed. It is a good idea to keep as many fields as possible optional and make only the most important fields required or suppressed. This kind of "control" will go a long way toward ensuring smooth postings in the system.

You'll recall from Chapter 2 that field status variants are assigned to company codes. Field status groups are assigned to field status variants. Field status variant 0001 is delivered with the system along with several standard field status groups. You can find a listing of these by following the configuration transaction shown in the Define Field Status Groups shortcut box. It is wise not to change the delivered field status groups but rather to copy the groups and make changes in your version. This way, you'll have a reference of how the groups originated. Alternatively (and probably best), you can copy the delivered field status variant and make changes to the field status groups in your new variant. This way, you do not have to reassign the field status groups in the G/L accounts. The menu path Financial Accounting ➢ Financial Accounting Global Settings ➢ Document ➢ Line Item ➢ Controls ➢ Define Field Status Variants will get you to the right screen for configuring field status groups.

Figure 3.12 displays all the field status variants that are already available in the system. Extreme Sports will make a copy of the delivered field status variant 0001. This copy will allow Extreme Sports to make changes to the field status groups and maintain a reference of the delivered field status groups in the delivered variant.

**FIGURE 3.12**    The field status group configuration screen

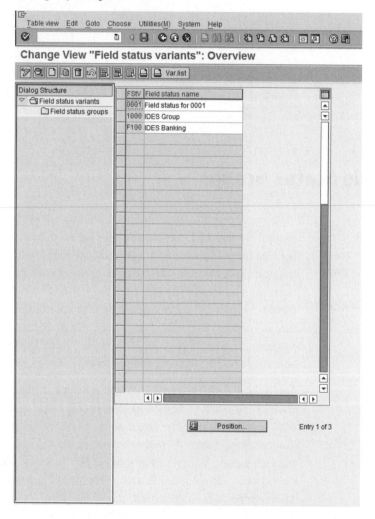

To create the new variant, select the entry for variant 0001 and click the Copy as… button. Then you will need to name your new variant and give it a description. After naming the variant, hit Enter; you will be presented with a pop-up box asking you if you want to copy the dependent entries. Select the Copy All button to copy the field status groups along with the variant. Once this step has been completed, you will be presented with the configuration screen as seen in Figure 3.13.

**FIGURE 3.13**    The configured variant screen

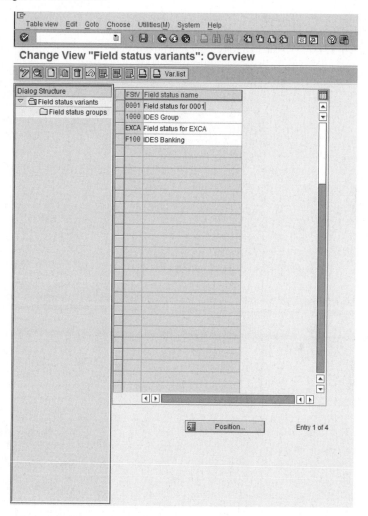

As discussed in Chapter 2, all of Extreme Sports's company codes are assigned to field status variant 0001. You will need to go back to the company code configuration screen and reassign the company codes to field status variant EXCA. Next, you will need to select the entry for variant EXCA on the screen in Figure 3.13. Then, select your field status group and double-click Field Status Groups. After doing this, you are presented with the screen shown in Figure 3.14. This screen displays all of the field status groups that belong to that particular field status variant. Select field status group G004. You will remember field status group G001 from the previous section on setting up G/L accounts. After selecting the field status group, you can either double-click the entry or click the Edit Field Status button. The screen in Figure 3.15 then appears.

**FIGURE 3.14**   The field status groups that belong to the field status variant EXCA

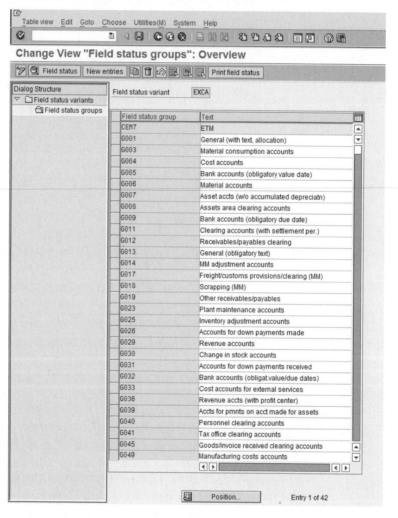

FIGURE 3.15    **FIGURE 3.15**    The field status variants in EXCA for field status group G004

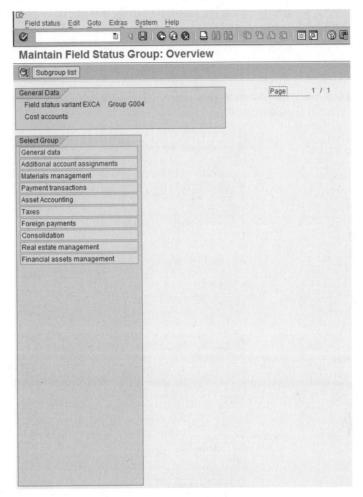

The individual fields are bound together in the groupings, as displayed in Figure 3.15. The highlighted groupings (*General Data* and *Additional Account Assignments* are shown in a different color text) represent groupings that have fields set to something other than optional. This highlight is used to point out the optional settings of groupings required for the transactions that SAP intended to be used with the group. After double-clicking the Additional Account Assignments group, you are presented with the screen for selecting the status of each individual field.

As you can see from Figure 3.16, you can choose to suppress each individual field (not available for posting) or make it required or optional. Your safest bet is not modifying the field status group at all, and the next best thing is to keep all fields optional. Extreme Sports wants to ensure that postings go to a business area, so the Business Area field will be changed to required.

**FIGURE 3.16**    The G004 field status modification screen for Extreme Sports shows Business Area as a required field.

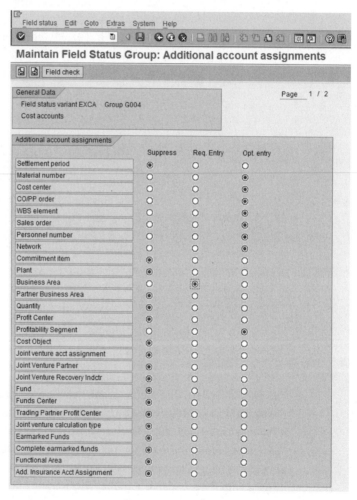

**EXTREME SPORTS FIELD STATUS GROUP CONFIGURATION ANALYSIS**

Extreme Sports has decided to copy the standard field status variant 0001 and create field status variant EXCA. All of Extreme Sports's company codes will be changed to point to the new field status variant. In the example presented, field status group G004 was modified because the accounting department at Extreme Sports wants to ensure that all postings receive a business area assignment. Because the business area balance sheet will be used to analyze capital requirements of the different business lines, the Business Area field was changed to *required*. This change will involve careful testing with Materials Management transactions (such as material price changes and inventory variances) that post to cost accounts to ensure that it does not adversely affect processing.

# Posting Key Configuration

*Posting keys* determine whether a line item entry is a debit or a credit as well as the possible field status for the transaction. Modifying the SAP-delivered posting keys is not recommended. You may be able to get by with some changes, such as making additional fields optional on payment-type posting keys, without adversely affecting the system. If a change to a posting key is required, the best possible action is to copy the posting key that needs to be modified and then modify the copy. With these rules in mind, the configuration steps for posting keys are presented here.

You can use the following menu path to get to the posting key configuration screen: Financial Accounting ➢ Financial Accounting Global Settings ➢ Document ➢ Line Item ➢ Controls ➢ Define Posting Keys.

Figure 3.17 displays all of the posting keys that are configured in the system. The screen reveals the posting key number, description, whether it is a credit or a debit, and the type of account that the posting key is used for (G/L, Customer, Assets, Vendor, and Material). To explain the configuration settings, we will create a posting key that is a copy of posting key 40 with modifications to the field status group. Posting keys 40 and 50 are the most commonly used posting keys in financial journal entry postings.

**FIGURE 3.17** This screen, define posting keys, displays all the available posting keys in the system.

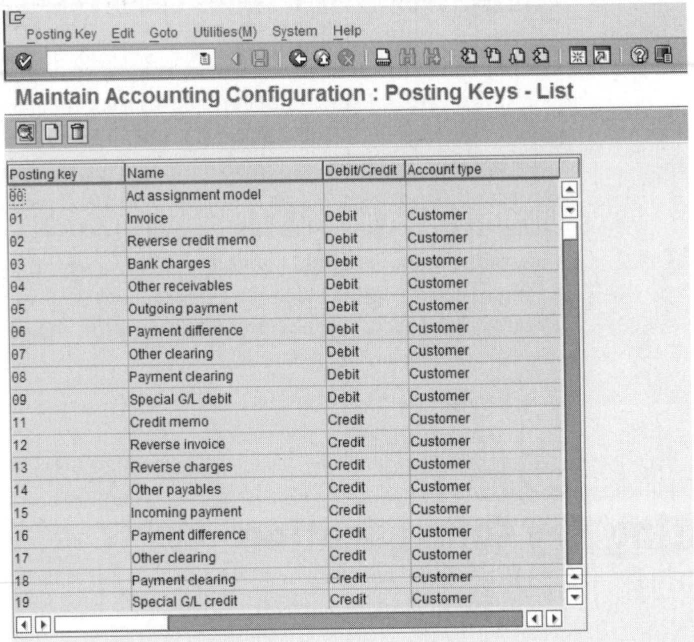


| Posting key | Name | Debit/Credit | Account type |
|---|---|---|---|
| 00 | Act assignment model | | |
| 01 | Invoice | Debit | Customer |
| 02 | Reverse credit memo | Debit | Customer |
| 03 | Bank charges | Debit | Customer |
| 04 | Other receivables | Debit | Customer |
| 05 | Outgoing payment | Debit | Customer |
| 06 | Payment difference | Debit | Customer |
| 07 | Other clearing | Debit | Customer |
| 08 | Payment clearing | Debit | Customer |
| 09 | Special G/L debit | Debit | Customer |
| 11 | Credit memo | Credit | Customer |
| 12 | Reverse invoice | Credit | Customer |
| 13 | Reverse charges | Credit | Customer |
| 14 | Other payables | Credit | Customer |
| 15 | Incoming payment | Credit | Customer |
| 16 | Payment difference | Credit | Customer |
| 17 | Other clearing | Credit | Customer |
| 18 | Payment clearing | Credit | Customer |
| 19 | Special G/L credit | Credit | Customer |

To create the copy of posting key 40 (the posting key most frequently used in journal entries as a debit entry), click the create icon on the toolbar. You are then presented with the pop-up box.

In the pop-up box, enter the ID for your posting key; the entry is alphanumeric. Then enter a description and press the Enter key. The configuration screen, shown in Figure 3.18, appears.

It is important to realize that you are not copying identical data but creating a new posting key. Therefore, you will need to fill in by hand the fields that need to be configured for posting key Z1. You must decide whether your posting key is for a debit or a credit. The next decision you must make is what type of account you'll be using with the posting key (Customer, Vendor, G/L, Assets, or Material). The other properties are as follows:

**Sales-Related** Select this indicator if the posting key is used when invoicing a customer.

**Special G/L** Choose this indicator if the posting key is used for special G/L transactions such as down payments. With this indicator selected, a valid special G/L indicator must be entered on the line item when a user is posting with this key.

**FIGURE 3.18**    The pop-up box to create posting key Z1 like posting 40

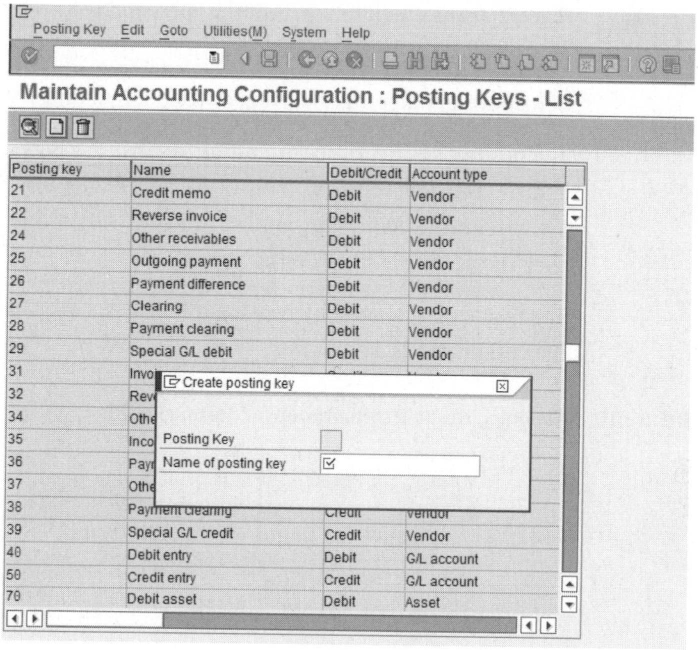

**FIGURE 3.19**    The fully configured posting key detail for Z1

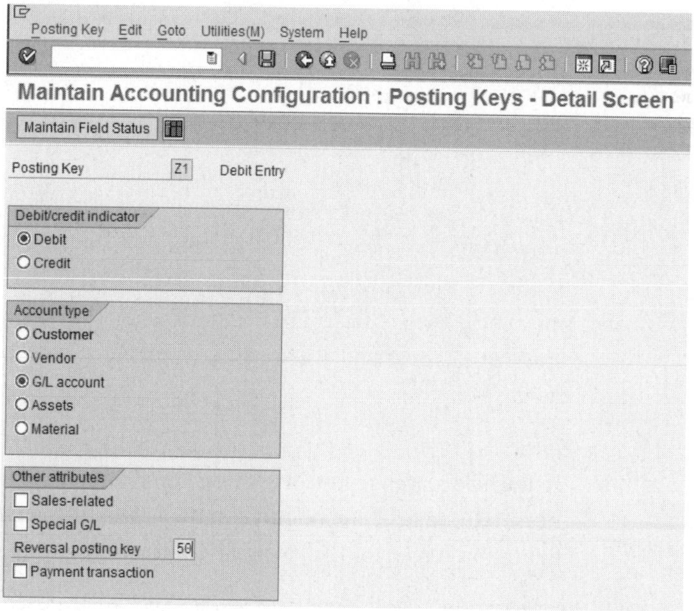

**Reversal Posting Key**   Select the ID of the posting key that will be used on the reversal transaction to back out the entry made by the current posting key.

**Payment Transaction**   Pick this indicator if the posting key is used for any type of incoming, outgoing, clearing, or residual postings of payments.

The posting key detail configuration settings are now the same for posting keys 40 and Z1. The next step is to modify the field status in posting key Z1 so that it's different than the field status in posting key 40. To configure the field status group, click the Maintain Field Status button.

The resulting screen, shown in Figure 3.20, is a display of the various categories for the various fields' field status.

**FIGURE 3.20**   Assigning the field status group for posting key Z1

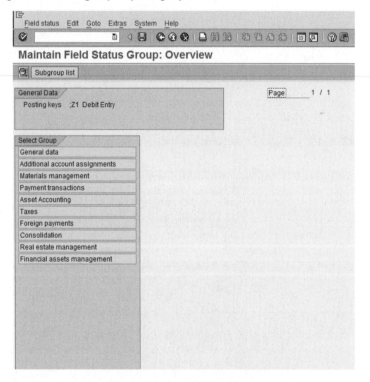

In the field status group for posting key 40, the Reason Code field is suppressed. The Reason Code field is configured in the Payment Transactions grouping. The configuration screen for the Payment Transactions group is displayed in Figure 3.21.

**FIGURE 3.21**    The Payment Transactions group configuration

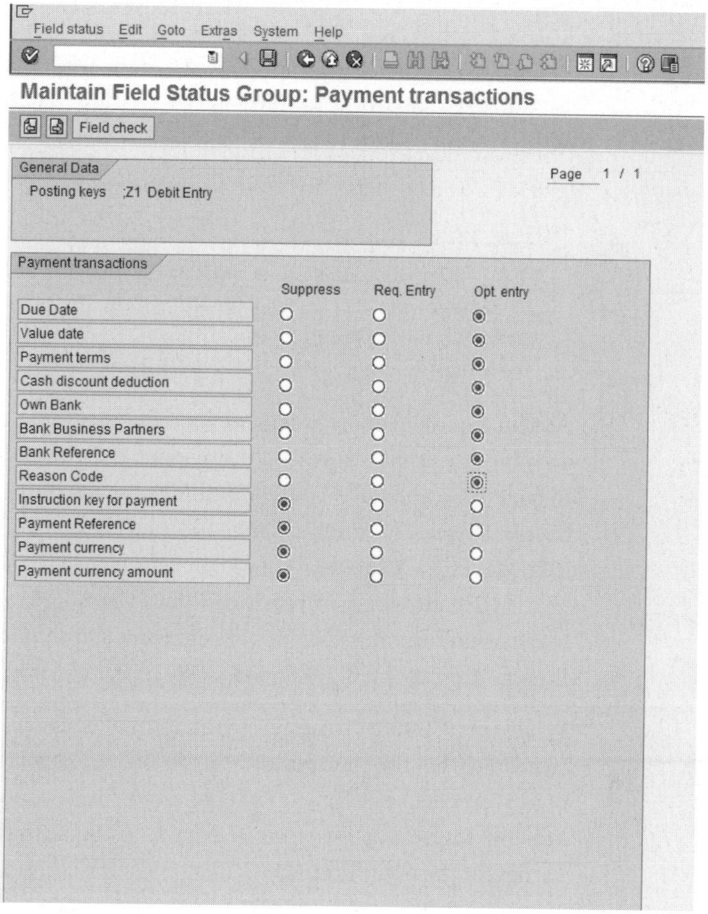

For now, the only change you will make is to click the Opt. Entry radio button for the Reason Code field.

## EXTREME SPORTS POSTING KEY CONFIGURATION ANALYSIS

Extreme Sports would like to be able to enter a reason code on a regular debit transaction. To accomplish this with the least risk for adverse system impact, a copy of the standard debit posting key 40 was made. For the new posting key Z1, the field status was changed to make reason code an optional entry.

# Automatic Account Determination

*Automatic account determination* is one of the most powerful tools in SAP. It allows the system to determine the correct G/L account to post to by considering the type of transaction and other factors. This feature provides a lot of flexibility and eliminates the need to hard-code the G/L account in source code.

> **TIP**  Automatic account determination is also known as both *automatic posting* and *automatic account assignment* in the SAP system. We will use these terms interchangeably throughout this book.

As stated in the section "Retained Earnings" earlier in this chapter, all automatic account determination (with the exception of Sales and Distribution) is configured in table T030 and table T001U (for intercompany postings). Table T030 is split into different objects for the various application areas and processing keys. Each object is known as *XXXYY* when viewed on your transport, where *XXX* represents the chart of accounts and *YY* represents the processing key. The processing keys used to determine automatic account assignment are supplied via standard SAP transactions and are updated in BSEG-KTOSL on each FI posting in the system.

When you're transporting automatic account determinations, it is important to remember that the transport is a whole table transport for that account assignment object (process key). For example, when you make an additional entry to processing key GBB (Offsetting Entry for Inventory Postings), the transport copies all of the entries for the processing key GBB, not just the additional entry that you make.

Whole table transport can become problematic in a multiple-project environment or when your system goes into maintenance mode because it allows someone with an older transport to overwrite changes made by someone with a newer transport. This situation can happen when Consultant X creates and releases a transport on June 15 and Consultant Y then creates and releases a transport on July 22. Consultants Y's transport moves immediately into the production environment on July 22 to fix a production problem. On July 30, Consultant X's transport moves out of the QA environment into production, overwriting all of the configuration that was included in Consultant Y's transport. As you can see, it is very important to have tight control over automatic account assignment in order to avoid problems.

The configuration of automatic account determination is located at various places throughout the IMG to correspond with the application area of the automatic account determination. There is a shortcut transaction code, FBKP, which allows you to configure all automatic account assignments from the same screen. There is no menu path to get to this screen.

Figure 3.22 displays the configuration screen that is presented from the transaction code listed in the shortcut box. Please note that there are additional areas that can be maintained. To get to the automatic account determination area, you will first need to select Automatic Postings. There are two pages of account determinations; they will appear on the screen after you page down. In the following sections, we will cover how automatic account determinations are configured. We will cover several examples of places in the system that require automatic account determination, but not all of them, because it's beyond the scope of this book. In the remaining chapters, we will cover some of the most important automatic account determinations that relate to the topic of the chapter. Because not all automatic account determinations will be explained in this book, it is important to review the IMG for the areas that you are configuring to look for the places that need automatic account assignment. If you miss an automatic account assignment and attempt to execute a business transaction, the system will issue you an error message telling you what processing key needs to be maintained. So, it's pretty easy to catch all of them.

**FIGURE 3.22**    The configuration screen for accounting configuration

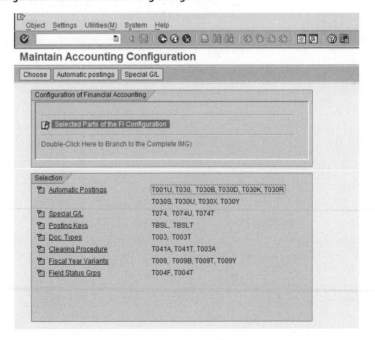

## Sales/Use Tax Automatic Account Assignment

As you can see in Figure 3.23, automatic account determination takes place in many areas throughout the system. The first area we'll cover is taxes, which is where we left off in Chapter 2. The tax accounts can be configured by double-clicking the tax group on the screen shown in Figure 3.23 (you'll need to page down to see it) or by following the menu path Financial Accounting ➢ Financial Accounting Global Settings ➢ Tax on Sales/Purchases ➢ Posting ➢ Define Tax Accounts.

**FIGURE 3.23**    The automatic account determination configuration screen

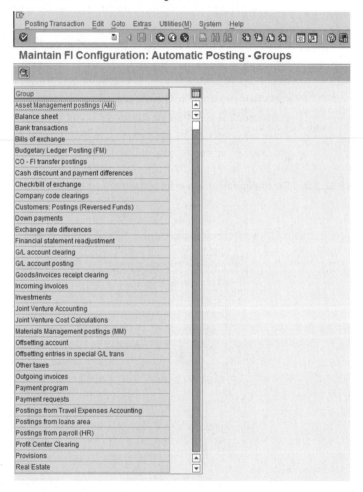

You can use the following menu path to access the define tax accounts configuration screen: Financial Accounting ➢ Financial Accounting Global Settings ➢ Tax on Sales/Purchases ➢ Posting ➢ Define Tax Accounts. You can also use transaction code OB40.

As you can see in Figure 3.24, the account determinations are separated via processing keys that the system uses for different transactions. We will use processing key MW1 as our example of tax automatic account determination.

**FIGURE 3.24**    The account determinations are separated by processing keys for various transactions.

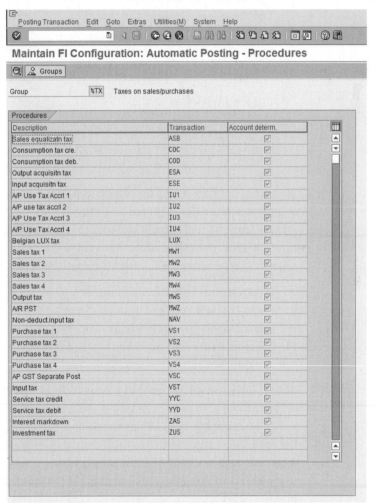

The main use of processing key MW1 is for sales tax that you charge to your customers on invoices. To begin configuring, double-click the processing key MW1. You will be presented with a pop-up box asking which chart of accounts you would like to use. After entering the appropriate chart of accounts (EXCA), you are presented with a screen like the one shown in Figure 3.25. You will then need to click the Rules button to get to the rules screen.

**FIGURE 3.25**   The rules configuration screen for MW1

The screen in Figure 3.25 is the rules screen. The rules define at which level the account determination takes place. For tax accounts, the rules can be defined at two possible levels: the debit/credit level and the tax code level. It is important to think carefully about the level at which you want to set your rules because once they are set, they cannot be changed unless all account determinations are first erased.

As you can see, the Debit/Credit indicator is grayed out, so it cannot be maintained for this process key. You are able to set the tax code level, which you will do for this example to provide greater flexibility. Once you set this indicator, you should select the save icon to save your rules. You are then presented with the account determination assignment screen, shown in Figure 3.26.

This is where you will assign your account determinations. As you can see, you are required to fill in the Tax Code field as well as the G/L Acct field. This is because you set up the rule for this process key to use tax codes when you the account rules in the preceding section. In this example for Extreme Sports, the tax codes I0 (for A/R sales tax) and U1 (amongst others) for use tax are configured to accrue liabilities to separate accounts. (This configuration for Extreme Sports was shown earlier in Figure 3.26.)

**FIGURE 3.26**    The account determination assignments for Extreme Sports

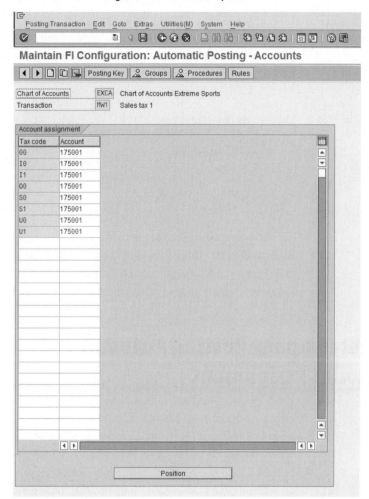

The final step for configuring this processing key is to configure the posting keys that will be used when processing this type of transaction. To do so, click the Posting Key button from either the rules screen or in the G/L account assignment screen. You are then presented with the screen for assigning debit or credit to your assigned posting key (shown earlier in Figure 3.27).

**FIGURE 3.27** The posting key needs to have its Debit and Credit settings assigned.

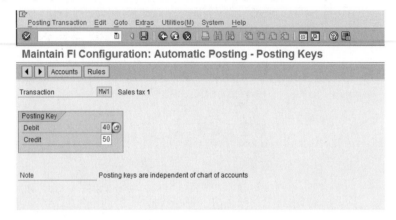

It is important to be aware of the note that the posting keys are independent of the chart of accounts. This means that, if your SAP solution includes more than one chart of accounts, the debit and credit posting keys set here will be valid for all charts of accounts. Extreme Sports will use the standard posting keys 40 (debit) and 50 (credit).

# Intercompany Posting Automatic Account Assignment

*Intercompany postings* (also called cross-company code transactions) occur in the system when a single transaction is posted to one or more company codes (this must occur on separate line items). For these postings, an intercompany clearing (payable/receivable) account must be maintained. The configuration screen for determining codes for intercompany accounts can be reached by following the menu path Financial Accounting ➤ General Ledger Accounting ➤ Business Transactions ➤ Prepare Cross-Company Code Transactions.

After finding the configuration transaction screen, you'll get a pop-up box for entering company codes, as shown in Figure 3.28.

In the pop-up box, enter the company codes that you want to configure for intercompany transactions. The screen for configuring the posting keys to specific accounts appears; Figure 3.29 displays the configured intercompany clearing configuration screen for company codes 1100 and 1110.

**FIGURE 3.28**   The intercompany pop-up window

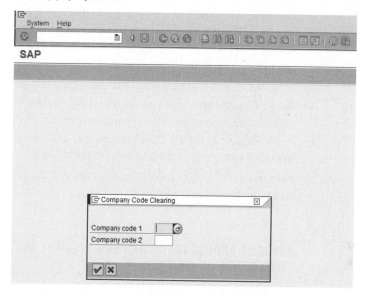

**FIGURE 3.29**   The configured intercompany clearing configuration for Extreme Sports

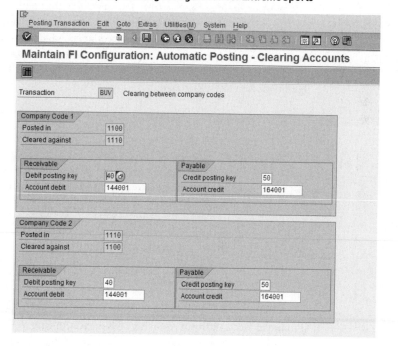

In the configuration screen, you configure the posting keys and intercompany accounts to post to. You will notice that there are two groupings on the screen, one for each combination of intercompany relationships. You need to pay particular attention to the Posted In company code. The Posted In company code represents the company code that the intercompany G/L accounts you designate will be posted *to* for the given Cleared Against company code (for example, the company code for which you are configuring the accounts). You have the option of creating both an intercompany receivable and an intercompany payable account or using a single intercompany account for both the payable and the receivable. It is a good idea to use the same G/L account number for both company codes because, in addition to making the clearing less confusing, this will cut down on the number of G/L accounts that are needed.

### EXTREME SPORTS INTERCOMPANY ACCOUNT DETERMINATION CONFIGURATION ANALYSIS

The controller of Extreme Sports has determined that there is a need for Extreme Sports to keep track of intercompany payables and receivables separately. Because of this, both an intercompany payable and an intercompany receivable account were set up. Both company codes in an intercompany transaction will use the same G/L account number, thus reducing the number of accounts needed in the chart of accounts. The project team at Extreme Sports will configure the remaining intercompany relationships in the same fashion, as demonstrated in the next section, "Materials Management Automatic Account Assignment."

# Materials Management Automatic Account Assignment

Materials Management (MM) automatic account determination is a major integration point between FI and MM. It is very important to work with your MM counterparts when configuring this part of the system. Accurate configuration takes a good working knowledge of the different movement types, valuation classes, and transactions that take place in the MM module. A detailed explanation of MM is beyond the scope of this book.

To configure MM's automatic account determination, follow the menu path Financial Accounting ➢ General Ledger Accounting ➢ Business Transactions ➢ Integration ➢ Materials Management ➢ Define Accounts for Material

Management. This menu path will take the user to a screen that is essentially built off of the same functionality as explored for the account assignment for sales tax in the previous section, as shown in Figure 3.30.

**FIGURE 3.30**    The configuration screen for MM account assignments

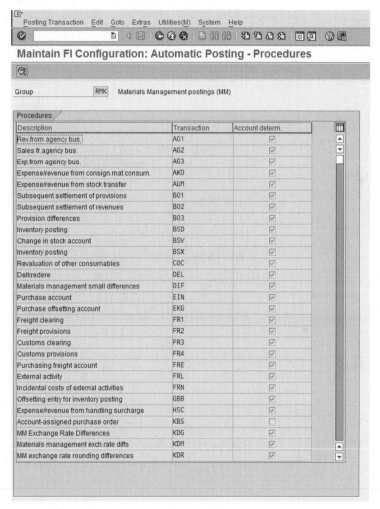

In this example, we will configure the account assignment for the processing key BSX. Processing key BSX is used to determine the inventory account to which MM transactions are posted. For example, you could use it to determine which inventory account to use to increase inventory through a goods receipt or which inventory account to use to decrease inventory through a goods issue. Double-click the processing key BSX, and you are presented with a pop-up screen asking you for the chart of accounts for which you wish to configure the automatic account assignment. After entering the appropriate chart name (EXCA), you are presented with the Automatic Posting – Accounts screen. To get to the rules screen, you have to use the Rules button. This will take you to the posting procedure rules screen, shown in Figure 3.31. This is the configuration screen for the rules to be used in the automatic account assignment for this processing key (BSX). There are three different control indicators that you can set in your rule: Debit/Credit, Valuation Modif., and Valuation Class.

**FIGURE 3.31**     The configured posting procedure rules for Extreme Sports

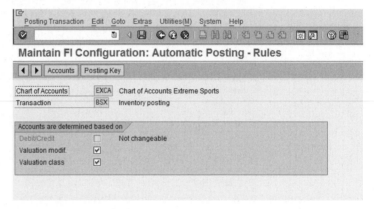

By setting the Debit/Credit indicator, you can assign different accounts to be used by the processing key depending on whether the transaction is debiting or crediting the account. By setting the Valuation Modif. (valuation modifier) indicator, you can use valuation grouping codes to distinguish your account determination. Valuation grouping codes are assigned to production plants; thus, if you want to post the same material to different accounts based upon division assignments, the valuation grouping code will allow you to make these different postings. By setting the Valuation Class indicator, you can assign different G/L accounts based upon the valuation class. Valuation classes are assigned to the material master of each material and signify the type of inventory that material represents, such as a finished good, semi-finished good, or maintenance part.

On other processing keys, such as GBB, there is an additional indicator, General Modification, that you can select. The General Modification indicator allows you to configure account modifiers along with the G/L account. Account modifiers are assigned to different movement types, thus allowing you to post to various G/L accounts based on the movement type that is used in the transaction. The configured rules for Extreme Sports's BSX processing key appear in Figure 3.31.

After making the settings, click the Accounts button and the screen in Figure 3.32 appears.

**FIGURE 3.32**  The account determination screen for valuation (modifier) grouping code, valuation class, and account has been configured for Extreme Sports.

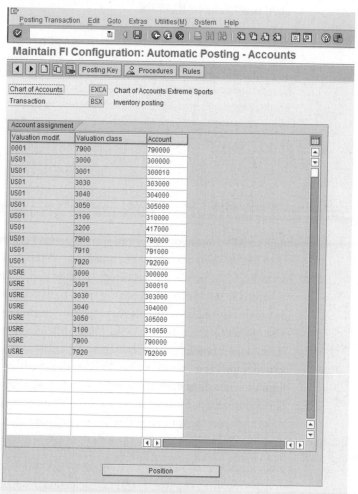

As you can see, you have three columns to configure. You'll set the valuation modifier (grouping) code (which appears because of the valuation modifier settings in the rules), the valuation class (which appears because of the valuation class setting in the rules), and the account. (Only one column appears for the account because the Debit/Credit indicator was not set in the rules. If it had been set, two Account columns would appear.)

## EXTREME SPORTS MM AUTOMATIC ACCOUNT DETERMINATION CONFIGURATION ANALYSIS

Extreme Sports needs to keep track of its finished inventory (valuation class 7920) and its raw materials (valuation class 7900) in different accounts based upon whether the account is for apparel or sporting goods. All of the apparel production plants have been assigned to valuation grouping code 0001, and all of the sporting equipment production plants have been assigned to valuation grouping code US01. The ability to use valuation classes and valuation grouping codes was set in the configuration for the rules of the processing key.

# Sales and Distribution Automatic Account Assignment

As with MM, one of the main integration points between FI and the Sales & Distribution (SD) module is the *automatic account assignment*. SD automatic account assignment is different from all other account assignments in the system. SD account assignment does not use table T030. SD account assignments depend on condition tables and access sequences to determine the correct G/L account. You can set up the condition tables to use different characteristics such as customer class, plant, material group, and account modifiers. Account modifiers are attached to condition types, which are used in the SD pricing procedure. Account modifiers are what allow you to assign different G/L accounts to various condition types. Condition types can be set to be accrual condition types that allow you to make debit and credit postings from a single condition type.

Typically, you will use several different condition tables. After determining which characteristics you need and setting up the condition tables, you configure the access sequence. The access sequence determines the order in which the condition tables are read. Generally, you should go from the most-specific condition table (the one with the most characteristics) to the least-specific condition table (the one with the least number of characteristics). Some clients choose to have a "General" condition table that has no conditions for G/L accounts only so that all billings are allowed to go through (or post to) the system. There are arguments both for and against this practice; just be aware that it can be very time consuming to fix billings that have gone through the system with the wrong account assignment. If you want to catch all problems before a billing is posted and an invoice is sent to the customer, do not use a "General" condition table. The configuration of condition tables and access sequences is beyond the scope of this book. You can get to the six steps of setting up account determination for SD by using the IMG menu: Sales and Distribution ➢ Basic Functions ➢ Account Assignment/Costing ➢ Revenue Account Determination.

The configuration path takes you to the area in the IMG where you configure condition the various steps of revenue account determination. The configuration path Financial Accounting ➢ General Ledger Accounting ➢ Business Transactions ➢ Integration ➢ Sales and Distribution ➢ Prepare Revenue Account Determination also takes you to the account determination screen.

# Financial Statement Versions

*Financial statement versions* group together related accounts into balance sheet and income statement format for financial reporting purposes. SAP uses the financial statement version assigned to the company code when preparing the standard balance sheet and income statement reports in the system. The grouping in your financial statement version may or may not correspond to the account groupings that were configured earlier. You can assign accounts from different account groups in the same hierarchy nodes (groupings) in the financial statement version.

You can use the following methods to get to the financial statement versions definition screen: Financial Accounting ➢ General Ledger Accounting ➢ Business Transactions ➢ Closing ➢ Document ➢ Define Financial Statement Versions.

You will recall from Chapter 2 that we've assigned all of Extreme Sports's company codes to financial statement version EX01. After clicking the record for EX01 in the screen shown in Figure 3.33, you are presented with the general specification screen, shown in Figure 3.34.

**FIGURE 3.33**    The listing of the financial statement versions

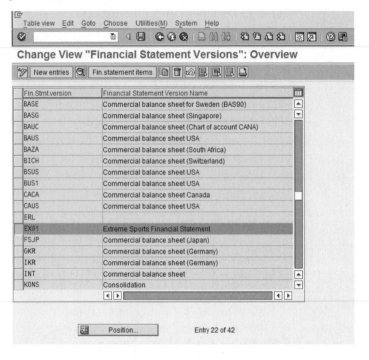

**FIGURE 3.34**    The general specification screen

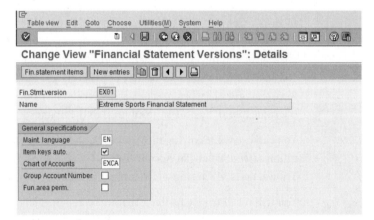

You will notice that there are five configuration settings that can be grouped under the heading General Specifications. They are as follows:

**Maint. Language**    The maintenance language determines the language in which the financial statement version is kept. For Extreme Sports, the maintenance language entry is EN for English.

**Item Keys Auto.**    This indicator specifies whether item keys are assigned automatically or manually. Item keys are tied to the hierarchy nodes (financial statement items) in the financial statement version itself. It is recommended that you set this indicator so that item keys are assigned automatically.

**Chart of Accounts**    Enter the chart of accounts that this financial statement version relates to. In our case, the chart of accounts is EXCA.

**Group Account Number**    Set this indicator if you wish to assign numbers from the group chart of accounts instead of the chart of accounts that was configured in the Chart of Accounts indicator. Group charts of accounts are part of the consolidation function. This setting is valid only if you are using the consolidation functionality of SAP.

**Fun. Area Perm.**    This setting allows you to use the functional area organizational element. Functional areas are used for cost of sales accounting and reporting. It allows the user to create yet another alternative grouping of costs.

Once you have made all your configuration settings, as shown for Extreme Sports in Figure 3.34, you are ready to configure your financial statement items. Financial statement items are similar to hierarchy nodes. To configure the financial statement items, click the Fin. Statement Items button. You are then presented with a screen like the one shown in Figure 3.35.

**FIGURE 3.35**    The Extreme Sports financial statement configuration

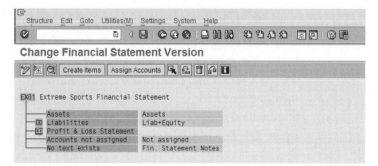

As you can see, only a base skeleton is given to you to work with. Right now, there are no subgroupings or accounts assigned to any of the financial statement items. In our example, the Assets financial statement item will be configured. To start, double-click the Assets financial statement item (hierarchy node). You are presented with the Change Texts dialog box, shown in Figure 3.36.

**FIGURE 3.36**  The Change Texts dialog box is used to add details to the Assets financial statement.

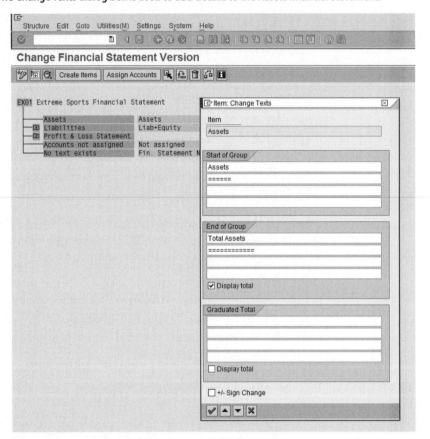

In this dialog box, you are able to control the textual description of the financial statement item as well as whether totals are shown for the item and whether the sign should be reversed when displaying the balances in accounts. Reversing the sign of an account causes a credit balance account to display as a debit and vice versa. Figure 3.36 shows the fully configured screen for the Assets financial statement item.

As you can see, the item was named Assets in the first line. When this financial statement item is used, the term *Assets* will be shown at the beginning of the grouping of Assets accounts. At the end of the group, the term *Total Assets*, underscored with a double line, will be shown. The end of the group will also display the total account for the financial statement item. There is no need to display graduated totals because graduated totals are relevant only for income statement accounts. Extreme Sports would also like to display assets using their natural debit balance, so there is no need to set the +/- Sign Change indicator. Now that the Assets financial statement item has been configured, you are ready to assign other subitems to it. To do so, select the Assets financial statement item by clicking on it once. Then click the Create Items button. You are presented with the screen shown in Figure 3.37.

**FIGURE 3.37    Creating subitems under Assets**

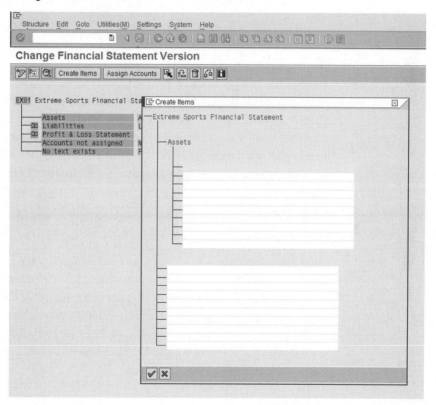

In this screen, enter the subitems you would like to appear under Assets. The subitems can have accounts assigned directly to them or have other subitems attached to them so that they act as hierarchy nodes. The configuration for Extreme Sports appears in Figure 3.38.

**FIGURE 3.38**     The configuration of some Assets subitems for Extreme Sports

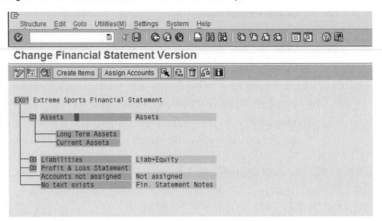

As you can see, only two additional items were attached directly to the existing assets. These two items, Current Assets and Long Term Assets, will have additional items attached to them, and you can have yet more additional items attached to them or, in turn, have G/L accounts assigned to them. You are now ready to configure the items that will appear under the Current Assets item. To attach more items to it, click the Current Assets item and then click the Create Items button, as was done before. You are again presented with the Create Items screen, as shown in Figure 3.39.

After you enter the additional items needed under Current Assets, the main configuration screen appears, as in Figure 3.40.

Although normally you would want to break out each of the lowest-level items even further later in your project, in this example, we are now ready to assign G/L accounts to the lowest-level financial statement items under Current Assets. To assign G/L accounts, select the item that you want to assign accounts to by single-clicking it (in our example, Cash and Cash Equivalents). After selecting the item, click the Assign Accounts button. The screen in Figure 3.41 appears. Yours won't have the elements filled in.

**FIGURE 3.39** Creating subitems under Current Assets

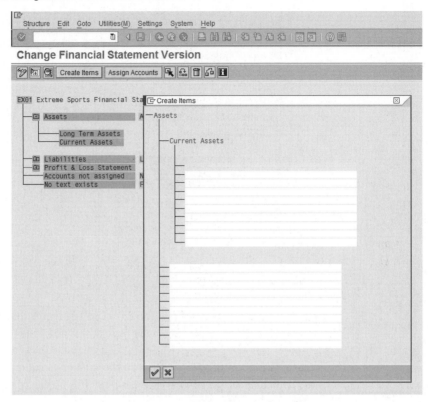

**FIGURE 3.40** The configured items now show under Current Assets.

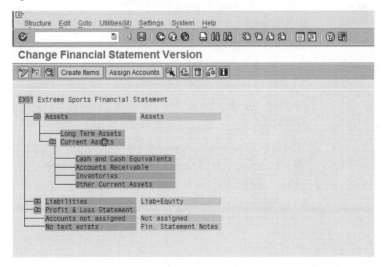

**FIGURE 3.41**    The Change Accounts dialog box

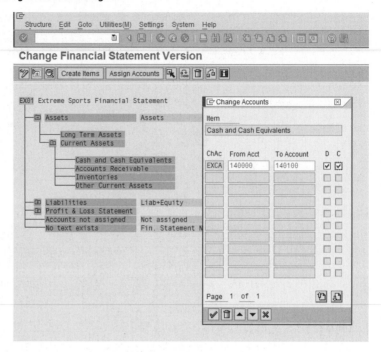

Enter the G/L account number range in the Change Accounts dialog box to display either debit balances, credit balances, or both. It is normally a good idea to set both the debit and credit indicators so that you are picking up all activity in your financial statements. There's nothing that gets the accounting staff more riled up than when the balance sheet doesn't balance. Figure 3.41 displays the configuration for Extreme Sports's Cash and Cash Equivalents grouping on the balance sheet.

Figure 3.42 displays the fully configured Cash and Cash Equivalents portion of Extreme Sports's balance sheet. As you can see, the Cash and Cash Equivalents item now has a range of G/L accounts assigned to it. You can display all the G/L account numbers by clicking on the hierarchy expand/collapse icon next to the range of accounts.

The implementation team will use the technique demonstrated in this section to finish configuring the rest of the financial statement version for both the balance sheet and income statement.

**FIGURE 3.42**    The configured balance sheet for Extreme Sports

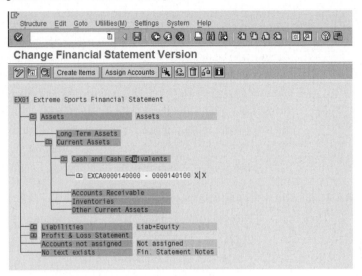

# G/L Display Configuration

Now that you have an understanding of the various settings that can be made in G/L accounts, it is time to learn how to incorporate the use of these settings into G/L display functionality. The following sections will be used specifically to create line item layouts, sort variants, and totals variants to be used in G/L line item display. In addition to these functions, there are other components of line item display that can be configured, such as selection fields, additional fields, and search fields. You will recall from the previous sections that accounts can be set to display line items. Posting and displaying items in an account with line item display turned on allows you the most flexibility in analyzing an individual account.

## Line Item Layouts

The first piece of configuration that will be done is a line item layout. Line item layouts display the value of different fields that come from the field status group of the G/L account posted to and fields populated via the G/L company code screen as well as fields from the accounting document headers and other special fields. Line item layouts are used in the G/L line item display transaction from the application (user) menu.

Follow the menu path Financial Accounting ➤ General Ledger Accounting ➤ G/L Accounts ➤ Line Items ➤ Display Line Items ➤ Define Line Layout to get to the initial configuration screen.

As you can see in Figure 3.43, SAP comes delivered with several line item layouts. A *check* in the far right column (Special Variant) denotes that the line item layout uses a special field for its display. Special fields display additional information from places other than the line item display tables (RFPOS), such as the document header, check register, or document line item. Because it is reading from another table, performance may be slower than on other line item layouts that do not use special fields. Special fields will be covered in more detail later in this section.

**FIGURE 3.43**    The define line layout screen

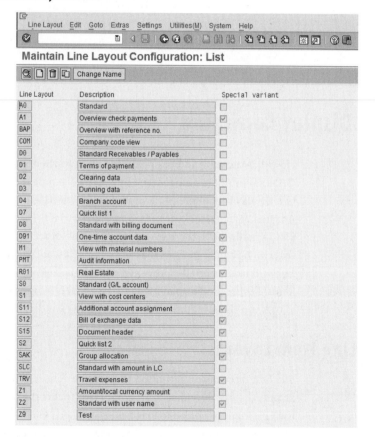

To create a new line item layout, click the create icon. You are presented with the pop-up box, as shown in Figure 3.44, to enter the identifier for the line layout.

**FIGURE 3.44**    The initial pop-up box for your new line layout

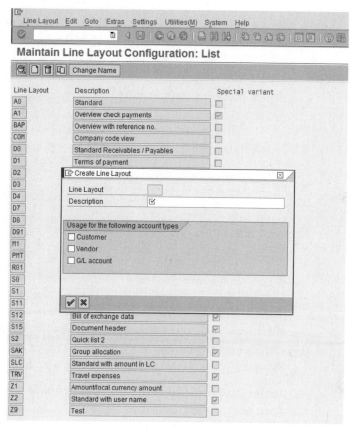

Enter a line item layout identifier in the line layout box. The identifier can contain up to three characters. The next step is to give the layout a description and choose whether the line item layout will be used on Customer, Vendor, or G/L accounts. In this example, you will be configuring a G/L line item layout. After entering all of the information in the pop-up box and pressing Enter, you are presented with the blank configuration screen for your line item layout, as shown in Figure 3.45.

**FIGURE 3.45**    The blank configuration screen for line item layout

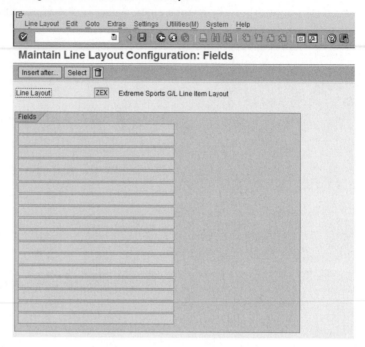

On this screen, select the fields that you would like included on the line item layout. To add fields, click the first of the blank entries under the Fields header. After clicking the entry to select it, click the Insert After button. The screen shown in Figure 3.46 presents you with a list of fields available for selection.

The list window defaults to show the normal fields you can select from the line item table. Take special notice of the Field Names and Special Fields buttons at the bottom of the window. If you click the Field Names button, the actual field names from the table are presented next to the description. This feature can be quite helpful because some of the descriptions for different fields are exactly the same. The Special Fields button brings up a list of additional fields that are not in the regular line item tables. As mentioned earlier, special fields may decrease the performance of the line item layout. Once you find the field you want to select, double-click it to add it to your line item layout. When the field name is added, repeat the process by continuing to click the Insert After button. Line item layouts can contain a maximum of 15 fields and/or a maximum of 130 characters. The fields selected to be displayed in the line item layout default to the maximum size of the data element for the field, with a one-character displacement between fields. You can customize the size of the field, the offset for display, and the character displacement between fields by double-clicking the field. When you do so, you are presented with the Display Format dialog box, which is shown in Figure 3.47.

**FIGURE 3.46**    Field selection screen

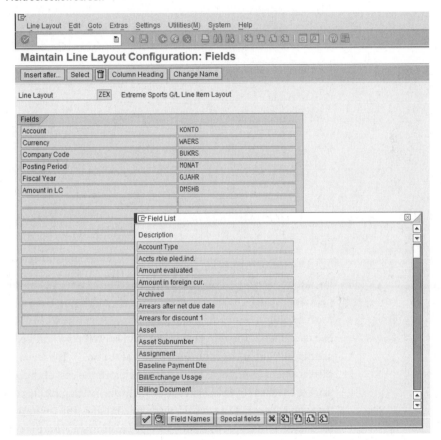

**FIGURE 3.47**    The display format screen for individual fields in your screen layout

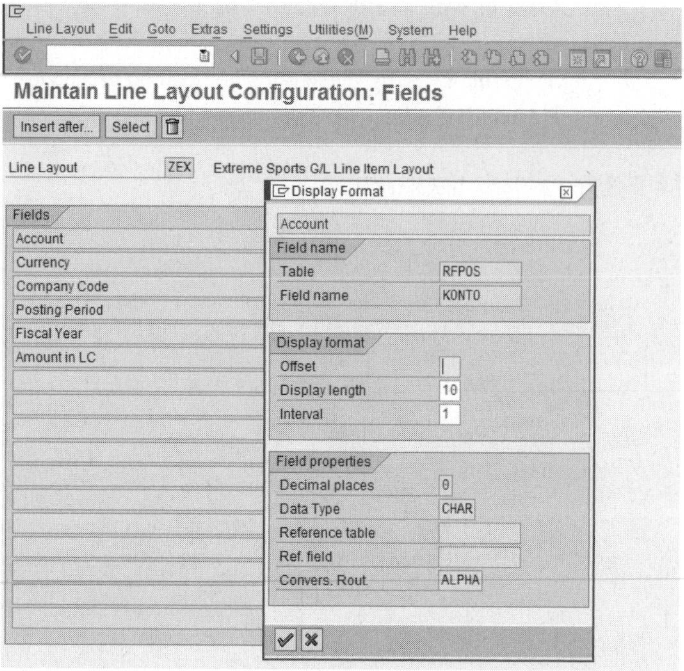

The Display Format fields control the length and display of the field in your screen layout. By entering a number in the Offset field, you can control the position in the field from which the start of the display should begin. For example, placing a 5 in the field will make the field start displaying from the sixth character (it will skip five characters). The Display Length field controls the number of characters that are displayed (cutting off from the end of the field). The Distance field controls the displacement (number of characters) between the end of the preceding field and the start of the current field. After setting the formatting display options for the fields that you have selected, you are ready to configure the column headings of the line item layout. To do so, first click the save icon. Then click the Column Heading button, and the screen displayed in Figure 3.48 appears.

From the screen in Figure 3.48, you can see the fields that were selected for the line item display in the previous steps. Each field is assigned a letter from A to F, which corresponds to the column heading letters for the fields. In the Column Heading section, enter a description for each of the fields next to the assigned field letter. These are the column headings that will be displayed on the screen when the line item layout is used. Figure 3.48 displays the configured column heading screen for Extreme Sports.

**FIGURE 3.48**    The column heading configuration screen

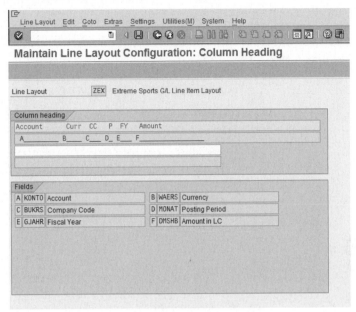

Once you have entered the descriptions, click the save icon. Then use the green arrow to back out to the field configuration screen for the line item layout. Click the save icon once more to save the entire line item layout. If a special field was selected, you will receive an informational/warning message informing you of its selection. Press Enter to complete the save process.

## Special Fields

Special fields were used in the line item display subsection. In addition to being used in line item displays, special fields can be used for selecting, finding, and sorting (sort variants) data. SAP comes delivered with several special fields that can be used with no additional configuration. To add additional fields to the special field lists, additional configuration must be undertaken. The configuration transaction for creating additional special fields is begun by following the menu path Financial Accounting ➤ General Ledger Accounting ➤ G/L Accounts ➤ Line Items ➤ Display Line Items ➤ Define Special Fields for Finding and Sorting Data.

This particular configuration transaction (OBVU) uses table (view) V_T021S. V_T021S is a client-independent table. Refer to Chapter 1 for an explanation of the difference between client-dependent and client-independent tables and transports.

In the configuration screen, shown in Figure 3.49, you are required to enter the table and the field name of the special field you want to add.

**FIGURE 3.49**   **The configuration screen for entering the table and field name of the special field you want to add**

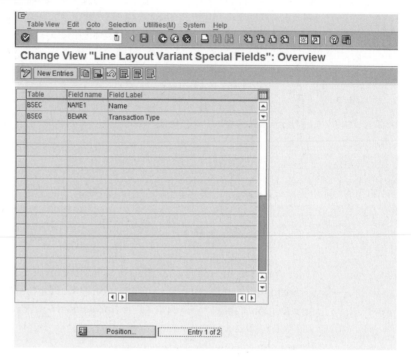

You can choose fields from the following tables:

- ► BKPF Accounting Document Header

- ► BSEC One-Time Account Data Document Segment

- ► BSED Bill of Exchange Fields Document Segment

- ► BSEG Accounting Document Line Items Segment

- ► PAYR Payment Transfer Medium File

It is important to note that not all fields from these tables can be selected. You must select one of the fields from the drop-down list. When you decide to use BSEG, you can't select any field that is within BSEG; you must select one of the BSEG fields shown in the drop-down list in the field on the screen.

# Sort Variants

*Sort variants* are used to determine the order in which line items are displayed on the screen when you're using a line item layout without a totals variant. SAP comes delivered with standard sort variants, but you are also afforded the flexibility to create your own. You can choose or create configuration commands for sort variants by following the menu path Financial Accounting ➢ General Ledger Accounting ➢ G/L Accounts ➢ Line Items ➢ Display Line Items ➢ Choose Sort Variants. Figure 3.50 is the configuration screen that allows the user to customize how the screen, and therefore the data, is presented.

**FIGURE 3.50**     The configuration screen for sort variants

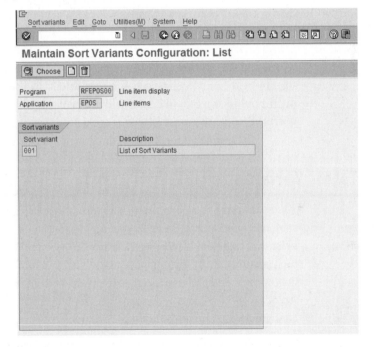

To create a new sort variant, click the create icon. Next you will be asked to enter a three-character identifier for the sort variant as well as a description. After entering the identifier and description and pressing Enter, you are presented with a screen like the one shown in Figure 3.51.

**FIGURE 3.51**    The sort field configuration screen allows you to set the order in which the fields will be displayed.

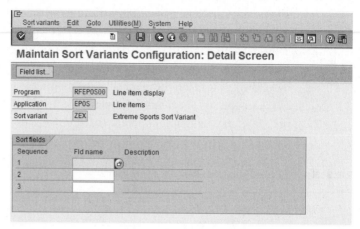

As you can see, you are allowed a maximum of three fields to sort by. The system sorts by field 1 first, then field 2, and then field 3. To select your fields for sorting, use the pull-down button on the field (the pull-down menu will appear when you select the field). You must select one of the fields in the pull-down list. After you've selected the fields that meet your requirements, click the save icon.

## Totals Variants

*Totals variants* are used in lieu of sort variants to display line items and to total and subtotal amounts. For example, you might use a totals variant to total by document type and then by posting date. The described totals variant would subtotal each posting date by document type and display a total for each document type. Follow the menu path Financial Accounting ➢ General Ledger Accounting ➢ G/L Accounts ➢ Line Items ➢ Display Line Items ➢ Define Totals Variants to get to the configuration commands for totals variants.

To create a new totals variant, click the create icon, shown in Figure 3.52. You are then presented with a pop-up box asking for a three-character totals variant identifier as well as a description for the variant. After entering this information and pressing Enter, you are presented with a screen like that in Figure 3.53.

**FIGURE 3.52**     The totals variant configuration screen

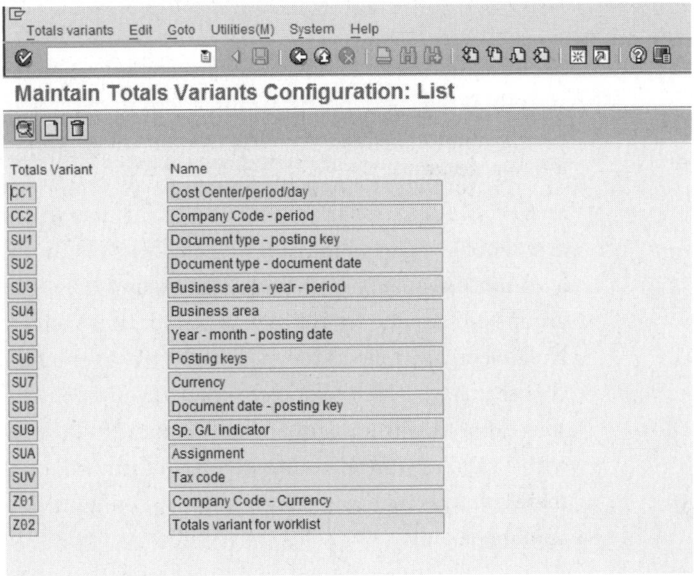

**FIGURE 3.53**     You are allowed to select the way you want the results of a totals variant configuration presented.

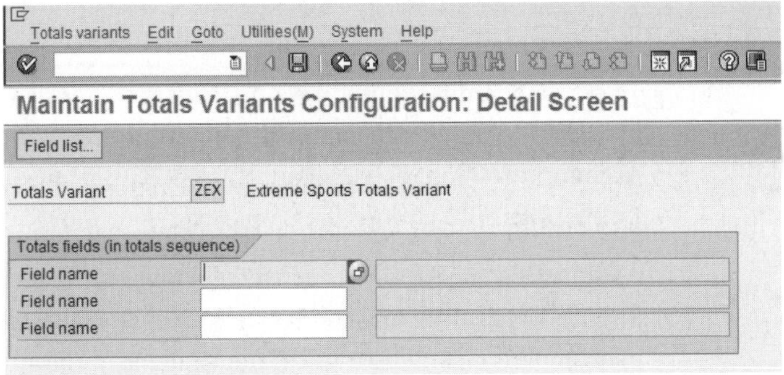

Like sort variants, totals variants allow you to select up to three fields by which to total. You must select one of the fields from the pull-down box. The system will total by the first field, then the second field, and then the third field; as you can imagine, it is best to go from less detail to more detail when ordering the fields to be used. After entering the fields, click the save icon to record your variant.

# Posting Amount Defaults and Tolerance Groups

Now that the entire chart of accounts configuration has taken place, it is time to start thinking about posting transactions in the system. The next step is to set up *posting amount defaults*. Posting amount defaults are stored in *tolerance groups*. Tolerance groups, in turn, are assigned to user IDs. You will need to do a careful analysis of the various tolerance groups that you will need in the system. This process should be part of the overall security and authorization setup of your system. If a tolerance is not explicitly assigned in a user ID, the tolerance group defaults to the group Null (empty) for the company code. It is therefore very important to have the Null tolerance group as the most restrictive tolerance group in your system if you choose to have a Null tolerance group. If you want to ensure that unauthorized persons cannot make postings, do not create a Null tolerance group; then only user IDs with a valid tolerance group assigned to them will be able to make postings. With these concepts in mind, you are ready to configure tolerance groups and posting amount defaults.

**NOTE** It is very important to have the Null tolerance group as the most restrictive tolerance group in your system if you choose to have a Null tolerance group. Otherwise, it is possible for unauthorized users to post large amounts to the G/L.

To get to the initial configuration screen for defining tolerance groups (see Figure 3.54) and posting amount defaults, follow the menu path Financial Accounting ➢ Financial Accounting Global Settings ➢ Document ➢ Line Item ➢ Define Tolerance Groups for Employees.

As you can see, SAP comes delivered with a standard tolerance group for the SAP-delivered company code 0001. You must create at least one tolerance group per company code. Postings cannot be made in the system until a tolerance group is configured. In our example we'll create the Null tolerance group for Extreme Sports's company code 1100. From the configuration screen for defining tolerance groups, click the New Entries button. You are presented with the screen in Figure 3.55.

**FIGURE 3.54**   The configuration screen for defining tolerance groups

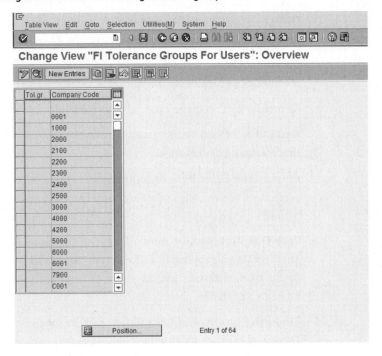

**FIGURE 3.55**   The configuration screen for creating a Null tolerance group for Extreme Sports

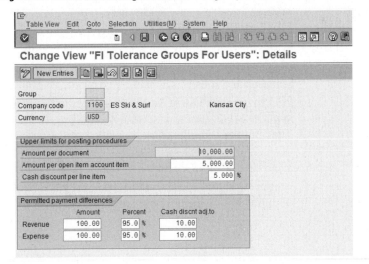

The fields that appear in Figure 3.55 are explained here:

**Group**   Enter the four-character alphanumeric identifier of the group. In this example for Extreme Sports, we will leave the group field blank (Null).

**Company Code**   Enter the four-character identifier of the company code to which the tolerance group being configured belongs.

**Currency**   The company code currency defaults into this field.

**Amount per Document**   Enter the maximum amount that can be posted in a single accounting document.

**Amount per Open Item Account Item**   Enter the maximum amount that can be posted to a vendor or customer account. This field restricts the amount that can be paid to a vendor or cleared from receivables for a customer.

**Cash Discount per Line Item**   Enter the maximum percentage for a cash discount that can be applied to a line item in this field. For example, a cash discount rate of 5% would mean that the maximum cash discount that can be granted on a $100 line item is $5.

**Amount, Percent, and Cash Discnt Adj. To (both Revenue and Expense)**
These fields have to do with the handling of customer overpayments and underpayments to the company. In the Amount field, enter the maximum amount of customer overpayment (revenue fields) or the maximum amount of customer underpayment (expense fields) that can be processed by this tolerance group. In the Percent field, enter the maximum percent of the total payment that can be applied by this tolerance group. The system looks at both the Amount and Percent fields when making postings. The system will post differences up to the maximum percent specified as long as it does not go over the amount specified in the Amount field. In the Cash Discnt Adj. To (cash discount adjustment) field, enter the amount of the difference that is to be posted to the cash discount account. Typically, this field is set to be a lower figure than the amount field.

To assign user IDs (employees) to tolerance groups, follow the menu path Financial Accounting ➤ Financial Accounting Global Settings ➤ Document ➤ Line Item ➤ Assign Users/Tolerance Groups, and set the configuration transactions.

**EXTREME SPORTS POSTING AMOUNT DEFAULT AND TOLERANCE GROUP CONFIGURATION ANALYSIS**

Extreme Sports has decided to use several different tolerance groups and assign them to users based on their position in the company. They have also decided to configure the Null tolerance group. This will give Extreme Sports the flexibility to assign tolerance groups only to higher-level accounting staff, with the accounting clerks defaulting to the Null tolerance group. Because of this, the Null tolerance group is the most restrictive tolerance group created for Extreme Sports. Employees assigned to the Null tolerance group can post accounting documents up to $10,000 and clear customer and vendor accounts on items up to $5,000. Employees can grant cash discounts up to 5% of the line item amount. Both revenue and expense payment differences (customer overpayment and underpayment) are set to a maximum of 95.0% up to a total of $100. Amounts up to $10 of the total difference will be applied to the cash discount account.

# Number Ranges and Document Types

There is one final piece of configuration that is needed before you can post entries in the system. The final step is setting up *document types* and assigning them to *number ranges*. SAP comes delivered with several different document types that are assigned to different transactions in the system. Each document type must have a number range assigned to it. The number ranges are what determine the document number. The document number, along with fiscal year, is the audit trail that is used in the system. As you are well aware, SAP utilizes the document principle, meaning that every posting in the system is done through a document, thus providing detailed drill-down to the source of all posting entries in the system. Each document in the system must balance before it is posted and cannot be deleted from the system until it is archived to other storage media.

## Number Ranges

The first configuration step for this section is to set up number ranges. Because of the nature of number range objects in the system, number ranges are not automatically included in transport requests, even when automatic recording of changes is activated in the client. It is very easy to overlay number range objects and get existing ranges out of sync when you transport number ranges. It is recommended that you do not transport number ranges. Number ranges should be set up individually in each client. Doing so will save a lot of headaches as your project progresses. You set up number ranges by company code and year. Specifying the year as 9999 makes the number range valid for any year.

You can get to the screen for defining number ranges by using the following menu path: Financial Accounting ➤ Financial Accounting Global Settings ➤ Document ➤ Document Number Ranges ➤ Define Document Number Ranges. Figure 3.56 shows the first screen, where you select which company code's number ranges you would like to work with.

**FIGURE 3.56**    The define document number ranges screen

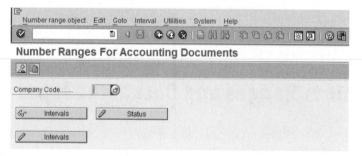

On this screen, enter the company code for which you want to configure number ranges. In our example, we will use company code 1100. After entering the company code, click the change interval button or follow the menu path Interval ➤ Change. You are then presented with the configuration screen shown in Figure 3.57.

As you can see, Extreme Sports has already configured quite a few number ranges. Each interval is assigned a number, a year, a range of numbers, and an indicator to signify whether the interval should be externally assigned. Externally assigned number ranges require the user or a user exit to provide the document number to SAP. For internally assigned number ranges, the system determines and fills in the document number based upon the next available number in the range. Let's create a number range to be used by the company code. First, click the insert interval icon. You are presented with the pop-up configuration screen.

**FIGURE 3.57** The configuration screen for Extreme Sports's number ranges

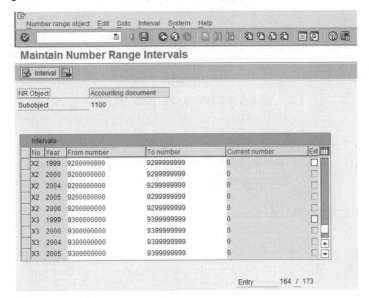

In the configuration dialog box, you are required to fill in the following fields:

**Number**  Enter the two-character alphanumeric identifier for the number range.

**Year**  Enter the year through which this number range is valid. You can have several different entries for a number range, assigning it to different years. If you enter the year 9999, the number range is valid for all years.

**From Number**  Enter the first number to be used in the range (lower limit). You can also specify a range to use all characters instead of numbers.

**To Number**  Enter the last number to be used in the range (upper limit).

**Current Number**  This field defaults to 0. Do not make an entry in this field unless you do not want the first number that is assigned to be the same as the From Number setting on the interval.

**Ext (Externally Assigned)**  Select this indicator if you do not want the system to automatically assign a number to the document. Selecting this field makes the user input the document number manually (or a user-exit could possibly populate the field).

After entering information for the fields in the Insert Interval dialog box, press Enter or click the insert icon. Your entry will now appear in the overall number range list that was shown earlier.

## Document Types

Different document types are used for different transactions throughout the system. The document type controls many things, including the type of account that can be posted to, the number range assigned to it, and required document header fields. SAP comes delivered with several standard document types. For the most part, all you have to do is assign number ranges to each document type. You do have the option of creating new document types if your requirements determine that you need it.

To set the initial configuration screen for document types, shown in Figure 3.58, follow the menu path Financial Accounting ➤ Financial Accounting Global Settings ➤ Document ➤ Document Header ➤ Define Document Types.

**FIGURE 3.58    The document types available listing**

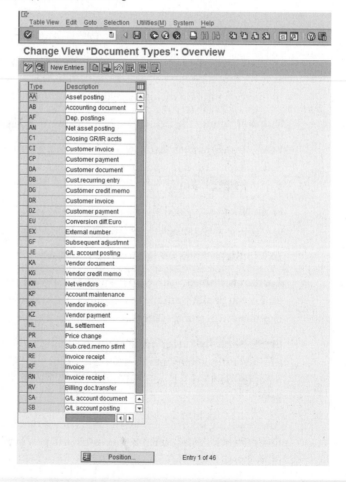

As you can see, there are numerous document types delivered with the system. From this screen, you can change the configuration of an existing document type or create a new document type. In our example, we will look at the configuration for one of the existing document types, SA, a G/L account document. To enter the configuration screen for the document type, double-click the document type identifier. You are presented with the screen shown in Figure 3.59.

**FIGURE 3.59** The document type configuration screen for SA G/L account document

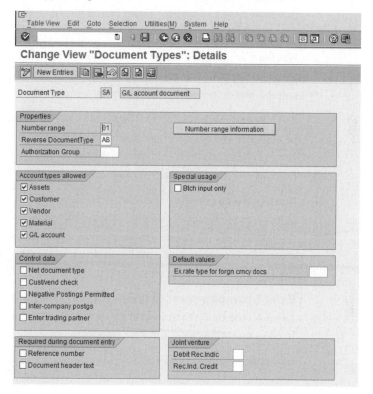

Let's examine the configuration fields:

**Number Range** Enter a valid number range that you configured in the preceding section. The number range assigned to a document type is valid for all company codes, but the number range must be set up in all company codes before it can be posted to. The number range can be assigned different number intervals in each company code. A number range can be assigned to more than one document type.

**Reverse DocumentType** In this field, enter the identifier of the document type that should be used to reverse this type of document. The document type specified here will be used when a reversal transaction is undertaken in the system. The reversal document type can be the same document type as the document type being configured or it can be a different document type.

**Authorization Group**   If you want to restrict the document type so that it can be used by only certain users, assign it to an authorization group. Authorization groups are assigned to user IDs via authorization objects. You will need to work closely with your Basis group to determine authorization groups.

**Account Types Allowed**   Select one of the following account types: Assets, Customers, Vendors, Materials, G/LAccount.

**Net Document Type**   This field is only valid for document types used for vendor invoices. Selecting this indicator will reduce the total amount due by the cash discount amount specified by the payment terms on the invoice.

**Cust/Vend Check**   Select this indicator if only a single customer or vendor should be allowed to be posted to on the document type. Setting this indicator on A/P and Invoicing document types is usually a good idea so that individual transactions exist for each customer or vendor account.

**Inter-company Postgs**   Select this indicator to allow postings for more than one company code on the document. When a document contains entries for more than one company code, a cross-company code accounting document is automatically created by the system using the automatic account determination that was configured earlier in the cross-company code automatic postings discussion.

**Enter Trading Partner**   If this indicator is selected, the user is allowed to manually enter the trading partner on the document. Normally, trading partners default in off of one of the vendor master records.

**Reference Number**   Select this indicator to make the reference number in the document header a required entry. Normally, this indicator is set on document types used for A/P invoices.

**Document Header Text**   Select this indicator to make the document header text field a required entry.

**Btch Input Only**   Select this indicator if you want to keep this document type from being used on manual postings. If this indicator is set, only batch input sessions can create documents of this type.

**Ex. Rate for Forgn Crncy Docs**    The system uses exchange rate type M (average rate) for documents posted in a foreign currency. The foreign currency translation is automatically done at this rate. If you want to use an exchange rate type other than M (average rate), enter it here. This field contains a pull-down list with all available exchange rate types.

## Transaction Default Document Type and Posting Key

The standard accounting transactions delivered with SAP enable you to customize a default document type and posting key for each transaction. SAP comes delivered with standard document types and posting keys. If you wish to change these settings, SAP has the flexibility to allow you to do so. Depending on your requirements, you might find it useful to create several new documents to be used by different transactions. The following configuration will allow you to assign a new document to the proper transaction. Changing the default posting key is not recommended unless you are very experienced in the system and it is absolutely necessary.

You can use the following menu path to get to the screen for defining document types and posting keys: Financial Accounting ➢ Financial Accounting Global Settings ➢ Document ➢ Default Values for Document Processing ➢ Define Default Values. Or you can use transaction code OBU1.

You'll get a screen like the one shown in Figure 3.60. Double-click the appropriate entry. You will then be able to select another document type and posting key from their respective pull-down menus. Please note that this is a client-independent configuration setting. (For more on client-dependent and client-independent settings, see Chapter 1.)

## Fast Entry Screens

G/L document fast entry is a popular function with end users. Fast entry screens allow transactions to be posted at a more rapid pace than the usual method. In this section, we will demonstrate how to configure G/L fast entry screens. The configuration transaction for G/L fast entry screens is reached by following the menu path Financial Accounting ➢ Financial Accounting Global Settings ➢ Document ➢ Line Item ➢ Maintain Fast Entry Screens for G/L Account Items.

**FIGURE 3.60** The configuration screen for defining documents and posting keys

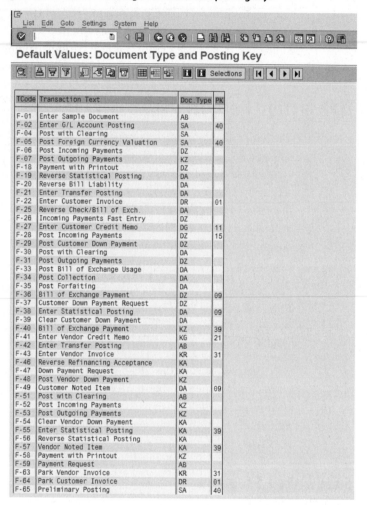

To create a new fast entry screen, click the create icon, shown in the screen in Figure 3.61.

After clicking the create icon, you are presented with a pop-up box asking for a variant name, a description, and the number of lines for the variant. The number of lines defaults to one, and you can have a maximum of three lines. The number of lines determines the number of rows on which the fields for the variant are placed. After entering the required information, you are presented with the screen that shows the array of field names available. You can see the screen for Extreme Sports in Figure 3.62.

**FIGURE 3.61** The fast entry configuration screen

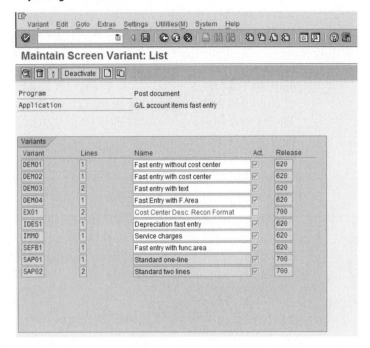

**FIGURE 3.62** The fields available for fast entry in Extreme Sports

SAP presents you with the names of the fields that can be added. To add a field to your fast entry screen, double-click it. This will move the field over to the Current Fields column. After a field is moved to the Current Fields column, an indicator for the column number appears, as does a configurable field for offset. The offset of a field determines from what position the field starts, beginning from the left margin of the line in the fast entry screen. A fast entry screen line can have a maximum of 82 characters, which means that an entire fast entry screen can have a maximum of 246 characters because each fast entry screen can have up to three lines. The field posting key is required for each fast entry screen. If you set your fast entry screen to have more than one line, once you have entered all of the fields for the first line, click the Insert before button. After entering all of the fields you need, click the save icon.

After saving the fast entry screen, you must activate it in order for it to be available for use. To activate it, select the fast entry screen ID, as shown earlier. After selecting the proper fast entry screen ID, click the Activate button. The Activate button is the one that looks like a magic wand.

The configured Extreme Sports fast entry, as it would be used in a G/L account posting transaction, is shown in Figure 3.63. Notice that the available fields for posting appear on two different lines.

## EXTREME SPORTS G/L FAST ENTRY SCREEN CONFIGURATION ANALYSIS

Extreme Sports has decided to configure an all-encompassing G/L fast entry screen for regular G/L entry transactions. Knowing the overall system design and requirements, they selected the appropriate fields for the fast entry screen (Account, Amount, Posting key, Assignment, Business Area, Cost Center, Profit Center, Text). Because fast entry screens are limited to 82 characters and the fields required for the screen contained more than 82 characters, the variant was set up to use two line items. Accounting clerks at Extreme Sports will use the configured fast entry screen when making normal journal entries in the system.

**FIGURE 3.63** The results of configuring Line 1 for fast entry as you'd see in a G/L account posting

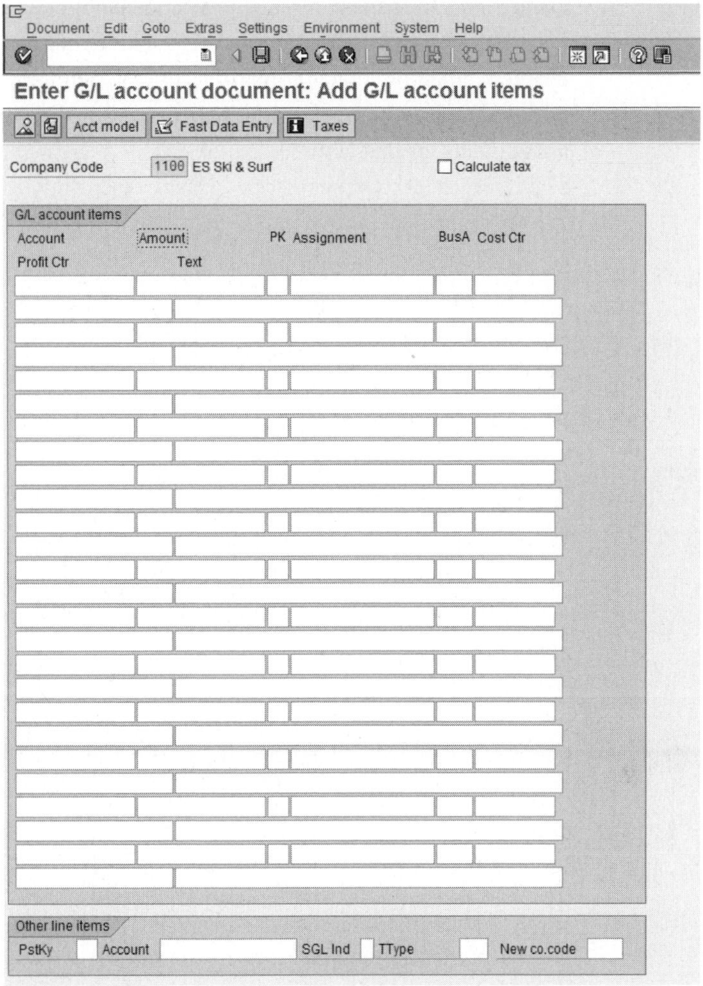

# Summary

This chapter covered a combination of configuration and master data maintenance. We finished the configuration of our chart of accounts and created a G/L account. The important concept of automatic account determination was introduced in this chapter. As you work through other chapters, be sure to look for automatic account assignments in the IMG because it would be impossible to cover every needed automatic account assignment in this book. If you remember one thing from this chapter, remember that automatic account assignments act like a whole table transport and that changing the rules on a processing key wipes out all existing account assignments for that key.

# Accounts Payable

**A**ccounts Payable (A/P) is the first subledger that we'll discuss in this book. The A/P module is tightly integrated with the Materials Management (MM) module, the Treasury module, and the Accounts Receivable (A/R) module. The A/P module allows you to manage the most complex of A/P transactions. With SAP's A/P system, a company can easily manage its payables to provide the maximum cash discount and available cash position on its liabilities. All types of payments can be used, as well as the additional function of A/P and A/R netting for vendors that are also customers. In addition to configuring the A/P module, we'll discuss how to configure house banks and accounts.

# House Banks and Accounts

The first step in configuring the A/P submodule is to create *house banks*, which are the banks your company uses for banking purposes. A house bank can have several bank accounts linked to it. As part of the reengineering phase of your project, it is important to analyze which and how many banks and bank accounts your company uses. As part of your SAP implementation, and the typical review of business process, now is a great opportunity to rationalize your bank account population.

A unique bank key identifies each house bank. Bank keys vary in form from country to country. In the United States, the bank key is known as the American Bankers Association (ABA) number. Normally, the system is set up so that each house bank has its own company code. Lately, with the large number of mergers in the U.S. banking industry, it may be necessary to set up for a single banking institution two house banks within a company code. This need arises because some of the larger banks use one ABA number for paper transactions (your company's checks) and another ABA number for electronic transactions. For this scenario, two house banks would be set up for a single physical bank, and two bank accounts linked to the same G/L account would also be created for the single bank account. Once again, this is the exception and not the rule; a thorough understanding of the system is necessary in order to implement this technique successfully.

Configuring the house banks is relatively simple. It is much like setting up master data in the system. To get to the house bank configuration screen, follow the menu path Financial Accounting ➤ Bank Accounting ➤ Bank Accounts ➤ Define House Banks. Figure 4.1 shows the initial configuration screen for house banks.

**FIGURE 4.1** The initial house banks configuration screen

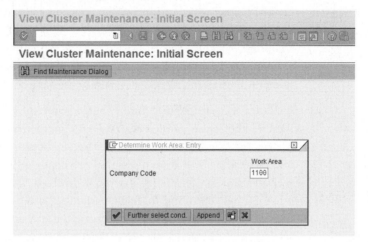

As you can see, a house bank is tied to a company code, and each bank account is tied to a house bank. The first configuration step is to enter the company code for which the house bank is being configured and click the Enter button. After you enter the company code, you will be presented with the screen with a listing of all your house banks. To link your banking company (house bank) to the company code, you will have to hit the New Entries button on the upper-left side of the screen. The screen you are now presented with is shown in Figure 4.2.

**FIGURE 4.2** The house bank data configuration screen

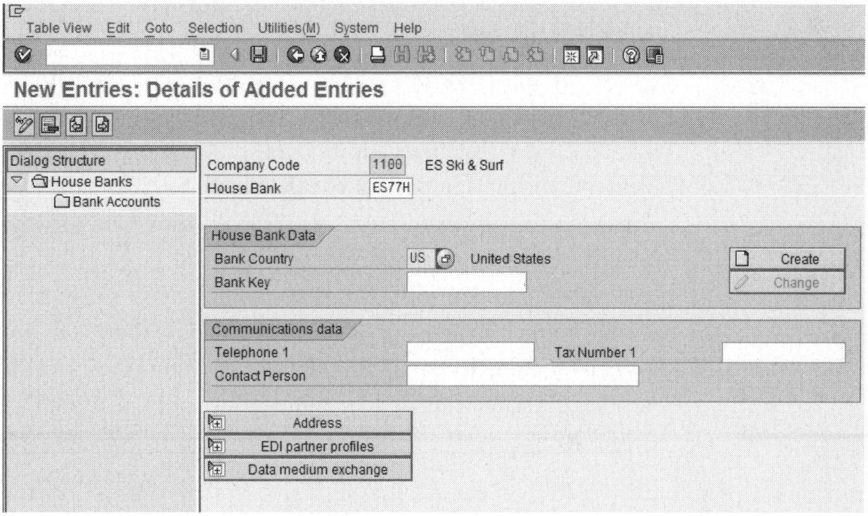

The house bank identifier is used by the system as part of the key for the house bank. It is determined by you and should follow the naming standards developed for your project. The house bank identifier is alphanumeric and can be up to five characters in length. The bank country is the country where the bank and your accounts reside. A pull-down menu is available to choose the allowable entries. Enter the house bank identifier and the house bank country.

Bank Key is a required field. In the United States, the bank key (also known as the ABA number) is a nine-digit field; the ABA number along with your account number and check number is printed at the bottom of your checks and is known as the micro-encoding (MICR) number. SAP uses an algorithm to ensure that the entry is a valid bank key for the country you've specified. The check algorithm, as well as other settings controlling the bank master data, can be controlled in the global settings of the IMG for your specific country. The settings made here are the default settings for the United States. Enter the bank key, and press Enter. There are three buttons on the left side of the screen:

- ▶ Address

- ▶ EDI Partner Profiles

- ▶ Data Medium Exchange

If have used this house bank before, the Address button should house the address details of the bank. If not, then you have to hit the Create button on the right side of the screen. This is where you will enter the address details. After entering the information in the pop-up screen, you are returned to the configured house bank data configuration screen (shown in Figure 4.3).

Next, enter the name of the bank in the Bank Name field. In the Region field, enter the state where the bank is located. The Street, City, and Bank Branch fields are self-explanatory. Within the Control Data section, the SWIFT Code and Bank Group fields are the most important. SWIFT stands for Society of Worldwide Interbank Financial Telecommunications. SWIFT codes are used throughout the world to identify banks in international transactions. It is a good idea to enter the SWIFT code of your bank if you want to conduct international business. You define the Bank Group field. You can set up bank groups to meet your project's needs and help optimize bank selection in the payment program. You can also enter information for the contact person for your company at this bank as well as telephone and tax code information (not required in the United States). After entering this information and clicking the Bank Accounts folder on the left side of the screen, you are taken to the list of bank accounts configuration screen, shown in Figure 4.4.

**FIGURE 4.3**     The configured house bank data configuration screen

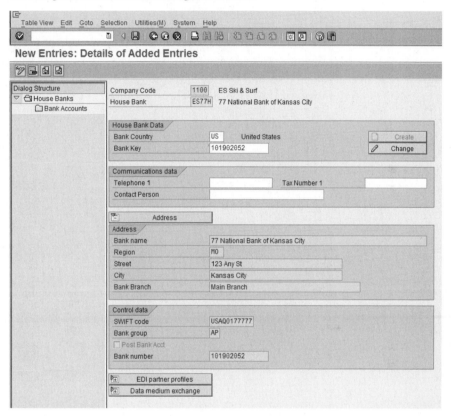

Now that the house bank is fully configured, it is time to create the accounts that go with it. As was stated earlier, each bank account is tied to one house bank. To create a bank account, click the New Entries button. The Create Bank Account screen appears. Enter the account ID, a text description for the bank account. Press Enter and the system will validate the entries you just made, presenting you with the bank account data configuration screen shown in Figure 4.5. You are free to define the identifier; it is alphanumeric and can be up to five characters in length.

**FIGURE 4.4**    The list of bank accounts configuration screen

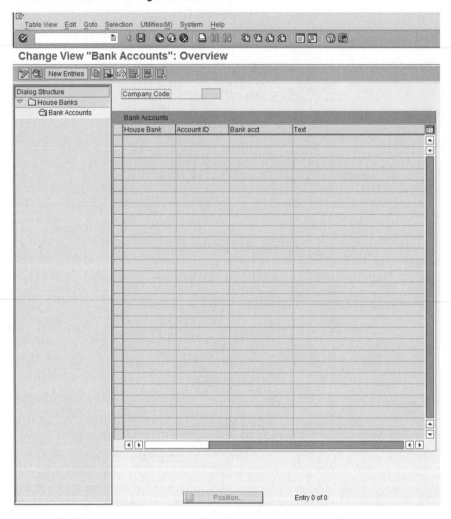

Let's take a look at the fields on the bank account data configuration screen:

**Bank Account Number**    Enter the identifying number of your account at the bank. This entry should correspond to the account number that is given to you on your bank statement.

**Alternative. Acct No.**    This field should be used only when accounts at the same bank have the same account number. Normally, the only way two different accounts will have the same account number is if the bank manages your company's accounts in more than one currency. Do not make an entry in this field unless it is required by your banking relationship. The alternative account number must be different than your normal bank account number.

**FIGURE 4.5**    The bank account data configuration screen

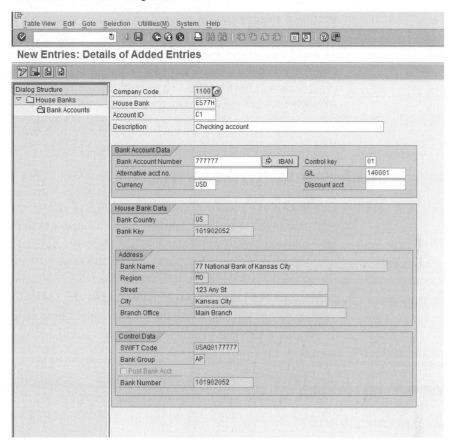

**Currency**    Enter the currency in which this account is managed. A listing of all valid currencies is available in a drop-down box.

**Control Key**    For U.S. banks, this is used to identify whether the account is a checking account (01) or a savings account (02). If an entry is not made in this field, the system defaults to checking account (01).

**G/L**    Each bank account has to be tied to a valid G/L account number. The bank account updates the G/L account entered here. The G/L structure for bank accounts will be explained in more detail later.

**Discount Acct**    If your company utilizes bill of exchange functionality, enter the cash discount account for credit memo postings that this bank account should update.

## EXTREME SPORTS HOUSE BANK AND ACCOUNT CONFIGURATION ANALYSIS

Because Extreme Sports has several trading partners outside of the United States, the SWIFT code for the house bank was entered. This will greatly enhance Extreme Sports's ability to conduct electronic banking transactions with the partner banks of its vendors and customers. The use of bank accounts will be configured in a later section.

# Bank Account G/L Structure

One of the many benefits that the flexibility of SAP offers is the ability to determine how much confirmed cash, floating cash out, and floating cash in there is for your company on any particular day. To accomplish this, you must form a strategy for the bank account G/L structure. For this to work, there must be *only one* confirmed cash G/L account, with several bank-clearing accounts. For example, a checks outgoing clearing, wire outgoing, ACH out, and deposits clearing need to be set up for each bank account. It is also important to leave yourself room for additional clearing accounts that you may need in the future for additional functionality.

The most flexible and best solution is to have a range of 10 G/L account numbers for each bank account. This solution will give you maximum flexibility; though you probably won't need 9 clearing accounts for each bank account at the outset, it gives you the ability to add more in the future should the need arise. This solution also allows you to simplify electronic bank statement transactions. (Electronic bank statement transactions will be explained in detail in Chapter 6.) For Extreme Sports, each confirmed cash balance will end with 1 (for example, G/L account 140001), each deposit clearing account will end with 2 (for example, G/L account 140002), each outgoing check clearing account will end with 3, each outgoing ACH account will end with 4, and each outgoing wire account will end with 5. You will notice in Figure 4.5 that Extreme Sports's A/P bank account was assigned to G/L account 140001. Even though it is an account designated for A/P, it still has a confirmed cash balance (140001) and clearing accounts for the different ways in which A/P transactions can be paid.

**EXTREME SPORTS BANK ACCOUNT G/L STRUCTURE CONFIGURATION ANALYSIS**

Extreme Sports wants the ability to see its confirmed cash balance as well as any incoming deposits or outgoing payments. For this reason, several bank-clearing accounts are set up for each bank account. This functionality is explained in more detail in Chapter 6. The Extreme Sports bank account G/L structure is as follows (the + symbol is a wildcard):

▶ **Confirmed Cash: +++++1**

▶ **Deposit Clearing: +++++2**

▶ **Outgoing Check Clearing: +++++3**

▶ **Outgoing ACH Clearing: +++++4**

▶ **Outgoing Wire Clearing: +++++5**

## Check Lots and Void Reason Codes

The final step in configuring the A/P bank account is to assign it to a check lot. Extreme Sports has purchased a micro-encoding (MICR) printer so that blank check stock can be used for payables. The check lot will determine the check number that is used on payments. To get to the check lots configuration screen, follow the menu path Financial Accounting ➢ Accounts Receivable and Accounts Payable ➢ Business Transactions ➢ Outgoing Payments ➢ Automatic Outgoing Payments ➢ Payment Media ➢ Check Management ➢ Define Number Ranges for Checks or use transaction code FCHI. Figure 4.6 shows the Check Lots screen.

**FIGURE 4.6**    The Check Lots screen

Enter the company code, house bank, and account for which you are creating the check lot, and then click the Change Status button. The Maintain Check Lots screen, shown in Figure 4.7, fully configured for Extreme Sports, appears.

**FIGURE 4.7**    The Maintain Check Lots screen

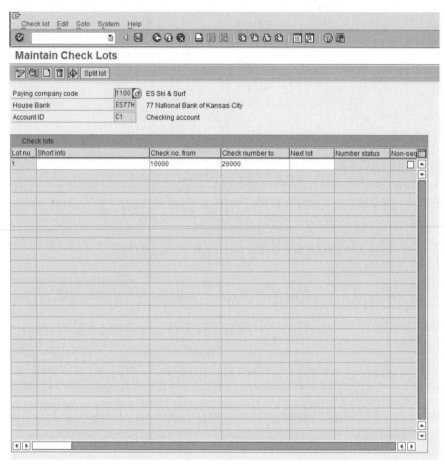

The system does not default to the create mode, and therefore the create icon and menu path (Edit ➤ Create) are not available and grayed out, respectively. To get past this, you should use the change/display icon on the upper-left side (the glasses and pencil icon) and alternate between change and display mode. Once you're back in change mode, the create icon appears. To create a new check lot and assign it to this account, click the create icon. In the pop-up box that appears, enter an identifier for the lot number (numeric only), the check numbers that the lot should begin and end with, and the next lot number (if needed). After entering these fields, press Enter.

The next step is to create void reason codes. SAP does not allow the user to void a check without a valid void reason code. You can have as many or as few void reason codes as you need, but you must have at least one. You can display the void reason codes configuration screen by using the menu path Financial Accounting ➤ Accounts Receivable and Accounts Payable ➤ Business Transactions ➤ Outgoing Payments ➤ Automatic Outgoing Payments ➤ Payment Media ➤ Check Management ➤ Define Void Reason Codes or using transaction code FCHV. Figure 4.8 shows the void reason codes configuration screen.

**FIGURE 4.8**    The void reason codes configuration screen

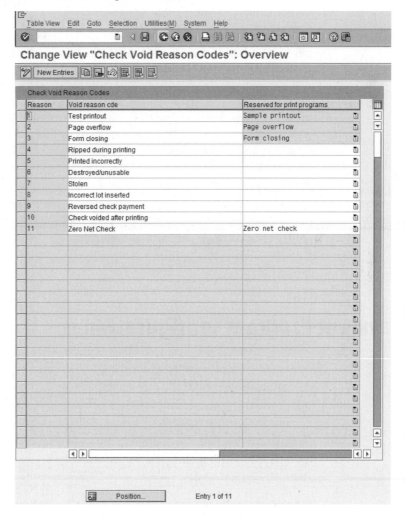

SAP comes delivered with void reason codes 1, 2, 3, and 4 in this version. The payment program uses these void reason codes when it encounters problems with the printer. As you can see from the indicators on the right side of the screen, a void reason code can be used manually or by the print program that is used by the payment program. Any void reason codes you create are automatically set to the manual indicator, which cannot be overwritten (Extreme Sports has configured void reason code 4). To create a new void reason code, click the New Entries button. In the new entries screen that appears, enter a new void reason code identifier (two-digit numeric) and a description. The system activates the manual check box for you.

### EXTREME SPORTS CHECK LOTS AND VOID REASON CODES CONFIGURATION ANALYSIS

Check lot 1 was created for one of Extreme Sports's A/P accounts. The lot number is specific to the bank account, so it is not of great importance. The beginning number of the check range was set to what the next check number should be once the cutover is made to SAP. Because Extreme Sports has invested in a MICR printer and will be using blank check stock, the last check number was set to the highest possible limit allowed by the system.

The manual void reason code 4 was created for Extreme Sports. This void reason code can be used after checks are printed to void a check number from the system. The project team will create additional void reason codes.

# Payment Program Configuration

Configuring the payment program allows you to determine exactly how and when vendor invoices get paid. You can configure many settings in the payment program; this provides you with a lot of flexibility in how you process payables in your production system. SAP allows both vendor and customer line items to be paid through the payment program. The ability to pay customers comes in handy when used in conjunction with some of SAP's other standard functionality, such as Sales & Distribution (SD) rebates.

Payment program configuration is a series of steps that are configured within one program (in the older versions of SAP, the configuration screen was housed on one main configuration screen). The specific steps that need to be undertaken will be shown in the order needed for configuration. The configuration transaction for the payment program is shown in the following sections. It occurs in table T042 and other variations of table T042 whose names have a letter as an extension (for example, T042Z, T042E, and so on). To get to the payment program configuration screen, follow the menu path Financial Accounting ➢ Accounts Receivable and Accounts Payable ➢ Business Transactions ➢ Outgoing Payments ➢ Automatic Outgoing Payments ➢ Payment Method/Bank Selection for Payment Program ➢ Set Up All Company Codes for Payment Transactions. Figure 4.9 displays the configuration screen for setting up the companies that will be performing payment transactions.

**FIGURE 4.9**    Paying company code configuration screen

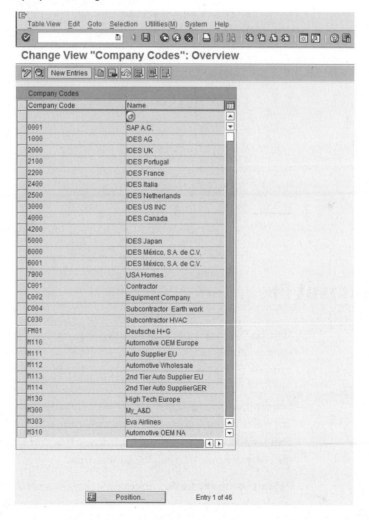

# Company Code Data

The first configuration step is to set up your company code (or codes) so it is available to the payment program. In addition to making the company code available to the payment program, this setting specifies a lot of the general control data for the company code. To carry out this step, click the New Entries button on the configuration screen. You are presented with the screen shown in Figure 4.10.

**FIGURE 4.10**   The New Entries: Details of Added Entries screen

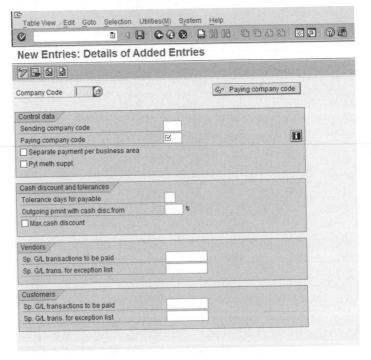

Here is where you enter the company code you want to make available to the payment program.

These are the fields that appear in the company code data configuration screen:

**Sending Company Code**   Enter the company code identifier by which the vendor you're paying knows your company. This will almost always be the same as the company code you are setting up. Leaving this field blank is the same as entering the company code that you are configuring.

**Paying Company Code**   Enter the company code identifier of the company that is actually paying the invoices. This is a required entry, even if the paying company code is the same as the company code you are configuring. A lot of companies, such as Extreme Sports, have a centralized A/P function set up in a shared services company. For this type of organizational structure, enter the company code of the shared services company that is actually paying the invoice for the configured company code. When you use this functionality, an intercompany posting is automatically created when invoices are paid.

**Separate Payment per Business Area**    Select this if you would want to have separate payments made by each business area within a company code.

**Pyt Meth Suppl.**    Usage of payment method supplements is functionality that allows the user to determine how customers and vendors are to be paid. This field is editable at the time of a payment run and is specific to a vendor within a company code.

**Tolerance Days for Payable**    If your company wants to grant itself "grace days," enter the number of days here. For example, if you enter a 5 in this field, the invoice won't be paid until the due date plus five days.

**Outgoing Pmnt with Cash Disc. From**    Unless a minimum percentage rate is entered here, SAP will make the payment at the time in which your company would receive the maximum cash discount amount related to its terms of payment on the invoice. If you enter a percentage here, SAP will only take cash discounts equal to or greater than the amount entered. Any cash discount below the entered rate will be ignored, and payment will be made on the next due date. For example, Extreme Sports earns 6% annually (0.5% monthly) on its deposits at the bank. Because most of Extreme Sports's terms are at X% discount rate, net 30 days, it would not want to accept a cash discount below 0.5%.

**Example 1**    Suppose there is an invoice amount of $5,000 and terms of 2% cash discount if paid in 10 days; otherwise the full amount is due in 30 days. Keeping the money to pay the invoice in the bank for 30 days would allow Extreme Sports to earn $25 in interest ($5,000 * 1.005). Taking the cash discount would save Extreme Sports $100 ($5000 * .02). Clearly, the benefit of the $100 cash discount far exceeds the $25 in interest that could be earned by keeping the money in the bank.

**Example 2**    Suppose there is an invoice amount of $5,000 and terms of 0.25% cash discount if paid in 10 days; otherwise the full amount is due in 30 days. Keeping the money in the bank for 30 days would allow Extreme Sports to earn $25 in interest ($5,000 * 1.005). Taking the cash discount would save Extreme Sports $12.50 ($5000 * .0025). Clearly the benefit of the $25 earned in interest by not paying the invoice until the end of 30 days far outweighs the cash discount amount of $12.50.

**Max. Cash Discount**   When this indicator is selected, the cash discount amount is always deducted when invoices are paid, even when the payment is after the maximum date specified in the terms to allow a cash discount. For example, an invoice has a baseline date of January 1, 2000, and terms of 2% cash discount if paid in 10 days; otherwise the full amount is due in 30 days. According to the terms, a cash discount can be taken on the invoice only up to January 10th. If this indicator is selected, and the invoice mentioned earlier was paid after January 10th, the cash discount would still be subtracted from the payment, and the full amount of the invoice would be cleared on the paying company's books. Selecting this indicator makes any entry in the Outgoing Pmnt with Cash Disc. From field invalid.

**Sp. G/L Transactions to Be Paid (under Vendors)**   In this field, enter the letter(s) of the special type of G/L postings that can be paid for vendors. The available special transactions are as follows:

**A**   Down Payment Request

**B**   Financial Assets Down Payment

**D**   Discount

**E**   Unchecked Invoice

**F**   Initial Down Payment Request

**G**   Guarantee

**H**   Security Deposit

**I**   Intangible Asset Down Payment

**M**   Tangible Asset Down Payment

**O**   Amortization Down Payment

**P**   Payment Request

**S**   Check/Bill of Exchange

**V**   Stocks Down Payment

**W**   Bill of Exchange (rediscountable)

**Z**   Down Payment for an Order or Project

**Sp. G/L Trans. for Exception List (under Vendors)**   In this field, enter the letter(s) of the special type of G/L postings that should be output to the exception list when the payment program is run. If a type of special G/L transaction is not entered in this field or in the Sp. G/L Transactions to Be Paid field, the payment program will totally ignore these transactions. The listing of special G/L transactions is the same as the list for the preceding field.

**Sp. G/L Transactions to Be Paid (under Customers)**   In this field, enter the letter(s) of the special type of G/L postings that can be paid for customers. The available special transactions are as follows:

A   Down Payment

B   Bill of Exchange Receivable

E   Reserve for Bad Debt

F   Down Payment Request

G   Guarantee

H   Security Deposit

P   Payment Request

Q   B/E Residual Risk

R   B/E Payment Request

S   Check/Bill of Exchange

T   Down Payment

U   IS-RE Adjustment Payment Sales Based Rent

W   Bill of Exchange Receivable

Z   Interest Receivable

**Sp. G/L Trans. for Exception List (under Customers)**   In this field, enter the letter(s) of the special type of G/L postings that should be output to the exception list when the payment program is run. If a type of special G/L transaction is not entered in this field or in the Sp. G/L Transactions to Be Paid field, the payment program will totally ignore these transactions. The listing of special G/L transactions is the same as the list for the preceding field.

## EXTREME SPORTS PAYMENT PROGRAM COMPANY CODE DATA CONFIGURATION ANALYSIS

The shared services organization of Extreme Sports (company code 1400) will be in charge of A/P for Extreme Sports's U.S.-based operations. Extreme Sports Mexico (company code 1300) will be responsible for its own A/P process. Because the shared services organization will be paying all invoices, company code 1400 (Extreme Sports Services) was entered as the paying company code for company code 1000 (Extreme Sports Ski & Surf). Utilizing this approach will cause SAP to automatically create an intercompany posting between company code 1000 and company code 1400 when payments are made.

The minimum cash discount amount to be taken was set to 0.5%. Please refer to the explanation of the Outgoing Pmnt with Cash Disc. From field for a review of why this setting was made.

Because Extreme Sports is utilizing business area functionality, the indicator was set to group and pay invoices by business area. This will help with the clearing and reconciliation of business area liabilities.

Some of Extreme Sports's business partners require down payments on materials. Because of this, special G/L transactions of A (Down Payment) and F (Down Payment Request) were configured so that these transactions would be paid on vendor line items. Extreme Sports does not currently have any special G/L transactions that should be paid for customers, so the customer special G/L transaction field was left blank.

# Paying Company Code Data

The second step to configuring the payment program is to set up parameters for the *paying company codes*. You will recall from the preceding section that the sending company code does not necessarily need to be the paying company code. For our example, company code 1400 is the paying company code for all of Extreme Sports's U.S.-based operations. Because of this, you need to set up only company code 1400 as a paying company code. The project team at Extreme Sports will set up company code 1300 (Extreme Sports Mexico) as a paying company code for Mexican-based operations at a later date.

To be able to configure the next step, follow the menu path Financial Accounting ➤ Accounts Receivable and Accounts Payable ➤ Business Transactions ➤ Outgoing

Payments ➤ Automatic Outgoing Payments ➤ Payment Method/Bank Selection for Payment Program ➤ Set Up Paying Company Codes for Payment Transactions.

The initial screen is a display of all existing paying company codes. Figure 4.11 shows the paying company codes.

To create company code 1400 as a paying company code, click the New Entries button. The configuration screen, shown in Figure 4.12, appears.

**FIGURE 4.11**   The list of paying company codes configuration screen

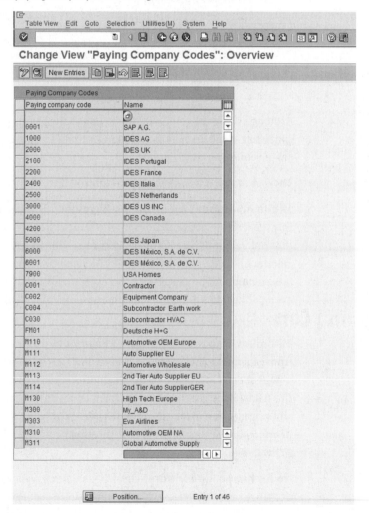

**FIGURE 4.12**    The paying company code data configuration screen

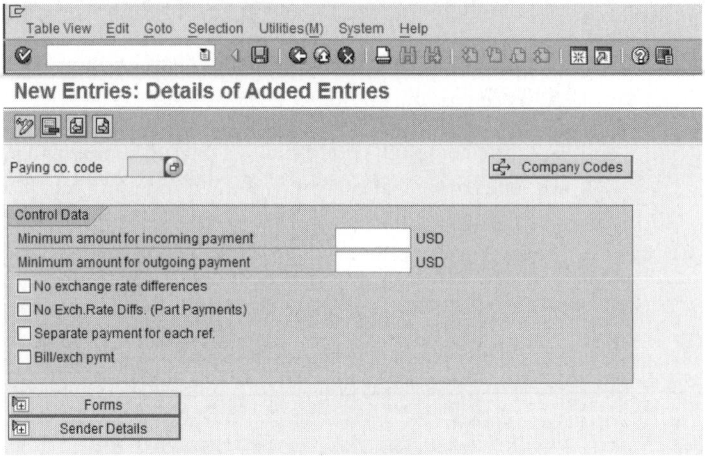

Although company code 1400 was set up as the paying company code for company code 1100 in the first payment program configuration step, it is still not set up as a paying company code.

These are some of the key fields in Figure 4.12:

**Minimum Amount for Incoming Payment**    If you want to stop the system from generating debit memos for amounts below a certain threshold, enter the threshold amount here. Only debit memos with an amount equal to or above the amount entered in this field will be generated by the system. All debit memos under this amount will be generated in an exception list after processing. Once there are enough line items to put the customer over the threshold amount, all line items will be included in the debit memo.

**Minimum Amount for Outgoing Payment**    If you want to stop the system from generating checks for amounts below a certain threshold, enter the threshold amount here. Only checks with an amount equal to or above the amount entered in this field will be generated for payment by the system. All checks under this amount will be generated in an exception list after processing. Once there are enough line items to put the customer over the threshold amount, all line items will be included in the check.

**No Exchange Rate Differences**    If you do not want the system to generate exchange rate differences when paying invoices, set this indicator. If this indicator is left blank, exchange rate differences will be posted for each individual transaction affected by foreign currencies.

**No Exch. Rate Diffs. (Part Payments)**   If you do not want the system to generate exchange rate differences when paying partial amounts on an invoice, set this indicator.

**Separate Payment for Each Ref.**   This indicator should be selected if the user wants to separate out payments by lines that have different reference values.

**Bill/Exch Pymt**   This indicator displays the Bill of Exchange field, if this field is selected, then use of bills of exchange will be permitted.

You'll see the following fields when you click the Forms button.

**Form for the Payment Advice**   Enter the identifier of the SAPScript to be used for creating payment advices. Payment advices are sent to vendors along with checks to explain the product or service for which the check is issued. (The creation of SAPScripts is beyond the scope of this book. SAP does deliver for each form several standard SAPScripts that can be used or referenced to create a custom form.)

**EDI Accompanying Sheet Form**   Enter the identifier of the SAPScript that is to be used to create the correspondence sheet that accompanies EDI transactions.

The remaining fields on the screen in Figure 4.12 all have to do with bills of exchange. Each setting is self-explanatory if you are using the bill of exchange functionality.

---

### EXTREME SPORTS PAYING COMPANY CODE DATA CONFIGURATION ANALYSIS

Extreme Sports has determined that it is too costly to process payments less than $5. For this reason, $5 was set as the minimum amount for incoming and outgoing payments. Extreme Sports does not want to recognize foreign currency gains and losses on individual payment transactions, so the No Exchange Rate Differences indicator was set. Layout set F110_US_AVIS was set as the form for the payment advice. Later, an ABAP project team member will copy and then modify the layout set to meet Extreme Sports's requirements. Bill of exchange functionality is not utilized by Extreme Sports.

---

## Country Payment Methods

The third step in configuring the payment program is to set up *country payment methods*. Country payment methods specify which payment methods (checks, wires, ACH, etc.) can be used by company codes in a specific country. The country payment method configuration specifies the general control parameters for a payment method. To configure the country payment methods, follow the menu path Financial Accounting ➢ Accounts Receivable and Accounts Payable ➢ Business Transactions ➢ Outgoing Payments ➢ Automatic Outgoing Payments ➢ Payment Method/Bank Selection for Payment Program ➢ Set Up Payment Methods per Country for Payment Transactions. The screen shown in Figure 4.13 appears.

**FIGURE 4.13**   The country payment methods configuration screen

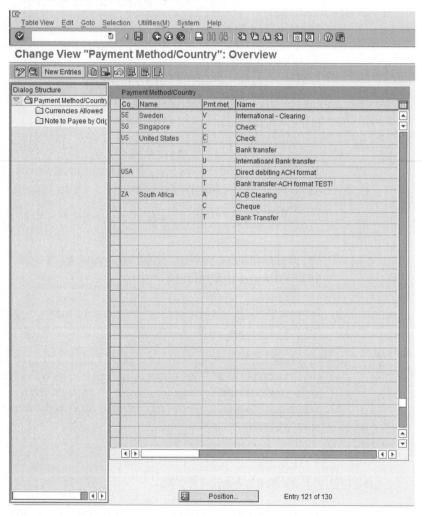

As you can see in Figure 4.13, several payment methods are configured for United States company codes. In Figure 4.14, we have selected C for check as a payment method in the United States. You select a payment type by double-clicking its identifier. When you double-click, the appropriate country screen appears.

**FIGURE 4.14**    The country payment methods detail screen

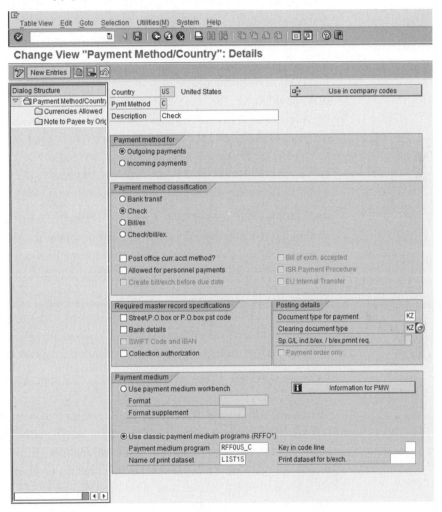

The fields in the country payment methods detail screen are grouped into four categories; the category explanations as well as the most important fields in each category are listed here:

**Payment Method Classification**   These fields control the type of payment that is made as well as special country-specific processing methods that are used by the payment type. The most important indicators for normal payment types are Check and Allowed for Personnel Payments. If the payment type is supposed to create a physical check, the Check indicator must be activated.

For payment types that are set up for incoming payments, the Payment Method for Incoming payments indicator must be active (this is used primarily with other treasury activities). To allow the SAP Human Resources module to use a payment type, the Allowed for Personnel Payments indicator must be activated. It is a good idea not to allow the normal check payment type (C) to be used for payroll transactions. So that you can better reconcile and control A/P and payroll checks, a new payment type for payroll checks (P) should be created. Payment type P should be a copy of C with the Allowed for Personnel Payments indicator activated.

**Required Master Record Specifications**   These fields specify what master data must be filled out on the individual customer or vendor master record for a payment to be made by this payment type. If the master data fields activated in this grouping are not filled out on the customer or vendor master record, the line items are output to an exception list.

**Posting Details**   These fields control how payments update (post) in the system. The document types for payment and reversal of payments are specified here as well as the special G/L indicator that is updated when bills of exchange are processed.

**Payment Medium**   These fields control how the output of the payment program is created. The most important field in this grouping is Payment Medium Program. To find the correct print program for your payment type in your country, do a search of SAP programs that begin RFFO*. The programs for your country are usually RFFO++*, where ++ is the two-character identifier for your country. The check printing program for the U.S. is RFFOUS_C, and the program for wires and ACH transfers is RFFOUS_T. The name of the print dataset is used when the checks are spooled instead of immediately printed.

**EXTREME SPORTS COUNTRY PAYMENT METHODS CONFIGURATION ANALYSIS**

The U.S. payment type for checks (C) was configured in this section. Because physical checks will be created with this payment type, the Check indicator was activated. Extreme Sports wants the ability to easily see what checks are A/P and what checks are payroll, so the Allowed for Personnel Payments indicator was not activated.

Extreme Sports will make important fields required in the actual setup of vendor master records, not in the payment types. For this reason, none of the fields in the Required Master Record Specifications section were activated. Making fields required in the actual setup for master records will cut down on exception processing by Extreme Sports's staff.

Document type KZ (Vendor Payment) was set for both the payment document type and the clearing document type. Any document type that allows postings to both vendor and G/L accounts can be used.

The SAP standard U.S. check printing program (RFFOUS_C) was set for use by this payment type. If the standard SAP program does not meet all of your requirements, the program can be copied and modified. The name Checks was used for the print dataset so the print job can be easily found if the checks are spooled instead of immediately printed.

## Company Code Payment Methods

The fourth step to configuring the payment program is to make further specifications to the payment types that were created in the preceding section (country payment types). The *company code payment methods* allow further control of how the payment method works in the system. To configure the company code payment methods, use the following menu path: Financial Accounting ➤ Accounts Receivable and Accounts Payable ➤ Business Transactions ➤ Outgoing Payments ➤ Automatic Outgoing Payments ➤ Payment Method/Bank Selection for Payment Program ➤ Set Up Payment Methods per Company Code for Payment Transactions. Figure 4.15 shows the screen that appears.

**FIGURE 4.15**    The list of company codes payment methods screen

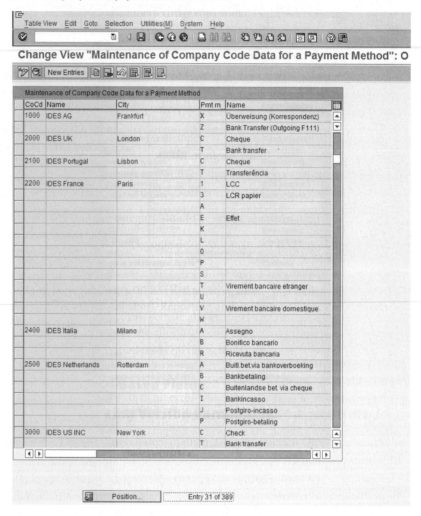

We once again set up company code 1400, this time to extend country payment methods to it. From the screen in Figure 4.15, select Edit ➤ New Entries, or merely click the New Entries button. The screen in Figure 4.16 appears.

**FIGURE 4.16**    The company code payment methods configuration screen

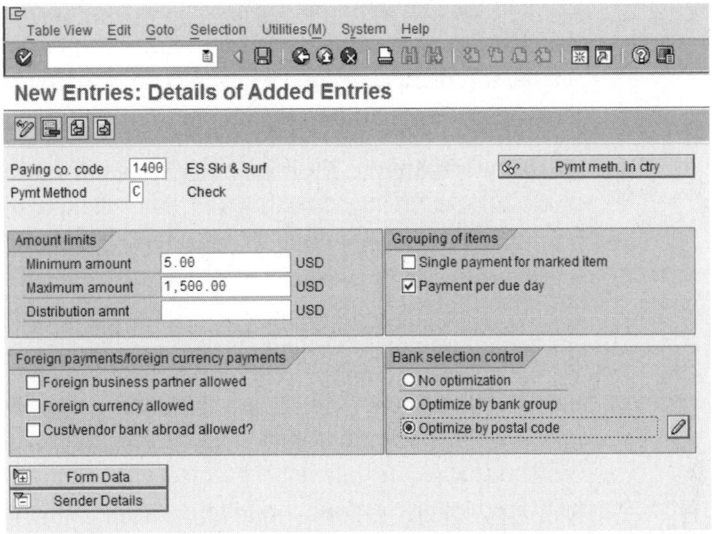

Here's an explanation of the fields (with the exception of Bill of Exchange fields) that appear in the company code payment methods general data configuration screen:

**Minimum Amount**    You will recall from the subsection on company code data that a minimum amount for payment was already configured. The Minimum Amount field on this screen controls the minimum amount for the payment method on items that are not explicitly assigned a payment type. This field has no effect on items that are assigned a payment type on the document or vendor master record. The following table shows whether the payment method Minimum Amount field would work on each line item, assuming a minimum amount entry of $4.

| Vendor Master Record | | | | |
|---|---|---|---|---|
| Payment Type | C | - | - | - |
| Document Payment Type | - | C | - | - |
| A/P Amount | $2.00 | $2.00 | $2.00 | $4.25 |
| Payment Method Minimum | | | | |
| Amount Field Used? | No | No | Yes | No |

**Maximum Amount**    Enter the maximum amount that can be paid by this payment method on items that are not explicitly assigned a payment method. This field has no effect on items that are assigned a payment type on the document or vendor master record. Review the explanation of the minimum amount field to determine how the processing will work.

**Distribution Amnt**    The functionality employed here is to limit payments to the maximum set. The functionality is further enhanced by matching remaining allowable amounts with other smaller open items. This is the most efficient way of pairing open items with payment methods.

**Single Payment for Marked Item**    Activate this field if you want to create an individual payment for each line item assigned this payment type. If this field is not activated, the payment program will group together all open items for a vendor or customer and pay them on a single payment. If you have only a small group of vendors that require individual payment for each invoice, an easier method is to activate the single payment field in the vendor master record of the affected vendors. This approach is much easier than creating a new payment method for single payments; this will be explained further in "Vendor Master Data" later in this chapter.

**Payment per Due Day**    Activate this field if you want to group together items by payment date. This features means that only items with the same due date for a vendor will be grouped together for payment. Normally, all items, regardless of due date for vendors, are grouped together. The functionality of this field is better explained in the following example, in which Extreme Sports has six individual line items with vendor A:

| DUE DATE | AMOUNT | PAYMENT GROUPING | | |
|----------|--------|------------------|--------|--------|
| 10/03/1999 | $500 | 1 | - | - |
| 10/19/1999 | $200 | 3 | - | - |
| 10/03/1999 | $700 | 1 | $2.00 | $4.25 |
| 10/04/1999 | $876 | 2 | | |
| 10/03/1999 | $589 | 1 | Yes | No |
| 10/19/1999 | $250 | 3 | | |

If the Payment per Due Day functionality was activated, there would be three separate payments to vendor A because the six line items are due on three separate days. Payment 1 (10/03/1999 due date) would be in the amount of $1,789, payment 2 (10/04/1999 due date) would be in the amount of $876, and payment 3 (10/19/1999 due date) would be in the amount of $450.

**Foreign Business Partner Allowed**    Select this indicator if you want to allow the payment method to be used with vendors and customers who do not reside in the home country of the company code.

**Foreign Currency Allowed**    Select this indicator if you want the ability to pay invoices in a currency other than your company code currency. Be careful not to allow payments in foreign currency on checks if your check stock denominates in your home currency.

**Cust/Vendor Bank Abroad Allowed?**    Select this indicator if you want to be able to use bank-to-bank payment communication for customer and vendors who reside abroad and wish to be paid at a bank in their home country. The bank must be set up in the vendor master record in order for the bank-to-bank communication to occur.

**Optimize by Bank Group**    Activate this indicator if you want SAP to determine the paying bank based on the best match of your company's house banks and the vendor's banks. You will recall from the section on house banks that there was a Bank Group field on the house bank master data. SAP will look at the entries in the Bank Group field for all affected banks (paying company and vendor) and determine the best match for quicker processing of payments. This functionality is particularly useful in electronic payment types (wires, ACH, etc.).

**Optimize by Postal Code**    Activate this indicator if you want SAP to determine the paying bank by looking at the zip code of the vendor being paid. This functionality will be configured in the next section.

## EXTREME SPORTS COMPANY CODE PAYMENT METHOD CONFIGURATION ANALYSIS

The payment method C (for checks) was configured in this section. Extreme Sports decided to keep the minimum overall payment amount for items not explicitly assigned to this payment method. A maximum of amount of $1,500 was configured.

To make sure cash discounts are maximized, the Payment per Due Day indicator was activated. This will allow invoices to be held as long as possible before payment.

This payment method is also allowed for payments to customers and vendors that are not based in the company code's country (US) because of a reciprocity agreement with some Canadian banks, allowing Extreme Sports's Canadian vendors to cash U.S. checks.

Bank selection will be optimized by postal code. SAP will look at the vendor's zip code and determine the appropriate house bank to use for payment based on configuration settings that map ranges of zip codes to house banks.

## Bank Selection

The next step in configuring the payment program is determining the *bank selection* procedure. This step is actually a series of smaller steps that build upon one another. Follow the menu path Financial Accounting ≻ Accounts Receivable and Accounts Payable ≻ Business Transactions ≻ Outgoing Payments ≻ Automatic Outgoing Payments ≻ Payment Method/Bank Selection for Payment Program ≻ Set Up Bank Determination for Payment Transactions. The initial bank selection configuration screen, shown in Figure 4.17, appears.

**FIGURE 4.17**   The initial bank selection configuration screen

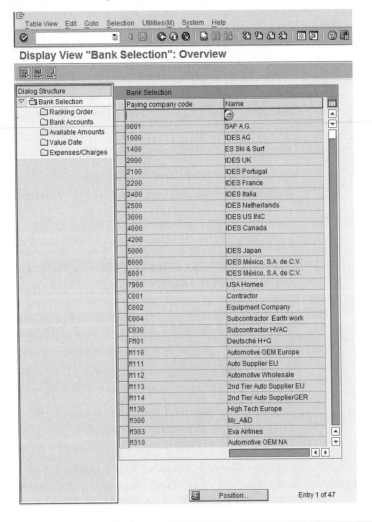

## Payment Method Bank Selection

On the initial bank selection configuration screen, select the paying company code (1400) for which you wish to configure bank selection. The Dialog Structure section on the left-hand side contains the menu options you will follow. The first step in the setup process is to create a ranking order from which the payment program can make a payment. Double-click the Ranking Order folder on the left. Figure 4.18 shows the bank account ranking screen that appears.

**FIGURE 4.18**    The bank account ranking screen

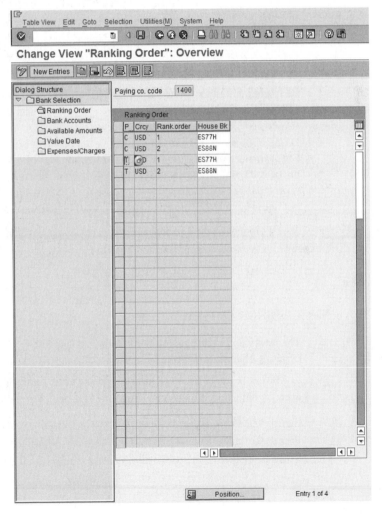

The payment method has been configured for Extreme Sports, but when the screen first appears, there will be no existing information for the company code you are configuring. To configure the information, click the New Entries button. The blank screen that was grey is now white, which is the standard indicator that a field is in an editable status. Insert the appropriate payment method (C), currency (USD), ranking order, and house bank in the proper fields. The ranking order determines which bank should be selected for the given payment method if the other forms of bank selection fail. For example, if postal code bank optimization is being used and the vendor has a zip code that does not fall within a configured range, SAP will use the bank with the highest ranking order (starting from 1) with the available funds to pay the invoice. You must utilize bank selection optimization by either bank group or postal code, as this is the only way SAP knows how to select the bank.

## EXTREME SPORTS PAYMENT METHOD BANK SELECTION CONFIGURATION ANALYSIS

Extreme Sports utilizes two different banks for payment activities (ES77H and ES88N). For payment method C, house bank ES77H should be the first bank selection if the postal code optimization is unable to select a bank; house bank ES88N should be the second bank selected. The only way house bank ES88N would be selected in this case is if house bank ES77H did not have the available funds to make the payment.

As you can see from the screen in Figure 4.18, an additional payment method was created for company code 1400: T for wires.

## Bank Account Determination

The next step in configuring bank selection is to configure the accounts that are to be used by the house banks you just set up for payment method bank selection. To configure the bank accounts, double-click the Bank Accounts folder. The bank account determination screen shown in Figure 4.19 appears.

Figure 4.19 shows the screen configured for Extreme Sports, but when the screen first appears, there won't be any bank accounts set up for the company code you're using. To make the proper bank accounts available, click the New Entries button.

**FIGURE 4.19**    The bank account determination screen

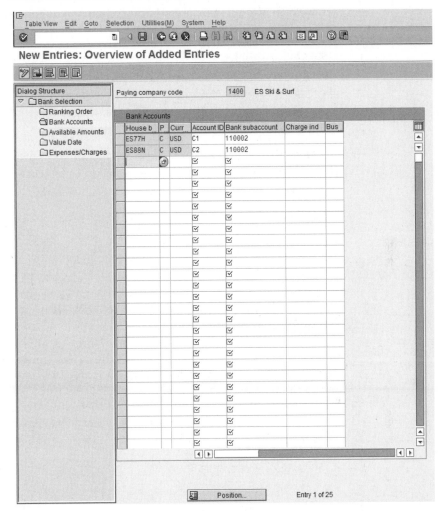

The fields that appear in Figure 4.19 are explained here:

**House Bank**    Enter the identifier for the house bank where the bank account you wish to configure resides. Make sure all accounts configured in this screen belong to house banks that were set up in the payment method bank selection screen.

**Payment Method**    Enter the payment method with which the bank account is to be used. Payment methods were configured in the preceding section, "Payment Method Bank Selection."

**Currency**    Enter the currency identifier used by the bank account.

**Account ID**    Enter the identifier for the bank account that is to be configured. House bank IDs were configured in the section "House Banks and Accounts" earlier in this chapter.

**Bank Subaccount**    Enter the G/L account to which the payment posting for the bank account is to be made. This account should be the clearing account that should be used by the payment method for which you are using the account. Refer back to "Bank Account G/L Structure" earlier in this chapter for an explanation of the different bank clearing accounts used by Extreme Sports.

**Charge Ind**    Some payment methods, such as bills of exchange, utilize charges on payments. If your payment requires a charge, enter a charge indicator here. Generally, this field is not used for U.S. payment methods.

**Business Area**    Enter the business area that is to be posted to for this bank account. If you configured separation of payment per business area in the company code configuration of the payment program, this entry is ignored.

### EXTREME SPORTS BANK ACCOUNT DETERMINATION CONFIGURATION ANALYSIS

The bank accounts that are to be used by Extreme Sports were configured in this section. Notice the bank subaccounts that were used and how they relate to the information in "Bank Account G/L Structure" earlier in this chapter. Also be aware that some of the bank accounts, such as those used for payment methods C and T, are physically one bank account with several G/L subaccounts to simplify bank statement processing.

## Amounts

Now that the appropriate bank accounts have been configured, it is time to maintain the available amounts they can use. To configure the amounts for bank accounts, double-click the Available Amounts folder on the left (shown in Figure 4.19). You are presented with the available amounts configuration screen, shown in Figure 4.20.

As you can see, information has not been maintained for company code 1400. To configure the amount per bank account information, click the New Entries button. The available amounts screen will be editable; enter the identifiers for the house bank and account ID as well as the days and currency of the bank account. The Days (until Value Date/Charge) field is generally only used for bill of exchange payment methods; this allows you to post payment before the due date. For payment methods other than bill of exchange, enter **999** in the Days (until Value Date/Charge) field. The 999 entry in effect nullifies this field when processing is taking place. Enter the maximum amount of money in the configured bank account that you want to be available to the payment program. You can enter all 9s in this field to make all amounts in the account available for use by the payment program.

**FIGURE 4.20** The planned amounts screen

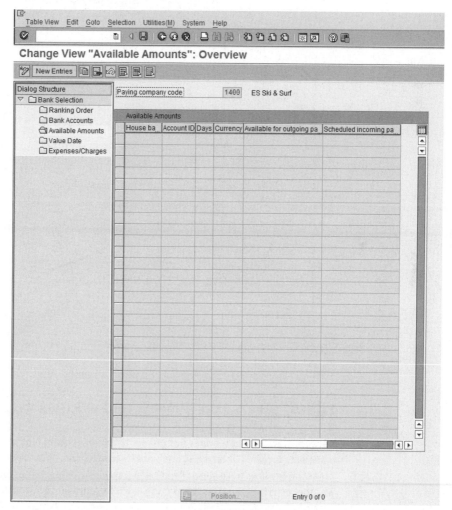

The fully configured planned amounts screen for Extreme Sports is shown in
Figure 4.21.

**FIGURE 4.21**   The fully configured planned amounts screen for Extreme Sports

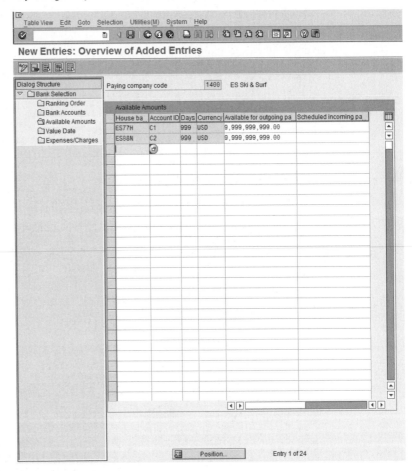

## EXTREME SPORTS BANK AMOUNTS CONFIGURATION ANALYSIS

Because Extreme Sports does not utilize the bill of exchange payment method, the
value date for all of Extreme Sports's bank accounts was set to 999. Extreme Sports's
cash strategy is to have separate A/P and payroll accounts that are segregated from
all other activities. For this reason, the available amount for outgoing payment was
set to $9,999,999,999.00 so that all funds in these accounts are available for use by
the payment program.

## Value Dates

Another important step in configuration of the payment program is to maintain *value dates* for the payment methods used by your company. A value date is used as an average of the number of days it takes for a payment to clear the bank. The value date is important because it determines the amount available per due date to the payment program. It's also important for cash management and liquidity forecasting in the Treasury module. To configure value dates, double-click on the Value Date folder on the left as can see in Figure 4.21. The value date configuration screen appears (Figure 4.22).

**FIGURE 4.22**    The value date screen

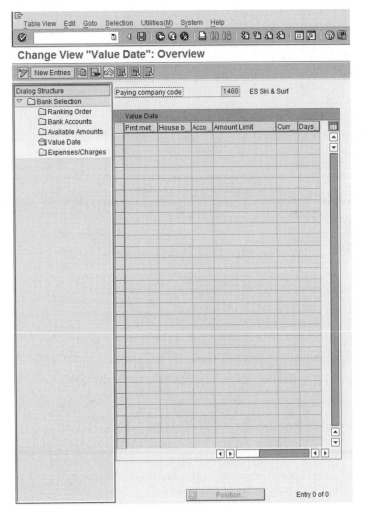

Value dates have not yet been maintained for company code 1400. To configure value dates, click the New Entries button. You will be able to tell from the configuration screen that value dates are unique per payment method, house bank, account ID, and amount limit. The amount limit is the maximum amount up to which the value date is valid. This functionality is useful if a payment that is over a certain amount takes longer to process through the bank than payments of lower amounts. The number of days entered in the Days to Value Date field is added to the payment date to derive the value date. The fully configured value date screen for Extreme Sports is shown in Figure 4.23.

**FIGURE 4.23**    The fully configured value date screen for Extreme Sports

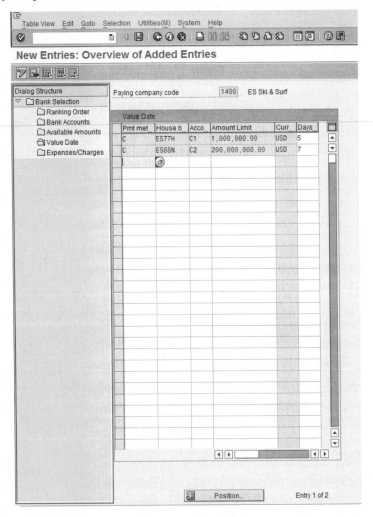

## EXTREME SPORTS VALUE DATE CONFIGURATION ANALYSIS

On average, Extreme Sports has determined that it takes three days for A/P checks under $150,000 to be cleared through the bank. For A/P checks over $150,000, it generally takes five days. It takes an average of two days for payroll checks to clear the banks. The bank clears all U.S. wire transactions on the next business day.

The value date will be used to forecast available cash balances to the payment program as well as cash management and liquidity forecasts in the Treasury module. Once there is more history in the system, SAP has the functionality to determine value dates for each individual vendor. When this information is in the system, the value date here will be used only if there is no information for a vendor.

## Bank Optimization via Postal Codes

You will recall from the configuration of the paying company code that bank selection optimization via postal codes was activated. The functionality for selecting a bank from the zip code on the vendor master record will be configured in this section. To configure postal code functionality, you will have to follow this menu path: Financial Accounting ➤ Accounts Receivable and Accounts Payable ➤ Business Transactions ➤ Outgoing Payments ➤ Automatic Outgoing Payments ➤ Payment Method/Bank Selection for Payment Program ➤ Set Up Payment Methods per Company Code for Payment Transactions.

From the initial configuration screen, select company code 1400 and you will be presented with the screen shown in Figure 4.24.

To optimize postal code (zip code) functionality, click the pencil icon next to the Optimize by Postal Code radio button. Once you have selected this icon, you will be presented with the configuration screen in Figure 4.25 (note that the screen has already been configured for Extreme Sports). To enter the necessary data to use this functionality, click the New Entries button. The fields to configure in the screen are for country, postal code (zip code) lower limit, postal code (zip code) upper limit, and the house bank that is to be used for the range of zip codes in the country being configured. This configuration is very simple and self-explanatory.

**FIGURE 4.24**    The maintenance of company code data for a payment method

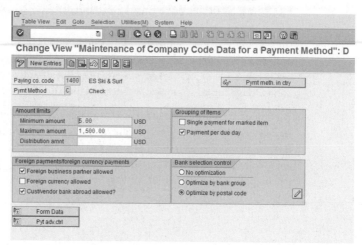

**FIGURE 4.25**    The bank selection by postal code screen

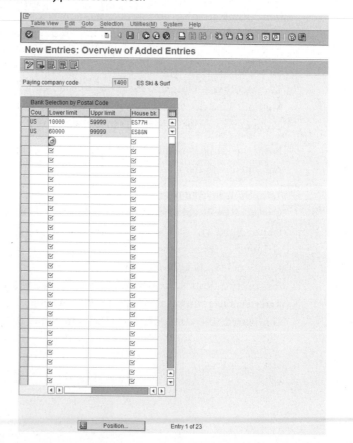

## EXTREME SPORTS BANK OPTIMIZATION VIA POSTAL CODES CONFIGURATION ANALYSIS

Extreme Sports has opted for a simplified bank optimization via zip codes at this time. For purpose of this book, it is assumed that all zip codes from 10000 to 59999 lie east of the Mississippi and all postal codes from 60000 up lie west of the Mississippi, with house bank ES77H based in Kansas City and house bank ES88N based in New York. This allows Extreme Sports to match bank payments to geographic regions as an added benefit to its vendors (which will allow vendors to cash Extreme Sports's payments faster).

# Vendor Master Data

Before you begin configuration of *vendor master* data, it is necessary to have a strategy. You should know ahead of time how you would like to use your vendor master data and how you will convert vendors from your legacy system, as well as the integration points that vendor master data has with MM, Treasury, and A/R. Much like the G/L, vendor master data is a combination of configuration and master data maintenance.

A key concept in the configuration of vendor master data is *vendor groups*. Vendor groups allow you to have separate purposes and field statuses for different types of vendors. For example, you could have a group for regular vendors, a group for 1099 vendors, and a group for one-time vendors. By separating these different types of vendors into different vendor groups, you can make different fields required, optional, or suppressed for each of the groups.

## Vendor Groups

The first step in configuring vendor master data is to create your vendor groups. Once you have gathered all of your requirements and know what the groups should be, you are ready to begin. You can display the configuration screen for creating vendor groups by using the menu path Financial Accounting ➤ Accounts Receivable and Accounts Payable ➤ Vendor Accounts ➤ Master Records ➤ Preparation for Creating Vendor Master Records ➤ Define Account Groups with Screen Layout (Vendors).

After entering the configuration transactions, you are presented with the screen shown in Figure 4.26.

**FIGURE 4.26**   The initial vendor groups configuration screen

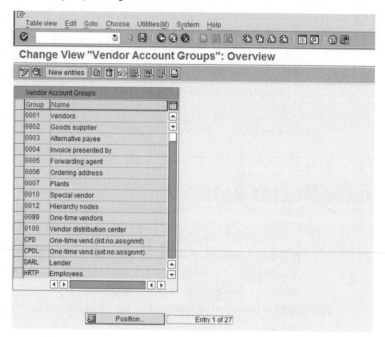

From the initial vendor groups configuration screen, click the New Entries button to access the screen shown in Figure 4.27.

**FIGURE 4.27**   The vendor groups new entries screen

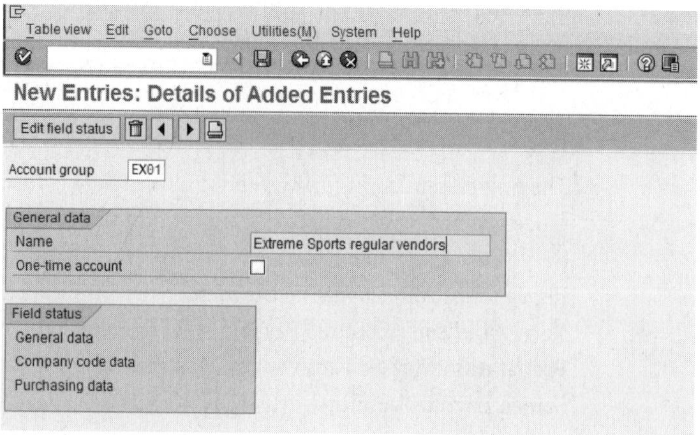

Here is a list of the fields that appear in the vendor groups new entries screen:

**Account Group**    Enter a four-character alphanumeric identifier for the vendor group you are creating.

**Name**    Enter a descriptive name for the vendor group you are creating.

**One-Time Account**    Select this indicator if you want this vendor group to be used for one-time vendors. One-time accounts are used for vendors that you may use only once and for which you do not want to store a unique vendor master record. Only one vendor master record is needed for all one-time vendors. The name, address, and other important information needed for payment are entered on the document when you specify a one-time vendor number. You should only need one one-time vendor account group for your company.

**Field Status**    The concept of field statuses should be familiar to you from your work on the general ledger in Chapter 3. The field statuses on this screen control which fields are optional, required, and suppressed when a vendor master record is created.

The first page of the configuration screens and the most important fields for each category of vendor group field status are covered in the following sections.

## Vendor Group Field Status

Now we will explore in detail the different kinds of data that you configure from the Field Status section of the vendor groups new entries screen. To access a field status group, double-click the field status group name on the lower-left corner of the screen.

The first screen for the configuration of the *General Data* section of the vendor group field status appears in Figure 4.28. The fields in this section are valid for the vendor master data regardless of the company code using it.

The subsections of the general data field status, as well as some of the most important fields to consider in each subsection, are listed here:

**Address**    The Address section contains the fields that capture the mailing address information about the vendor. It is generally a good idea to make the Name, Location (city), Region (state), and Country fields required so that you don't have incomplete information about your vendors.

**Communication**    The Communication section contains fields that capture information such as telephone numbers, fax numbers, and so on. These fields are relatively self-explanatory, and it's easy to determine if you need to fill them out.

**FIGURE 4.28**    The initial general data configuration screen

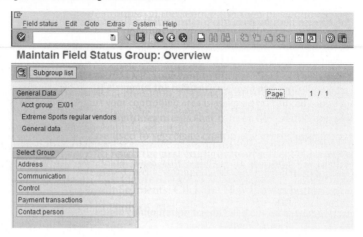

**Control**    The Control section contains many important fields that capture how the vendor master record is processed. Here's a listing of the most important fields in this section:

**Customer**    In this field, you can tell the system that this vendor is also a customer (by entering the customer number). This allows you to do A/P-A/R netting if you so desire.

**Tax Codes**    These fields are important in determining the type of tax used on invoices for these vendors (sales or use tax) and in specifying 1099 vendors.

**Payment Transactions**    The fields in this section help with the processing of the payment program:

**Bank Details**    The fields pertaining to bank details allow you to specify where the vendor's bank wishes to receive payment. This helps with payment program optimization by bank group as well as electronic payment transactions.

**Alternative Payee Account**    If you have some vendors you do not pay directly, this field helps to facilitate that transaction.

**Company Code Data**    The first screen for the configuration of the *Company Code Data* section of the vendor group field status appears in Figure 4.29. All fields in this section are valid at the company code level only. This means that, as vendors are extended across several company codes, the fields in this section can have different values based on the company code using the vendor master data.

**FIGURE 4.29**    The initial company code data configuration screen

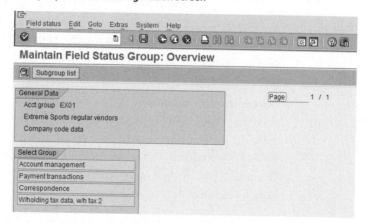

The subsections of the company code data field status, as well as the most important fields to consider in each subsection, are listed here:

**Account Management**    The Account Management fields control how vendor master data updates the general ledger. They are as follows:

**Reconciliation Account**    As you are aware, the A/P system is a subledger. The reconciliation account is the G/L account updated by A/P transactions using this vendor account. Different vendors or vendor groups can update different reconciliation accounts.

**Planning Group**    The planning group is a major integration point between A/P and Treasury. The planning group updates the payable section in the liquidity-forecast functionality of the Treasury module. (The liquidity-forecast report will be covered in Chapter 6.) If you want to utilize the treasury functions within SAP, make this field mandatory.

**Previous Account Number**    This field can be used to capture the legacy vendor number in SAP. It is especially useful in the initial time after Go-Live when the system is looking up vendors. A match key can be created to look up vendor numbers based on this field.

**Payment Transactions**    The fields in this section help with the processing of the payment program based on specific settings for the company code in which the vendor can be used. The settings for these fields can vary from company code to company code, whereas the settings for the fields in the payment transaction subgrouping in the General Data section cannot. Here are the settings and their definitions:

**Terms of Payment**    You can specify the default payment terms that the vendor grants your company in this field. The default terms of payment can be overridden at the document level when the invoice is entered.

**Double Invoice Validation**    When this indicator is set, the system checks to see if the invoice being entered has previously been entered. It is a good idea to make the reference document field required on the document type that is used for A/P invoices. The vendor's invoice number should be entered in the Reference Document field. The use of the Reference Document field allows this indicator to work for non-P.O.-related invoices

**Payment Block**    Using this field, you can block all invoices for this vendor from being paid automatically by the payment program.

**Payment Methods**    You can specify which payment method (or methods) is valid for this vendor's invoices. Payment methods were configured in the payment program.

**Clearing with Customer**    Select this indicator if you want to clear open A/P accounts with open A/R accounts for this vendor if the vendor is also a customer. The customer number can be specified in the General Data section.

**Cashed Checks Duration**    The system updates this field based on the history of how long it takes for checks cut to this vendor to clear the bank. The program that updates this field is contained in the Treasury module.

**Individual Payment**    Select this indicator if individual checks should be cut for each invoice that relates to this vendor.

**Correspondence**    The fields in this section allow you to store additional information for contact with the vendor as well as enable and specify dunning information with the vendor:

**Account at Vendor**    Your customer number at the vendor is stored in this field. This can greatly help your A/P clerks in researching open A/P issues.

**Purchasing Data**    The first screen for the configuration of the Purchasing Data section of the vendor group field status appears in Figure 4.30. These fields deal mainly with MM functionality. How you configure the fields in this section will depend greatly upon the purchasing strategy that is designed and agreed upon between you and your MM group. These fields are another major integration point between FI and MM.

**FIGURE 4.30**    The initial purchasing data configuration screen

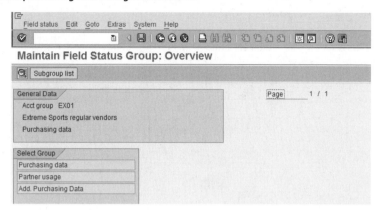

## EXTREME SPORTS VENDOR GROUP CONFIGURATION ANALYSIS

The regular vendor account group for Extreme Sports was configured in this section. The vendor group identifier EX01 was configured for this group. The One-Time Account indicator was not activated because a separate one-time vendor account group will be configured for Extreme Sports.

## Assigning Number Ranges to Vendor Account Groups

In this section, you will create a new number range and assign the number range to the vendor account group that was just configured. Number ranges can be set up as external (user assigns a number) or internal (system assigns a number).

**TIP**    It is a good idea to initially make all of your vendor account groups externally assigned. This will help in the conversion of your vendor accounts from your legacy system to SAP. This way, the conversion program can be run into each client and you know that the vendor numbers will be the same for production. After your final conversion run into your production client, the number range can be changed to internal.

To get to the vendor account number ranges configuration screen, follow the menu path Financial Accounting ➢ Accounts Receivable and Accounts Payable ➢ Vendor Accounts ➢ Master Records ➢ Preparation for Creating Vendor Master Records ➢ Create Number Ranges for Vendor Accounts or use transaction code XKN1.

After entering the configuration transaction, you are presented with the screen shown in Figure 4.31.

**FIGURE 4.31**    The vendor account number ranges configuration screen

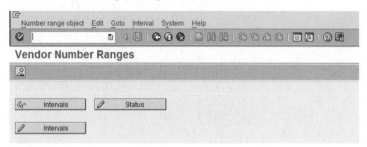

Click the Intervals button (with the pencil, which indicates you are going to maintain mode). The screen shown in Figure 4.32 appears.

**FIGURE 4.32**    The number range intervals screen

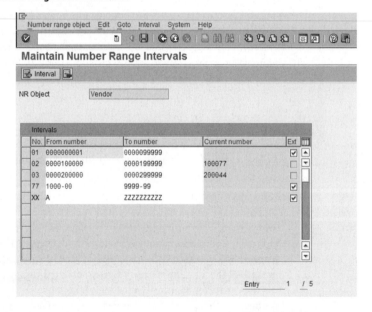

From the screen displayed in Figure 4.32, click the insert interval icon. The pop-up box shown in Figure 4.33 appears.

**FIGURE 4.33**    The Insert Interval pop-up box

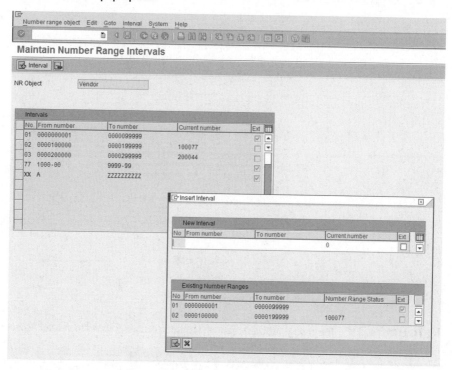

In the fields in Figure 4.33, enter an identifier for the number range, the number where the range should start (From Number), and the number where the range should stop (To Number). Update the current number (if internal number assignment is used), and activate the external indicator if you want the user to specify the vendor number. After entering this information, click the insert icon. The configured number range for Extreme Sports is shown in Figure 4.34.

The next step is to assign the number range that was just created to the vendor group just created. Remember that number ranges are not automatically included in transports and should be created manually in each client. The configuration transaction for assigning number ranges to vendor groups is displayed using the menu path Financial Accounting ➢ Accounts Receivable and Accounts Payable ➢ Vendor Accounts ➢ Master Records ➢ Preparation for Creating Vendor Master Records ➢ Assign Number Ranges to Vendor Account Groups.

Figure 4.35 shows the configuration screen for assigning number ranges to vendor account groups. Enter the number range you would like to assign to the vendor group.

**FIGURE 4.34** The configured number range intervals screen for Extreme Sports

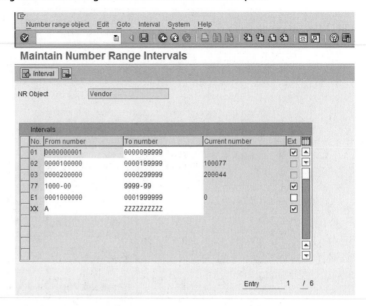

**FIGURE 4.35** The configuration screen for assigning number ranges to vendor account groups

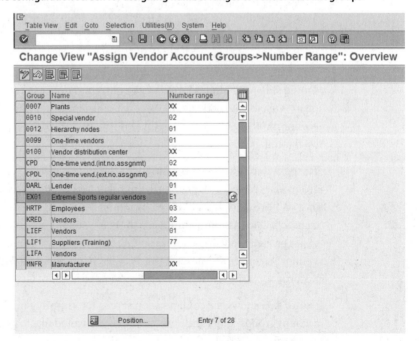

## EXTREME SPORTS VENDOR GROUP NUMBER RANGE ASSIGNMENT

Extreme Sports created number range E1 with internal number assignment to be used for vendor group EXO1, which is for normal vendors. Utilizing internal number assignment for normal vendors will speed up the process of creating new normal vendors.

## Creating Vendor Master Data

There are several ways to create vendor master data in the system. In particular, there are two ways to create vendor master data in the FI-AP area. Vendor master records can be created for the company code or centrally. When you select company code creation, only the general and accounting screens are available for data population. When you select the option to create them centrally, all the general, accounting, and MM purchasing screens are available for configuration. Creating vendor master data centrally requires a good amount of coordination with your MM group.

Just as there are two ways to create vendor master data, there are two ways to enter invoices in the system. You can enter non-P.O.-related invoices directly in the A/P system. Non-P.O.-related invoices are usually for services such as utilities and telephone and for insurance bills. The other way to enter invoices is through the MM module. Invoices entered through the MM module are P.O.-related invoices. The MM module can be configured to require either two-way or three-way matching. Three-way matching ensures that each P.O. has matching G.R. (Goods Receipt) and I.R. (Invoice Receipt). P.O.-related invoices are usually done for production and maintenance materials. Using P.O.-related invoices allows you to use a lot of functionality included in the MM module.

SAP delivers two programs that allow you to extend vendor master records to company codes other than the company code where the vendor master record was created. These programs are very similar to the programs that are used to extend G/L accounts. You can get to the program that copies vendor master records from company code to company code by using the application menu path Accounting ➤ Financial Accounting ➤ Accounts Payable ➤ Master Records ➤ Compare ➤ Company Codes ➤ Send or by using transaction code FK15.

Figure 4.36 shows the screen for the vendor master record copy program (RFBIKR10).

**FIGURE 4.36**    The vendor master record copy program (RFBIKR10) screen

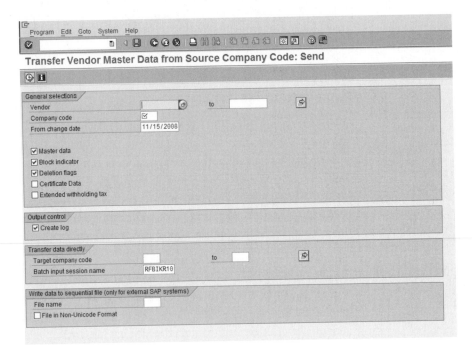

As we mentioned earlier, this program works in much the same manner as the G/L copy program (RFBISA10). Using this program (RFBIKR10), you can either create a batch input session that can be executed in the same client or create an external file that can be run into other clients.

You can get to the program that imports the file created by the vendor master copy program (RFBIKR20) using the application menu path Accounting ➢ Financial Accounting ➢ Accounts Payable ➢ Master Records ➢ Compare ➢ Company Codes ➢ Receive or using transaction code FK16.

Figure 4.37 shows the vendor master copy file import program (RFBIKR20) screen.

**FIGURE 4.37**    The vendor master copy file import program (RFBIKR20) screen

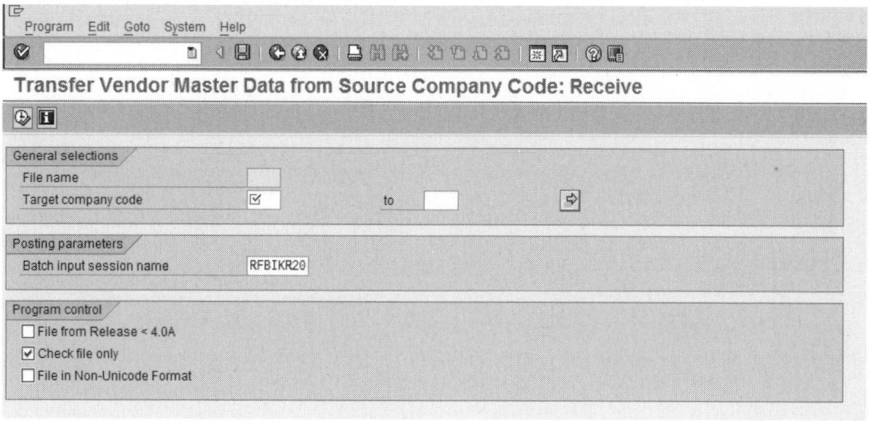

# Summary

In this chapter, we covered the configuration of the Accounts Payable module. You learned that the proper master data configuration (house banks, bank accounts, and vendor master data) is vital to a finely tuned A/P module. The paramount of A/P configuration is the payment program. We covered configuration of the payment program step by step, allowing you to learn how to best configure the program for your company.

# Accounts Receivable

**FEATURING:**

▶ TERMS OF PAYMENT AND INTEREST CALCULATION

▶ REASON CODES

▶ DEFAULT ACCOUNT ASSIGNMENTS

▶ OVERALL A/R AND EMPLOYEE TOLERANCES

▶ CREDIT MANAGEMENT

▶ CUSTOMER MASTER RECORDS

The Accounts Receivable subledger (A/R) allows you to effectively manage your customer accounts and unpaid invoices. The A/R submodule has lots of options and is very flexible. In addition to strictly A/R topics, we'll also cover credit management in this chapter. Credit management allows you to grant customers' credit according to your business terms and risk aversion.

# Terms of Payment and Interest Calculation

*Terms of payment* involve the discount amounts and the related time frames for payment you send to your customers. The configuration for terms of payment is the same for both A/R and A/P. The same terms of payment can be used for both A/R (customer) and A/P (vendor) accounts. To configure terms of payment, follow the menu path Financial Accounting ➢ Accounts Receivable and Accounts Payable ➢ Business Transactions ➢ Outgoing Invoices/Credit Memos ➢ Maintain Terms of Payment.

After using this menu path, you are presented with the terms of payment overview screen, shown in Figure 5.1.

**FIGURE 5.1**     The terms of payment overview screen

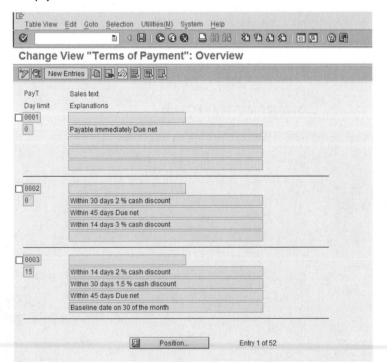

To create a new payment term, click the New Entries button. The payment terms new entry screen, shown in Figure 5.2, appears.

**FIGURE 5.2**        The payment terms new entry screen

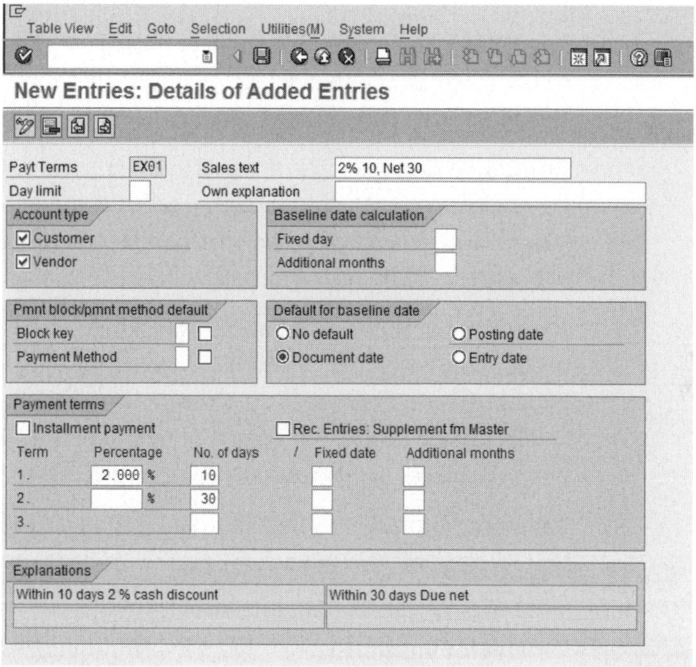

Here is an explanation of the fields in the payment terms new entry screen:

**Payt Terms**    Enter a four-character alphanumeric identifier for your payment-term key.

**Sales Text**    Enter a short text explanation of the key. Your entry is limited to 30 characters.

**Day Limit**    This field is valid only if your terms of payment depend on the day of the month. For example, an invoice billed on or before the 10th of the month is due on the 25th of the same month, and an invoice billed after the 10th is due on the 5th of the next month. Given this example, a 10 would be entered in this field because the terms are good until the 10th day of the month.

**Own Explanation**    This field is used to give a detailed explanation of the payment terms. This field should be used only if you want to override the explanation that is automatically generated by the system. The system explanation is shown in the bottom fields, in the Explanations section.

**Customer**    Select this indicator if you want the payment term to be used for customer accounts (A/R).

**Vendor**    Select this indicator if you want the payment term to be used for vendor accounts (A/P).

**Fixed Day**    Use this field if you want to override the default baseline date proposed by the system. If you want to utilize this functionality, enter the calendar day that should be used for the baseline date.

**Additional Months**    Use this field in conjunction with the Fixed Day field. Enter the number of months that should be added to the calendar month of the proposed baseline date. The baseline date then becomes the combination of the Fixed Day field and the Additional Months field.

**Block Key**    If this term of payment should propose a block key—which blocks goods issued for delivery (A/R) or payment (A/P)—enter the block key here. The block key takes effect only if the terms-of-payment key is entered in the customer or vendor master record. If this payment term is inserted in the line item of the document, the block key is not defaulted in.

**Payment Method**    If you want to specify a specific payment method (other than that specified in the customer or vendor master record) with this term of payment, enter the payment method identifier here.

**Default for Baseline Date**    Select the radio button that corresponds to the baseline date you want to default to when using this term of payment. You can choose between No Default, Document Date, Posting Date (the date that the document posts in the system; this can be the same or it can vary from the document date), and Entry Date (the system prompts you for the baseline date when the document is entered).

**Installment Payment**    Select this indicator to allow the system to automatically break out a single line item into multiple line items with different due dates based on the payment term. The system prompts you for the breakout when an FI document is entered.

**Rec. Entries: Supplement fm Master**    When this setting is selected, the system will derive the terms of payment from the master record if the terms are not present on the original entry.

**Percentage**    Enter the percentage rate that is to be used for the discount.

**No. of Days**    Enter the number of days out from the baseline date for which the percentage discount is valid.

**Fixed Date**   Enter the day of the month on which the discount ends if you do not want to use the baseline date.

**Additional Months**   If you want to add a month or months to the baseline-date month to determine the length of time the discount is valid, enter the number of additional month(s) in this field.

**Explanations**   The system defaults an explanation of the payment term in this field based on of the percentage discount and length of time the discount is valid. An entry in the Own Explanation field overwrites the system-derived explanation.

## EXTREME SPORTS' PAYMENT TERMS CONFIGURATION ANALYSIS

The terms-of-payment key, EX01, was configured to meet one of the terms it grants for cash discount. Both customer and vendor accounts can use EX01. This way Extreme Sports can use the key on the invoices it sends out, and if a vendor uses the same terms for Extreme Sports' invoices due, this key can be used in the vendor master record. The default baseline date for this key is the document date. This means that the calculation for cash discount and overall due date will begin from the document date entered in the system. You can see in the Payment Terms section that a cash discount of 2% is granted if the invoice is paid within 10 days (of the document date of the invoice). If the invoice is not paid within 10 days, the full amount of the invoice is due in 30 days. The sales text is set to read "2% 10, Net 30," so that when invoices and customer master records are created, the user can easily determine what type of cash discount this terms-of-payment key is granting. The system automatically generates the Explanations section at the bottom of the screen based on the configuration that was done in the screen.

# Interest Calculation

The next feature that will be configured for Extreme Sports is the *interest calculation* procedure. Interest calculation allows you to charge interest on overdue customer accounts. The system keeps track of the date of the last interest run and stores it in the customer master record.

The first step to configuring interest calculation is to create an *interest indicator*. For interest to be calculated on a customer, the interest indicator must be stored in the customer master record. Interest can be calculated by using line items or overall account balances. The line-item calculation will be used in this example.

If you want to calculate interest on a G/L account such as confirmed cash, you would calculate the interest based on the account balance. To get to the configuration screen for interest indicators, follow the menu path Financial Accounting ➢ Accounts Receivable and Accounts Payable ➢ Business Transactions ➢ Interest Calculation ➢ Interest Calculation Global Settings ➢ Define Interest Calculation Types.

The interest settlement (calculation type) overview screen, shown in Figure 5.3, is displayed after following that menu path.

**FIGURE 5.3**    **The interest settlement (calculation type) overview screen**

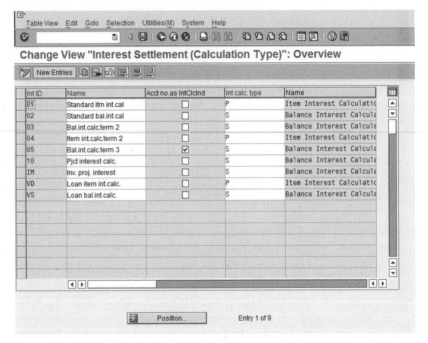

To create a new interest indicator, click the New Entries button. You are then presented with the new entries configuration screen, shown in Figure 5.4.

Here is a list of explanations for the fields in the new entries configuration screen:

**Int ID**    Enter a two-character alphanumeric identifier to be used for your interest indicator.

**Name**    Enter a descriptive name for your interest indicator.

**Acct No. as IntClcInd**   If you want to use the customer account number as the interest indicator, activate this field. The field must contain 10 characters, so you may have to enter leading zeros.

**Int Calc. Type**   Select either P or S from the drop-down box. P signifies that this interest indicator will calculate interest based on line items. S signifies that this interest indicator will calculate interest based on account balances.

**FIGURE 5.4**     The new entries configuration screen

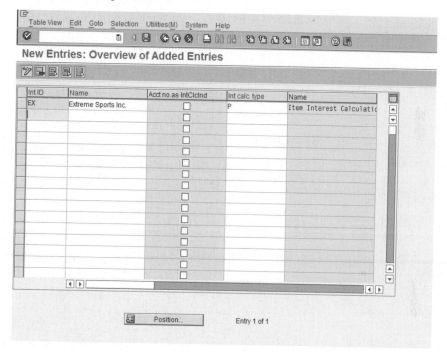

## EXTREME SPORTS INTEREST INDICATOR CONFIGURATION ANALYSIS

The interest indicator EX was configured for Extreme Sports. It will be used for overdue accounts-receivable interest calculations. Therefore, the interest-calculation type of P was used so that the interest would be calculated off of individual line items. Because interest indicators can also be used on normal G/L accounts such as confirmed cash, the S option is provided so that interest can be calculated off of account balances.

Now that the interest indicator has been created, the next step is to make it available to the interest run program. When you make the interest indicator available to the interest run program, you also specify additional characteristics about how you want the indicator to function. Follow the menu path Financial Accounting ➤ Accounts Receivable and Accounts Payable ➤ Business Transactions ➤ Interest Calculation ➤ Interest Calculation Global Settings ➤ Prepare Interest on Arrears Calculation to get to the configuration screen to make the interest indicator available to the interest run program.

Figure 5.5 shows the configuration screen for making the interest indicator available to the interest run program.

**FIGURE 5.5**    The initial interest run program configuration screen

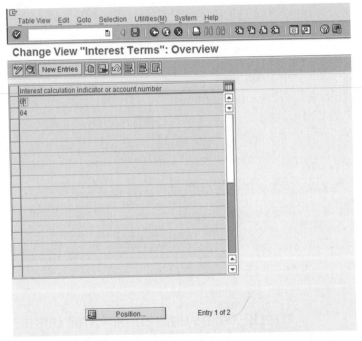

To make your interest indicator available to the interest run program, click the New Entries button. The screen shown in Figure 5.6 is displayed.

Here is an explanation of the fields in the interest run program configuration screen:

**Int. Calc. Indicator**    Enter the identifier of the interest indicator you created earlier (shown earlier in Figure 5.4).

**FIGURE 5.6**        The interest run program configuration screen

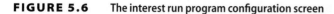

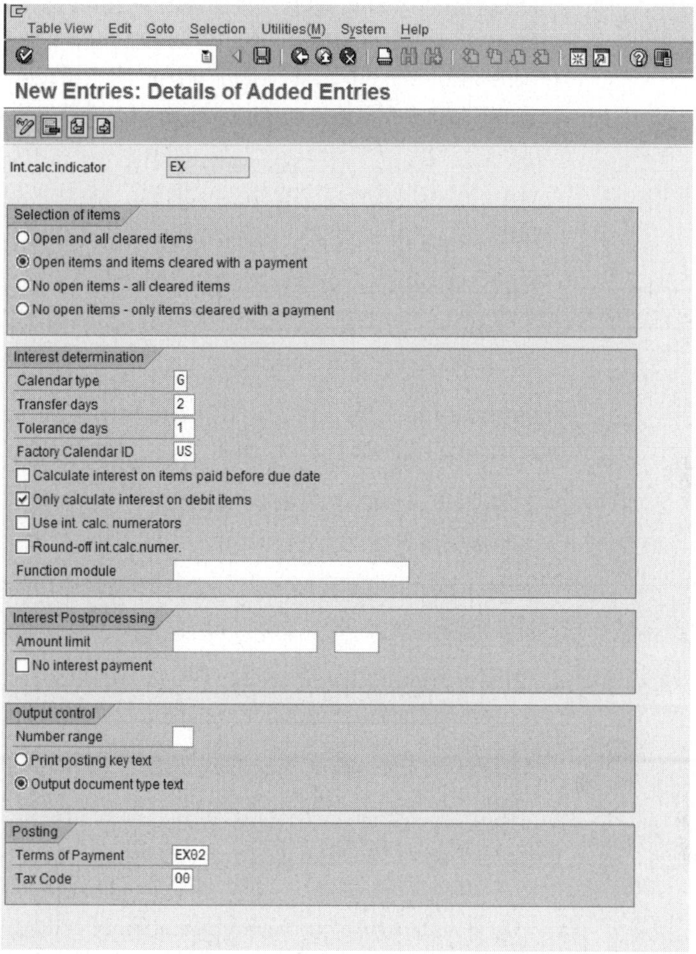

**Selection of Items**    The radio buttons in this section determine the line items on which interest is calculated. The program will try to select all available line items that have become past due since the date of the last interest run based on the parameter selected here. The available entries are as follows:

**Open and All Cleared Items**    If you select this radio button, all line items (both open and cleared), regardless of the clearing method, are selected for interest calculation—this option is all-inclusive. For example, if an invoice has already been cleared by a payment but the payment did not fall within the terms of payment, interest is still calculated on the invoice. The same rule applies for invoices cleared with a credit memo.

**Open Items and Items Cleared with a Payment**    If you select this radio button, all open line items and line items cleared by a payment transaction are selected for interest calculation. In this example, invoice line items cleared by a credit memo would not be selected for interest calculation—only those invoice line items cleared by a payment would be selected.

**No Open Items—All Cleared Items**    If you select this radio button, only cleared items are selected for interest calculation. All cleared items are selected regardless of how they were cleared. Open items are not selected with this option.

**No Open Items—Only Items Cleared with a Payment**    If you select this radio button, only line items cleared by a payment will be selected for interest calculation. Line items cleared by any other method and open line items are ignored.

**Calendar Type**    The calendar type determines the number of days per period that interest is calculated. The available options are as follows:

**B (Bank Calendar)**    The bank calendar uses 360 days as the basis for a year and 30 days as the basis for a month.

**F (French Calendar)**    The French calendar uses 360 days as the basis for a year and the exact number of days in the month as the basis for a month.

**G (Gregorian Calendar)**    The Gregorian calendar uses 365 days as the basis for a year and the exact number of days in the month as the basis for a month.

**J (Japanese Calendar)**    The Japanese calendar uses either 365 or 366 days (depending on leap years) as the basis for a year and 30 days as the basis for a month.

**Transfer Days**    Transfer days represent the number of days it takes for the customer's payment to reach your company and be applied. For example, you can use transfer days to figure out the average number of days it takes a customer's check to reach your company or your company's lockbox through the mail. Transfer days are deducted from overdue up until the point that they would result in a late payment being paid early. Transfer days affect only cleared line items; they have no effect on open line items. Assume, for example, that an invoice is paid four days late. If two transfer days have been granted in this configuration step, when interest calculation is run, SAP treats the invoice as being only two days late (four days overdue minus two tolerance days). If an invoice was cleared with a payment two days late and three transfer days have been granted in this configuration step, when interest calculation is run, SAP treats the invoice as being paid on the due date (not before the due date as the calculation of two days overdue minus three tolerance days might lead you to believe).

**Tolerance Days**    Tolerance days are also known as the grace period, or grace days. They are subtracted from overdue days to determine whether interest should be calculated. For example, if an item is one day overdue and one tolerance day is granted, it will be treated as paid on the due date, and no interest will be calculated. However, if an item is five days overdue and one tolerance day is granted, the item is treated as four days overdue, but five days' worth of interest would be calculated. Transfer days are subtracted before grace days when interest calculation is run.

**Factory Calendar ID**    This calendar is used to differentiate from working and non-working days.

**Calculate Interest on Items Paid Before Due Date**    If you select this indicator, interest is also calculated on items paid before their due date. The result of this calculation is credit interest, which will decrease the customer's A/R balance. This is the opposite of the most common reason for calculating interest—debit interest that increases the customer's A/R balance.

**Only Calculate Interest on Debit Items**    If you select this indicator, interest is only calculated on debit line items (invoices and debit memos). If you do not select this indicator, interest is also calculated on credit line items (credit memos), and this credit interest is offset against the debit interest from invoices.

**Use Int. Calc. Numerators**    This option is not normally needed. If this indicator is activated, the system first determines the numerators that are to be used for the calculation and then carries out the rest of the interest calculation.

**Round-off Int. Calc. Numer.**    If you have activated interest calculation numerators in the preceding field, you can activate this indicator to allow the system to automatically round off the numerators that are used in the calculation.

**Function Module**    If you do not want to use the standard interest-calculation procedure in SAP, you can program your own function module to calculate interest. Enter the name of the module in this field.

**Amount Limit**    You can keep the system from posting insignificant amounts of interest by entering a minimum/maximum amount here. If the amount of interest calculated is larger than the minimum/maximum amount entered here, the interest is posted. If the amount of interest calculated is smaller than the minimum/maximum amount entered here, the interest is not posted.

**No Interest Payment**    If you are calculating interest on credit items as well as debit items, you can select this indicator if you do not want to create an interest settlement when credit interest is paid back to the customer.

## EXTREME SPORTS—MAKING THE INTEREST INDICATOR AVAILABLE TO THE INTEREST RUN PROGRAM CONFIGURATION ANALYSIS

In this step, we have made interest indicator EX, which was configured earlier, available to the line-item interest-calculation program. There is a separate configuration step to make interest indicators available to the account-balance interest-calculation program. Interest indicator EX will select all open items and only cleared items that were cleared with a payment. This means items cleared by a credit memo or other means will not be selected for interest. This fits in well with Extreme Sports' customer-service philosophy because items cleared with a credit memo normally arise due to some type of dispute with the customer, in which case Extreme Sports has decided that the customer is correct. Extreme Sports decided that calculating interest on an invoice that was disputed and might later be issued credit would not work well with its business model.

The Gregorian calendar is used as the basis for calculating interest. Analysis done by Extreme Sports has determined that it normally takes two days for a check to travel from the customer's office to Extreme Sports' lockbox. Because of this, Extreme Sports has granted two transfer days. Extreme Sports has also decided to grant one tolerance day per invoice and to calculate interest only on debit items (invoices and debit memos) because this is the standard U.S. business practice followed by all of Extreme Sports' subsidiaries. The payment term EX02 was configured for use with interest postings. Payment term EX02 does not grant any cash discount—all line items with EX02 are due in full in 30 days. Tax code O0 was configured for use with interest postings. Tax code O0 is maintained with a 0% rate. This will work well because interest postings are nontaxable in the U.S.

**Number Range**    SAP will post interest using a normal accounting document. However, you have the option of also creating an interest form that becomes a reference document to the interest posting. If you wish to create an interest form, enter the document number range the form should use. Use transaction code OB84 to define the form that your company code should use for interest forms.

**Print Posting Key Text**    If you decide to use interest forms, you can activate this indicator to output the posting-key text on the line item that is created on the interest form.

**Output Document Type Text**    If you decide to use interest forms, you can activate this indicator to output the document type text on the line item that is created on the interest form.

**Terms of Payment**    Enter the terms of payment that should be used for the interest posting. The interest posting does not automatically take on the terms of payment for the line item causing the interest posting.

**Tax Code**    Enter the tax code the system should use when making the interest posting. Normally you should enter an exempt tax code (a tax code maintained with a 0% rate).

Now that the interest indicator has been made available to the interest-calculation program, the next step is to determine the interest rate that the calculation will use. The first step in determining the interest rate is to define a reference interest rate. Reference interest rates are keys by which specific interest rates are assigned to specific periods. Examples of reference interest rates include LIBOR, Prime, Fed Funds Rate, and 30-Year Bond Rate. To create a reference interest rate, follow the menu path Financial Accounting ➢ Accounts Receivable and Accounts Payable ➢ Business Transactions ➢ Interest Calculation ➢ Interest Calculation ➢ Define Reference Interest Rates or use the transaction code OBAC.

After executing the transaction listed in the Define Reference Interest Rates shortcut box and clicking the New Entries button, you are taken to the reference interest rate new entries screen, shown in Figure 5.7.

**FIGURE 5.7**    The reference interest rate new entries screen

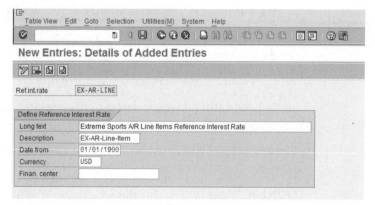

The fields on the reference interest rate new entries screen are as follows:

**Ref.Int.Rate**    Enter a 10-character identifier to be used for the reference interest-rate key.

**Long Text**    Enter a long text description that can be used to give detailed information about the reference interest-rate key.

**Description**   Enter a short text description that can be used to give information about the reference interest-rate key.

**Date From**   Enter the first date that the reference interest rate can be used. Like most things in SAP, reference interest rates are time-dependent. Make sure you set this date so it is available in all periods in which you may want to use it. It is always safer to make it available much earlier than you think you will need it.

**Currency**   Enter the currency identifier key that this reference interest-rate uses.

**Finan. Center**   If you are utilizing the cash budget-management functionality within the Treasury module, enter the financial center that this reference interest rate belongs to.

Now that a reference interest rate has been created, the next step is to assign our interest indicator to our reference interest rate. The relationship between interest indicator and reference interest rate is time-dependent. Because it is time-dependent, you can configure your interest indicator to use different reference interest rates in the future. You can assign interest indicators to reference interest rates by following the menu path Financial Accounting ➢ Accounts Receivable and Accounts Payable ➢ Business Transactions ➢ Interest Calculation ➢ Interest Calculation ➢ Define Time-Based Terms.

Following the configuration methods for assigning a reference interest rate to interest indicators takes you to the screen shown in Figure 5.8.

After clicking the New Entries button, you are taken to the time-based interest terms configuration screen, shown in Figure 5.9.

The fields on the screen in Figure 5.9 are listed here:

**Int.Calc.Indicator**   Enter the interest-indicator identifier to which you wish to assign a reference interest rate.

**Currency Key**   Enter the currency-key identifier that is to be used in the interest calculation.

**Eff. From**   Enter the first date this relationship is valid. If in the future you want to assign the interest indicator to a different reference interest rate, you can create a new record with a Valid From date that is later than the Valid From date in the first record. In this case, the Valid From date on the first record will be valid only until the Valid From date on the second rate. Beginning at the Valid From date on the second record, the new reference interest rate is used.

**FIGURE 5.8**       The reference interest rate configuration screen

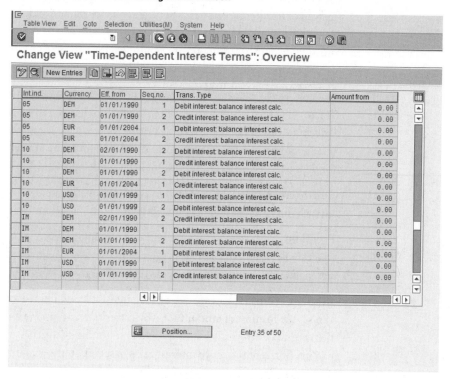

**FIGURE 5.9**       The time-based interest terms configuration screen

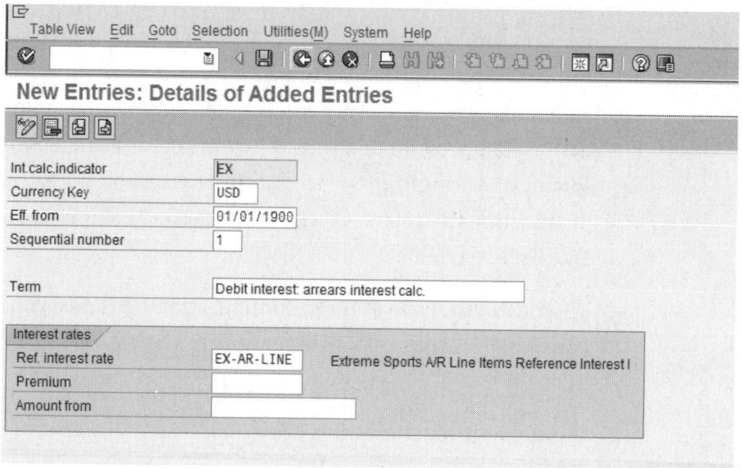

**Sequential Number**   If you are calculating interest based upon account balances instead of line items, you can enter the sequence number that is to be used. This field, in combination with the Amount From field, allows you to use more than one interest rate based upon the account balance and the sequence in which reference interest rates are assigned. If you are using line-item interest calculation, always enter 1 in this field.

**Term**   Use the pull-down box on this field to select the appropriate entry. This field determines what the interest indicator/reference interest-rate relationship is used for (credit interest for days overdue, credit interest for account balances, debit interest for days overdue, or debit interest for account balances).

**Ref. Interest Rate**   Select the reference interest-rate key you want to assign to the interest indicator entered in the first field.

**Premium**   You can charge an additional percentage rate on top of the reference interest rate by entering a percentage rate in this field. If the reference interest rate is not maintained or contains 0%, only the surcharge rate is used in interest calculation.

**Amount From**   If you are calculating interest based upon account balances, you can set the minimum amount for which this reference interest rate is valid. You can then create new records with different amounts and sequence numbers so that you can use different reference interest rates based upon the account balance.

The final configuration step needed to make the interest-calculation program work is to determine how and to which accounts the interest program will post. The interest-calculation program does not use the automatic account-determination features that we discussed in Chapter 3. It uses its own posting interface to determine the accounts instead of using process keys. However, the posting interface functions in the same way account determination via process keys function. To define your account determination for interest calculation, execute the menu path Financial Accounting ➤ Accounting Receivable and Accounts Payable ➤ Business Transactions ➤ Interest Calculation ➤ Interest Posting ➤ A/R: Calculation of Interest on Arrears, or use OBV1.

After executing one of these configuration methods, you are taken to the interest calculation account assignment screen, shown in Figure 5.10.

The screen in Figure 5.10 might look like hieroglyphics at first, but once you understand how it functions, it is not difficult at all. Instead of directly indicating G/L accounts, it uses symbols that represent different G/L accounts. To create or view the symbols that can be used, click the Symbols button. You are then taken to the account symbols configuration screen, shown in Figure 5.11.

**FIGURE 5.10**     The interest calculation account assignment screen

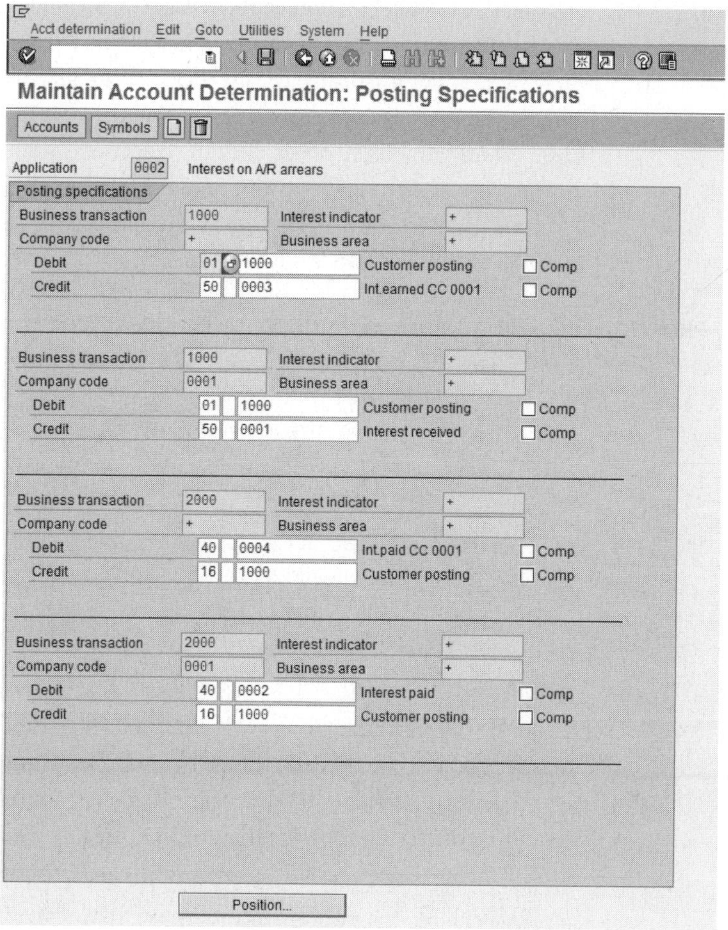

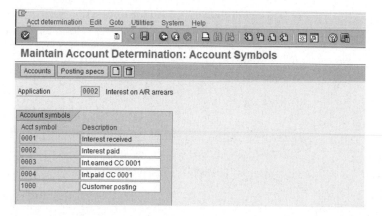

**FIGURE 5.11**     The account symbols configuration screen

SAP is delivered with some standard symbols. The most important are 1000 for customer and vendor (vendor screen can been seen only in the vendor calculation screen) postings. G/L accounts do not need to be assigned to symbol 1000 because they will post automatically against the correct master record. Extreme Sports will use the delivered account symbols. The next step is to assign G/L accounts to the account symbols. To do so, click the Accounts button. A pop-up box asks you for the chart of accounts you want to use. After you enter the appropriate chart of accounts (EXCA), you are presented with the account determination accounts configuration screen, shown in Figure 5.12.

**FIGURE 5.12**    The account determination accounts configuration screen

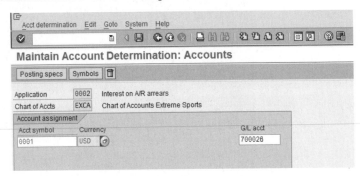

Assigning G/L accounts to account symbols is very straightforward. All you need to do is select the account symbol, specify the currency, and assign the account symbol to an existing G/L account. We are now ready to complete our account determination. From the screen shown in Figure 5.12, execute the menu path Goto ➤ Posting Specs. You are taken back to the interest calculation account assignment screen shown in Figure 5.10. From this screen, click the create icon. The pop-up box shown in Figure 5.13 appears.

The Business Transaction field is the first that needs to be filled in. You have two options: 1000 and 2000. Business transaction 1000 is for interest *received* by your company and business transaction 2000 is for interest *paid* by your company.

The next field to be configured is Company Code. You can either enter a specific company code or the wildcard character + to symbolize all company codes.

**FIGURE 5.13**    The create new posting procedure pop-up box

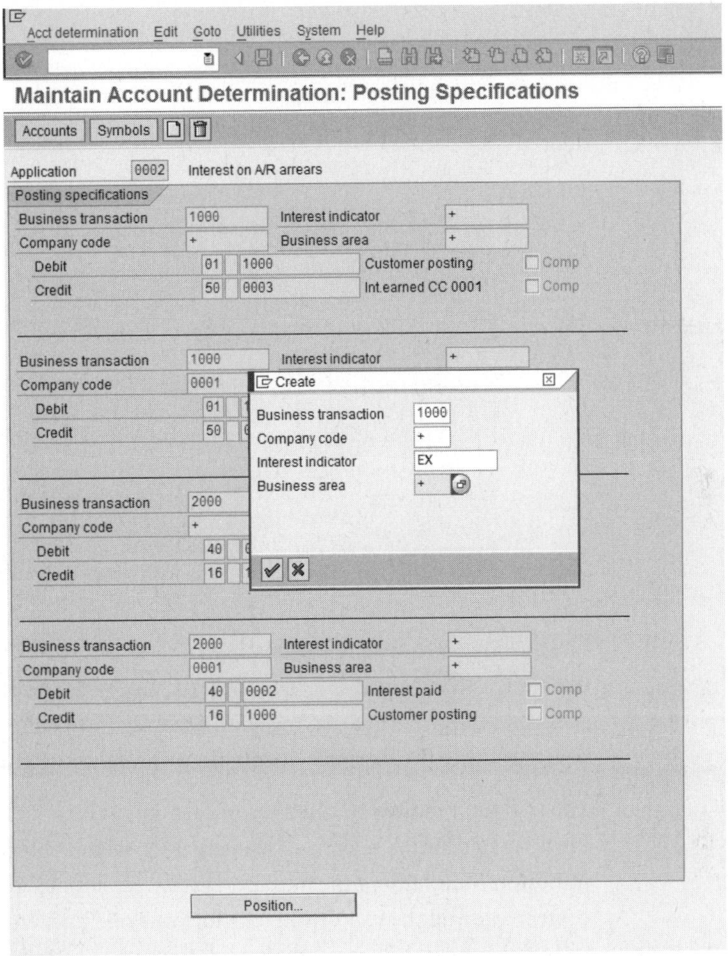

After making your settings in the Company Code field, you need to select the interest indicator that this account assignment is for. Once again, you can enter a specific interest indicator or use the + wildcard character.

The last field to be configured is Business Area. As before, you can enter a specific business area or the + wildcard character. After filling in all the fields in the pop-up box, press the Enter key. You are taken to the account determination posting specification details screen, shown in Figure 5.14.

**FIGURE 5.14**    The account determination posting specification details screen

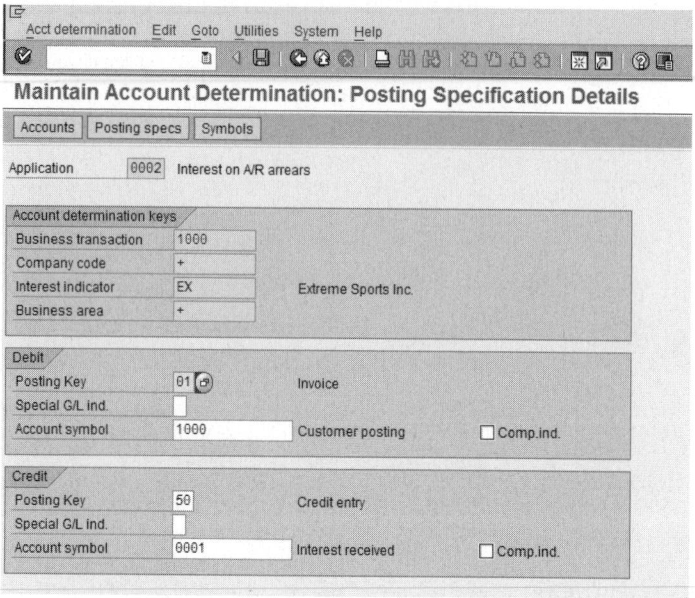

Next you need to specify the posting key and account symbols to be used for the debit and credit for the interest-calculation posting. You have the option of using a special G/L indicator. Selecting the Comp. Ind. indicator compresses the line items before posting (for example, it combines several line items into one per account).

The last step required to run interest calculation for A/R line items is to maintain the interest rates for the reference interest rate to which you have assigned your interest indicator. Maintaining the interest rates is very simple. You need only to enter the correct rate and the valid-from date for your reference interest rate. Maintaining the reference interest rate is not truly a configuration activity. You would not want to transport the interest rates from your development to your production client because this would be too tedious and time-consuming. Therefore, SAP has made maintaining the reference interest rate a current setting, much like opening and closing posting periods, entering exchange rates, and so on. To maintain your reference interest rate, follow the SAP application menu path Accounting ➢ Financial Accounting ➢ General Ledger ➢ Environment ➢ Current Settings ➢ Enter Reference Interest Values.

## EXTREME SPORTS INTEREST CALCULATION AUTOMATIC ACCOUNT-ASSIGNMENT CONFIGURATION ANALYSIS

The standard account symbols 0001 and 1000 were used for Extreme Sports' automatic account-assignment procedure for the interest posting. Account symbol 1000 always represents the customer master record and is not assigned to a specific G/L account for this reason. Extreme Sports configured account symbol 0001 to map to G/L account 700026 (interest received). The standard customer debit posting key 01 was used to debit (increase) the customer account balance. The credit posting key 50 was used to credit (increase) the interest received G/L account 700026. This automatic account assignment is available for use by all company codes and business areas, but it is valid only for the interest indicator EX. The business transaction 1000 represents the interest received transaction.

# Reason Codes

*Reason codes* are used to segregate different reasons for underpayment and overpayment on A/R line items. With a reason code, you can define whether the difference should be charged off to a G/L account or if a residual posting should be made. Residual postings clear the line item being paid and create a new open line item for the difference between the total amount of the line item and the payment amount.

The following is an example of a residual posting: A customer pays $700 against invoice #123, which has a total due amount of $1,000. Invoice #123 with a total due amount of $1,000 is cleared against the customer account, and a new residual posting for $300 ($1,000 invoice amount – $700 payment amount) is created. Residual postings made via reason codes are treated as disputed amounts and therefore do not figure against the customer's available credit. (Credit management will be discussed later in this chapter.) Reason codes are valid for only one company code. They also can be configured to generate correspondence to the customer, informing the customer of the residual item and how it is being treated by your company or should be treated by their company. To create reason codes, follow the menu path Financial Accounting ➢ Accounts Receivable and Accounts Payable ➢ Business Transactions ➢ Incoming Payments ➢ Incoming Payments Global Settings ➢ Overpayment/Underpayment ➢ Define Reason Codes, or use OBBE.

After executing this configuration transaction, you are presented with a pop-up box asking you for the company code for which you want to configure reason codes. Remember that reason codes are valid for only one company code. After entering the appropriate company code (1100 in our example), you are taken to the reason code configuration screen shown in Figure 5.15.

**FIGURE 5.15** The reason code configuration screen

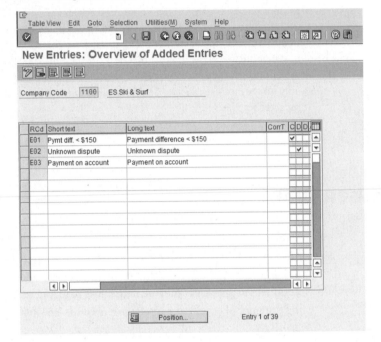

As you can see, three reason codes have already been configured for Extreme Sports' company code 1100. The fields shown in Figure 5.15 are explained here:

**RCd** Enter the three-character identifier of your reason code. This field is alphanumeric.

**Short Text** Enter a short text description for what this reason code represents. This field can be 20 characters long.

**Long Text** Enter a long text description for what this reason code represents. This field can be 40 characters long.

**CorrT** Select one of the correspondence identifiers from the pull-down window if you wish to generate a letter to your customer for line items with this reason code. SAP comes with several correspondence types that can be used or copied and changed. The creation of new correspondence types is usually the responsibility of an ABAPer who is knowledgeable in SAPscript. The creation of correspondence types is beyond the scope of this book.

**C**   Activate this indicator if you want line items assigned to this reason code to charge the difference between the payment amount and the invoice amount to a G/L account. This indicator will take any payment difference (over or under) to a miscellaneous income and expense account and totally clear the customer line item. The assignment of the G/L account will be explained later in this chapter.

**D**   Activate this indicator if you want line items assigned to this reason code to create a residual posting on the customer account. As explained earlier, a residual posting clears the original line item in total and creates on the customer account a new line item for the difference between the invoice amount and the payment amount.

**D**   This indicator is selected if you do not want the reason code text to be copied into the line item. This then allows you the flexibility to enter text of your own.

## EXTREME SPORTS REASON CODE CONFIGURATION ANALYSIS

Extreme Sports has created three reason codes (E01, E02, and E03) to use with company code 1100. Reason code E01 is used for payment differences (overpayments and under-payments) of less than $150. These differences are written off to a G/L account. Reason code E02 is used for unknown payment differences. It is configured to create a residual posting and send out a letter (correspondence) to the customer inquiring about the difference. Reason code E03 is used for payments on account. This reason code is not configured to write off to a G/L account or create a residual line item because the invoice that it is supposed to clear is unknown.

## Reason-Code Conversion Versions

Some industries, such as the apparel industry, have a large amount of customer deductions on invoices that are paid. Deductions are in essence an underpayment of an invoice. There are numerous business reasons for deductions. In the industries where deductions (short-pays) are common practice, it is customary to clear the underlying invoice and create a residual item to follow up. The residual item is then either written off to a G/L account based on the type of deduction, or the customer is informed via correspondence that they are still liable for the underpayment (an invalid deduction). In deduction situations, it would be very cumbersome to have a large number of on-account postings when using lockbox (autocash) functionality. SAP's lockbox functionality will be covered in Chapter 6.

The short version of lockbox functionality is that payment differences on an invoice result in an on-account posting for the entire check without clearing a line item, or if the payment amount doesn't match the invoice amount, the payment is distributed across the oldest invoices. It is a good idea to configure a reason code that will be used for creating deductions (residual postings) that can be used by the lockbox. This is accomplished through reason code conversion versions, which allow customer reason codes to be mapped to your SAP reason codes to create the desired effect (residual postings or G/L account write-offs) and to mark the line item with your proper reason code. It is also a good idea to write a lockbox preprocessing program to include a generic reason code on every line item that doesn't already have a reason code. This will allow for smooth processing of your lockbox cash application.

The first step is to create a reason code conversion version to be used by your customers. The reason code conversion version is assigned to the customer master record in your system. You can have more than one reason code conversion version per company code. The fields to be updated in the customer master record will be covered later in this chapter. To create a reason code conversion version, follow the menu path Financial Accounting ➤ Accounts Receivable and Accounts Payable ➤ Business Transactions ➤ Incoming Payments ➤ Incoming Payments Global Settings ➤ Overpayment/Underpayment ➤ Define Reason Code Conversion Version or use transaction code OBCR.

The reason code conversion version configuration screen shown in Figure 5.16 is displayed after following one of the previously mentioned configuration methods.

The configuration of reason code conversion versions is very simple. You need only to create a three-character identifier and a textual description of your version.

The final configuration step that is needed to make reason code conversion versions work is to map customer (external) reason codes to your SAP (internal) reason codes. To do so, follow the menu path Financial Accounting ➤ Accounts Receivable and Accounts Payable ➤ Business Transactions ➤ Incoming Payments ➤ Incoming Payments Global Settings ➤ Overpayment/Underpayment ➤ Define Conversion of Payment Difference Reason Codes, or use transaction code OBCS.

After executing one of these configuration methods, you are presented with the reason code conversion screen shown in Figure 5.17. Before the screen is actually displayed, you are prompted to enter the company code you are mapping.

**NOTE**   The mapping of reason codes is done on a company-code level.

**FIGURE 5.16**    The reason code conversion version configuration screen

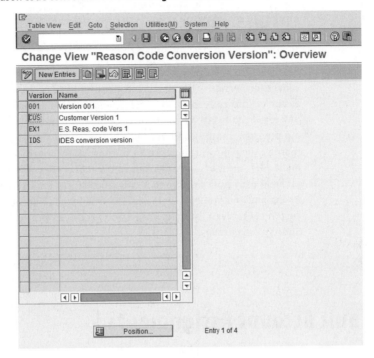

**FIGURE 5.17**    The reason code conversion screen

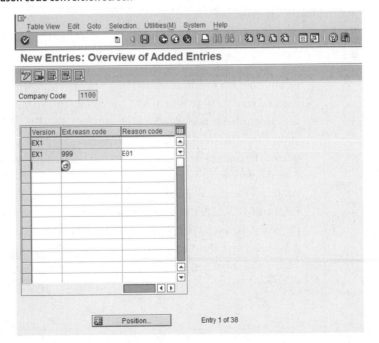

## EXTREME SPORTS REASON CODE CONVERSION VERSION CONFIGURATION ANALYSIS

Reason code conversion version EX1 was created for Extreme Sports. The reason code conversion version will be set up in Extreme Sports' customer master records to allow easier lockbox cash application processing. External reason code 999 was mapped to SAP reason code EO1 for company code 1100. In Extreme Sports' lockbox preprocessing program, reason code 999 will be inserted on any line item that doesn't have a reason code. This will allow the lockbox program to create residual postings for payment differences of over $150. Remember that there is another reason code that will automatically post any payment difference of less than $150 to an expense account. As the implementation progresses, Extreme Sports will communicate with its major customers to get a listing of their reason codes so they can be mapped to Extreme Sports' reason codes.

# Default Account Assignments

In this section, we will cover some of the most important automatic account determinations that relate to A/R. Automatic account determinations for G/L functionality were covered in Chapter 3.

## Overpayments/Underpayments

Recall from the previous section that you can configure a reason code to create a residual posting or to post to a G/L account. You are now ready to determine what G/L accounts are posted to for each individual reason code. The payment differences that arise from the use of reason codes are referred to as overpayments/underpayments in the system (as well as in real life). To assign G/L accounts to post reason codes to, follow the menu path Financial Accounting ➢ Accounts Receivable and Accounts Payable ➢ Business Transactions ➢ Incoming Payments ➢ Incoming Payments Global Settings ➢ Define Accounts for Overpayments/Underpayments. Or follow the menu path Financial Accounting ➢ Accounts Receivable and Accounts Payable ➢ Business Transactions ➢ Incoming Payments ➢ Incoming Payments Global Settings ➢ Overpayment/Underpayment ➢ Define Accounts for Payment Differences. Alternatively, you can use transaction code OBXL.

After executing one of these configuration methods, you are prompted to enter the chart of accounts that you want to use for the automatic account determination. After entering the appropriate chart of accounts (EXCA), you are presented with the reason code to account mapping screen. For the sake of logical progression we will move on directly to the rules for posting of differences in payments by selecting the Rules button, which will present you with the screen in Figure 5.18.

**FIGURE 5.18**    The payment differences by reason automatic posting rules screen

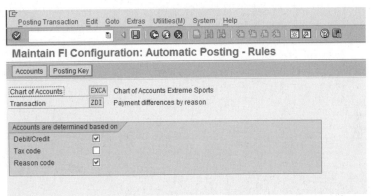

Overpayment/underpayment automatic account assignment uses processing key ZDI. You have the option of assigning G/L accounts based on debit/credit postings, tax code, reason code, or a combination thereof. In addition, account determination is always done via the chart of accounts first. Using the chart of accounts to distinguish account determination is nonconfigurable. After selecting the indicators you wish to use (Debit/Credit and Reason Code in our example), you must maintain the posting keys that are to be used. To set the posting keys, click the Posting Key button. (The process of setting the posting keys was shown in detail in Chapter 3; please refer to that chapter for a detailed explanation.) Once you have set your posting keys, you are ready to assign your G/L accounts. You can assign the G/L accounts by clicking the Accounts button shown in Figure 5.18. Alternatively, once the rules for the processing key and the posting key have been maintained, when you enter one of the configuration methods for this step, the G/L assignment screen for overpayments/underpayments, shown in Figure 5.19, is defaulted.

You'll notice that we have maintained the missing configuration for reason codes by assigning reason code E01 to G/L account 750000 for debits and G/L account 750001 for credits. This configuration will allow Extreme Sports to track all underpayments in G/L account 750000. An underpayment will result in a debit on this account and will allow Extreme Sports to track all overpayments in G/L account 750001 because an overpayment will result in a credit on this account.

**FIGURE 5.19**     The G/L assignment screen for overpayments/underpayments

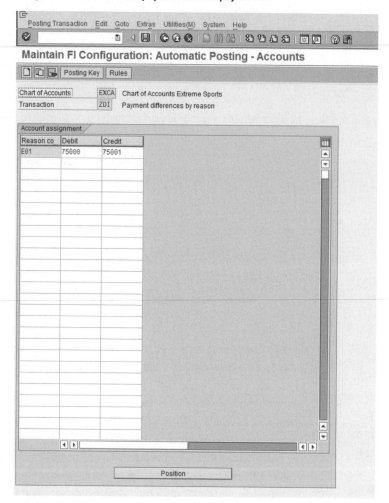

# Cash Discounts

If your company grants cash discount terms to its customers, it is necessary to define the cash-discount account that will be used by automatic account assignment. The cash-discount account is debited when payments of the gross amount less the cash-discount amount are received within the specified time period for which the cash discount is allowed. This happens to the customer account clearing transaction (applying the cash against the appropriate customer invoice). To configure the cash-discount account, follow the menu path Financial Accounting ➢ Accounts Receivable and Accounts Payable ➢ Business Transactions ➢ Incoming Payments ➢ Incoming Payments Global Settings ➢ Define Accounts for Cash Discount Granted, or use transaction code OBXI.

Figure 5.20 shows the account determination configuration screen for cash discount granted. The rules for the processing key SKT and the posting key are not shown in this example. The only option you have for rules is to assign G/L accounts based on tax codes. As you can see, all cash discounts taken by Extreme Sports' customers will be posted to account 888000.

**FIGURE 5.20**  The account determination configuration screen for cash discount granted

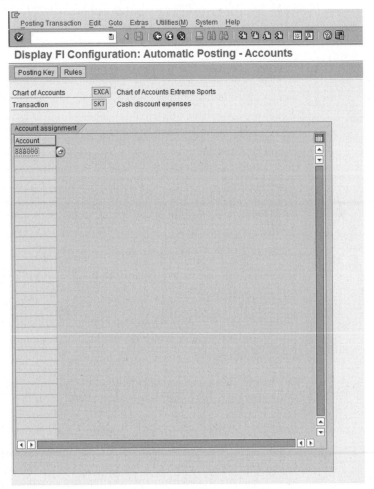

# Overall A/R and Employee Tolerances

Recall from Chapter 3 that the employee tolerance group null was configured for Extreme Sports. In the configuration of tolerance groups, you can set the maximum amount that employees can clear against a customer account, the maximum cash-discount percentage that can be applied to a customer invoice, and the maximum payment difference in percentage terms up to an overall dollar amount. Please review the "Posting Amount Defaults and Tolerance Groups" section in Chapter 3 for more information on employee tolerance groups.

In addition to employee tolerance groups, there are *customer tolerance groups*. Customer tolerance groups are assigned to customer master records, which will be covered later in this chapter. Customer tolerance groups allow you to specify the maximum payment difference that can be charged to a G/L account, the maximum cash-discount percentage, and the maximum allowable payment difference in percentage terms up to a total dollar amount. As with employee tolerance groups, you can specify a null customer tolerance group that will be valid for all customers that do not explicitly have a different tolerance group assigned to them via their customer master record. To configure customer tolerance groups, follow the menu path Financial Accounting ➢ Accounts Receivable and Accounts Payable ➢ Business Transactions ➢ Incoming Payments ➢ Manual Incoming Payments ➢ Define Tolerances (Customers), or use transaction code OBA3.

After following one of these configuration methods and then clicking the New Entries button on the screen that appears, you are taken to the create new customer tolerance group configuration screen, shown in Figure 5.21.

The fields in the create new customer tolerance group configuration screen are explained here:

**Company Code**    Enter the four-character value for the company code you want this customer tolerance group assigned to. A tolerance group can be assigned to only one company code.

**Currency**    The currency-key identifier defaults into this field based on of the company code (company-code currency).

**Tolerance Group**    Enter the four-character value to distinguish this customer tolerance group. The naming convention of the tolerance group is up to you. It you leave this field blank (or null), this tolerance group is valid for all customer master records that are in this company code and aren't explicitly assigned a named tolerance group.

**FIGURE 5.21**    The create new customer tolerance group configuration screen

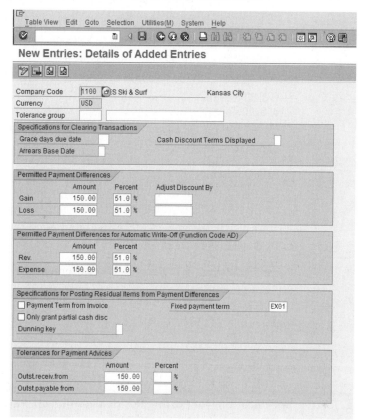

**Grace Days Due Date**    If you wish to grant grace days to your customers (beyond the grace days granted in the payment term), enter the number of grace days here.

**Cash Discount Terms Displayed**    You can change the cash-discount terms that are displayed when the line item is cleared by entering the appropriate indicator here. Leaving the field blank makes the cash-discount term default to the cash-discount term on the line item.

**Arrears Base Date**    This is the date that should be used for calculating days in arrears. There are two options: the date of the invoice or the value date.

**Permitted Payment Differences**    The fields are explained here:

**Amount**    Enter the maximum payment difference that can be written off to a G/L account. You will recall from earlier in the chapter that we configured a reason code and assigned the reason code to the proper G/L accounts for payment differences of less than $150. You can specify different amounts for overpayments (Gain) and underpayments (Loss).

**Percent**    For small-dollar invoices, you can enter a percentage in this field to limit the maximum amount that can be written off. The system will take the total invoice amount times this percentage to come up with the maximum allowable amount up to $150. For example, if 51% is entered in this field and an invoice of $200 is being paid, the maximum allowable amount to write off would be $102 ($200 * 51%). You can specify different percentages for overpayments (Gain) and underpayments (Loss).

**Adjust Discount By**    In this field, you can enter an amount that is equal to or less than the number that was entered in the Amount field. The amount entered in this field will be treated as a cash discount as long as the cash-discount rules you set up in the employee tolerance group allow the amount entered to be handled as a cash discount.

**Permitted Payment Differences for Automatic Write-Off**    The fields are explained here:

**Rev.**    Payment differences in your favor (revenue) are limited to either an absolute amount or a percentage of the value received.

**Expense**    Payment differences to your deficit (expense) are limited to either an absolute amount or a percentage of the value received.

**Specifications for Posting Residual Items from Payment Differences**    The fields are explained here:

**Payment Term from Invoice**    Activate this indicator if you want the residual posting that is created during clearing to assume the payment term on the invoice from which the residual item was created.

**Only Grant Partial Cash Disc**    Activate this indicator if you do not want to grant the full cash-discount amount when a residual item is paid.

**Fixed Payment Term**    You can establish a specific payment term that should be used on all residual postings by entering the payment-term identifier in this field.

**Dunning Key**    If you are using dunning (sending out past-due letters), you can enter the dunning key to be used by all residual postings.

**Tolerances for Payment Advices**    The fields are explained here:

**Amount**    A residual item is automatically created for any payment-difference amount greater than the amount entered here. Normally, the amount entered in the field should equal the amount entered in the Amount field in the Permitted Payment Differences section. Different amounts can be specified for overpayments (outstanding receivables) and underpayments (outstanding payables).

**Percent**    You can enter a percentage rate that is used in conjunction with the Amount field when the system is deciding to generate residual items. This means that a residual item can be created for less than the amount entered in the Amount field, depending on the invoice amount. For example, if 52% is entered in this field and an invoice in the amount of $200 is being a paid, a residual-item posting would be created for any payment difference of $104 ($200 * 52%) or greater.

### EXTREME SPORTS OVERALL A/R AND EMPLOYEE TOLERANCES

Accounts Receivable tolerances comprise two parts: employee tolerances and customer tolerances. Employee tolerances were covered in detail in Chapter 3. The customer tolerance group Null (blank) was configured for Extreme Sports company code 1100 in this section. The Null customer tolerance group for Extreme Sports was configured so that any payment difference equal to or less than $150—only payment differences that exceed 51% of the invoice amount—are eligible to write off the entire $150. The fixed payment term EX02 was configured for use on all residual postings. Payment term EX02 does not grant a cash discount and is due within 30 days. Any payment differences greater than $150 will automatically create a residual line item posting to the customer account.

# Credit Management

SAP's *credit management functionality* allows you to grant credit terms according to your business practices. Based on the credit limit and open A/R value for your customer, SAP can automatically block deliveries from being sent to customers who exceed the credit limit you have set for them. There is a question as to who really owns credit management on a project—FI or SD. According to SAP, both do. There are vital pieces of credit-management configuration in both modules. We will only be covering the configuration of the FI related credit management in this chapter.

As with some of the other SAP areas that we have looked at, there are several separate pieces of interrelated configuration that must be completed. There is not a set order in which these components must be configured—we will show them in the order that we feel makes the most sense to the flow of the book. With this in mind, the first piece of credit management that will be configured is the credit control area.

A company code can only be assigned to one credit control area. A credit control area can, however, be assigned to more than one company code. To create a credit control area, follow the menu path Enterprise Structure ➢ Definition ➢ Financial Accounting ➢ Define Credit Control Area or use OB45.

After following one of the configuration methods and clicking the New Entries button on the overview screen that is displayed, you are presented with the create new credit control area configuration screen, shown in Figure 5.22.

**FIGURE 5.22**    The create new credit control area configuration screen

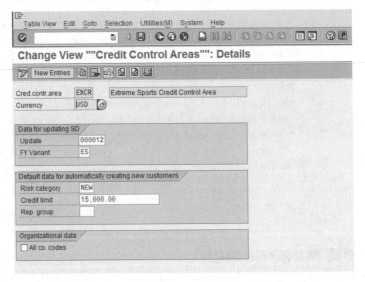

Here is a detailed list of the fields that appear in the create new credit control area configuration screen:

**Cred. Contr. Area**    Enter a four-character identifier for your credit control area.

**Description**    Enter a long text description for your credit control area.

**Currency**    Enter the currency identifier for the monetary unit that this credit control area will use.

**Update**    The equation for available credit is credit limit less the sum of open orders, open deliveries, open billings, and the A/R account balance. Open billings are used because it is possible for a billing (invoice) to be created and not be passed to accounting due to a posting error. Once a billing is passed on to accounting, the open billing balance decreases and the A/R balance increases. This field controls how SAP updates the values for open orders, open deliveries, and open billings from SD documents. The following choices are available in this field:

**Null (Blank)** Leaving this field null (blank) causes SAP to ignore SD documents when determining available credit. If this option is selected, available credit equals the credit limit less the customer's A/R account balance.

**000012** This option is the most robust. If the system cannot use the algorithm due to the way master data is set up (a material on the order is not relevant for delivery), the system will determine the best remaining algorithm to increase the value elements for available credit. This algorithm causes the open-orders value to increase with SD sales orders (for delivery-relevant items only); once the sales order has a valid delivery against it, the open sales-order value is decreased and the open delivery value is increased. Once the delivery has been billed (invoiced), the open delivery value decreases and the open billing value increases. Once the billing is posted successfully to accounting (this is instantaneous unless there is a problem with the invoice), the open billing value is decreased and the A/R balance is increased.

**000015** If this algorithm is used, sales orders are ignored. When a delivery is created, the open delivery value and the open billing value increase. Once the billing document is posted in accounting, the open billing value and open delivery value decrease while the A/R balance increases.

**000018** If this algorithm is used—when a sales order is created—the open delivery value increases. When the billing occurs, the open delivery value decreases and the open billing value increases. Once the billing document is posted in accounting, the open billing value decreases and the A/R balance increases.

**FY Variant** Enter the identifier of the fiscal-year variant that this credit control area will use. Remember that a credit control area can be assigned to more than one company code. Therefore, all company codes assigned to the credit control area must have the same fiscal-year variant (the one that matches this entry).

**Risk Category** If you want all new customer master records to default in a risk category, enter the appropriate risk category here. Risk categories will be explained later in this section.

**Credit Limit**    If you want all new customer master records to default in a credit limit, enter the appropriate credit limit here.

**Rep. Group**    If you want all new customer master records to default in a credit representative group, enter the appropriate credit representative group here. Credit representative groups will be explained later in this section.

**All Co. Codes**    Select this only if you would like the credit control area to evaluate credit exposure for all company codes set up in the system. I prefer not selecting this option, because the setting may be relevant for today's business environment but may no longer apply if/when acquisitions are made in different geographies or industries.

**NOTE**    Until credit master data has been entered for a customer, the customer has no credit limit. Credit master data is not created until one of the main credit elements is maintained for the customer: risk category, credit limit, and/or credit representative group. If you want to ensure that all new customers have a credit limit, it is a good idea to make one of the main credit elements default in from the credit control area configuration.

Now that you have created your credit control area, the next step is to assign the newly created credit control area to the company codes that you would like use with it. Remember, a credit control area can be assigned to several company codes, but a company code can be assigned to only one credit control area. You assign credit control areas to company codes in the global parameters configuration of company codes (transaction code OBY6). You can revisit Chapter 2 for an in-depth explanation of company-code global parameters and see where this field is assigned.

An alternative way of assigning a credit control area to a company code is by following the menu path Enterprise Structure ➤ Assignment ➤ Financial Accounting ➤ Assign Company Code to Credit Control Area.

After assigning your credit control area to the proper company codes, you are ready to define credit risk categories for your credit control area. Recall from the explanation of credit control area configuration that we have already assigned a credit risk category of New to the credit control area. As mentioned at the beginning of this section, there is no set order for the configuration steps, with the exception of creating the credit control area. Do not be confused; we have not already assigned a credit risk category to the credit control area. Credit risk categories provide a way to group together customers with a similar credit rating (credit risk). You can run credit reports off of credit risk categories to analyze how well your credit-management policies are working with each risk category. You assign the credit risk category to the credit-management screens of the customer master record. To create credit risk categories, follow the menu path Financial Accounting ➢ Accounts Receivable and Accounts Payable ➢ Credit Management ➢ Credit Control Account ➢ Define Risk Categories, or use transaction code OB01.

## EXTREME SPORTS CREDIT CONTROL AREA CONFIGURATION ANALYSIS

Credit control area EXCR was created for Extreme Sports. Credit control area EXCR is configured to use U.S. dollars as its currency and Extreme Sports fiscal year variant ES. Algorithm 000012 was selected for the credit update controls. This algorithm provides the most updates to open values that are in the system and is used to determine available credit. If the system cannot use algorithm 000012 for any reason, it will select the next most encompassing algorithm to update open values. All new customer records will default in with risk category New and a credit limit of $15,000. In addition to ensuring that all customers have a credit limit in the system, defaulting in this information causes credit master data to automatically be created for the customer. If a customer does not have a credit limit, it is impossible for SAP to perform credit checking.

After following one of these configuration methods and clicking the New Entries button on the screen that appears, you are presented with the define new credit management risk categories configuration screen, shown in Figure 5.23.

The configuration of credit risk categories is very simple. You need only to create a three-character risk category, select the credit control area you want to assign it to, and then give the credit risk category a description.

You are now ready to create credit representative groups. You assign credit representative groups in the credit management screens of the customer master record. The credit representative groups relate to the credit representative or credit manager that is assigned to the customer account. To create credit representative groups, follow the menu path Financial Accounting ➢ Accounts Receivable and Accounts Payable ➢ Credit Management ➢ Credit Control Account ➢ Define Credit Representative Groups, or use transaction code OB02.

The create new credit representative groups configuration screen, shown in Figure 5.24, appears after you follow one of the configuration transactions and click the New Entries button.

**FIGURE 5.23**   The define new credit management risk categories configuration screen

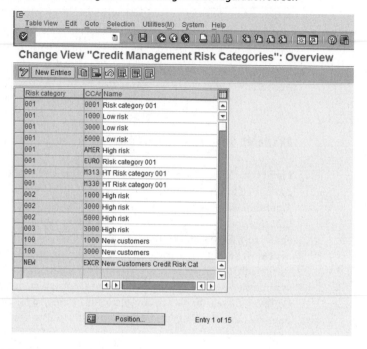

**FIGURE 5.24**   The create new credit representative groups configuration screen

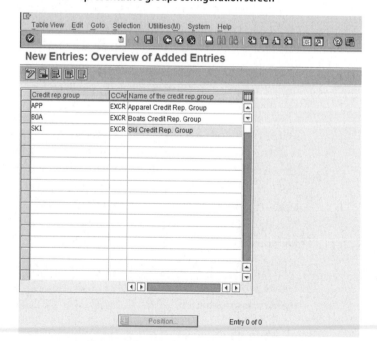

As you can see, the configuration for credit representative groups is straight-forward. You need only to create a three-character credit representative group identifier, assign the identifier to your credit control area, and give the credit representative group a long text name.

Once you have created your credit representative groups, you can assign employees to them. To do so, follow the menu path Financial Accounting ➤ Accounts Receivable and Accounts Payable ➤ Credit Management ➤ Credit Control Account ➤ Define Credit Representatives, or use transaction code OB51.

The assign employees to credit representative group configuration screen, shown in Figure 5.25, appears when you follow one of these configuration transactions and then click the New Entries button.

**FIGURE 5.25**    The assign employees to credit representative group configuration screen

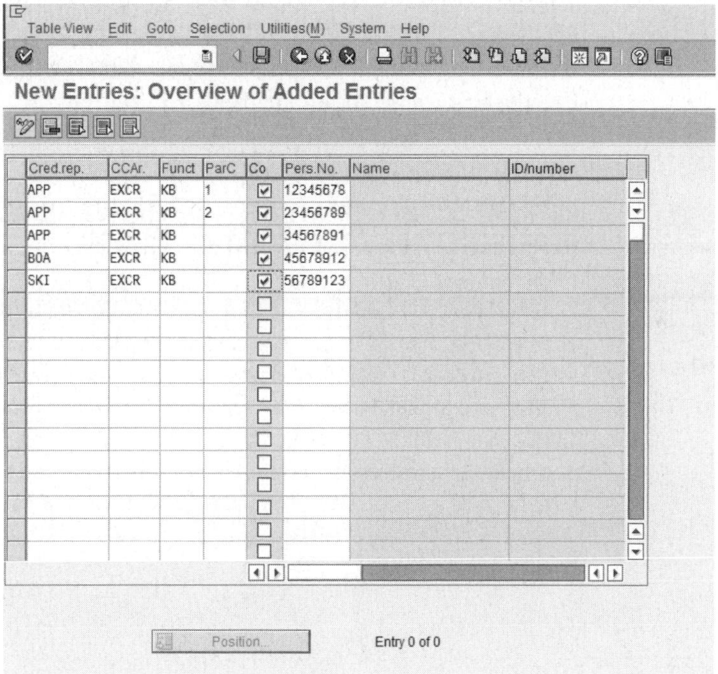

Here's an explanation of the fields that are displayed in Figure 5.25:

**Cred. Rep.**    Enter the credit representative group to which you want to assign an employee. Credit representative groups were created in the preceding step.

**CCAr.**    Enter the credit control group that the credit representative group belongs to.

**Funct**    Enter the SD partner function that assigns the employee as the credit representative for your company. The two standard delivered SAP partner functions that are used for this purpose are KB (credit representative) and KM (credit manager). A credit representative group can have both a credit representative and a credit manager assigned to it.

**ParC**    If you have assigned the same partner function more than once to a credit representative group, several employees are assigned to the credit representative group. You can enter the numerical sequence (1, 2, 3, etc.) that the system should use when assigning them.

**Co**    Activate this indicator if you want the ability to copy the employee number into SD documents.

**Pers. No.**    Enter the employee number of the person you wish to assign to this credit representative group for this partner function. The employee number is the personnel number assigned to the employee in the HR module. After you enter the personnel number, the employee's last name and R/Mail user ID default into the Name and ID/Number fields, respectively.

## EXTREME SPORTS CREDIT REPRESENTATIVE GROUP AND CREDIT REPRESENTATION CONFIGURATION ANALYSIS

Extreme Sports created credit representative groups for its three major business lines: apparel (APP), boats (BOA), and ski equipment (SKI). Employees of Extreme Sports were assigned to each credit representative group. Credit representative group APP has two employees assigned to the credit representative partner function. Employee number 12345678 is assigned first and employee number 23456789 is assigned second in each document. In addition to the two credit representatives, a credit manager (partner function KM) is also assigned to the apparel credit representative group (APP). The remaining credit representative groups (BOA and SKI) have employees assigned as credit representatives.

The final step on the FI side of credit management is to define your days-in-arrears calculation. SAP allows you to set the grouping of days outstanding and how the due date is calculated for analysis purposes. To create a days-in-arrears calculation, follow the menu path Financial Accounting ➤ Accounts Receivable and Accounts Payable ➤ Credit Management ➤ Business Transaction: Credit Monitoring ➤ Define Intervals for Days in Arrears in Credit Management, or use transaction code OB39.

The define new days-in-arrears calculation configuration screen is shown in Figure 5.26. This screen appears when you enter one of the configuration transactions and click the New Entries button.

**FIGURE 5.26**     The define new days-in-arrears calculation configuration screen

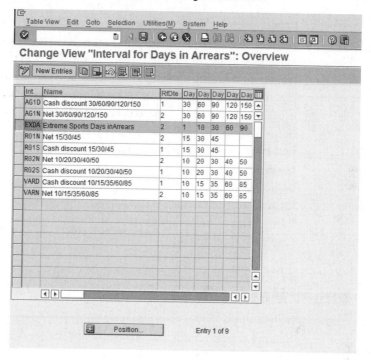

Here are the explanations of the fields that are displayed in Figure 5.26:

**Int**     Enter a four-character identifier for your days-in-arrears calculation. You will select this identifier when running custom SAP A/R and credit-management reports.

**Name**     Enter a textual description of your days-in-arrears calculation indicator.

**RfDte**     This field defines the reference date that is used as the due date in the calculation. You have two options:

1     The cash-discount due date

2     The net due date

**Day**     There are five Day fields. In the first Day field, enter a number that represents the last day of the days outstanding that you want to analyze. For example, if you enter 15 in the first Day field, SAP will group items that are 0–15 days overdue. Because there are five Day fields, there are six day groupings because the last Day field serves as the lower indicator. If you enter 90 in the last Day field, a grouping of all items that are at least 90 days past due is created.

Once you have completed the FI configuration of credit management, it is time to take a look at the SD configuration of credit management. As an FI configurer, you may or may not be responsible for the SD configuration of credit management. Whether you are responsible or not, it is important to work closely with the SD team in configuring the remaining pieces. So, what are the remaining pieces? In the SD configuration (configuration that falls under SD in the IMG), you can use sales-order type and delivery type to define whether automatic credit checking should occur. You can then use risk category and order or delivery type to further define how stringent the credit check should be and whether a warning message, a warning message with a delivery block, an error message, or just a delivery block should be created automatically if the customer's credit limit is exceeded. If you want to know more, you can look at the activities that fall under the menu path Sales and Distribution ➢ Basic Functions ➢ Credit Management/Risk Management ➢ Credit Management.

# Customer Master Records

Before you begin configuration of customer master data, it is necessary to have a strategy. You should plan how you would like to use customer master data and how you will convert customers from your legacy system, as well as the integration points that vendor master data has with SD Treasury and A/P. Much like the G/L, customer master data is a combination of configuration and master data maintenance.

A key concept in the configuration of customer master data is customer groups. Customer groups allow you to have separate purposes and field statuses for different types of customers. SD uses partner functions, which segregate different purposes for customer master data, such as the sold-to party, the ship-to party, the bill-to party, and so on. It is important to work closely with SD and have a good design between FI and SD so that master data fulfills the needs of both modules. Also, by separating these different types of customers into different customer groups, you can make different fields required, optional, or suppressed for each of the groups.

We will not go into detail in this section on how to create the customer master record, but will instead focus on the configuration that allows you to create customer master records. However, it is important to remember that customer master records can be maintained from the FI point of view or centrally (just like vendor master data). It is also important to note that when you maintain customer accounts centrally, you are still not able to maintain the credit screens for the customer. To create the credit views of the customer, you must specifically select the Maintain Credit option on the A/R master data menu.

## Customer Groups

The first step in configuring customer master data is to create *customer groups*. As mentioned earlier, customer groups are used to segregate different types of customers as well as segregate customers by SD partner function. To create customer groups, follow the menu path Financial Accounting ➢ Accounts Receivable and Accounts Payable ➢ Customer Accounts ➢ Master Data ➢ Preparations for Creating Customer Master Data ➢ Define Account Groups with Screen Layout (Customers), or use transaction code OBD2.

The create new customer account group configuration screen shown in Figure 5.27 is displayed after you enter one of the configuration methods and click the New Entries button. SAP comes with some standard customer account groups for SD partner functions and other needed groupings. We will explore a custom customer account group for demonstration purposes.

**FIGURE 5.27** The create new customer account group configuration screen

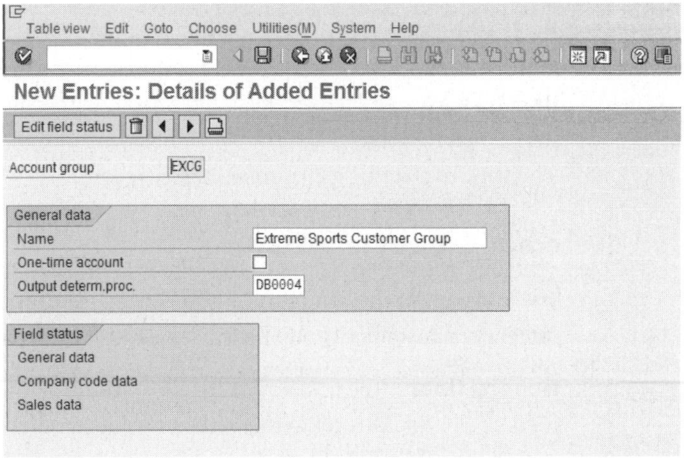

The fields shown in Figure 5.27 are explained here:

**Account Group**    Enter a four-character identifier by which to distinguish your customer account group.

**Name**    Enter a long text description of what this customer account group is used for.

**One-Time Account**    Select this indicator if you want this customer group to be for one-time customers—those you may use only once and for whom you do not want to store a unique customer master record (such as miscellaneous cash sales). Only one customer master record is needed for all one-time customers per company code. The name, address, and other important information needed for creating an invoice are entered on the document when you specify a one-time customer number.

**Output Determ. Proc.**    The billing process produces different outputs that are sent to the customer, such as invoices, past-due notices, order acknowledgement, and so on. Using the output determination procedure, you can determine which fields are available for output and in what order they can be output. You can select from the following options when populating this field:

> **Null (Blank)**    No output determination procedure is used.
>
> **DB0001**    This output determination procedure is used for sold-to parties.
>
> **DB0002**    This output determination procedure is used for ship-to parties.
>
> **DB0003**    This output determination procedure is used for bill-to parties.
>
> **DB0004**    This output determination procedure is used for payers of the invoice.
>
> **DBJ1A1**    This output determination is similar to DB0001 (sold-to parties) but specifically used for Argentina.

**Field Status**    The concept of field statuses should be familiar to you from your work on the general ledger in Chapter 3 and with vendors in Chapter 4. The field statuses on this screen control which fields are optional, required, and suppressed when you're creating a customer master record.

## Customer-Group Field Status

The first page of the configuration screen, and the most important fields for each category of customer-group field statuses, will be explained here.

**General Data**    The first screen for the customer-group field status appears in Figure 5.28. You can get to this screen by double-clicking the General Data text or clicking the Edit Field Status button—both shown in Figure 5.27. The settings made in the General Data field status are valid for customer master records created in this customer account group regardless of company code or sales organization.

**FIGURE 5.28** The first general data field status screen for customer groups

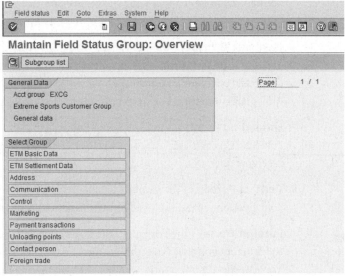

Explanations of the subsections of the general data field status as well as the most important fields to consider in each subsection are listed here:

**ETM Basic Data**   There are two fields available for entry: the mobile telephone and ETM (Electronically Transmitted Message) basic data fields.

**ETM Settlement Data**   This field status group has only one field called ETM Settlement Data. This is the data that will be used for ETM functionality.

**Address**   The Address section contains fields for name, street address, P.O. box, and so on. It is a good idea to make the customer name and address fields required for entry.

**Communication**   The Communication section contains fields that capture such information as telephone numbers and fax numbers. These fields are relatively self-explanatory, and it's easy to determine if you need them based on your requirements.

**Control**   The Control section contains many important fields that capture how the customer master record is processed. Here's a listing of the most important fields in this section:

> **Vendor**   By utilizing this field, you can tell the system that this customer is also a vendor (by entering the vendor number). This allows you to do A/P-A/R netting if you so desire.

> **Tax Codes**   These fields are important in determining the tax and tax jurisdiction from which sales taxes on invoices are generated.

**Marketing**    The Marketing section contains fields that can help you capture marketing information about your customers. Some of the included fields are Nielson ID, Industry Sector, and Fiscal Year of the Customer.

**Payment Transactions**    These fields help in receiving payment from customers. You can capture information about the customer's banks and accounts to help with electronic payment transactions. You can also specify alternate payers if the customer has more than one partner function that may pay an invoice.

**Unloading Points**    The Unloading Points fields help you to determine where customers receive shipments, as well as the times the customers' docks are open for receiving goods.

**Contact Person**    The Contact Person fields allow you to keep information about your frequent contacts as well as their function in their organization.

**Foreign Trade**    The Foreign Trade fields allow you to capture information about the different countries that this customer may have you ship goods to or buy from. You can specify by country whether the customer is blocked for export due to government regulations such as denial orders, specially designated nationals, or overall boycotts.

**Company Code Data**    The first screen for the configuration of the Company Code Data section of the customer-group field status appears in Figure 5.29. All fields in this section are valid at the company-code level only. This means that, as customers are extended across several company codes, the fields in this section can have different values based on the company code using the customer master data.

**FIGURE 5.29**    The first company code field status screen for customer groups

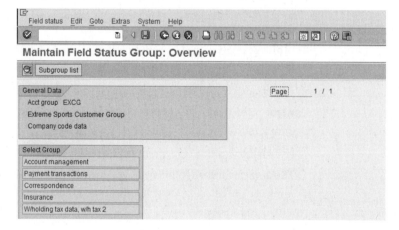

Here's a listing of the subsections of the company code data field status as well as the most important fields to consider in each subsection:

**Account Management**    The Account Management fields control how vendor master data updates the general ledger:

**Reconciliation Account**    As you are aware, the A/R system is a subledger. The reconciliation account is the G/L account updated by the A/R transactions using this customer account. Different customers or customer groups can update different reconciliation accounts.

**Cash Management Group**    The cash management group is a major integration point between A/R and Treasury. The planning group updates the receivable section in the liquidity-forecast functionality of the Treasury module. The liquidity-forecast report will be covered in Chapter 6. If you want to utilize the treasury functions within SAP, make this field mandatory.

**Previous Account Number**    This field can be used to capture the legacy customer number in SAP. This field is especially useful in the initial time after Go-Live, when users are looking up customers. A match key can be created to look up customer numbers based on this field.

**Payment Transactions**    The Payment Transactions fields help in processing customer payments. Some of the most important customer payment transactions are explained here:

**Terms of Payment**    Use this field to give the customer a default terms-of-payment key to occur on all invoices. The terms-of-payment key can be overridden in the document line item.

**Clearing with Vendor**    Activating this field allows you to activate A/P-A/R netting. If a customer is both a customer and a vendor, you can net the two accounts to create either one payable or one receivable.

**Tolerance Group**    Using this field, you can indicate the customer tolerance group you would like to assign this customer to. Customer tolerance groups were covered earlier in the chapter.

**Lockbox**    If you are going to use lockbox, whereby one can use the functionality to apply cash and clear receivables, you can enter the lockbox that this customer is assigned to in this field. Lockboxes will be explained in Chapter 6.

**Correspondence**   The fields in this section allow you to store additional information for contact with the customer as well as enable and specify dunning information with the customer.

**Account at Customer**   Your vendor number at the customer is stored in this field. This can greatly help your A/R clerks in researching open A/R issues.

**Insurance**   The Insurance field group allows you to use fields to store information about export credit insurance.

**W/holding Tax Data, w/h Tax 2**   There are four fields available to the user for capturing withholding tax.

**Sales Data**   The first screen for sales data field status appears in Figure 5.30. The fields stored in the sales data field status are valid for combinations of sales organizations, distribution channels, and divisions. These fields have an impact on the functionality of the SD module, so it is a good idea to work in close coordination with your SD group when defining rules for these fields.

**FIGURE 5.30**    The first screen of the sales data field status for customer groups

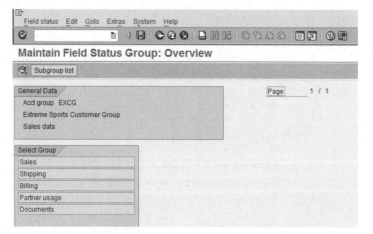

## EXTREME SPORTS CUSTOMER ACCOUNT GROUP CONFIGURATION ANALYSIS

The customer account group EXCG was created for Extreme Sports. The output determination procedure DB0004 was used because payer partners will be set up using this customer account group. The One-Time Account indicator was not activated for this customer account group because a separate one-time customer account group will be created for Extreme Sports at a later time.

# Summary

In this chapter we covered the configuration of the A/R subledger, including credit management. Like all aspects within SAP, master data is vital to ensuring that processing goes smoothly. You can see yet again how configuration settings have an impact on transaction processing. Before we can configure an area of functionality, we need to consider all of the upstream and downstream aspects to the business process. This chapter demonstrated that payment terms cannot be set without some idea of what our customer risk profile looks like, nor can we set credit limits for our customers (when setting up the master data) without understanding our tolerance levels for risk. All of these decisions depend on a good understanding of the business processes and environment within which we operate. Any one of these design questions can adversely affect the processing of business events.

# Financial Supply Chain Management

## FEATURING:

- ▶ BILLER DIRECT

- ▶ CASH AND LIQUIDITY MANAGEMENT

- ▶ LIQUIDITY PLANNER

- ▶ COLLECTIONS MANAGEMENT

- ▶ CREDIT MANAGEMENT

The Financial Supply Chain Management module helps a business manage how cash flows through a business. You can optimize cash in several ways, including for cash outflows (such as vendor payments) as well as for reduced cycle time for when you receive cash (customer payments, for example). Improvements in how quickly cash flows into a business—or how slowly cash flows out of a company—result in a better cash flow.

After all, one of the biggest reasons why companies fail is not because they are not making profits but because they are not liquid enough. In other words, they did not manage their cash and the resulting cash flow adequately. In this chapter, you will learn about SAP's solution to a business's cash management needs.

# Biller Direct

Biller Direct is a relatively new functionality, offered only with mySAP ERP (SAP 5.0). It is SAP's solution to electronic invoicing and payment collection. At first glance this may not seem like an exciting development, but this application offers a business many advantages and operating efficiencies. SAP achieves this by linking AR and AP to a web-based tool that can both present invoices to customers and allow customers to process payments online.

The efficiencies that you can derive from Biller Direct start with the processing of invoices electronically. Instead of having to mail an invoice to your customer, your customer now receives the invoice instantaneously. The savings are threefold. First, Biller Direct reduces the cost of production of the invoice and the cost of getting it to its destination. Second, you save costs in the process of evaluating the invoice for payment and dispute management, all of which can be done online and much more quickly and accurately than using faxes, mail, and the phone to communicate the discrepancies. The third area of savings lies in the reduction of data entry, which reduces time required for both initial entry and data entry error correction.

This chapter covers a lot of functionality; therefore, we'll cover only the key configuration steps and fields. The steps that we're not covering have similar requirements to those examined in the previous chapters (such as account determination).

# Process Integration with Accounts Receivable Accounting

The first step in the configuration process is to identify what additional payment methods will be available for payment of invoices. To open the configuration screen shown in Figure 6.1, choose Financial Supply Chain Management ➤ Biller Direct ➤ Process Integration with Accounts Receivable Accounting ➤ Release Credit Cards. The screen is a simple identification of available payment methods.

**FIGURE 6.1**     The Change View "Additional Payment Method Classes": Overview screen

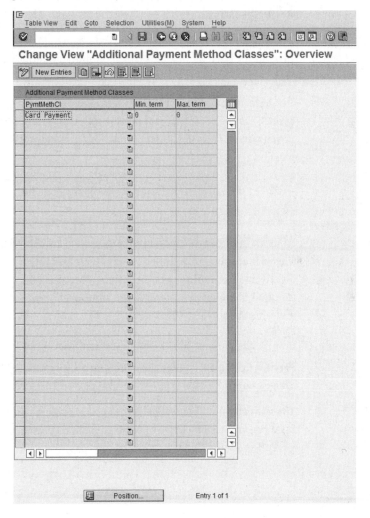

The following fields are relevant to the configuration step:

**PymtMethCl**   The Additional Permitted Payment Method Classifications per Client field is merely a means to identify valid payment methods. SAP delivers two standard types of payment: card (credit) payment and Orbian. Orbian is a software solution developed in conjunction with SAP and Citibank, which provides hosted electronic payment service.

**Min. Term**   This field contains the number of days after the current date that would be included in the selection process; if as in the example the value is zero, all items are selected.

**Max. Term**   The selection criteria would include items with a maturation date of prior to the current date plus the maximum date stipulated by this field.

The next step is to identify the payment methods available to the Electronic Bill Presentment and Payment (EBPP) process. Before this step in the configuration process can be complete, you need to follow these configuration steps, which are covered more fully in Chapter 5, "Accounts Receivable":

1. Set up payment methods per country for payment transactions.

2. Set up payment methods per company code for payment transactions.

3. Set up bank determination for payment transactions.

You can find the relevant configuration steps by choosing Financial Supply Chain Management ➢ Biller Direct ➢ Process Integration with Accounts Receivable Accounting ➢ Edit Payment Methods. Figure 6.2 illustrates a fully configured company code with the additional permissible payment type for Extreme Sports.

The following fields are relevant to the configuration step:

**Paying Co. Code**   Enter the company code processing the Biller Direct transactions.

**Classification**   This field tells the system what payment type can be expected for a specific transaction. Three options are delivered with SAP: Credit Card, Collection, or Collection in Master Record.

**FIGURE 6.2**    The permissible payment types by company code

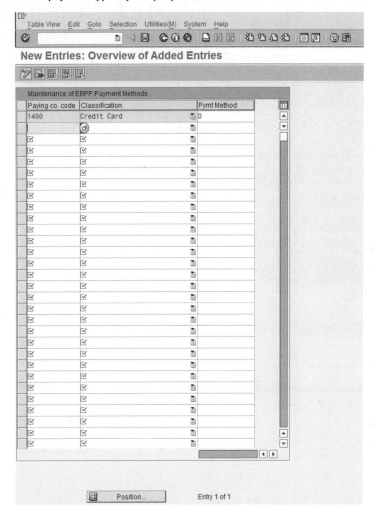

**Pymt Method**    This field is covered in Chapter 5.

The next step is to configure the applicable entries for tracking/logging activity of web users. Before completing this task, check that your settings do not infringe on any privacy protection laws. We find this a useful (optional) step to take as this can be an invaluable tool if there is ever a need to reconcile between SAP and the web interface. To access the screen shown in Figure 6.3, choose Financial Supply Chain Management ➢ Biller Direct ➢ Process Integration with Accounts Receivable Accounting ➢ Define Entries for the Logging of the Activities of Web users.

**FIGURE 6.3**    An example of an activity that is being logged for a period of 10 days

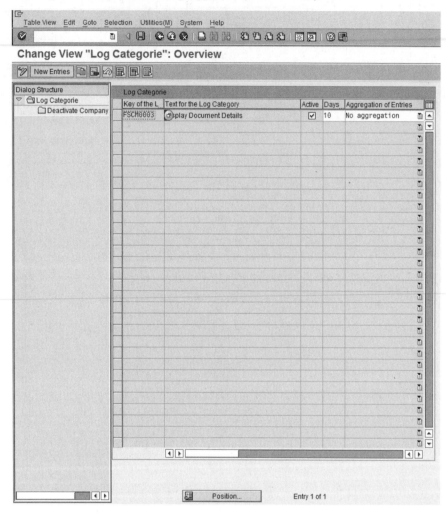

The following fields are relevant to the configuration step:

**Key of the Log of Category**    This field provides the identifier of the activity that will be logged by SAP. SAP delivers 15 system activities, among them:

- ▶ Display Document Header
- ▶ Display Document Details
- ▶ Payment of a Bill

**Text for the Log Category**    Enter a description in this field.

**Active**    This field indicates if the log is active or inactive.

**Days to Deletion**    This field specifies the number of days the log will be retained.

**Aggregation of Entries**    This field has three options:

> ▶ No Aggregation means that the individual entries will be kept without summary.

> ▶ Retain Older Entry means the older entry for the particular period will be retained.

> ▶ Overwrite Older Entry will result in the most current entry being retained.

The next step in setting up Biller Direct functionality is to define what the system should do with partial payments. This is an important step because the choices made here have an impact downstream in the process. Assuming we choose to use this functionality and elect to accept partial payments, then the first two effects that come to mind are the reconciliation process and the analysis of open items. These topics will be explored as we explain your choices in the next step. The following menu path will get you to your next configuration screen: Financial Supply Chain Management ➢ Biller Direct ➢ Process Integration with Accounts Receivable Accounting ➢ Define Partial Payment and Currency.

Figure 6.4 shows the fully configured screen that reflects the settings required for Extreme Sports's shared service company.

**FIGURE 6.4**    The fully configured screen for partial payments and currency for Extreme Sports

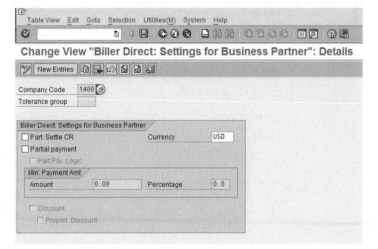

The following fields are relevant to the configuration step:

**Company Code**    Enter the company code in this field.

**Tolerance Group**    This field has been covered in both Chapters 4 and 5. Here the field is intentionally left blank because it serves as our default group used for all of our vendor and customer account setup.

**Part. (Partial) Settle CR**    If you select this option, the system will allow for partial payments for credits via the Internet.

**Partial Payment**    Select this option if you want to allow for partial payment of invoices by a customer. This functionality is also available for incoming payments in AR. The functionality offered here is more powerful than the simple check mark may imply. This allows a business to accept partial payments on an invoice. A resulting decision must be made as to how to account for the remaining portion of the invoice. Do you want the system to keep the original document, which has an effect on the aging of outstanding invoices, or would you prefer to have the system create a new document and therefore a new document date?

**Part. Pay. Logic**    This selection allows the system to reflect the partial payment in the open item history. If you don't select this option, you will only see the open item portion of the invoice.

**Amount**    This field contains an absolute amount that limits the smallest amount that can be accepted in partial payments.

**Percentage**    This field specifies a minimum amount as calculated by a percentage of the open item. Either the amount field or percentage field should be used.

**Discount**    By selecting this option, you ensure that the customer will be entitled to discount, based on the payment terms, for the partial payment on an invoice. If you don't select the following field, there will be a limit to the first partial payment receiving the discount.

**Proport. Discount**    By selecting this option, you ensure that the customer will be entitled to the portion of the discount available, based on the payment terms, for the partial payment on an invoice.

The next step in setting up Biller Direct is a quick one and is purely optional. This functionality (all online with Biller Direct) allows the customer to separate out the function of reviewing and approving invoices for payment.

You can access the payment block configuration screen by choosing Financial Supply Chain Management ➤ Biller Direct ➤ Process Integration with Accounts Receivable Accounting ➤ Define Payment Block for Release Process.

The configuration screen shown in Figure 6.5 is the fully configured screen that uses one of several payment block reasons supplied by SAP.

**FIGURE 6.5**     The fully configured screen for partial payments and currency

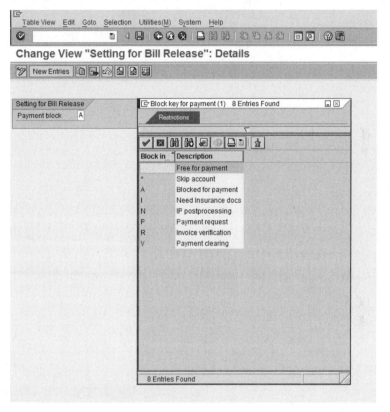

The next step in setting up Biller Direct is to create reference users. They are required if you want to be able to manage how your customers process transactions on Biller Direct.

Access the reference user configuration screen by using the choosing Financial Supply Chain Management ➤ Biller Direct ➤ Process Integration with Accounts Receivable Accounting ➤ Define Reference User.

The configuration screen shown in Figure 6.6 contains the two types of users that Extreme Sports's customers will be able to segregate business activities into.

**FIGURE 6.6**    The reference user screen for Extreme Sports

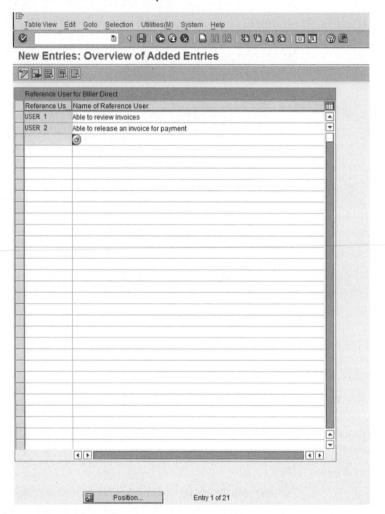

The following fields are relevant to the configuration step:

**Reference User**    This is the key identifying field.

**Name of Reference User**    This description field lets you categorize the functionality and access the user will receive.

**EXTREME SPORTS HOUSE BILLER DIRECT CONFIGURATION ANALYSIS**

Extreme Sports has decided to use Biller Direct to help improve cash flow and customer satisfaction. The functionality enables customers to pay their account and review, query, or dispute any invoices online—resulting in an improvement in customer satisfaction.

This immediate sharing of information reduces the cycle time between issuing and invoice and receipt of the payment for that invoice. Extreme Sports has also enabled customers to pay their accounts with a credit card.

# Cash and Liquidity Management

*Cash and Liquidity Management* contains two separate areas of functionality: Cash Management and Liquidity Planning. Cash Management focuses on cash movements between bank accounts and looks at cash flows in the short term. Liquidity Planning encompasses activity in the subledgers (accounts receivable, accounts payable, and the materials ledger) that have an impact on cash flow in the mid to long term.

Here's an example of how analyzing one of the subledgers impacts a company's cash flow. Assume a company has on average two months' worth of inventory (as it relates to sales turnover) in its warehouse at any given time. This inventory level is valued at $2 million, which translates to $2 million in cash being tied up in inventory (working capital). Assume that Extreme Sports implemented an ERP system that allowed for more accurate forecasts of inventory movements and that it was determined that they could reduce inventory levels down to the equivalent of one month's revenue. This reduction in cash invested in inventory results in a cash flow of $1 million.

The first step in configuring the Cash Management submodule is to set up the master data required. We'll cover the currency setup first. This, of course, is not relevant to those organizations that will not be trading with other countries. To access the next configuration screen, choose Financial Supply Chain Management ➢ Cash and Liquidity Management ➢ Cash Management ➢ Market Data ➢ Master Data ➢ Currencies ➢ Check Currency Codes.

You are presented with an SAP standard-delivered table that reflects the international ISO standard codes for currencies, as shown in Figure 6.7. This configuration involves reviewing this screen and ensuring that your currency codes are in line with the ISO standard. This check is important because Cash Management rely heavily on external data and services. Therefore, you should use industry-standard naming conventions.

**FIGURE 6.7**    The check currency code screen

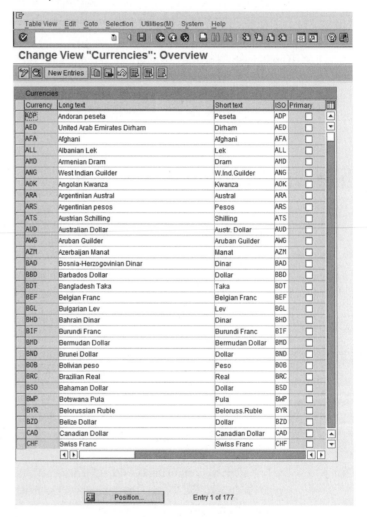

The next step is to create the currency exchange rate types. The exchange rate types will dictate what algorithm SAP should use when translating one currency to another. The most commonly used and standard-delivered exchange rate type is M—Average Rate. This algorithm will calculate the average between the bank buying and bank selling rate. This will then be the rate used to translate one currency to the desired currency.

Choose Financial Supply Chain Management ≻ Cash and Liquidity Management ≻ Cash Management ≻ Market Data ≻ Master Data ≻ Currencies ≻ Check Rate Types. The configuration screen shown in Figure 6.8 is an example of different exchange rate types.

The SAP-delivered rate types are as follows:

▶ B: Bank Selling Rate

▶ G: Bank Buying Rate

▶ M: Average Rate

We'll discuss how these rates affect the translation of a transaction in one currency to the desired currency when we evaluate the fields in the following section, as shown in Figure 6.8.

**FIGURE 6.8**    The change currency type screen

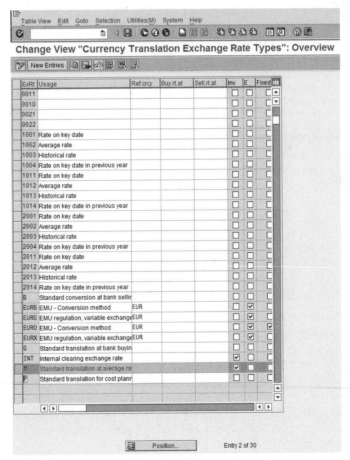

The following fields are relevant to the configuration step:

**ExRt**   This field contains the exchange rate type, which is the key that will dictate what algorithm is to be employed when translating currencies. The system will translate a transaction based on the exchange rate type. Take, for example, the various SAP-delivered currency rate types.

Say a transaction takes place in Mexican Peso and you want to translate it into USD. The transaction amounted to 100 MXN. There are three scenarios that the USD equivalent can result in:

> ► MXN to USD using the exchange rate type B, which is MXN 1: 0.2USD: the result is $20USD.

> ► MXN to USD using the exchange rate type G, which is MXN 1: 0.1USD: the result is $10USD.

> ► MXN to USD using the exchange rate type M, which is MXN 1: 0.15USD: the result is $15USD.

As you can see, the exchange rate type can greatly affect the financial results of a company.

**Usage**   This is a description field.

**Ref.crcy**   This is a key field; if your company is trades with several countries, and therefore many currencies, this field can save your database many table entries. The reference field is a central currency that allows the system to calculate an exchange rate derived from the reference currency. For example:

> ► USD = 1.3 EUR

> ► USD = 0.8 CAN

Therefore, the system can deduce that CAN = 0.6 EUR. The key currency in this example is USD. The advantage of using this functionality is that you can significantly reduce the size of the table (by the number of the entries on the table) and therefore improve the performance of currency evaluations and data management.

**Buy.rt.at**   This field contains a rate based on the calculation derived by determining the average and *subtracting* the spread.

**Sell.rt.at**   This field contains a rate based on the calculation derived by determining the average and *adding* the spread.

**Inv (Inverted)**   This field allows you to save table space. If, for example, 1 USD = 0.1 MXN (Mexican Peso), the inverted result is 1 MXN = 10 USD.

Using this functionality means that you do not have to include an entry for every permutation of a currency translation.

**EMU**    This indicator is only applicable for those countries that are part of the EMU agreement. If this is applicable, a reference currency is required.

**Fixed**    This selection is only applicable to those currencies that have a fixed exchange rate.

Once you've set up the master data for the successful translation and management of currency exchange, you can learn about the actual translation of foreign currency table. Larger companies are trending to automatic updates to this table via financial services companies.

You can access the configuration step by choosing Financial Supply Chain Management ➢ Cash and Liquidity Management ➢ Cash Management ➢ Market Data ➢ Manual Market Data Entry ➢ Enter Exchange Rates.

Figure 6.9 shows the configuration decisions you will make in this section. The decisions have a direct impact on how large this table will become. The two fields lost affected are Ref.crcy (reference currency) and the inverted fields mentioned earlier in this chapter. Figure 6.9 shows an example of the foreign currency translation table.

In Figure 6.9, there are 771 entries. This may seem like a large number, but you can reach this number in a relatively short period of time. Assume the following scenario:

- There are 100 currencies you transact with.
- You maintain currency exchange rates on a monthly basis.

Under this very simple model, you would have 10,000 lines for month one alone. After 1 year you would have 120,000 entries, and so on. After only a few years your table would contain more than 1 million lines. This can severely impact the speed at which the system can perform currency revaluations (used in open item calculations).

The following fields are relevant to the configuration step:

**ExRt**    This field contains the exchange rate type (covered in the previous section).

The following fields are relevant to the configuration step:

**ValidFrom**    This field contains the date from which an exchange rate is valid.

**FIGURE 6.9**    The Currency Exchange Rates screen

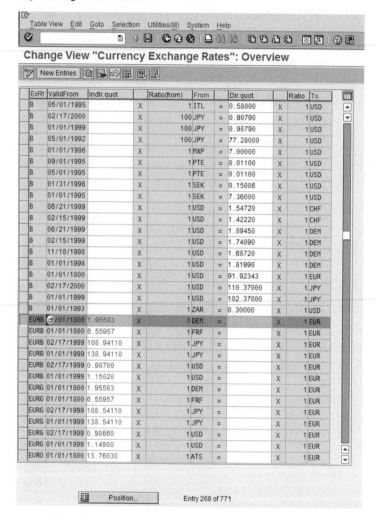

**Indir.quot**   This is a derived field, based on your setup of the exchange rate type in the previous section. You can specify that a currency's exchange rate be derived from a central currency—in this example, the European Euro.

**Dir.quot.**   This field is updated manually and is the actual exchange rate that would be used to translate the transaction currency (from) to the reporting currency (to).

As we alluded to earlier in this section, SAP does have functionality that allows for exchange rates to be updated automatically. To access the screen, you choose

Financial Supply Chain Management ➤ Cash and Liquidity Management ➤ Cash Management ➤ Market Data ➤ Datafeed. We will not be exploring these configuration steps.

Now that you've set up the exchange rate table for the successful translation of foreign currency–based transactions, let's take a brief look at setting up the bank master data used in this module.

To access the configuration screen for the setup of master data, choose Financial Supply Chain Management ➤ Cash and Liquidity Management ➤ Cash Management ➤ Master Data ➤ G/L Accounts ➤ Define Account Groups. This menu path at first glance can appear to be out of place. The reference to G/L Accounts here is accurate. By following these configuration steps, you'll reach the settings that will be required for the master data referenced by bank accounts. This is one of many examples of where you can reach the same configuration tables via multiple configuration paths. In Chapter 3, for example, we covered account groups and reached the configuration screen by choosing Financial Accounting ➤ General Ledger Accounting ➤ G/L Accounts ➤ Master Data ➤ Preparations ➤ Define Account Group.

**NOTE**   Defining account groups and field status groups is no different from the steps covered in Chapter 3.

The next step is to set up groupings or, as SAP refers to it, *structuring*. Larger companies quite often have many bank accounts established for specific business objectives. They range from short-term investments to accounts dedicated to paying vendors or employees. There are many advantages to having specialized bank accounts, but whatever the reasons are, this is the area where we group like accounts together. In addition to the grouping of bank accounts, you can group all accounts that are cash related. They are typically your A/R and A/P accounts. These can vary in terms of cash flow nature. For example, your customers could have the terms of 30 days net, but your vendors extend only 15 days credit. It is for this reason that you have to group accounts together based on their typical cash behavior.

Begin by choosing Financial Supply Chain Management ➤ Cash and Liquidity Management ➤ Cash Management ➤ Structuring ➤ Groupings ➤ Define Groupings and Maintain Headers. You will be presented with the screen in Figure 6.10, where you create the structure for account groupings in cash management.

**FIGURE 6.10**    The groupings and header screen

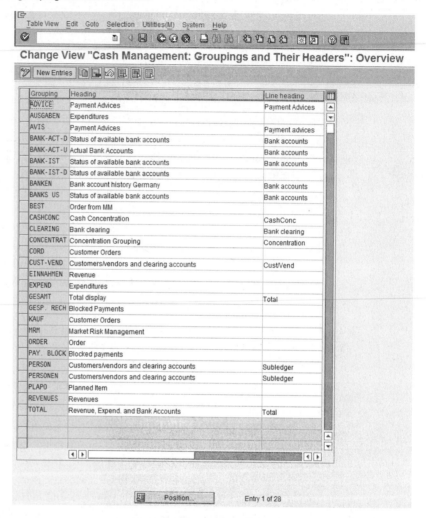

The following fields are relevant to the configuration step:

**Grouping**    This is the identifier field used to link grouping headers to accounts.

**Heading**    This field specifies the text that will be used as descriptors in the forecasting reports in cash management.

After you have created the headings, it is now to time to select the appropriate accounts for these groupings. Choose Financial Supply Chain Management ➤ Cash and Liquidity Management ➤ Cash Management ➤ Structuring ➤ Groupings ➤ Maintain Structure to open the screen shown in Figure 6.11, where you will map accounts to groupings.

**FIGURE 6.11**    The groupings to accounts screen

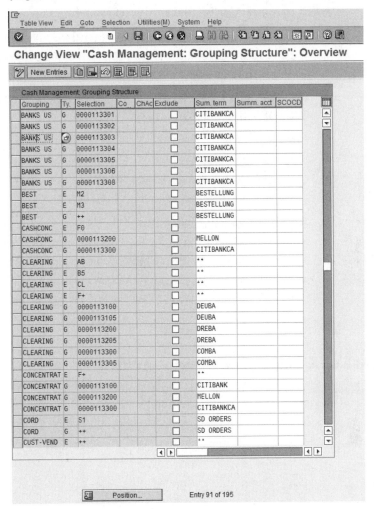

The following fields are relevant to the configuration step:

**Grouping**    We covered this field in the previous section.

**Ty.**    This field contains an indicator that is either a group or a level entry.

**CoCD**    This field contains the company code. Use this field if you want the grouping to be specific to a company code. Often large companies will want to see their cash flow position across various company codes; if this is the case, you would not use this field.

**ChAc**   This field specifies the chart of accounts, which is similar to the company code field. Use this field only if you want the grouping to be specific to a chart of accounts.

**Sum. Term**   By using this field, you can combine the group and level lines as one summarized line item in the liquidity forecast.

**Summ. Acct**   This field allows for summarization of all cash accounts in the selection line to be summarized at this account.

**SCOCD**   This field, the summarization for company code cash concentration, is similar to the previous field; use it when you would like to summarize cash across company codes. This functionality is commonly used when the holding company receives all excess cash from the subsidiaries on a daily (or regular) basis.

After you have added the accounts to the groupings, define the distribution of the various cash-related transaction types. Various transaction types such as checks or wire transfers have different rates of converting into cash. The following menu path will get you to your next configuration screen: Financial Supply Chain Management ➤ Cash and Liquidity Management ➤ Cash Management ➤ Structuring ➤ Define Distribution Function. You will see the screen shown in Figure 6.12, where you map a cash event to a probability.

**FIGURE 6.12**   The Distribution for Cash Position and Liquidity Forecast screen

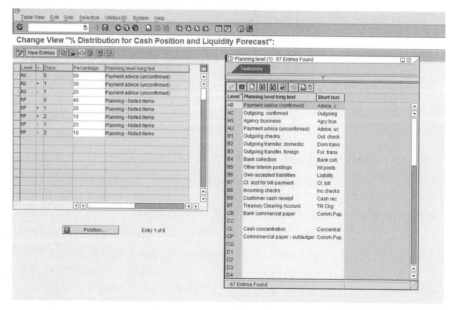

The following fields are relevant to the configuration step:

**Level**    Planning level is used to categorize types of transactions that will affect the cash position of a company. Various cash-related transactions have different time-lines with respect to actually impacting the cash reserves in a company.

**+-**    The field is +, -, or blank, indicating that the transaction will have a cash impact before, after, or on the expected date, respectively.

**Percentage**    This field specifies the probability of an event occurring.

The next area of functionality that you'll explore is that of cash concentration, or the pooling of cash across business divisions/company codes. Begin by choosing Financial Supply Chain Management ➤ Cash and Liquidity Management ➤ Cash Management ➤ Business Transactions ➤ Cash Concentration ➤ Define Intermediate Account, Clearing Accounts, and Amounts. After clicking the New Entries button, you will see the screen shown in Figure 6.13, which stipulates how accounts within a company code will be pooled (concentrated).

**FIGURE 6.13**    The concentration of cash configuration screen

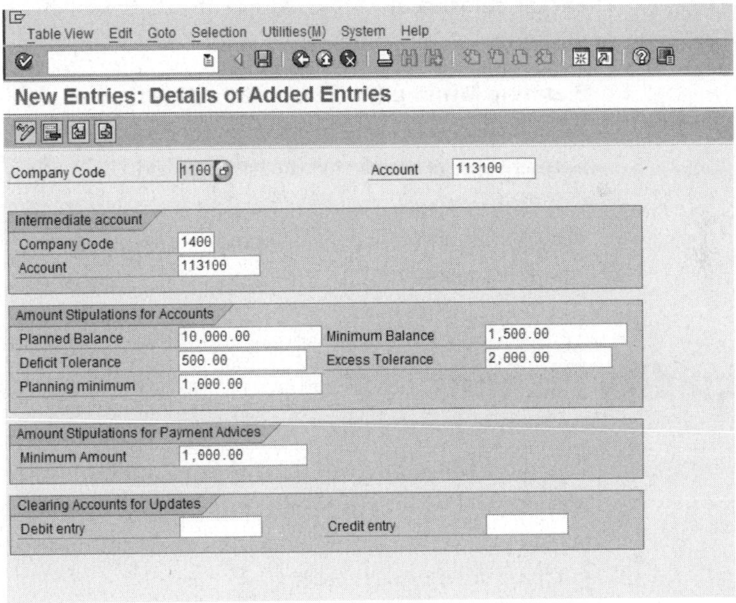

The following fields are relevant to the configuration step:

**Company Code**    This field specifies the company code where the money will be pooled.

**Account**    This field specifies the account where the money will be consolidated to.

**Company Code**    This field contains the company code from which the money will be pooled.

**Account**    This field specifies the account where the money will be consolidated from.

**Planned Balance**    This field specifies the minimum amount that the account can have before excess cash will be swept to the central/concentrated account.

**Minimum Balance**    This field specifies the minimum balance that the account should contain.

**Deficit Tolerance**    This field specifies the level below the planned balance that a transfer to or from this account will be permitted.

**Excess Tolerance**    This field specifies the level above the planned balance that a transfer to or from this account will be permitted.

**Planning Minimum**    This field specifies the amount over or under the planned balance that must occur before cash concentration will take affect. In this example, Extreme Sports has elected the balance deviation to be within $1,000. This means that the balance can be either $1,000 less than the planned value before cash is swept to this account, or $1,000 greater than the planned balance before cash is swept out of this account.

# Liquidity Planner

*Liquidity Planner* forecasts the cash flow impacts of business activity looking forward, typically over a horizon of more than one month. The system focuses on business events that do not directly generate or consume cash, such as creating a purchase order or sales order.

Liquidity Planner looks at all transactions that result in either an inflow or an outflow of cash, and the impact is either immediate or sometime in the future. The key to this module is that it can forecast a company's future cash position based on business rules. One of the leading causes for companies declaring bankruptcy is not that they are not profitable but because they are not liquid enough. Effective management of cash (cash flow) avoids this, and the credit crunch of 2008 provided ample examples of where cash flow became a serious issue.

Liquidity Planner monitors and collates three sources of data to form a comprehensive picture of your company's cash position:

**Bank statements**    Liquidity Planner can be mapped to all of your electronic bank statements. This enhances the timeliness of the cash in and outflows.

**Finance data**    Here we map general ledger accounts that are related to cash, such as bank accounts. This will then enhance how we account for checks that are not yet cleared, via our check clearing account.

**Logistics data**    Logistics data is primarily in the form of invoice data. This allows the system to extend the horizon of cash in and outflow projections.

## EXTREME SPORTS CASH AND LIQUIDITY MANAGEMENT CONFIGURATION REVIEW

Extreme Sports has decided to take advantage of several of the functionality options offered in the Cash and Liquidity submodule. As Extreme Sports has operations in both Mexico and the United States, they must accurately reflect the results of business activity in both the Mexican Peso and the U.S. Dollar. Extreme Sports has decided to use the functionality that will automatically revalue open items (such as open customer invoices). Extreme Sports considers timely and accurate cash flow and cash forecasts an important tool for effectively managing its business. It is for this reason they are using the cash forecasting tools that help to group cash-related accounts together. The grouping is based on the type of financial activity that takes place in the accounts.

In this section, you learned how using functionality like indirect quotes, which allows the system to derive the effective exchange rate for a currency, helps improve performance. We also used the cash distribution functionality that increases the accuracy of our cash flow forecasts. inally, to take full advantage of interest earned on our cash, we used cash concentration to consolidate our cash holdings.

# Collections Management

*Collections Management* helps the collections department within the accounts receivables function to identify, prioritize, and manage the collections opportunities. In this section, you'll learn how to prioritize collections activities. You will also learn how to manage customers by grouping them together based on market segment, business unit, or risk profile.

Once you have identified and organized those customers, you will learn how to manage the data that results in the collections activities. This area of functionality helps a company to become more effective in its collections activities, which results in a greater percentage of accounts receivable invoices turning into cash.

The first step in configuring the Collections Management submodule is to identify which company codes will be participating in collections management. Begin by choosing Financial Supply Chain Management ➤ Collections Management ➤ Basic Settings for Collections Management ➤ Basic Data ➤ Define Company Codes for SAP Collections Management to open a simple screen where you'll list the company codes participating in Collections Management. Figure 6.14 is configured for Extreme Sports so that company codes 1100 through 1400 will be taking advantage of the Collections Management submodule. Be careful when entering company codes on this screen; this is one of the few areas within SAP where there is no validation of the entries. The good news is there is a validation step later (when the company code is assigned to collection segment—you'll learn more about this topic later in this chapter).

The next step in configuring Collections Management is to define your collection strategies. SAP delivers several collection strategies, and of course, you can create your own. The strategies refer to Business Add-Ins (BAdi), which are programs that evaluate customer data depending on your business environment. Choose Financial Supply Chain Management ➤ Collections Management ➤ Basic Settings for Collections Management ➤ Collection Strategies ➤ Basic Rules ➤ Define Basic Rules, and you will be presented with a warning message that says, "Caution: The table is cross-client." Press Enter to dismiss the warning. You will then be presented with the configuration screen shown in Figure 6.15, which displays the preconfigured and SAP-delivered collection strategies.

**FIGURE 6.14** The Company Codes in Collections Management screen

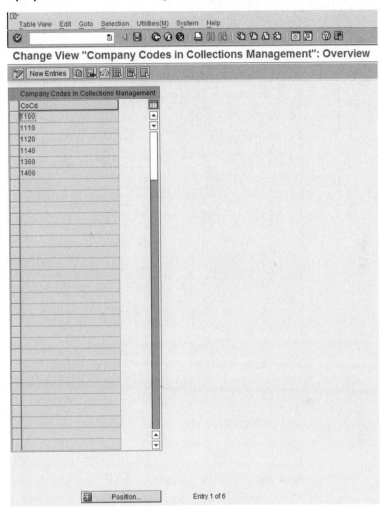

**FIGURE 6.15**   The collections strategy screen

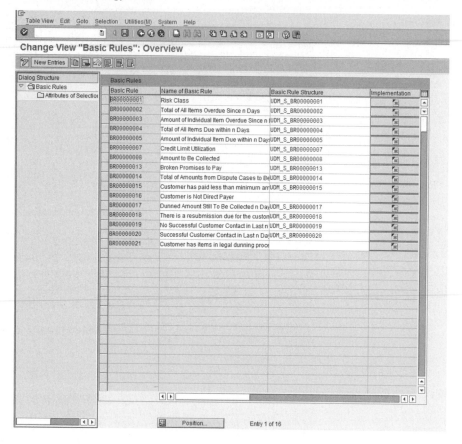

The following fields are relevant to the configuration step:

**Basic Rule**   This is the identifier field. The field is free form. Remember to use either a Y or Z as the prefix to indicate it is not a standard SAP collection strategy rule.

**Name of Basic Rule**   This is the description field for the collection strategy.

**Basic Rule Structure**   Here you specify which fields are to be evaluated and in what order.

Once you have set up the strategy for selecting customers to be a part of the collections process, you need to create collection rules. Customers will be selected based on the rules; base your selection priorities on how many of the criteria the customer meets. To open the screen shown in Figure 6.16, choose Financial Supply Chain Management ➢ Collections Management ➢ Basic Settings for Collections

Management ➤ Collection Strategies ➤ Collection Rules ➤ Define Collection
Rules. On this screen you define a collection rule for slow payers. The next step is
to select your collection rule and assign it to the basic rules created in the previous
step. Select the Assignment of Basic Rules to Rules menu option on the left. You will
see the configured screen shown in Figure 6.17.

**FIGURE 6.16**  The define collection rules screen

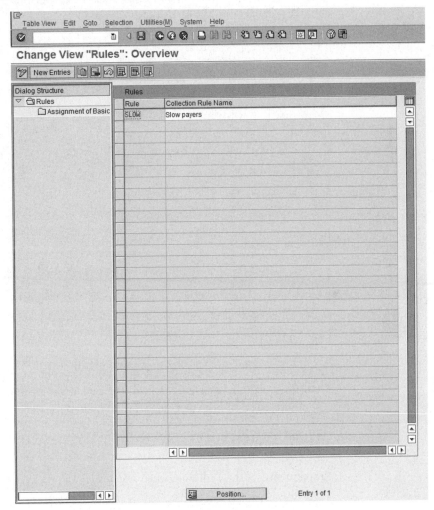

**FIGURE 6.17**   The Assignment of Basic Rules to Rules screen

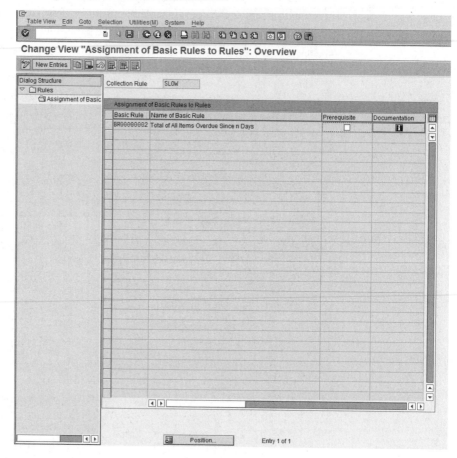

The following fields are relevant to the configuration step:

**Basic Rule**   This is the identifier field. The field is free form. It can contain the SAP-delivered set of rules or a custom rule you have created.

**Name of Basic Rule**   Enter a description of the basic rule defaults from the previous step.

**Prerequisite**   This indicator, when selected, allows the system to treat the rule as a prerequisite; when this field is unselected, the rule is treated as a condition.

The next step in setting up your collections strategy is to prioritize the conditions that will result in a customer being a high-priority collections candidate. Because all businesses have different business conditions and practices, you have a lot of flexibility here. The system comes with four levels of priority; you can access them (see Figure 6.18) by choosing Financial Supply Chain Management ➤ Collections Management ➤ Basic Settings for Collections Management ➤ Collection Strategies ➤ Priorities ➤ Define Priorities.

**FIGURE 6.18**   The Priority of Worklist Item screen

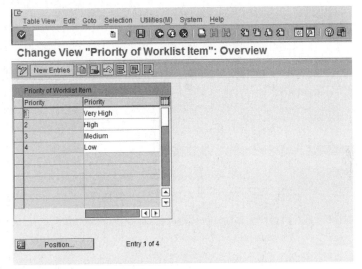

The following fields are relevant to the configuration step:

**Priority**   Enter a numeric value, corresponding to the order in which customers will be worked on in the collections process.

**Priority**   The second priority field is the description field and is free form.

The next step in the process is to define how priorities are met. The priority with which a customer is going to be allocated, in terms of collections activity, is completely configurable and is based on the number of tests met. The value of the priority, is directly proportional to the level of urgency with which that customer will be dealt with. Generally, the higher risk customers (and therefore those less likely to pay) with the greatest outstanding sum will result in the highest priority values.

SAP has a value system where the highest priority is awarded the value of 30. The number of tests you define in your collection strategy will depend on how points are awarded. To access the screen shown in Figure 6.19 (where you can see how priority is ranked based on the percentage of points awarded), choose Financial Supply Chain Management ➤ Collections Management ➤ Basic Settings for Collections Management ➤ Collection Strategies ➤ Priorities ➤ Define Derivation of Priority.

**FIGURE 6.19**    The define derivation priority screen

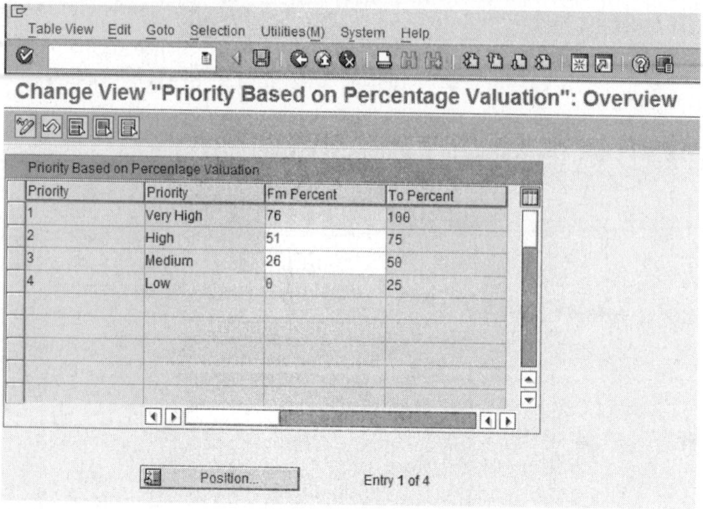

The following fields are relevant to the configuration step:

**Priority**    This field contains a numeric value corresponding to the order in which customers will be worked on in the collections process.

**Priority**    This second priority field is the description field and is free form.

**Fm Percent**    This specifies the minimum percent of the maximum score to be considered for a particular priority level.

Let's walk through an example. Assume there are five tests and each test is equally weighted. Each test carries a value of 6 points (with the maximum being 30 points). If a customer is to qualify as a high priority, it would have to pass at least four out of the five tests to gain sufficient points to qualify as "Very High." The math is as follows: 4 tests @ 6 points a test = 24 points, which is greater than the minimum points required to qualify as a high priority, which is 76 percent of 30 points = 22.8 points.

**To Percent**    This represents the upper limit of the range that defines a priority group; above this value the customer gets "bumped" to the next level of elevated priority.

Your next task is to set up the organizational data. This tool is powerful because it offers you the ability to consolidate customer account analysis across company codes. As you may recall, most functionality and reporting is segregated by company code, the legal entity. Access the configuration screen by choosing Financial Supply Chain Management ➤ Collections Management ➤ Basic Settings for Collections Management ➤ Organizational Structure ➤ Define Collection Segments.

Two configuration steps are involved. The first is to create a collection segment. You may create different segments if your business segments are vastly different in the way you allocate credit and terms. One industry can have very different industry standards in terms of how invoices are paid, and therefore, it would make little sense to have both industries evaluated with the same tests.

The second step is to assign company codes to the collection segment. Figure 6.20 shows the collections segment created for Extreme Sports, which combines both the customers from the Apparel and Equipment segments of the market.

**FIGURE 6.20**     The Define Collection Segments screen

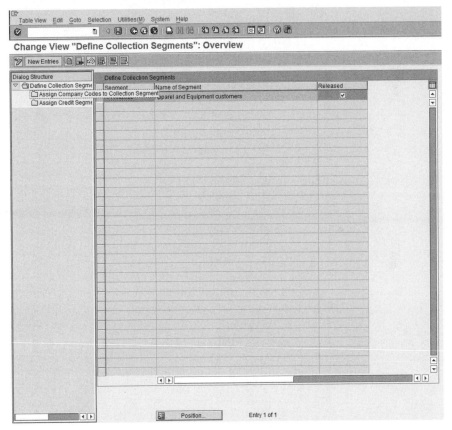

The following fields are relevant to the configuration step:

**Segment**     This key field/identifier is used to name the segment; this field is free form.

**Name of Segment**     This field contains a description; the field is free form.

**Released**     If this field is checked, the segment is active, which means the collections tests will take effect for those companies that you assign to this segment.

The next step is to select the segment and then click the Assign Company Codes to Collection Segment menu option on the left. This opens a configuration screen like the one in Figure 6.21, where we've assigned the company codes that represent Extreme Sports to the collection segment.

**FIGURE 6.21** The Assign Company Codes to Collections Segment screen

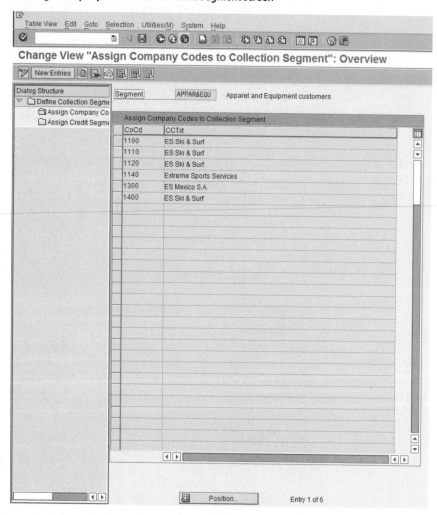

The following fields are relevant to the configuration step:

**CoCd**   Contains the company code for only those companies that were identified in the configuration step "Define Company Codes for SAP Collections Management" above.

**CCTxt**   The company code text field, which is defaulted in from the T001 table.

Next, you'll explore how the system keeps track of the actions that have taken place and the status of the customer. Begin by choosing Financial Supply Chain Management ➢ Collections Management ➢ Basic Settings for Collections Management ➢ Customer Contacts ➢ Define Result of Customer Contact. Figure 6.22 shows an example of the type of contact that would result from collections activities.

**FIGURE 6.22**   Use this screen to define the results of customer contact.

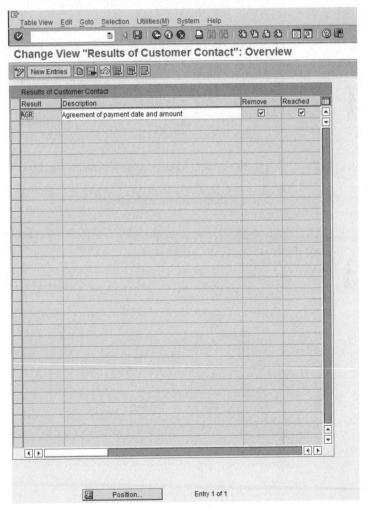

The following fields are relevant to the configuration step:

**Result**   This field specifies a three-character field used as an identifier.

**Description**   This field provides a description for the result field.

**Remove**   If this field is checked, it means that the customer has been reached and the task is completed on the worklist and can therefore be removed from the worklist.

**Reached**   If this field is checked, it means that the customer has been reached and therefore is the equivalent of completed on the worklist; the system will check the customer contacts for evaluating the worklist.

The next step is integrating collections management with dispute management, a topic that will be covered later in this chapter. To access the screen shown in Figure 6.23 (where you link a case in dispute management to cases that need to be collected), choose Financial Supply Chain Management ➢ Collections Management ➢ Basic Settings for Collections Management ➢ SAP Dispute Management Integration ➢ Define Status for Dispute Cases to Be Collected.

**FIGURE 6.23**   Here you define status for dispute cases to be collected.

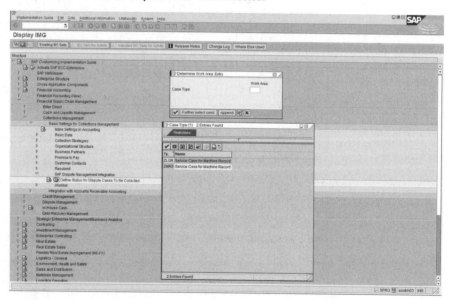

## EXTREME SPORTS COLLECTIONS MANAGEMENT CONFIGURATION REVIEW

Extreme Sports was fast to realize that without an effective collections strategy, money was being left on the table, as the saying goes. With an effective collections strategy, a company can ensure that the collections professionals focus on those accounts that have the highest ratio of effort to dollars retrieved.

The first thing that Extreme Sports decided to do was include all company codes under the collections management submodule. This is a powerful decision, because it allows the system to review all customers across all company codes. This means that a customer account, when viewed in a consolidated picture, may result in a different priority in terms of collections urgency.

Extreme Sports is using the system to perform tests against the customer account. The number of tests applicable to the customer will have an impact on how the customer is prioritized.

With the implementation of these tools, Extreme Sports has been able to take all of the guesswork out of its collections function. Because the data is available automatically, they are able to rely on up-to-date and accurate data for decision making.

# Credit Management

*Credit Management* is the submodule that significantly helps a company reduce its credit exposure by using tools that increase the probability of customer invoices being paid. In Chapter 5 we covered the A/R portion of credit management, which involved setting up credit limits and monitoring customers against their credit limits. This functionality is relatively manually intensive and not dynamic. Decisions regarding customers' credit limits should not be arbitrary; you will learn in this chapter how this need not be the case.

Credit Management, from Financial Supply Chain Management, offers you functionality that utilizes external sources of data, such as credit rating providers, to help you manage the process of extending credit to customers. Credit Management offers you several tools to decide how credit limits are changed or updated, including change logs and workflow that enforces management approval before limits can be changed.

The next step is to set up credit segments. As you learned in Chapter 5, you set up three credit representative groups:

► Apparel

► Boats

► Ski

In this chapter, you'll set up credit segments that mirror the credit representative groups. Credit segments are used to segregate customers' credit management by major industry segment. To reach the first configuration screen, choose Financial Supply Chain Management ➤ Credit Management ➤ Credit Risk Monitoring ➤ Master Data ➤ Create Credit Segments. Click the New Entries button to open a screen similar to the one in Figure 6.24.

**FIGURE 6.24**   Creating credit segment data

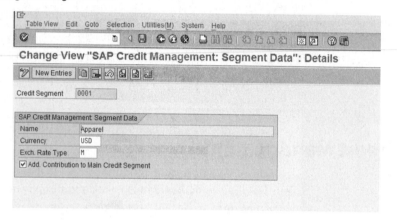

The following fields are relevant to the configuration step:

**Credit Segment**   The naming convention is to start with a "Z"; this is a standard SAP insists upon to augment the process of upgrading.

**Name**   This field contains the description of the credit segment.

**Currency**   This field specifies the currency you want to use for managing your credit segment.

**Exch. Rate Type**   This field specifies the exchange rate type—the way in which foreign currency–based transactions will be translated.

**Add. Contribution to Main Credit Segment**   This indicator, if selected, will result in the credit activity being rolled up to the main credit segment, typically credit segment 0000.

Next you set up your rating systems. A typical example of a rating system or service is Moody's. The purpose of this step is to create a mapping to the service and your ranking system. To open the next configuration screen, choose Financial Supply Chain Management ➢ Credit Management ➢ Credit Risk Monitoring ➢ Master Data ➢ Define Rating Procedure. Figure 6.25 shows a fully configured screen with several rating services; select one of the line items and then the menu option on the left to see the details of the mapping. Figure 6.26 shows the mapping of the rating system to the ranking system.

**FIGURE 6.25**    Defining rating procedure

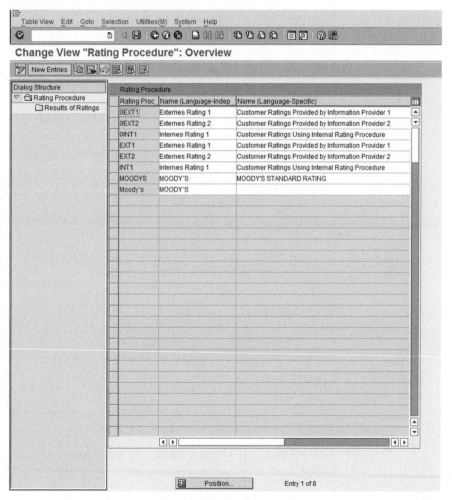

**FIGURE 6.26** Rating to ranking mapping

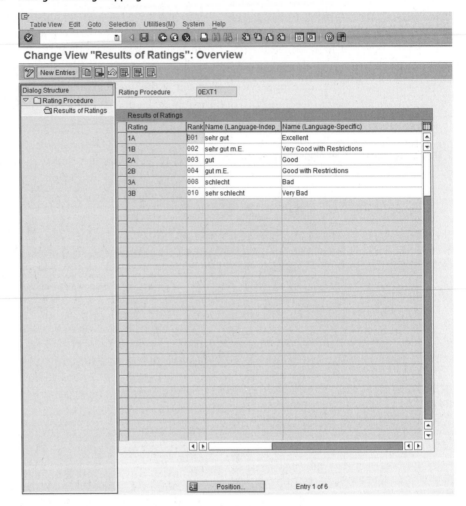

The following fields are relevant to the configuration step:

**Rating** This field contains the rating provided by the business partner or rating service.

**Rank** This represents the rank for the rating.

**Name (Language-Independent)** This field contains the description of the rank, independent of the language of the user.

**Name (Language-Specific)**    This field contains the description of the ranking, specific to the log-on language of the user.

The next step is grouping customers based on their creditworthiness. Begin by choosing Financial Supply Chain Management ≻ Credit Management ≻ Credit Risk Monitoring ≻ Master Data ≻ Define Customer Credit Group. Figure 6.27 shows the three customer credit groups that Extreme Sports will use to manage their credit accounts.

**FIGURE 6.27**    Customer Credit Group screen

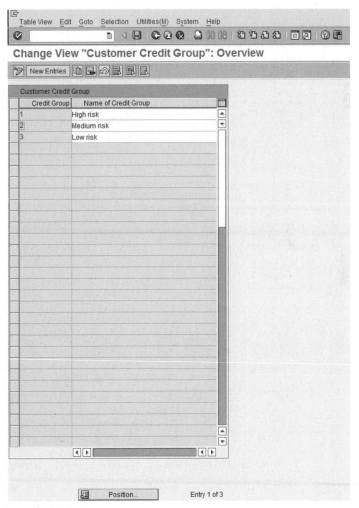

The following fields are relevant to the configuration step:

**Credit Group**    This numeric field is used to identify your customer credit groups.

**Name of Credit Group**    This description field lets you provide some context to the numeric value for your credit group.

Next, you'll look at what SAP's standard delivered formulas are for calculating credit risk. If the standard formulas are not adequate for your needs, you can use the Formula Editor (a BAdi) to define your own. Choose Financial Supply Chain Management ➢ Credit Management ➢ Credit Risk Monitoring ➢ Master Data ➢ Define Formulas. The resulting screen, shown in Figure 6.28, shows you the four standard formulas.

**FIGURE 6.28**    Defining formulas

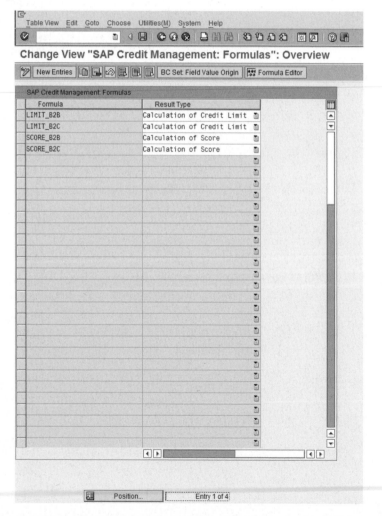

Let's look at the fields on this screen:

**Formula** This field contains the name of the BAdi that is used to perform the calculation.

**Result Type** There are only two result types: credit score and credit limit.

Now let's tie all these steps together: we'll create a rule for the calculation of credit scores and credit limits. Begin by choosing Financial Supply Chain Management ➢ Credit Management ➢ Credit Risk Monitoring ➢ Master Data ➢ Create Rule for Scoring and Credit Limit Calculation. Figure 6.29 has four rules set up; you can see on the left that there are three steps that you will follow before this configuration is complete.

**FIGURE 6.29** Rule for Scoring and Credit Limit Calculation screen

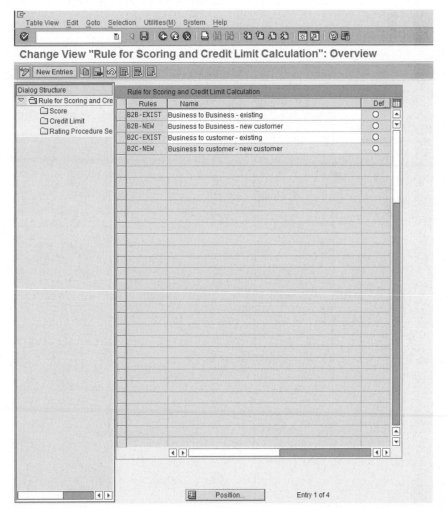

Let's look at the fields on this screen:

**Rules** This field contains an alphanumeric key used to identify the rule for calculating credit limits and scores.

**Name** This is the description field for the rule.

**Default** If this field is selected, the rule will be used as the default rule when new customers are created.

The next step is to select the rule, and by using the Score menu on the left, you can assign a formula to the rule. Figure 6.30 shows how the formula is assigned to a rule.

The following fields are relevant to the configuration step (remember only those fields that are in white are fields where you can edit):

**Rule** The entry in this field is based on your selection in the previous step.

**FIGURE 6.30** Assigning a formula to a rule

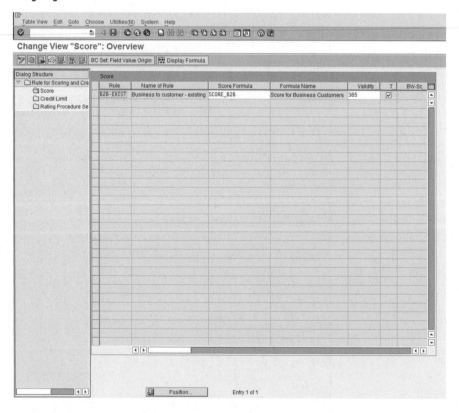

**Score Formula**   Select one of the formulas set up in the previous configuration step.

**Validity in Days**   This field stipulates how long the result from a formula will be valued. In other words, the system will reevaluate a customer's credit score once this period has expired.

**Trace**   When this field is selected, the results of the formula calculation will be recorded in the customer's account.

The next step is to assign credit limits for the credit segments within a rule; do this by selecting the Credit Limit option on the left (see Figure 6.31).

**FIGURE 6.31**   Assigning credit limits to credit segments and formulas

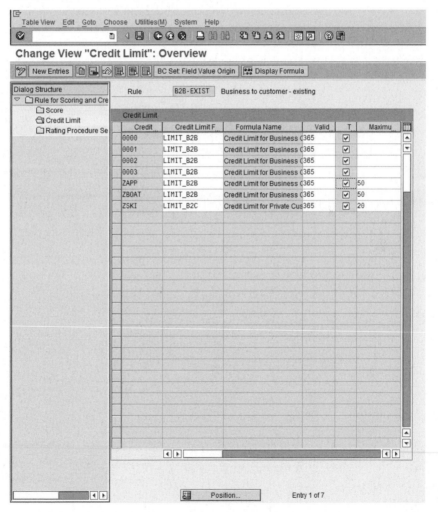

The following fields are relevant to the configuration step:

**Credit Segment**    This field specifies the mapping of the credit segments created in the earlier step and is now mapped to a formula and the rule.

**Credit Limit Formula**    In this field, you map the formula to the credit segment.

**Validity in Days**    The number of days the calculation is valid before a customer's account needs to be reevaluated for creditworthiness.

**Maximum Credit Limit Increase**    This field specifies the maximum amount, in percentage terms, a customer's account can have an increase in credit limit.

The next step is selecting rating procedures and assigning a validity period. Do this by selecting Rating Procedure Selection in the left window. Figure 6.32 shows the four rating systems and their validity periods.

**FIGURE 6.32**    Rating Procedure Selection screen

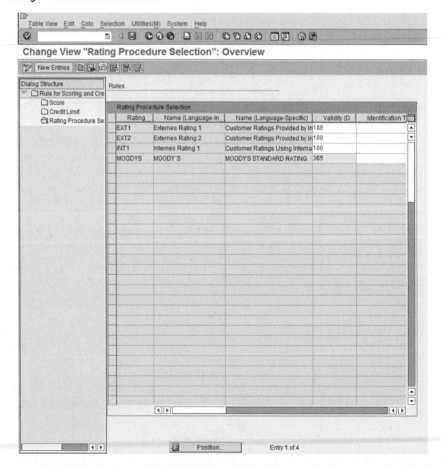

These fields are relevant to the configuration step:

**Rating Procedure**    Select the rating procedures we created earlier in this step.

**Validity (Days)**    This field specifies the number of days the procedure will be valid before a recalculation will be required.

**Identification Type**    This contains the type of ID used; it can be an ID card or commercial registry. This is not a required field.

The final step, with respect to master data, is the assignment of risk classes to credit scores. You can access the configuration screen by choosing Financial Supply Chain Management ➤ Credit Management ➤ Credit Risk Monitoring ➤ Master Data ➤ Create Risk Classes. Figure 6.33 shows three credit risk classes based on FICO (Fair Isaac Corporation) scores.

**FIGURE 6.33**    Assigning risk classes to a score

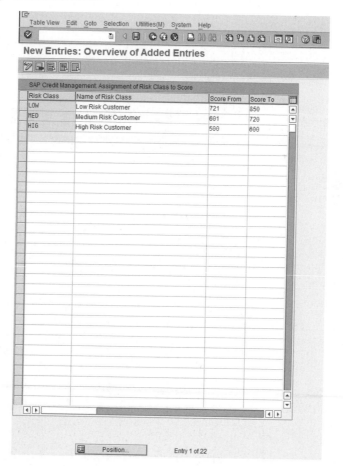

The following fields are relevant to the configuration step:

**Risk Class**   This is a three-character field, used to identify risk classes.

**Name of Risk Class**   This is the description field for the risk class.

**Score From**   This field specifies the lower limit a customer can achieve before the customer will be assigned the next (lower) credit risk category (higher risk).

**Score To**   This field specifies the upper limit, above which the customer qualifies for a better category.

You have now finishing setting up the credit master data; the next task is to create reasons when credit management will block a customer from transacting. Choose Financial Supply Chain Management ➢ Credit Management ➢ Credit Risk Monitoring ➢ Credit Limit Check ➢ Define Blocking Reasons. Figure 6.34 shows an example of when a customer's account would be blocked.

**FIGURE 6.34**   Reasons for locks in credit management

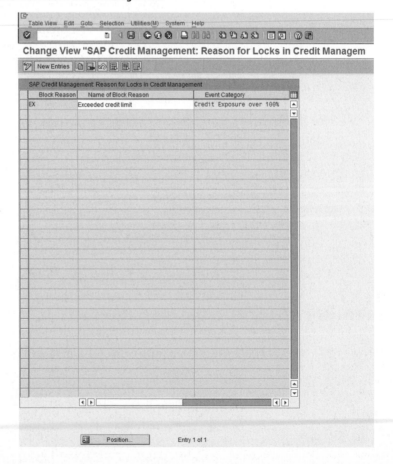

The following fields are relevant to the configuration step:

**Block Reason**    This is a two-character field, identifying the blocking reason.

**Name of Block Reason**    This field contains the description for the block reason.

**Event Category**    The event category is the activity that has to occur before a customer's account is blocked. This means that the customer will no longer be able to order goods or services.

---

### EXTREME SPORTS HOUSE CREDIT MANAGEMENT CONFIGURATION ANALYSIS

The Credit Management submodule within the Financial Supply Chain module is an extension of the original credit management functionality we explored in Chapter 5. In future releases of SAP, the functionality found in the A/R module will be assumed here in the Financial Supply Chain module. The functionality offered has more automation in the credit management process and uses external, third-party service providers to achieve this level of automation.

Extreme Sports took advantage of external services like Moody's to provide credit scores for its future customers. This helps eliminate the guesswork with respect to granting credit.

---

In Chapter 5 we created credit representative groups that grouped together customers with a category supported by credit representatives in the credit function. In Chapter 6 we continued with this theory and applied it to credit segments. Credit segments can span multiple company codes and are a way of identifying groups of customers with similar risk profiles.

Finally, we explored ways in which we can systematically prohibit further transactions from occurring. You also learned how to reduce further credit exposure by creating blocking rules.

# Summary

In this chapter we covered some of the most often used processes in financial supply chain management. SAP delivers this functionality to augment the original FI/CO module and is primarily focused on improving cash flow management. We covered the four submodules:

**Biller Direct**    This feature provides functionality that reduces the amount of manual entry (and therefore errors) and increases the speed of converting customer invoices to cash by presenting invoices to customers via the Internet.

**Cash and Liquidity Management**    You learned how to better forecast a company's cash position, maximize interest earned, and reduce bank charges through cash concentration.

**Collections Management**    We eliminated the guesswork from our collections activities through automated data analysis and prioritization tools, thereby ensuring the most effective use of our collections resources.

**Credit Management**    Here we continued to build on what we developed in Chapter 5. You learned how to make use of external credit rating systems to make more informed credit risk decisions.

Unfortunately, we are not able to cover every configuration option in this book, but two submodules that are worthy of recognition are Dispute Management and In-House Cash.

Dispute Management is the logical next step in collections management and is therefore it's no surprise that they are closely integrated.

In-House Cash is functionality generally only available to large organizations. It allows a company to facilitate its own banking function in house. For further information on these topics, visit `http://help.sap.com/`. You can find explanations of specific functionality of Dispute Management at `http://help.sap.com/saphelp_erp60_sp/helpdata/en/30/88c2c466631f46862f8928b1d6cde5/frameset.htm`.

You can find additional information about In-House Cash at `http://help.sap.com/saphelp_erp60_sp/helpdata/en/39/239739f4e38a2ce10000000a11402f/frameset.htm`.

Configuration documentation is always available at almost every step of the IMG.

# New GL Accounting

**FEATURING:**

- ▶ **OVERVIEW OF THE CONCEPTS OF NEW GL**

- ▶ **INITIAL CONFIGURATION REQUIREMENTS OF THE NEW GL**

- ▶ **MASTER DATA OF THE NEW GL**

The New GL module, as the title indicates, is the new option of configuration and implementation within the ECC system for the General Ledger Accounting module. This new approach was developed to accommodate the numerous requirements for legal, managerial, country, and local accounting practices. Basically, this approach brings together much of the reporting and analysis completed separately by several different components in the ECC system. In this chapter, we will cover the activation of the New GL, additional configuration of the Ledgers and Master Data that is required, and some additional concepts about parallel accounting that will be of use to you. After this, you will have to work with the FI team and understand any additional requirements that would enhance the overall GL process. Please see some of the reasons for the New GL to discuss any additional configuration with your business users.

## Overview of the New GL

With the activation and use of the New GL, you can incorporate additional functionality that will offer you information that you would normally obtain from the areas of the classic FI module, the Cost of Sales Ledger, the reconciliation ledger used to validate and reconcile data between FI and CO, the managerial reporting handled by the CCA and PCA modules (segment reporting) within ECC, and the reporting and analysis available by using the Special Purpose Ledger process. Therefore, the process of activating and implementing the New GL requires all of the same integration between the different areas in SAP ECC, such as the FI-AR, FI-AP, MM, FI-AA, CO-CCA, CO-PCA, HCM (Human Capital Management), TRM (Treasury and Risk Management), FI-TV (Travel Management), and PSM-FM (Funds Management) and the Special Purpose Ledger. However, in the past for you to obtain the specific information from each of these areas and validate and compare this information to the appropriate FI areas, it took additional effort and reporting processes. With the New GL module, all of these different reporting integration activities are eliminated, and the New GL can generate a standard report with all of the information already integrated together.

As a result, the New GL offers the ability to create reports that can view information from a group level or company-specific level. It allows automatic and simultaneous posting of all subledger items in the appropriate general ledger accounts (reconciliation accounts). It offers simultaneous updating of the parallel general ledgers and of the cost accounting areas. In addition, it offers real-time evaluation of and reporting on current posting data, in the form of account displays, financial statements, and different balance sheet versions and with the use of the segment field(s) allows for additional analysis using multiple dimensions.

> **NOTE**  A *Dimension* in the New GL is defined as one of the sections of the coding block that makes up the overall string of characteristic values that are used for integration purposes within the New GL. For example, some dimensions are Profit Center, Segment, Company Code, and so on.

In this way, the New GL Accounting serves as a complete record of all business transactions. It is the central and up-to-date component for reporting. All posted transactions can be checked at any time in real time by displaying the original documents, line items, and debit/credits posted at different levels in the accounting information, journals, summary, and balance sheet/profit and loss levels. See Figure 7.1 for a graphical view of this information.

**FIGURE 7.1**    Possibilities with the New General Ledger Accounting

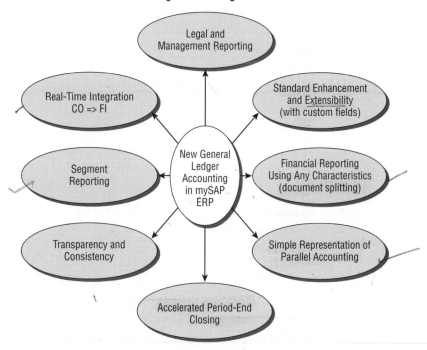

Breaking this down a bit more into specific areas of accounting for general use in the new General Ledger, you can display the parallel accounting using parallel accounts (as in R/3) or using parallel ledgers. The FI standard functions and reports are available for all parallel ledgers. The Segment entity and the relevant reporting that are required for segment reporting according to IAS (International Accounting Standards), IFRS (International Financial Reporting Standards), and US GAAP are available in the new General Ledger (this requires the Segment dimension).

In addition, you can enhance the new General Ledger flexibility; therefore, you can enter user-defined fields and update the relevant totals. Many standard reports can evaluate the information from the user-defined fields. Another option is to use the new Document Splitting function (online split); you can create financial statements at company code level and, if required, for entities, such as the segment. For each document, the system then creates a zero balance for the relevant entity, for example, for the segment. The Document Splitting functionality will be discussed later in this chapter.

Another benefit of the New GL is that as a result, you no longer have to carry out time-consuming reconciliation tasks between FI and CO for the end of the period since cross-entity processes are transferred in real time to the new General Ledger in Controlling. In addition, you can, for example, navigate from the financial statements report results or the profit and loss statement report results to the relevant CO report. Because of the new multidimensional aspect in the General Ledger, all data that is relevant for the General Ledger is stored in one environment. As a result, reconciliation tasks—for example, between the general ledger and Profit Center Accounting or the consolidation staging ledger, and processing steps that have to be carried out repeatedly in the individual applications (for example, balance carryforward)—are no longer required. When you use the new General Ledger, you may not have to use the special ledger anymore depending on the different types of reports required. But as you will realize, the New GL tables look similar to the table structure of the Special Purpose Ledger. The nice thing about the New GL is that it uses the same interfaces as the Classic GL in R/3. Therefore, business users do not know that they are posting to a different set of tables for the New GL.

As you can see, there are numerous advantages of using the New GL accounting approach, including integration of managerial and financial accounting, such as segment reporting, easy extensibility of the coding block for enhanced reporting purposes, new procedures for parallel accounting, acceleration of the period-end closing (fast close) process, improved transparency, corporate governance enhancements, and reduced TCO due to the reduced number of steps for reconciliation and analysis of data.

**NOTE**  In new installations, the new General Ledger Accounting is activated by default in SAP ERP. SAP does not recommend that new customers use the classic general ledger accounting since using the classic general ledger accounting requires additional migrations at a later stage. As a result, new customers require explicit authorization from SAP to use the classic general ledger accounting. If you want to use the classic general ledger accounting, create and send a CSS message to SAP before you start using the system. When you upgrade an R/3 system to SAP ERP, the classic General Ledger remains active at first. If you want to convert your system to the new General Ledger, you can do so, and we recommend that you use a project process after you have completed the upgrade.

# Initial Configuration Requirements of the New GL

The following sections discuss the initial configuration requirements of the New GL. We will work through the basic configuration needed to use the New GL process within the ECC environment.

## Configuring the New General Ledger Accounting

As mentioned earlier, any existing customer of SAP will not be required to activate the New GL and the Classic GL will remain active and available. However, we strongly suggest that you move to the New GL in the future to take advantage of the benefits and to streamline your FI process. In a new installation of SAP ECC, the New GL tables will default be active and available. As mentioned earlier, to use the Classic GL tables you would have to discuss this directly with SAP. In any case, you can use this chapter to familiarize yourselves with the different tasks, menu paths, and parameters necessary to implement the New GL. We will work through the tasks and screens to show you the setup of the New GL Accounting.

Before you can start working with the functions of New General Ledger Accounting, you have to activate them and make the general settings for Accounting. In addition, you have to configure the ledgers you use in General Ledger Accounting. On the basis of this data, you set up the integration with Controlling (CO) and, where applicable, the parallel accounting process.

To make the settings and use the functions in General Ledger Accounting, you have to activate it. To do this, in Customizing choose Financial Accounting ➢ Financial Accounting Global Settings ➢ Activate New General Ledger Accounting, or you can use the transaction code FAGL_ACTIVATION. You'll see the screen shown in Figure 7.2.

**FIGURE 7.2**    Change View "Activation of New General Ledger Accounting": Details screen

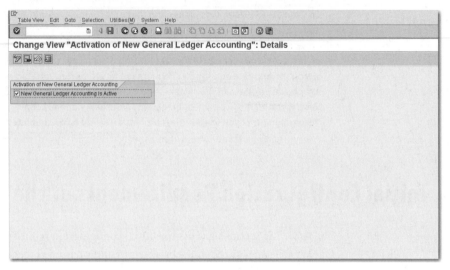

As you can see, the New GL Accounting is Active. The effect of this is that the customizing settings for General Ledger Accounting appear in the SAP Reference IMG. You access the settings under Financial Accounting (New) ➢ Financial Accounting Global Settings (New) and General Ledger Accounting (New) (see Figure 7.3). The General Ledger Accounting functions appear in the SAP Easy Access menu under Accounting ➢ Financial Accounting ➢ General Ledger, such as the General Ledger Reports (New) option (see Figure 7.4). And the most important is that the tables for new General Ledger Accounting are activated and updated. Therefore, the FAGLFLEX* tables have been activated and updated. In the standard system, the tables from classic General Ledger Accounting (GLT0) are updated as well as the tables in new General Ledger Accounting during the activation. This enables you to perform a ledger comparison during the implementation of new General Ledger Accounting to ensure that your new General Ledger Accounting has the correct settings and is working correctly. To compare ledgers, in Customizing choose Financial Accounting Global Settings (New) ➢ Tools ➢ Compare Ledgers, or you can use the transaction code GCAC (see Figure 7.5).

SAP recommends that you deactivate the update of tables for classic General Ledger Accounting once you have established that new General Ledger Accounting is working correctly. To do this, in Customizing choose Financial Accounting Global Settings (New) ➢ Tools ➢ Deactivate Update of Classic General Ledger by removing the check mark from the appropriate box (see Figure 7.6). As you can see, you are affecting the GLT0 table.

**FIGURE 7.3**   Additional menu paths activated by the New GL Accounting

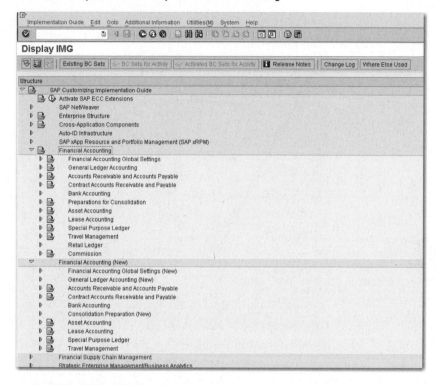

**FIGURE 7.4**   SAP Easy Access main menu displaying new folders for the New GL Reports

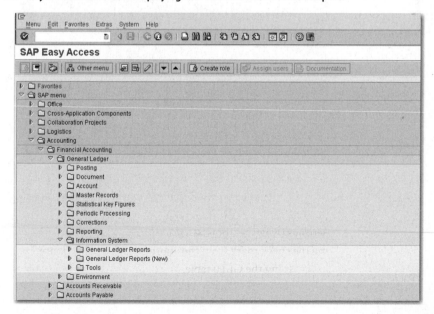

**FIGURE 7.5**    Ledger Comparison initial screen for the New GL vs. the Classic GL tables

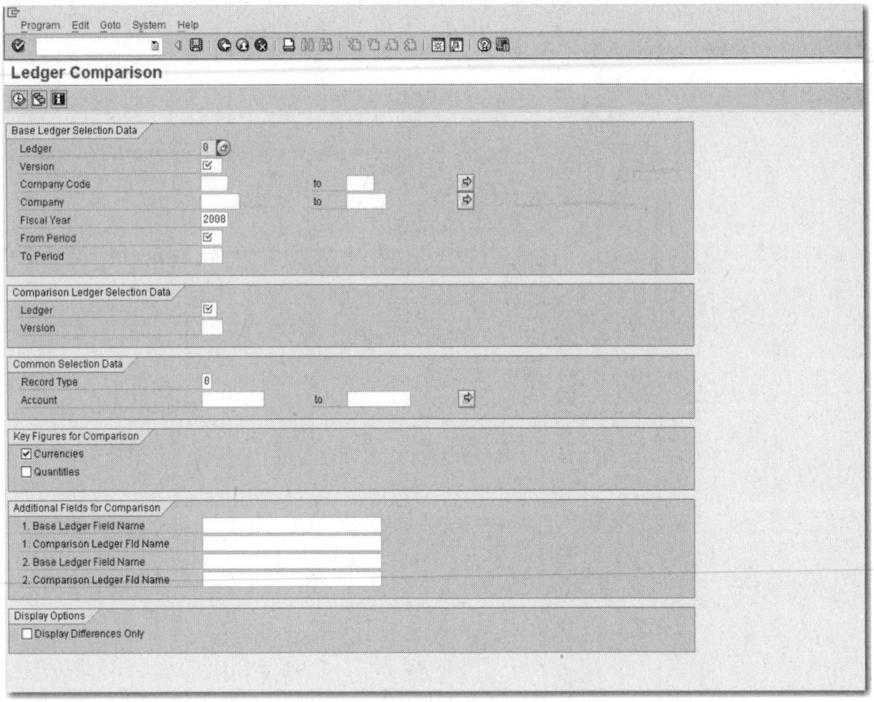

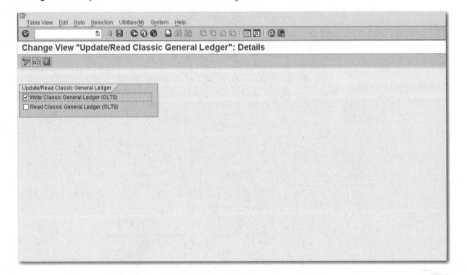

**FIGURE 7.6**    Change View "Update/Read Classic General Ledger": Details screen

In all, when you activate the New GL accounting process, you are affecting tables from the Classic FI (GLT0), the Cost of Sales Ledgers (GLFUNCT), the reconciliation ledger for FI to CO (COFIT), and the EC-PCA classic profit center accounting (GLPCT). The New GL has activated tables that you can find by using the prompt *FAGLFLEX* via transaction code SE12 or any of the transaction codes to review tables. You will see that there are several tables available that have been activated since you activated the New GL (see Figure 7.7).

**FIGURE 7.7**    ABAP Dictionary: Initial Screen displaying New GL Tables for FAGLFLEX*

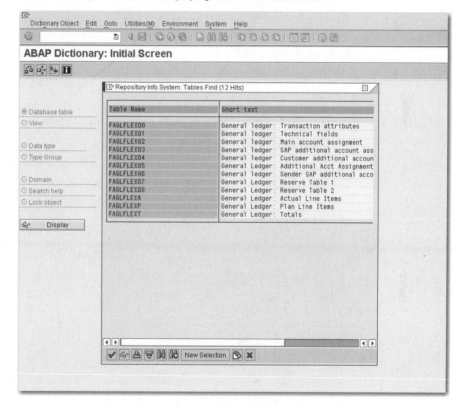

**NOTE**    Once you have become familiar with the paths for the New GL Accounting (in many of the cases the paths are the same as the Classic GL), you can run the program RFAGL_SWAP_MENU_OLD to hide the classic FI paths.

Before you start reviewing the new tables that have been created, you can make sure that some of the basic settings have been defined. In this chapter, we will focus on

**332**     **CHAPTER 7  •  NEW GL ACCOUNTING**

*FA(new) → FAGL(NEW) → Ledger → Ledger*

*Path for completion & add'n settings for activation*

*G/L for FY, currencies PP are set*

the tasks that are specific to the New GL Accounting. Those that overlap from areas such as the Classic GL accounting or Profit Center Accounting will be covered in the appropriate chapters for each module. You will also notice that once you review the New GL menu paths that certain nodes have been changed and that many are exactly the same. Much of the initial work can be found in the area in customizing under Financial Accounting (New) under Financial Accounting Global Settings (New) ≻ Ledgers ≻ Ledger, and this is where you complete the additional settings for the activation. You need to make sure that the general settings for the fiscal year, the posting periods, and the currencies are set. You find the settings for the fiscal year and posting periods in Customizing for Financial Accounting (New) under Financial Accounting Global Settings (New) ≻ Ledgers ≻ Fiscal Year and Posting Periods (see Figure 7.8). The currencies are under the folder above this in the Financial Accounting Global Settings (New) ≻ Ledgers ≻ Ledger area (see Figure 7.8).

**FIGURE 7.8**     **IMG display of additional settings for the New GL Accounting setup**

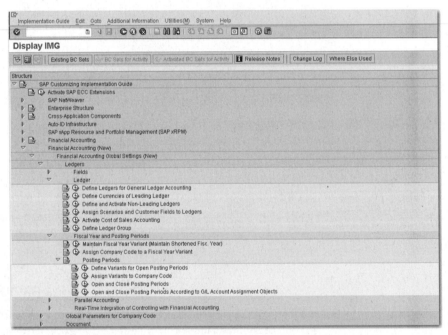

*FY, FYV, P.P - are configured in the same way as the Classic G/L*

*Assign currency in a diff way*

In terms of the fiscal-year variant, fiscal year, and posting periods tasks, these are all configured in the same way as in the Classic GL; therefore, refer to Chapter 2 for this configuration. In terms of the currencies, you can see that you need to assign a currency to the Leading ledger. If you review the list of activities below the node for Ledger in the customization screen, you can see that the first node is for Define Ledgers for General Ledger Accounting. One of the other activities completed via the activation of the New GL is that one ledger is created—this is the Leading ledger (0L). This is the New GL Leading Ledger and at this point, the only ledger that has been created. You can access this ledger by choosing Financial Accounting Global Settings (New) ➢ Ledgers ➢ Ledger ➢ Define Ledgers for General Ledger Accounting. Once you execute this, you will see the initial Leading Ledger 0L (see Figure 7.9).

**FIGURE 7.9**   Change View "Define Ledgers in General Ledger Accounting": Overview, Leading Ledger 0L screen

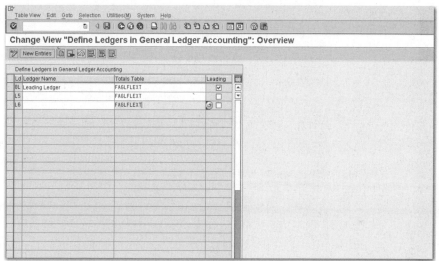

There can be only one leading ledger for the New GL, but you can develop a number of nonleading ledgers. As you can see, two nonleading ledgers have already been created. We will get into the development of nonleading ledgers shortly. The leading ledger is based on the same accounting principle as that of the consolidated financial statements. If you use the accounting approach for parallel accounting, you post all data to the leading ledger. This leading ledger is integrated with all subsidiary ledgers and is updated in all company codes. This means that it is automatically assigned to all company codes and there is only *one* leading ledger for the New GL Accounting.

Now that you have seen the leading ledger, you can now assign the currencies to this by using the executable directly below the previous task (refer to Figure 7.8). Once you run the Define Currencies of Leading Ledger executable, click the New Entries button to access the appropriate screen (see Figure 7.10). As shown, you can assign multiple currencies to your company code for the leading ledger. The first local currency is set by the settings assigned to the company code EX01 during the configuration of the company code. The remaining two currencies can be defined here.

**FIGURE 7.10** New Entries: Details of Added Entries screen showing currencies by company code for the Leading Ledger screen

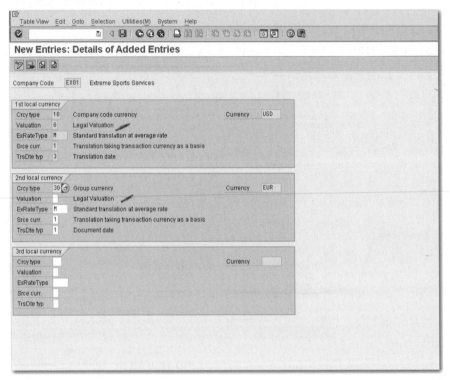

On this screen, you have several fields to assign parameters to the following:

**Crcy Type** The currency type defines the role of the parallel currency. A distinction is made between the following types of currencies:

- ▶ Company code currency
- ▶ Group currency
- ▶ Hard currency
- ▶ Index-based currency
- ▶ Global company currency

*[Handwritten note at top: 3 ways - 1) Group/Legal (3) Individual Corporate Enterprise/Legal (1) 2) Profit Center (2)]*

**Valuation**   You can use valuation views to represent different ways of viewing business transactions in a company. You can look at a business transaction from the following viewpoints: Group, Profit Center, and Individual Enterprise. *[handwritten: /Legal valuation]*

**ExRate Type**   The exchange rate type determines the exchange rate (which is stored in the system) that is applied in calculating the additional amount fields. As in the case of the local currency, you can use exchange rate type M (average rate) or any other exchange rate types. The exchange rate type is used in Cost Center Accounting to post calculated imputed costs.

*[Handwritten left margin: Source Cur. for Transl. Curren.]*

**Srce Curr.**   The calculation of the amounts in parallel currencies can be determined using the document currency or the local currency. *[handwritten: transaction (2)]*

**TrsDte Typ**   The rate for translation amounts can be based on the translation date, the document date, or the posting date. *[handwritten: 3 choices - Doc. date, Postg Dt, translation date]*

Now that you have defined some of the basic settings for the New GL Accounting process, you can start to do some analysis of the posting process. It all comes down to the tables that are being posted to. We mentioned that the leading ledger table has been defined and that, if you notice in Figure 7.9, the table that is feeding Leading Ledger 0L is the FAGLFLEXT table. If you take a quick look at this table, you will see that it has many more fields included in it than each of the other classic tables have separately. However, if you review all of the classic tables, you will see that it is a combination of them and the setup of the special purpose ledger tables. We will use any transaction code that allows you to see the details of a table—SE12 is our favorite (see Figure 7.11).

Notice that in this short list of the FAGLFLEXT table—a total of 142 fields—that you are seeing fields such as Cost Center, Profit Center, Functional Area, Business Area, Controlling Area, as well as Account Number, Company Code, and Segment all included in one table, and depending on the types of activities, you would like to capture in the New GL, you can fill all or part of this table with values for each posting within the ECC system. In addition, there are the normal fields for Record Type, Fiscal Year, Period, and of course all the posting fields by period. We don't want to turn this into a technical analysis of the table structures, but it's important that you realize what is happening behind the scenes with these tables. It will definitely make it easier for you to understand the different processes that are happening. You can also extend this FAGLFLEXT table with additional fields, either predefined SAP fields or new customized fields.

**FIGURE 7.11**    Dictionary: Display Table screen of the FAGLFLEXT table and some fields involved

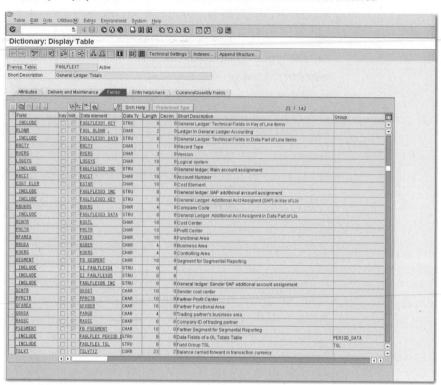

Now you can review the different posting processes that occur to these tables. You review this process by looking at another executable in the list under Ledger— Financial Accounting Global Settings (New) ➤ Ledgers ➤ Ledger ➤Assign Scenarios and Customer Fields to Ledgers. Once you execute this option, you will choose the Leading Ledger (0L) by using the field to the left of the Ledger and then view the Scenarios options available by double-clicking the folder Scenarios to the left of the ledgers (see Figure 7.12 and Figure 7.13).

**FIGURE 7.12**    Display View "Ledgers": Overview screen with 0L being reviewed

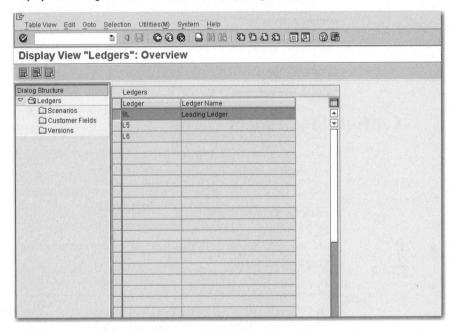

**FIGURE 7.13**    Change View "Scenarios": Overview screen of the scenarios assigned to 0L

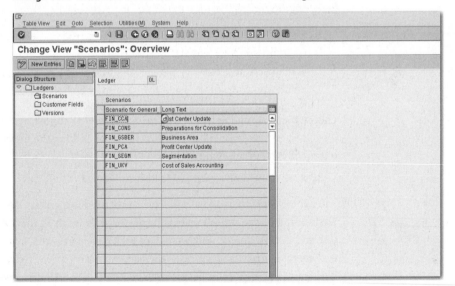

*[handwritten margin note: define scenarios]*

This shows that defaults assigned to the leading ledger are all possible scenarios. A scenario determines what fields in a ledger are updated when it receives posting from other application components. If you look behind the scenarios, you will see that each is assigned groups of posting tasks in accounting documents for both FI and CO activities. We will return to this screen once we show you how to create the nonleading ledgers.

## Configuring Ledgers

Before you can start working with the functions of new General Ledger Accounting, you have to configure the ledgers. Initially, you will need to have planned the data structure for General Ledger Accounting. Once this is complete, you can take the concepts that you've designed and then incorporate it/them when customizing your SAP system. We covered initially the Leading ledger, but let's review the ability to set up additional ledgers to manage other reporting needs such as additional accounting standards.

**NOTE**   The term *ledger* describes a technical view of a database table, and it is used in this documentation as a synonym for a general ledger.

To configure the ledgers for General Ledger Accounting, proceed as follows:

1. Define the standard fields that you require. You make the settings in Customizing for Financial Accounting (New) under Financial Accounting Global Settings (New) ➤ Ledgers ➤ Fields ➤ Standard Fields. You can also define your own fields using the Customer Fields option in customizations, but before doing this, you should review the standard delivered fields to see whether they will do the trick.

*[handwritten margin note: define standard fields]*

2. Create your ledgers and ledger groups, and configure them.

3. Assign the desired scenarios to your ledgers.

*[handwritten margin note: create ledger define scenarios]*

After these three basic steps, you have configured ledgers in General Ledger Accounting and can now create your master data (such as chart of accounts, G/L accounts, segment, and profit center). As you have seen, a totals table is used in General Ledger Accounting as the basis for your parallel ledgers. It offers a number of dimensions or fields in the coding block. SAP delivers the totals table FAGLFLEXT for General Ledger Accounting in the standard system. When you activate the New General Ledger Accounting, the totals records in General Ledger Accounting are updated in the standard totals table FAGLFLEXT. This totals table is deployed in functions such as planning and reporting.

> **NOTE**   SAP recommends working with the delivered standard totals table. In this way, you ensure that you can use the functions based on the standard totals table.

For our purposes we will use the SAP delivered Totals Table and work with the development of the nonleading ledgers. A *ledger* is a section of a database table. A ledger contains only those dimensions of the totals table that the ledger is based on and that are required for reporting. In General Ledger Accounting, you can use several ledgers in parallel. As an example, this allows you to produce financial statements according to different accounting principles. You create a ledger for each of the general ledgers you need. A ledger uses several dimensions from the totals table it is based on. Each dimension of the totals table represents a subset of the coding block. You can also include customer fields in your ledgers. To do this, you have to add the customer field to the coding block and then include this field in the totals table that the ledger is based on. You define your ledgers in Customizing for Financial Accounting (New) under Financial Accounting Global Settings (New) ➤ Ledgers ➤ Ledgers. When you create a ledger, the system automatically creates a ledger group with the same name.

Let's use these steps and configure a nonleading ledger. First access the Financial Accounting (New) under Financial Accounting Global Settings (New) ➤ Ledgers ➤ Fields ➤ Standard Fields. In this section we can maintain transaction types for consolidation and assign the functional area to the different master data items such as the GL account, Cost Center, and so on. To see a list of standard fields involved in the overall process that could be used in the coding block for the New GL accounting, we can select Financial Accounting Global Settings (New) ➤ Ledgers ➤ Fields ➤ Customer Fields ➤ Edit Coding Block. After executing this option, you will see that two folders are available: Standard Account Assignments and Customer-Defined Account Assignment. If you open the Standard Account Assignments folder, you will see the list of possible fields that you can include in your coding block for use in the posting process (see Figure 7.14).

This is not the full list but a good portion of the group. If you decide that you need more than what the current standard coding block has, you can enhance the totals table by using the next executable down the list: Include Fields in Totals Table.

**FIGURE 7.14**     Maintain User-Defined Codling Block Fields: List screen of Standard Account Assignments

Maintain User-Defined Coding Block Fields: List

Add Fields | Field Information | Technical View

SAP Standard Account Assignments

| Field | Description |
|---|---|
| AFPOS | Item Number |
| ANBWA | Transactn Type |
| ANLN1 | Asset |
| ANLN2 | Sub-number |
| AUFNR | Order |
| BEMOT | Accounting Indicator |
| BUKRS | Company Code |
| BWTAR | Valuation Type |
| BZDAT | Reference Date |
| CONDI | CondKey |
| CRPCAL | CRP Calculation |
| EGRUP | Equity group |
| ERLKZ | Set to 'Done' |
| FIKRS | FM Area |
| FIPEX | Commitment Item |
| FIPOS | Commitment Item |
| FISTL | Funds Center |
| FKBER | Functional Area |
| GEBER | Fund |
| GRANT_NBR | Grant |
| GSBER | Business Area |
| IMKEY | Real Estate Key |
| KBLNR | Earmarked Funds |
| KBLPOS | Document item |
| KDAUF | Sales Order |
| KDEIN | Sales Order Schedule |
| KDPOS | Sales Order Item |
| KOKRS | Controlling Area |
| KONTT | Acct Assignment Cat. |
| KOSTL | Cost Center |
| KSTRG | Cost Object |
| LSTAR | Activity Type |
| MATNR | Material |
| MAT_KDAUF | Sales Order |
| MAT_KDPOS | Sales Order Item |
| MAT_POSID | WBS Element |
| MAT_PSPNR | WBS Element |
| NPLNR | Network |
| PAOBJNR | Profitab. Segmt No. |
| PARGB | Trading part.BA |
| PERNR | Personnel Number |
| PPRCTR | Partner Profit Ctr |
| PRCTR | Profit Center |
| PRODPER | Production Date |
| PRZNR | Business Process |
| PSEGMENT | Partner Segment |
| PS_POSID | WBS Element |
| PS_PSP_PNR | WBS Element |
| RECID | Recovery Indicator |
| RMVCT | Transaction Type |
| SAKNR | G/L Account |
| SEGMENT | Segment |
| VBUND | Trading Partner |

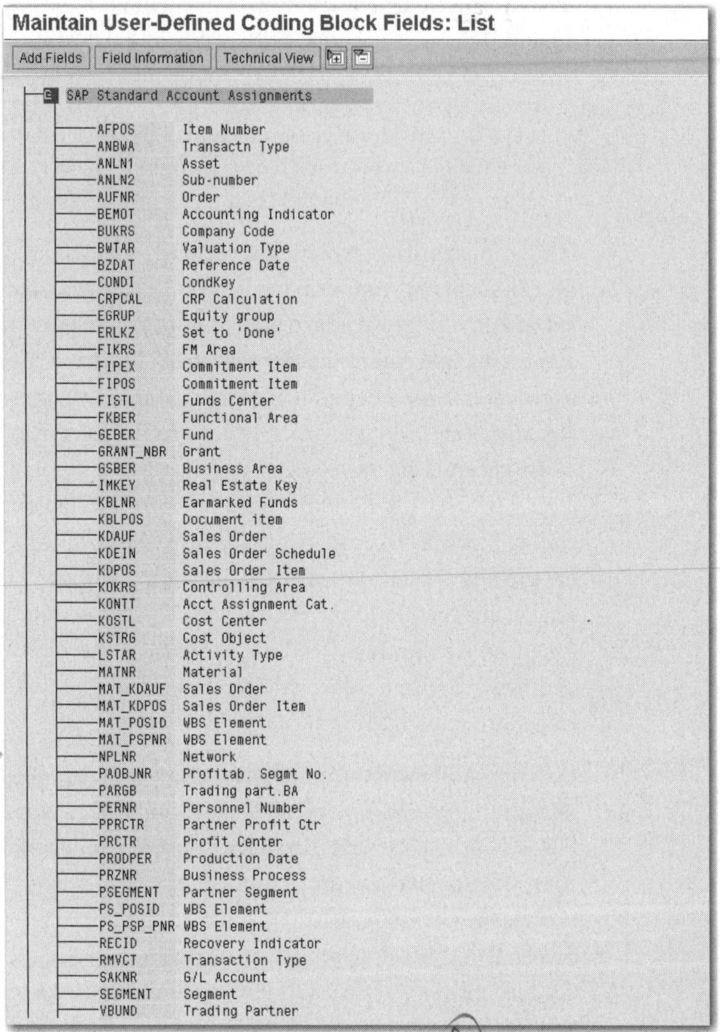

Now you can create the nonleading ledgers. The nonleading ledgers are parallel
ledgers to the leading ledger. In contrast to the leading ledger, you have to activate
a nonleading ledger for the individual company codes. Posting procedures with
subledger or G/L accounts managed on an open item basis always affect all ledgers.
This means that you cannot perform ledger-specific postings to subledger or G/L
accounts managed on an open item basis. If you manage G/L accounts on an open
item basis to monitor accounting aspects such as reserve allocations and reversals,
you need to take additional measures in your internal controls system. Nonleading

ledgers can have different fiscal-year variants and different posting period variants per company code to the leading ledger of this company code. The second and third currency of the nonleading ledger must be a currency that is managed as second or third currency in the respective company code. However, you do not have to have a second and third currency in the parallel ledgers; these are optional. Alternative currencies are not possible. The process of setting up the nonleading ledger would be to use the executable Define Ledgers for General Ledger Accounting, which is the first item in the list. Once you execute this option, you will see a list of ledgers, including the leading ledger. You must first define the ledger with a technical name. Click the New Entries button to access the create screen (see Figure 7.15).

**FIGURE 7.15**    New Entries: Overview of Added Entries screen with new ledger defined

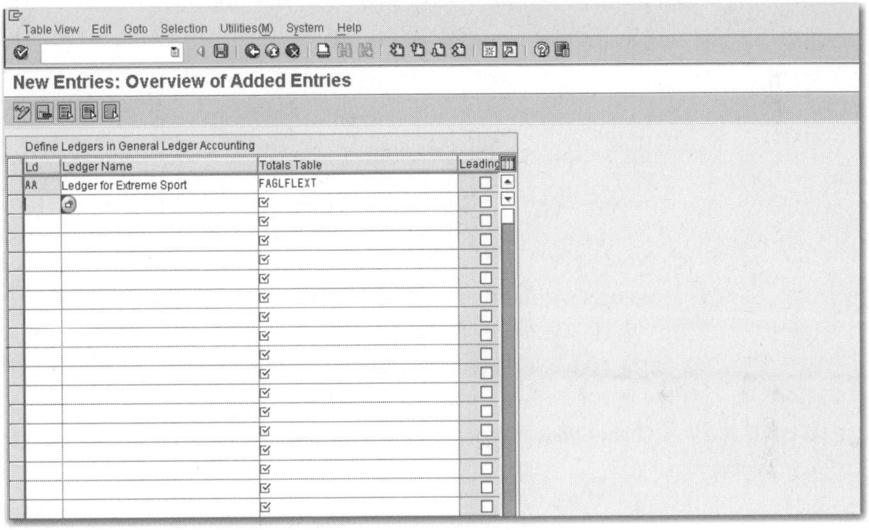

For this example, we have created a nonleading ledger AA for Extreme Sports, and the only totals table we can use is the FAGLFLEXT table. Once you have completed this process, you can assign and activate settings for each of the company codes against this ledger. Using the executable Define and Activate Non-Leading Ledgers, you can then set up the company codes that will be able to use this nonleading ledger and the currencies that will be used in each (see Figure 7.16). In the first dialog box, choose the ledger AA to process. Then click the New Entries button to open the screen for assigning company codes. For this example, we have assigned the Extreme Sport company code EX01 to this nonleading ledger AA. In this way, as we post data to the company code EX01, these postings will be saved in the Leading Ledger 0L and also the nonleading ledger AA.

FT(new) →FIGL(new)
Ledgers → Ledgers

Define &
actuate non.
leading ledgers

**FIGURE 7.16**   New Entries: Overview of Added Entries for Settings for Non-Leading ledgers in General
Ledger assigning EX01 to currencies    T882G (TCode)

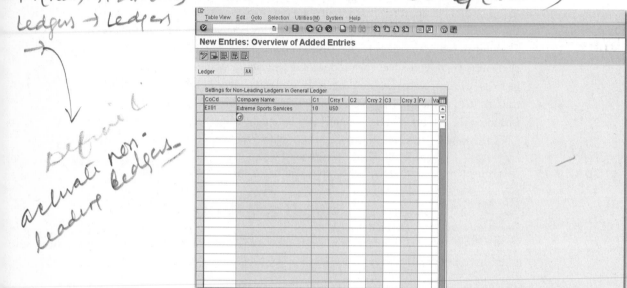

Now we will review what has happened in the Ledger Group area. You access this
using a similar menu path, but the last executable is Define Ledger Group. Once you
run this, you will see that a ledger group has already been created for the ledger AA.
The Ledger Group is AA (see Figure 7.17).

**FIGURE 7.17**   Change View "Ledger Group": Overview screen    — Define Ledger Group

TCode
V_001

ledger
assignment

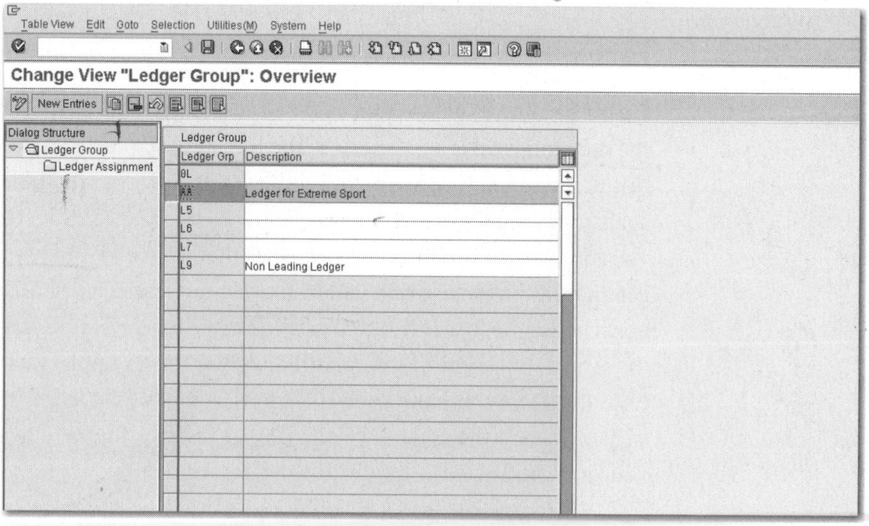

If you then access the assigned ledger using the folder Ledger Assignment, you see that the Ld is AA and the Rep (Representative) Ledger has been checked (see Figure 7.18).

**FIGURE 7.18**    Change View "Ledger Assignment": Overview of Ledger Assignment for AA

*Assign the Scenarios in Ledger*

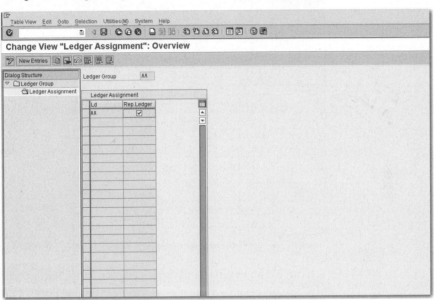

*We can't create new scenarios for in New G/L*

*Total to be so*

The last step in this process is to assign the scenarios to the ledger. To complete this task, you go to the area under Ledgers ➤ Ledger ➤ Assign Scenarios and Customer Fields to Ledgers. Execute this option and then choose your ledger (AA in this example) and double-click the folder Scenarios. Using the New Entries button, you will be able to assign scenarios to your ledger. Remember that you can't create any additional scenarios for the New GL Accounting, but you can assign customer created fields to the totals table (see Figure 7.19).

In the New GL Accounting, you have a total of six scenarios:

**FIN_CCA**   Updating for Sender cost center and receiver cost center fields

**FIN_CONS**   Updating of consolidation transaction type and trading partner fields

**FIN_GSBER**   Updating of sender business area and receiver business area fields

**FIN_PCA**   Updating of profit center and partner profit center fields

**FIN_SEGM**   Updating of the segment, partner segment, and profit center fields

**FIN_UKV**   Updating of the sender functional area and receiver functional area fields

**FIGURE 7.19**   New Entries: Overview of Added Entries screen showing the assignment of scenarios to ledgers

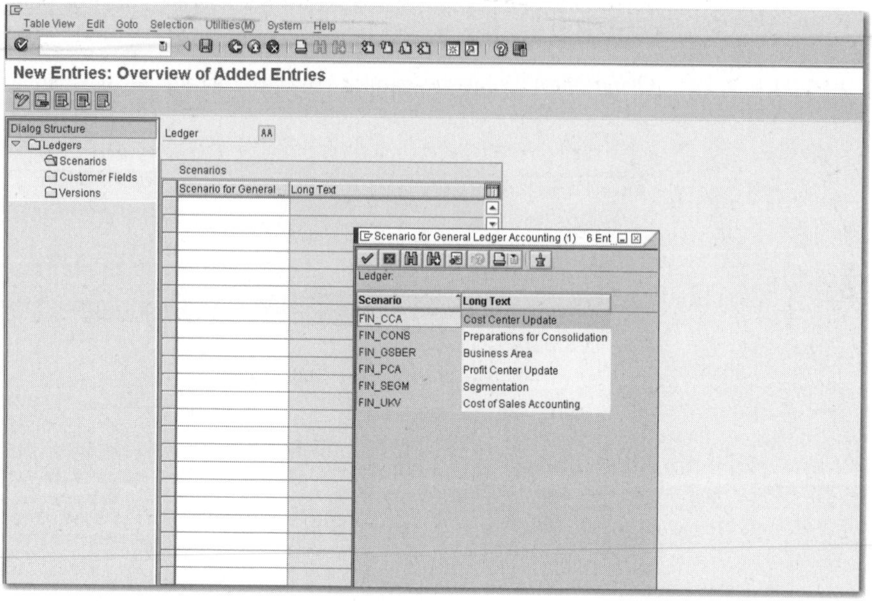

You can use all or just one of these scenarios for each ledger. You do not necessarily have to define nonleading ledgers, and you also don't need a ledger for each scenario. In addition to your parallel ledgers, you can define a rollup ledger for special reporting purposes. In a rollup ledger, you can combine summarized data from other ledgers in General Ledger Accounting. This enables you to compile cumulated reports on different ledgers. You use a day ledger to create a day ledger if you want to create reports for average balances (reports for displaying average daily balances). You can activate the day ledger for drill-down reporting. You may not define day ledgers as the leading ledger or as the representative ledger in a ledger group. For example, you create your consolidated financial statements in accordance with the IAS accounting principles. Your individual company codes apply the local accounting principles US GAAP or German HGB to produce their financial statements. You therefore create three ledgers:

► Ledger LL (a leading ledger), which is managed according to the group accounting principle

► Ledger L1 (a nonleading ledger), which you activate for all company codes that apply US GAAP

► Ledger L2 (a nonleading ledger), which you activate for all company codes that apply HGB

## Ledger Groups

A *ledger group* is a combination of ledgers for the purpose of applying the functions and processes of General Ledger Accounting to the group as a whole. You can combine any number of ledgers in a ledger group. In this way, you simplify the tasks in the individual functions and processes of General Ledger Accounting. For example, you can make a posting simultaneously in several ledgers. In some General Ledger Accounting functions, you can only specify a ledger group and not individual ledgers. This has the following consequences for the creation of your ledger groups:

▶ Each ledger is also created automatically as a ledger group of the same name. You can use these automatically created ledger groups to process an individual ledger.

▶ You only have to create those ledger groups that you want to process together in a function using processing for several ledgers.

▶ If you do not enter a ledger group, processing is performed automatically for all ledgers. You therefore do not need to create a ledger group for all ledgers.

You define your ledger groups in Customizing for Financial Accounting (new) under Financial Accounting Global Settings (New) ➢ Ledgers ➢ Ledgers ➢ Define Ledger Group.

When you define each ledger group, you have to designate one of the assigned ledgers as the representative ledger for that ledger group. The system uses the representative ledger to determine the posting period during posting and to check whether the posting period is open. The posting is then made to the assigned ledgers of the ledger group using the appropriate fiscal-year variant for each individual ledger. When the posting periods of the representative ledger are open, the postings are made to all other assigned ledgers, even if their posting periods are closed. In addition to this information if the ledger group has a leading ledger, the leading ledger must be designated as the representative ledger but if the ledger group does not have a leading ledger, you must designate one of the assigned ledgers as the representative ledger. During posting, the system uses the fiscal-year variant of the company code to check whether the selection is correct. If all ledgers in the ledger group have a different fiscal-year variant to that of the company code, you can designate any ledger as the representative ledger. If one of the ledgers in the ledger group has the same fiscal-year variant as that of the company code, you must designate that ledger as the representative ledger.

## Day Ledger

*[handwritten: —Totals table with FYV → 366 Per + original posting for GIL]*

A *day ledger* is a totals table with a fiscal-year variant of 366 periods and containing all original postings for the general ledger. You create a day ledger if you want to create reports for average balances (reports for displaying average daily balances).

*[handwritten: Use of day Led.]*

You can activate the day ledger for drill-down reporting. You may not define day ledgers as the leading ledger or as the representative ledger in a ledger group. You'd specify a ledger group, for example, when defining a cycle for a ledger. You can define a group so that it contains the source ledger and the day ledger. An example of what the postings will look like based on the different ledgers would be something similar to the Table 7.1. Let's assume you have made the postings shown in Table 7.1.

**TABLE 7.1**     Postings During One Period of Time to the New GL

| Date | Amount in EUR |
| --- | --- |
| January 6 | 200 |
| January 10 | 300 |
| January 20 | 400 |
| February 4 | 500 |

This results in the balances shown in Table 7.2 in the ledgers.

**TABLE 7.2**     Results of Postings During One Period of Time to the New GL Leading Ledger and Day Ledger

| Leading Ledger (16 Periods) Period/Amount | Day Ledger Period/Amount |
| --- | --- |
| 1 / 900 | 6 / 200 |
| 2 / 500 | 10 / 300 |
|  | 20 / 400 |
|  | 35 / 500 |

# Parallel Accounting

You can portray parallel accounting in your SAP system. This enables you to perform valuations and closing preparations for a company code according to the accounting principles of the group as well as other accounting principles, such as local accounting principles. Parallel accounting is necessary for a German subsidiary of an American group. The German subsidiary has to create financial statements according to the accounting principles of the group (such as US GAAP) as well as according to German commercial law (HGB). To simplify matters, this documentation assumes two parallel accounting principles. You can use the following approaches to portray parallel accounting in the SAP system:

▶ Portrayal using additional accounts

▶ Portrayal using parallel ledgers

You can also continue to use the option for portraying parallel accounting using an additional company code. However, this approach is not supported by all application components. To configure the use of parallel accounting, begin by selecting Financial Accounting Global Settings (New) ➢ Ledgers ➢ Parallel Accounting ➢ Define Accounting Principles. In the resulting screen, you specify the name and description of the accounting principles (see Figure 7.20).

**FIGURE 7.20**    Change View "Accounting Principles": Overview screen for creating accounting principles

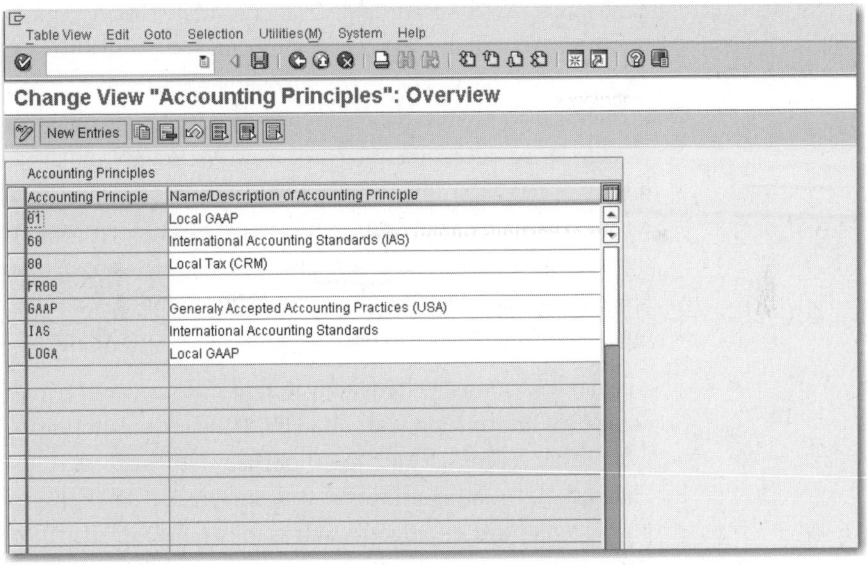

Here you specify the accounting principle and the name/description. Once this is complete, click the option Assign Accounting Principle to Ledger Groups. Then click the New Entries button to create the assignment. Using the available accounting principles, we assign 60—IAS to Ledger AA (see Figure 7.21).

**FIGURE 7.21**    New Entries: Overview of Added Entries screen for assigning accounting principles to ledger

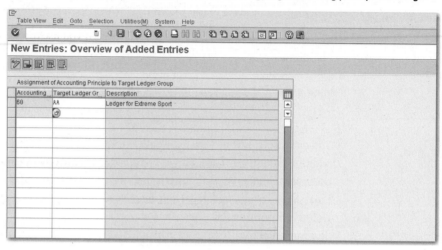

Parallel accounting is supported by the following application components: Financial Accounting, Asset Accounting, Treasury and Risk Management, Controlling, and Inventory Accounting (MM). The ability to have parallel accounting for any of these areas requires that you have customized the application components you are using. Customization can be a detailed process since you are configuring each of these areas to allow for parallel accounting processes. For example, in the area of Controlling, the display of data according to different accounting principles is not a classic requirement for the Controlling application (CO). Generally, CO represents the leading valuation. But to help with the parallel accounting process, we can activate the use of Real-Time Integration of Controlling with Financial Accounting. One area that is affected by the option to set up parallel accounting is allocations in CO and the effect on FI.

Allocations within CO frequently lead to shifts between segments and functional areas. This information is required in Financial Accounting for segment reporting or to reflect cost of sales accounting. The values for these shifts are transferred to Financial Accounting using real-time integration. With this transfer, data can be posted to the leading ledger as well as to parallel ledgers. The calculation of work in process and the results analysis in CO are generally performed using different valuations methods dependent on the accounting principle. You can post the results to additional accounts or parallel ledgers. Different methods are represented in parallel in different results analysis versions. You can assign an accounting principle to each results analysis version in the posting rules. If you want to post to additional accounts, you do not have to assign an accounting principle to the results analysis version. If you want to post to parallel ledgers, an accounting principle must be assigned to the results analysis version and the relevant ledger group must be assigned to this accounting principle.

During the transfer of posting from CO to FI, if you use the portrayal using additional accounts you will only need to transfer values from the accounts of the leading valuation in FI into CO. However, you can also transfer values from other accounts into CO. In this case, you have to consider these additional accounts in all CO-internal allocations. Since actual price calculation always considers all accounts, it therefore cannot be used together with additional accounts. If you are using the portrayal using parallel ledgers all CO-relevant values in the leading ledger are transferred. Postings that are updated exclusively in parallel ledgers are not available in Controlling. If you include additional CO account assignments (such as cost centers) in the line items and totals records of a parallel ledger, you can perform simple controlling using this parallel ledger.

# Master Data of the New GL

The three items that are listed as master data for the New GL Accounting area are the G/L Account, Profit Center and Segment. As mentioned earlier, if the configuration is similar to what is explained in another area of this book, we will not cover it in detail. Therefore, if additional information is required around the configuration of the master data objects G/L Account and Profit Center, refer to the appropriate chapters, Chapter 2 for G/L Accounts and Chapter 13 for Profit Centers.

The only master data object that we've haven't discussed in detail is the segment, and it is not a difficult concept. A *segment* is another field assigned to the transaction to help with the process of reporting in a different and more detailed manner.

A segment can be a division of a company for which you can create financial statements for external reporting. The accounting principles US GAAP and IFRS require companies to perform segment reporting. You can define segments in your SAP system for this purpose. You find the appropriate IMG activity in Customizing under Enterprise Structure ➤ Definition ➤ Financial Accounting ➤ Define Segment (see Figure 7.22).

Here you define a segment for the purposes of reporting transactions based on a specific value. Once this is complete, you can then go to each of the other objects master data screens and assign the segment to that object. For example, on the profit center master data screen, you assign a segment for a more detailed reporting capability (see Figure 7.23).

**FIGURE 7.22**    Change View "Segments for Segment Reporting": Overview screen

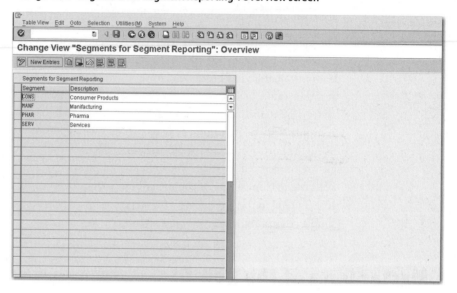

**FIGURE 7.23**    Change Profit Center screen showing the field for segment assignment

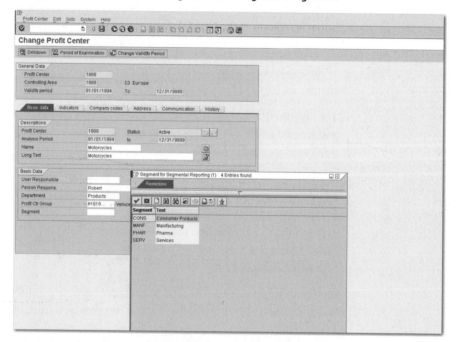

The characteristic segment is released only in combination with the characteristic profit center. If no segment is specified manually during posting (only possible for transactions in Financial Accounting), the segment is determined from the master record of the profit center. This profit center can also be assigned manually or derived. If you want to apply different rules to derive the segment during posting, you can define your own rules for this. You find the corresponding settings in Customizing under Financial Accounting (New) ≻ Financial Accounting Global Settings (New) ≻ Tools ≻ Customer Enhancements ≻ Business Add-Ins (BAdIs) ≻ Segment Derivation ≻ Derive Segment. The document splitting procedure is the prerequisite for creating financial statements at any time for the *Segment* dimension. For this, you need to set up a zero balance setting for the *Segment* characteristic. You find the document splitting settings in Customizing under General Ledger Accounting (New) ≻ Business Transactions ≻ Document Splitting.

# Summary

At this point in the process of configuration, you are able to use the New GL Accounting method in the ECC environment. In this chapter, we discussed the initial activation of the New GL Accounting system, which included a review of all the standard activities that occur during the activation, including new menu paths, new menu path for reports, new tables that were created, and other indicators that are available for the move from the old GL tables to the new GL tables and postings. You can see that much of the configuration that you do in other areas is usable by the New GL accounting system, and therefore none of the other valuable information that you find in this book will go to waste. You use most of it. You also need to remember that this is another approach to reporting and consolidating the transactional data so that you can validate and confirm the data in a more consistent manner and that allows you to move toward a consolidation process more quickly. All of the concepts that have been supported by an ERP system have not gone away. So, if you have posted $1 million in revenue in FI, you should see postings of $1 million in any other area or report being run with master data from FI or CO. That being said, all of these additional postings do not create additional data.

As mentioned, at this point you can use the New GL Accounting process and tables to run reports being sourced by the leading and nonleading ledgers, but there are many more possible options in the configuration of the New GL that are possible, such as document splitting where you can set up the ability to split a document (for example an AP document) between two different reporting values or segments.

This is helpful with the ability to report on different accounting principles. This is probably the next most popular configuration item in the New GL besides the use of parallel accounting or adding nonleading ledgers. You also have the whole process of setting up real-time integration with Controlling, FI Subledgers, or Materials Management. Document splitting is part of this real-time integration in an area such as accounts payable, and you can also effectively turn on real-time integration to help with the overall closing process in the areas of accounts receivable, asset accounting, controlling (the most popular), and material management. Another topic of interest is the use of the allocation of costs within the FI and CO areas. This process sometimes requires that you run a reconciliation run at period end to sort out any issues with postings between FI and CO. By using this integration process, you can eliminate the period end task of reconciliation. Again, remember that this is a relatively new environment in the ERP/ECC system, and additional functionality is continuing to be added to this module.

Finally, if you are using an older version of R/3 and you are looking to migrate to the newer ECC versions that support the New GL, remember to treat this as a full project since the process requires all of the historical data to be loaded and tested after the migration is complete. Once you start to use the New GL Accounting approach, we believe you will be satisfied with the functionality and overall easy of use of the New GL. Also remember that the experience to business users is not affected, and therefore users are unaware that the posting process has been enhanced to offer more detailed reports that are sliced and diced with more fields and values.

# Controlling Enterprise Structure

## FEATURING:

▶ **THE CONTROLLING AREA**

▶ **THE OPERATING CONCERN**

The enterprise structure is the foundation upon which all SAP components are configured and built, and we discussed and presented configuration for the FI Enterprise Structure in Chapter 2. It is not necessary to complete the Controlling (CO) Enterprise Structure if the CO module is not in your work plan.

As described earlier, the configuration covered in the book will include most of the CO module; one of the areas of CO not covered in this book is the Product Costing component of CO. As you know, the Product Costing area of CO covers an incredible amount of information and content; essentially, it would require an entire book to offer complete coverage of the different areas of it, such as Product Cost Planning, Cost Object Controlling, and Actual Costing/Material Ledger. Therefore, in this chapter we will cover two organizational elements of the CO Enterprise Structure: the controlling area and the operating concern.

This chapter will show you in detail how to establish both sections. We use the word *establish* here because the configuration work is done piecemeal and is covered in more than one chapter of this book. SAP requires that you perform configuration tasks in a specific order for the development of the controlling area and operating concern. In fact, you'll see this type of process in many areas of the SAP architecture. In these instances, we use the "define and then assign" approach. In other words, in most cases, you define the object, and then later, once you start the actual configuration, you assign the parameters to the object.

# The Controlling Area

The controlling area is the central organizational unit within the CO module. It is representative of a contained cost accounting environment where costs and revenues can be managed. If you utilize CO, you must configure at least one controlling area.

Prior to beginning any configuration, it is important to understand the relationships between FI and CO and between the controlling area and the operating concern. The operating concern will be explained in greater detail later in this chapter, but briefly, it is the environment within which CO-PA, or Profitability Analysis, operates. The operating concern is the first step in completing CO-PA configuration.

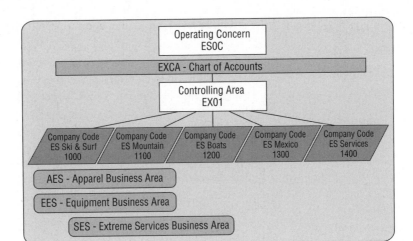

You can see that the link between FI and CO is established through the assignment of company codes to a controlling area. A controlling area can contain multiple company code assignments (which is a one-to-many relationship). Note that, in contrast, a single company code can be assigned to only one controlling area. We will talk about the parameters that define this one-to-many relationship a bit later in this chapter in the section "Activating Component/Control Indicators."

The relationship between the controlling area and operating concern is established in much the same manner. An operating concern may contain multiple controlling areas, but a controlling area may be assigned to only one operating concern (again, a one-to-many relationship), and again you have specific parameters that will define which controlling areas will be assigned to the specific operating concern.

Also, if you are thinking of creating more than one controlling area, keep in mind that there can be no cross-controlling-area or cross-operating-concern postings standard within the system. A cross-controlling-area or cross-operating-concern posting would be similar in nature to a cross-company-code posting. Unlike the ability to post entries cross-company code then execute a reconciliation of those postings, the ability to reconcile cross controlling area postings is not available. Each side of a debit/credit entry would take place in a different controlling area or operating concern. In terms of SAP best practices, the recommendation is to establish only one controlling area. You should have a strong overriding reason to establish more than one controlling area; one example would be that you have more than one business line and these business lines have absolutely no integration between them.

## Controlling Area Definition · OX06

Establishing the controlling area is the first step in completing the CO configuration. Additional steps include activating the components you will use within the controlling area and assigning company codes. To get to the controlling area maintenance screen, you must first access the Implementation Guide (IMG), and to do this you can either use one of our favorite transaction codes, SPRO, or from the main menu SAP menu select Tools ➢ Customizing ➢ IMG ➢ Execute Project. (We will be working in the IMG quite a bit from now on, so this will be the only time we give that menu path. As you go through your configuration, you will probably just include this transaction code as part of your favorites.) If you are going to configure any components of ECC, you will probably be using the tcode SPRO. Once you are in the IMG screen, go to SAP Reference IMG ➢ Enterprise Structure ➢ Definition ➢ Controlling ➢ Maintain Controlling Area ➢ Maintain Controlling Area in the dialog box that appears or just use the transaction code OX06. After you enter the configuration transaction listed in the shortcut box, the controlling area maintenance screen, shown in Figure 8.1, appears.

**FIGURE 8.1**    The controlling area maintenance screen

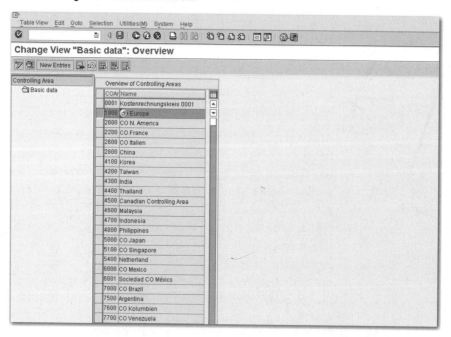

Click the New Entries button to access the controlling area details configuration screen, shown in Figure 8.2.

**FIGURE 8.2**    The controlling area details configuration screen

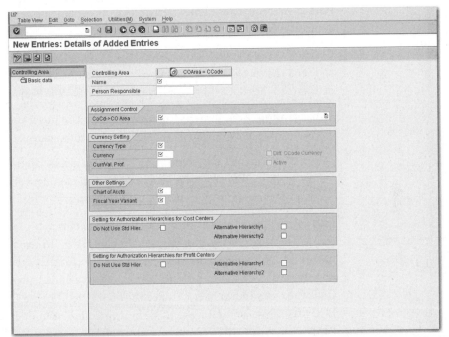

**NOTE**    You can identify the required fields as those that have a check mark in the field space. As you know, the check mark is the SAP indicator that an entry is required.

Let's examine the fields:

**Controlling Area**    Enter the four-digit alphanumeric identifier of your controlling area. If your controlling area will contain just one company code, select the option for the controlling area, which is a one-to-one relationship to the company code. When prompted, enter the company code ID. Realize that if you indicate that there is more than one company code to a controlling area, then assigning only one will not cause any system issues. However, if you do indicate that there is a one-to-one relationship between the CO area and company code, then going back and having to change this setting will be difficult. Therefore, it would be better if you just confirm that it will be a one-to-many relationship so that if you need it, it will be available for your use.

**Name**   Enter a description of your controlling area.

**Person Responsible**   Enter the name of the person responsible for this configuration.

**CoCd->CO Area**   This field is used to define the relationship between the company code and the controlling area. You will have identified this relationship when you determined the controlling area ID. The options for this field are as follows:

**Controlling Area Same as Company Code**   Use this if you have a one-to-one relationship between company code and controlling area.

**Cross-Company Cost Accounting**   Use this if your controlling area will have two or more company codes assigned to it. This setting will activate cross-company cost accounting within the controlling area.

**Currency Type**   This setting defines the type of currency used throughout the controlling area. Currency settings can be confusing. Remember that the combination of the Assignment Control selection and the currency type define the controlling area currency, and depending on the settings defined, then the Other Company Code Currency Indicator is activated. If you selected 1 in the CoCd->CO Area field, ECC uses the default setting of 10, Company Code Currency. If you selected 2, or Cross-Company Cost Accounting, your choices expand. Use the pull-down menu and the following options will appear:

**10 (Company Code Currency)**   Use this only if all the company codes assigned use the same currency.

**20 (Controlling Area Currency)**   This selection offers the use of a possible group currency for the controlling area. It allows the controlling area to identify a specific currency for only that controlling area. All other selections impose artificial constraints.

**30 (Group Currency)**   This is currency maintained at the client level. Use this option to reconcile FI and CO ledgers.

**40 (Hard Currency)**   This can be used if the assigned company codes are from the same country and use the same index-based or group currency. This option is often used in countries where inflation is very high.

**50 (Index-Based Currency)**    This is often used in countries where inflation is high or unstable. The currency is fabricated and is used to support external (outside the company) reporting only.

**60 (Global Company)**    Use this only if you have global companies configured. In addition, each of the companies assigned to the controlling area must belong to the same Global Company or use the same currency.

**Currency**    The entry made for currency type may influence your selection of a currency. Remember that you are defining the default currency for the controlling area only.

**Diff. CCode Currency**    This is used if the company code currency is going to be different than the currency currently assigned to the company code.

**Curr/Val. Prof.**    With this indicator, the currency and valuation profile determines which valuation views can be stored in which currencies. You will need to assign a currency and valuation profile to the controlling area only if you are looking to store multiple valuation views in the system.

**Active**    This indicator shows whether a controlling area allows transfer prices for a company code or profit centers.

**NOTE**    In many cases, and in the case of Extreme Sports, currency type 20 is selected.

**Chart of Accts (COA)**    Each controlling area can utilize only one chart of accounts. If you selected 1 in the CoCd->CO Area field, the system populates this field automatically with the company chart. If not, you must manually enter the chart name. Remember that all company codes assigned to the controlling area must use the same chart the controlling area uses.

**Fiscal Year Variant**    The variant must be the same for the assigned company codes and the controlling area.

The previous options are the required parameters between the company code and controlling area. Basically these are the required indicators or parameters to allow a company code to be linked to a controlling area.

**NOTE**    These definitions are unique to the controlling area. Company code currency assignments, exchange rates, and currency translation are covered in Chapter 2.

### Setting for Authorization Hierarchies for Cost Centers (and Profit Centers)

Since the initial introduction of the new authorization concept after release 4.0, you can inherit authorizations within a hierarchy. If a user is authorized for one of these groups, then they are also authorized for all objects in these groups. This logic applies only to the standard hierarchy, but now you can also have these settings apply to two additional alternative hierarchies that are used in the authorization check process. These indicators also allow you to deactivate the standard hierarchy and use the alternative hierarchies. This applies to both the cost center and profit center hierarchies. Authorizations are checked in the sequence starting with the current calendar year and the valid hierarchies—standard hierarchy, then alternative hierarchy 1, then 2.

Once you have completed the configuration on this screen, notice the additional button called Distribution that appears at the top-right side of the controlling area technical name, as shown in Figure 8.3.

**FIGURE 8.3**    The controlling area detailed configuration screen for distribution

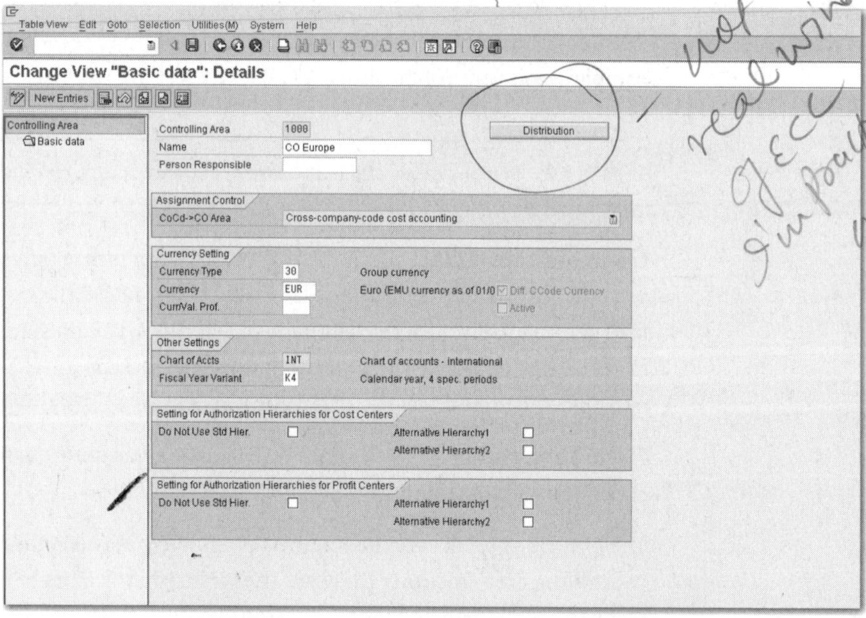

If you click this button, you will default into a screen where the settings for the ALE distribution for cost accounting overview are determined, as shown in Figure 8.4.

**FIGURE 8.4** The Change view "ALE Distribution for Cost Accounting: Overview" detailed configuration screen for distribution

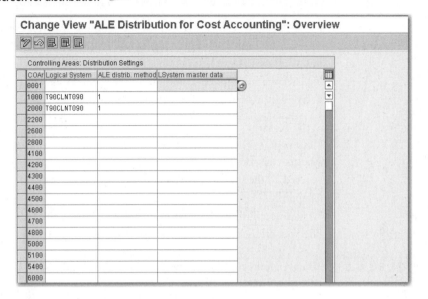

Here are the options on this screen:

**Logical System** This is relevant only if ALE is utilized. If you are using the distribution methods of managing master data, then you would be filling in this information. In this field you would enter the name of the central system for the controlling area. This would be the system of standard for all master data for the cost accounting area.

**ALE Distrib. Method** This field is relevant only if you are using SAP's Application Link Enabling (ALE) to link multiple R/3 systems together. If you are not using ALE, leave this field blank. There are three options for this field:

**No Distribution to Other Systems** If you select this, you are not using any other decentralized system for management of master data.

**All Cost Centers Centralized** If you select this, you are using the ALE distribution approach. All of the cost center master data processing is being distributed to other systems and the management of the transactional activities are being managed by the logical home system—so transactional data is being managed by the central system of the controlling area.

**Cost Centers Decentralized or Centralized** If you select this, you are using the ALE distribution approach. All of the cost center master data processing is being distributed to other systems but all transactional data is being managed by the individual systems and the settings in the controlling area for those systems.

**LSystem Master Data**    This field is relevant only if you are using SAP's Application Link Enabling (ALE) to link multiple R/3 systems together. If you are not using ALE, leave this field blank. This field allows you to identify an alternative logical system for management of the cost center master data. If you are interested in having the master data of your system be managed by another system, you can assign the logical system name here as the alternative.

*New GL Activated*

Once you have completed this information and you exit this screen, you will receive a notice that the new General Ledger Accounting is active (Figure 8.5). We already covered all the information you need regarding the new GL Accounting process in Chapter 7, "The New GL Accounting." So for now, we will refer you to that chapter for additional information as to the implications of this functionality. Once you've filled out all the fields, save the controlling area definitions.

**FIGURE 8.5**    Warning information for the new GL Accounting activation

Figure 8.6 shows the controlling area details configuration screen configured for Extreme Sports.

## EXTREME SPORTS CONTROLLING AREA DEFINITION CONFIGURATION ANALYSIS

The organizational structure for Extreme Sports includes multiple company codes and therefore needs to maintain cross-company cost accounting. Extreme Sports is a U.S.-based company and maintains its books in U.S. dollars. It has a Mexican subsidiary that operates in pesos, and it is anticipating a foreign sales expansion into Europe. The company's SAP solution does not include ALE.

**FIGURE 8.6**       The controlling area details configuration screen configured for Extreme Sports

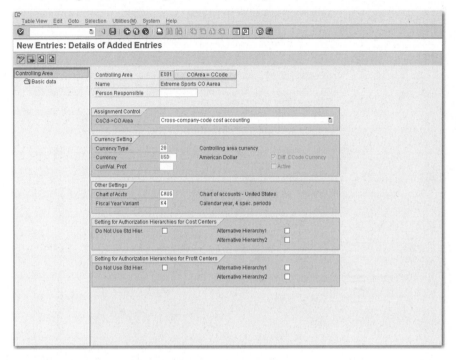

# Activating Component/Control Indicators

After establishing the controlling area, it becomes important to activate the components of CO that are relevant to your project. To do so, you must move to the Controlling section of the IMG. Do this by following the menu path Controlling ➤ Controlling General ➤ Organization ➤ Maintain Controlling Area. You can also use the transaction code OKKP. When you follow the menu path or enter the transaction code, the controlling area maintenance screen, shown in Figure 8.7, appears.

This screen looks similar to the one you used to create the controlling area. In fact, it is the same screen with a few additions. The Activate Components/Control Indicators and Assignment of Company Code(s) options now appear in the Controlling Area portion of the screen.

Components are activated and defined within the controlling area through a fiscal year assignment. You decide whether to establish one parameter that covers all years (for example, from 1999 to 9999) or to maintain a new variant each year (for example, from 1999 to 1999).

**FIGURE 8.7**    The controlling area maintenance screen

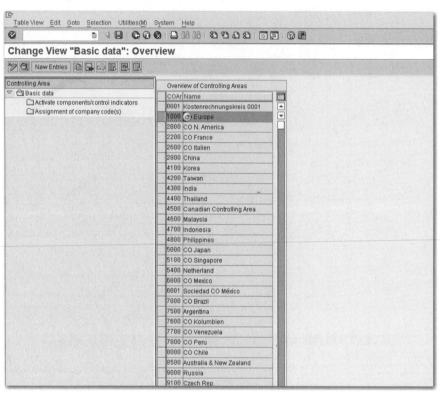

The next step is to finish the basic data configuration for the new controlling area. Once you've completed that, you'll assign a cost center standard hierarchy. The hierarchy will not be completed until Chapter 10, "Cost Center Accounting," but to complete the controlling area, it's important to define the hierarchy.

Choose the newly created controlling area found in the Overview of Controlling Areas portion of the screen; it's the field to the left of the controlling area. Then click the Details button on the toolbar. The controlling area details configuration screen, shown in Figure 8.8, appears.

In the CCtr Std. Hierarchy field, enter the name you want to give your cost center standard hierarchy. If the hierarchy you enter is new, a box will pop up and ask you if you want SAP to create the hierarchy for you. Select Yes. If you select No, the screen will revert to the original setting and the standard hierarchy will not be defined. It is important that this step be completed before you move on to the next step.

**FIGURE 8.8** The controlling area details configuration screen

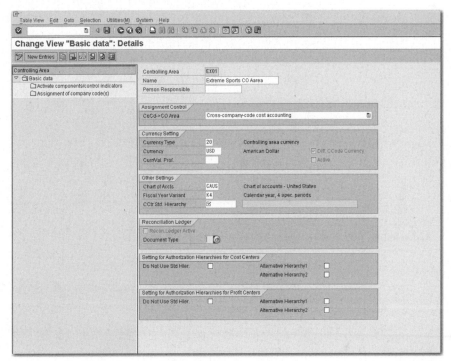

When you've defined the hierarchy, save the controlling area. Click the green arrow to move back to the controlling area maintenance screen. Double-click Activate Components/Control Indicators. The control indicators configuration screen appears (see Figure 8.9).

**NOTE**  You may find that you will have to assign a company code to your controlling area before going through this assignment. If so, please see the next section ("Assigning Company Codes to Controlling Area") for additional information.

Click the New Entries button to access the control indicators detail configuration screen, shown in Figure 8.10.

**FIGURE 8.9**    The control indicators configuration screen

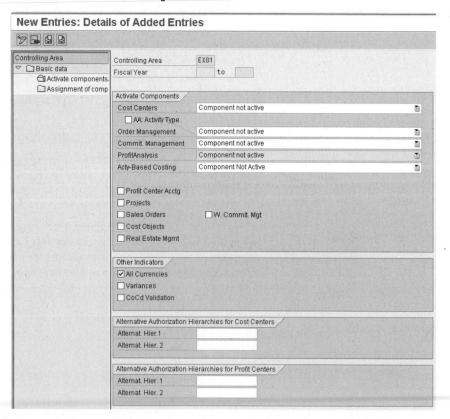

**FIGURE 8.10**    The control indicators detail configuration screen

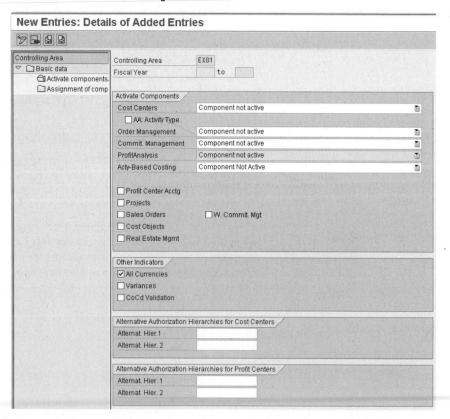

Here are the fields on this screen:

**Fiscal Year**   Enter the fiscal year when the activation settings become valid. Realize that the To field will automatically fill with the year 9999. If you decide that you need to adjust this ending field, the approach is to come back into this screen and using the change process, enter in the ending year in the From field. Once that occurs, the To field will again be filled in with 9999. So you will have created a sequential change in the parameters of your controlling area. This approach is similar to making the changes needed for a cost center or other costing objects.

**Cost Centers (Activate Components section)**   Cost Center Accounting (CCA) will be inactive until this field parameter is changed. The possible entries from the drop-down list are as follows:

**0**   Component not active.

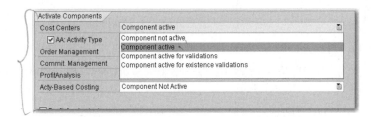

**1**   Component active.

**2**   Component active for validations—CCA is not activated, but you can use cost centers as account assignment objects. The cost center is validated/checked against the master data table. CO is not updated. Utilize this setting if you do not want CCA active today but may want to activate it with the same cost center master data at some point in the future. You can then subsequently post all the cost center data to the CO files. Cost centers must be created in full.

**3**   Component active for existence validations—CCA is not activated, but you can use cost centers as account assignment objects. The main difference is that cost centers do not have to be completed in full.

**AA: Activity Type**   If you check this box, the activity types will be available for posting against primary cost elements.

**Order Management**   Internal Order Accounting will be unavailable until you change the initial entry in this field. Here are the other options for this field:

**1**   Internal Order Accounting component is not active.

**2**    Internal Order Accounting is fully activated.

**3**    Internal Order Accounting is not activated, but you can use orders as account assignment objects. The order is then validated/checked against the master data, including whether the order has been released for postings. CO is not updated. Utilize this setting if you do not want internal orders active today but may want to activate them at some point in the future. You can then subsequently post all the internal order data to the CO files.

**4**    Internal Order Accounting is not activated, but you can use internal orders as account assignment objects. The system doesn't check internal orders to see whether postings can occur; it only checks to see if they exist.

**Commit. Management**    Use this field to determine whether commitments (for example, purchase requisitions and purchase orders) are updated for the controlling area. Here are the other options for this field:

**1**    Commitment Management is not activated.

**2**    Commitment Management is fully activated.

**ProfitAnalysis**    Use this field to define whether and how Profitability Analysis (CO-PA) is activated. SAP provides two types of CO-PA: account-based and costing-based. Of the two, costing-based is more flexible and therefore more popular. Originally, only costing-based CO-PA existed. However, many accountants thought that it is important to easily tie to the G/L, so SAP developed account-based CO-PA. Leave this field as the default for CO-PA will validate that CO-PA should not be activated. The options from the drop-down list are as follows:

**0**    Component is not active.

**1**    Component for only costing-based CO-PA is activated.

**2**    Component for only account-based CO-PA is activated.

**3**    Components for both account- and costing-based CO-PA is activated.

**Acty-Based Costing (ABC)**    With this field, you can choose whether activity-based costing should be activated within your system. (ABC will not be discussed in detail within any chapter of this book. However, we will provide an explanation of the settings. It is our recommendation that anyone interested in learning more about ABC, or product costing, attend a relevant SAP course or review the additional information available from SAP help files.) Leave this field as defaulted

(Component Not Active) if ABC should not be activated. There are two other options for this field:

**1**   Component Active for Parallel Calculations. ABC is activated with restrictions. Allocations are posted as statistical entries on the cost object. The real posting would go to another CO object, like a cost center. (The differences between real and statistical postings are covered in Chapter 10.)

**2**   Component Active for Parallel and Integrated Calculations. ABC is activated without restrictions. All postings to ABC Accounting are posted as real postings to the appropriate ABC object. Other costing objects received the statistical postings.

**Profit Center Accounting (PCA)**   Select this field if you want PCA to be activated. (Profit Center Accounting will be discussed and configured in Chapter 13.)

**Projects**   If you are utilizing Project System, this setting becomes important. Project System integrates with CO through work breakdown structure (WBS) elements and networks. (Project System will not be covered in this book. For further information on the impact of Project System to the controlling area, we recommend that you attend an SAP course on the matter.) If you activate Projects in the controlling area, you can use WBS elements and networks as real account assignment objects and CO data is recorded. If this field is not activated, project data within CO is not updated. Note that even though you don't select this parameter, master data for additional account assignments to a WBS element will be validated within the system.

**Sales Orders**   If you are utilizing make-to-order production, this setting becomes important. If you are not, leave this blank. If it's activated, all revenues and costs will post to the sales order item. Therefore the system will create a costing object for the sales order and CO will be able to track the revenue and costs assigned to the sales order number. Also, production orders, networks, and other objects settle to a sales order item. In this case the account assignment category plays a very important role.

**Sales Orders (and W. Commit. Mgt)**   This controls whether commitments are updated to the sales orders.

**Cost Objects**   If you are using repetitive manufacturing within your product cost environment, this setting becomes relevant. Repetitive manufacturing uses cost objects to plan and track production costs.

**Real Estate Mgmt**   This will define if Real Estate Mgmt is another cost object that can be posted to for actual data. This will allow postings such as financial accounting, cost center assessments, CO transfer postings, and other account assignments to a real estate object in CO.

**All Currencies (Other Indicators section)**   This setting will often default from your controlling area definition. If it's activated, the system will update CO values in the transaction currency and the object currency. If it's inactive, only the controlling area currency is used to update CO values. Be very careful with this indicator. If you decide to deactivate it, you can't reactivate it until the next fiscal year and in the current year all of the CO postings will not be available in multiple currencies. Also, if you do change this indicator, please check any additional information and requirements with SAP information.

**Variances**   Activate this if you want SAP to calculate and post as a line item variances from each primary cost posting. Variances occur when the actual costs are less than or greater than planned costs. Actual and planned cost variances result when the actual price of the resource is less than or greater than the planned price.

**CoCd Validation**   This setting will automatically activate if cross-company-code cost accounting is activated in the controlling area definition. If active, the setting will ensure that both sides of an accounting or purchasing transaction generate from a cost center in the same company code. And, using the same criteria, it ensures that all inventory activities are posted properly in both company codes.

There are additional settings on this screen, and we will discuss these a bit later in the chapter. For now, these are the settings that are critical for the completion of the configuration of the controlling area.

When you're finished configuring the control indicators, save your settings. You will notice that SAP has filled 9999 in the "To" field of the fiscal year range. The settings are valid until year 9999 or until you make an entry for a new fiscal year.

If you want to make a change to any of the settings for the next fiscal year, create a new entry in the Control Indicators table. By entering a new fiscal year in the table, you ensure that the validity date for the prior entry becomes the last fiscal year before the new entry. Table 8.1 provides you with an example of multiple fiscal year assignments. The first entry for 1999 was originally valid until the aforementioned year 9999. A new fiscal year entry was then defined for 2002, which immediately changed the prior setting's validity period end date to 2001.

**TABLE 8.1**     Control Indicator Validity Period

| Maintain Fiscal Year | Validity Period |
| --- | --- |
| 1999 | 1999–2001 |
| 2002 | 2002–2005 |
| 2006 | 2006–9999 |

Component activation is complete and you can now begin to assign your company codes.

### EXTREME SPORTS COMPONENT/CONTROL INDICATOR ACTIVATION CONFIGURATION ANALYSIS

Extreme Sports will be using Cost Center Accounting, internal orders, Profit Center Accounting, and repetitive manufacturing. Because the company will be using Cost Center Accounting, we had to identify a standard hierarchy, EX01. In addition, the company wants to track purchase order commitments. Extreme Sports has decided not to include Project System or ABC in this rollout of SAP. Because it is not interested in ABC, it has no desire to track variances.

## Assigning Company Codes to Controlling Area

The FI-to-CO integration occurs when you assign a company code to a controlling area. If, in your controlling area definition, you determined that there would be no cross-company-code cost accounting, the company code assignment would default from the entry made. Remember that you entered a company code when you decided on a controlling area ID (see the section "Controlling Area Definition" earlier in this chapter). The configuration of the company code is done in the FI area and specifically in the general setup of the company configuration.

If you are using cross-company-code cost accounting, proceed with the configuration steps that follow. Many of the initial steps are similar to those taken when activating the controlling area components. To get to the proper screen, follow the menu path Controlling ➤ Controlling General ➤ Organization ➤ Maintain Controlling Area. You can also use the transaction code OKKP to access this screen.

Either click the controlling area you want to maintain, or click the button next to your controlling area.

 **TIP**    Do not double-click the controlling area. If you do, the basic data details screen will appear. Click the green arrow to back out of the screen if necessary.

Click the Assignment of Company Codes button. The initial assignment of company codes screen appears (see Figure 8.11).

**FIGURE 8.11**    The initial screen to assign company codes to the controlling area

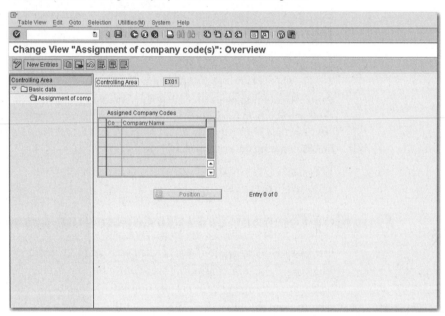

Click the New Entries button in the header. The screen shown in Figure 8.12 appears. You will notice that the company code entry column in the assignment box is empty and ready for postings, either by using the F4 help to supply the list of company codes that are available or just manually entering the company codes that you want to assign to this controlling area. In either case, enter company code IDs that you want assigned and save your entries.

**FIGURE 8.12**    The completed assignment of company codes to controlling area

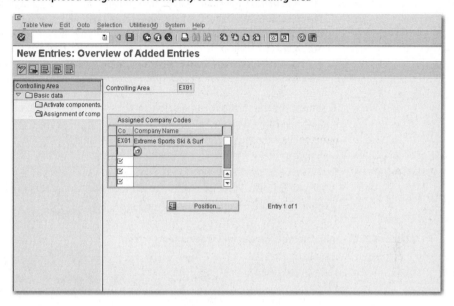

## EXTREME SPORTS COMPANY CODE ASSIGNMENT CONFIGURATION ANALYSIS

Extreme Sports maintains five separate legal entities. They are company codes EX01, Extreme Sports Ski & Surf; EX02, Extreme Sports Mountain; EX03, Extreme Sports Boats; EX04, ES Mexico, S.A.; and EX05, Extreme Sports Services.

# Assigning Number Ranges to Controlling Area

Within SAP, all postings are tracked through the assignment of a document number. The document number assigned is dependent upon a couple of factors: the activity used to update the CO file and the number range assigned within the controlling area. Number range assignments can be internally generated by SAP or flagged to allow external (manual) updates. We recommend letting SAP generate the numbering internally.

**WARNING**    You should not be transporting your number ranges between clients. There is a potential to accidentally wipe out an existing document range or to accidentally reset the interval status. If this were to occur, your system could possibly contain two documents with the same number in the same fiscal year. Manually entering the ranges in each client prevents any inadvertent duplication.

To maintain the number ranges, follow the menu path Controlling ➢ Controlling General ➢ Organization ➢ Maintain Number Ranges for CO Controlling Documents. You can also use the transaction code KANK to access this configuration screen.

After you follow the menu path or use the transaction code, the initial Number Ranges for CO Document screen (see Figure 8.13).

**FIGURE 8.13    Initial number ranges for CO documents screen**

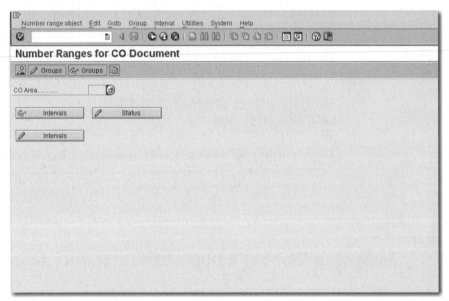

In the following sections, you'll perform these tasks:

1. Set up number range assignment groups.

2. Assign activities as necessary.

3. Create number range intervals.

There are two methods for creating your assignment groups: copy from an existing controlling area or create a new group from scratch. It is far easier to copy a group, so we recommend this approach. Any defaults carried over with the copied group can be augmented later. These augmentations would be necessary if you wanted a specific activity, like assessments, to post to a document number range other than the SAP default.

## Setting Up Number Range Assignment Groups: Copy

In the Number Ranges for CO Document screen, you'll select the proper areas for copying. Follow these steps to set up for copying:

1. In the CO Area field, enter the ID of the controlling area to be copied. Controlling area 0001 is delivered with the system and can be used to copy.

2. Click the copy icon. The pop-up box shown in Figure 8.14 appears.

**FIGURE 8.14**    **The copy pop-up box**

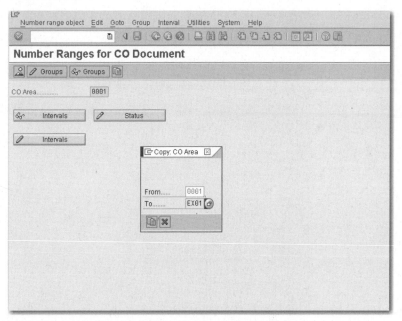

3. In the To box, enter the name of the receiving controlling area and press Enter. If the copy was successful, you will receive a message at the bottom of the screen that reads, "CO area 0001 copied to *XXXX*," where *XXXX* refers to the recipient controlling area.

**4.** To maintain your number range groups, select the group maintain icon (icon that has the "change" pencil next to the Groups) on the Number Ranges for CO Document screen (shown earlier in Figure 8.13). The Maintain Number Range Groups screen appears (see Figure 8.15). You will notice that all the activity assignments are copied from CO area 0001.

**FIGURE 8.15**    The Maintain Number Range Groups screen

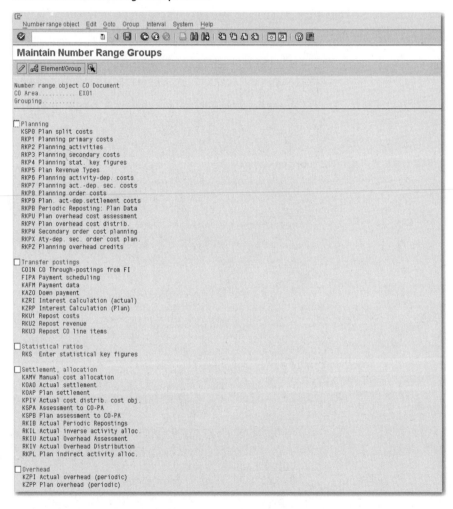

**5.** Scroll to the bottom of the screen. As you do so, review the activity assignments. At the bottom, you will find all the activities that have not yet been assigned, as shown in Figure 8.16. Depending on your solution, some of these unassigned activities may be relevant.

**FIGURE 8.16**     The Not Assigned section of the Maintain Number Range Groups screen

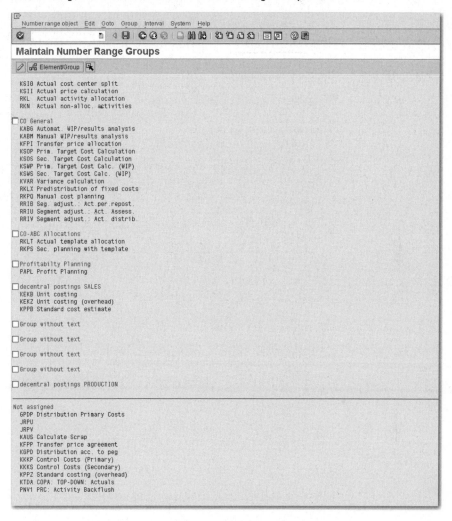

6. To move an unassigned activity to a range group, place your cursor on the activity and choose the select element icon (the icon that looks like an arrow pointing at a box). You will notice that the activity becomes highlighted.

7. Place a check next to the activity group to which you want to assign the activity. Select the Element/Group button. The activity moves from the Not Assigned section to your new activity group. Repeat this assignment as often as necessary.

## Setting Up Number Range Assignment Groups: Manual

To create a new range group, select Group ➤ Insert (F6) on the Maintain Number Range Groups screen. The Insert Group window appears (see Figure 8.17).

**FIGURE 8.17**    The Insert Group window

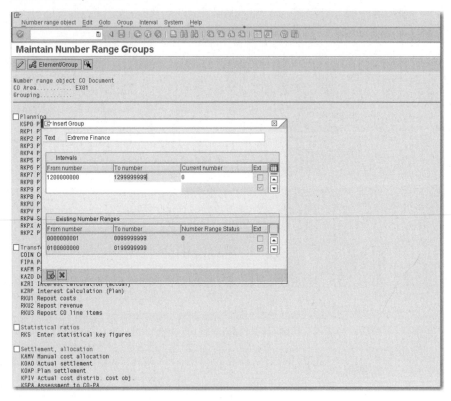

Follow these steps to create a new range group:

1. In the Text field, enter the name of the new group.

2. Enter the number range that will support the new range group in the From Number and To Number fields. Be sure that the new number range does not overlap an existing range. SAP will do a check automatically. To view the existing number ranges, drop to the Existing Number Ranges section and scroll using the + and – keys. When you're finished entering the number ranges, press Enter. The insert box disappears and you are returned to the Maintain Number Range Groups screen.

> **NOTE**  If you copy from group 0001, the first number range interval you enter will default to the range group named Finances. Repeat steps 1 and 2 again to get a new group and number range assignment.

Review the new number range by scrolling down until you see your new group. If you place your cursor on the new group and select the Maintain button, the number range assigned to the group will appear. When all number range groups have been created, save the assignments.

To get a listing of activities, assigned and unassigned, grouped by controlling area, be sure you are at the Number Ranges for CO Document screen. Click the Overview button found on the icon bar and an activity overview screen will appear. To exit, just green arrow back once.

## Changing the Number Range Status

From this same screen (Number Ranges for CO Document, shown earlier in Figure 8.13), it is possible to review and maintain the number range status for any number interval in the controlling area. To do so, follow these steps:

1. Enter a controlling area ID in the CO Area field.

2. Select the maintain status icon found in the center of the screen (it is identified with a pencil symbol and the word *Status*). A list of the number intervals appears (see Figure 8.18). From this list, you can reset any range to 0 or adjust the number to something more appropriate.

> **NOTE**  Resetting number ranges is not recommended in your live production client. If this occurs, it will have a significant impact on your overall posting process, and the possibility of the system attempting to post additional records to a document number that has already been used is a major concern. It is also recommended that you create number ranges for actual and planned data. Also make sure that as you create number ranges you are using these specific posting assignments frequently and are actively in these areas of the posting process.

Once you are satisfied with the number range groups and number interval assignments, the controlling area number assignment process is complete.

**FIGURE 8.18**    The Maintain Number Range Intervals screen

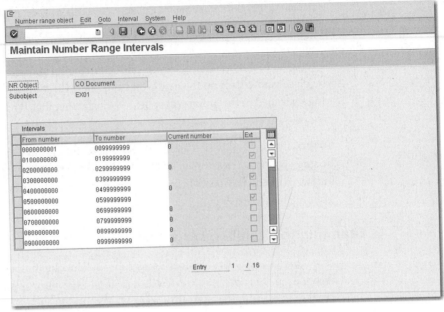

## EXTREME SPORTS CONTROLLING AREA CONFIGURATION ANALYSIS

Upon reviewing the activity groupings, Extreme Sports determined that it could maintain its controlling operations by using most of the standard range and number interval definitions taken from the copy of 0001. Any maintenance to the activity assignments will be minimal.

# The Operating Concern — *Main org. unit in CO-PA*

*Analyze specific market or busi concern*

If you have chosen to implement either account-based or costing-based Profitability Analysis (CO-PA), you must configure an operating concern. The operating concern is the main organizational unit within CO-PA. It is utilized as a management tool to analyze specific markets or business segments. As with the controlling area, we will complete the configuration in two steps. With this first step, you will establish a name and description for the operating concern. We'll show how to do the complete configuration in Chapter 12, "Profitability Analysis."

Be aware that much of your operating concern configuration is client independent. The configuration completed in one client will have an impact on all clients in your development instance.

## Operating Concern Definition — ORKE

*[handwritten: KEP8]*

To change the operating concern using the maintain operating concern screen, follow the menu path Enterprise Structure ➢ Definition ➢ Controlling ➢ Create Operating Concern. You can also use transaction code KEP8 to access this configuration screen. There is also a unique transaction code, ORKE, that will access an Implementation Guide format that only includes COPA in the configuration, and you can also access this information from that transaction code.

In the Define Operating Concern: Overview screen, shown in Figure 8.19, click the New Entries button. An empty operating concern entries table will appear with the following fields requiring entry:

**Operating Concern**    Enter a four-character alphanumeric key.

**Name of Operating Concern**    Enter the description of your operating concern.

**FIGURE 8.19**    The maintain operating concern screen

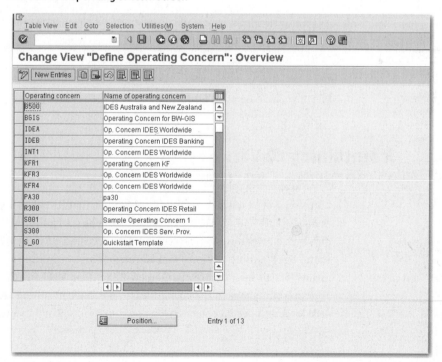

Figure 8.20 provides you with the definition for Extreme Sports's operating concern.

**FIGURE 8.20**    The saved operating concern data

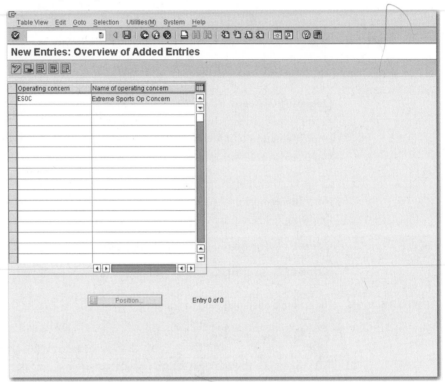

When you've entered the information, save the operating concern data. The first phase of the operating concern configuration is complete.

## Maintaining CO Versions — *For transactional data*

Prior to entering transactional data into your production system, you must maintain a version to support planned and actual activity. Version 0 is generated automatically within the system when you create the controlling area. Version 0 is the only version where actual transaction data is posted. SAP allows you to maintain numerous planning versions, and all versions are controlling area independent. This means that all versions are maintained at the client level and thus are available to any controlling area in the client. Please note that controlling area, operating concern level, and profit center version configuration settings can be different.

*Version 0 + for actual data*

*Diff settings*

**NOTE**   Basically, the system holds the  actual version of data as 000, but the business user will normally see the actual version as 0. In the case of CO-PA the actual and planned data is identified a bit differently and this will be covered in the chapter on CO-PA.

To complete the base CO enterprise configuration, you will need to configure version 0 for the current fiscal year and Profit Center Accounting. Additional version configuration will take place when Profitability Analysis is addressed in Chapter 12.

*OKEQ*   *maintain contr...*

To maintain the version, follow the menu path Controlling ➤ Controlling General ➤ Organization ➤ Maintain Versions. You can also use the transaction code OKEQ. The General Version Definition configuration screen, shown in Figure 8.21, is divided into two sections: a navigation section and a General Version Overview section. In the navigation section there are several areas to maintain:   *SPRO*

▶ General Version Definition

▶ Settings in Operating Concern

▶ Settings for Profit Center Accounting

**FIGURE 8.21**   The General Version Definition configuration screen

*Overview section*

*nav section*

| Version | Name | Plan | Actual | WIP/RA | Variance |
|---------|------|------|--------|--------|----------|
| 0 | Plan/actual version | ☑ | ☑ | ☑ | ☑ |
| 1 | Plan version: change 1 | ☑ | ☐ | ☑ | ☑ |
| 2 | Plan version 2 | ☑ | ☐ | ☑ | ☑ |
| 3 | Plan version 3 | ☑ | ☐ | ☑ | ☑ |
| 4 | Plan version 4 | ☐ | ☐ | ☐ | ☐ |
| 6 | Cost Estimate Maint. Orders | ☑ | ☐ | ☐ | ☐ |
| 10 | Plan version: integration OPA | ☑ | ☐ | ☐ | ☐ |
| 20 | Plan Reconcil. CO-OM Basis | ☑ | ☐ | ☐ | ☐ |
| 21 | Plan Reconcil. CO-OM Result | ☑ | ☐ | ☐ | ☐ |
| 40 | ABC Version | ☑ | ☑ | ☐ | ☐ |
| 50 | ABC Version | ☑ | ☑ | ☐ | ☐ |
| 70 | Planning Integration LMRP | ☑ | ☐ | ☐ | ☐ |
| 0K0 | IDES Delta for TP: Group View | ☐ | ☑ | ☑ | ☑ |
| 0PC | IDES Delta for TP: PrCtr View | ☐ | ☑ | ☑ | ☑ |
| 100 | CO-PA IDES plan version | ☑ | ☐ | ☐ | ☐ |
| 101 | CO-PA plan version SOP | ☑ | ☐ | ☐ | ☐ |
| 102 | CO-PA Plan w/ Plan Structure | ☑ | ☐ | ☐ | ☐ |
| 110 | Sales Planning | ☑ | ☐ | ☐ | ☐ |
| 111 | CO-PA Current Forecast | ☑ | ☐ | ☐ | ☐ |
| 112 | CO-PA Planning Management | ☑ | ☐ | ☐ | ☐ |
| 113 | CO-PA Planning Sales Personnel | ☑ | ☐ | ☐ | ☐ |
| 125 | CO-PA: top-down distribution | ☑ | ☐ | ☐ | ☐ |
| 130 | PS: Plan/actual version | ☑ | ☐ | ☐ | ☐ |
| 131 | PS: Fixed prices | ☑ | ☐ | ☐ | ☐ |
| 132 | PS: Earned value analysis | ☑ | ☐ | ☐ | ☐ |
| 133 | PS: Cost forecast | ☑ | ☐ | ☐ | ☐ |
| 140 | CO-PA ref version for ratios | ☑ | ☐ | ☐ | ☐ |

Dialog Structure
▽ General Version Definition
  ☐ Settings in Operating Concern
  ☐ Settings for Profit Center Accounting
  ▽ ☐ Controlling Area Settings
    ☐ Settings for Each Fiscal Year
    ☐ Delta Version: Bus. Transactions from Ref. Version
  ☐ Settings for Progress Analysis (Project System)

General Version Definition

General Version Overview

► Controlling Area Settings

► Settings for Each Fiscal Year

► Delta Version: Bus. Transactions from Ref. Version

► Settings for Progress Analysis (Project System)

To make the controlling area functional for version 0, you need to define the CO version and maintain activities for the fiscal year. Begin the process by setting the default controlling area:

**1.** Choose Extras ➣ Set Controlling Area. Figure 8.22 shows this menu option.

**FIGURE 8.22**   Setting the controlling area

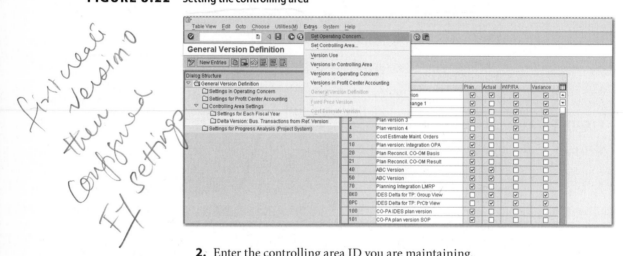

**2.** Enter the controlling area ID you are maintaining.

Because version 0 is generated within the controlling area, the settings for the fiscal year will be configured next. When version 0 is generated, SAP makes the version available for five years by default. Should the need arise, additional years can be added once the last year expires.

## Fiscal Year Version Parameters

To maintain the version parameters, select version 0 in the General Version Overview section of the General Version Definition configuration screen. Look at the navigation section and choose Settings for Each Fiscal Year, found in the middle of the list in the navigation section. Double-click the line item, and the Version Settings for Each Fiscal Year screen appears. Click New Entries, and a new fiscal-year-dependent version screen appears (see Figure 8.23). From here you need to choose the year—for example, 2008—and then click the details icon (the magnifying glass) to see the Change View "Settings for Each Fiscal Year": Details screen, as shown in Figure 8.24.

**FIGURE 8.23**   The new fiscal-year-dependent version details screen

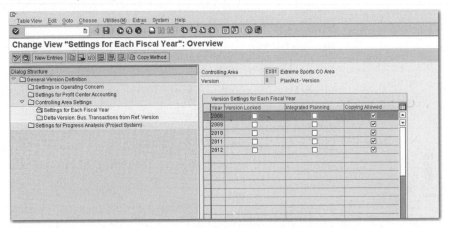

**FIGURE 8.24**   The Change View "Settings for Each Fiscal Year": Details screen

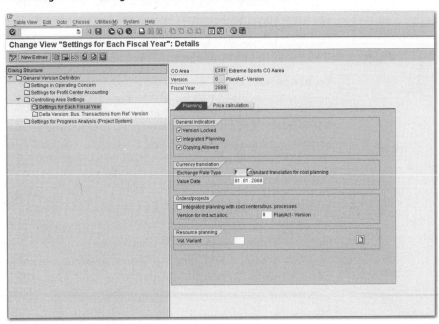

Let's look at the fields in the fiscal year version detail screen; the following options are on the Planning tab:

**Fiscal Year**   The fiscal year is already defaulted in the screen since we have identified the year ranges for controlling area EX01. If we were going to identify the actual years from this screen, we would have to fill in the year. Best practices suggest that we have already set up the year ranges and therefore have to deal only with the parameters for each year. You will have to maintain a version for each year.

**Version Locked**   If this field is active, planning is locked. This setting is useful if you want to freeze plan values after a certain date.

**Integrated Planning**   Activate this field if you want to transfer plan data from cost centers to Profit Center Accounting or to special ledgers. Since no plan data exists in this version yet, you can change this setting. If plan data has been posted, the integration indicator can be activated through transaction KP96: Activate line items and planning integration. Once this field is activated, SAP posts previously planned line items.

**Copying Allowed**   Select this field if you want to copy plan versions to one another. We recommend that you activate the setting because of the flexibility it adds to your planning capabilities. With Copying Allowed activated, a company could easily maintain multiple planning scenarios, copying the information from one to another and then making version-specific changes. Upon completion and approval of the plan, the final version could quickly be copied back to version 0 and used in reporting and analysis.

**Exchange Rate Type**   Enter the key for how you will value transactions. For planning, the P rate—Standard translation for cost planning—is used most frequently.

**Value Date**   Enter a date in the Value Date field if you want the same date used for all planning translations. If this field is left blank, SAP will determine the exchange rate on a period-by-period basis. Leave this blank if you want SAP to track any exchange rate fluctuations.

**Integrated Planning with Cost Centers/Bus. Processes**   This field refers to integration with internal orders and WBS elements. If this field is activated, any planned order settlements will be picked up in Cost Center Accounting. In addition, any planned assessments, distributions, or indirect activity allocations from cost centers to orders/WBS elements will be permitted. Also, if Planning Integration with CCA is activated, integration could occur between orders/WBS elements and PCA and/or special ledgers.

*IAA — Indirect activity allocation*

**Version for Ind. Act. All. (IAA)**    IAA stands for indirect activity allocation. This field can be set only if Planning Integration with CCA is inactive. The default version from SAP is 0.

*Use for detailed level plan*

**Resource Planning – Val. Variant**    Val. Variant can be used if the detailed-level planning process for resource planning is being used. This option allows the user to assign a valuation variant to the specific year and version prior to the use of this version in the planning process. The valuation variant assigns, among other things, the method used to valuate specific resources to be used during resource planning, such as equipment and materials.

The following options are on the Price Calculation tab:

**Pure Iterative Price**    This field should be activated if you wish to maintain parallel activity prices within one version. The requirement for activation is that you must manually set the allocation prices during your activity type planning. If this field is not activated, SAP calculates only the prices resulting from your activity planning.

*Use for price plan*

**Plan Method**    Use this field to choose a method for activity price planning. SAP provides three methods: periodic, average, and cumulative (only possible in the actual method). Each of these methods is unique in the posting that is generated. The periodic method is the basic approach—the postings that are created are posted in the period that they are incurred. The average method posts the same amount to each period no matter what the actual posting has occurred. The cumulative method generates the amount posted by summing all postings to date and then generates an average for each period.

**Actual Method**    Similar to Plan Method, use Actual Method to choose the type of activity for price calculations. SAP offers three types of actual activity price calculations: periodic, average, and cumulative.

**Revaluation**    Use this field to decide whether actual activities are revaluated or not. If it's checked, you can determine whether actual activity is revaluated using only an actual price or both the actual and the planned price. There are three options available: Do Not Revaluate, Own Business Transaction, and Original Business Transaction.

**Cost Comp. Layt**    If activity pricing is used in Product Costing or Cost Center Accounting and you are using a cost component layout, enter the desired layout key in the Cost Comp. Layt box.

When you have completed your settings, save the version (see Figure 8.25). The next step is to maintain the version settings for Profit Center Accounting.

**FIGURE 8.25**   Extreme Sports's CO

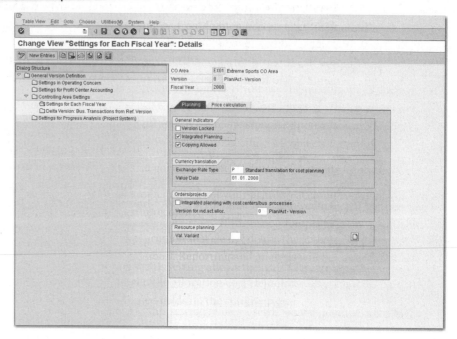

## Profit Center Accounting Version Parameters

While in the CO Versions change maintenance transaction OKEQ, select the version you want to maintain and choose Settings for Profit Center Accounting. The Change View "Settings for Profit Center Accounting": Overview screen appears. If you are looking to maintain the current settings for a version, you would complete that configuration from this screen. If you are changing the information at the year, level then choose the New Entries button and the New Entries: Overview of Added Entries screen appears. Figure 8.26 shows this screen configured for Extreme Sports.

**FIGURE 8.26** The EC-PCA fiscal year dependent version parameters

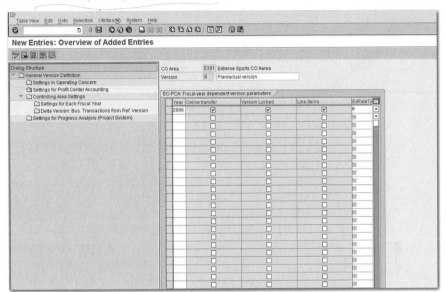

Select New Entries. In the version parameters box, there are several fields to complete:

**Fiscal Year**   Enter the fiscal year for which the settings are valid.

**Online Transfer**   If this field is activated, all transactions will update PCA automatically. If it's not activated, postings will have to be transferred manually through special transactions.

**Version Locked**   Activate Version Locked if the version should be protected from entries or changes.

**Line Items**   Activate Line Items if you want to use line item postings for all planning transactions.

**ExRate Type**   Save an exchange rate type assigned to this year and PCA Planning. This would be the default exchange rate for PCA but can be changed during the setup of the PCA planning process either in the planning layout or the planning profile.

**Value Date**   This will identify the date that the exchange rate type will refer to during the process of posting the transactions during planning or actual processes.

**Variant for TP**    If you have activated the transfer pricing process, you can assign a variant to valuate the transfer pricing process during PCA planning and actual posting. This will also determine the order for the pricing process. This is all determined in the transfer pricing procedure.

When finished, save your settings. That screen concludes the version maintenance for now. As stated earlier, additional maintenance will be covered in later chapters.

---

### EXTREME SPORTS CO VERSION CONFIGURATION ANALYSIS

Extreme Sports requires that only cost center planning roll to the assigned profit center for P&L reporting. The company would like to recognize exchange rate fluctuations in its plan versus actual estimates. The company would also like to have the ability to copy any version. Extreme Sports anticipates having multiple planning versions to support various "what-if" scenarios. When planning is complete, version 1 will be locked and used for Plan to Forecast comparisons. Plan version 0 will then become a forecast version to be changed periodically.

---

# Summary

This chapter is probably one of the most important chapters that we will cover in CO configuration. Within this chapter, we developed the foundation for the entire CO structure. All other chapters from this point forward will use the configuration discussed here. It may be necessary, as you get further into the system development, to revisit some of the topics covered in this chapter for additional configuration and specific unique parameters.

Much of the SAP configuration is trial and error. It is not uncommon to develop two or three controlling areas or operating concerns before the right mix of settings is found. Do not be afraid to try different ideas. People find more solutions on the fifth attempt than the first, but realize that we are focusing on having only *one* controlling area and operating concern at the end of this configuration.

# Cost Element Accounting

**FEATURING:**

▶ COST ELEMENT TYPES

▶ AUTOMATIC COST ELEMENT CREATION

▶ MANUAL COST ELEMENT CREATION

▶ IMPUTED COSTS

▶ RECONCILIATION LEDGER

▶ EXPLANATION OF CO UPDATES

1) Co. Elements  5) Statistical keys.
2) Co Centers
3) Activity types

Master
4 data types in Co

Prim. Co. Elem
|
Linked to FI
in G/L

1. Co. Elem    like Co comm
1. Co. Object   ~ Int Or.

Within the Controlling (CO) module are four distinct master data types: cost elements, cost centers, activity types, and statistical key figures. Each is tightly integrated with the others to provide the basis for transactional postings in Controlling. At the center of all the transactional activity are cost elements.

Each posting in cost accounting is linked to a cost element and at least one controlling object, such as a cost center or internal order. Cost elements, specifically primary cost elements, are links to the general ledger in the FI module because no primary cost element can exist without its identical twin first being created in FI. The exception to the rule is the relationship that imputed cost elements share with the chart of accounts and the ledger within FI. Imputed cost elements are primary elements, but they are created only in Controlling.

SAP also accommodates internal CO activity through secondary cost elements. Although not linked to general ledger accounts, they are just as important because to use the ability to track costs via multiple postings to cost objects, we have to have secondary cost elements to assign the costs. To keep all the internal CO activity in sync with the FI ledger, Cost Element Accounting utilizes the reconciliation ledger. We will explain this in detail later in this chapter.

To begin, you need to establish the primary cost elements in the CO module. We will work our way through this process using a number of different approaches. Each approach has its place in the process, and examples of these different situations will be shown as we go along.

## Cost Element Types

Prim. — Posting via other module like FI/SD
second. — acted upon other elem.

See
posting

Prim Co. Elem
must be
creation in
FI

There are two distinct cost element types within the Controlling module: primary and secondary. In simple terms, primary cost elements can be directly posted to via the posting that occurs in another module, such as a posting to FI or SD, whereas secondary cost elements must be acted upon by another transaction that will determine the cost element for you, therefore posted only within CO. An example of such a transaction is a cost center assessment where, for the ability to track costs at different levels, you choose to charge other cost objects part or all of the original costs. Again, this concept will be further explained as we move through each of the different cost object chapters. Another technical distinction is that a primary cost element is linked to a G/L account that must be created first in the FI chart of accounts. A secondary cost element can be created only in Controlling.

*(handwritten margin notes: Prim. Cost Elem / Prim. Cost Elem Categories; Secc. Cost-Ele / Sec. Cost Elem Cate.)*

Both primary and secondary cost element types can be broken down further to cost element categories. Categories allow SAP to determine when a cost element should be uniquely utilized within Controlling.

# Primary Cost Element Categories

The primary cost element categories will be the first to be defined (recall that the primary cost elements are used for direct postings and must be accompanied by a G/L account in FI). If you look at any activity in the CO area, this is one that has some added enhancements from the R/3 version 3.0 to the ECC version 6.0, but the fundamental concepts are the same. You can't really change the basic structure that allows you to track and move costs around the CO module. Therefore, much of this information for Cost Element Accounting will hold well for you no matter what version of SAP CO you are working with.

The categories are as follows:

**01: General Primary Cost Elements**   Used to capture all primary cost accounting transactions.

**03: Imputed Cost Elements, Cost Element Percentage Method (Accrual/Deferral per Surcharge)**   Used in Cost Center Accounting to post calculated imputed costs. Create in CO only and used for accrual calculations when you are using the percentage method.

**04: Imputed Cost Elements, Accrual Calculation Target = Actual Method**
Used in Cost Center Accounting to post calculated imputed costs. Create in CO only and used during accrual calculations when you are using the Target = Actual method.

**11: Revenue Elements**   Used to post revenue in Controlling. Revenues are tracked in Profitability Analysis within Controlling and in Profit Center Accounting in Enterprise Controlling. In some cases you'll find that companies use cost elements to post revenues against cost centers, and this can be done but will not allow the system to track the debit/credit process for revenue correctly.

**12: Sales Deductions**   Used by CO to track any sales adjustments or deductions.

> **NOTE**   If you open revenue postings on a cost center, you can use categories 11 and 12 to update the cost center balance. The cost center balance will be updated statistically. SAP will still require a real cost object, either a profitability segment or a sales order.

**22: External Settlements**    Used to post any settlement to an object outside of Controlling. An example of such a transaction is settlement from an internal order to a G/L account.

**90: Cost Elements for Balance Sheet Accounts in FI**    Used to post costs statistically (we will discuss this a bit later in the chapter) to asset reconciliation accounts. These are automatically assigned when you create cost elements for accounts within FI that are of this type.

## Secondary Cost Elements Categories

Secondary cost elements are used strictly for internal CO postings like assessments and settlements. We will discuss the concepts of assessments, distribution, and settlements in Chapter 10, "Cost Center Accounting." The categories for each type are as follows:

**21: Internal Settlements**    Used to track internal settlement activity. An example of internal settlement is settlement from an internal order to a cost center.

**31: Order/Project Results Analysis**    Used to track results analysis activity from an internal order or project.

**41: Overhead**    Used to allocate indirect costs from cost centers to orders or from cost object to cost object.

**42: Assessment**    Used during assessment to allocate costs.

**43: Internal Activity Allocation**    Used to allocate costs, like labor and overhead in a maintenance order, during internal activity postings.

**50: Incoming Orders: Sales Revenue**    Used to track internal revenue allocations within CO coming from incoming sales orders.

**51: Incoming Orders: Other Revenues**    Used to track other revenues such as imputed revenue values.

**52: Incoming Orders: Costs**    Used to track costs from sales orders.

**61: Earned Values**    Used for tracking values from Project System.

# Creating Cost Elements Automatically

Primary cost elements can be created either manually or through an automatic batch run. The automated approach is recommended when you're first creating

*Steps of Automatic*
*1) Define Relationship bet. A/c Range & Category*
*2) Create Batch input session*
*3) execute, the session*

your cost elements because it is the quickest solution and because you are probably creating your GL accounts at the same time and also using the automatic batch creation. We'll cover the three-step process in the following sections. The first step is to define the relationship between the account range and category. The second step is creating a batch input session, and the third step is executing the session.

## Defining the Default Settings — *OKB2   ask for COA →*

To define the default settings, follow the menu path Implementation Guide ➢ Controlling ➢ Cost Element Accounting ➢ Master Data ➢ Cost Elements ➢ Automatic Creation of Primary and Secondary Cost Elements ➢ Make Default Settings. Or you can use transaction code OKB2 to access this screen. If you have accessed this screen before, the system will automatically allow you to access it directly, but if not, you will initially get a dialog box asking for the specific chart of account (COA) that you will be creating these accounts within (see Figure 9.1).

**FIGURE 9.1**     Dialog box for specific chart of accounts

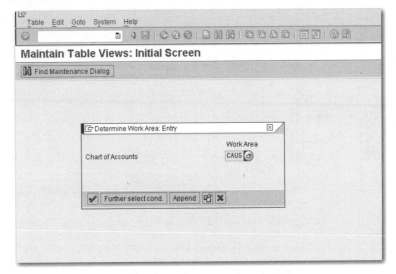

After you use one of the COA options in the dialog box, the transaction configuration's automatic cost element generation screen appears (see Figure 9.2).

**FIGURE 9.2**    The blank automatic cost element generation screen

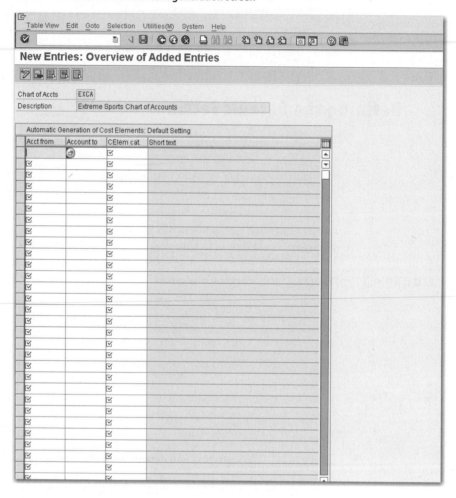

Figure 9.3 shows the fields configured for Extreme Sports.

Here are the fields on the screen in Figure 9.3:

**Acct From**    Enter the beginning account range for a specific category.

**Account To**    Enter the ending account range for a specific category.

**NOTE**    The account ranges do not have to be in numerical order. The system will adjust them accordingly.

**FIGURE 9.3**     The automatic cost element generation default setting screen for Extreme Sports

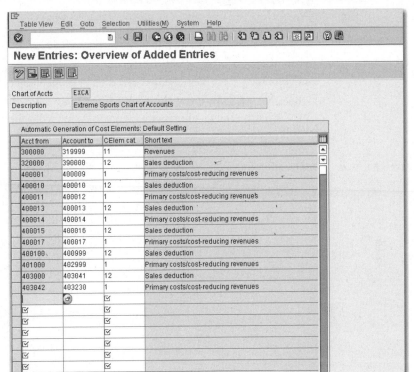

**CElem Cat.**    Enter the cost element category that relates to the corresponding account range (see "Cost Element Types" earlier in this chapter).

**Short Text**    The short text will default from the category assignment in the preceding field.

Remember to use the possible entries key (F4) or the drop-down menu on the field to search for accounts. To add new lines, use the path Edit ➤ New Entries. When you're finished, save the default settings.

**TIP**    Remember, you can copy only revenue and cost elements from the chart of accounts. No balance sheet accounts can be copied to Controlling.

# Defining a Batch Input Session   ~OKB3

Once the default settings are complete, you must create the cost element creation batch run session. To do so, follow the menu path Controlling ➢ Cost Element Accounting ➢ Master Data ➢ Cost Elements ➢ Automatic Creation of Primary and Secondary Cost Elements ➢ Create Batch Input Session. Or you can use transaction code OKB3 to access this screen. The Create Batch Input Session to Create Cost Elements screen appears (see Figure 9.4). You will want to change most of the default settings.

**FIGURE 9.4**     The Create Batch Input Session to Create Cost Elements screen

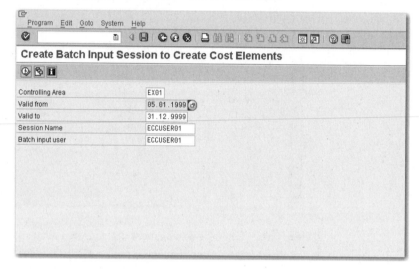

Let's examine the fields:

**Controlling Area**     Enter the ID of the controlling area in which the cost elements should be created.

**Valid From**     Enter the date from which the cost element will be valid.

**WARNING**     Be sure the From date is set early enough to provide an adequate time frame for any historical loads or allocations. You may have noticed by now that we have time dependency on the cost elements being created. This is a bit different than the counterpart FI GL accounts. If you look around CO, you will find that time dependency is linked to specific CO objects and one of them is the cost elements.

**Valid To**    The date you enter here will be the last date the cost element will be valid.

**Session Name**    The user ID of the person creating the session will default as the name of the batch session. Because of the specific use of the batch session, any session name you use will be sufficient.

**Batch Input User**    The user ID of the person creating the session will default as the name of the batch session. As with Session Name, any entry will be sufficient.

You have the option to save the session as a variant. The Variant Attributes save screen will appear (see Figure 9.5).

**FIGURE 9.5**    The Variant Attributes save screen

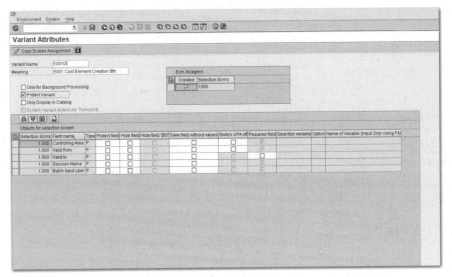

 **NOTE**    Saving the settings as a variant is an option. It may be useful if you anticipate using the settings more than once or using them as an automated batch task.

Here are the fields on the Variant Attributes screen:

**Variant Name**    Enter the name of the variant.

**Meaning**    Enter a description of the variant.

**Environment**    Select as many of the boxes as are relevant for your variant. An entry is not required. The options are as follows:

**Only for Background Processing**    If this check box is selected, the variant can run only in the background.

**Protect Variant**    If this check box is selected, the variant can be changed only by the person who created it or by the last person to change it.

**Only Display in Catalog**    If this field is selected, the variant view is restricted to only the variant directory.

**Field Attributes**    Select as many of the boxes as are relevant for your variant. An entry is not required. The options are as follows:

**Protect Field**    If this check box is selected, the value of the field cannot be altered at runtime. For example, if this field is activated for the Controlling Area field, the value of the controlling area is displayed but cannot be changed in the session.

**Hide Field**    If this check box is selected, the field is not visible when the variant is used.

**Save Field without Values**    If this check box is selected, the values of the field are provided through a variable. Selections manually applied to the variant on the selection screen will be overwritten with the variable value.

When all decisions are made, save the variant. The screen will return to the Create Batch Input Session to Create Cost Elements screen (shown earlier in Figure 9.4).

Create the batch input session by selecting the execute icon. A session log detailing the cost elements to be created will appear (see Figure 9.6). Be sure to review the log for anything that may have been left out. Or, more important, check for cost elements that have been accidentally included. Once master data has been created in the system, it will be available for use until the validity period expires.

**NOTE**   There is an approach to deleting a cost element that has been created by mistake and it seems a bit of a workaround, but due to the time dependency, it's the best approach. Basically, you would need to access the cost element in the Change mode and adjust the ending date (Date To) to the next day. In that way, you have eliminated any ability to post to this cost element after the current day.

**FIGURE 9.6**     The session log for the batch input session needs to be carefully checked.

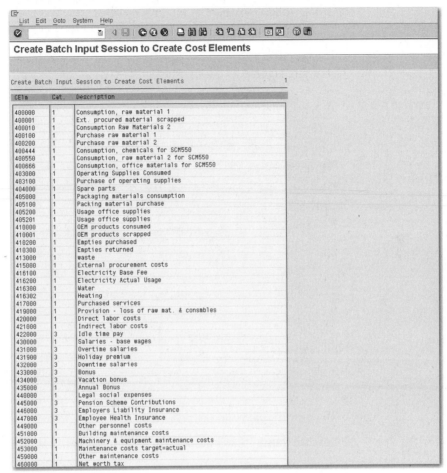

## Executing a Batch Input Session

You can run the batch job online or in the background. For performance reasons, it is recommended that the program be run in either background or display-error-only mode. Correct any fallout or errors after processing. When running a batch online, you can correct any errors as they appear.

Follow the menu path Controlling ➢ Cost Element Accounting ➢ Master Data ➢ Cost Elements ➢ Automatic Creation of Primary and Secondary Cost Elements ➢ Execute Batch Input Session. Or you can use the transaction code SM35 to access this screen.

**TIP**  You can use the SM35 transaction to run any batch session; it is not limited to just cost element creation.

Use the menu path or transaction code to access the batch input execution screen, shown in Figure 9.7.

**FIGURE 9.7**  The batch input execution screen

These are the options on this screen:

**Session Name**  Enter the name of the cost element creation batch.

**Created By; Date From/Time**  This option is used to restrict the batch sessions by date and time. If you have multiple batch sessions, this allows you to narrow the choices of which session should run.

**Status**  These settings help to limit the number of sessions that appear in the overview. The settings represent the six potential statuses of a batch session. The default settings are appropriate.

Double click the Session Line to display the batch session. A listing of potential batch sessions appears (see Figure 9.8).

Select the session you want to run and then execute the batch session. In Extreme Sports's case, we have created one session to choose. A Process Session box requesting information on how to run the session will appear (see Figure 9.9).

**FIGURE 9.8**    A listing of potential batch sessions appears when you double click on the Overview Line.

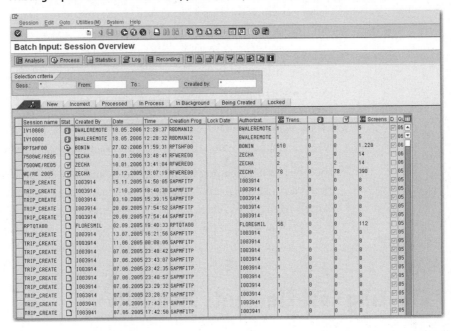

**FIGURE 9.9**    The Process Session dialog box

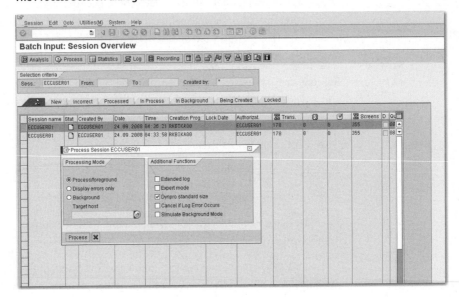

To run the batch in the background, select Background from the dialog box and enter a target system in the Target Host box. Use the drop-down arrow if you are not sure of your system IDs. If the Target Host box is left blank, SAP will select the next available system. Leave all other settings as they defaulted and click the Process button.

To review the job status, select Goto ➢ Background ➢ Job Overview. If an error occurs when the batch is run in the background, the job will terminate. If that happens, correct the error online and continue processing the session. To analyze the session from the Job Overview screen, click the Analyze Sess. button. From the screen that appears, you can review the transactions that occurred.

Once the batch has completed without error, automated primary cost element creation is complete. There will be a need to manually create additional primary and all the secondary cost elements to support your configuration. The manual creation process is not found in the configuration menu in the IMG; it is processed though the user menu in the Cost Element Accounting module.

# Creating Cost Elements Manually

SAP allows you to create primary and secondary cost elements from many places within the system. The most direct location is the user menu in the Cost Element Accounting module. Because primary cost elements were created earlier in batch sessions, in this section we will describe creating secondary cost elements. In either case, the processes are identical for creating primary and secondary cost elements.

Remember that secondary cost elements are used to track internal CO movements and are not tied to the chart of accounts. Here are some potential uses for secondary cost elements:

- ▶ Cost center assessments

- ▶ Internal order settlements

- ▶ Internal allocation of overhead to maintenance orders

Secondary cost elements are not restricted to a number range, so be aware of the number you are using.

To create a secondary cost element, follow the SAP (not IMG) menu path Accounting ➢ Controlling ➢ Cost Element Accounting ➢ Master Data ➢ Cost Elements ➢ Individual Processing ➢ Create Secondary (or Primary). Or you can use the transaction code KA06 (KA01 for primary elements).

After you use one of the configuration transactions, the initial create secondary cost element screen appears (see Figure 9.10).

FIGURE 9.10 The initial create secondary cost element screen

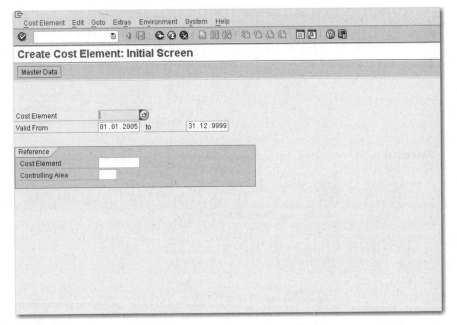

**NOTE** Be sure that you have predetermined the proper controlling area. If it has not been previously set, SAP will offer a prompt to set one. If you want to change the designated controlling area, from the Cost/Revenue Element Accounting main screen (transaction code CEMN), use the menu path Environment ➤ Set CO Area. You can find Environment in the toolbar at the top of the screen.

Here are the fields on this screen:

**Cost Element**    Enter the number of the secondary cost element.

**TIP** It will be helpful to segregate the secondary cost elements from the primary by using distinct account ranges for each. For example, internal settlement elements could fall into a 900000 range.

**Valid From/To**    Enter the validity period of the cost element. You cannot delete the element while it exists within this period of time.

**Cost Element**    Enter the number of the cost element to copy.

**Controlling Area**    Enter the ID of the controlling area where the reference cost element exists.

> **NOTE**    For primary cost elements, the reference element and controlling area must be assigned to the same chart your controlling area is assigned to. You can copy a secondary cost element from any controlling area in the client.

When you've filled in the fields, press Enter. The create secondary cost element configuration screen appears (see Figure 9.11).

**FIGURE 9.11**    The create secondary cost element configuration screen filled out for Extreme Sports

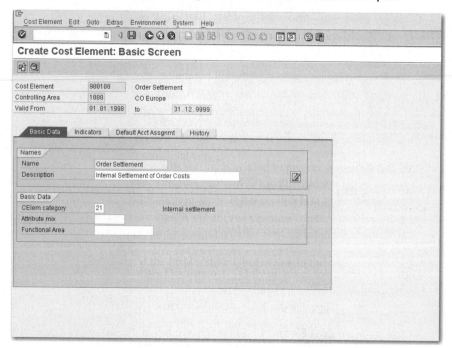

You need to fill in these fields on the Basic Data tab:

**Name**    Enter the name of the cost element.

**Description**    Enter a description of the cost element.

**CElem Category**    Enter the category of the cost element. Use the drop-down box or refer to "Cost Element Types" earlier in this chapter for a listing of possible entries. Remember that the cost element category limits the account's use to specific business transactions, so choose carefully.

**Attribute Mix**    This field is optional. Attributes help to further classify cost elements, but they have no control functionality. That is to say, the attributes do not limit business transactions. Cost element attributes are maintained in the IMG.

**Functional Area**    There are numerous companies that are using functional areas and will link these cost elements to a specific functional area.

Fill in these options on the Indicators tab:

**Record Quantity**    Select this check box if you want to track quantities, as well as currencies, for the cost element.

**Unit of Measure**    If you select Record Quantity, you must provide a unit of measure with which to track the quantities.

Fill in this option on the Default AcctAssignment tab:

**Cost Center or Internal Orders**    This is used if the cost element will be defaulted to a specific cost center and/or internal order for tracking specific costs.

When configuration is complete, save the cost element. Figure 9.12 shows the screen for the filled-out version for Extreme Sports.

**FIGURE 9.12**    Configuration screen for creating a secondary cost element

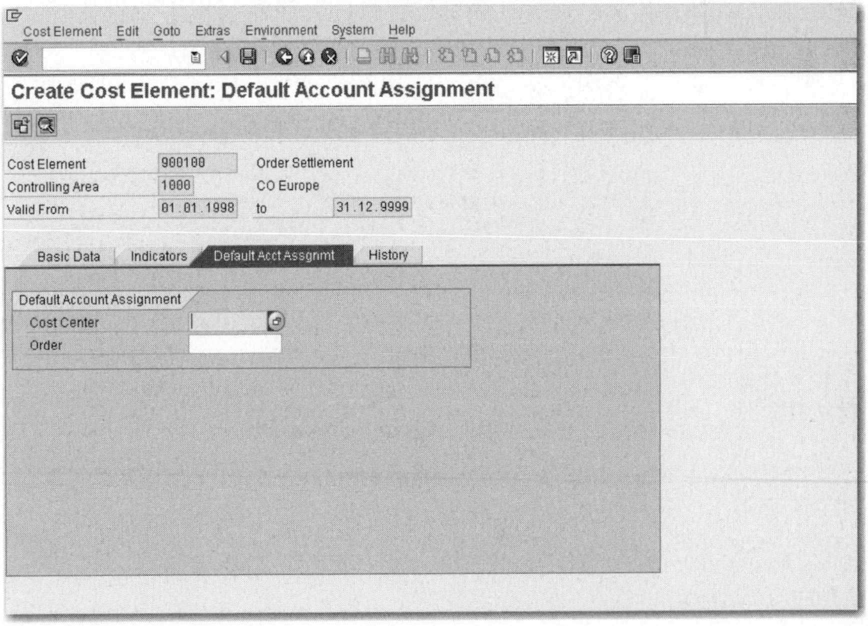

You might be interested in executing another configuration activity, especially if you are looking to report on the cost elements in a certain format. This is the creation of a cost element group (or groups). This approach allows you to organize the cost elements in a formatted hierarchy that can be accessed anytime from the underlying field. To start, you need to access the configuration screen. You can do this by following this menu path from the main menu: Accounting ➤ Controlling ➤ Cost Element Accounting ➤ Master Data ➤ Cost Element Group ➤ Create. Figure 9.13 shows the menu path for the creation of primary and secondary cost element groups. Once this screen is accessed, you would identify a top root node. Normally this is a TEXT entry; then all of the controlling objects, in this case cost elements, would be assigned to this hierarchy. Within the cost element hierarchy, additional summary (text) nodes would be created with the appropriate cost elements assigned to them for reporting purposes.

**FIGURE 9.13**   Menu path to create cost element group(s)

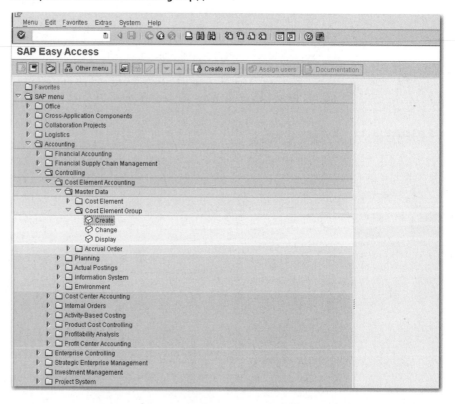

**EXTREME SPORTS COST ELEMENT CONFIGURATION ANALYSIS**

The Extreme Sports FI/CO configuration and master data team decided to not use cost element attributes to classify their cost elements. There was no present need for differentiation in this manner. In addition, the team made a decision to not track quantities in any cost element, whether it is a primary or a secondary element. They chose to use other cost objects, like cost centers and orders, to meet their quantity-tracking requirements.

# Imputed Costs

*[handwritten: X]*

*[handwritten: – 2 Methods – for the expenses which don't accrue in a timely manner]*

Throughout a fiscal year, certain expenses may not accrue in a timely manner, whether they relate to a project, an employee bonus, or a tax bill. To assist in smoothing these irregular costs across multiple periods within the cost accounting environment, SAP provides two methods:

- Recurring entries *[handwritten: = in FI module]*
- Imputed cost calculation *[handwritten: – in CO - module]*

*[handwritten: Diff – ① Origin of Posting]* The distinct difference between the two methods stems from the origin of the postings. The recurring entry posting originates in the FI module, and the imputed cost calculation originates within the CO module. Although both methods are appropriate, a benefit of the imputed cost calculation is its use of actual costs to generate the posting. The recurring entry is fixed at the time of its creation and and the account, posting key, or amount cannot be changed.

Simply stated, the imputed cost calculation accrues a cost based on some surcharge percentage and posts to the cost object (cost center or order) of your choice. No FI update is made at the time of the actual CO imputed cost calculation. When the actual irregular cost is incurred, the transaction will initiate in FI and credit CO for costs already imputed and posted. The net effect in this activity is smoothed over any number of periods and offset with a one-time charge. Any differences in the total amount of imputed charges in CO will be taken against the operating profit of the entity charged.

SAP provides two types of imputed cost calculations:

► Cost element % method

► Target = Actual method

Of the two processes, the cost element % method is easier to maintain and understand, and it will be described in detail. The Target = Actual method is more difficult and requires some level of activity-based planning. The configuration for Target = Actual will not be demonstrated, but basically speaking, the Target = Actual is an iterative process for assigning costs that takes the actual values into account and replaces the estimated values with the actuals once they have been posted.

# Cost Element % Method *– 2 step procen*

The configuration of the cost element % method is a two-step process:

**1.** Create the imputed cost element that will be used to post the costs.

**2.** Maintain the overhead costing sheet for the controlling area.

## Imputed Cost Element Creation *— Primary cost. clem.*

An imputed cost element is a primary cost element and thus requires a G/L account prior to its creation. Refer to Chapter 4, "Accounts Payable," for the exact configuration steps to manually create a G/L account.

> **NOTE**  The G/L account(s) should be set up as an expense account(s). Also, remember to extend the account(s) to all the company codes that will use the calculation.

For the steps necessary to manually create the primary cost element, refer to "Creating Cost Elements Manually" earlier in this chapter. The cost element category to be applied here is 03. Be sure to create the cost elements first because the accounts are necessary to complete the overhead costing sheet.

> **TIP**  It is likely that multiple accounts will be required in most circumstances. Thinking ahead about how and to what level of detail you want the activity tracked will speed up the process.

## Overhead Costing Sheet Creation: Manual

The overhead costing sheet configuration is tied directly to a controlling area because of the link to cost elements, cost centers, and internal orders. All of these are controlling-area-specific objects. During the configuration process, you will assign your controlling area to a costing sheet. You may assign more than one controlling area to a costing sheet because the master data configuration is controlling area specific.

**N O T E** There can be only one active costing sheet per controlling area. If you require multiple versions, you can use subsheets.

To assist you with the manual configuration of the costing sheet, in this section we'll discuss the costing sheet requirements for Extreme Sports.

### EXTREME SPORTS COSTING SHEET DEFINITION CONFIGURATION ANALYSIS

Extreme Sports has decided to use imputed costs to help cost center managers plan taxes and benefits for its staff. Additionally, it wants to accrue a charge on each of its sales cost centers for a bonus to be paid at different points throughout the fiscal year. The bonus is calculated as a percentage of salaries and is charged to the cost center.

Follow the menu path in the IMG – Controlling ➢ Cost Element Accounting ➢ Accrual Calculation ➢ Percentage Method ➢ Maintain Overhead Structure to create the overhead costing sheet. You can also use the transaction code KSAZ to access this information.

After you use one of the transaction configurations, the overhead costing sheet configuration screen appears (see Figure 9.14).

If the table has not been maintained for any other controlling area or costing sheet, only the SAP-delivered sheet, SAP000, will be present. Rather than augment the existing template, we recommend you either copy SAP000 to something you can update or create your own.

To create a new costing sheet, select the create overhead structure icon (F7).

An ID box will appear to ask for the overhead structure ID and description, as shown in Figure 9.15. The ID is alphanumeric and can be up to six characters long. Enter the information and click Save. An empty screen will appear (see Figure 9.16).

**FIGURE 9.14**     The overhead costing sheet configuration screen

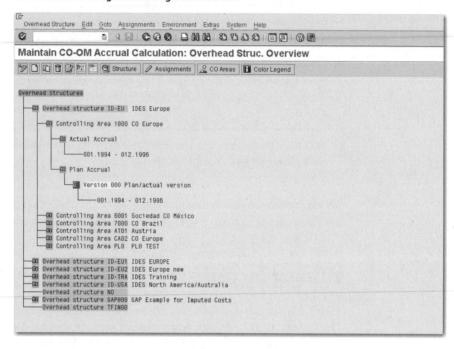

**FIGURE 9.15**     You can create a new costing sheet using the dialog box generated by pressing F7.

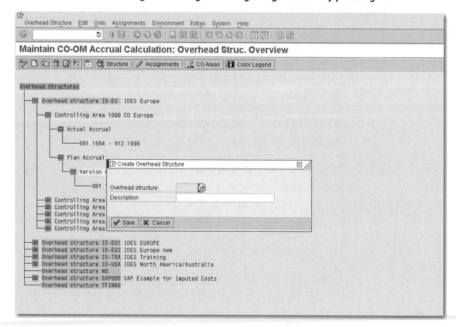

**FIGURE 9.16**    An empty costing sheet detail configuration screen

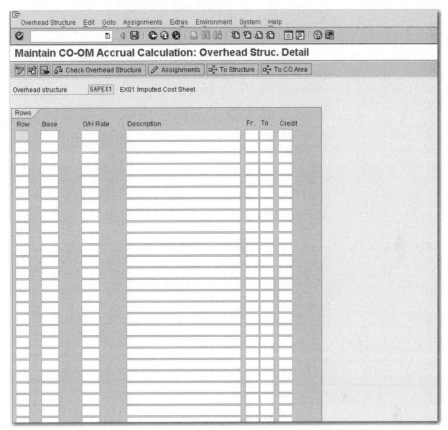

Let's review the columns found within the Row section:

**Row**    Enter a three-digit numeric ID. Be sure to make the frequency of the line items large enough to accommodate for the insertion of additional line items (for example, 010,020,030).

**Base**    Enter a four-character ID denoting the calculation base for the costing sheet. The calculation base determines the cost elements to be used.

**O/H Rate**    Enter a four-character ID denoting the overhead surcharges. It is here that cost centers and surcharge percentages are applied to the formula.

**Description**    Enter a text description of the line, base, or overhead item.

**Fr/To**    Enter a range of reference rows to be used in conjunction with the surcharge percentages.

**Credit**    Enter a three-character ID. The credit is used to assign the offset to the imputed cost posting, once it's calculated, to a company code, business area, and cost center/order. The imputed cost element to be charged is assigned to the credit.

After you create the costing sheet, you'll build upon it as you go along. First, define your calculation base. Then, define your percentage charges, and finally, define what objects will receive the charge.

A few bases are delivered with the system. Use the drop-down box to review and choose one. For Extreme Sports, we will calculate a new base called A-B1—Wages. Enter **A-B1** in the Base field and press Enter.

Because A-B1 is a new base, a Create Calculation box appears after you choose the value in the Restrict Value Range pop-up box (see Figure 9.17). Give the base a name and select Create.

**FIGURE 9.17**    The Restrict Value Range pop-up box

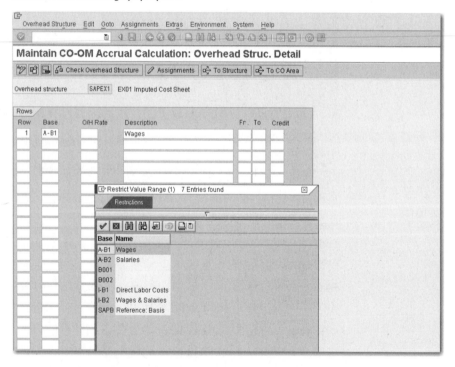

Notice that the new base appears in the detail screen (also shown in Figure 9.17). From the configuration requirements stated earlier, we know that Extreme Sports does not require additional bases. It is a good idea to place a total line in your costing sheet. A total line clearly defines where the calculation base ends, and it can be used as a reference row for surcharge calculation. To enter a total line, enter a line number, a description, and a range of rows, if applicable, in the Fr./To columns. After pressing Enter, you will notice that the line turns red.

As with the base, certain overhead surcharges were delivered with the system and can be used. In the case of Extreme Sports, two new overhead IDs will be created: EXBN (Benefits) and EXBS (Bonus). Enter **EXBN** in the Overhead column field, and press Enter. The Create Overhead screen appears, as shown in Figure 9.18.

**FIGURE 9.18**    The Create Overhead screen

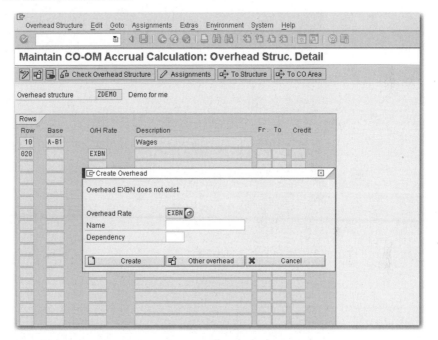

Enter a description of the surcharge and a dependency. Dependencies define the access sequence of the surcharge calculation. Many useful dependencies come predefined. For example, by selecting the dependency KST2 (Cost Center/Controlling Area), you will be able to assign an overall controlling area rate, as well as a varying rate, to individual cost centers. When all your selections are complete, select Create.

**TIP**    For a quicker process, repeat the surcharge creation steps for additional overhead charges now. Maintenance will be easier later.

Enter the line item(s) to be used for the calculation base in the Fr./To columns. In Extreme Sports's case, line 100 is selected for all bases.

The credit will supply the costing sheet with the object to be posted with the credit entry during the planning/actual posting process. Some credit IDs are supplied with the system. To create a new ID, enter the ID number, such as EX1 for Extreme Sports, in the Credit field and press Enter. The Create Credit box appears, as shown in Figure 9.19. Enter a description and click Create.

**FIGURE 9.19**     The Create Credit dialog box

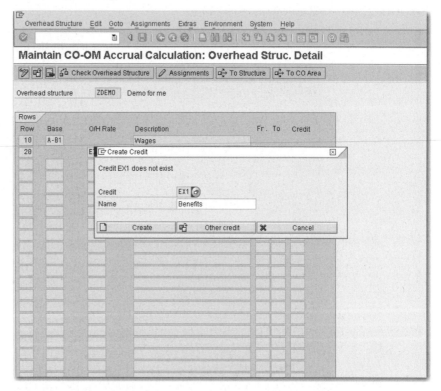

Repeat the process as often as required for your solution. In the case of Extreme Sports, the credit EX2 (Bonus) will also be created. The basics for the overhead costing sheet are now complete. Before you continue, save the sheet. You are now ready to assign the costing sheet and maintain the detail configuration.

**NOTE**   A warning may appear, stating that a controlling area has not been defined. You will be assigning the controlling area next. It's a really good idea to just be safe and save as you go.

## Assign the Costing Sheet to a Controlling Area

At the overhead costing sheet detail configuration screen (shown earlier in Figure 9.14), click the Assignments button. The Select Assignments dialog box appears (see Figure 9.20).

**FIGURE 9.20**　The Select Assignments dialog box

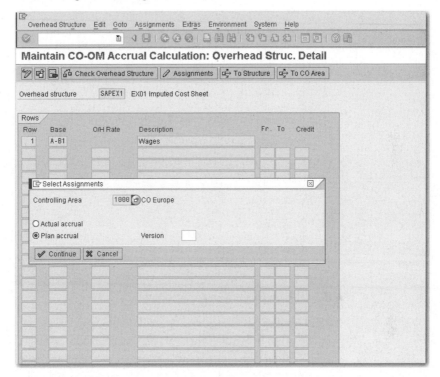

There are four fields to fill out on this screen:

**Controlling Area**　Enter the controlling area that will receive the costing sheet.

**Actual Accrual and Plan Accrual**　Imputed costs can be used for posting plan or actual activity. The assignments are made individually; if you want to maintain both actual and plan postings, you must make two assignments.

**Version**　For the plan assignment, enter a version you would like posted.

Click Continue. The assignments detail screen appears (see Figure 9.21). Validity periods for the costing sheet assignment are determined here.

**FIGURE 9.21**    The assignments detail screen

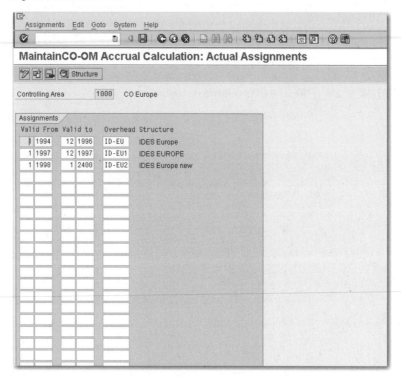

The fields on this screen are as follows:

**Valid From/To**    Enter the range of dates for which the costing sheet assignment will be valid. Remember that only one costing sheet can be valid at any one time for a controlling area. If you want to assign more than one costing sheet, be sure the validity periods do not overlap.

**Overhead**    Enter the ID of the costing sheet to be assigned.

When all the assignments are complete, save the settings. Click the green arrow to move back to the costing sheet detail screen. Repeat the steps, if necessary, to assign validity periods for both the actual and planned imputed cost calculations. For Extreme Sports, both will be made.

## Maintain the Base Calculation

To make the cost element assignment to the base calculation ID (A-B1), double-click the ID. The cost element assignment screen, shown in Figure 9.22, appears.

**FIGURE 9.22**    You can review your settings after clicking the save icon in the cost element assignment screen.

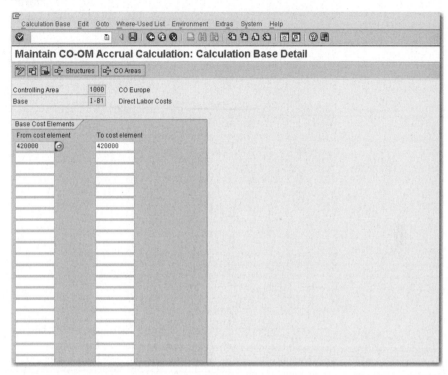

Enter either a single cost element or a varying range of cost elements in the Fr./To Cost Element fields and then save the settings. Click the green arrow to move back to the costing sheet detail configuration screen.

## Maintain the Overhead Surcharge

To assign the overhead rates and make any cost-center–specific percentage assignments, double-click the overhead ID (for example, EXBN or EXBS or any other overhead surcharge ID, in this case IZ11). The surcharge assignment screen appears, shown in Figure 9.23. Notice in the Header section that there's a Controlling Area/ Overhead Rate setting and there could also be a Controlling Area/Overhead Rate/ Cost Center setting.

If you want to have a blanket rate for all cost centers in the controlling area, maintain only the Controlling Area/Overhead Rate section. However, if you would like to override the rate with a special rate for specific cost centers, maintain the Controlling Area/Overhead Rate/Cost Center section. You will find both buttons in the Condition section of the screen (see Figure 9.23).

**FIGURE 9.23**    The saved settings for controlling area/surcharge

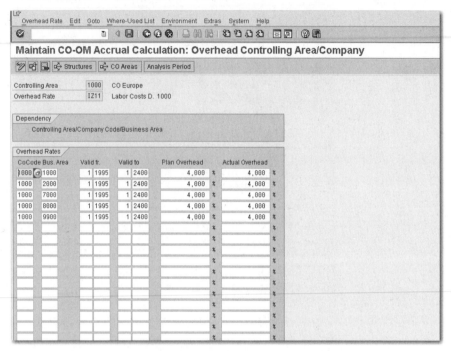

The fields on the controlling area/surcharge screen are as follows:

**Valid Fr./To**    Enter the valid period range for the surcharge percentages.

**Plan Overhead**    If you will be using the plan imputed cost calculation during planning, enter the monthly rate at which you want overhead charged to a cost center.

**Actual Overhead**    If you will be using the actual imputed cost calculation during period end closing, enter the monthly rate at which you want overhead charged to a cost center.

Save the settings when you're finished. To apply specific rates to select cost centers, select the Controlling Area/Surcharge Type/Cost Center condition button.

**NOTE**    If you want to apply specific rates to cost centers, you will have to save the controlling area rates first.

You'll find the following fields on the controlling area/surcharge/cost center screen:

**Cost Center**    Enter the number of the cost center to receive the special rate. Enter as many lines as you need.

**Valid From/To**    Enter the validity period for the cost center/rate relationship. It is possible for a single cost center to have multiple rates within a fiscal year if you properly sequence the validity periods.

**Plan Overhead**    If you will be using the planned imputed cost calculation during planning, enter the monthly rate at which you want overhead charged to a cost center.

**Actual Overhead**    If you will be using the actual imputed cost calculation during a period end closing, enter the monthly rate at which you want overhead charged to a cost center.

Figure 9.24 shows the saved controlling area/surcharge/cost center configuration. Save the settings and click the green arrow to move back to the costing sheet detail configuration screen to maintain the credit IDs.

**FIGURE 9.24**    The saved controlling area/surcharge/cost center configuration

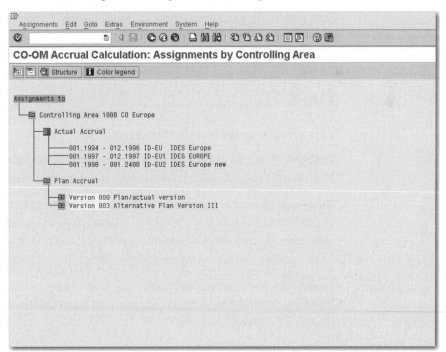

## Maintain Credit Calculations

The credit assignment determines which cost object will receive the offsetting credit entry when the imputed costs are posted. Double-click any of the credit IDs created. The credit detail configuration screen appears (Figure 9.25 shows the screen filled out for Extreme Sports).

**FIGURE 9.25**   The credit detail screen filled out for Extreme Sports

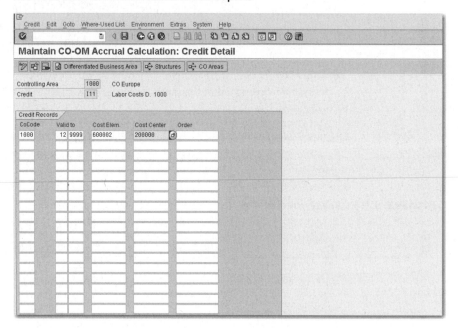

Let's take a look at the fields on this screen:

**CoCode**   Enter the company code ID of the company to receive the credit entry. The company code should correspond with the cost center assignment in the low.

**Bus. Area**   Enter the business area ID if you are tracking activity in this manner. Remember that business areas can receive cross-company code postings. In our particular case, the business area is not being used for this tracking process. Notice that you need to select the Differentiated Business area Button to use this parameter.

**Valid To**   Enter the fiscal month and year that represents the last valid period for the credit assignment.

**Cost Elem.**    Enter the imputed cost element that will receive both the credit and debit imputed cost posting. The cost element chosen here will post to the cost centers selected in the preceding section (see Figure 9.21).

**Cost Center**    Enter the ID of the cost center, if used, that will receive the offsetting credit posting. The cost center chosen should be the same one that receives the debit cost object assignment when the actual expense is incurred in FI.

**Order**    Enter the ID of the order, if used, that will receive the offsetting credit posting. The order category of the object will be 02 and must be configured specifically for this purpose. Be sure that the same order receives the debit cost object assignment when the expense is incurred in Fl.

**TIP**    You can have only one unique combination of cost element to cost center or order per validity period.

When configuration is complete, save the settings. The imputed cost calculation settings are complete and ready for testing. Experiment with different combinations of settings until the desired posting results are achieved. To test the settings, run the imputed cost calculation for either cost center/order planning or actual postings.

## Overhead Costing Sheet Creation: Copy

An alternative to creating a new costing sheet is to copy the SAP-delivered sheet SAP000 and use it as a template.

**TIP**    Copying SAP-delivered objects and making adjustments to the copies is always recommended.

To copy the SAP-delivered sheet SAP000, follow the menu path Controlling ➢ Cost Element Accounting ➢ Accrual Calculation ➢ Percentage Method ➢ Maintain Overhead Structure. You can also use the transaction code KSAZ to offer access to the end user.

In the cost maintenance screen that appears, place the cursor on the overhead structure line and click the Copy Costing Sheet button (F6). The Copy Overhead Structure input box appears (see Figure 9.26). Enter an alphanumeric ID and description for your costing sheet. You can use up to six characters. When finished, select Save.

**FIGURE 9.26**    The Copy Overhead Structure dialog box

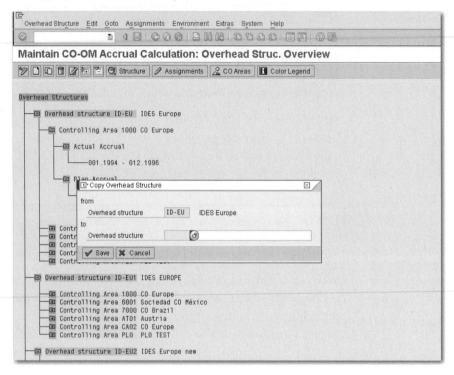

The imputed costing sheet detail screen will appear. Because you copied an existing sheet, some default entries show up. If the entries do not meet your requirements, they can be easily deleted. From this point, refer to the sections earlier in this chapter on manual costing sheet creation for assistance in maintaining the copied template.

# Reconciliation Ledger

One of the more important areas of CO configuration is the development of the reconciliation ledger. Among its many uses is the ability to keep activity within the FI G/L in balance with the CO module. The reconciliation ledger tracks all activity within the CO module at a summarized level (to be used for reporting and reconciliation purposes). Activities that occur in CO can be reported by object class and/or object type (shown in Tables 9.1 and 9.2). This process is affected by the NEW GL process. This will be discussed in Chapter 7, "New GL Accounting."

**TABLE 9.1**  Object Classes

| Object Classes | Description |
|---|---|
| OCOST | Overhead costs |
| INVST | Investments |
| PRODT | Production |
| PROFT | Profit and sales |

**TABLE 9.2**  Object Types

| Object Types |
|---|
| Cost center |
| Order |
| Cost object |
| Network |
| Reconciliation object |
| Sales document item |
| Project structure |
| Business process |

It is important to understand how each classification can be used. Object types are used within the various CO information systems to report summary and line item activity. Some object types can support many different object classes, and others can support just one. The object types cost center, cost object, reconciliation object, and sales document item all have fixed class assignments that cannot be varied. All other object types can have classes assigned by the users. There are a few rules to keep in mind:

- ▶ Cost center will always be associated with OCOST.
- ▶ Cost object will always be associated with PRODT.
- ▶ Reconciliation object will always be associated with PROFT.
- ▶ Sales document will always be associated with PRODT.

Like the object type, the object class is also used for reconciliation ledger reporting. By correctly identifying the object class on all object types, you can get an accurate view of all operating activity within the CO module. A good example of the need for accuracy in the assignment is the INVST class.

INVST can be used to identify and report all capitalization activity for a controlling area. When costs are capitalized through an investment internal order in CO, depending on the settlement configuration, the original debited account may not receive the offsetting credit during settlement. The result on the FI side is a trial balance with some capitalized costs reported in its operating account balances. If the object class INVST is used properly, an accountant could use the reconciliation ledger to determine how much of an operating account balance was capitalized.

The reconciliation ledger is utilized as a conduit for the FI G/L to access the cost accounting assignment on all its operating postings. Remember that the only organizational unit posted to in FI is the company code.

## PURPOSES OF THE RECONCILIATION LEDGER: EXAMPLE 1

When you need to drill back from the FI G/L to find which cost center was posted to on an expense account, the reconciliation ledger is accessed.

The need to have a CO-to-FI reconciliation process is a result of cross-company code, cross-business area, or cross-functional area activity that may occur in the CO module. Order settlement or confirmation, cost center assessment, or other internal CO movement may initiate these postings. When costs are moved internally within CO, the FI G/L is not updated because of CO's use of secondary cost elements to facilitate the postings.

The first two steps in reconciliation ledger configuration are to activate the ledger within the controlling area and assign a document type. If you have an existing controlling area that does not have the reconciliation ledger activated, follow the instructions in the next section. For all newly created controlling areas, the reconciliation ledger is automatically activated.

## PURPOSES OF THE RECONCILIATION LEDGER: EXAMPLE 2

A goods receipt posting of $100 has occurred on internal order 1, which is assigned to company code 1. One hundred percent of the value of internal order 1 is settled to internal order 2, which is assigned to company code 2. A settlement cost element is used for the settlement posting. When an order settlement is run, internal order 1 is credited ($100) and internal order 2 is debited $100. The balances of internal order 1 and internal order 2 are $0 and $100, respectively. However, the balances of company code 1 and 2 remain as they were prior to settlement. The reason: The settlement activity was internal to CO. No FI update occurred.

To place the FI company codes back in balance, the CO-FI reconciliation posting transaction should be run. The resulting FI postings would credit company code 1 for ($100) and debit company code 2 for $100. The internal CO activity will now have been accounted for in FI, and the company codes are now in balance.

# Activate Reconciliation Ledger

To get to the Activate Reconciliation Ledger screen, follow the menu path Controlling ➢ Cost Element Accounting ➢ Reconciliation Ledger ➢ Activate/ Deactivate Reconciliation Ledger or use the transaction code KALA.

The Activate Reconciliation Ledger screen is shown in Figure 9.27.

**FIGURE 9.27**    The Activate Reconciliation Ledger screen

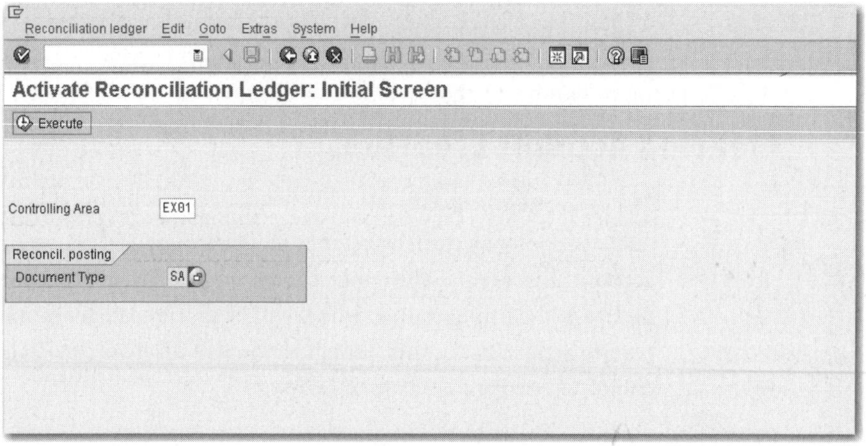

The fields in this screen are as follows:

**Controlling Area**   Enter the ID of the controlling area in which you want to activate the reconciliation ledger.

**Document Type**   Enter the ID of the document type with which you want all reconciliation postings marked. Review the section on document types found in Chapter 4 for some insight into document type configuration. It may be helpful, for analysis purposes, to provide reconciliation postings with their own document type.

Execute the settings when complete. If you were unsure and attempted to activate a previously activated reconciliation ledger, the system will return an error. If not, the ledger is now activated.

For newly created controlling areas, the reconciliation ledger will have been automatically activated, but a document type will not yet be maintained. The assignment of the reconciliation document type to the controlling area will complete the controlling area and basic data settings. To maintain the assignment of the controlling area, follow the menu path Controlling ➤ Controlling General ➤ Organization ➤ Maintain Controlling Area. You can also use the transaction code OKKP to access this screen.

The basic data overview screen appears. The screen should look familiar; it was accessed during the base controlling area configuration in Chapter 8, "Controlling Enterprise Structure." Double-click the controlling area to be maintained. On the screen (Figure 9.28), scroll down until you find the field Document Type. Enter the ID of the reconciliation document type you prefer. The document type selected will provide the number range for the FI update, so choose carefully. If you like, you can configure a new document type to allow for the analysis of reconciliation postings in this manner (see Chapter 4). Save the settings when complete.

## Clearing Account Creation

The reconciliation ledger requires, at minimum, two clearing accounts to post: one intercompany clearing balance sheet account and one reconciliation expense account. There is also the option to add varying layers of account assignment complexity to the configuration, which will be discussed later in this chapter. The intercompany clearing account configuration was discussed in Chapter 4 and should be complete. See Figure 9.29 for a review.

**FIGURE 9.28**  The basic data screen

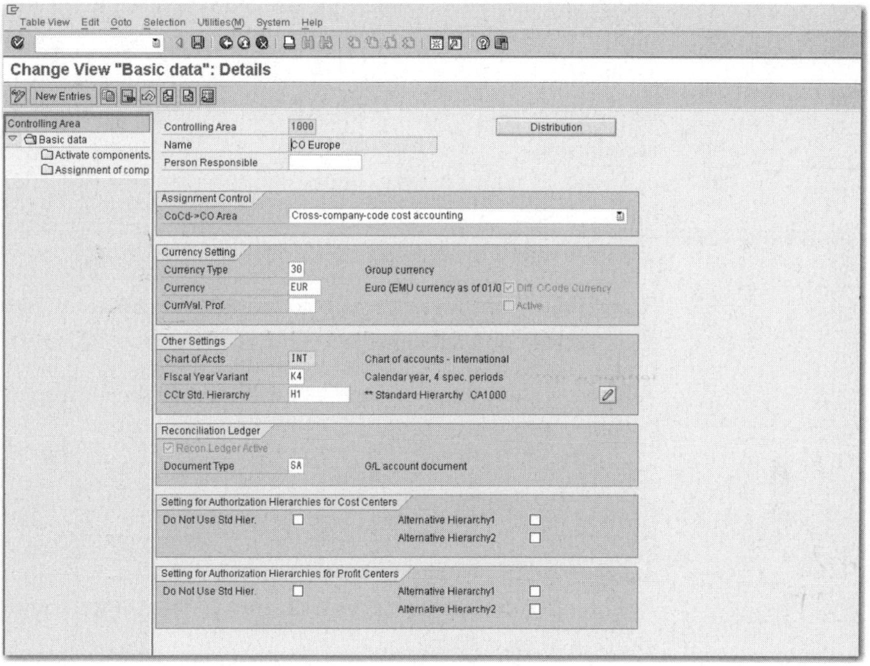

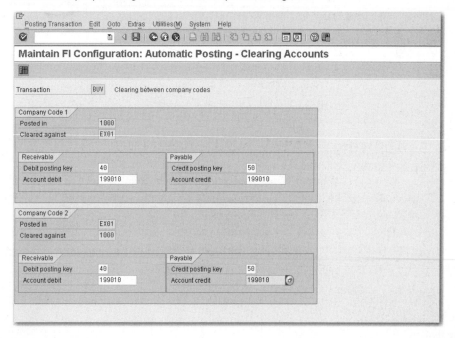

**FIGURE 9.29**  The intercompany clearing account has already been configured.

During the CO-to-FI reconciliation process, the intercompany clearing accounts will be automatically credited and debited. The offset to the intercompany clearing will be the expense account you are about to create. Keep in mind that the account(s) must be represented in the FI P&L (Profit and Loss) for the operating activity to be properly reported. Ask yourself some questions before creating the accounts:

- ► How does management want to see reconciliation activity reported?

- ► Do I need to segregate the reconciliation postings by activity or object class?

- ► How much cross-company code, cross-business area, or cross-functional area activity do I anticipate?

Answering these questions up front will ease the remaining configuration process.

Extreme Sports has decided to add some complexity and track reconciliation activity with three accounts: the first will be used to report investment settlement postings, the second will report production activity, and the third will catch everything else.

Refer to Chapter 4 for the steps to create a G/L account. Here are some notes to be aware of when creating the account:

- ► It is recommended that you use a special account group when creating the reconciliation accounts. The unique account range will make it easier to pick up the activity in reporting.

- ► The account should be created as a P&L account.

- ► Remember to extend the account to all the company codes within the controlling area.

- ► Do not create a corresponding cost element. Reconciliation postings occur only in FI.

Figure 9.30 shows an example of one of the accounts to be used by Extreme Sports.

When all accounts have been created and extended to the company codes, you can begin defining the accounts for automatic posting.

**FIGURE 9.30**    One of the accounts in Extreme Sports's G/L

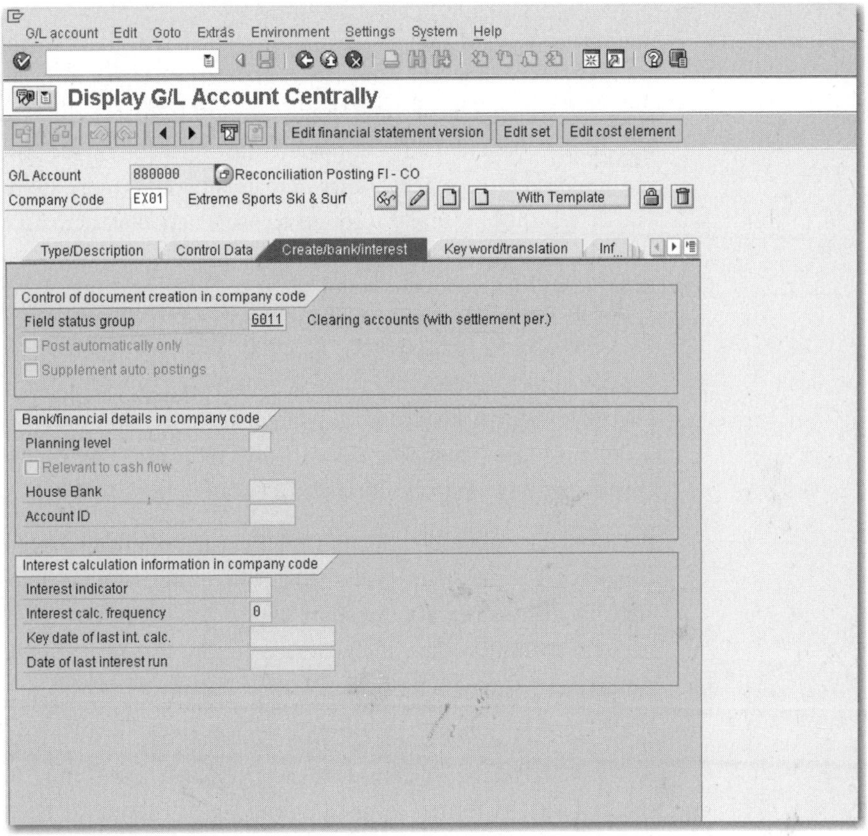

## EXTREME SPORTS RECONCILIATION ACCOUNTS CONFIGURATION ANALYSIS

Extreme Sports will be using three accounts to track reconciliation activity:

- ▶ 880000Investment Reconciliation
- ▶ 880100Production Reconciliation
- ▶ 880110CO-FI General Reconciliation

Management prefers to see the activities segregated on the company code P&L.

# Maintain Accounts for Automatic Reconciliation Posting

Automatic account assignment was discussed in detail in Chapter 4. The same concepts apply to automatic reconciliation postings. Depending on the level of detail required, adjustment account usage can vary from just one account to over one hundred accounts for all postings. In most cases, one is too few, and in all cases, one hundred is too many. Somewhere in between is more appropriate. But how do you determine how many accounts to use? A good place to find the answer is to look at the rules applicable to the process key.

Rules are indicators that you set to control how automated postings can occur in the system. Refer to Chapter 3, "General Ledger," if you need to, for a detailed discussion of process keys and rules. A process key provides a unique set of rules that control how the system can be updated. The process key for reconciliation ledger activity is CO1. Potentially, there are four indicators that can be set for CO1: debit/credit, costing scope (object class), CO Transaction (activity), and Default.

In addition, any combination of the rules can be activated to provide even greater complexity. More will be explained as the configuration is described. Begin by entering the reconciliation account assignment repository after following the menu path Controlling ➤ Cost Element Accounting ➤ Reconciliation Ledger ➤ Define Adjustment Accounts for Reconciliation Posting ➤ Define Accounts for Automatic Postings, or use the transaction code OBYB.

A pop-up box appears asking for the chart of accounts to be entered. Adjustment account activity for the reconciliation ledger is maintained at the chart level and is thus active for the entire client. Keep this in mind when account choices are being made.

**NOTE**  The settings for the reconciliation adjustment accounts are maintained at the chart of accounts level—they are controlling area independent.

Enter the name of the chart of accounts in the field requested and press Enter. The automatic posting configuration screen appears (see Figure 9.31).

Because no rules indicators have been set, the default rule of one account setting is active. If only one adjustment account is desired for all reconciliation activity, enter the account on this screen and click the save icon. If not, select the Change Account Determin. button. The automatic posting rules configuration screen appears (see Figure 9.32).

**FIGURE 9.31**    The automatic posting configuration screen

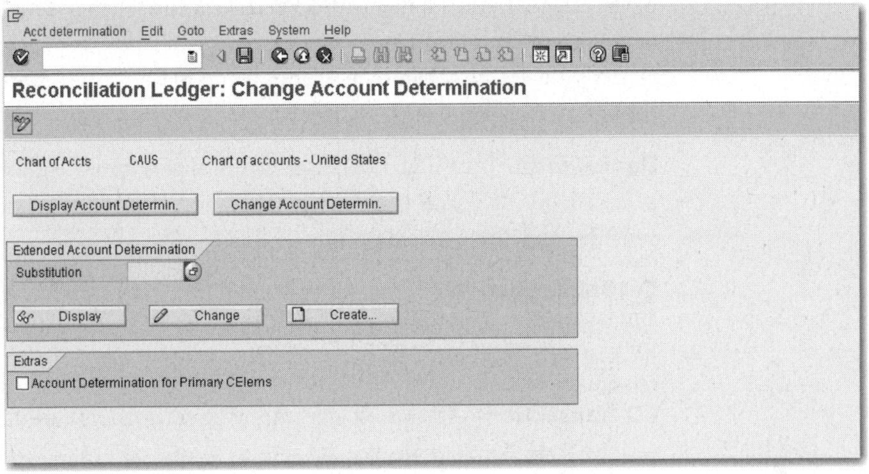

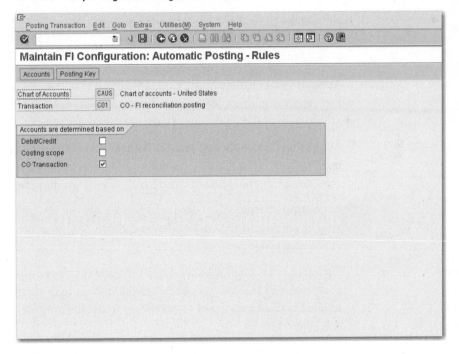

**FIGURE 9.32**    The automatic posting rules configuration screen

Any one of the rules indicators can be set individually or in combination with any of the others. In the following descriptions of the settings, *level* refers to the amount of detail associated with an account assignment rule. The highest level can be associated with a minimal amount of choice and maintenance. Here are descriptions of the various settings:

**Debit/Credit**   At a high level, this setting allows for potentially two accounts to be assigned: one debit account and one credit account. If Debit/Credit is set, SAP will provide you with two fields to fill.

**Costing Scope**   The next level of detail down from Debit/Credit. You define an adjustment account for each of the four object classes: Investment, Production, Profitability, and Overhead Cost.

**CO Transaction**   The lowest level. Adjustment accounts are assigned at the CO activity level. An example of a CO activity would be KOAO: Order Settlement.

When activating combinations of these rules, keep in mind the maintenance level involved:

**Activating Debit/Credit and Costing Scope**   You must maintain an adjustment account for both the debit and credit posting for each object class. There are eight assignments in total.

**Activating Debit/Credit and CO Transaction**   You must maintain an adjustment account for both debit and credit postings for each CO activity. With 25 CO activities times the 2 debit/credit indicators, there are 50 assignments in total.

**Activating Costing Scope and CO Transaction**   You must maintain an adjustment account for each unique grouping of CO activity and object class. With 25 activities times 4 object classes, there are 100 assignments in total.

**Activating all rules**   You must maintain adjustment accounts for each unique grouping of Debit/Credit indicator/object class/CO Transaction. The total number of potential assignments is 200.

The complexity certainly builds quickly. Whatever you decide, select one, some, or none, and click the save icon. In the case of Extreme Sports, Costing Scope will be selected to allow tracking by object class. The account assignment screen appears (see Figure 9.33).

**FIGURE 9.33**    The account assignment screen

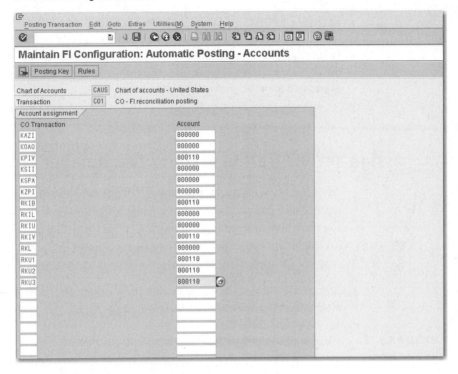

Make the following entries:

**Costing Scope**    Enter the relevant cost objects one time each in a field.

**Account**    Enter the proper adjustment account.

When you're finished, save the settings. At this point, reconciliation ledger account assignment activity is complete. The final step in the CO-FI reconciliation ledger configuration is assigning a number range.

**WARNING**    Once you make the adjustment account settings, you should think through the changes. Until you make postings with these settings, you can change them. After activity has occurred and you make a rule change, all prior account assignments are lost forever.

## Assign Reconciliation Activity to a Number Range

As with every activity in the CO module, a number range must be assigned to the reconciliation postings. The number range assignment is at the controlling area level. Use the following menu path to begin: Controlling ➤ Cost Element Accounting ➤ Reconciliation Ledger ➤ Specify Document Number Range for Reconciliation Postings. Or you can use the transaction code OK13 to access this screen.

After you use one of the configuration transactions, the reconciliation ledger document number range screen appears (see Figure 9.34).

**FIGURE 9.34**    The reconciliation ledger document number range screen

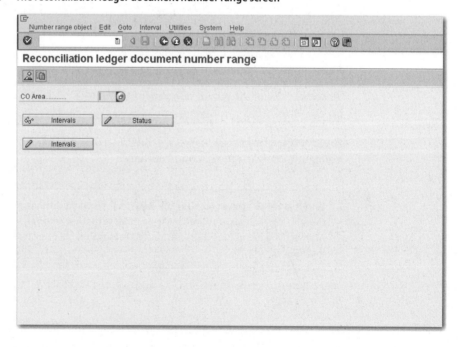

There are two methods to assigning a number range interval: create your own or copy an existing range. The recommended approach is to copy from an existing controlling area if one is available. To copy the interval, select the copy icon. A pop-up box labeled Copy: CO Area appears (see Figure 9.35).

**FIGURE 9.35**    The Copy: CO Area dialog box

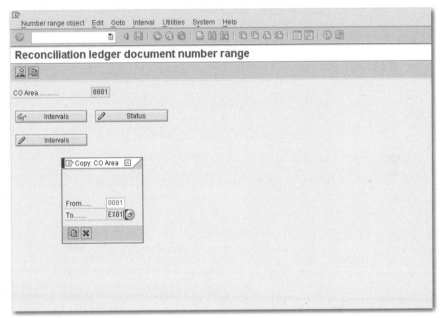

Enter the following data:

**From**    Enter the ID of the controlling area to provide the range.

**To**    Enter the ID of the controlling area to receive the number range interval.

Click the copy icon when complete. A memo box may appear, warning you that number ranges should not be transported but rather maintained manually within each client. Press Enter to complete the transaction. The number range has been copied.

If you are maintaining the first controlling area in your client, you must manually create the interval. A similar process occurred when you maintained the controlling area document number range in Chapter 8. In the reconciliation ledger document number range screen, enter the ID for the controlling area to receive the interval in the CO Area field.

Select the Change Intervals button (with the pencil icon) found in the middle of the screen. The maintain number range intervals screen appears. Select the Insert

Interval button (icon with the plus sign) to maintain the number range, and an interval entry box will appear (see Figure 9.36).

**FIGURE 9.36** The Insert Interval dialog box

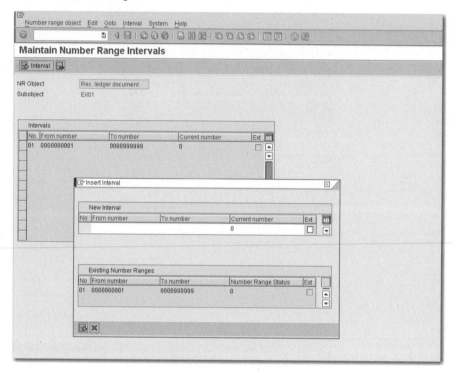

Here are the fields in the Insert Interval dialog box:

**No.** Enter the two-digit alphanumeric ID of the number range.

**From Number** Enter the lower end of the number range. Use up to 10 digits.

**To Number** Enter the upper limit of the number range. Again, use up to 10 digits.

**Current Number** If you would like to start at a number other than the From number, enter that number here.

**Ext** Select whether you would like the user to determine the document number at the time of entry.

**TIP** Whenever possible, allow the system to determine the number range.

When the settings are complete, click the Insert button or press Enter. The number range interval will appear (see Figure 9.37). Save the settings when complete.

**FIGURE 9.37**    The number range object screen

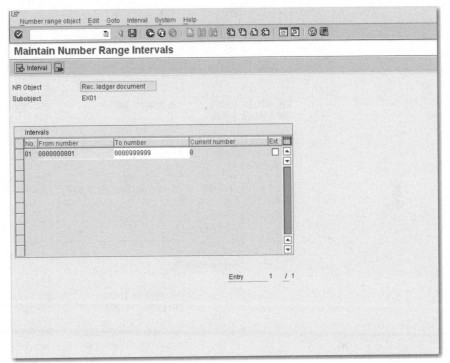

Reconciliation ledger configuration is finished. The system is now capable of successfully running the CO-FI reconciliation transaction. Although understanding how to configure the CO-FI reconciliation is important, it is equally important to know how the resulting transactions flow. The next section will touch briefly on this subject.

## Reconciliation Ledger Cost Flows

When thinking about reconciliation postings, remember that updates occur only in the FI module. No postings will occur in CO as a result of the CO-FI transaction. The reason is that the cross-company, cross-business area, or cross-functional area activity has already happened in CO. The purpose of the reconciliation ledger is to put FI back in balance with CO, not the other way around. To illustrate, Figure 9.38 gives an example of how a cross-company order settlement in CO is balanced in FI.

**FIGURE 9.38** The cross-company order settlement flows from CO to FI and balances.

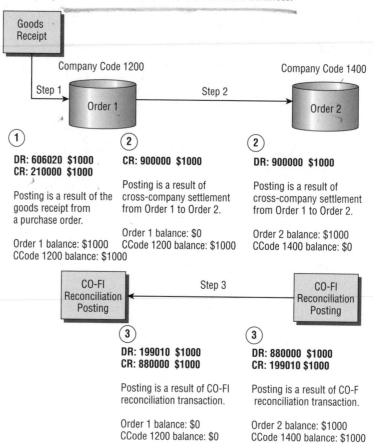

Notice how the cross-company settlement, step 2, does not require a posting to an intercompany account. CO tracks only cost accounting activity. All balance sheet activity is maintained in the FI ledger only. CO will allow a two-sided entry, with each side residing in a different company code. The same scenario could be detailed for both business area and functional area postings. When the CO-FI reconciliation transaction is run, as seen in step 3, the intercompany postings are made automatically. There is no need to keep the companies in balance through manual journal entries.

Now that the reconciliation postings have been detailed, a further discussion of CO cost accounting updates is in order.

# Explanation of CO Updates

*how costs flow through to module* [handwritten annotation]

One of the more difficult and critical SAP topics to learn is how costs flow through the CO module. The concepts of object type, object class, and real versus statistical postings are foreign to most individuals. The key to understanding this is to recognize that CO activity is tracked for management reporting only. It is not subject to statutory accounting or reporting requirements. The CO module is governed by the rules of cost accounting assignments and internal/external movements. Of these concepts, internal CO activity movements are possibly the most difficult to understand. Just remember that if you have posted $1,000,000.00 into CO and assigned a cost object and cost element to these postings, if you run a CO report you will not increase or decrease the total amount that you have posted. CO doesn't create any additional postings.

Internal CO movements include, among others, order settlement, cost center assessments, and internal activity allocations. Internal movements are defined as those activities that move cost from one object type to another, without any FI update. External movements can involve movements from an object type in CO to an object in FI. An example would be a settlement from an internal order to a fixed asset. Because the movement is external to CO, a real G/L account would have to be involved for an FI update to occur.

## Real vs. Statistical Postings

The flexibility of SAP can be observed when you look at the software's ability to track cost accounting information. A complete account assignment in CO includes both a cost element and a real cost object. It is the cardinal rule in SAP that every cost accounting transaction must have one, and only one, real cost object assignment. Only real postings are reported in the CO reconciliation ledger. Here are some examples of real cost objects:

- ▶ Cost center
- ▶ Real internal order
- ▶ Profitability segment
- ▶ Sales order

Extending its reporting capabilities, SAP also allows you to assign a second cost object (or more) to any cost accounting transaction. Now, the cardinal rule doesn't change when you add the second cost object. Only one of the objects will receive a real posting. The second object's posting is not real but instead is considered statistical. The uses for statistical activity are limited to analysis and reporting. They cannot be acted upon directly by any other SAP transaction. All updates must occur in conjunction with a real object posting. The total number of statistical postings are directly related to the number of different ways that you are looking to track the information.

## AN EXAMPLE OF REAL VS. STATISTICAL POSTINGS

Say a journal entry is made to correct some expense activity on cost center 1000. Within the transaction, costs are credited to cost center 1000 and debited to both cost center 2000 and internal order 3000 (assuming that the internal order is "real").

Two real cost objects are included in the debit side of the transaction. Only one of these objects can receive the posting in the CO reconciliation ledger. The other will receive a statistical posting. In this case, cost center 2000 will be the recipient of the statistical update. We have seen where a company will track specific postings using as many as four different postings; only one is real and the others are statistical.

To support two real objects being included in a single transaction, SAP has hard-coded the real-versus-statistical relationship. SAP will determine which object receives the real update and which receives the statistical update. The relationship is fixed and cannot be acted upon by the user. The following are some of these posting relationships:

**Cost center and internal order (real)**   The order receives the real posting.

**Cost center and sales order**   The sales order receives the real posting.

**Cost center and project**   The project receives the real posting.

**Profitability segment and any other object**   The profitability segment *always* receives the real posting.

**Internal order and sales order**   To post to both, the internal order must be statistical.

With any rule, there are always exceptions. In many instances, you will find that a transaction has more than two postings, and this is, as mentioned, dependent upon the tracking objects that have been turned on in the system. For example, if you were to create a journal entry to debit a cost center, profitability segment, and a statistical internal order, the transaction would post because the internal order is statistical. A statistical object maintains special properties that preclude it from being recognized during the transaction.

Like a real object, a statistical object can be used in all reporting and analysis functions. It cannot be posted to directly, however. The differences between a statistical posting to a real object and a statistical posting to a statistical object are minimal. The main variance is the object type. Real objects can be used individually. Statistical objects must be accompanied by a real object assignment in any transaction.

*Value Types*

SAP differentiates real versus statistical posting by tagging each CO transaction with a value type. There are numerous value types available in the system, many of which will be discussed in later chapters. Here is a quick list of recognized types:

- ► Actual costs
- ► Plan costs
- ► Actual statistical costs
- ► Plan statistical costs
- ► Commitments
- ► Variances
- ► Target costs

Notice that SAP segregates statistical postings. In this manner, the system allows for distinct reporting of actual real and actual statistical costs.

**TIP**   When line item activity within CO is analyzed, the value type can be displayed for each item. Actual line items will have a value type of 04. Statistical items will have a value type of 11.

## Corrections and Other Topics

When you're making corrections that involve statistical updates, it is always recommended that you reverse the original document. If reversal is not possible, it is important that any manual corrections include all the objects originally posted. If you are tracking activity through statistical postings, you must have a unique reporting requirement. If an object is missed during the correction, the reporting will be inaccurate. These will be critical steps in the next set of chapters when we link the actual postings to the cost objects.

A second recommendation is to not post operating expenses directly to Profitability Analysis (CO-PA). Remember, when posting to a cost center in Cost Center Accounting (CCA), and a segment in CO-PA, the CO-PA posting is always real. If an error was found, the manual correction activity can be cumbersome because of the level of detail required to properly update CO-PA. The recommended approach to transferring costs to CO-PA from CCA is through cost center assessments. Of course, there are exceptions to this rule—for example, if a specific expense is not being posted to a cost center but needs to be used for analysis and validation, then you can post the expense directly to CO-PA. An example of this might be some exceptional expense against a sales order—freight or special handling. Assessments will be covered in detail in Chapter 10.

# Summary

This chapter provided a solid background into the basics of overhead cost controlling and cost element accounting. Understanding the cost accounting effects of the various settings will be invaluable as you continue your configuration. Remember to pay attention to object types when creating new cost objects. The benefit from proper definition will be seen in the reconciliation ledger reporting. Also keep in mind the established cost object relationships when posting to two cost objects simultaneously in a single transaction.

Remember that without the correct cost element architecture the posting process will be very challenging. The cost element assignment is the one core object within Cost Accounting that will follow the posting through the process and also create the link between CO and FI postings. Make sure you look to create both cost and revenue elements since both are used quite frequently and trying to post revenue to a fake cost element will be difficult to work with. The overall maintenance of this situation outweighs the amount of time it takes to work through the appropriate configuration initially.

# Cost Center Accounting

**FEATURING:**

▶ **INTRODUCTION TO COST CENTER ACCOUNTING CONFIGURATION**

▶ **COST CENTER ACCOUNT STANDARD HIERARCHY**

▶ **CONTROLLING AREA/PROFIT CENTER ACCOUNTING MAINTENANCE**

▶ **COST CENTER BASICS**

▶ **ACTIVITY TYPES AND STATISTICAL KEY FIGURES**

▶ **ASSESSMENTS, DISTRIBUTIONS, AND REPOSTINGS**

▶ **COST CENTER ACCOUNTING: PLANNING**

▶ **ASSIGNING ACCOUNTS AUTOMATICALLY IN CO**

Cost Center Accounting (CCA) is utilized within SAP to collect and report operating activity within an organizational unit. Within CCA, three separate master data objects can capture operational expenses: cost centers, activity types, and statistical key figures. Cost centers are maintained within a hierarchy that is representative of the implementing company's internal reporting/accountability structure. The hierarchy development is central to all cost-accounting reporting within the CO module and will be discussed early in this chapter.

Understanding the differences between master data and transactional data is important, and we'll outline the key topics in this chapter. Another important concept is the data flow within CO objects and how they are posted and processed; therefore, we will discuss this in detail in this chapter. A key piece of functionality within CCA is the ability to process allocations quickly. Through the use of the two methods of allocations, assessments, and distributions, the user has the ability to quickly process hundreds of cost allocations across numerous organizational units. This can be completed either automatically or manually. In addition, one of the key responsibilities of CO is the planning process and its entire infrastructure, which is vital to an effective operational accounting environment and will be dealt with in detail. Lastly, we'll introduce the concept of CO automatic account assignment and document its configuration.

The process will begin with an introduction to Cost Center Accounting.

# Introduction to Cost Center Accounting Configuration

Besides the configuration of Cost Element Accounting, Cost Center Accounting is the most used component of CO when it comes to tracking costs. Configuring the Cost Center Accounting (CCA) module is a combination of table settings and master data development. The key to properly marrying the two is a good understanding of the organization's reporting requirements. How are operating costs supposed to flow through the organization? Does the company collect costs centrally and allocate at the end of the month, or should costs flow directly to the responsibility center? How detailed of an analysis process is there? As with most things dealing with SAP, it depends.

The key development area within the CCA module is the *standard hierarchy,* which will become your main tool for reporting operating costs. All cost centers must be assigned to a node on the standard hierarchy. In addition to cost centers, you can develop activity types to assist in calculating internal activity costs. Activity types

*Cardamom hill* (handwritten)

are assigned to a cost center and, with the help of the activity rates, utilize actual activity quantities to determine the activity cost per cost center. Again, regardless of whether you are charging your costs by a rate or by an amount, you will be using one or more of these objects to see the data post into Cost Center Accounting.

A third piece of master data (after cost centers and activity types) used in CCA is the statistical *key figure*, which is used to track quantities and values for various operating activities. The statistical nature of the master data allows the user to manipulate the data without causing inconsistencies. Uses for key figures range from reporting/analysis to utilization as a tracing factor in allocations and planning processes.

*Statistical key figure* (handwritten margin note)

# Cost Center Accounting Standard Hierarchy

Prior to creating any cost centers within your controlling area, you must first complete the standard hierarchy, which is the central cost center hierarchy created in your system and acts as the one repository for all cost centers. You can create additional, or alternative, hierarchies to meet additional planning or reporting requirements and for possible use in the allocation process. The hierarchy name is defined automatically, or you can define the naming convention yourself when the controlling area is created (see "The Controlling Area" in Chapter 8) and is utilized as the top node. You cannot assign cost centers at this level, so the standard hierarchy will require further development.

Keep in mind that you should develop the standard hierarchy with the initial intent of supporting your reporting environment. If certain cost centers should be uniquely grouped to support management reporting, then you should reflect this in your hierarchy design. Cost centers can be assigned only at the lowest node level within the hierarchy. Each time you create a cost center, a hierarchy node assignment is required on the master record. The requirement of an assignment thus assures you that all cost centers will be applied to one and only one node within your hierarchy.

**TIP**   Before beginning development, spend time querying management about any upcoming changes to their organizational structure. Then develop a hierarchy outline on a spreadsheet and seek sign-off. This may save needless development time.

*✗ SH2*

You can develop the standard hierarchy, like most master data, from either the user
menu or the Implementation Guide (IMG). To begin, follow the user menu path
Accounting ➤ Controlling ➤ Cost Centers ➤ Master Data ➤ Standard Hierarchy
➤ Change or use the transaction code OKEON. Alternatively, you can use the older
transaction code KSH2, but that will point you to a screen that initially offers a
field for entering a single hierarchy, and only upon execution do you get to the full
hierarchy view. In either case, this process eventually gets you to the same screen for
data entry. We prefer using OKEON since it will allow you to see all hierarchies as a
list; then you can pick and choose what ones you want to see.

*Easy access*

The standard hierarchy for cost centers change screen will appear (see Figure 10.1).

**FIGURE 10.1**    **The standard hierarchy for cost centers change screen**

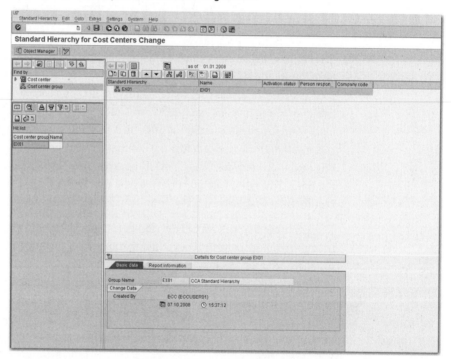

If the hierarchy has not yet been maintained, only the top node will be displayed.
Enter a standard hierarchy description into the empty field next to the node, if
applicable.

# Adding New Hierarchy Nodes

The next step is to add new hierarchy nodes. On the standard hierarchy for cost centers change screen, begin adding nodes by placing the cursor on the node that will be augmented. In the case of a new hierarchy, place the cursor on the top node. By placing your cursor on a node, you are identifying that node as the focal point. Click the create icon to start the insert process for additional Cost Center nodes. Use the tab item on the icon to choose the drop-down list of options. Choose the positioning of the node—either Lower-Level Group or Group at Same Level to insert the new Group folder. Click the Lower-Level Group option, and the Details for Cost Center Group dialog box will appear at the bottom (as shown in Figure 10.2).

**FIGURE 10.2**   Standard hierarchy for cost centers change screen with Lower Level Group change menu

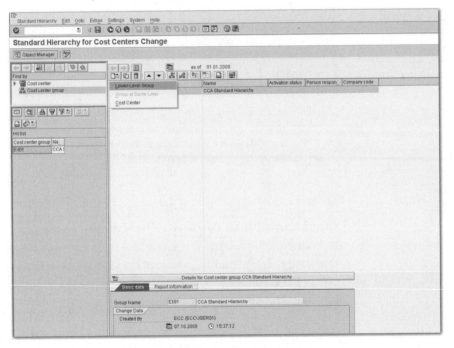

Notice that the ID of the node you selected with your cursor appears in the screen as the Superior-Node. The Superior-Node becomes the basis for the new node's assignment to the hierarchy (see Figure 10.3).

**FIGURE 10.3**   Standard hierarchy for cost centers change screen with a new node being developed

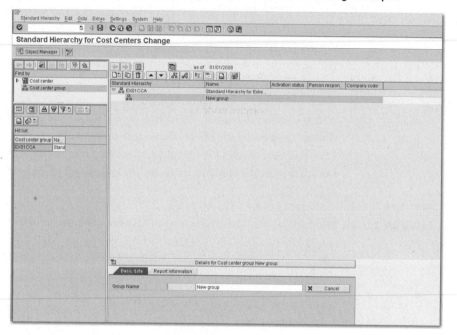

**TIP**   The node IDs are maintained at the client level and therefore must be unique across all controlling areas within the client.

Let's take a look at the fields in this screen. Here are the fields on the Basic Data tab:

**Group Name**   Enter the character ID of the new node group. The ID can be up to 11 characters in length. Remember that the group node ID can be used later in reporting and/or planning, so be sure to use an ID name that easily identifies the cost center group.

**Description**   Enter the description of the node group.

**Created By**   The Change Data reflects the time and date that it was created and the person that created this hierarchy node.

Here are the fields on the Report Information tab:

**Symbolic Name**   If you are looking to use this hierarchy node in the Report Writer process as an available node, you can use this to help enhance this process.

**Format Group**   Used for printing purposes.

**Representative Value** This can be used as a presentation title for this hierarchy node. Therefore, if you are using this hierarchy node in a report and you need to have a description other than what the actual node is titled, you can insert a description here.

**Authorization Group** Used for the purposes of assigning additional authorization options to a specific hierarchy node. This will help manage who has the ability to use this hierarchy node and the values assigned.

The next step in creating the full hierarchy is to use the node you just created and use the context menu (by right-clicking) from the lower node to access the additional options (see Figure 10.4).

**FIGURE 10.4** Creating additional hierarchy nodes from the standard hierarchy for cost centers change screen

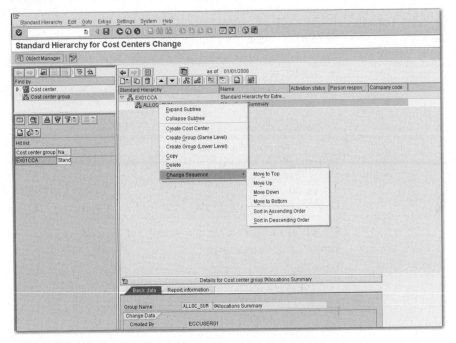

The relevant fields in this menu are as follows:

**Create Group (Same Level)** If the node you are adding is to be represented on the same level as the superior node, select Same Level.

**Create Group (Lower Level)** If the node is to be represented subordinate to the superior node, select Lower Level.

**Copy**  Allows the ability to make a copy of the existing node and use the configuration that has already been developed.

**Delete**  Allows the deletion of the hierarchy nodes.

**Change Sequence (Move to Top, Move Up, Move Down, Move to Bottom, Sort in Ascending Order, and Sort in Descending Order)**  This offers the option to move the current hierarchy node around the current hierarchy structure.

After selecting one of the options, the appropriate create screen will appear for additional configuration.

**TIP**  It is recommended that the hierarchy be built from the top down; that is, build each level completely, and then continue to the next. You will find it quicker to add a string of Same Level nodes than to repeatedly build depth with lower-level nodes.

**Save icon**  Click the save icon to complete an insertion step. You will notice that the nodes have been added to the standard hierarchy, as shown in Figure 10.5.

**FIGURE 10.5**  Displays the nodes that have been added to the standard hierarchy for cost centers change screen

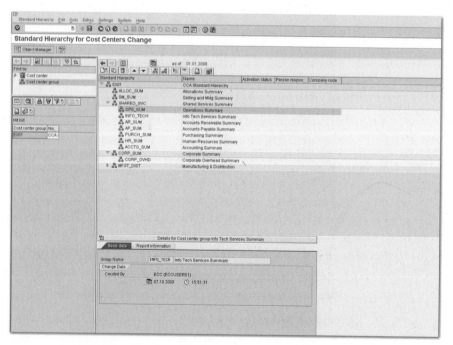

Continue adding nodes until the hierarchy is complete. Be sure to save when complete.

## Changing, Moving, and Deleting Hierarchy Nodes     *OKEON*

In the same way that you can add nodes, you can move, alter, and delete them. The process is simple and repeatable, even after cost centers have been assigned. To move an existing node, select the node from the standard hierarchy change screen. You can access that screen by using the path Application Menu Path of Accounting ➤ Controlling ➤ Cost Centers ➤ Master Data ➤ Standard Hierarchy ➤ Change or by accessing the transaction code OKEON. Alternatively, you can use the older transaction code KSH2.

Once in this screen, you will see that you have the same functionality as before. If you need to access an alternative hierarchy, you can click it in the navigation pane on the right side of the screen. Once you do this, it will appear in the main screen for you to make any changes. The initial hierarchy is shown in Figure 10.5.

The available options are as follows:

**Copy (double page icon)**   Use this icon to copy a hierarchy node with all attributes.

**Delete (trash can icon)**   Use this button to delete the node.

**Change Sequence: Move Up (up-arrow icon)**   If you place your cursor on a new node and select this button, the selected node will move so that it moves up in the list in the same upper node, same level.

**Change Sequence: Move Down (down-arrow icon)**   If you place your cursor on a new node and select this button, the selected node will move so that it moves down in the list in the same upper node, same level.

**One Level Up: Move up based on a Hierarchy node**   Place your cursor on the node to which you want to move the upper node, and select this icon. The selected hierarchy node moves above the next node in the list. Therefore this moves the nodes up levels rather than just moving them up a list as the "change sequence" buttons do.

**One Level Down: Move down based on a hierarchy node**   Place your cursor on the node to which you want to move the upper node and select this icon. The selected hierarchy node moves below the next node in the list. Therefore this moves the nodes down levels rather than just moving them down a list as the "change sequence" buttons do.

The remaining icons in this list are specific to changing the screen format. In Figure 10.5, the node OPS_SUM is subordinate to SHARED_SVC. It was selected and moved so that it's now subordinate to the CORP_SUM node. The result, shown in Figure 10.6, is that OPS_SUM now rolls up into CORP_SUM. When your changes are complete, be sure to save the hierarchy.

**FIGURE 10.6**    Movement of hierarchy node OPS_SUM using the standard hierarchy for cost centers change screen

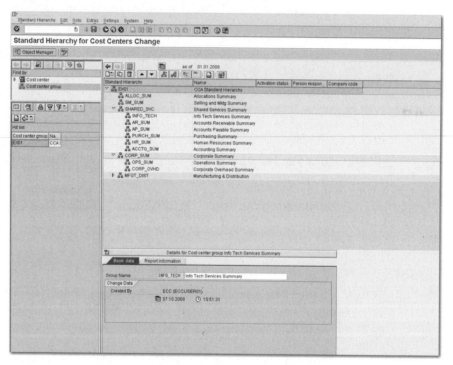

**TIP**    All changes, except for node removal, can take place after cost centers have been assigned. To remove a node from the hierarchy, it must not have any cost center assignments.

**EXTREME SPORTS COST CENTER STANDARD HIERARCHY CONFIGURATION ANALYSIS**

Extreme Sports has an uncomplicated operating structure. The majority of overhead expenses are captured within the shared service organization and assessed at a period close to the respective profitability centers. An overhead allocation will occur within Cost Center Accounting to ensure that an audit trail exists. Another option for Extreme Sports would be to allocate somewhere between a portion of and ail of its costs through Profit Center Accounting.

# Controlling Area/Profit Center Accounting Maintenance —OKE5

If Profit Center Accounting is active within your controlling area, as it is within Extreme Sports's EX01, you must first create a standard hierarchy and assign a dummy profit center. (We'll further discuss hierarchy development in Chapter 13, "Profit Center Accounting.") Before proceeding, be sure to set the controlling area to the one you will be maintaining. To do so, follow the IMG menu path Enterprise Controlling ➤ Profit Center Accounting ➤ Basic Settings ➤ Controlling Area Settings ➤ Maintain Controlling Area Settings or use transaction code OKE5.

After you use one of these transaction configurations, the change view "EC-PCA: controlling area settings": overview screen appears, as shown in Figure 10.7.

Notice that two fields, Standard Hierarchy and PCtr Local Currency Type, are required. The others are optional:

**Dummy Profit Center**    The field is grayed out. The dummy profit center is the default profit center for the entire controlling area. It will capture all postings that do not have a profit center account assignment. Additionally, the dummy will serve as the default for assignment on the cost center master record if one is not manually assigned. An entry cannot be made into the field from this screen. The assignment is made when the master record is created. A special transaction is used to create the dummy profit center. There can be only one dummy profit center per controlling area.

**FIGURE 10.7**    The change view "EC-PCA: controlling area settings": overview screen

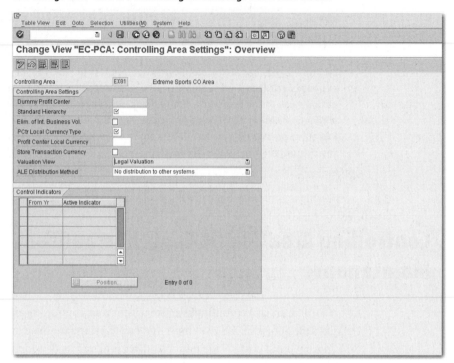

  **TIP**    The standard hierarchy must be defined and built prior to creating the dummy profit center. The dummy, like all profit centers, must have a node to reside upon.

**Standard Hierarchy**    Just as you did for the CCA standard hierarchy, enter the name of the EC-PCA hierarchy. The name can be up to 10 characters in length.

**Elim. of Int. Business Vol.**    Activate this field if it you desire to eliminate internal activity between two or more account assignment objects that are assigned to the same profit center. For example, a profit center, P1000, has assigned to itself a production order, O2000, and a cost center, C2000. Standard direct labor is confirmed on the order, with the associated labor credit going to cost center C2000. By eliminating internal activity volumes, no PCA document will be produced.

**PCtr. Local Currency Type**   Select the currency type in which all PCA transactions will be maintained. The currency options include the following:

**10**   Controlling area currency

**20**   Group currency

**90**   Profit center currency

If you select 90, profit center currency, you must identify the currency type. You assign the currency for type 90 in the Report Currency field. In addition, all standard EC-PCA reports will display information in the default currency type identified here.

**Profit Center Local Currency**   This field is required if you selected currency type 90. If either the controlling area or group currency type is selected, leave the field blank. If this field is completed, SAP will store transaction data in the currency identified here.

**Store Transaction Currency**   If you want the transaction currency stored in EC-PCA, flag this field. Data volumes will increase, but if the transaction currency is different from the controlling area or profit center currency, it may be important for reporting.

**Valuation View**   Use the Valuation view to represent different ways of viewing business transactions in a company. You can look at a business transaction from the view of a Group, Profit Center, or Individual Enterprise approach. These valuation views are directly linked to the use of Transfer Pricing to view postings at different levels. The options here are Legal, Group, and Profit Center Valuation.

**ALE Distribution Method**   This is used based on the distribution of information to other ECC systems. ALE = Application Link Enabling allows the ability to link several ECC systems to one another for the purposes of sharing the master data (profit center list) and allowing postings across systems. The options here are No Distribution to Other Systems, Method 1: Centralized Profit Center Accounting, and Method 2: Decentralized Profit Center Accounting.

The last item that needs to be assigned is the Control Indicators From Yr. This will assign the information identified above to the years that follow the year indicated in this list. When this screen is configured, save the settings. Figure 10.8 shows the completed EC-PCA controlling area settings. You can now maintain the EC-PCA standard hierarchy.

**FIGURE 10.8**    The completed change view "EC-PCA: controlling area settings": overview screen

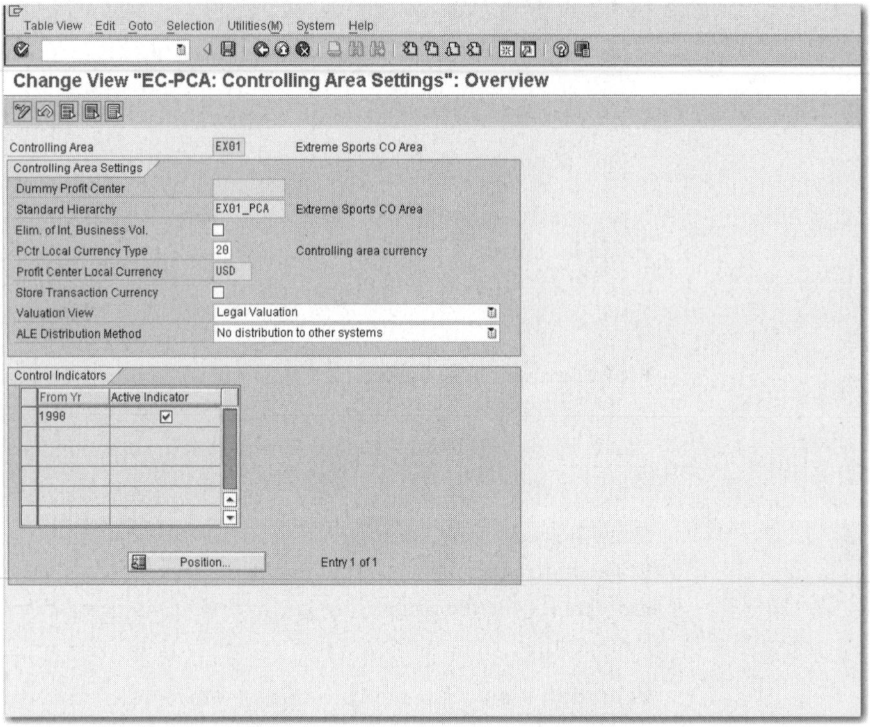

# Profit Center Accounting: Creating the Standard Hierarchy

The method for creating and maintaining the PCA standard hierarchy is identical to the processes involved in upkeep of the CCA hierarchy. The keystrokes and movements for adding, moving, and deleting nodes are the same for both hierarchies. Just as there is one CCA standard hierarchy, there is only one PCA standard hierarchy.

Another similarity is that you can create or maintain the PCA hierarchy from either the IMG or the user menu. The IMG menu path is Enterprise Controlling ➢ Profit Center Accounting ➢ Master Data ➢ Profit Center ➢ Define Standard Hierarchy, and the transaction code is KCH1. Transaction code KCH2 takes you to the change screen for the standard hierarchy and also the Profit Center Group hierarchy change screen.

Please refer to "Changing, Moving, and Deleting Hierarchy Nodes" earlier in this chapter for tips on how to maintain hierarchy nodes.

# Creating the Dummy Profit Center

You create the dummy profit center by using a special transaction code (KE59). Although it shares many of the same attributes as a normal profit center, the indicator flag identifying it as the dummy can be activated only by using either this special transaction code or the menu path Enterprise Controlling ➢ Profit Center Accounting ➢ Master Data ➢ Profit Center ➢ Create Dummy Profit Center.

A window will appear asking whether you want to create the dummy or change a profit center. Select the Create the Dummy Profit Center option. The initial create dummy profit center screen appears. Enter the name of the dummy, and press Enter. The create dummy profit center: basic screen configuration screen appears.

Notice that the Valid From and Valid To dates have defaulted into the master record. Because there is only one dummy profit center, the valid dates must cover the entire existence of the active system. Complete the remaining open fields:

**Name**   Enter the name of the dummy profit center.

**Description**   Enter a description of the dummy profit center.

**Person Responsible**   Enter the name of the individual assigned the responsibility of managing the dummy.

**Department**   Enter the name or a description of the department to which the person in charge belongs, if desired.

**Profit Center Group**   Enter the node ID on the PCA standard hierarchy where the dummy is to be assigned.

**Segment**   This is an additional assignment of a value to the attributes of a dummy profit center if further detailed reporting is required. This field has been added to the profit center master record to provide financial segment reporting to meet the new accounting standards. It is used in conjunction with the new general ledger.

When the fields are filled in, save the master record. The dummy is now active, as shown in Figure 10.9, and postings can begin to occur within PCA.

## EXTREME SPORTS PROFIT CENTER ACCOUNTING MAINTENANCE CONFIGURATION ANALYSIS

Extreme Sports is using Profit Center Accounting to capture and report its profitability by division. Therefore, because it is active within the controlling area, the profit center standard hierarchy was developed and a dummy profit center was created.

**FIGURE 10.9**     Create dummy profit center: basic screen; dummy profit center is now active

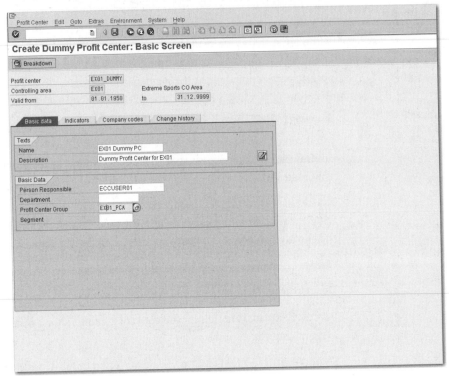

# Cost Center Basics

Before creating the cost center master record, you must consider a few configuration settings:

- ► Cost center categories or types

- ► Time-dependent fields

- ► Profit Center Accounting (PCA) relevance

The relevance of PCA stems from the activation settings found on the controlling area. If PCA is active for your controlling area, SAP expects a profit center assignment on the cost center master record. If you attempt to save the cost center without this assignment, the system will give you a warning and as mentioned the dummy profit center will be used. Complete Profit Center Accounting configuration will be covered in detail in Chapter 13, but PCA-relevant controlling area configuration must be completed prior to adding any cost centers.

**TIP**   If PCA is active, it is highly recommended that you always assign a profit center to the cost center master record. Inconsistencies will surely occur if the assignment is not made. In addition, this will affect the validation and analysis of the final Profit Center reports, and at period end, the task of sorting out the postings and assigning them to the appropriate Profit Center will have to occur.

Additionally, the following two tables are relevant when maintaining cost center master data (you can review all necessary setting for each table using the Data Browser/transaction code SE12, then enter the table name):

**CSKS**   Contains all cost center master data field settings (for example, Cost Center Category, Hierarchy Assignment)

**CSKT**   Contains all cost center text field settings (for example, Cost Center Description, Short Text)

## Cost Center Categories

The uses of cost center categories are threefold:

▶ They deliver default control indicator values to the cost center master record during cost center creation.

▶ They are assigned to the activity type master record as the key to which types of cost centers can use a given activity type.

▶ They can be used during functional area assignment, reporting, and evaluations and as search criteria.

SAP delivers standard categories like Sales, Administration, and Production, for your immediate use. You can, however, make changes to the standards, or you can create as many of your own categories as you like. To create/change/display the cost center categories, use the menu path Controlling ➢ Cost Center Accounting ➢ Master Data ➢ Cost Centers ➢ Define Cost Center Categories, or use transaction code OKA2.

The cost center category configuration screen appears (see Figure 10.10). Notice the various table settings. To create a new category, click the New Entries button. An empty category table will appear.

**FIGURE 10.10** The change view "cost center categories": overview configuration screen

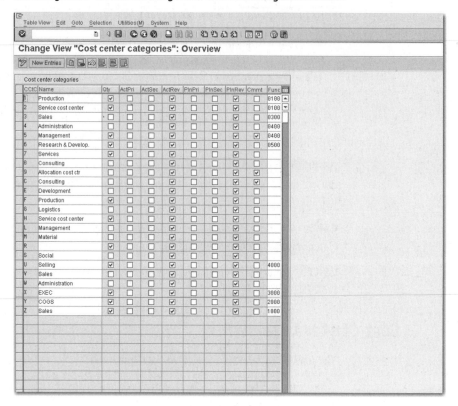

**N O T E** Remember, when you begin to make the block indicator settings, a check in the column signals that you want that activity blocked. Leave the column field empty if the posting described is desired.

Here are the fields you need to configure on this screen:

**Category Indicator** Enter the category ID. This field is alphanumeric, but only one character in length.

**Name** Enter a description that corresponds to the category indicator.

**Qty** If this field is checked, the cost center will retain quantity information.

**ActPri** This field determines if actual primary costs are blocked. Usually left empty for most categories.

**ActSec**   This field determines if actual secondary costs are blocked. Also almost always left empty.

**ActRev**   If this field is activated, revenues cannot be posted to the cost center with this category. If it's not active, revenues can be posted to the cost center, but only statistically.

**PlnPr**   If this field is activated, the cost center category is blocked from planning costs.

**Pln Sec**   If this field is activated, the cost center category is blocked from planning secondary costs.

**PlnRev**   If this field is activated, the cost center category cannot be planned with revenue.

**Cmmt**   This field determines if commitments can be tracked on the cost center. If commitment management is activated for the controlling area, you should strongly consider allowing commitment update postings.

**Func**   This field determines the functional area that is assigned to the Profit Center category. The functional area is required to create a P&L in Finance using the cost-of-sales accounting.

Something to remember about the categories is that a new cost center will absorb the control indicator settings as they were configured at the moment of creation. Any future changes to a category will not have a retroactive impact on previously created cost centers. To affect an existing cost center, you must make desired changes manually. For example, a change to disallow secondary cost element planning on all production cost centers is made. Any future cost centers created from that time forward will be subject to this restriction. Any existing cost centers in the environment will not be affected. Each of the production cost centers will need to have its control indicators adjusted manually.

# Time-Based Fields

With the use of the time dependency table, shown in Figure 10.11, SAP has regulated how often a field on the cost center master record can be changed. In addition to the dependency settings, the table provides for the ability to configure whether SAP should retain all historical settings.

**FIGURE 10.11** Change: time-based fields (cost centers): the time dependency table

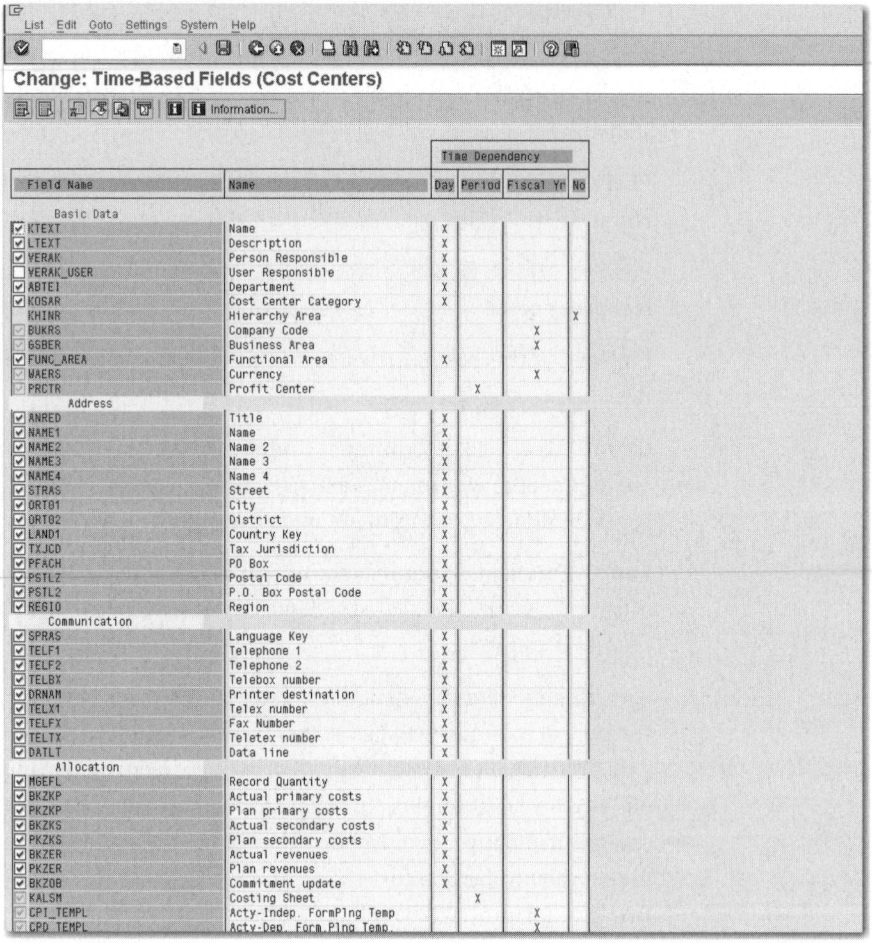


| Field Name | Name | Day | Period | Fiscal Yr | No |
|---|---|---|---|---|---|
| Basic Data | | | | | |
| KTEXT | Name | X | | | |
| LTEXT | Description | X | | | |
| VERAK | Person Responsible | X | | | |
| VERAK_USER | User Responsible | X | | | |
| ABTEI | Department | X | | | |
| KOSAR | Cost Center Category | X | | | |
| KHINR | Hierarchy Area | | | | X |
| BUKRS | Company Code | | | X | |
| GSBER | Business Area | | | X | |
| FUNC_AREA | Functional Area | X | | | |
| WAERS | Currency | | | X | |
| PRCTR | Profit Center | | X | | |
| Address | | | | | |
| ANRED | Title | X | | | |
| NAME1 | Name | X | | | |
| NAME2 | Name 2 | X | | | |
| NAME3 | Name 3 | X | | | |
| NAME4 | Name 4 | X | | | |
| STRAS | Street | X | | | |
| ORT01 | City | X | | | |
| ORT02 | District | X | | | |
| LAND1 | Country Key | X | | | |
| TXJCD | Tax Jurisdiction | X | | | |
| PFACH | PO Box | X | | | |
| PSTLZ | Postal Code | X | | | |
| PSTL2 | P.O. Box Postal Code | X | | | |
| REGIO | Region | X | | | |
| Communication | | | | | |
| SPRAS | Language Key | X | | | |
| TELF1 | Telephone 1 | X | | | |
| TELF2 | Telephone 2 | X | | | |
| TELBX | Telebox number | X | | | |
| DRNAM | Printer destination | X | | | |
| TELX1 | Telex number | X | | | |
| TELFX | Fax Number | X | | | |
| TELTX | Teletex number | X | | | |
| DATLT | Data line | X | | | |
| Allocation | | | | | |
| MGEFL | Record Quantity | X | | | |
| BKZKP | Actual primary costs | X | | | |
| PKZKP | Plan primary costs | X | | | |
| BKZKS | Actual secondary costs | X | | | |
| PKZKS | Plan secondary costs | X | | | |
| BKZER | Actual revenues | X | | | |
| PKZER | Plan revenues | X | | | |
| BKZOB | Commitment update | X | | | |
| KALSM | Costing Sheet | | X | | |
| CPI_TEMPL | Acty-Indep. FormPlng Temp | | | X | |
| CPD_TEMPL | Acty-Dep. Form.Plng Temp. | | | X | |

To access the screen with the time dependency table, follow the IMG menu path Controlling ➢ Cost Center Accounting ➢ Master Data ➢ Cost Centers ➢ Define Time-Based Fields for Cost Centers, or use the transaction code OKEG.

As you can see in Figure 10.11, entering a check mark in the box to the left of the field name sets the historical tracking flag.

There are four related areas of time dependency:

**Day** A field with this setting can be changed daily without any warning.

**Period**  A field with this setting can be changed at any time. If the change occurs within a period, a warning may be given. The change can still be made, but caution should be used if the field is marked as historical.

**Fiscal Yr**  A field with this setting can be changed only at the beginning of a new fiscal year. Any attempt to change the setting for the current validity interval will result in an error being returned by SAP.

**No**  Only the Hierarchy Area field is set with this dependency. There are no restrictions to making changes to the field.

SAP has hard-coded the time dependency settings for all cost center master record fields. There is no standard way of altering these settings. You can, however, through the activation of the historical flag, adjust whether changes to the record are tracked.

If it is important to track changes to the master record, each change will need to correspond to a new analysis period. The default analysis period on the master record is the original validity period given to the cost center. New periods can be configured directly on the same master record. (See "Establishing a New Analysis Period" later in this chapter for details.)

## Creating and Changing Cost Centers

You can create the cost center master record from either the IMG or the user menu path. The IMG path is Controlling ➤ Cost Center Accounting ➤ Master Data ➤ Cost Centers ➤ Create Cost Centers, and the transaction code is KS01. Remember, when you create a piece of CO master data, it cannot be deleted easily, so plan your steps appropriately.

The create cost center: initial screen request screen will appear, prompting you for input of a cost center number and validity period (see Figure 10.12).

The fields you need to configure on this screen are as follows:

**Cost Center**  Enter an alphanumeric identifier for the cost center. The ID can be up to 10 characters in length.

**Valid From/To**  The validity period of the master record is the time frame within which postings may occur. Be certain that the period is significant in length to not interrupt activity within a given fiscal period. Additionally, be certain that the range is sufficient to support any history loads.

**FIGURE 10.12** The create cost center: initial screen request screen

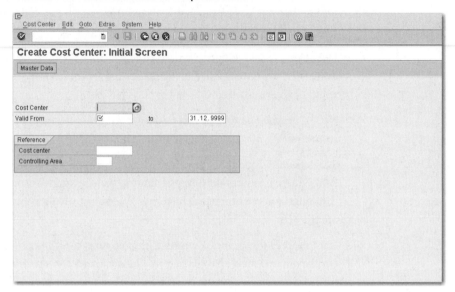

**TIP**   To save yourself potential rework, before you begin have in mind the number-ing methodology you will be using and review the length of time that your cost centers should be available for postings.

When configuration is complete, press Enter. The create cost center: basic screen appears (see Figure 10.13). Notice the number of fields that are required. You can see that the information from the request screen has carried forward into the basic screen and is now grayed out. To make a change to the ID or validity period now, you must exit the update prior to saving, and restart.

Let's take a look at the fields on the basic screen:

**Name**   Enter a name for the cost center. This field is required.

**Description**   Enter a description for the cost center.

**User Responsible**   Enter the ID of the user in charge of the cost center. This field is required.

**Person Responsible**   Enter the ID of the person in charge of the cost center. This field is required.

**Department**   Enter the name or ID of the department to which the cost center belongs.

**FIGURE 10.13**  The create cost center: basic screen

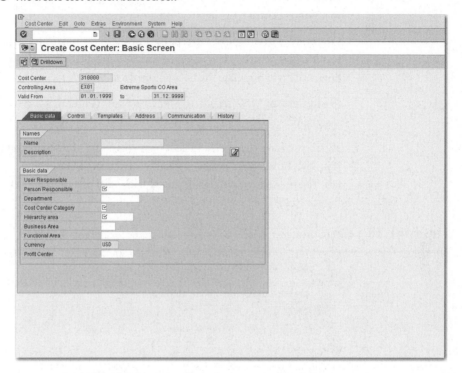

**Cost Center Category**    Enter the category ID (see "Cost Center Categories" earlier in this chapter for details). This field is required.

**Hierarchy Area**    Enter the CCA standard hierarchy node to which the cost center will belong. This field is required.

**NOTE**   Remember that the cost center, or profit center in PCA, can be assigned only to the lowest node on the standard hierarchy. If you attempt to enter a master record at the summary level, SAP will stop the assignment with an error.

**Company Code**    Assign the cost center to a specific company code. This is necessary for proper FI integration of operating costs. This field is required. In our particular case, the controlling area for Extreme Sports has only one company code, and therefore this field does not show up on this screen; however, if you have multiple company codes for one controlling area, you will be required to assign a value here.

**Business Area**    Enter a business area if you are utilizing the areas and expect to report with them.

**Functional Area** Enter a functional area if you are utilizing the areas and expect to report on these cross application groups.

**Currency** In this case, Currency is grayed out. Controlling area currency, USD, was identified as the currency type for the controlling area. When you press Enter now, USD will populate the field automatically.

**Profit Center** If PCA is active, enter a profit center to which the cost center is assigned.

When you have completed the entry, you can save the cost center (see Figure 10.14). It is wise, however, to review the control indicators before saving. Select the Control tab. The next screen will be displayed with a list of activities that can be blocked (see Figure 10.15).

**FIGURE 10.14** The create cost center: basic screen configured for Extreme Sports

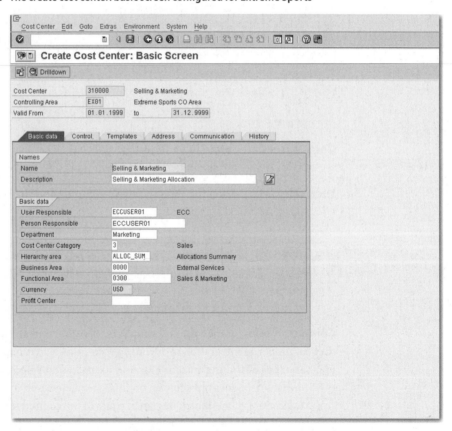

**FIGURE 10.15** The Control tab on the create cost center: indicators screen

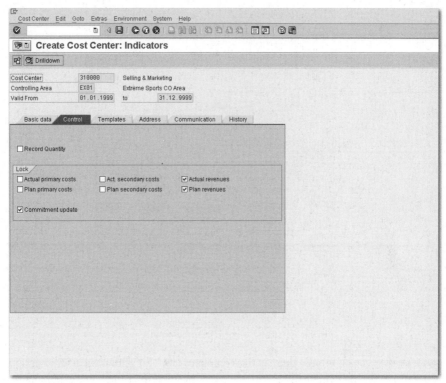

Remember from the previous section that the reason for configuring the category settings first was to have the information automatically flow to the cost center upon creation. However, you can make control changes to specific cost centers on the master record.

The same categories appear on the master record and in the category table. Make any necessary changes to the indicators and press Enter to return to the basic screen.

To enter a name, street address, and tax jurisdiction code for the cost center, select the Address tab (see Figure 10.16). All fields are optional and can be changed at any time. Each can be set as time dependent, and changes can thus be tracked. When you have completed the address, press Enter and save the cost center.

**FIGURE 10.16** The Address tab

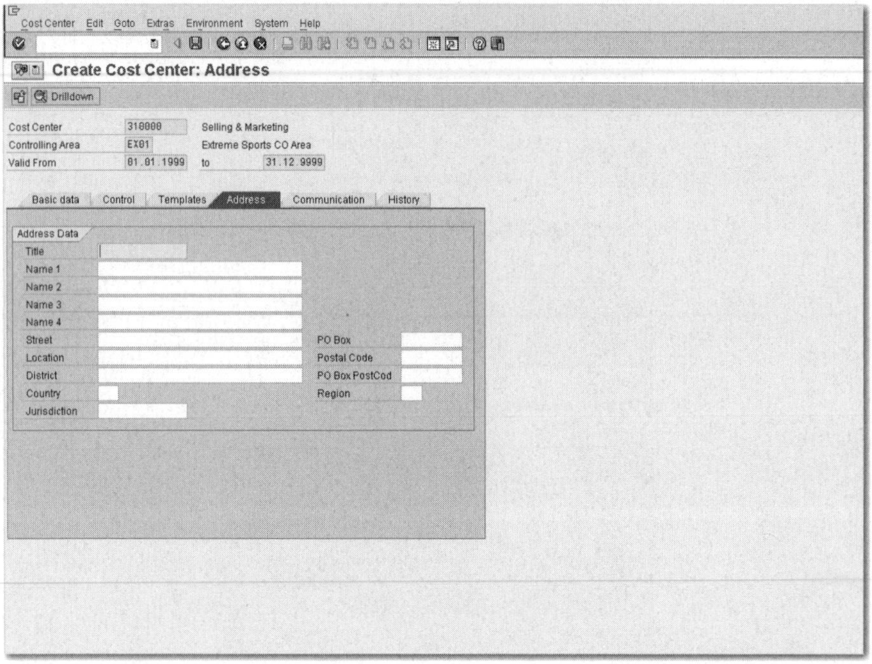

Finally there is the Templates tab. This allows the user to assign to the cost center any Plan or Actual allocation structures and/or Costing Sheet. We will discuss these concepts in detail shortly in the section titled "Assessments, Distributions, and Reposting." Basically this allows the assignment of a allocation method at the time of creation of the cost center rather than having to assign these tasks to the cost center later in the process (see Figure 10.17). All fields are optional and can be changed at any time, but realize that any change in the future will not affect the past postings. This is relatively new to the cost center master data but will have been used frequently if the company is using either the cost center planning or allocation of actual postings.

**FIGURE 10.17** Create cost center: templates

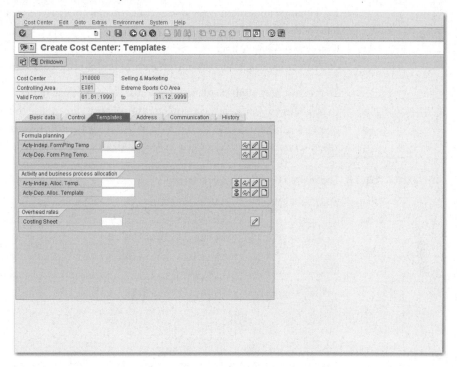

## Establishing a New Analysis Period

If you flagged certain master data fields as historically relevant when you were maintaining the time dependency table, a new analysis period may be appropriate. The default analysis period for any CO master record is the original validity period established when the object was created (see "Creating and Changing Cost Centers" earlier in this chapter). As was mentioned in earlier sections, if you change a time-relevant field on the master record and do not create a new analysis period, the change will overwrite the previous setting. If a second analysis period is created, the change is maintained uniquely. These types of changes are not unusual but are probably more infrequent. If a cost center changes tasks or responsibilities, we are normally drawn to creating a new cost center rather than changing a cost center. If there is a change in the owner or another field such as description, then a change to the cost center can be discussed.

For example, cost center 310000 has an original validity period of 01/01/1999 to 12/31/9999 and carries cost center type M. If you were to change the type to H and not define a new analysis period, the cost center will be represented as always being H. A change document is generated, but you cannot analyze what activity may have occurred on the cost center when the center was type M versus when it was H. Conversely, if you establish a new analysis period, 07/01/1999 to 12/31/9999, then you can analyze activity for both the current and prior period range.

To create a new analysis period, you must be in the cost center master record that is to be changed. Once in the change master record screen, use the following path to open the analysis period screen: Edit ➢ Analysis Period. The analysis time frame: select screen appears, as shown in Figure 10.18.

**FIGURE 10.18**  The analysis time frame: select screen

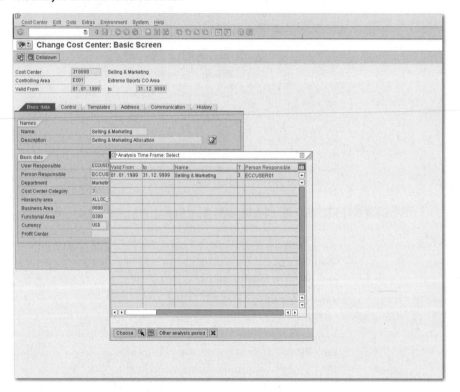

If you have not previously entered an analysis period, only the default settings will appear. If other periods have been established, they will be visible. To enter a new period, select the button labeled Other Analysis Period. A new Other Analysis Period box appears, providing the opportunity to enter a date range (see Figure 10.19). Prior to entering a range, be aware of the time dependency of the field you are changing. Also make sure that you do not miss any days in this process. If the cost center is split by a missed day, many processes, such as posting from FI and allocations processes, will fail.

**FIGURE 10.19**  The Other Analysis Period pop-up box

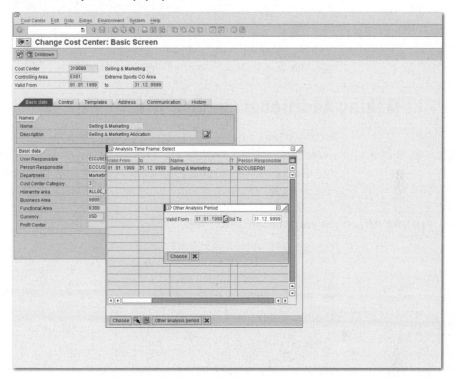

Referring back to the section on time-based fields, the following time dependencies have been established within SAP:

**Day**    A field with this setting can be changed daily without any warning.

**Period**    A field with this setting can be changed at any time. If the change occurs within a period, a warning maybe given.

**Fiscal Year**    A field with this setting can be changed only at the beginning of a new fiscal year. The only fields with this setting are Company Code, Business Area, and Currency.

**No**    Only the Hierarchy Area field is set with this dependency. There are no restrictions to making changes to the field.

When establishing the range, be sure to keep these items in mind. After entering the new range, click Choose. The analysis period has replaced the default validity period on the basic screen.

If, for example, you want to change the company code assignment, which carries a time dependency of fiscal year, the new range must begin on the first day of the next fiscal year.

With the new analysis period active, make the changes to the master record and save. The changes will become effective on the first day of the new period range.

## Making Additional Changes After New Analysis Period

Because you have two or more potential validity periods on that cost center, when you go to change the record again, a box will appear asking you to select an analysis period (see Figure 10.20). If you are currently in the master record, use the path Edit ➤ Analysis Period to switch between period ranges.

**FIGURE 10.20** Analysis time frame: select screen

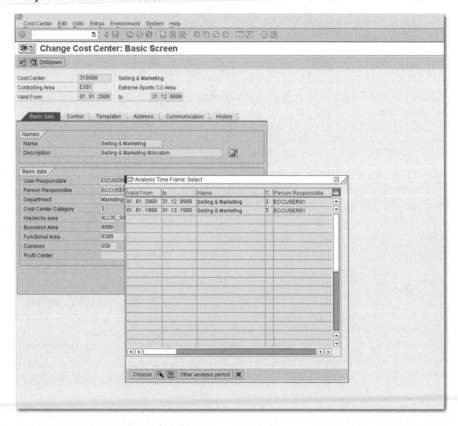

**EXTREME SPORTS COST CENTER BASICS CONFIGURATION ANALYSIS**

The majority of information provided in the "Cost Center Basics" section of this book was for the benefit of the accounting department and master data team. Extreme Sports controls both activities through its Shared Services organization.

# Activity Types and Statistical Key Figures

Activity types and statistical key figures are the last two types of master data maintained within Cost Center Accounting. Each type is important to tracing and allocating internal activity within the Controlling-module environment. Activity types are used by SAP to allocate, both directly and indirectly, expenses based upon an amount of output for a given cost center. The activity type becomes the vehicle through which the quantities are tracked. Examples of activity quantities include the following:

► Production hours

► Lbs. produced

► Energy consumed in kWh

Statistical key figures help the user track activity in another manner. Key figures are designed to be used in reporting and analysis and assist in the assessment or distribution of costs throughout the CCA environment. Key figures are statistical in nature and thus are invisible to the FI environment. Postings to a key figure do not integrate with PCA either. They are, however, powerful when utilized properly. Examples of key figures include the following:

► Units sold

► Number of employees

► Production hours

► Square footage of office space

This section will outline statistical key figures first, followed by activity types.

# Creating and Maintaining Statistical Key Figures

Creating and maintaining key figures is far simpler than creating and maintaining activity types, but that's because key figures have less functionality. However, with the proper development, a key figure can become invaluable to you from a reporting and allocation viewpoint. Key figures are exclusive to Cost Center Accounting (CCA) within CO, but they can be picked up and utilized by Profit Center Accounting. You will see later that much of the SAP master data is transferable to PCA (see Chapter 13). As with all CCA master data, you can create the record from either the IMG or user menu. Follow the IMG path Controlling ➢ Cost Center Accounting ➢ Master Data ➢ Statistical Key Figures ➢ Maintain Statistical Key Figures or use transaction code KK01.

Use one of the transaction configurations to access the initial create statistical key figure screen, shown in Figure 10.21.

**FIGURE 10.21** The initial create statistical key figure screen

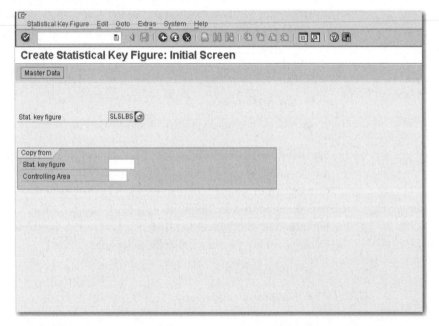

**TIP**    Before continuing, be sure that the controlling area is set properly. You can set the controlling area through the path Extras ➢ Set Controlling Area.

The fields on this screen are as follows:

**Stat. Key Figure**   Enter the name of the key figure that you will be creating. The name can be up to six alphanumeric characters in length.

**Copy From**   Fill in the following fields in the Copy From section:

**Stat. Key Figure**   If you choose to copy from a key figure in your controlling area or another, enter the name of the source key figure here.

**Controlling Area**   Enter the ID of the controlling area where the source key figure can be found.

Press Enter; the create statistical key figure basic configuration screen appears (shown in Figure 10.22 configured for Extreme Sports). Notice that the name of the key figure and the assigned controlling area were brought over from the initial screen and grayed out. You can no longer change these assignments on the master record. Your only recourse at this point, if you want to change the name or controlling area is to not save the figure, and start over.

When you are happy with the information, begin completing the master record:

**Name**   Enter the descriptive name of the key figure. The name can be up to 40 characters in length.

**FIGURE 10.22** The create statistical key figure: master data screen

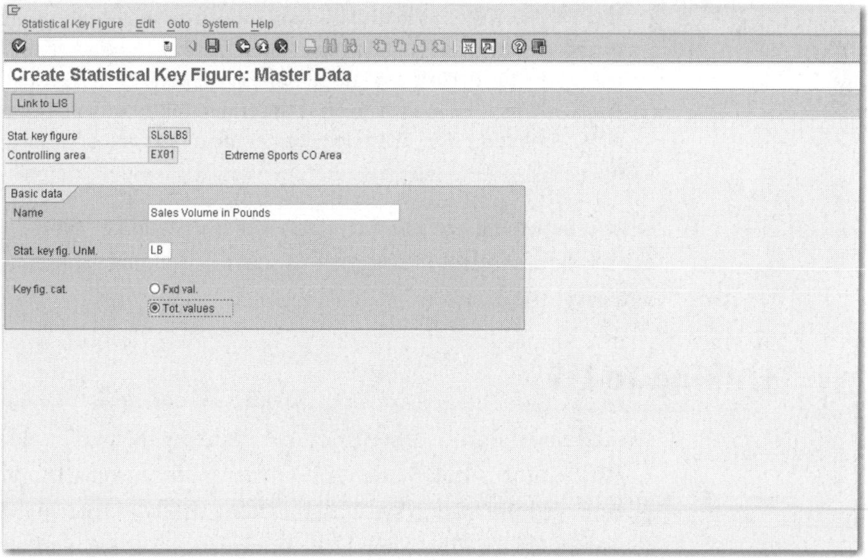

**Stat. Key Fig. UnM.**    Enter the unit of measure by which entries will be measured. Use the pull-down list for a view of possible entries. Don't worry if you do not find the unit of measure you like; the unit is configurable. Examples include the following:

**LB**    Pounds

**EA**    Each

**H**    Hours

**Key Fig. Cat.**    With this setting, you can determine how the key figure will be utilized. You have two choices:

**Fxd Val.**    Fixed indicates that the amount entered will be consistent over all periods within a fiscal year and should be carried forward to each period. Examples of a fixed value might include the square footage of a building or the number of employees in a department. The amount does not change period to period.

**Tot. Values**    Total Values indicates that the amount could change from period to period and therefore should not be carried forward into any future periods. Examples include the number of kilowatt hours of electricity used or the number of units sold within a period.

**NOTE**    Corrections to the Fixed and Total Values key figures are handled differently. To correct an entry in a Fixed Type key figure, simply enter a new fixed value, and the correction will be carried forward into all subsequent periods. Corrections to an entry in a Total Type key figure require you to erase the original entry with one of the same value but with a reversed ± sign. Then simply enter the correct value for the period.

When the settings are complete, save the statistical key figure. If you desire to attach the key figure to an LIS structure (discussed in the next section), the next section will cover the details to establish the link.

## Linking to LIS

An additional feature of statistical key figures is their ability to be linked to a Logistics Information System (LIS) structure for automatic update. The LIS consists of multiple information systems, including the Sales Information System (SIS), Inventory Controlling, Shop Floor Information System, and others. A structure within LIS is similar to a table in reporting, within which you can control what and how activity updates. A structure can combine three types of information: characteristics, time reference or period units (weeks, days, months), and key figures (currency or quantities).

When it's linked to an LIS structure, the statistical key figure gains the ability to update automatically rather than require manually entered values. So if you are using the total number of sales orders for a report or allocation, this will eliminate the need to enter data manually. Updates occur by running a special transaction within Cost Center Accounting:

**KVA5**   This is the screen that will execute a transfer of data from LIS to the cost centers and statistical key figures.

**KVD5**   This is the screen that will execute a transfer of data from LIS to the cost center/activity type and statistical key figures.

To establish the link, select the Link to LIS button. The first box to appear will ask how you want to search for the LIS key figure to link with (see Figure 10.23).

**FIGURE 10.23**  Selecting the search strategy for key figures

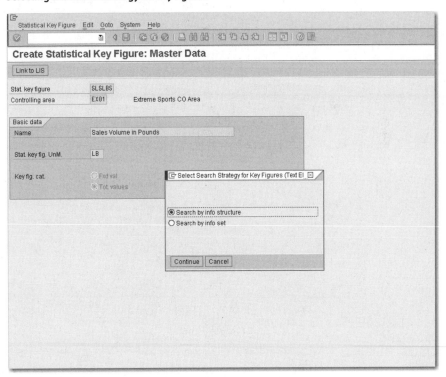

The two choices offered are similar, but distinctions are made:

**Search by Info Structure**   To search by information structures, you must have some knowledge of which module generates the data. Information structures will transfer both currency amounts and quantities.

**Search by Info Set**   Similar to information structures, info sets provide greater depth in the information by which they can search. However, as of version 3.1 only currency amounts can be transferred automatically.

The following examples will follow the path of searching by information structures.

The next screen to appear, shown in Figure 10.24, will ask you to select an application from which the information structure will update. It is vital that you select the proper application if you are to find the necessary structure and key figure. Select the desired application and continue. In the case of the Extreme Sports example, application 01, Sales and Distribution, was selected.

**FIGURE 10.24** Selecting an application

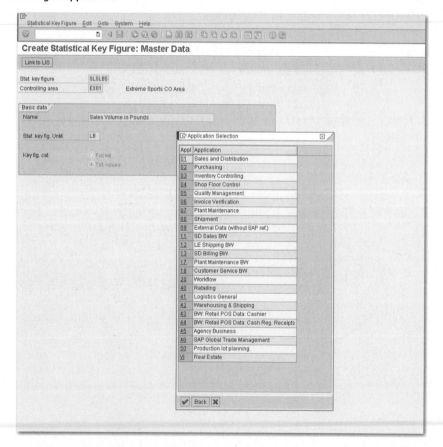

A list of available information structures will appear. The list will include both SAP-delivered and client-defined structures used for standard analysis. Review the list to determine the structure to which you want to attach your statistical key figure. The link is actually at the key-figure level on the information structure. When an information structure is selected, a list of potential key figures will appear, as shown in Figure 10.25. The key figure is the object that contains the data and is the lowest level of the assignment.

**FIGURE 10.25**   A list of potential key figures

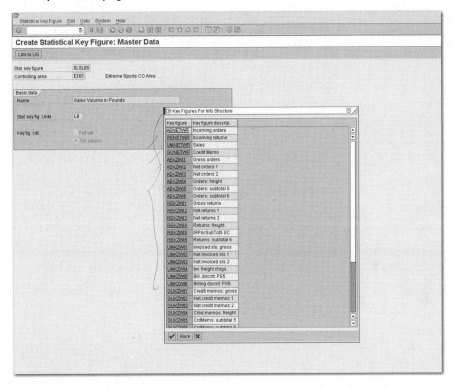

If you see the key figure you need in the list, select the object, and SAP will establish the link automatically. If the key figure is not present, click Back, and the information structure list will reappear. After you've selected the key figure, the basic screen will appear with the LIS link information established at the bottom of the master record, as shown in Figure 10.26. The information is grayed out because the link was established automatically by SAP and cannot be changed.

Here are the LIS Data fields on this screen:

**Value Origin**   The A in the field indicates that the statistical key figure will be determined automatically. SAP establishes the setting automatically.

**Info Structure**   This field contains the ID of the information structures you just selected. It may be helpful later if someone else needs to quickly identify how the statistical key figure is updated.

**LIS Key Figure**   This field contains the key figure on the information structure that updates the statistical key figure. Remember that the key figure is the object that holds the data within the information structure.

When configuration is complete, save the statistical key figure.

**FIGURE 10.26** The LIS Data link information

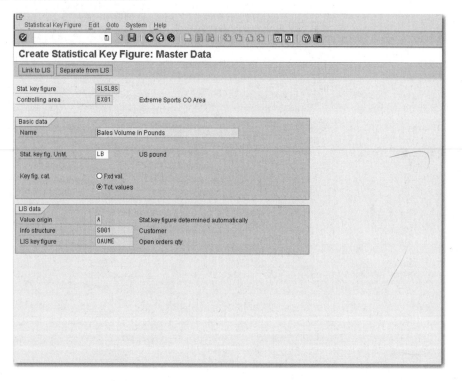

## Changing the LIS Link

If you need to make changes because you need to assign a new information structure or you don't want the statistical key figure to update automatically, you can break the link. Enter the statistical key figure master record and click the button Separate from LIS. The link will disappear from the bottom of the master record, and you can begin again.

# Creating and Maintaining Activity Types

Activity types are used within the SAP system to track activity, or output, within a cost center. Other objects within the controlling area will pull from a given cost center's resources and use them as their own. To ensure that proper credit is given at the proper rate and for the proper output type, activity types should be built at the proper level of detail. Examples of activity types include labor hours, overhead rate, electricity used, and consulting hours.

The function of activity types is to provide credit to the resource cost center at a specific rate multiplied by an amount of activity. To achieve this goal, activity types are assigned and planned on the sending resource cost center. As output is confirmed, the formula [rate * output type (hours)] is used to calculate a dollar credit/debit. A simple example follows.

Cost Center 1000 contains all the resources, or employees, that are used to support the plant-maintenance functions. Cost Center 2000 requires service to a piece of its machinery; the service utilizes 40 hours of labor at a rate of $10/hr. At the end of the period, Cost Center 1000 is credited for $400 of labor, whereas Cost Center 2000 is debited for $400. The posting occurred as a result of the assignment of an activity type called Labor, which was planned with a rate of $10, to Cost Center 1000. The maintenance activity was allocated internally within Controlling. No Financial Accounting updates occurred.

The next section will provide you with the steps to set up an activity type within Cost Center Accounting. Because activity types are used throughout production execution and plant-maintenance execution as well as by other modules, some comments may step outside the CCA boundary.

Additionally, the ideas of internal activity allocation and activity-type planning will be touched upon. Prior to creating the first activity type, you will need to create an allocation account within the controlling area.

## Creating the Allocation Cost Element

The allocation account is a secondary cost element and exists only in CO. The cost element is assigned on the activity-type master record and is the cost element that will be posted to during the credit/debit confirmation process. The cost element can be created from either the IMG or the user menu. Keep in mind the number of unique activities you will need to track, and be sure to create an accommodating number of cost elements.

Included here will be the IMG path and some simple guidelines for creating the allocation cost element. Refer to Chapter 9, "Cost Element Accounting," for detailed steps.

You can use the following methods to create an allocation cost element by using the menu path: Controlling ➢ Cost Center Accounting ➢ Master Data ➢ Activity Types ➢ Define Cost Elements for Activity Allocations, or use transaction code KA06.

A transaction selection screen will appear if you use the menu path as opposed to the transaction code. Select Create Allocation Cost Element. The create secondary cost element screen will appear. Here are some key points to creating the cost element:

▶ The cost element category should be 43, Internal Activity Allocation.

▶ Use an account number outside of your primary account range. It will make the account easier to recognize.

▶ Use a name and description that clearly define the activity (Maintenance Labor versus Production Labor). Reporting and analysis will be easier this way.

When you have completed the allocation cost element creation process, move on to maintaining the time-based fields on the activity types.

## Maintaining the Time-Based Fields

The concepts of time-based field settings are the same for activity types as they are for cost centers. As you make changes to fields on the activity-type master record, keep in mind the time-based settings. Additional analysis periods may be required. Use the following IMG menu path: Controlling ➢ Cost Center Accounting ➢ Master Data ➢ Activity Types ➢ Define Time Based Fields for Activity Types to maintain the fields, or using the transaction code OKE1.

The change: time-based fields (activity types) screen will appear (see Figure 10.27).

You will notice that the majority of the fields are flagged for historical tracking. The four not automatically set are described here:

**Name**   Enter the name of the activity type.

**Description**   Enter a description of the activity type.

**FIGURE 10.27** The change: time-based fields (activity types) screen

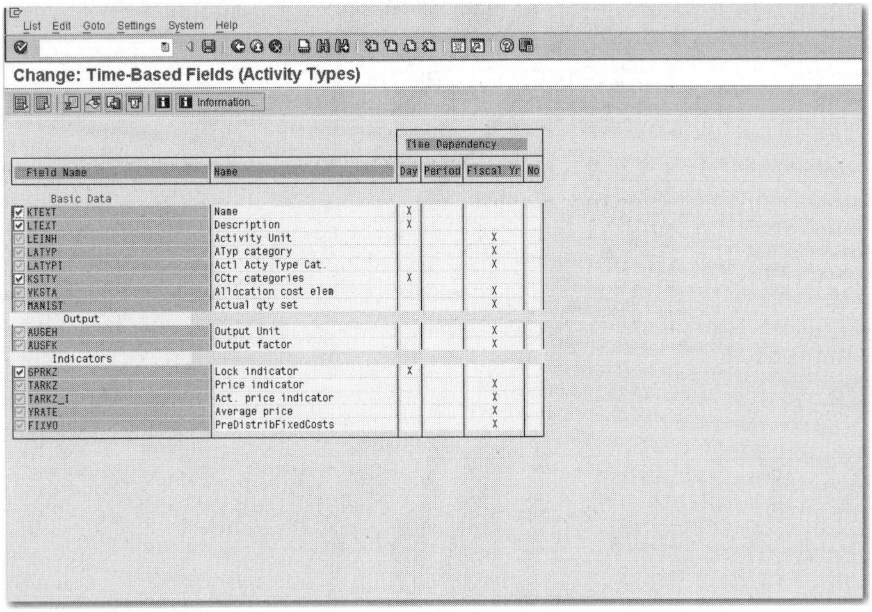

**CCtr Categories**   On the master record, you can limit the type of cost center the activity type can be assigned to by establishing a cost center category.

**Lock Indicator**   Use this field to determine whether the activity type is blocked from planning.

Make the historical flag settings as needed and save. You will, however, want to review the time dependency of each of the fields before creating or changing an activity-type master record. Once the settings are complete, you can move on to create the activity-type master record.

## Creating and Maintaining the Activity Type

You can create the activity type, which is master data, through either the IMG or user menu. The IMG path is Controlling ➢ Cost Center Accounting ➢ Master Data ➢ Activity Types ➢ Create Activity Types, and the transaction code is KL01.

The initial create activity type screen will appear (see Figure 10.28).

**FIGURE 10.28** The initial create activity type screen

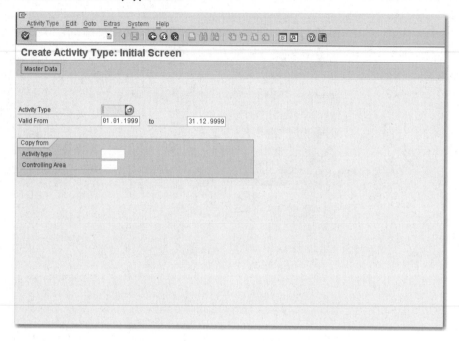

Here are the fields on this screen:

**Activity Type**    Enter the ID of the activity type you are creating. The ID can be up to six characters long.

**Valid From/To**    Enter the validity period of the activity type.

**TIP**    When maintaining the validity period, pay attention to the beginning date. If you are implementing midyear but want to plan for the entire year, including prior months, the activity type must be made valid for all prior periods. This is true for each of the objects in master data, including the cost elements and cost centers.

Press Enter when the ID and validity period have been created. The basic create activity type screen appears (see Figure 10.29).

**FIGURE 10.29** The basic create activity type screen

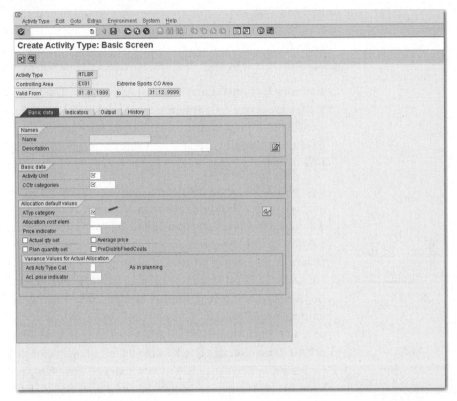

The first thing to notice is that the proper controlling area has been set and defined on the record. Next review the record for which fields are required. These are the minimal settings necessary to make the record available for use:

**Name**    Enter the name of the activity type. This field is required.

**Description**    Describe the activity in greater detail.

**Activity Unit**    Enter the unit of measure in which the activity type is measured (hours, minutes, or gallons per minute). Use the drop-down list to display possible entries. This field is required.

**CCtr Categories**    Enter the cost center type for which the activity type is valid for planning and internal activity allocations. If you enter an asterisk, the activity type is valid for all cost center types. It is recommended that changes to this category not be made within a fiscal period. The potential for inconsistencies is too great. This field is required.

**ATyp Category**     There are two separate sections to complete for the activity type category for Plan and Actual allocation. The first, seen in the Default Values section of the screen, is used to denote the default method for both plan and actual activity allocations. The category determines how the activity may be planned and how actual activity may be allocated. There are four potential categories to choose from:

**Category 1: Manual Entry, Manual Allocation**     Use this category if you desire to measure actual activity against a planned activity rate. For example, to process a credit for overhead activity OHLBS, you enter at the end of a period the actual production quantity in pounds. During the internal allocation process, SAP will take the actual amount entered and multiply it by the planned activity price.

**Category 2: Indirect Calculation, Indirect Allocation**     Categories 2 and 3 are both related to indirect allocation of activity. Category 2 should be used if, within your business, you deem it too difficult to accurately calculate the actual quantity of activity on a given cost center. In these cases, tracing and weighting factors on the receiver are used to determine the amount of credit to the sender. For example, Cost Center 100 is the central maintenance center for a production facility. Cost Centers 101, 201, and 301 all have had standard work provided for their respective cost centers by Cost Center 100. Activity MTLBR is planned on Cost Center 100 with a rate of $25/hr. One thousand hours of activity have occurred over the last period. So the total amount of credit coming to Cost Center 100 is $25,000, or $25 * 1,000 hours. In this example, it is impossible to know the exact number of hours that were applied to Cost Center 101, 201, and 301. In addition, there was activity from three other cost centers that contributed to the cost. It is determined that only 70% of the cost should be applied to 101, 201, and 301.

To facilitate the internal allocation, a tracing factor of # of Jobs Started is used to track activity. The number of jobs begun for each of the three cost centers is 10, 15, and 20 respectively. A weighting factor of 70% will ensure that only the appropriate percentage of costs will be allocated during the processing. Based upon the tracing factors, the following postings will occur:

- Cctr 101: [($25,000/50 jobs) * 10 jobs] * .70 = $3,500

- Cctr 101: [($25,000/50 jobs) * 15 jobs] * .70 = $5,250

- Cctr 101: [($25,000/50 jobs) * 25 jobs] * .70 = $8,750

**Category 3: Manual Entry, Indirect Allocation**    When you can accurately determine the amount of activity on the sender, the use of Category 3 becomes important. Similar to Category 1, the formula, (actual activity * a planned rate) is used to determine the amount of sender credit. Tracing factors are used during the allocation process to determine the cost each receiving center is to be posted with. For example, Cost Center 100 has a planned labor rate of $25. At the end of the period, the center is posted with 1,000 hours of actual maintenance hours. A tracing factor, # of Jobs Completed, is used to determine the cost that is to be allocated to each of the three maintenance cost centers: 101, 201, and 301. Cost Center 101 completed 10 jobs, Cost Center 201 completed 15 jobs, and Cost Center 301 completed 25, for a total 50 jobs completed.

During processing, the following calculations occur to provide for the proper allocation amounts:

► Cost Center 101: (10 jobs/50 jobs) * $25,000 = $5,000

► Cost Center 201: (15 jobs/50 jobs) * $25,000 = $7,500

► Cost Center 301: (25 jobs/50 jobs) * $25,000 = $12,500

**TIP**    The sender rule must use the setting Posted Quantities. Any of the receiver rules can be used, except Fixed Quantities.

**Category 4: Manual Entry, No Allocation**    All planned and actual activity is entered manually. It is not possible to allocate activity with this category. Values are entered in Cost Center Accounting using the following menu path: Actual Postings ➤ Manual Cost Allocation. The category is used when a cost center accrues costs that cannot be allocated to other CO objects using internal activity allocation. For example, a shipping cost center accrues activity costs for all marketing cost centers based upon the amount of daily shipments. These costs cannot be allocated internally.

**Allocation Cost Elem**    Enter the allocation cost element that both the sender and receiver will be posted with (see "Creating the Allocation Cost Element" earlier in this chapter for details).

**WARNING**   Be certain that the validity period of the cost element is equal to or greater than the validity period of the activity type to which it is being assigned. If there is a discrepancy, SAP will not allow the cost element to be used.

**Price Indicator**   As with the ATyp Category field, there are two locations to enter an activity price indicator. The first setting, found in the Default Values section, is used to determine how the plan and actual activity price is calculated. There are three choices:

**Option 01: Plan Price, Automatically Based on Activity**   The activity price is calculated automatically based upon plan activity and costs of the cost center in question. Both the fixed and variable portions of the variable price are calculated in the same manner. The combination of the fixed and variable prices adds to the total activity price.

**Option 02: Plan Price, Automatically Based on Capacity**   The activity price is calculated automatically based upon planned costs and capacity. The main difference between option 02 and option 01 is in the calculation of the fixed portion of the price. Planned capacity on the cost center, in conjunction with planned costs, is used to determine the fixed activity price.

**NOTE**   If you determine that option 01 or 02 is necessary for your solution, then you will be required to calculate the planned activity price (transaction code KSPI). Refer to the Version/Fiscal Year settings on the controlling area version to determine the activity-price calculation setting.

**Option 03: Determine Manually**   The activity price is determined manually.

**Actual Qty Set.**   If this field is activated, you must post a manual quantity in addition to the quantity with which the object is credited.

**Plan Quantity Set**   If this field is activated, the planned activity quantity is not changed by plan reconciliation.

**Average Price**   This indicator determines that activity prices for cost centers/ activity types remain constant for the entire fiscal year.

**PreDistribFixedCosts**   This indicator allows for the activity type or business process to be used in fixed cost predistribution.

The Variance Values for Actual Allocation section allows you to differentiate Actual allocations from the actual/plan settings established in the Allocation Default Values section.

**Actual Acty Type Cat.**   This is used for variance analysis for Actual allocations, not planned. Therefore this is a repeat of the AtTyp category from earlier. This is one of the four categories plus the options—as in planning—that are available. In the Allocation Default Values section, one additional category is found here:

**Category 5: Target-to-Actual Allocation**   Target-to-actual activity allocation uses the receiving cost center's operating rates to determine the actual activity quantities. No manual entry is allowed.

**Act. Price Indicator**   There are three methods for calculating the actual activity price; they are different from the plan method established in the Allocation Default Values section:

**Option 05: Actual Price, Automatically Based on Activity**   The actual price is calculated automatically based upon actual activity. To utilize the option, you must run the actual activity price calculation.

**Option 06: Actual Price, Automatically Based on Capacity**   The actual price is calculated automatically based upon capacity. The variable portion of the price will be determined based upon actual activity, whereas the fixed portion will be based upon capacity.

**Option 07: Manually Determined for Actual Allocations**   In this situation you would set the price of the activity type manually. Using this price indicator, you can set a price manually that is independent from the plan price.

When configuration is complete, save the activity type (see Figure 10.30). The activity type can now be planned on the appropriate cost center. Because activity-based costing (ABC) is not covered, much of the extensive activity type functionality is not demonstrated. If ABC is in scope for your project, we recommend that you attend one of the SAP courses on the subject matter prior to beginning.

The next section will cover the development of the following periodic allocations: assessments, distributions, and periodic repostings.

**FIGURE 10.30** The basic create activity type screen configured for Extreme Sports

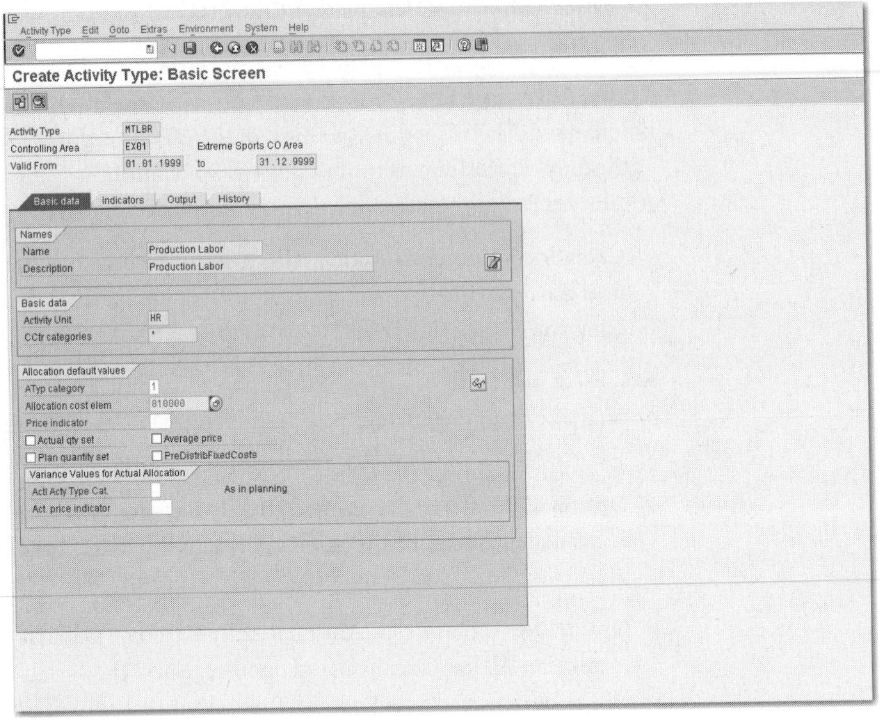

# Assessments, Distributions, and Periodic Repostings

In the past, accounting departments spent numerous hours manually allocating operating activities among their Strategic Business Units (SBUs) to get a more accurate profitability picture. Although we won't debate the worth of such allocations, we'll discuss SAP's capabilities in this area. We've already covered imputed cost calculations and indirect activity allocations in prior sections. The three remaining allocation methods we'll describe are assessments, distributions, and periodic repostings.

All CO allocations, or *periodic allocations* as SAP refers to them, act in a similar manner. Costs posted to an original object called a *sender* are allocated via a set of rules to an object called a *receiver*. With respect to assessments and distributions in Cost Center Accounting, the sender will always be a cost center. But the receiver can be any other CO object, like an order, a cost object, or a cost center. Periodic repostings allow for any CO object to be a sender or a receiver.

Another differentiating feature among the three is how each posts within the CO module. Because of the way in which they post, both periodic repostings and distributions will allocate primary costs only. Assessments can allocate both primary and secondary costs. Keep this in mind when determining which method is appropriate.

This section will discuss the configuration elements necessary to create the assessment, distribution, and periodic reposting cycles and segments. We'll also cover how to create an allocation cycle and segment. You have numerous options when making your settings, with many unique ways of grouping tracing factors, sender values, and receiver weighting. Experimentation will be important when building your solution. The process you use has a lot to do with the amount of information that is known about the process and what each area—sender and receiver—know about the process that it is trying to execute. You may find that the receiver of the cost/activity knows more about their ongoing needs, process, and requirements than the receiver knows about their own activities and what they are going to be able to support. So, based on this situation you lean on the receiver for the necessary information to do the allocations, therefore driving the process from the opposite end versus the source.

The first allocation type we'll discuss is assessments. However, the concepts covered, such as cycle/segment creation and allocation rules, will be applicable to all three types. We'll note where differentiation occurs.

## Periodic Allocations: Overview

When it is unimportant or not possible for the user to know the breakdown of costs that a cost center will receive in an allocation, assessments are a good, functional solution. Allocating general and administrative costs to an SBU is a good example of when assessments will work. In this scenario, it is probably unimportant for the SBU manager to know the specific detail behind the allocation; they need to know only the total amount of Goods & Administrative costs they have received. Further analysis is available through CCA reporting. If it is important that original cost elements be posted on both sender and receiver, distributions or periodic repostings methods are the solution.

Allocation configuration at the smallest level is defined as a *segment*. Segments are the individual rules through which an allocation determines what and how to assess. Primary and secondary costs are combined at the cost-center level and assigned in some way to receiver cost centers. Related segments are grouped together in what is called a cycle. This would be a great spot to open cycle run groups for parallel processing.

The *cycle* is the object that is run during the period/month-end processing. It is possible to have just one cycle for a given controlling area, with all allocation segments assigned. This would be impractical, however, due to the performance issues that would inevitably occur. Rather, multiple cycles should be created and run sequentially.

A key feature to all periodic allocations is the ability to reuse the settings repeatedly over many periods or years. The first step in defining an allocation is establishing the allowed receiver types, followed closely by developing the assessment cost element, if applicable, and then creation of the segments and cycles. Begin by looking at the SAP-delivered allocation receiver types.

## Allocation Receiver Types

SAP allows you to determine the receiver settings for each of the three types of allocations. Allowing differentiation between the Actual and Plan allocation types provides additional flexibility. The allocation type determines how the allocation is used. These settings act in the same manner as field-status variants in how they control what fields are made available for entry and what data may be included. All of the settings in this table are controlling area–dependent, so feel comfortable in experimenting with what works well for your solution.

We will review the cost center settings for the allocation type Actual. Remember that receiver type settings can be made only for repostings, distributions, and assessments. To eliminate needless redundancy, only the receiver type settings for an assessment will be detailed. The concepts are transferable to both distributions and periodic repostings. Again, realize that the assessment summarizes the allocation postings but the distribution, and periodic repostings generate detailed postings for both the sender and receiver.

---

**TIP**   The contents of this section are informational only. It is quite possible that you'll never have to augment the SAP-delivered settings.

---

To maintain the receiver type settings, follow the IMG menu path Controlling ➢ Cost Center Accounting ➢ Actual Postings ➢ Period End Closing ➢ Assessment ➢ Specify Receiver Types for Assessments, or use the transaction code KCAU.

The change view "customizing field attributes: allocation": details overview screen appears (see Figure 10.31).

Scroll down the screen and select the Actual allocation type with Cost Center as the field. The details screen for the cost center appears (see Figure 10.32).

**FIGURE 10.31** The Change View "Customizing Field Attributes: Allocation": overview screen

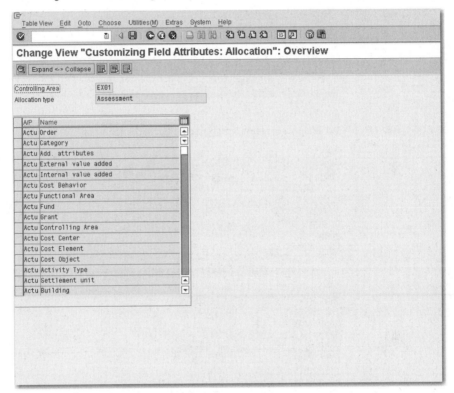

The characteristics detail screen will provide different options depending on the field you are maintaining. Some fields can be used as a sender object, a receiver object, or a tracing factor object. In our example, the cost center can be utilized as both a sender and a receiver. The concepts will be easier to understand if an example of an allocation is provided. In this case, an assessment is used.

See Figure 10.33 for an example of an assessment segment. As settings are changed in the allocation field characteristics screen, you will see the segment fields for the cost center appear or disappear. In the example, the SAP-delivered settings are being used.

**FIGURE 10.32** The change view "customizing field attributes: allocation: details field characteristics screen

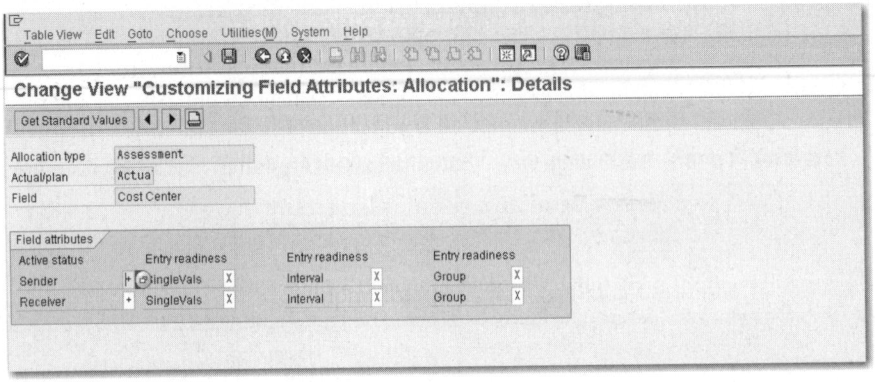

**FIGURE 10.33** An example of create actual assessment cycle: segment

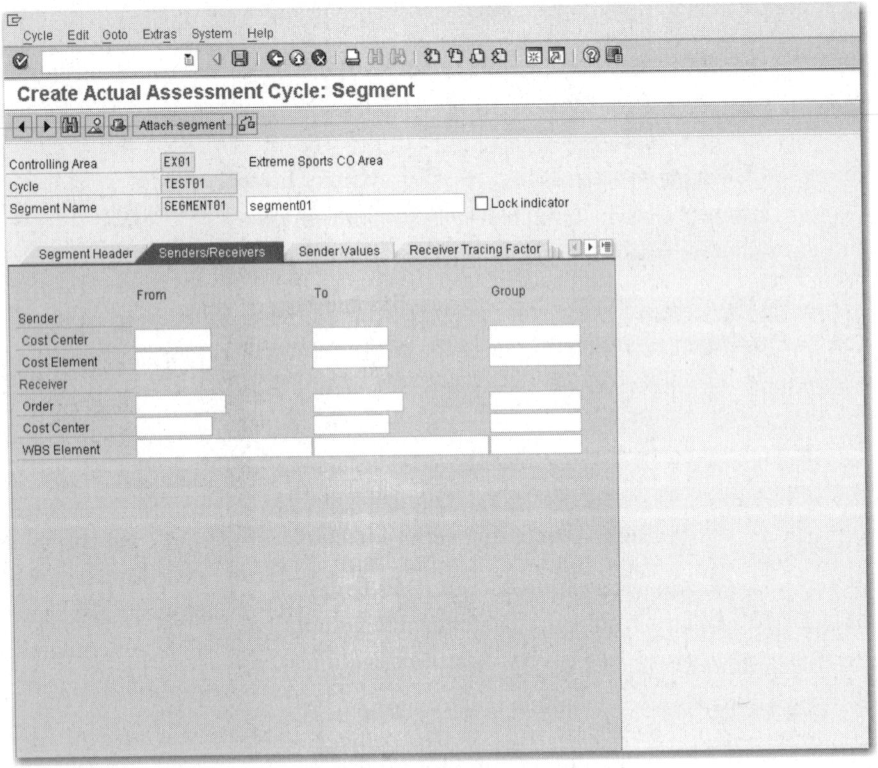

Referring back to Figure 10.32, you'll see these columns:

**Active Status (Sender and Receiver)**   Determines if the field is required, optional, or hidden during allocation maintenance.

**Entry Readiness (SingleVals)**   Determines whether you can enter a value in the From column on the allocation segment screen.

**Entry Readiness (Interval)**   Determines whether you can enter a value in the To column on the allocation segment screen.

**Entry Readiness (Group)**   Determines whether you can enter a value in the Group column on the allocation segment screen.

> **TIP**   In this example cost center, it is possible to remove a field from the assessment screen entirely. To accomplish this, remove all the settings from each of the Entry Readiness columns.

Returning to Figure 10.33 and the assessment-segment-screen example, see what happens when the Entry Readiness SingleVals and Interval fields for the sender are set to not allow entry. Figure 10.34 is an example of the allocation field characteristics screen, and Figure 10.35 shows the results of the settings on the assessment segment screen.

**FIGURE 10.34** The allocation field characteristics screen with the Entry Readiness SingleVals and Interval fields for the sender set to not allow entry

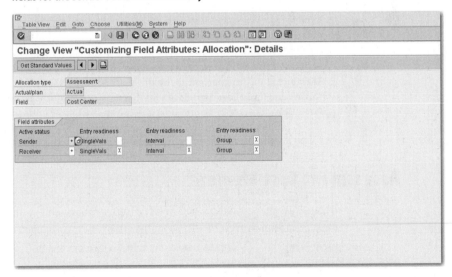

**FIGURE 10.35** The results of the settings on the create actual assessment cycle: segment screen

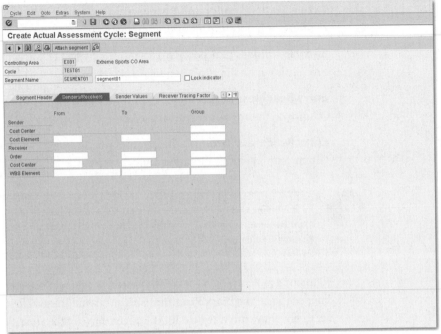

Notice in Figure 10.35 that the From and To fields disappear from the segment screen for the sender cost center. If you determine at a later date that you want the columns returned, simply reset them for entry.

**NOTE** Any changes made to the allocation field characteristics screen will be active for all allocations, both new and previously created. For the previously created allocations, the fields will be removed from sight, but the settings, if any, will remain valid. Therefore, if the field had entries before it was removed, the entries are still good. Keep this in mind if you have any allocations that require constant maintenance.

The next step in allocation development is creation of the assessment cost element.

## Assessment Cost Element

Because assessments allow you to settle both primary and secondary costs, you must create a new type of cost element called an *assessment element*. The assessment element is a secondary cost element used to post to both the sender and receiver during processing. Similar to the allocation cost element created in the "Activity Types and Statistical Key Figures" earlier in this chapter, you can create the assessment cost element from either the IMG or user menu. The user-menu path is Accounting ➢ Controlling ➢ Cost Elements ➢ Master Data ➢ Cost Element ➢ Individual Processing ➢ Create Secondary, and the transaction code is KA06.

The create secondary cost element screen appears. Because the details have been covered in previous chapters, we'll provide only some key points to creating the cost element here:

- ► The cost element category should be 42, Assessment Cost Element.

- ► Use an account number outside your primary account range. It will make the account more easily recognizable but make sure that these account numbers are used only for this activity.

- ► Use a name and description that clearly define the activity (Advertising Assessment, Selling & Marketing Assessment). Reporting and analysis will be easier this way.

Save the assessment cost element. The next section will cover the development of an Actual allocation.

## Allocation Creation

You can create the allocation from either the IMG or the user menu. For demonstration purposes, we'll show how to build a cost center assessment. Where a unique field setting for a specific type of allocation may occur, it will be noted. The IMG paths for all three types are listed here:

You can get to the screen to create cost center reposting by using the following menu path: Controlling ➢ Cost Center Accounting ➢ Actual Postings ➢ Period End Closings ➢ Periodic Reposting ➢ Define Periodic Repostings, or by using the transaction code KSW1.

To create a cost center distribution use the menu path Controlling ➢ Cost Center Accounting ➢ Actual Postings ➢ Period End Closings ➢ Distribution ➢ Define Distribution, or use the transaction code KSV1.

Finally the third approach to creation of the cost center assessment is via the menu path Controlling ➢ Cost Center Accounting ➢ Actual Postings ➢ Period End Closings ➢ Assessment ➢ Maintain Assessment, or by using the transaction code KSU1.

After executing the maintain assessment option in the menu path, you have to choose the appropriate option: either create or change. The initial create actual assessment cycle screen appears. Give the cycle a name and a valid start date. When entering the start date, it is best to provide the first day of a fiscal period. That way, all postings within the period will be selected. Press Enter, and the Create Actual Assessment Cycle: Header Data screen appears (see Figure 10.36).

**FIGURE 10.36** The create actual assessment cycle: header data screen

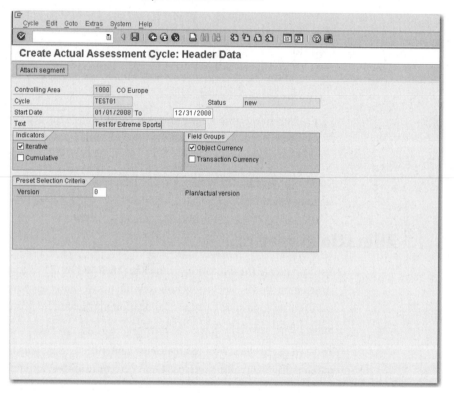

The allocation, or assessment, cycle header provides settings that are valid for all attached segments. Here you will find a listing of the pertinent fields on the header, and definitions of how they should be utilized:

**Start Date**    You provided the starting date of the cycle on the initial screen. Within the header, you have the ability to provide the ending date for the validity period range.

**Text**    Enter a high-level description of what the cycle will accomplish.

The fields in the Indicators section are as follows:

**Iterative**   This indicator controls whether iterative sender/receiver relationships are considered when this cycle is processed. The iteration repeats until each sender is fully credited. An example of this would be the use of water to generate heat, then the use of heat to generate water. This could become an iterative process that might go on for quite some time. Setting this indicator would allow the iterative process to be executed.

Let's look at an example. In Segment 1, cost center 1000 wants to allocate $1,000 to cost centers 2000 and 3000, 50% to each. In turn, in Segment 2, cost center 2000 wants to allocate 100% of its posted amount to cost centers 1000 and 3000, also 50% each. Table 10.1 shows the steps taken during an iterative cycle.

**TABLE 10.1**   Calculation Base for Iterative Cycle

| Step | Cost Center 1000 | Cost Center 2000 | Cost Center 3000 |
|---|---|---|---|
| 1. $1,000 from cost center 1000 | $0 | $500 | $500 |
| 2. $500 from cost center 2000 | $250 | $0 | $250 |
| 3. $250 from cost center 1000 | $0 | $125 | $125 |
| 4. $125 from cost center 2000 | $62.50 | $0 | $62.50 |
| 5. $62.50 from cost center 1000 | $0 | $31.25 | $31.25 |
| **Net Allocation Amount** | $0 | $0 | $1000 |

In the example, the iteration would continue until the entire $1,000 was allocated to cost center 3000. If there is no similar link between the segments in a cycle, do not activate iteration. The processing time for this type of cycle is considerably more than one in which iteration is not required.

**Cumulative**   If this indicator is set, the allocation will be executed with cumulative values rather than values of the current period. The sender amounts posted up to the current period are allocated based on tracing factors, which are cumulated from period 1 onwards.

**Object Currency**   Controlling-area currency is the default currency for CO allocations. By activating this setting, you are requesting that the object currency be taken into account during the calculation and posting. SAP will calculate and post the object currency results and controlling-area results separately. A precondition to using object currency is that all sender and receiver objects must use the same currency type. If a discrepancy arises, SAP ignores the setting and posts using only the controlling area currency.

**Transaction Currency**   If this setting is activated, the allocation values are calculated in the transaction currencies on the sender and then posted to the receivers. If the setting is not activated, all postings occur in controlling-area currency only.

Let's look at another example. Cost center 1000 has activity in two currencies: $1,000 in DEM and $1,500 in MXP. You want to allocate 75% of the activity to cost center 2000 and 25% to cost center 3000. If Transaction Currency is activated, the allocation postings will produce the line items shown in Table 10.2.

**TABLE 10.2**    Transaction Currency Postings

| Cost Center 1000 | Cost Center 2000 | Cost Center 3000 |
|---|---|---|
| $1,000 MXP | | |
| $1500 DEM | | |
| ($1,000) DEM | $750 | $250 |
| ($1,500) MXP | $1,125 | $375 |

The results of the allocation include six line-item postings with Transaction Currency active rather than three if it were not active. Keep in mind that having Transaction Currency active will increase the number of line items posted.

Use the path Cycle ➤ Check ➤ Formal Check or Formal Check in Batch to have SAP review the master data validation.

**Preset Selection Criteria: Version**   This will identify the version of the postings that will be used in the allocation process. If the version is 0, then the postings allocated will be the actual postings. A number of versions can be used, but all are segments of planned data except for version 0.

When you have completed the header detail, begin to add the segments to the cycle. Select the Attach Segment button. The create actual assessment segment detail configuration screen appears (see Figure 10.37).

Begin the segment definition by filling in the following fields:

**Segment**   Enter a unique 10-character ID defining the segment.

**Text**   Describe the function of the segment.

**Lock Indicator**   If this box is checked, the segment will be excluded from cycle processing.

**FIGURE 10.37** The segment detail configuration screen

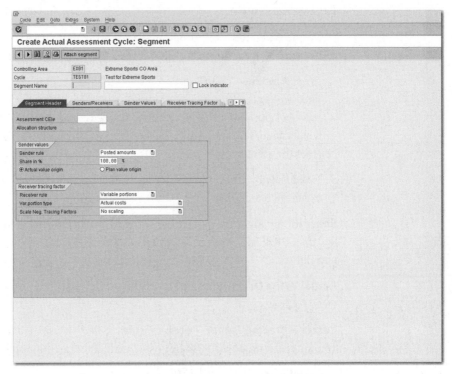

**Assessment CEle**   (Used by assessments only.) Enter the assessment cost element that will be used to post to the sender and receiver. See the section on "Assessment Cost Element Creation" in Chapter 9.

**Allocation Structure**   If your allocation is more complex than just having one assessment cost element to allocate the posted values, then you may need to create an allocation structure. This will allow you the flexibility to have more than one cost element for allocation purposes. If the allocation structure is used, all of the information required for the creation of the cycle will be configured within this structure. Therefore the structure will house the sender rules, tracing-factor format, sender and receiver values, additional details around the sender values, and any receiver weighting factors.

**Sender Values: Sender Rule**    Select how the sender values will be calculated. Here are the options:

**Posted Amounts**    If this option is selected, SAP will use the amounts posted to the sender object through whatever transactions have occurred.

**Fixed Amounts**    If this option is selected, SAP will ask you to maintain the fixed amounts with which the sender objects (cost center) will be posted. Each receiver's portion will be determined by the tracing factors. A button called Sender Values will appear in the icon bar. Select it; a screen will appear for you to enter the amount per object.

**Fixed Rates**    This option is similar to Fixed Amounts, but you enter fixed prices rather than amounts.

**Share in %**    Enter the percentage of sender activity you want to allocate. Anything less than 100% will result in a portion of the sender value remaining on the sender object.

**Actual Value Origin/Plan Value Origin**    Select which type of sender values you wish to allocate.

**Receiver Tracing Factor: Receiver Rule**    Select the method that calculates the amount receiving objects will be posted with. There are four options:

**Variable Portions**    When using variable portions, SAP determines the allocation amount automatically, based on the tracing factor selected. (See the setting for Scale Neg. Tracing Factors for details on the impact of this selection.) The use of variable portions is appropriate if you want to always derive the posting from the actual or planned activity on a cost center. For example, suppose you allocate your actual G&A expense based on the planned ratios. Additionally, you have the opportunity to add a receiver weighting to the receiving objects by selecting the Receiver Weighting button. The default setting is 1. Select the Tracing Factors button and enter the appropriate information. See Figure 10.38 for a view of the screen.

**Fixed Amounts**    If you choose Fixed Amounts in the Rule field, select the Tracing Factors button, and within the receiver tracing factor screen, enter the amounts that should be posted to each receiver. The amount of the sender credit will be the sum of the fixed amounts posted to the receivers. See Figure 10.39 for a view of the screen.

**FIGURE 10.38** The receiver tracing factor screen with the Variable Portions option chosen

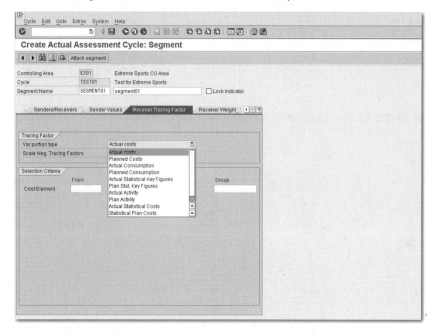

**FIGURE 10.39** The receiver tracing factor screen with the Fixed Amounts option chosen

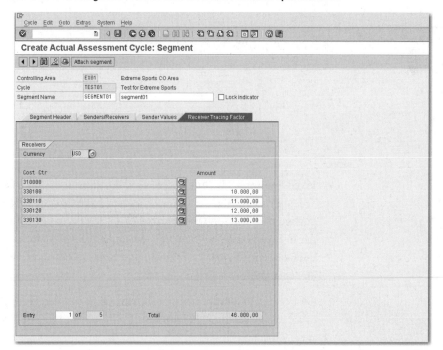

**Fixed Percentages**    If you choose Fixed Percentages in the Rule field, select the Tracing Factors button, and within the receiver tracing factor screen, enter the percentage of cost allocation to be posted to each receiver. The total percentage is not to exceed 100%. If the tracing factor percentage is less than 100%, the percentage of cost less than 100 will be left on the sender. See Figure 10.40 for a view of a completed percentage screen.

**FIGURE 10.40**  The receiver tracing factor screen with the Fixed Percentages option chosen

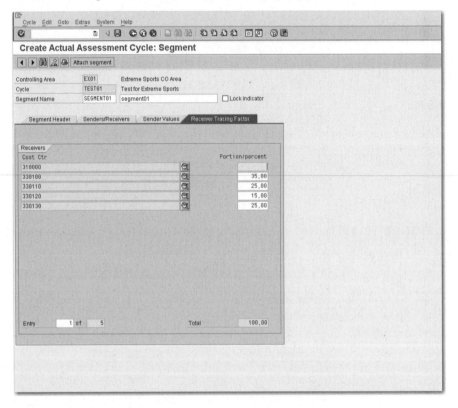

**Fixed Portions**    If you choose Fixed Portions in the Rule field, select the Tracing Factors button, and within the receiver tracing factor screen enter the portion of allocation with which each receiver is to be posted. This option is similar to Fixed Percentages except you can exceed 100% for the portion allocated to the receivers. Review the following portions and the accompanying formula for an explanation.

Cost center 1000 wants to allocate $10,000 to cost center 2000 with a portion of 75, to cost center 3000 with a portion of 75, and to cost center 4000 with a portion of 100. The total portion amount is 250 (75 + 75 + 100). The amount each cost center is to receive is calculated here:

Cost center 2000: $10,000/250 * 75 = $3,000

Cost center 3000: $10,000/250 * 75 = $3,000

Cost center 4000: $10,000/250 * 100 = $4,000

Net allocation = $10,000

See Figure 10.41 for a view of the completed receiver tracing factor screen with the Fixed Portions option chosen.

**FIGURE 10.41** The receiver tracing factor screen with the Fixed Portions option chosen

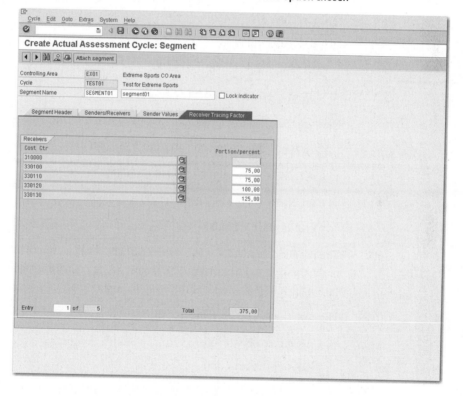

Once you have completed the segment, additional segments can be added quickly by selecting the Attach Segment button. As you add the segments, keep in mind processing speed and cycle integration. See the next section, "Allocation Development Issues."

**Scale Neg. Tracing Factors**    Negative tracing factor may come into play if you determine that a segment will use actual posted values rather than fixed amounts or rates. Within the allocation, tracing factors are used to determine the amount to be posted to the receiver. The factors can include amounts from key figures, activity types, or actual/plan costs. Negative tracing factors are important when the tracing factor selected involves variable portions. The following is an example of the impact of negative tracing factors on an allocation.

Suppose that sender cost center 1000 wants to allocate $10,000 to three receiving cost centers: 2000, 3000, and 4000. The tracing factor is set to Variable Portions and uses actual postings CO statistical key figure PROD, net production activity.

Here are the actual key figure values for each cost center:

Cost center 2000 = 100

Cost center 3000 = 50

Cost center 4000 = –50

Net tracing factor = 100

Here are the calculations without negative tracing factors active:

Cost center 2000: $10,000 * 100/100 = $10,000

Cost center 3000: $10,000 * 50/100 = $5,000

Cost center 4000: $10,000 * –50/100 = –$5,000

Net allocation = $10,000

The net allocation value is accurate at $10,000, but on an individual cost-center basis, the amounts are wrong. The largest negative factor is set to zero, and the absolute value is added to each of the other factors.

Here are the key figure values for each cost center:

Cost center 2000 = 150

Cost center 3000 = 100

Cost center 4000 = 0

Net tracing factor = 250

Here are the calculations with negative tracing factors active:

Cost center 2000: $10,000 * 150/250 = $6,000

Cost center 3000: $10,000 * 100/250 = $4,000

Cost center 4000: $10,000 * –0/250 = $0

Net allocation = $10,000

Cost center 4000, with the negative tracing factor of –50, does not receive any value. Be certain to activate the setting if you feel there is any opportunity to have a negative tracing factor.

To further handle negative tracing factors there are six choices with varying scenarios based on the previous example:

► No Scaling

► Standard Scaling

► Absolute Value (Negative to Positive)

► Negative Tracing Factors to Zero

► Smallest Negative Tracing Factor to Zero

► Smallest Negative Tracing Factor to Zero, but Zero = Zero

The next section to configure in the segment detail configuration screen (see Figure 10.42) is the senders/receivers section. There are two subsections, Sender and Receiver:

1. Enter in this section the ranges of valid sender/receiver objects. The objects can vary from cost centers to WBS elements, depending on the type of allocation you are creating. The key is to include only objects that are required. Object groups, like cost center groups, are a good exclusionary tool.

2. If you want to allocate all costs assigned to your sender objects, do not limit the cost elements included within the allocation. Leaving the Cost Element range blank is the easiest way to include all cost element postings in an allocation calculation.

3. Once the senders and receivers have been identified, you can maintain all tracing factors and receiver weights.

**FIGURE 10.42** Senders/receivers screen for the From and To values

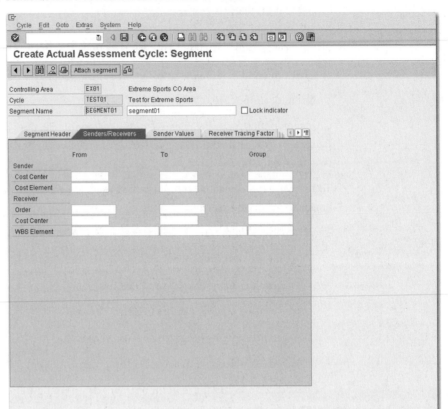

**Consumption**   This field is used by distributions and periodic repostings only. If it's selected, consumption quantities will be allocated along with the dollars. A precondition to using this setting is that all senders must have quantities posted on them. If the condition is not met, SAP will deliver a warning and the allocation will be stopped.

The final portions of the assessment cycle to configure are the sender values and receiver weighting factors. In both cases, the fields on each of these screens will vary based on the information and values assigned in the previous screens:

**Sender Values**   On this screen the share of the total amounts are defined for the allocation process. Therefore the sender can define that only a portion of the total values is to be allocated at a given time. This is quite valuable in terms of smoothing the allocation process if you are allocating by periods. Rather than having large amounts allocated in one period and smaller amounts allocated in another period, the sender can identify a fixed amount to allocation or a percentage of the total to allocate. Further filtering of the values to be allocated can be accomplished using the additional selection criteria for versions and characteristic values.

**Receiver Weighting Factors**    On this screen the amount assigned to each receiver can be controlled. The effect of configuring this screen is that each of the receivers can be assigned a percentage or fixed amount of the values being allocated. Therefore a weighting factor can be used in this process to distribute the costs more effectively and accurately across the different receivers. This can be based on any sort of statistical key figure process.

When you have completed the allocation, run a quick master data check. Use the menu path Cycle ➤ Check ➤ Formal Check or Formal Check in Batch, and SAP will validate the master data included within the allocation. When configuration is complete, save the allocation.

# Allocation Development Issues

The preceding section took you through the creation of a single cycle and segment. It is very possible that your solution will require multiple cycles containing multiple segments. This is not unusual. Before building a cycle, however, identify any dependencies that may need to exist at either the segment or cycle level.

Dependencies will determine the order with which a cycle/segment will process. A dependent cycle is one that requires the results of another previously run cycle or cycles before it can successfully process its allocation. The same meaning covers any dependent segments. Selecting the Iterative indicator on the cycle header will ensure that the attached segments are processed as dependent. Cycles do not have the advantage of an iterative indicator.

You must force the execution of each cycle in the proper order by either entering them properly on the execute actual assessment screen (see Figure 10.43) or running them individually in order.

A second development issue deals with the proper number of cycles and segments to build. SAP will support a 1-cycle, 100-segment allocation, but it is completely impractical. There are two things to keep in mind when deciding how many cycles and segments to build:

➤ You have the ability to correct a single segment's posting within an allocation cycle. If an error occurs within a segment posting, that specific segment can be reversed and rebooked. For example, go into Distribution ➤ Segment Adjustment.

**FIGURE 10.43** The allocation execution screen

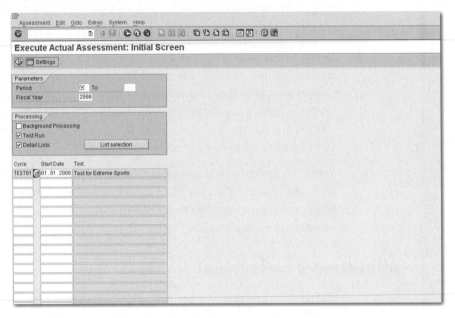

▶ Consider the timing of your closing cycle. If too many segments are tied together, you may negatively influence the closing and reporting schedule. An example would be a cycle with all SBU-specific allocations contained within. If one SBU is not ready to process, no SBU allocations can occur. You should always consider breaking apart unrelated cycles and segments.

**TIP** The cycle can be reversed via the Assessment ➤ Reverse menu path from the execute actual assessment: initial screen.

Remember that it will be important to experiment with allocations to find the proper mix. Expect to make changes periodically throughout the year to tweak for performance and timing.

Another helpful tool in the allocation process is the use of the Runtime Analysis. This will allow the processor to review the process and progress of all cycles from a single screen, offering additional insight into the overall cycle process, individual cycles, and individual segments within a cycle (see Figure 10.44). To access this component from the Execute Actual Assessment: Initial Screen ➤ Goto ➤ Runtime Analysis.

**FIGURE 10.44** Display runtime analysis CCA: actual assessment screen

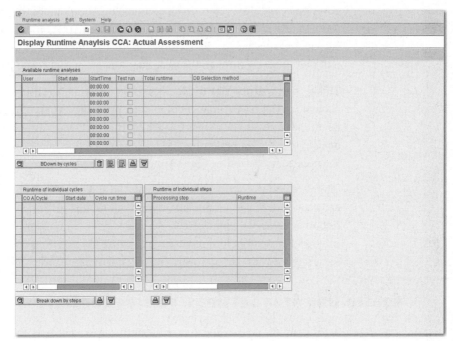

The next section will take you through some of the relevant planning topics for Cost Center Accounting.

## EXTREME SPORTS PERIODIC ALLOCATIONS CONFIGURATION ANALYSIS

Extreme Sports will utilize cost center assessments to allocate its general and administration costs from its Shared Services organization to each of its operating divisions. Distributions will be utilized for the purpose of reorganizing actual postings. As the cost center structure is modified, actual activity to date may need to be moved to the new area. Distributions will be the tool of choice.

# Cost Center Accounting: Planning

Much of the theory for planning and budgeting within Cost Center Accounting will not be discussed in this section. Rather, the topics covered will enhance some basic functionality. Some general theory will inevitably come out, but it is impossible to cover every industry's planning methodology. Additionally, the goal of this section is not to provide detailed analysis of SAP planning integration. Since the overall subject area of planning, budgeting, and forecasting could fill a book on its own, we will work our way through the basic components of cost center planning.

This section will describe the configuration necessary to ensure that integration occurs if desired. Development of manual planning layouts and how allocations can be utilized will also be covered. Much of what SAP offers as preconfigured tools will be used to meet your planning needs. The first section relates to version control and the necessary controlling area settings.

There are many options and components of CCA planning, and even though we can't cover all of the components and functions, it is very important to review and test other areas of planning in CCA, such as full integrated planning, resource planning, and allocation. It is possible to configure the planning side at just about the same level of granularity at which we track actuals.

## Controlling Area Settings/Version Control

Settings on the controlling area will determine to what level planning integration will occur within Cost Center Accounting. Figure 10.45 is a view of the fiscal-year parameters of the controlling area for version 0. The details behind the settings are covered at length in the "Maintain CO Versions" section of Chapter 8, "Controlling Enterprise Structure." Review the section so you can be aware of each field's impact in the planning process.

For a quick reference, however, here are two fields that you should consider deciding on the level of planning integration:

**Planning Integration**    This field should be activated if you want any planned activity on the cost center to integrate with other modules.

**Planning Integration with CCA**    Activate this setting if you want to have internal order/WBS-element plans integrate with Cost Center Accounting. The integration is a two-way door; cost center plans can affect orders, and order planning can affect cost centers.

These settings are controlling area/version/fiscal year–specific. If you desire, you can have multiple versions, each with unique settings. Version control and the concept of multiple versions are discussed in the next section.

**FIGURE 10.45** The change view "settings for each fiscal year": details parameters of the controlling area for version 0

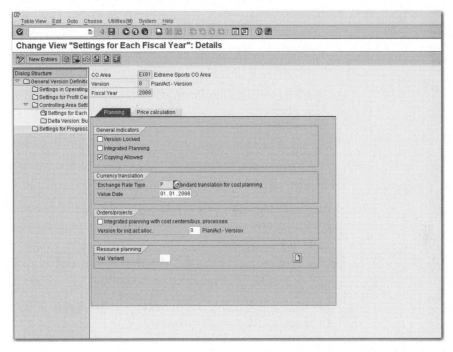

## Planning Versions

Utilization of version control, or maintaining multiple planning versions, can enhance a company's ability to build complex planning scenarios. To make better use of SAP's flexibility, it is recommended that you have more than one planning version. The de facto version from which you will draw your actual/plan comparisons is version 0, because only version 0 is updated in real time with actual transactional data. Prior to creating a controlling area–specific version in Cost Center Accounting, you must define the general version ID. The creation of the general version ID is covered in Chapter 8, in the section "Maintain CO Versions" (review the section for more detailed analysis).

By creating a general CO version, you have made the ID available for use by all controlling areas. The assignment to controlling area is not automatic, meaning that all versions are not available to all controlling areas upon creation. However, when you are defining the controlling-area settings, SAP will ask you if you want to copy the new version to the controlling area that is set at that time. If you answer yes, the version—along with its controlling area, fiscal year, and delta version settings—is copied to your controlling area. The necessary steps and transaction code for defining a new planning version are as follows:

1. Create a general version ID for CO (transaction code OKEQ).

2. Define settings for the controlling area. (Version 0 setting is automatic for all controlling areas and is available during controlling area creation.)

3. Define settings for the fiscal year.

4. Define settings for the delta version (if applicable).

Once a plan version is created, plan data can be entered. SAP provides you with a tool that allows you to copy plan data from one version to another. The next section will elaborate on this feature.

**Copying Plan Data**   One key feature of version control is the ability to copy one version to another, as long as the configuration is set to support the activity (see Figure 10.46). To use the copy planning functionality, follow the user menu path Accounting ➢ Controlling ➢ Cost Center Accounting ➢ Planning ➢ Planning Aids ➢ Copy Plan to Plan or use the transaction code KP97.

The initial copy planning screen will appear (see Figure 10.46). Any of these settings can be changed at any time between copies.

**FIGURE 10.46** The initial copy planning screen

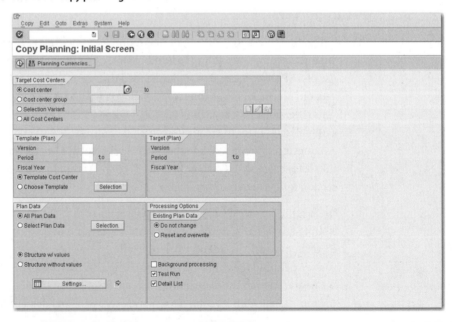

The key fields in the Target Cost Centers section are as follows:

**Cost Center**    You can select to copy to the cost centers that were identified in the Copy From section in the previous dialog box or augment the range of centers. There are certain copy relationships SAP will not support in the copy process. Sending data from all cost centers to a single cost center is one of these relationships. You can choose to use a cost center group (hierarchy) or all cost centers.

The key fields in the Template (Plan) section are as follows:

**Version**    Enter the version you want to copy.

**Period and Fiscal Year**    Enter the period range and year of the data to be copied. There is no limitation to copying across fiscal years.

**Cost Center Selection**    You have a choice of including all cost centers within a controlling area in the copy or including a smaller subset.

Here are the key fields in the Target (Plan) section:

**Version**    Enter the version you want to receive the copy.

**Period and Fiscal Year**    The period range must equal the range entered in the Copy From section. If you're copying to a future fiscal year, be sure to have the year defined for the controlling area.

Here are the key fields in the Plan Data section:

**All Plan Data and Select Plan Data**    Use these fields to determine whether postings from all planning transactions can be copied, or only specific planned postings.

**Structure w/without Values**    Select Structure w/ Values if you want to copy the planned postings to the target version. If you want the copy to erase plan data in the target version and replace it with all $0s, select Structure without Values.

The key fields in the Processing Options section are listed here:

**Existing Plan Data**    If you have existing plan data in your target version and you do not want the entry erased with the copy, select Do Not Change in the Existing Plan Data box. If data is to be replaced with the copy regardless of any existing data, select Reset and Overwrite.

**Background Processing/Detailed List**    If the plan-data records coming from the sender cost centers are significant, run the transactions in the background. If not, the choice is yours. Select the Detail List check box to receive detail about the copy.

When you've completed your settings, execute the transaction. You cannot save the settings as a variant, so each time you want to copy, the entries will have to be remade. When completed, a detailed report will appear, offering statistics specific to the copy.

**NOTE** Cost Center Accounting planning has changed and is not limited to copying only plan data across versions; you have the ability to copy actuals to plan in CCA as well as in Profit Center Accounting (PCA). You will see PCA's ability to copy across value types in Chapter 12, "Profitability Analysis."

## Plan Revaluation

Another nice feature of cost center planning is the ability to revalue existing plan data without rekeying. SAP allows the user to adjust, by percentage, any existing plan data within any version. Revaluation will come in handy during "what-if" analysis and when making broad but general plan adjustments. An example of revaluation use might be to increase salaries, taxes, and benefits in all shared services cost centers by 5%. For 150 cost centers, the change may take hours. But with the proper cost center and cost element sets, revaluation could handle the change in seconds.

Be aware that, as with most of the planning configuration, the revaluation can be created from both the user menu and IMG. The IMG menu path is Controlling ➤ Cost Center Accounting ➤ Planning ➤ Planning Aids ➤ Define Revaluation ➤ Create Plan Revaluation, or you can use the transaction code KPU1.

The initial create plan revaluation screen will appear (see Figure 10.47).

**FIGURE 10.47** The initial create plan revaluation screen

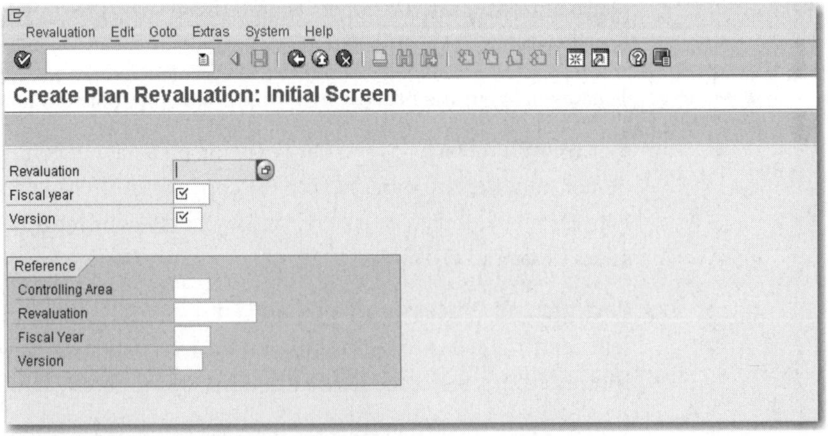

Begin defining the revaluation by establishing the ID/fiscal year/version relationship:

**Revaluation**    Enter a 10-character ID for your revaluation. This field is required.

**Fiscal Year**    Enter the fiscal year for which the revaluation is valid. The validity period is limited to a single fiscal year. This field is required.

**Version**    Enter the version that you want the revaluation to affect. This field is required.

When you've filled out these fields, press Enter. The create plan revaluation: select screen will appear (see Figure 10.48). Within the screen, you define which cost centers and cost elements the revaluation will impact.

**FIGURE 10.48**  The create plan revaluation: select screen

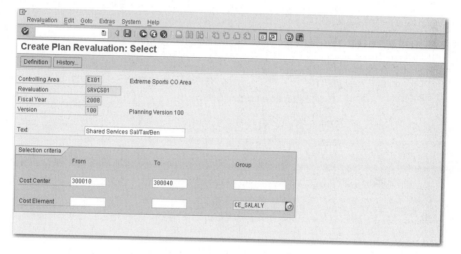

 **WARNING**    All cost centers included in the revaluation will be augmented, so be careful when entering the object ranges.

Begin by providing the revaluation with a text description:

**Text**    Enter a description for the revaluation. It is likely that you will have more than one revaluation, so be clear in your description.

**Cost Center**    Enter a single cost center or a range/group of cost centers that should be augmented by the revaluation.

**Cost Element**    Enter a single cost element or a range/group of cost elements that should be augmented by the revaluation. Only primary cost elements can be revalued. Secondary and assessment cost elements are excluded.

> **TIP**    A properly developed cost element group can provide flexibility in your ability to define revaluation percentages.

In the example provided (see Figure 10.48), a range of Extreme Sports's shared services cost centers was entered, as well as a cost element group comprising salary, tax, and benefit accounts.

Click the Definition button on the create plan revaluation screen to establish the percentage changes for the cost element range/group by period. The create plan revaluation: definition screen will appear (see Figure 10.49).

**FIGURE 10.49** The create plan revaluation: definition screen

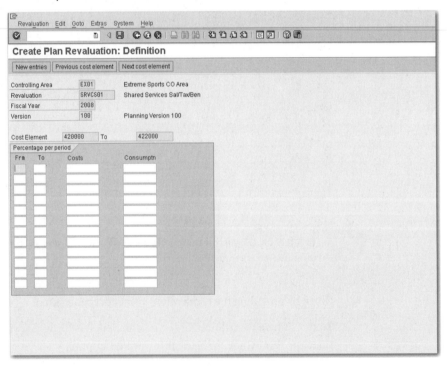

The definition screen allows you to enter percentage changes, either up or down, for the cost elements selected in the prior screen. Notice the range of cost elements that appears in the middle of the screen. In the example provided, a cost element group was defined to encompass a range of salary, tax, and benefit accounts. The cost element group can be seen in Figure 10.50. The same group of accounts could have been added easily as one From/To range of 420000 to 422000 on the selection screen, but the impact would have been different on the definition screen.

**FIGURE 10.50** The cost element group used in planning revaluation

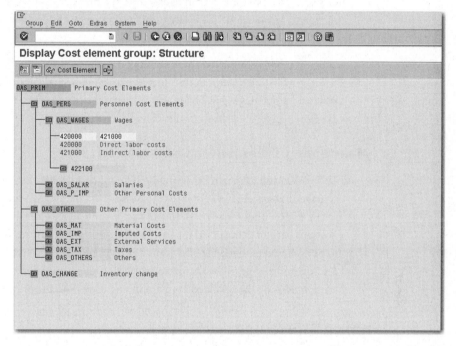

If a single range of accounts is included, there can be no differentiation between cost elements when assigning percentages, meaning that a 5% increase to cost element 500000 and a 10% increase to cost element 503001 would not be possible. Although across-the-board increases are acceptable in many cases, in the example provided, the increases required a different percentage adjustment for administrative labor and direct labor. The only way to achieve this differentiation is through a cost element group.

By building a cost element group that applies both cost elements on separate lines, and not in a range like cost elements 420000–422000, you gain the ability to enter percentages uniquely. Referring back to the create plan revaluation: definition screen (see Figure 10.49), begin completing the revaluation by deciding which period range you want the percentage increase to affect and entering it into the Frm and To columns:

**Frm/To**   Enter the range of periods the percentage change is to affect. You can have a unique percentage change for each fiscal period.

**Costs**   Enter a percentage change, positive or negative, for the specific cost element(s) in question. The change will affect dollars only, not quantities.

**Consumptn**   Enter a percentage change, positive or negative, for the specific cost element(s) in question. The change will affect consumption quantity planned for the cost center(s)/cost element(s).

When you have completed the screen but other cost elements exist within the range, select the Cost Element + button to move to the next element or range of elements. When all percentages have been applied, save the revaluation. The plan revaluation can now be executed through the CCA user menu.

### Maintaining/Deleting Plan Revaluation

The plan revaluation can be maintained for all cost centers, cost elements, and percentage changes entered. Be careful, however, to not delete or make a change to a revaluation without first reversing any prior runs. Once a revaluation is deleted, the postings cannot be reversed for that same definition. A new revaluation would have to be designed to mask the effects of the prior one. The same principle applies to any revaluation changes. Always reverse the effects from the prior run. Otherwise you are augmenting the revalued plan amounts rather than the original postings.

## Planning Allocations

The development of periodic allocations like assessments and distributions was covered earlier in the chapter. These same tools can be developed for use during cost center planning. The concepts that are applied to allocate actual expenses can be used to develop planning allocations. Tools like plan distributions and plan imputed costs are used for primary cost element planning, and plan assessments are used in secondary cost planning. You might want to add that actual cycles can be copied to plan cycles, and also that planning cycles are usually run for all 12 months at once.

Based on the normal planning process the use of planning allocations should not occur until after the manual planning and revaluations have occurred. Review the

"Activity Types and Statistical Key Figures" section earlier in this chapter for development detail.

## Planning Layouts: Overview

During cost planning, users enter information into SAP through the use of planning layouts. The layouts represent the options the user has on the screen when entering the data. Choices may include, among others, whether they can enter activities, cost elements, key figures, or some combination of all three. Additionally, layouts may limit the version or period a user can plan. Layouts provide you with a tool to tailor the planning environment to meet your exact business requirements. Since the planning layouts are the component of choice to offer the planners in your company the ability to manipulate the planned data once the planning process has begun, it is important that these planning layouts are user-friendly and the planners have input into the functionality and configuration of these screens. Not to say that the financial planners will be creating their own layouts (although that's not out of the question), but that the ability to complete this task, manual planning, as quickly and effectively as possible is critical to the planning process. We all realize that in most cases the planners have been working in an Excel-based environment and to shift to another toolset to do the planning process is a challenge on its own. We don't really need to have additional issues around the usability of the SAP CCA planning front end.

SAP delivers a number of planning layouts with the software that will meet the majority of your planning needs. However, your solution may require that a unique new layout be created. The following section will take you through the necessary development steps.

**TIP**    Review the SAP-delivered planning layouts before building your own. It will be helpful to copy an existing layout rather than develop one from scratch. You will find it easier to delete unnecessary formatting than to build new layouts.

Planning layouts use the same design platform that accompanies the report development tool Report Painter. Concepts like general data selection, columns, rows, and variables are all as relevant with planning layouts as they are with reports. Because of the variety of solutions available, a simple example of a cost element–planning layout will be provided. Review the following screen shots of a SAP cost element–planning layout, Cost Element Standard 1-101.

Figure 10.51 is the basic layout view. It comprises columns and rows that make up the enter screen. Rows may be made up of various characteristics, like cost elements, that will hold the data when planned. These are represented by the two characteristics Activi and Cost Eleme, located in the far-left column. The columns may be made up of key figures or key figures and characteristics, and can determine the form in which the data is held. Examples include fixed versus variable costs, CO currency versus object currency, and dollars versus quantity units. In this example, an attribute, Distribution Key (DK), was added. The attribute provides additional flexibility to planning.

**FIGURE 10.51** The Report Painter: display cost centers: planning layout view for the SAP cost element–planning layout

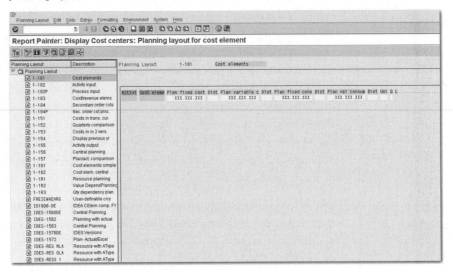

Figure 10.52 is a view of the general data selection screen for this planning layout. The general data selection screen provides characteristic settings available for the entire layout. The four characteristics chosen here—Version, Period, Fiscal Year, and Cost Center—have been assigned variables, meaning the user will be prompted for entry during planning. It is just as easy to hard-code the values for these characteristics. An example of this would be entering the value of 2000 directly into the Fiscal Year field in place of the variable. The Fiscal Year value for this layout would then always be 2000. When you provide for user entry through the use of variables, the layout becomes more flexible and more long-lasting.

**NOTE**   All planning layouts are controlling area–independent.

**FIGURE 10.52** The element definition: general data selection screen for the SAP cost element-planning layout

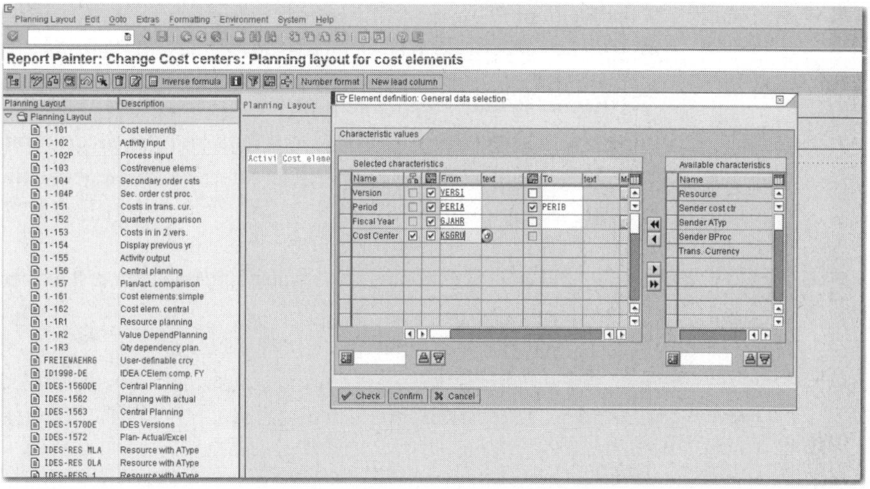

## Planning Layouts: Creation

Similar to creating a new report, it is often more expedient to build a new planning layout if it is created from a copy. If, however, your layout is too unique and would require extensive rework, then we recommend that you start from scratch. The example provided here is rather simple but will be built from scratch. For the sake of the demonstration, the parameters in the sidebar "Extreme Sports Cost Element Planning Layout Configuration Analysis" will apply to the layout.

### EXTREME SPORTS COST ELEMENT PLANNING LAYOUT CONFIGURATION ANALYSIS

Extreme Sports needs to develop a quarterly cost element–planning layout called EX01QTRPLAN. Although entered on a quarterly basis, the cost should spread evenly to each of the periods within the quarter. To add flexibility, the users should be allowed to enter such variables as cost center, cost element, plan version, and fiscal year. The layout of the data-entry screen should have each of the four quarters represented by columns and the cost elements represented in rows. As stated earlier, Extreme Sports has decided to track its activity only at the object-class level. Capitalized cost transfers between companies are now easily segregated from the production cost transfers.

The IMG menu path Controlling ➤ Cost Center Accounting ➤ Planning ➤ Manual Planning ➤ User Defined Planning Layouts ➤ Create Planning Layouts for Cost Element Planning ➤ Create Planning Layout for Cost Elements will take you to the cost element–planning layout screen, as will the transaction code KP65.

The Report Painter create planning layout screen will appear. At the create planning layout screen, provide the layout with an ID, a description, and the ID of the planning layout to be copied. Click Create, and the Report Painter form screen will appear (see Figure 10.53).

**FIGURE 10.53** The Report Painter: create cost centers: planning layout for cost elements screen

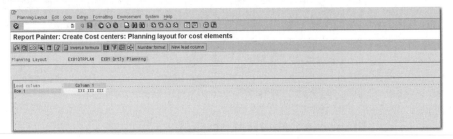

Begin development by establishing the characteristics you wish to plan. In the example description, cost element is the only characteristic the user is to enter. Additionally, it is defined that the cost elements should be entered in the rows. This is an important piece of information because it determines which area of the report (columns or rows) will hold the characteristic value. The first step in the example will be to define the general data selections.

**NOTE** The order of the steps taken is not important; it's important only that all is accomplished before saving.

**General Data Selection** Settings defined in the general data selection (GDS) screen become default values for the entire planning layout. Keep this in mind when creating your columns and rows. By first establishing a variable in the GDS, you will eliminate the need for definition elsewhere, which can save you development time (case in point, the fiscal-year definition for Extreme Sports's planning layout) and improve the performance of the planning layout.

The development decision to define a single fiscal year, version, and cost-center range for the entire layout has been made. When defined centrally, each of these characteristics will be maintained only once and will have just one value.

**TIP** Utilizing the general data selection to define your characteristic values ensures consistency in the value definition. If, however, you want a unique value defined per column or row do not use the general data selection as your definition point.

Begin the process by using the following menu path from the planning screen: Edit ≻ General Data Selection ≻ General Data Selection. The general data selection characteristic values screen will appear (see Figure 10.54). In this selection window that you decide which characteristics will be defined within the GDS. Based upon the Extreme Sports planning example, Fiscal Year, Version, and Cost Center will all be selected. When the values are filled in and the screen has been completed, select the left arrow and the GDS characteristics values screen will appear (see Figure 10.55).

**FIGURE 10.54** The element definition: general data selection characteristic values screen

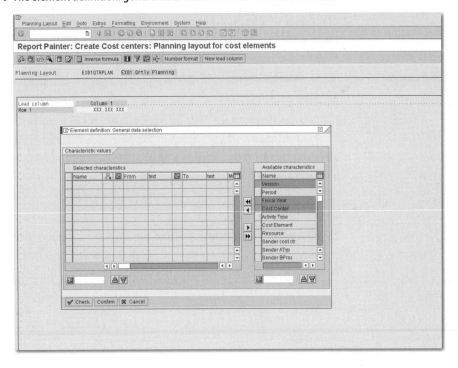

**FIGURE 10.55** The general data selection characteristic values screen

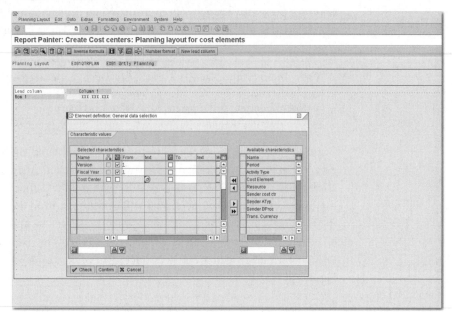

The values window is asking you to define the parameters for what can be planned when using this layout. To provide maximum flexibility, the layout should allow each user to enter the value ranges significant for plan entry each time they plan. This is accomplished by assigning variables to the value fields.

Check the box for the From field for both Version and Fiscal Year and in the Set field for Cost Center. SAP delivers default global variables that will populate the field automatically, as shown in Figure 10.55. Press Enter, and the general data selection is complete. The next phase in the layout development is the creation of the layout rows.

## Defining the Rows

Layout development requires you to run through a number of different windows before you are finished. To narrow the characteristic selection to only cost element, double-click the column block titled Lead Column.

**FIGURE 10.56** The element definition: lead column window

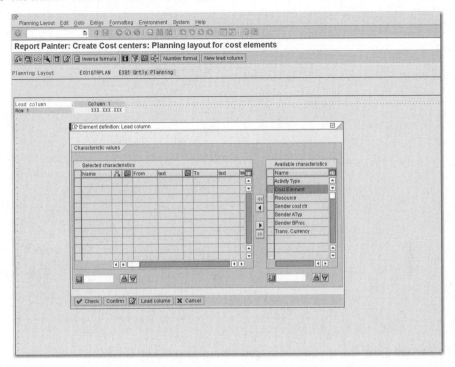

In the first window (characteristic values; see Figure 10.57), select Cost Element and the left arrow. Then define what values of the cost element can be planned. Notice that the default setting for Cost Element is an asterisk. If left alone, the planning layout will automatically allow all cost elements defined within the controlling area to be planned. The layout description stated that Extreme Sports wants to allow the users to determine which cost elements and cost centers are to be planned. A variable will have to be established for the Cost Element Group field. Place a check mark in the variable column to turn on the automatic variable feature. SAP delivers a default global variable for the cost element group, 1, that will populate the field automatically. Press Confirm when you're finished with this screen.

The second window (see Figure 10.58) to appear is used to define the characteristic display. Either leave the default set to characteristic value, or select one of the other three choices. Press Enter when you are finished.

**FIGURE 10.57** The characteristic values area

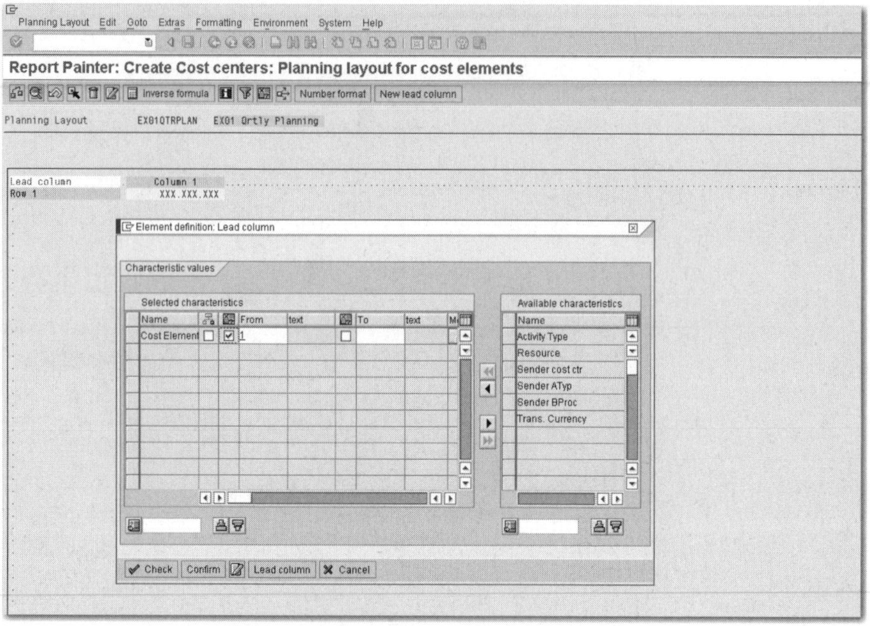

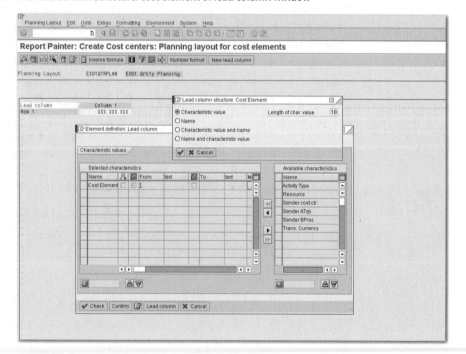

**FIGURE 10.58** The lead column structure: cost element of lead column window

The selection definitions are simple:

**Characteristic Value**   If this button is selected, only the value of the characteristic will be displayed during planning. In the example provided, a cost element value would be 500000.

**Name**   If this button is selected, the name of the characteristic selected will be displayed. Again using the example provided, instead of the cost element number 500000, the description of the cost element, Labor/Salaries, would appear.

**Characteristic Value and Name**   Both the value and name are displayed during planning (the value first).

**Name and Characteristic Value**   Both the name and value are displayed during planning (the name first).

Select whichever meets your requirements. For the demonstration, only Characteristic Value will be selected.

## Defining the Columns

The third phase within the layout development will be the addition of the Key Figure columns. Based upon the example description, Extreme Sports has asked that the layout allow for quarterly planning. Therefore, columns that represent each of the four quarters must be created. Begin the process by double-clicking the Column 1 field. A window will appear, asking you to select a key figure definition (see Figure 10.59). The list of standard key figures is extensive, but because you are planning on only cost element, only the key figures that capture plan costs are valid. Based upon Extreme Sports's requirements, the key figure Total Plan Costs in CO Area Currency will be selected. In some circumstances, planning fixed and variable costs separately may be appropriate. You must evaluate the unique needs of each instance. Press Enter when your selection is complete.

The second window in the column definition will ask you to define a characteristic to be associated with the key figure (see Figure 10.60). The characteristic assignment is used to ensure that only necessary information is available in the layout during planning. The example states that the user is to enter only quarterly amounts and that the Fiscal Year field is to be flexible. Based on the requirements, only Planning Period will be selected as a characteristic. When the selection is complete, press Enter; the characteristic values window appears (see Figure 10.61).

**FIGURE 10.59** The Key Figures window

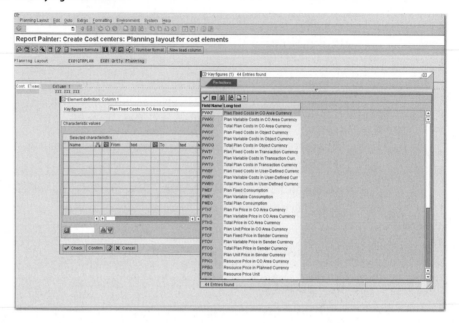

**FIGURE 10.60** The characteristic values: available characteristics window

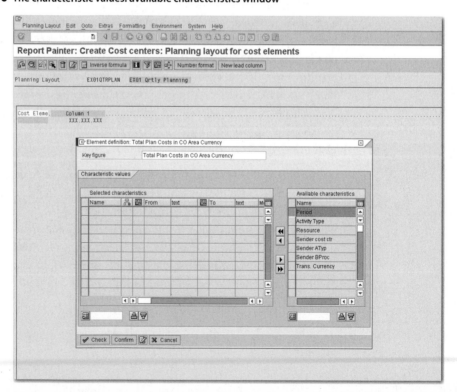

**FIGURE 10.61** The characteristic values: available characteristics values window

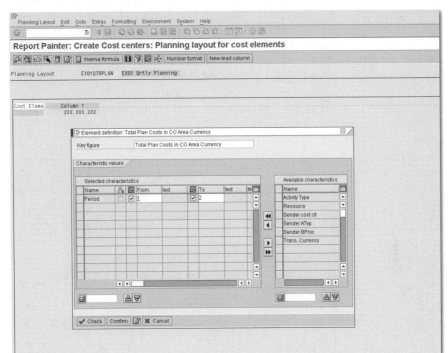

The values window gives you an opportunity to either define for the user the values of the characteristics selected or allow the user to decide by using a variable. Before completing the screen, think about the required uses for the layout. In the case of the planning-period values, the first quarter of each fiscal year will always be represented by the fiscal periods 1 through 3. Nothing will change this fact. Thus, hard-coding the first-quarter planning-period values into the fields is appropriate. Select the change-text icon (next to the Confirm button). A window will appear asking you to define the column text heading (Figure 10.62).

The column text window operates in the same manner as any text window. Enter the description of the column you are defining. For the example layout, the column has been defined as Qtr 1 (see Figure 10.62). Press Enter, and the column definition is finished. The column will appear on the layout definition screen. It will be necessary to repeat these steps for each of the four quarters within a fiscal year, changing the planning-period values accordingly. A quick way of adding columns is to copy them.

**FIGURE 10.62** The text maintenance window

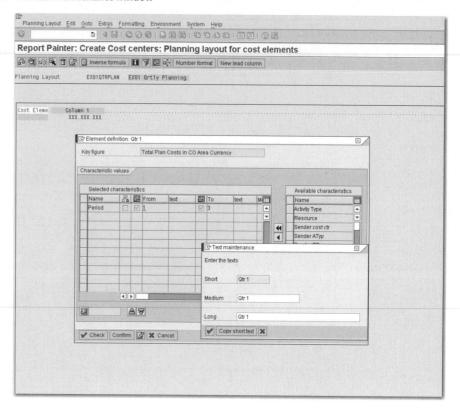

## Copying Columns

To copy a column, simply place the cursor on the column you wish to copy and click the select icon. You will notice that the column will change color and a new set of buttons will appear in the header. Next, either click the copy icon or select the F7 key on your keyboard to copy the column. You will notice that an exact duplicate of the column has appeared on the screen. To make the necessary changes to the copied column, double-click on the column header and cycle through the windows. In the case of the Extreme Sports example, only the planning-period values and the text window will need to change. When you're finished, you can save the layout and begin utilizing it during cost-center planning. However, in some cases additional detail is required. Attributes are designed for this purpose and are covered in the next section.

## Defining Attributes

Attributes provide additional flexibility to the planning screens by defining in greater detail the quantity or dollar amount being planned. Attribute values include, among others, unit, exchange-rate type, action, and distribution key. By adding the attribute action to the planning screen, the user would have the ability to determine whether the amounts being planned should replace, be added to, or be subtracted from any existing amounts. If the attribute were not present, the system would default with the replace option.

In support of the Extreme Sports planning layout, the attribute-distribution key is required. Because the planning periods are covering a range, a distribution key will be necessary to determine the exact amount that should post to each period within the range. By adding the distribution key, the user can select how the amounts will post. To place the attribute before the first column, place the cursor just to the left of the column and double-click. The select element type window will appear (see Figure 10.63), asking you to define the new column. Select the Attribute radio button and press Enter.

**FIGURE 10.63** The select element type window

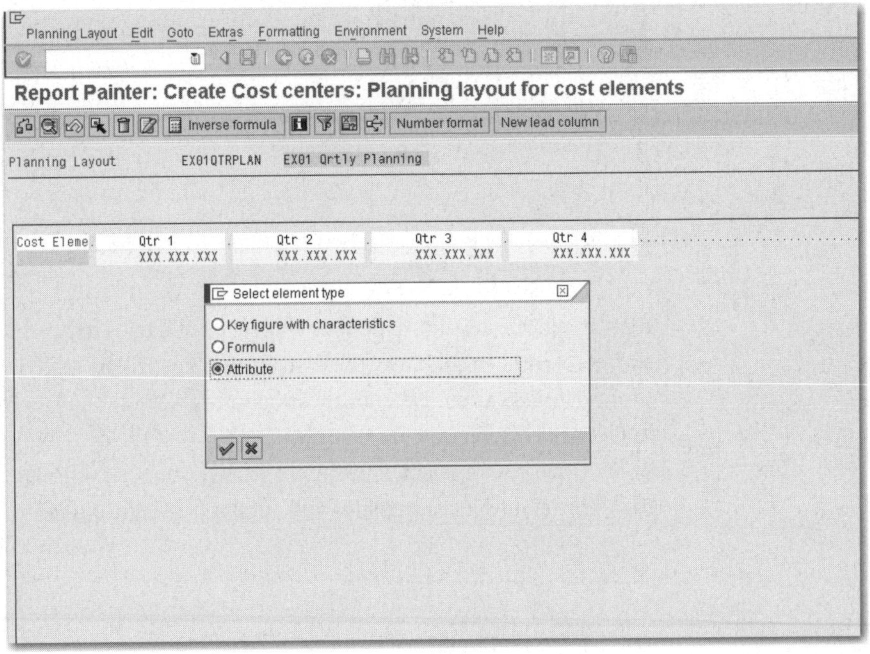

The second window to appear will ask for the attribute definition (see Figure 10.64). In the example, Distribution Key will be selected. Review the other attributes available for future reference. Once the selection is made, press Enter again. The third window will ask for the key figure definition.

**FIGURE 10.64** The choose attribute window

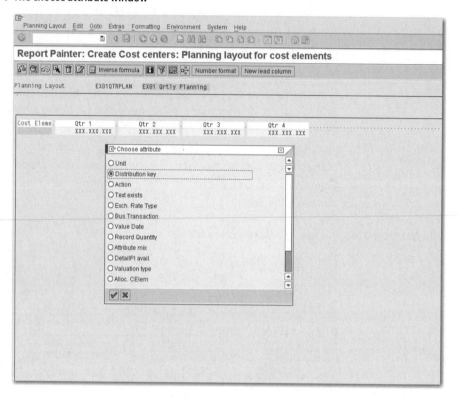

Remember, the key figure defines what type of data is to be utilized in or acted upon by the column. In this case, the distribution key will be affecting the planning columns defined earlier. Because these columns were defined as Total Planned Costs in CO Area Currency, consistency demands that the distribution key be defined the same. Once you've selected the appropriate option, press Enter; a window requesting the attribute characteristics will appear (see Figure 10.65).

**FIGURE 10.65** The element definition: dist window

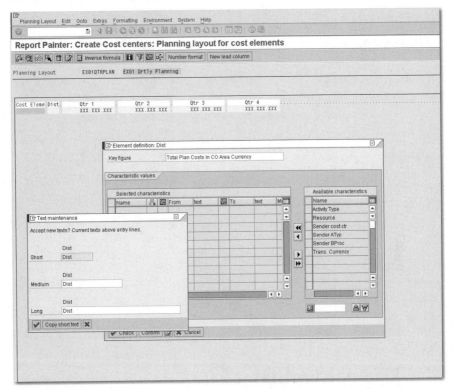

For the distribution key, only the Fiscal Year field must be maintained. Recall that the fiscal year was defined in the general data selection and so is not visible in this window. If, in your solution, you need further differentiation, please apply accordingly. After selecting the field, move to the next window and maintain the characteristic value. In the manner in which the columns and rows were maintained, set a variable for any necessary field's value. Because no characteristics were selected in the example, the characteristic values window was bypassed. The final window to process is again the text window. Keep the text-window requirements in mind when maintaining the value (see the preceding section "Defining the Columns" for detail). The attribute has now been created.

Because the same key figure, Total Planned Costs in CO Area Currency, was defined for each column and the attribute, only one has to be defined for the layout. The distribution-key value will be good for all columns. If each column had been defined differently, multiple distribution keys would have been necessary. Once the layout is complete, check it for errors by selecting the Check button. When it's error free, save the planning layout. For a view of the completed layout, see Figure 10.66. It is now available for use in cost center planning.

**FIGURE 10.66** The completed cost element–planning layout

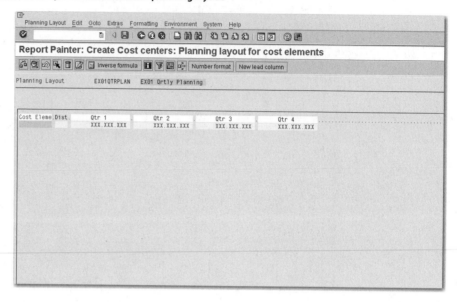

## Planning Profiles

Planning profiles within SAP marry a planning layout to an appropriate area of planning (for example, cost centers, orders, or profitability analysis). SAP delivers four standard profiles with the software:

**SAP101**   Primary Costs/Activity Types/Stat. Key Figures

**SAP102**   Activity Inputs/Activity Types/Stat. Key Figures

**SAP103**   Costs, Revenues/Activity Types/Activity Price/Stat. Key Figures

**SAP104**   Secondary Order Costs/Activity Types for Component Splitting/Activity-Dependent Key Figures

The majority of CO planning requirements can be covered with profiles SAP101 and SAP102. In the preceding section, the development of the planning layout EX01QTRPLAN was provided. To use the layout, it must be assigned to a planning profile. During the planning process, the profile is set prior to data entry.

The menu path Controlling ➤ Cost Center Accounting ➤ Planning ➤ Manual Planning ➤ Define User Defined Planning Profiles will take you to the planning profile development section of SAP, or you can simply use the transaction code KP34.

**TIP**  In some cases the menu path that is being described and the final transaction code are going to access the same screen, but the actual transaction code is going to be different. In this example, if you use the menu path you will notice that in the end the transaction code is still SPRO rather than KP34. This is not an issue, but you should know that the same screen can be executed using different approaches and methodology.

The CO planner profiles overview screen will appear (see Figure 10.67).

**FIGURE 10.67**  The CO change view planner profiles overview screen

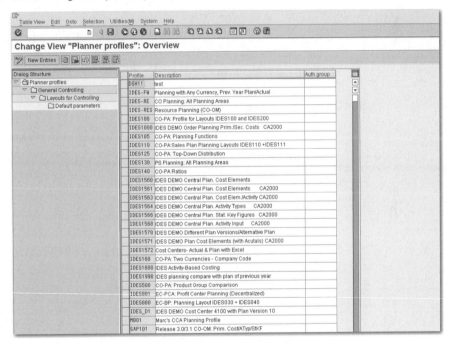

There are (up to) four sections that must be defined during profile creation:

**Section 1: Profile Overview**    Define the profile ID.

**Section 2: General CO Settings**    Determine planning-area settings.

**Section 3: General CO Layout**    Assign the CO planning layout to a specific planning area.

**Section 4: Default Parameter Settings for Layout (optional)**   If desired, you can preset values for the variables assigned in the planning layout.

During profile creation, these four sections are developed in order.

## Section 1: Profile Overview

To add a new profile, select the New Entries button and fill in the following fields:

**Profile**   Enter an alphanumeric ID for the new planning profile.

**Description**   Enter the profile description.

**Authorization Group**   If your company is using authorization groups to control system access, this field may be relevant. Five activities can be controlled with an authorization group: Create (01), Change (02), Display (03), Delete (06), and Execute (16).

The ZEXQTR-EX01 CCTR QTR planning profile was created for the example. Press Enter, and the new profile ID will become grayed out. Select the new layout ID and move to the General CO Settings section.

## Section 2: General CO Settings

SAP will automatically assign three planning areas with your new profile (see Figure 10.68). You can add other planning areas by selecting the New Entries button. When the new entry screen appears, use the drop-down box to select the additional areas.

Once all areas have been defined for the profile, you must assign a layout to each. The example layout EX01QTRPLAN is to be used in the planning of primary costs in Cost Center Accounting only. Additional areas will not be necessary for the example profile. Review the delivered planning areas to find one that may be appropriate for your solution. Select the planning area that is to receive your profile, and move to the General CO Layout section.

## Section 3: General CO Layout

You assign the layout simply by using the drop-down box in the Layout field to pull in the desired ID. You are allowed a number of layouts per planning area, depending on the need and definition, as denoted by the multiple layout field. In Figure 10.69, you will see the assignment of the example layout EX01QTRPLAN.

**FIGURE 10.68** The new entries: overview of added entries screen for the CO planning profile planning areas

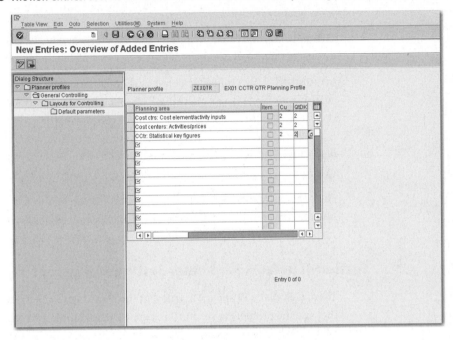

**FIGURE 10.69** The new entries screen for the planning layout assignment

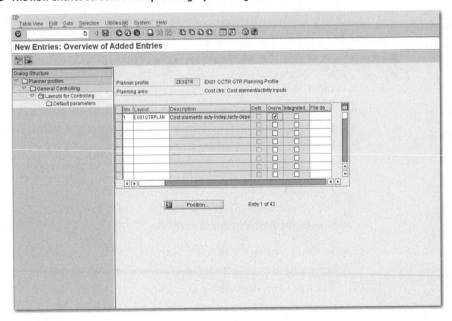

At the end of the layout line, you will notice two check boxes. Here are the definitions of those fields:

**Overw (Overwritten)**    This indicator denotes whether the user can overwrite the default parameter settings, maintained in step 4, during planning.

**Integrated**    This indicator denotes whether parameter settings make the layout available for Excel-based planning. This can be very useful since most planners are accustomed to using Excel for planning purposes and the ability to upload other Excel spreadsheets into this planning layout automatically is also available. The file description beside this column is for the description of the template layout for data uploads.

Once the assignment has been made, the profile can be saved and used during planning. However, if you want to establish some default values for the assigned layout's variables, select the layout and move to the next section.

### Section 4: Default Parameter Settings for Layout

The screen that will appear is a view of the planning screen the user will see when they use the profile. Figure 10.70 is a view of the planning screen for the layout EX01QTRPLAN. As stated earlier, the fields provided for input on this screen were designated in the layout by the use of variables (see "Planning Layout: Creation" for details). You may enter any valid default data within the field, and save. When you open the planning screen, the new parameter settings will default.

## Planning Profile Miscellanea

When you return to the General CO Layouts section, you will notice that both of the Overw buttons have been selected. Return to the General CO Settings section, and repeat the sections 2 through 4 above, as needed. Remember that each planning area must have a layout assignment if it is to be utilized for a specific area. However, the profile will work for the single planning area that has been completed.

With the completion of the planning profile, the cost center planning is finished. The next section will provide insight into CO's two methods of automatically combining cost elements and cost objects.

Again, this is not the functionality of CCA planning in its entirety but only the beginning. Review with your planners what functionality is required and use the different levels of planning available in CO to accommodate. We will be reviewing additional planning methods once we discuss Profit Center Accounting and Profitability Analysis in detail.

**FIGURE 10.70** The pre-parameterization screen for the planning layout

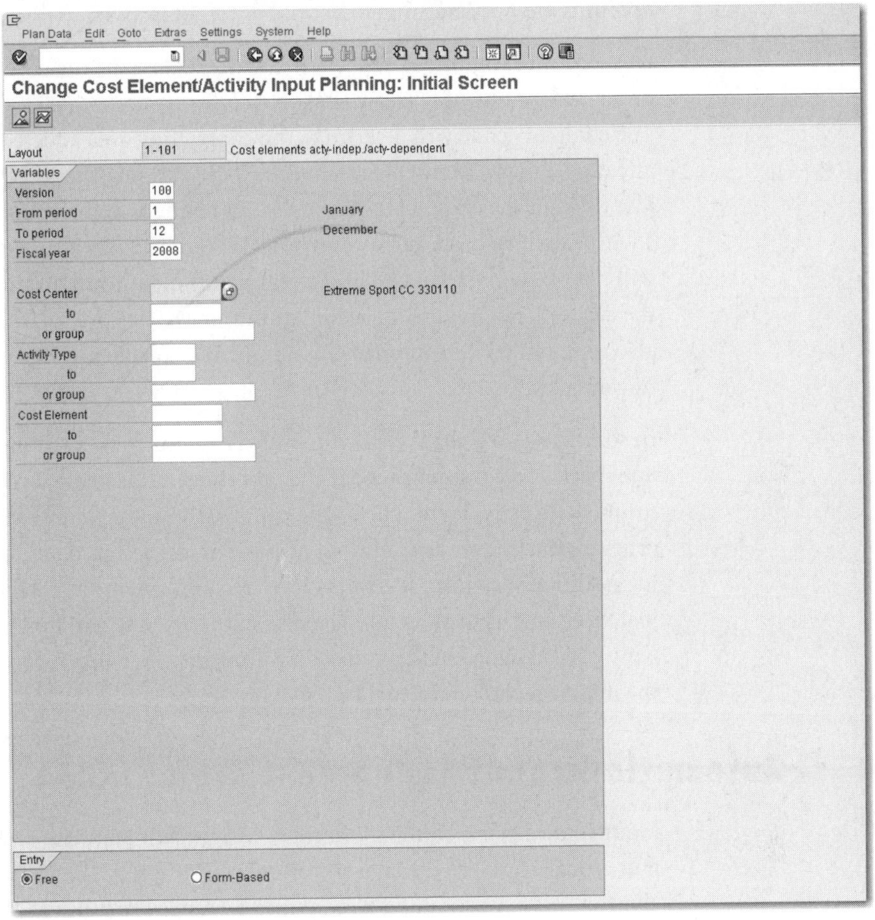

# Assigning Accounts Automatically in CO

At a high level, the logic applied to automatic account assignment in CO is similar to that in FI. During posting activity, SAP automatically determines coding block items based upon certain rules. In Chapter 4 you learned that these rules are defined for FI through activity processing keys like BSX (Inventory Postings). In the case of BSX, the company code/material valuation class involved in the material movement determines the account to be posted. For the CO account assignment, accounts are not determined, but rather CO objects are.

CO account assignment will automatically determine the cost center, profit center, order, and/or business area based on a company code/cost element relationship. The company code will determine the controlling area affected. When updates affecting a mapped cost element occur in SAP, if no other real CO object has been identified in the coding block, the default defined on the account assignment table, TKA3A, will be used. If, however, a real CO object has been defined previously, it will not be overwritten by the account-assignment configuration. The specifics of the account assignment table configuration will be covered in detail here. There is also a second level of automatic assignment available on the cost element/controlling area level.

In some cases, a general controlling-area assignment may be more appropriate than one specific to a company code. The cost element master record offers an opportunity to directly define a default account assignment for either a cost center or an order. Because there are only two possible object assignments, there is less flexibility. Additionally, the cost element level account assignment will be overwritten if a matching cost element mapping exists in the account assignment table for a company code assigned to the same controlling area. We'll also cover the details behind the master record maintenance in detail.

## Automatic Account Assignment Table: TKA3A

Maintenance of the automatic account assignment table can be accessed from numerous locations within overhead cost controlling. The IMG menu path Controlling ➤ Cost Center Accounting ➤ Actual Postings ➤ Manual Actual Postings ➤ Edit Automatic Account Assignment will take you through Cost Center Accounting, or you can use the transaction code OKB9.

The default account-assignment screen will appear (see Figure 10.71).

To better understand the example configuration settings, review the sidebar "Extreme Sports Automatic Account-Assignment Configuration Analysis" before proceeding.

**FIGURE 10.71** The default account assignment screen

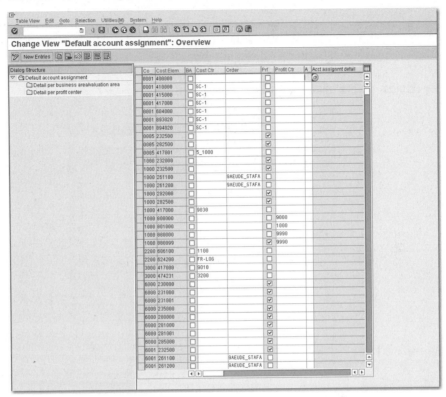

## EXTREME SPORTS AUTOMATIC ACCOUNT-ASSIGNMENT CONFIGURATION ANALYSIS

Extreme Sports has two immediate account-assignment requirements: The first is to assign all miscellaneous sales postings to the Misc. Sales profit center 140000. Misc. Sales generates most of its revenue from selling returned or traded-in equipment and should not affect the profitability of the other brands or divisions. One exception to the rule covers miscellaneous sales generated from contract services. These revenue dollars should route to the services Misc. Sales profit center 150000. The second assignment Extreme Sports requires is the routing of all maintenance activity to a central maintenance cost center for all company codes.

## Overview Screen

At the initial screen, select the New Entries button to begin defining your account assignments. The automatic account assignment default assignments overview screen appears (Figure 10.72).

**FIGURE 10.72** The default automatic assignment default overview screen

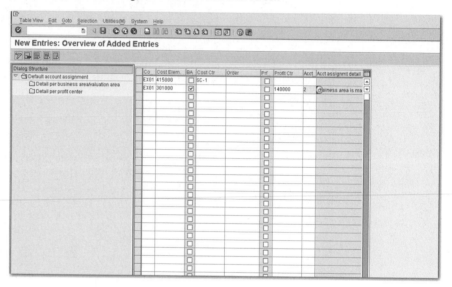

The fields are as follows:

**Company Code (CC)**   Enter the company code ID that is to be affected by the account assignment activity.

**Cost Elem.**   Enter the cost element used to derive the object assignment.

**Business Area Indicator (BArIn)**   If this field is active, the business-area assignment will override another business area defined in the posting. The priority assignment is important if costs must be forced into a single business area regardless of cost centers assigned elsewhere. If you are not using business area(s) in your solution, the setting is not functional.

**TIP**   You can have only one real CO account assignment in any posting.

**Cost Ctr.**   If applicable, enter the cost center ID that is to be defaulted into the coding block. Remember that there must be a relationship between the company code and cost center for the entry to be valid.

**Order**   If applicable, enter the order ID that is to be defaulted into the coding block. Remember that there must be a relationship between the company code and order for the entry to be valid.

**Prf...**   If applicable, check off this parameter to assign a profitability segment to the posting. This will automatically assign a system generated Profitability Segment to the record. By doing this you will be immediately processing the posting directly to Profitability Analysis.

**Profit Ctr**   If applicable, enter the profit center ID that is to be defaulted into the coding block. Only revenue elements can have a profit center default assignment. Unlike the cost center and order assignments, there is no relationship between profit center and company code. Instead, the validity check is at the controlling-area level. Both the company code and the profit center must belong to the same controlling area for a valid assignment.

**Acct - Acct Assignmt Detail (D)**   SAP allows for account assignment by valuation area and/or business in addition to company code. For example, the cost center to be assigned is 1000 unless the business area is AAA; then the cost center assignment is changed to 2000. There are four possible entries:

**0 (Default setting)**   Leave the field empty if you do not require additional assignment.

**1 (Valuation Area Obligatory)**   Select this option if you want to use the valuation area in the account assignment determination rule.

**2 (Business Area Obligatory)**   Select this option if you want to use the business area in the account assignment determination rule.

**3 (Valuation Area/Business Area Obligatory)**   Select this option if you want to use both in the account assignment determination.

If you have assigned a business area to the cost center or order master record, it will be difficult to differentiate account assignment by business area. The Extreme Sports solution will utilize the following setting to differentiate its Misc. Sales postings:

**Acct Assignment Detail**   Enter a text description describing the selection in the Acct Assignmt Detail field.

If your solution does not require the use of Acct Assignmt Detail, you can save the settings at this time. The account assignment is complete. In the Extreme Sports example, however, Acct Assignmt Detail is going to be used to route the miscellaneous sales from contract services to the proper profit center. Review Figure 10.72 for a view of the overview-screen settings necessary to route the general Misc. Sales to profit center 140000.

## Detail per Business Area/Valuation Area

At the automatic account assignment default assignments overview screen, select the row to which you want to add detail assignments to, and click the Detail per Business Area/Valuation button in the navigation box. The change view "Detail per business area/valuation area" window appears (see Figure 10.73).

**FIGURE 10.73** The Change View "Detail per business area/valuation area" window

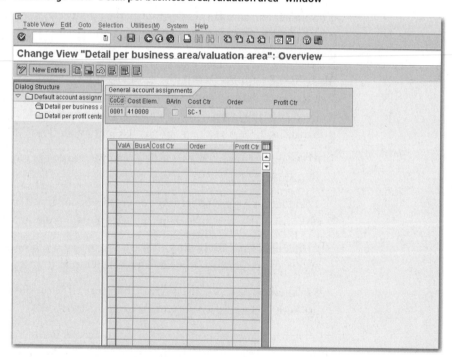

The fields on this screen are as follows:

**ValA**   If applicable, enter the valuation area to be used to route the posting to the proper CO object.

**BusA**   If applicable, enter the business area to be used to route the posting to the proper CO object.

**Cost Ctr/Order/Profit Ctr**   Enter the valid object ID to be used in the coding.

For the Extreme Sports solution, business area SES, Extreme Services, will be used to identify those miscellaneous sales postings that are to reroute to profit center 150000. Once the business-area assignments are set, when the user processes the invoice and enters the business area SES, 150000 rather than 140000 will default into the Profit Ctr field. See Figure 10.73 for a view of the Extreme Sports account assignment settings.

# Default Account Assignment: Cost Element Master Record Maintenance

The second method of CC account assignment is to maintain the cost element master record for a default object assignment. Referring to the second of the two Extreme Sports account assignment requirements, all maintenance costs in the controlling area are to be routed to a single cost center. Rather than set a rule in the account assignment table for each company code in the controlling area, it would be quicker and easier to maintain the assignment on the cost element.

Navigate to the Change View of the cost element master record (see Chapter 8 for details). Once at the master record, click the Default Acct Assgnmt tab (see Figure 10.74). A box will appear asking for a CO object entry. Enter either a cost center or internal order ID, and then press Enter (see Figure 10.75). Save the cost element, and the assignment is complete. When the user processes any activity for the cost element and does not enter a real account assignment object, the default will post automatically.

**FIGURE 10.74** The change view screen for cost element master record maintenance

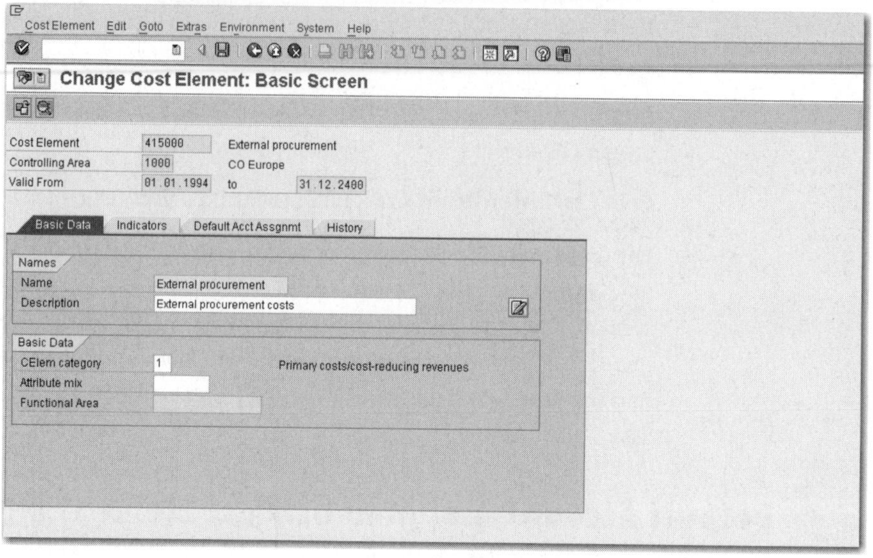

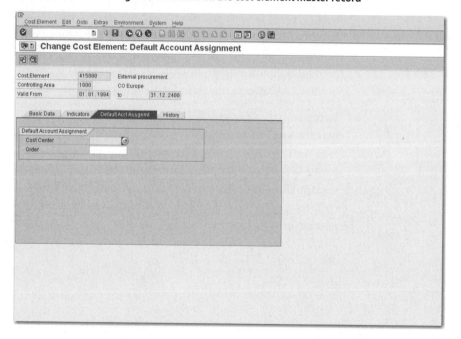

**FIGURE 10.75** The default account assignment window on the cost element master record

## Account Assignment Summary

CO automatic account assignment is complete. It is recommended that you experiment with each solution to find which will provide the proper fit for your company. One important thing to remember about CO automatic account assignment is that the default will not override an existing account assignment entry. Unlike the FI account determination activity, CO account assignment is effective only if the user is not manually overriding the activity. If your intention is to allow SAP to derive the CO object, be certain that you have identified the step in your procedure so that the user community is aware.

# Summary

As you can see by the amount of time spent discussing master data development, Cost Center Accounting is only partially maintained through table configuration. Although most of the menu paths provided routed you through the IMG, this approach was more for consistency than it was a requirement. You can access a lot of the work involved through the user menus and the application portion.

This chapter provided good breakdowns of which items were master data and which were configuration data. The sections dealing with controlling-area maintenance, version control, and planning mostly involved traditional configuration activity. Periodic allocation development, standard hierarchy creation, and activity type/statistical key figure creation were more master data–related. The combination of the two produced a fully functioning Cost Center Accounting module.

As you go through the process of configuration in this area—Cost Center Accounting—some of the key and critical items to remember are in the initial process of setting up the master data. We talked at length about the idea of making sure that your master data dates are in sync and validated across the company. Make sure that the dates for all master data are consistent and will not cause any issues during the data-flow process. Hierarchies in all areas are critical. They will be used extensively for reporting, planning and allocations. Take the time to do the analysis for this requirement, and it will be time well spent. As you work through the development of cost elements, confirm that you are using both the cost and revenue sides of the cost elements and that you are not trying to post a revenue to a cost type element. Number ranges are in all areas and need to be reviewed and validated early on. This is the type of activity that will lend itself to a corporate governance process of some sort since cost elements and other areas in CO use it.

Basically, this process is divided into two areas. The initial area is the actual configuration of the objects, and the second, and just as important, is the configuration of the objects that will affect the data-flow process. This includes areas such as allocations (assessments and distribution), and whether they are set up to execute automatically or manually is important. We didn't get very involved with the posting process other than the setup of the automatic account assignment for the cost objects, but this is an important area that will vary depending on a company's approach to posting records to the CO. If you are going to post records during any period, then execute period-end activity (in other words, the allocation process or the manual reposting process), then the overall validation process will work much better since you can initially view the original posting before the allocation. If you are going to immediately allocate postings at the time of the original posting, then the validation will be a bit tougher because the final posting will be the only information that is available. In either case, due diligence in the overall data flow is critical. This is where a toolset such as the Schedule Manager or the FI Closing Cockpit (see Chapter 15 "FI Closing Cockpit") comes in handy since they can track the closing process and use workflow in the ECC system to send out alerts and messages.

In conjunction with the above activities is the planning process. As you know, planning is critical to some companies to manage the costs and revenue. Planning can be accomplished in Cost Center Accounting with the help of plan revaluation, planning allocations, and all of the same toolsets that the actual postings have, and the planning can have as much detail as the original.

As you can see, it's important to have a very clear view of what Cost Center Accounting will be able to do for you and how it can impact the Controlling process within your company.

# CHAPTER 11

· · · · · · · · · · ·

# *Internal Order Accounting*

**FEATURING:**

▶ **INTERNAL ORDER CONFIGURATION**

▶ **CONTROLLING AREA MAINTENANCE FOR INTERNAL ORDER ACCOUNTING**

▶ **ORDER SETTLEMENT CONFIGURATION**

▶ **ORDER PLANNING AND BUDGETING**

▶ **INTERNAL ORDER STATUS MANAGEMENT**

▶ **ORDER TYPE DEVELOPMENT**

**O**rder Accounting is probably one of the most difficult areas within the CO module to understand. Whereas cost and profit centers have been in mainstream accounting for some time, internal orders (IOs) and their unique properties may be new to many developers and users.

In this chapter, we'll refer to settlement objects such as maintenance orders, production orders, and capital investment orders, but we'll spend the majority of this chapter defining the configuration steps for IOs only. The basic concepts supporting order type development—in particular, planning, budgeting, and settlement—are similar across all order types. Once you review this information, you'll see the advantages of using Internal Order Accounting. In terms of order types, about 75% of everything in the SAP world is affected by some sort of "type"—SD has sales document types, the production order processes have production order types, FI has document types…the list of "types" goes on and on. So, this setup in the Internal Order Accounting area is similar in some ways to many of the other areas of SAP, but having this level of flexibility in the CO world is what's good about IOs.

Internal Order Accounting allows you to manage and track information about costs at a granular level, and learning how to configure the Internal Order Accounting area can be well worth the effort. For example, let's say you have a pretty vast equipment pool. Specifically, you're managing the equipment for a large corporation with numerous locations and many different groups of equipment, including trucks of all types, bulldozers, heavy equipment, and so on. You've found that the budget for maintenance is always over the limit, and you need to analyze this area to determine exactly what is happening. By setting up Internal Order Accounting, you could assign an additional flag to the costs by group, or even by individual item, and track the budget or plan at a granular level to identify the source of the maintenance budget issues.

Sure, using Cost Center Accounting (CCA) will help you focus on the specific issues, but in terms of understanding and finding the true issue, CCA may be a bit too high level in terms of tracking information and costs. Internal Order Accounting is designed for detail-oriented analysis. It allows you to track information around a production order or set of production orders using IOs, break up costs at a granular detail to settle them to the appropriate cost object assignment, and do numerous other tasks. We'll discuss some of these options as we walk you through the configuration process of Internal Order Accounting.

# Configuring Internal Order Accounting

For some areas within SAP, such as Cost Center Accounting, you can do the configuration in any sequence. In other areas, though, you must complete the type of information required for a certain step in a prior step. Internal order development is one of those areas in which you must follow a specific order of configuration.

From a developer's viewpoint, the order type is the central figure in Internal Order Accounting. The order type determines what information can be held, how it will be settled, planning and budgeting parameters, authorizations, what order master data is required, and how it will be displayed on the screen.

Figure 11.1 provides a view of the detail screen in order type configuration. Note the number of field options available. When developing the order type, you should begin the process with the end in mind. This screen is one of those times when the initial view is just the beginning; behind the configuration of this screen are many more additional items to configure. In fact, when we look at all of the fields we can easily say there are 50% more objects required before you can complete the configuration on this screen. This is why we'll start with this process, move to configuring the necessary items to complete this information, and then find our way back to this screen at the end of the chapter.

Looking at the General Parameters section of the order, you can see fields for the settlement profile, planning profile, and budgeting profile. You have to configure and assign each of these prior to successfully completing the order type. Additionally, the Status Management section offers two options, one of which (General Status Mgmt) also has to be completed prior to being utilized by the order type. These status management sections will be displayed in this screen a bit later in the chapter. We mention them here to further explain the iterative nature of the order development cycle.

Much of the configuration you'll perform within Internal Order Accounting is independent of the controlling area and thus can be used universally within the client. Additional controlling area–specific development is almost always required, but the item itself is accessible to all controlling areas. In the next section, we'll begin the process of developing the Internal Order Accounting area by maintaining the controlling area.

**FIGURE 11.1**    The detail screen in order type configuration

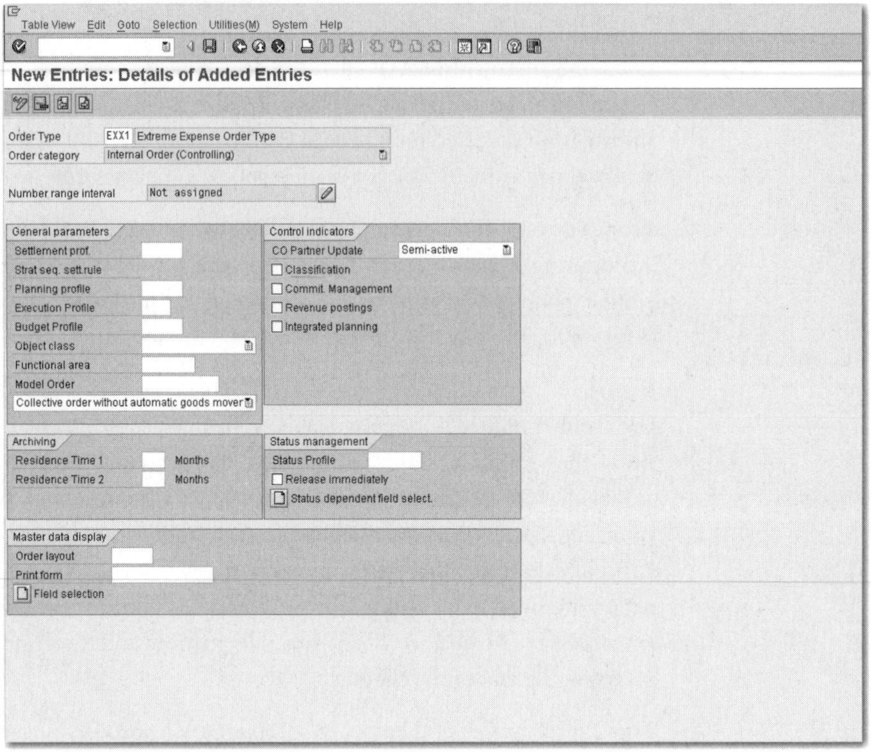

# Controlling Area Maintenance for Internal Order Accounting

As for each module in Controlling, you must activate Internal Order Accounting for the controlling area prior to beginning development. We covered how to activate the proper indicators in Chapter 8, "Controlling Enterprise Structure," but you can review Figure 11.2 for a refresher. As you can see, both order management and commitment management are active for the controlling area. The benefits of commitment management become evident later in the chapter.

Once you are satisfied with your controlling area settings, let's move on to the next section.

**FIGURE 11.2** Activating the proper indicators for Internal Order Accounting

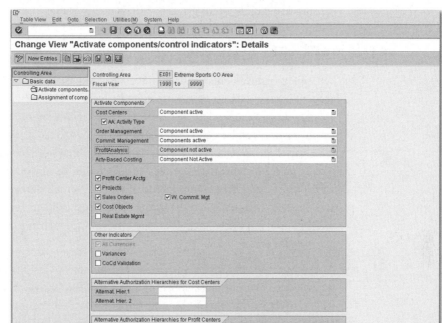

# Order Settlement Configuration

*Settlement* is the process of moving costs incurred on a sender object to one or more receiving objects. In the case of an internal order, costs are incurred on the order through goods issues or receipts, journal entries, internal activity allocations, or other settlements and settled to a cost center, order, fixed asset, or account, just to name a few. All offsetting postings on the sender are posted automatically, and the receiver will retain the history of the posting even if it in turn makes another settlement. The account(s) utilized in the posting activity is dependent on the settlement structure configuration and what type of account activity is maintained. Note that in the process of an IO settlement you may find that the costs are settled to a cost object outside of CO; therefore, it is possible that, unlike CCA, the settlement of an IO can be to a true account or object and have a true impact on FI. Basically, the settlement process for an IO doesn't have to be completely internal to CO. In this section we begin by looking at the settlement cost element.

## Settlement Cost Element

Settlement cost elements are used in specific cases to act as the sender and receiving account during settlement. If Settlement Element is selected within the settlement assignment (see the section "Settlement Cost Element" later in this chapter), either a primary or secondary cost element will be needed to facilitate the posting. The receiving object determines whether you use a primary or secondary element. The section on settlement structure development will cover the question in detail, but a brief description here is appropriate. If the receiver is external to CO, like a G/L account or fixed asset, you must use a primary cost element because of the necessary FI impact. If the receiver is internal within CO, such as a cost center, you must use a secondary cost element.

As for the settlement cost element, refer to Chapter 9, "Cost Element Accounting," for a detailed analysis on establishing a cost element. In the Implementation Guide (IMG), select Controlling ➢ Internal Orders ➢ Actual Postings ➢ Settlement ➢ Maintain Settlement Cost Elements and use the simple guidelines provided to create the settlement cost element, or use transaction code KA01 for Primary Cost Elements and KA06 for Secondary Cost Elements.

A transaction selection screen appears if you use the menu path as opposed to the transaction code. Select either Create Primary Cost Element or Create Secondary Cost Element. The cost element creation screen appears. Keep in mind these key points when creating the cost element:

▶ Cost Element Category should be either 21, for internal (secondary) settlement, or 22, for external (primary) settlement.

▶ Use an account number outside your primary account range—it makes the account easily recognizable.

▶ Use a name and description that clearly defines the activity (Capital Costs or Maintenance Expense or Settlement Cost Element). Reporting and analysis is thus made easier.

**NOTE**   Remember that secondary cost elements are relevant only for CO postings and do not require a corresponding G/L account in FI.

When creating a primary settlement cost element, be sure to create the G/L account in the chart of accounts first; if possible, use the automatic cost element creation process directly against the FI GL account. The system prompts you to assign the appropriate cost element category to the cost element. Depending on your settlement and reporting strategy, creating more than one settlement cost element may be necessary. Many companies prefer to see some level of segregation among material costs, overhead, and labor. The next section shows you how to accomplish this segregation.

# Allocation Structure

The settlement structure defines the "what and how" of the settlement process. It is the main component of the settlement profile, which will be discussed later in this chapter. Its purpose is twofold:

- ▶ To define which cost elements on the order can be settled. This group of cost elements is called the *origin*.

- ▶ To determine which cost element, called the *settlement cost element*, will be used to debit and credit the sending order and receiving object.

Each area, the origin and settlement cost element, is combined and uniquely defined within a *settlement assignment*. SAP lets you differentiate how you want costs settled through the use of multiple settlement assignments on a single settlement structure.

You can begin the allocation structure development process by selecting Controlling ➢ Internal Orders ➢ Actual Postings ➢ Settlement ➢ Maintain Allocation Structures or by using the transaction code OKO6.

The allocation structure overview screen, shown in Figure 11.3, appears, providing you with a look at the many settlement structures currently defined in your client. Remember that each new allocation structure is available for all controlling areas in the client.

Click the New Entries button. An entry screen appears, asking you to provide the new allocation structure with a two-character ID and description. Press Enter and click the green arrow to return to the settlement structure overview window. You are now ready to define the settlement assignment(s).

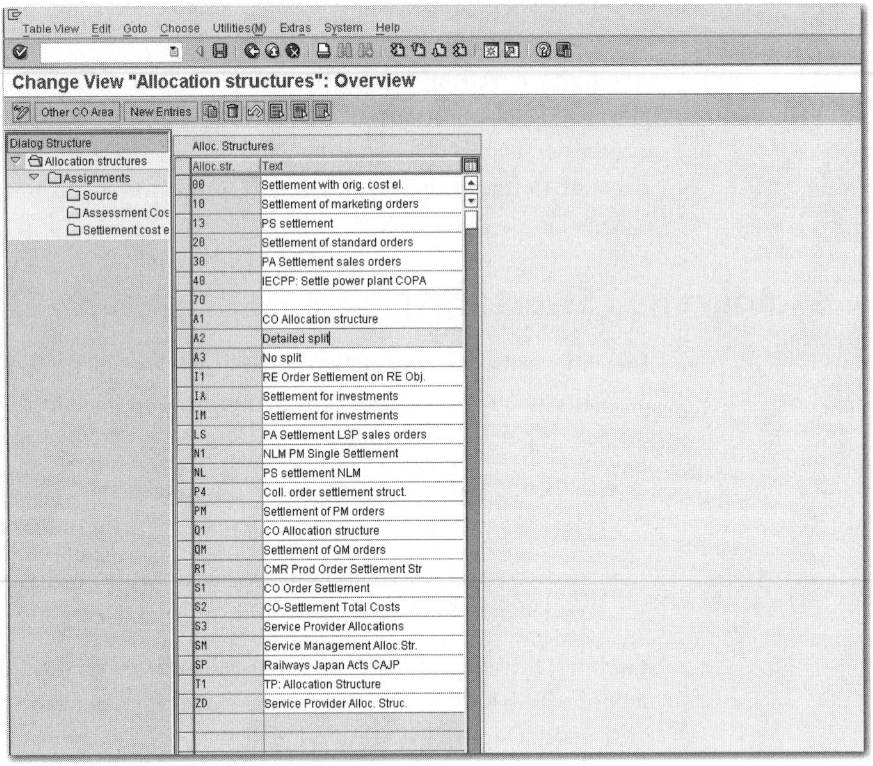

**FIGURE 11.3** Change View "Allocation Structures": Overview screen

| Alloc.str. | Text |
| --- | --- |
| 00 | Settlement with orig. cost el. |
| 10 | Settlement of marketing orders |
| 13 | PS settlement |
| 20 | Settlement of standard orders |
| 30 | PA Settlement sales orders |
| 40 | IECPP: Settle power plant COPA |
| 70 | |
| A1 | CO Allocation structure |
| A2 | Detailed split |
| A3 | No split |
| I1 | RE Order Settlement on RE Obj. |
| IA | Settlement for investments |
| IM | Settlement for investments |
| LS | PA Settlement LSP sales orders |
| N1 | NLM PM Single Settlement |
| NL | PS settlement NLM |
| P4 | Coll. order settlement struct. |
| PM | Settlement of PM orders |
| Q1 | CO Allocation structure |
| QM | Settlement of QM orders |
| R1 | CMR Prod Order Settlement Str |
| S1 | CO Order Settlement |
| S2 | CO-Settlement Total Costs |
| S3 | Service Provider Allocations |
| SM | Service Management Alloc.Str. |
| SP | Railways Japan Acts CAJP |
| T1 | TP: Allocation Structure |
| ZD | Service Provider Alloc. Struc. |

## Settlement Assignment

The settlement assignment, as stated earlier, uniquely defines the combination of the origin and the settlement cost element. It is important at this juncture to have your settlement strategy defined for the order type that will be using this settlement structure. Your strategy will have a direct impact on the depth of the assignment development. You can implement a simple strategy, resulting in all order costs being grouped under one origin and settled to one account. Or you may choose a complex strategy, with each unique cost type—such as labor, materials, and consulting, for example—being settled to separate settlement accounts. In either case, you achieve segregation with the number of settlement assignments defined and configured.

**NOTE** Remember that the settlement structure is independent of the controlling area and that other controlling areas can use the settlement assignment IDs you define. However, the origin and settlement cost element portions of the settlement assignment are controlling area *dependent* and thus require configuration specific to your solution and area.

On the allocation structure overview screen, begin defining the settlement assignment by selecting your newly created allocation structure ID and double-clicking the assignment navigation option on the left. The change view allocation assignment screen appears. Click the New Entries button on the toolbar, and the screen transfers to change mode and allows you to make new entries (see Figure 11.4).

**FIGURE 11.4**     The allocation assignment overview screen in change mode

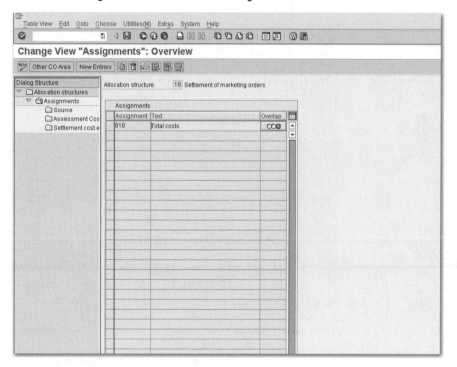

Fill in the following fields:

**Assignment (Settlement Assignment)**     This field is used by SAP to define the settlement activity. Enter an ID up to three characters long for the allocation assignment.

**Text (Description)**     Enter the Allocation assignment description.

When you've defined each assignment, save the configuration and click the green arrow to return to the overview screen.

## Source

Within the source, you can define through a cost element group or individual cost elements (range) which costs can be settled by the settlement assignment. Both primary and secondary cost elements can be contained within the group. To establish the origin, place your cursor on the settlement assignment being maintained and select the Source object. The source overview screen appears (see Figure 11.5).

**FIGURE 11.5**    The origin overview screen in change mode

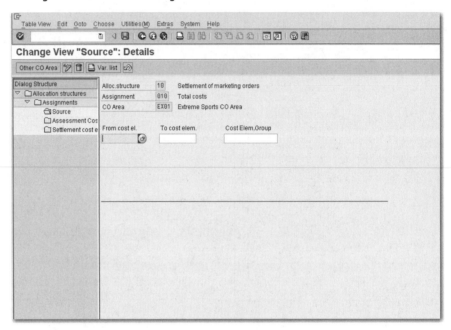

As you review the screen, notice the assignment information. Make sure that you are in the proper settlement assignment and that the correct controlling area is active. As you migrated to the source screen, you may have noticed that a new button labeled Other CO Area appeared on the toolbar. This button allows you to set and maintain another controlling area for that settlement assignment. Remember that the source and settlement cost element sections of the settlement assignment are the only controlling area–dependent sections of the settlement structure.

If the source cost element sections have not been maintained to date for your controlling area, the source field will be empty. To add a group, return to the previous screen by clicking the green arrow and then clicking the New Entries button. The Source (Cost Elem.) Group entry field converts to change mode (Figure 11.5 is a view of the screen in change mode). At this point, it is possible to enter a preexisting cost element group that you may have configured earlier. If you haven't configured one, SAP allows you to define the group from the entry screen. Simply enter the name you want to give your origin cost element group, select Extras ➤ Cost Element Group ➤ Change. You are prompted to confirm that you want to create a new cost element group; click Yes. The Create Cost Element Group: Structure screen then appears (see Figure 11.6).

**FIGURE 11.6**    The Create Cost Element Group: Structure screen, initial view

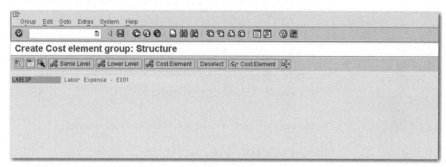

You have two choices when creating cost element groups: build a hierarchy with other defined groups or define individual cost elements and/or ranges of cost elements. In this example, we'll maintain ranges of cost elements. Click the Insert Cost Element button, and the Create Cost Element Group: Structure Single Values screen appears (see Figure 11.7).

**FIGURE 11.7**    The Create Cost Element Group: Structure screen, with fields filled in

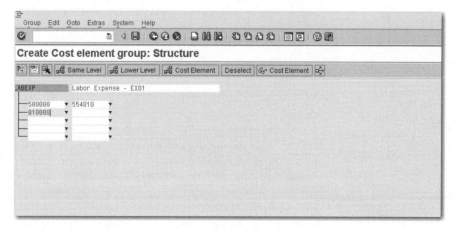

Complete the following fields:

**Description**    Enter a description of the cost element group.

**Cost Element From/To (blank fields available in screen)**    Enter a cost element or a range of cost elements to be included in the group. Include any relevant secondary cost elements (such as assessment elements, internal activity allocation elements, and other settlement cost elements).

Press Enter, and the cost element group structure appears. Save the group when you are satisfied, and the screen automatically returns to the original overview. Notice that the new cost element group has been defined for the assignment (see Figure 11.8). Save the changes, and click the green arrow to return to the settlement assignment screen and review the remaining assignments. When you've completed the source, move to the second step in settlement assignment development: maintaining the settlement cost element.

**FIGURE 11.8**    The source overview screen with a new cost element group

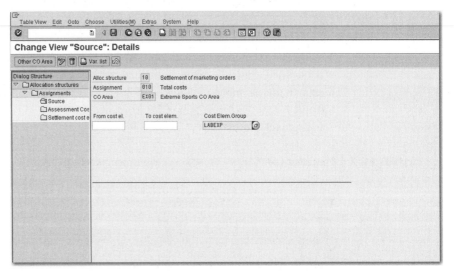

    **NOTE**    When transporting the settlement structure, be certain the cost element groups that the structure uses exist in the receiving client. You can easily determine whether the group is valid for the controlling area and the settlement assignment by verifying that a description appears in its designated field. If the group does not exist in the client, the name will appear in the ID field but the Description field will be empty. Once you create the cost element group in the controlling area, the Description field populates automatically.

## Settlement Cost Element

The settlement cost element is the section of the settlement assignment that determines the cost element(s) posted to both the sender and receiver during settlement. We recommend that you become familiar with the two types of settlement:

**Internal settlement**    This refers to the type of settlement in which postings are internal to CO. An example is any order settlement in which the receiver is another CO object, such as a cost center, cost object, CO-PA segment, or another order, to name a few. Because the postings never cross into FI, you must use a secondary cost element to facilitate the postings. The original account posting on the order, such as a goods receipt posting, is maintained and forms the bridge between CO and FI.

**External settlement**    This refers to the type of settlement in which postings are external to CO. An example of an external order settlement is one in which the receiver is a G/L account or fixed asset. Because the settlement results in a cross into FI, you must use a real or primary cost element. The original account posting is also maintained in this example, but a second posting would be added.

Take your time when educating yourself about order settlement. It is one of the more difficult concepts to grasp within SAP because of the uniqueness of the CO environment. Continue with the settlement cost element assignment by selecting one of the settlement assignments and clicking the Settlement Cost Element option in the left navigation pane. When the receiver type configuration screen appears, click the New Entries button. The grayed-out portion of the screen turns white, and you can maintain the assignment by filling in these fields:

**Receiver Category**    Define which object is a valid receiver for the settlement assignment. Click the pull-down button to see a complete listing of choices. If you forget to maintain the assignment category for a necessary object (cost center, G/L account) and then attempt to settle to that type of object, SAP will return an error.

**By Cost Element**    If the By Cost Element parameter is selected and the cost element is a primary element, SAP will always use the original cost element that is posted to the order as the settlement cost element. The rules change when the cost element posted to the order is a secondary element.

If, for example, an order is posted with a type 42 (internal activity cost element), used during labor confirmations, then OCE will be applicable only for CO objects such as cost centers. If settlement is required to a G/L account or Fixed Asset, you must use a settlement cost element.

If, however, an order is posted with a type 21 (settlement cost element), you cannot use the By Cost Element parameter with any object, CO or not. You have to use a settlement cost element every time.

You must use the source properly when a broad range of cost elements can be posted to an order. You have to segregate the posting activity by using multiple settlement assignments, with each assignment representing a unique cost element group. For example, you might have your labor confirmations in one group, all of your settlement activities that might be received on an order in a second group, and all of your primary account activity in a third.

Table 11.1 shows an example of the accounting impacts of By Cost Element using only primary cost elements.

**TABLE 11.1**   Impacts of Original Cost Element Settlement: Order 1000 Settles to Cost Center 2000

| Original Account Debits—Order 1000 | |
| --- | --- |
| Cost Element 600000 | $250 |
| Cost Element 610000 | $150 |
| **Total** | **$400** |
| **Settlement Account Credits—Order 1000** | |
| Cost Element 600000 | – ($250) |
| Cost Element 610000 | – ($150) |
| **Total** | **($400)** |
| **Settlement Account Debits—Cost Center 2000** | |
| Cost Element 600000 | $250 |
| Cost Element 610000 | $150 |
| **Total** | **$400** |

**Settlement Cost Element**   If applicable, enter a settlement cost element; refer to the section "Settlement Cost Element" earlier in the chapter for details. The By Cost Element parameter must not be active if a settlement cost element is to be defined. See Table 11.2 for a breakout of the accounting impacts when the settlement cost element is used.

**NOTE**   Remember, if you are settling to an object that will result in an FI posting, such as a fixed asset, an external settlement cost element is required.

**TABLE 11.2**    Impacts of Settlement Cost Element Settlement: Order 1000 Settles to Cost Center 2000

| Original Account Debits—Order 1000 | |
| --- | --- |
| Cost Element 600000 | $250 |
| Cost Element 610000 | $150 |
| **Total** | **$400** |
| **Settlement Account Credits—Order 1000** | |
| Cost Element 900000 | ($400) |
| **Settlement Account Debits—Cost Center 2000** | |
| Cost Element 900000 | $400 |

## Assessment Cost Element

The assessment cost element, the final section of the settlement assignment, determines the cost element(s) posted to both the sender and the receiver during settlement. You can use this section if you plan to use the Allocation Structure specifically for an assessment process rather than a distribution approach to settlement (see Figure 11.9).

**FIGURE 11.9**    New Entries: Overview of Added Entries—change view "Assessment Cost Element": screen

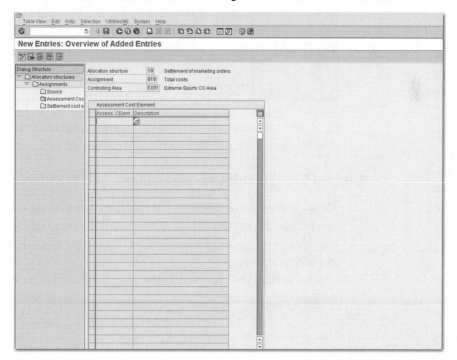

When you've completed the settlement cost element assignment, save the settings (see Figure 11.10). Click the green arrow to return to the settlement assignment screen and review the other assignments if necessary. When you've done so, save the settlement structure.

**FIGURE 11.10** The saved settings for the settlement cost element assignment

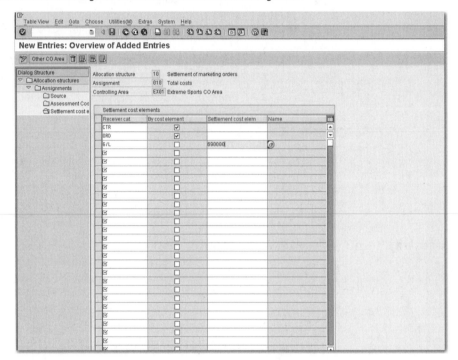

In the next section, we discuss the pros and cons associated with using either the By Cost Element or Settlement Cost Element parameter.

## Original Cost Element vs. Settlement Cost Element

Although there are no significant technical reasons for selecting the original cost element over the settlement cost element, SAP recommends using the settlement cost element to reduce the number of line items posted during order settlement. Probably the best reason that you should choose one solution over another is the likelihood of the user group being able to easily grasp the concepts surrounding settlement.

**EXTREME SPORTS SETTLEMENT STRUCTURE CONFIGURATION ANALYSIS**

For its projects, Extreme Sports wants to see the costs segregated into labor, materials, and consulting on its cost center statements. One way to ensure that this occurs is to define settlement assignments for each cost group. In Extreme Sports's case, three settlement assignments were defined: 10 (Labor Costs), 20 (Material Cost), and 30 (Consulting Costs). Additionally, Extreme Sports has chosen to use Original Cost Element instead of Settlement Cost Element. The decision was based on management's view that each cost center manager would like to see an account breakdown of any project settlement that hit their cost center. Because each origin group contained at least one secondary cost element, the settlement to G/L account required a settlement cost element because it is an external object.

# Source Structure

The source structure—or as it's sometimes referred to, the *origin structure*—is another component of the settlement profile. SAP uses the source structure during settlement rule creation to quickly segregate order activity. If you want the flexibility to uniquely define settlement rules per cost element group, the source structure is the tool to use. As with the settlement structure, you must create and maintain the source structure prior to its assignment in the settlement profile. Unlike the settlement structure, this is an additional option to use in setting up your settlement process. But if the scenario for your settlement doesn't require additional segregation of order postings, then you don't need to create this structure.

Here is how the source structure functions: A user determines that all consulting fees should be settled to cost center 1000, all labor costs should be routed to cost center 2000, and all material costs should be capitalized to an asset. The user can research the order postings and manually calculate that $1,150.73 of the total order costs is for consulting, $2,235.08 is for labor, and $4,893.45 is for material costs. Then, the user could maintain individual rules for each dollar amount. However, the process can get complicated if this example was a large project or if instead of applying to one project, the rules applied to many similar projects. Source structures can manage this separation automatically.

By establishing cost element groups that represent each of the major expense groups—consulting, labor, and materials—and assigning them to a source structure, the user can use the structure to reduce the settlement rule count to three. The settlement rules would state that all costs that fall in the consulting cost element group settle to cost center 1000, all costs that fall in the labor element group settle to cost center 2000, and all material costs identified by the material cost element group settle to the asset.

Figure 11.11 illustrates how source structures can be used in settlement rule creation. Initially you enter into a settlement rule based on an IO (see Figure 11.11). Once you have entered the settlement rule, you select Goto ➤ Settlement Parameters to display the assignment of the source structure (see Figure 11.12). The user has determined that all order costs that are labor related will settle to cost center 1000 by virtue of the source structure 20—Extreme Sports Expenses. All nonlabor costs will settle to cost center 2000 because of the source structure assignment NLB. The following configuration details take you step by step through the process of creating the source structure.

**FIGURE 11.11** Settlement rule creation with source structures

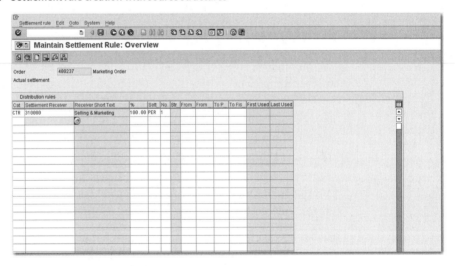

There are three steps to maintaining the source structure:

1. Create the source structure ID.

2. Create the source assignments.

3. Assign the source cost element groups to each origin assignment.

Begin the process by choosing Controlling ➤ Internal Orders ➤ Actual Postings ➤ Settlement ➤ Maintain Source Structure or by using transaction code OKEU.

The source structures overview screen appears. Click the New Entries button, and you'll see the source structure ID creation screen, shown in Figure 11.13.

**FIGURE 11.12**   Maintain Settlement Rule: Parameters screen

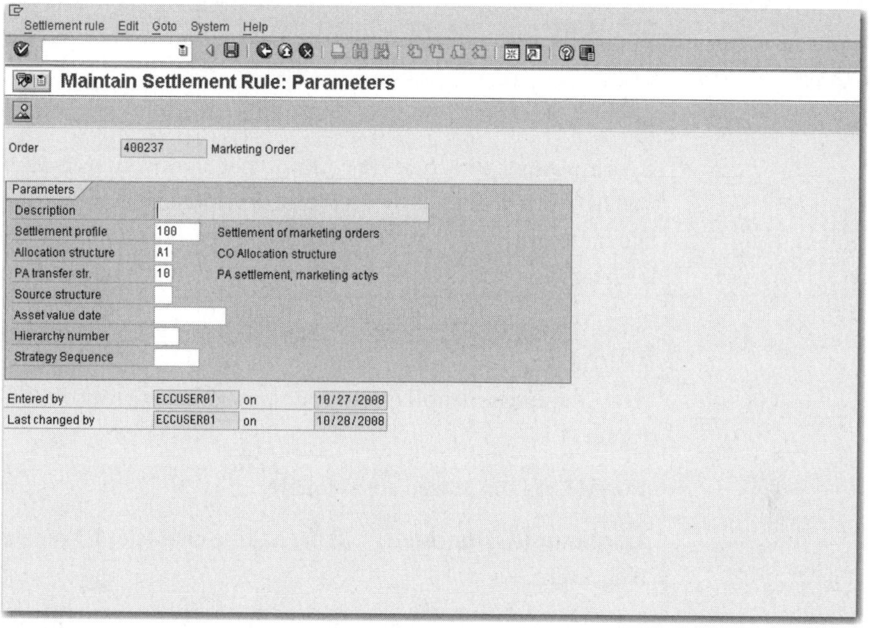

**FIGURE 11.13**   The source structure ID creation screen

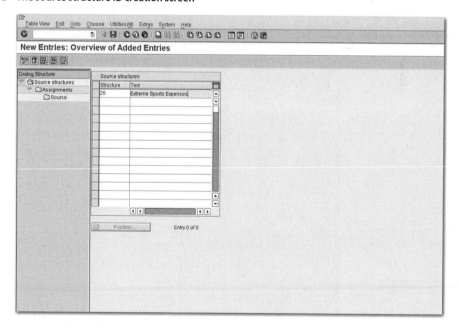

Fill in the following fields:

**Structure** Enter a two-character ID representing your origin structure. It is this ID that will be assigned to the settlement structure.

**Text** Enter a description of the origin structure.

Save the source structure ID. SAP will not allow you to continue development until you have saved. The source structure development continues with the creation of the source assignments. Referring to the earlier example, the assignments are either LAB (representing labor) or NLB (representing nonlabor activities).

Select the origin ID you want to maintain, and click Details on the toolbar. The Assignments to Original Layout screen appears. Click the New Entries button to create the assignment IDs. The source assignment creation screen appears (see Figure 11.14).

The fields on this screen are as follows:

**Assgnmnt (Assignment)** Enter a three-character ID representing the origin assignment.

**Text (Description)** Enter the description of the assignment ID.

**FIGURE 11.14** The source assignment creation screen

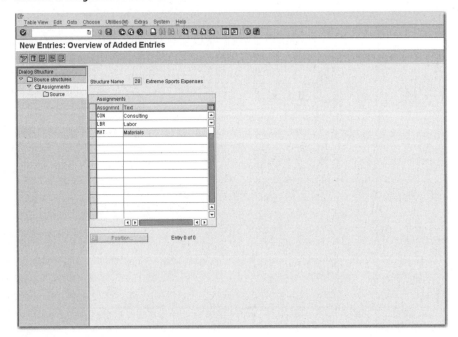

When you finish, save the settings. The next step is to create and assign the source assignment by selecting one of the assignments you just created and selecting the source option in the navigation pane. The Source Data for Assignment box appears, which includes the Field Label, From Value, and To Value for cost elements, and for faster assignments a Group field with the field label Cost Element (see Figure 11.15).

**FIGURE 11.15**  The New Entries: Overview of Added Entries screen for Source Data for Assignment

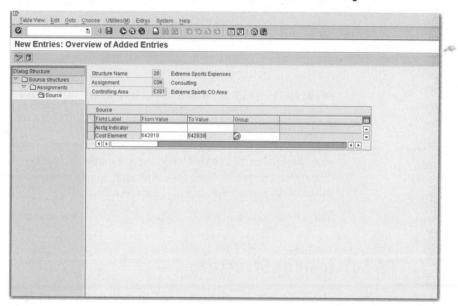

Notice that the assignment box outlines which source layout sheet you are maintaining, as well as the assignment and controlling area. Here are the fields you need to complete:

**Field Label**   The Field Label box in the upper-left corner allows you to toggle between assignments. However, each new assignment must be saved before you can maintain another. If you rotate to another assignment prior to saving the settings on the current assignment, the detail will be erased.

**From Value/To Value**   Enter a range of cost elements that relate to the assignment being maintained. In the example, a range of consulting cost elements is assigned.

**Group**   If an unbroken range of cost elements is not available, you can assign a cost element group. You have the option of using an existing group or creating a new group. If you want to create a new group, simply enter the name of the cost element group in this field and click the create group button at the bottom of the box.

The Create Group button will appear once you've entered the new group name. The familiar cost element group creation screen will appear. Complete, save the group, and click the green arrow to return to the assignment screen. It is also possible to display and change cost element groups that have been assigned by using the buttons found at the bottom of the box.

When you have maintained all the assignments in your source layout, save the screen. You can then use the source assignments while creating the settlement rule. In the next section, we continue our discussion of settlement structures by touching briefly on the PA settlement structure.

---

**EXTREME SPORTS ORIGIN STRUCTURE CONFIGURATION ANALYSIS**

To ease the burden on its project managers, Extreme Sports chose to configure an origin structure containing the breakout of its three main cost components: labor costs, material costs, and consulting costs. An order will contain numerous postings throughout a period, and using this approach, a project manager can easily establish the settlement rules necessary to break down the costs.

---

## PA Settlement Structure

The Profitability Analysis (PA) settlement structure is the link between costing-based PA and other modules such as the FI module or Production Orders. It is similar in function to the order settlement structure, which links order activity to both FI and CO objects. It comes into play in this example only when you are settling to a profitability segment. We'll discuss the PA settlement structure in greater detail in Chapter 12, "Profitability Analysis." For now, we'll touch on the areas in which it is relevant for internal order settlement, such as in the settlement profile assignment.

 **NOTE**   Many of the terms you'll see here will be reviewed and further developed in Chapter 12. So, although this section relates to the analysis in Internal Orders, you'll find this information valuable in the following chapter as well.

Costing-based Profitability Analysis, or CO-PA, is defined by two main components: characteristics and value fields. An example of a characteristic is a Material,

Distribution Channel, Profit Center, or Customer. Combinations of specific characteristic values, like Distribution Channel Southeast and Customer 101000-Acme Shoes, make up what are called profitability segments. Characteristics are used by both costing-based and account-based CO-PA.

A value field represents the quantity or value associated with any CO-PA transaction. Value field examples include Sales, Cost of Sales, Quantities, and Expenses. Account-based CO-PA has no need for value fields because all postings are maintained by account. Therefore, sales activity is maintained and posted to the sales account in CO-PA. But costing-based CO-PA requires specific mapping to a value field to facilitate posting activity from SD, MM, and FI. The vehicle through which FI postings are mapped to value fields is the PA settlement structure.

Simply stated, the PA settlement structure matches account-related postings resulting from FI activity (such as a goods receipt on an internal order) to a value field in Profitability Analysis. In this example, an order type is configured to support original cost element settlement. Account 60000-Materials is posted to an order through a goods receipt transaction. You now wish to settle the order activity to a profitability segment in CO-PA. In our example, the operating concern contains a value field called MATEXP (for material expense). For the settlement to process, the account 60000 must be mapped to the CO-PA value field MATEXP. All potential account postings must be mapped in some fashion to facilitate all settlement transactions.

Order accounting is unique in its relationship with CO-PA in that there can be more than one settlement structure used. For FI and SD, only one PA structure can be developed; the system will not recognize a second. What this means for you is that each order type you develop can settle its costs uniquely to CO-PA. In order type 1000, all material expenses settle to the value field MATEXP. However, because a different PA settlement structure is assigned to type 2000, all material expenses posted to an order of type 2000 settle to a value field called PROJECT.

As mentioned earlier, Chapter 12 covers the details of developing a surrounding PA settlement structure. It is a good idea to review that chapter if CO-PA is active within the controlling area.

Now that all preliminary settlement configurations are complete, you are ready to configure the settlement profile. Figure 11.16 shows an example of the PA Transfer Structures screen. As you can see, there is no noticeable difference between the Order Settlement Structure and the PA Transfer Structure.

**FIGURE 11.16**  PA Transfer Structures screen

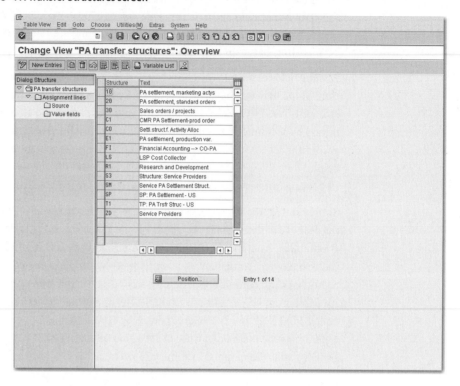

## Settlement Profile

The settlement profile is the component of order configuration that provides the order type with the details of how it can settle its costs. It accomplishes this by controlling how a settlement rule can be defined for a given order. The settlement profile is an accumulation of the other areas of settlement we previously configured in this chapter, as well as the addition of new pieces of customization not yet seen. Each order type can have a different settlement profile, but each must have one assigned. Use the following menu path to begin configuration of the settlement profile: Controlling ➢ Internal Orders ➢ Actual Postings ➢ Settlement ➢ Maintain Settlement Profile. Alternatively, use transaction code OKO7.

If you use the menu path, a screen appears asking whether you want to maintain the settlement profile or assign a profile to an order type. Select Maintain Settlement Profiles, and the settlement profile configuration screen appears. To create a new settlement profile, click the New Entries button to open the new entries detail screen. Figure 11.17 is a view of the completed settlement profile 90 that Extreme Sports will be using to track its expense-related project costs.

**FIGURE 11.17** The settlement profile configuration screen

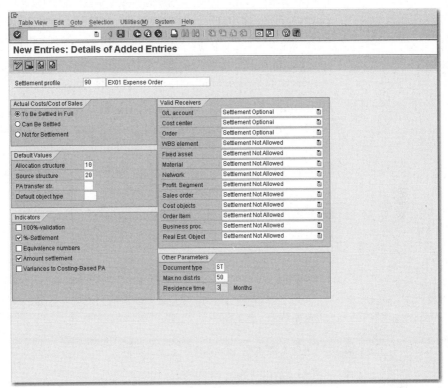

As with the other configuration screens, we'll describe this one in terms of its field groupings.

The fields in the Actual Costs/Cost of Sales section relate to overall control of the order in relation to when it may be closed and archived:

**To Be Settled in Full** This setting forces the value of the order to be $0 before it can be closed. SAP will return a hard error if a user tries to close the order with a balance. Because most companies prefer to see their operating expenses in CCA, the majority of internal orders fall into this category. Also, when integrating with Investment Management, it is important to choose this option so that balance sheet calculations are accurate.

**Can Be Settled** If you choose this setting, costs can be settled from the order, but it is not mandatory. If a user attempts to close an order with a balance and this setting is enabled, SAP will return a warning. Rarely would anyone want to leave balances on the order when closing. Again, most companies prefer to have their operating expenses reported consistently through one location, like CCA.

**Not for Settlement**     Actual costs cannot be settled if this setting is active. When the order is closed and has a balance, SAP will return a message indicating the balance. This might be used in conjunction with a sales-related order.

The fields in the Default Values section relate to how the order will determine what cost elements are valid for settlement and how the postings will occur:

**Allocation Structure**     We described this field in detail earlier. It is the only value that must be configured on the profile. Remember that the structure is independent of the controlling area and must be maintained accordingly.

**Source Structure**     We described this field in detail earlier as well. It is not a mandatory setting, but it can be helpful when you're creating settlement rules.

**PA Transfer Str.**     We also described this field in detail earlier. It is mandatory if you will be settling order-related costs to CO-PA.

**Default Object Type**     This field provides the order with a defaulting receiver object type during settlement rule creation. You can change the defaulting receiver object on the order settlement rule in production. Examples include the following:

**CTR**     Cost Center

**ORD**     Order

**PSG**     Profitability Segment

For certain order types (such as sales-related orders, repetitive collectors, and investment orders), specific default objects will be required. Examples of default objects include the following:

**Sales-related order types**     PSG is the default object.

**Repetitive collectors (orders)**     MAT, or material, defaults into the screen.

**Investment orders**     FXA is the default object.

Settings in the Indicators section relate to how you can define the dollar values to be settled:

**100%-Validation**     If you select this field, SAP will check to make sure all costs will be settled by the rules the user has established on the order. If less than or greater than 100% of the costs are not covered by the rules, SAP will return a warning when the order is saved. The user can still save the order, but SAP will return an error when attempting to settle. The setting is relevant for periodic settlements only. Overall settlements must always equal 100%.

**%-Settlement**　If this field is active, the user can maintain settlement rules on the order that determines the dollar value by percentage (see Table 11.3 for an example).

**TABLE 11.3**　　Percentage (%) Settlement Example

| Order Cost Total: $10,000 | | |
|---|---|---|
| Rule 1: Cost Center | 1000 | 60% |
| Rule 2: Cost Center | 2000 | 40% |
| **Total** | | **100%** |
| Settlement Breakdown | | |
| Cost Center | 1000 | $6,000 |
| Cost Center | 2000 | $4,000 |
| **Total** | | **$10,000** |

**Equivalence Numbers**　If you select this field, the user can use equivalence numbers as an alternative to percentages. If it is easier for the user to set up a proportion as opposed to calculating percentages, then equivalence numbers are appropriate. In the example in Table 11.4, the settlement rule apportion cost is based on the number of employees in each cost center.

**TABLE 11.4**　　Equivalence Number Settlement Example

| Order Cost Total: $10,000 | |
|---|---|
| Rule 1: Cost Center 1000—6 employees | |
| Rule 2: Cost Center 2000—13 employees | |
| Rule 3: Cost Center 3000—18 employees | |
| **Total: 37 employees** | |
| Settlement Breakdown | |
| Cost Center 1000 (6/37) | $1,621.62 |
| Cost Center 2000 (13/37) | $3,513.51 |
| Cost Center 3000 (18/37) | $4,864.87 |
| **Total:** | **$10,000** |

**Amount Settlement**    If this field is active, the user can establish settlement rules with dollar value amounts.

**Variances to Costing-Based PA**    Check this field only if you want to settle production-related costs to CO-PA. The setting should be used in conjunction with order-related and repetitive production order types. The system automatically creates a settlement rule for the profitability segment linked to the material being produced. For costing-based CO-PA, refer to the section "Costing Based CO-PA" later in Chapter 12 for an explanation of the relationship between cost elements and value fields.

The fields in the Valid Receivers section relate to what type of object(s) the user can create settlement rules for. The fields are specific SAP objects for which a settlement rule can be maintained (see Figure 11.17 for a complete listing). There are three potential settings for each receiver:

**Settlement Not Allowed**    With Settlement Not Allowed selected, the user cannot use a receiver to create settlement rules. If the user attempts to create a settlement rule for a receiver that hasn't been maintained, an error is returned.

**Settlement Optional**    This setting allows the user to create a settlement rule for the specific receiver.

**Settlement Required**    This setting makes a settlement rule mandatory for the specific receiver. If a settlement rule has not been maintained for a receiver marked as mandatory, SAP will return an error when the user tries to save the order.

You can see the power of maintaining a proper receiver list. Use these settings carefully, as a controlling influence over how your users are supposed to use the order type.

The fields in the Other Parameters section relate to order posting and archiving:

**Document Type**    You must provide the order with a document type with which the settlement documents will be labeled. We recommend that you use a separate document type for settlements; it will be easier to analyze and segregate the activity. Document Type is a mandatory setting.

**Max. No. Dist. Rls**    This setting provides the order with the maximum number of settlement rules the user can maintain. The maximum number is 999. Although 999 may not always be practical, you can do harm to your productivity if you do not maintain a high enough number.

**Residence Time**    This field determines how long, in months, the settlement document must be retained in the system before it can be archived. Consult the company policy for the proper setting. SAP will default the setting to three months.

> **TIP**   As you make changes to the settlement profile settings, they become retroactively on all existing orders. That means that all orders currently outstanding will become subject to the changes. Keep this in mind before proceeding.

Save the profile when you've finished. In the next section you'll learn how to configure pertinent number ranges.

---

## EXTREME SPORTS SETTLEMENT PROFILE CONFIGURATION ANALYSIS

For its expense-related projects, Extreme Sports created Settlement Profile 90-EX01 Expense Orders. Because all costs must be maintained on a cost center for reporting, it was important that the profile ensure complete settlement before closing the order. To prevent the users from settling to unwanted objects, the settlement structure and valid receivers would allow rules only for cost centers, orders, and G/L accounts. To provide a measure of flexibility, Extreme Sports wanted the profile to allow settlement rules to be created for both percentages and dollars. Finally, Extreme Sports decided to segregate its settlement activities with a unique document type, ST. This will make analyzing posting activity easier once all its plants are up and running.

---

# Maintaining Number Ranges for Settlement

Just as you assigned number ranges to activities in other areas of SAP configuration, you also must make a number range assignment for settlement documents. In the case of settlement documents, the number range assignment is at the controlling area level. You will notice that there are similarities in the assignment steps for settlement documents and the assignment for CO activities covered in Chapter 8. Because the steps are a little different, though, we will document them in detail. You can access the number range assignment location by choosing Controlling ➤ Internal Orders ➤ Actual Postings ➤ Settlement ➤ Maintain Number Ranges for Settlement Documents or by using the transaction code SNUM.

**TIP**   Transaction code SNUM directs you to a generic number range screen, and from there you will have to identify the specific number range object to work on that will be assigned to the CO component Internal Orders. If you use the menu path, you will arrive at the screen specific to IOs.

In the resulting number range for settlement documents CO objects screen, your first step is to create a group number range to which your controlling area can be assigned. Click the Maintain Groups button to display the Maintain Number Range Groups screen. SAP will deliver a default group for standard accounting documents that can be used for your controlling area. For performance reasons, SAP recommends that in environments with multiple controlling areas, each area receive its own number range. For the sake of demonstration, we'll create a new interval.

Select Group ➢ Insert to open the Insert Group box, shown in Figure 11.18.

**FIGURE 11.18**   Insert Group box

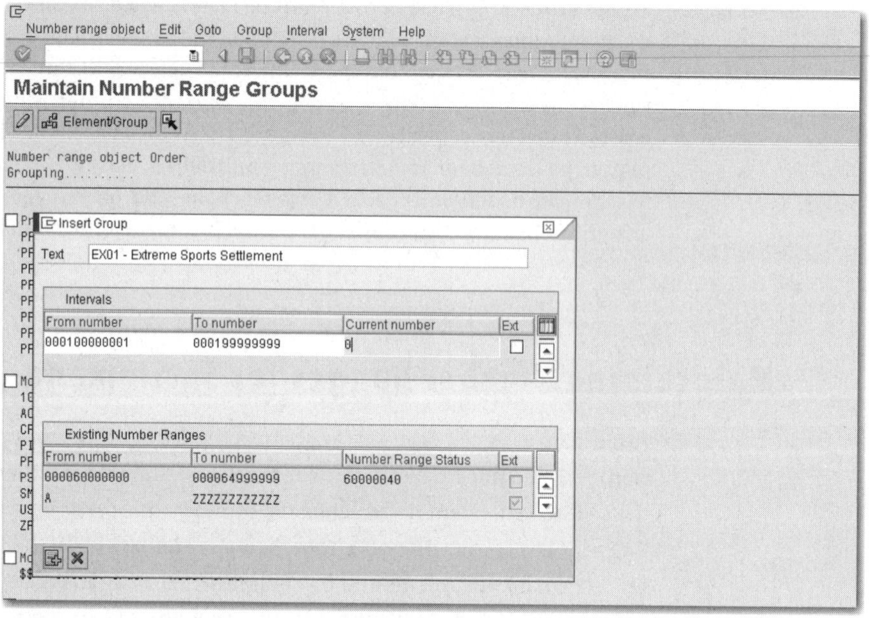

| | Number range object | Edit | Goto | Group | Interval | System | Help |

**Maintain Number Range Groups**

Number range object Order
Grouping. . . . . . . . .

| Insert Group | | | |
|---|---|---|---|
| Text | EX01 - Extreme Sports Settlement | | |

**Intervals**

| From number | To number | Current number | Ext |
|---|---|---|---|
| 000100000001 | 000199999999 | 0 | |

**Existing Number Ranges**

| From number | To number | Number Range Status | Ext |
|---|---|---|---|
| 000060000000 | 000064999999 | 60000040 | |
| A | ZZZZZZZZZZZZ | | ✓ |

Here are the important fields in the Insert Group box:

**Text**   Enter a description for the number range you are adding. Be certain to describe it uniquely and clearly.

**From/To Number**   Enter the number range you want for your settlements. If you anticipate multiple controlling areas, leave enough room in the range to accommodate the other areas. You will see any existing ranges noted at the bottom of the Insert Group box. Do not overlap the range or SAP will return an error.

Click the insert button at the bottom of the box. You will notice that the new interval appears on the Maintain Number Range Groups screen.

The second step is to assign your controlling area to the new range. You will find a listing of all unassigned controlling areas below the number range intervals in a section labeled Not Assigned. Place your cursor on the controlling area in question and click the select element button. Notice that the controlling area becomes highlighted. This is SAP's signal that the item has been selected.

To assign the selected controlling area to the number range, select the box next to the number range group and click the Element/Group button. The selected controlling area will move from the Not Assigned section to the new number range group (see Figure 11.19). Save the number range assignment.

**FIGURE 11.19**   The maintained number range group assignment for EX01, Extreme Sports

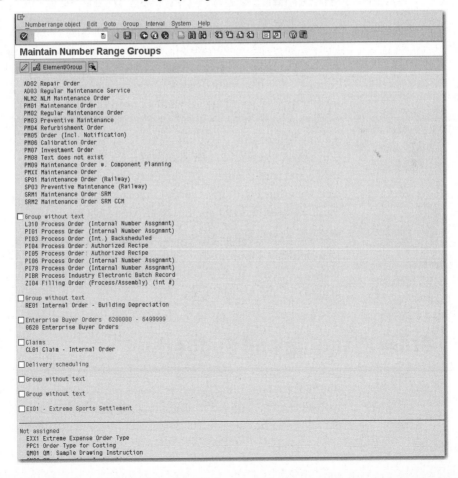

**WARNING**    Always remember to never transport your number ranges. Manually assign the ranges in each client to ensure the integrity of your document numbering.

---

### EXTREME SPORTS SETTLEMENT NUMBER RANGES CONFIGURATION ANALYSIS

Currently, only one controlling area will exist for Extreme Sports, so the need to segregate the document number ranges is not an issue. But if further expansion were to force a second controlling area, Extreme Sports would establish a second settlement document number range per SAP's recommendation. As we mentioned in Chapter 8, best practice is to have only one controlling area—only in unusual circumstances would you need to add another.

## Order Settlement Configuration Overview

We've now covered all the necessary order settlement configurations. It is important that you experiment with various settings before determining what works for your project. Engage your users as much as possible during the development process. The concepts of settlement will be completely foreign to many and could thus result in a lot of rework on your part. As we mentioned earlier, the configuration necessary for setting up Internal Order Accounting is a bit backward. So, a bit later in this chapter we'll circle around and go through the setup of an actual IO and the fields required during that process. We have started this process by reviewing the order type and the components required to set up that object, but we haven't gotten to the point in terms of using it during the configuration of master data. We still have that to cover. So, don't think that we have missed anything just yet.

The next section will examine order planning and budgeting configuration. Depending on your company's intended use for Internal Order Accounting, planning can be very simple or extremely complex. We'll cover unit costing, plan/budget profiles, and availability control.

# Order Planning and Budgeting

Internal order planning is another area in which one solution or type of planning will not fit all scenarios. For simple projects with a short life span, overall order planning may be the perfect solution. A more complex project spanning an entire year or longer may require a detailed unit cost planning approach. Further functionality provides the ability to fully integrate order planning with Cost Center Accounting, Profit Center Accounting, and special ledgers.

In the CO module, SAP makes a distinction between planning and budgeting. Planning implies that an iterative process may occur in which many different versions of the plan may be developed until one is decided upon. The budget, which can be defined as a detailed work plan describing how the approved amount will be allocated, is developed once the overall plan has been confirmed. The budget is the tool through which project management will approve and allocate costs within the internal order. Linked with the internal order budget is SAP's budget management system, known as availability control.

Availability control, its concepts of commitment and cost management, and its relationship to the budget are important for proper internal order development. Through proper configuration, availability control can assist your project manager by monitoring ongoing project variances and initiating specific actions when tolerances are reached. It is important to note here that not all configuration scenarios surrounding internal order planning and budgeting can be covered in this chapter. This chapter explores the basics necessary to get you started. The planning and budgeting toolset is very robust in the IO area. We are able to set up a planning process to create a planning object that can reflect the planning process of setting up a standard cost for a product. You can set up a planned standard cost for an object/material or product that is currently in existence or is a product that is being developed. This ties directly into the use of IOs against Production Orders in Production Planning. Therefore, the planning process allows integration from CO into the Logistics modules.

The following sections focus on functionality and explain specific configuration settings. You should concentrate on the concepts covered first and the explanation of the table views configured second. Both are important, and by the end, you will be able to apply these concepts when developing your own planning strategy. The development section begins with a brief description of the four available levels of internal order planning.

## Internal Order Planning/Budgeting: Basics

SAP provides you with four levels of internal order planning, with each level more detailed than the preceding:

**Overall planning**    This approach is the simplest form of internal order cost planning available. Plan costs are maintained at the order level and can be detailed on an overall and/or annual view. If the purpose of planning is to compare total actual project costs to plan, overall planning is a good solution. Another use may be to temporarily plan at an overall level and, when better information is available, plan at a more detailed level.

**Cost element/activity planning**   This approach is similar to the planning found in CCA. It is used for more detailed project tracking because it offers the user a cost structure view. Both costs and revenues can be planned for an internal order. Note that to plan revenues on an order, you must make specific order type settings (see the "Order Types" section later in this chapter).

With cost element/activity planning, you have the ability to integrate your planning efforts with CCA. A fully integrated order plan receives its activity prices from an assigned cost center plan. As activity rates change on the cost center, they are updated on the order. Activity planning on the order is available regardless of whether integration is active. In either case, there are implications for the controlling area maintenance screen in how SAP will determine the activity prices.

**Easy cost planning**   This cost-planning approach allows you to assign costing variant information, assign cost component structures to the planning process, and assign overhead to the planned data for additional details of the IO planning process. An advantage to using easy cost planning is that you can set up to automatically assign costs from purchase requisitions, purchase orders, reservations, good issues, and internal activity allocations directly to the planned values. This is called *execution services*, which is activated by using the easy cost planning methods.

**Unit costing**   Unit costing is related to cost element/activity planning, and is mainly used in circumstances in which you have access to more information, like quantities and rates of consumption. Expenses specific to the cost element level are broken down into greater detail through the use of costing sheets and valuation variants. Integrated planning is not available at the unit-costing level.

Here is an example of how unit costing is used: You have a project for which you want to track labor and material costs at a detailed level. The project work will be covered by three separate shifts of people, all working in the same cost center and using the same cost elements for salary and material consumption. Using unit costing, you can differentiate the plan allocation by each shift without using additional cost elements.

Keep in mind that you are not limited to one level of planning. It is entirely possible that you could have a project that begins at an overall planning level, moves to a cost element level of detail once more information is available, and finally moves to the unit costing level if even a greater level of detail is necessary. The first step in internal order planning is the maintenance of the CO versions within the controlling area.

**Controlling Area Version Maintenance**     Because versions are used in all areas of CO, it is important to always revisit them when configuring a new section like order accounting. Figure 11.20 and Figure 11.21 are views of the fiscal-year parameters of the controlling area for version 0. The details behind the settings are covered at length in Chapter 8. Review the section so that you can be aware of the impact each field has in the planning process. You can open the CO version control screen by choosing Controlling ➢ General Controlling ➢ Organization ➢ Maintain Versions or by using transaction code OKEQ.

**FIGURE 11.20**   Fiscal Year Dependent view for version 0—Planning

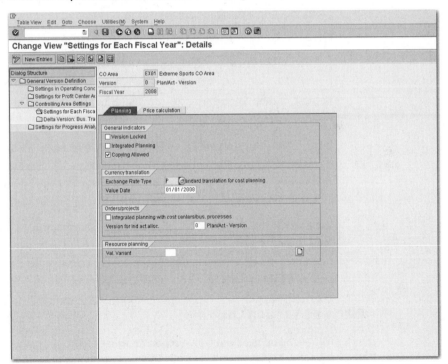

**FIGURE 11.21**   Fiscal Year Dependent view for version 0 – Price Calculation

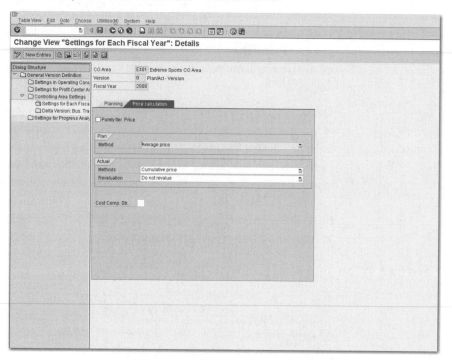

Because of their importance to order planning, pay close attention to the following two fields when reviewing the field definitions in Chapter 8:

**Integrated Planning with Cost Center/Bus Processes**   Choose this setting if you want to have internal order/WBS element plans integrate with Cost Center Accounting. The integration is a two-way street; cost center plans can affect orders and order planning can affect cost centers.

**Version for Ind. Act. Alloc.**   This setting is relevant only when Planning Integration with CCA is not active. Enter the version from which you want SAP to extract the activity price information for the activity types used as inputs to the orders/WBS elements.

## Planning Version Control

Although you need only one version to utilize CO planning, SAP provides the flexibility to use multiple versions during any planning cycle. Because order planning is different from Cost Center Accounting planning in that all orders may not always be developed at the time of planning, multiple versions may not always be necessary. If, however, you decide to use multiple versions, know that you have the same copy functionality found in Cost Center Accounting. The merits of multiple versions and configuration settings are covered in both Chapter 8 and Chapter 10, "Cost Center Accounting."

The next section describes the steps to completing internal order planning and budgeting.

# Internal Order Planning/Budgeting: Profile Development

Overall plan and budget profiles are used by SAP to control such aspects as planning views, formats, and detail planning sets. Additionally, unique to a budget profile is the ability to determine availability control activation. Although not required during order type development, profile assignments are necessary prior to any internal order planning or budgeting that is occurring. Both plan and budget profiles are maintained in a similar manner and can be configured and applied quickly.

 **WARNING**   Remember that all budget and plan profiles are controlling area independent. Any changes made to a profile will affect all orders that are assigned to the profile, regardless of the controlling area in which the orders reside.

Areas of concern when configuring the planning profile include how many years out will be planned and visible, whether cost element planning or unit costing will be used, and whether planning will occur for overall values, annual values, or both. Remember that circumstances will not always be the same for each order type you develop, so don't attempt to build one "universal solution." It will be far easier to build unique plan profiles for the more unusual internal order uses. Budget profile configuration is similar in the ease of development, but some of the questions or concerns that arise when developing are unique.

Budgeting within SAP is limited to just order accounting and project systems because of their unique project management properties. And not all internal order solutions include the use of budgeting as an option. Budgeting and budget profiles offer the developer an opportunity to control procurement by linking the profile with both a capital investment profile and availability control. From a version perspective, budgeting defaults to version 0 and cannot be rerouted. Like planning profiles, knowing the users' requirements relative to the time horizon and entry screen views is relevant. The next section describes the configuration processes for both plan and budget profiles.

## Plan Profile Development

Begin plan profile configuration by defining the profile ID. Select Controlling ➢ Internal Orders ➢ Planning ➢ Manual Planning ➢ Maintain Planning Profile for Overall Value Planning, or use transaction code OKOS.

If you use the menu path, a decision box appears asking whether you want to define the planning profile or assign a profile to an order type. Select the "Define planning profile for overall cost planning" line. The COST planning for CO orders screen appears. Two profiles—000001 (general budget/plan profile) and 000002 (CO production order profile)—are delivered with the system. You have the authority to change each of these profiles, but we recommend that you create your own.

Click the New Entries button and the details of created entries screen appears (Figure 11.22 shows the screen configured for Extreme Sports). Notice that only the Profile ID box is a required entry. It is possible to create a shell and fill in the other fields later. This approach may be a good idea when you're creating a new order type and you want a placeholder for the planning profile.

**FIGURE 11.22**  Display the New Entries: Details of Added Entries Screen for the completed Extreme Sports planning profile

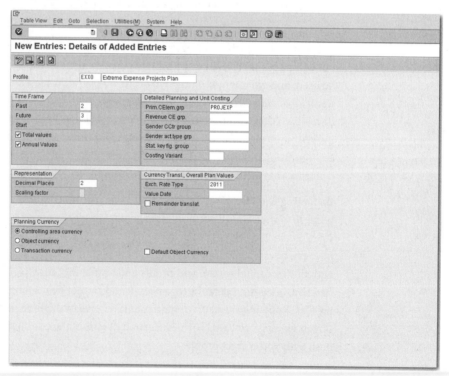

Begin the configuration by defining the profile's ID:

**Profile**    Enter an alphanumeric ID (up to seven characters) describing the planning profile.

**Text**    This is the blank field next to Profile. Enter a description of the planning profile. Be as clear as possible because the profile is controlling area independent and you do not want its use to be misinterpreted.

The fields found in the Time Frame section relate to the planning years available for user input and review:

**Past**    This field refers to the number of years before the start year the user will be able to plan/budget.

For example, if the number 2 is entered in the field and the current or start year is 2008, the user will be able to view or change the plan or budget back to 2006.

**Future**    This setting is similar to the Past setting. It refers to the number of years beyond the start year the user will be able to plan.

For example, if 3 is entered and the current or start year is 2008, planning will be allowed through 2011.

**Start**    This field refers to the first year that planning/budgeting will be accessible to the user. The number entered here will be added to the current fiscal year to determine the start year.

For example, suppose the current fiscal year is 2008. If you enter 2 in this field, the first year allowed for planning is 2010. Use caution when making the entry because this value becomes the basis for all future planning settings. If you want to default the current fiscal year as the start year, leave this field empty.

**Total Values**    Check this field if you want to allow the user to plan for overall values on the order. At the highest level, an order or project can be planned for total cost regardless of the year it is consumed.

For example, suppose an order has a total planned cost of $500,000. This would be considered its Total value. For capital investment orders, we recommend you enable this setting.

**Annual Values**    Check this field if you want to allow the user to plan annual expenditures for an order.

For example, suppose an order has a total planned cost of $500,000. This setting would allow the user to plan the cost expenditures across years. In the example, $200,000 would be planned for 2008, $200,000 for 2009, and $100,000 for 2010.

**NOTE**   Checking the Total Values and Annual Values fields does not make them required. If your project has no preference, we recommend that you select both.

Fields in the Representation section relate to the view the user will have on the planning entry screen:

**Decimal Places**   Enter the desired number of decimal places in which you want to plan.

**Scaling Factor**   If scaling is important when planning, enter the scaling factor here.

For example, if you want to plan in thousands, enter 3 in the Scaling Factor field. As you enter the plan, only the scaled amount will appear. The total amount is entered in the planning table.

With a scale of 3, a plan of $1,000,000 is entered as $1,000 on the planning screen.

If cost element-level detail or planning integration is desired, you can save time by entering the default master data sets in the Detailed Planning and Unit Costing section:

**PrimCElemGrp**   If desired, enter the primary cost element group to be the default for cost element-level planning. Entering a defined group of cost elements is a good way to limit the user's ability to plan.

**Revenue CE Grp.**   If desired, enter the revenue element group to be the default for revenue element-level planning. For revenues to be planned on an order, the order type must allow revenue postings. Planning entries must be entered as a negative, that is, with a preceding minus (–) sign.

**Sender CCtr Group**   If desired, enter the cost center group that you want to be the default for activity input planning. Planned activity is relayed from the cost center group, and as activity is recorded, the group is credited accordingly.

**Sender Act. Type Grp**   If desired, enter the activity type group that you want to be the default for activity planning. If maintained, when the user clicks the Activity Input button on the order-planning screen, this activity type group appears as the only option.

**Stat. Key Fig. Group**   If desired, enter the statistical key figure group to be the default for key figure planning. Entering a defined group of key figures is a good way to limit the user's ability to plan.

**Costing Variant**   If detailed planning is required, enter a costing variant. The costing variant ID is linked to the valuation variant that determines activity and material prices. The costing variant assigned here becomes the default for the user to enter the activity cost estimate.

If you aren't sure whether unit cost planning will be used, leave the field empty. You have the ability to enter a variant later if it becomes necessary.

Once you've entered these settings, save the profile. Figure 11.22 earlier in the chapter showed an example of profile EXXO (Extreme Expense Projects Plan). Remember that you can change these profiles on the fly, meaning that any setting changes resulting in some functionality addition or deletion will be immediately visible on all relevant orders. Any orders with the planning profile in question are relevant in this case. In the next section, we'll cover the subtle differences provided by budget profiles.

## EXTREME SPORTS'S ORDER PLANNING PROFILE CONFIGURATION ANALYSIS

Because of the diversity of Extreme Sports's internal order needs, multiple profiles will be developed to support various expense and capital project types. In the case of profile EXXO, it will be used to support cost element-level planning on all basic expense projects. All expense projects will be created at the beginning of the fiscal year at just an overall project level. As the projects are activated, a cost element-level plan will be developed for each project for just the accounts found in the cost element group PROJEXP. Unit costing will not be necessary for these project types. Though they are expense projects, they may still span multiple years—thus the need for the three-year visibility.

## Budget Profile Development

Budgeting in SAP offers enhanced project management capabilities not provided by internal order planning. Whereas an internal order plan is an estimate of expenditures made at the beginning of a fiscal year, a budget represents the actual approved amount of funding for a given order. Because the budgeted amount is maintained separately, you have the opportunity to do plan-versus-budget comparisons. Additionally, you can control spending through the use of availability control.

Because many of the same fields are described in the previous section, "Plan Profile Development," we'll describe only the unique budget profile fields in detail. Let's begin by reviewing the completed profile template shown in Figure 11.23. To access the configuration screen, choose Controlling ➢ Internal Orders ➢ Budgeting and Availability Control ➢ Maintain Budget Profile or use transaction code OKOB.

**FIGURE 11.23**　The completed Extreme Sports budget profile BUDGT1

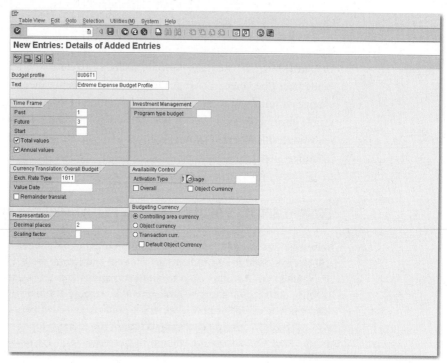

The budget profile for CO orders screen appears. Click the New Entries button to open a new profile entry screen. Immediately, you will notice the similarities between the budget profile and plan profile configuration screens. The Time Frame and Representation fields all have the same definitions.

Also notice that the Detailed Planning section is not present. Internal order budgeting is maintained at only the highest order level. Cost element budgeting is not available. There are two new sections of the profile that you should pay attention to:

► Program Type Budget

► Availability Control

After reviewing the plan profile field definitions for the related configuration fields, proceed to the two new sections.

The Program Type Budget section is related to Investment Management (IM). Enter the ID for a valid IM program type only if the orders using the profile will be assigned to a capital investment program. With this assignment, the only way these capital orders can receive budget allotments is through a direct distribution from the capital investment program. See Chapter 14, "Investment Management," for more details.

The fields in the Availability Control section are as follows:

**Activation Type**    This setting determines how availability control will be activated for a given internal order. There are three options:

**0**    Availability Control cannot be activated.

**1**    Availability Control will automatically activate upon assignment of the budget to an internal order.

**2**    Availability Control will be activated in the background.

**Usage**    This field is used in conjunction with background activation and funds commitments and is maintained as a percentage. When the percentage of funds entered in this field is achieved or exceeded, availability control is automatically activated.

**Overall**    Select this option if you choose to have the availability check occur against the overall budget of the project. If this field is deselected, availability checks will occur against the annual budget values.

**Object Currency**    Select this option if you choose to have the budget available in the local object currency.

**NOTE**    Keep in mind that, if availability control is to check against annual budget values, the next year's budget will have to be established before postings can occur. If you attempt to post a document without a budget in the future, SAP will return whatever failing action you have configured in Availability Control.

When you have completed the budget profile configuration, save the settings. The next section will continue the budget management development cycle by exploring the steps necessary to configure availability control.

## EXTREME SPORTS ORDER BUDGET PROFILE CONFIGURATION ANALYSIS

Budget profile BUDGT1 will be used to support expense-related projects for Extreme Sports. Availability control will be activated as soon as an order has been budgeted, which is Extreme Sports's signal that a project has been approved. This process fits in with its project management procedure of not allowing any procurement until the funds have been assigned.

## Availability Control Configuration

The idea behind availability control is that SAP should alert you when you are about to exceed some predefined percentage of project spending. You can do this by establishing spending tolerance levels for each budget profile/controlling area relationship. You must set up availability control for each profile individually—there is no opportunity to create a "universal" setting for all profiles.

SAP offers you much flexibility in establishing both the tolerance levels and the actions that result when those levels are exceeded. Once active, each setting can be changed without causing harm to previously budgeted orders. It may seem counter-intuitive, but the more complex the solution, the easier it is for you to understand how and when the budget was exceeded. The only step in configuring availability control is the creation of tolerance levels. You can reach the necessary table from the IMG by choosing Controlling ➤ Internal Orders ➤ Budgeting and Availability Control ➤ Define Tolerance Limits for Availability Control.

The availability control tolerance limits entry screen that appears (see Figure 11.24) is the only table entry screen necessary to complete availability control configuration. Notice the two entries on this screen. The same budget profile, BUDGT1, is defined twice in the table, with some differences in the Act. (Activation) and Usage columns. SAP establishes a relationship, called a key, between the profile, controlling area, activity group, and action. You are allowed only one unique value entry per this relationship. SAP will return an error otherwise.

Of the existing entries, you are allowed to make changes to only the Usage and Abs. Variance columns. To modify any of the key fields on an existing entry, you need to delete the entry and start anew by clicking the New Entries button. The created entries overview screen appears, allowing you to define your new tolerance limits (see Figure 11.25).

**FIGURE 11.24** The availability control tolerance limits entry screen

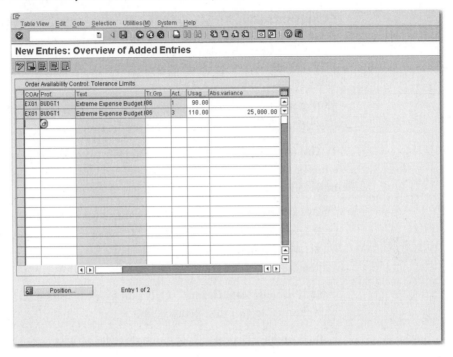

**FIGURE 11.25** The availability control settings for budget profile BUDGT1

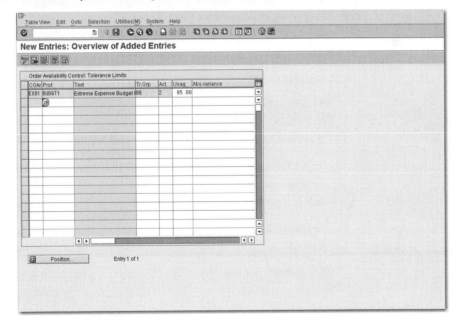

The key fields for availability control settings are as follows:

**COAr (Controlling Area)**     Enter the ID of the controlling area on which these settings will have an impact.

**Prof. (Budget)**     Enter the ID of the budget profile for which availability control is being set up.

**Text (Description)**     Manual entry is not allowed in this field. SAP takes the description from the assigned budget profile ID.

**Tr. Grp (Activity Group)**     Based on the setting in this field, SAP determines whether an activity against an order is relevant for availability check. There are 11 potential activity group settings:

**++ (All Activity Groups)**     All relevant activity against an assigned order is checked against the tolerance limit. The tolerance limits associated with the All Activity Groups setting are ignored if another activity group, like 01 (Purchase Requisition), is defined.

**00 (Purchase Requisition)**     Only purchase requisition activity against an order is checked against the tolerance limit.

**01 (Purchase Order)**     Only purchase order activity against an order is checked against the tolerance limit.

**02 (Orders for Project)**     This setting is related to project system. If this setting is selected, tolerance limit checks will occur during the planning process to ensure that the order plan does not exceed the stated limits.

**03 (Goods Issue)**     Only goods issued to the order will be subject to the tolerance limit checks.

**04 (Financial Accounting Document)**     Only postings to an order that result in a financial accounting document will be subject to the tolerance limit checks. Internal CO activity, like order settlement, will not be picked up.

**05 (CO Document)**     This setting is similar in concept to 04. Only postings to an order that result in a CO document, like settlement, will be subject to the tolerance limit check.

**06 (Budgeting)**     This setting is similar in concept to 02. During budget updates, SAP will check to see that the stated tolerance limits have not been exceeded.

For example, suppose the original budget on a project was $1,000. Current actual postings and stated commitments total $945 on the order. A tolerance limit has been set to return an error if 100% of the budget is exceeded. If someone attempts to reduce the budget on the order to $900, SAP will return an error because the current actuals + commitments will be 105% of the overall budget.

**07 (Funds Reservation)**     Only postings resulting from a manual funds reservation will be subject to the tolerance limit checks. Funds reservations are manual commitments you place on the order for costs that you expect to incur in the future.

**08 (Fixed Prices in the Project)**     This setting is related to project system. Only fixed-price costs will be subjected to tolerance limit checks.

**09 (Payroll)**     This setting is specific to assigning tolerance limits to a payroll account for budgeting purposes.

**Act. (Action)**     The setting in this field denotes the action SAP will take if a defined tolerance limit is exceeded. Three potential actions that can be taken:

**1 (Warning)**     SAP will return a warning at the time of system update. However, the user will be able to continue with the transaction, and the update will occur.

**2 (Warning with Mail)**     SAP will return a warning and send a SAP Mail message to the assigned budget manager. Additional configuration is necessary for this action to work (see the upcoming section, "Budget Manager Maintenance"). However, the user will be able to continue with the transaction, and the update will occur.

**3 (Error Message)**     SAP will return an error at the time of update, and the transaction will not be able to post.

**Usage**     Expressed as a percentage, this amount represents the threshold for total funds committed to an order. If the threshold percentage is exceeded, the assigned action is triggered.

For example, if the budget for an order is $1,000 and the usage percentage is set to 95%, when 95.1% of the budget is used, the appropriate action will be triggered.

**Abs. Variance (Absolute Variance)**     Expressed as a dollar amount, this setting represents the total permitted amount of budgeted overrun.

For example, if the budget for an order is again $1,000 and Abs. Variance is set at $150, SAP will trigger the appropriate action once the total commitment on the order exceeds $1,150.

When you are establishing the tolerance limits, SAP recommends an either/or scenario. However, maintaining both fields does no harm, and in some cases, it may be vital for proper control (see the Extreme Sports scenario). If both are maintained, the assigned action is triggered when one of the two limits is exceeded.

Once the tolerance limits have been assigned, configuration is complete and you can save the settings. Remember, if you want to change any of the key fields after pressing Enter, you will have to delete the entry and start again. Figure 11.25 earlier provides you with a view of the Extreme Sports availability control settings for budget profile BUDGT1. Notice that action 2 (Warning with Mail) was maintained for the profile. In the next section we cover the necessary configuration to ensure that the SAP Mail can be sent.

---

### EXTREME SPORTS AVAILABILITY CONTROL SETTINGS CONFIGURATION ANALYSIS

For the expense projects using this profile, Extreme Sports sought to use a three-tiered control system set at 90%, 95%, and 100%. A warning would be returned at the 90% level. Any new purchase requisitions or orders would trigger the warning and let the purchasing agent know that the budget ceiling was close. The budget manager, in this case the project manager, wanted to be made aware of any budgets exceeding 95%. The SAP Mail system is a good communication tool and would be developed to send mail messages. Because projects are allowed 5% (or $25,000) overrun, no errors would occur until these levels had been exceeded. If the budget is high enough, it is possible for a project to have an overrun greater than $25,000 and not yet be at 105% of the budget—hence the need for both tolerance limit settings. For simplicity, Extreme Sports chose the All Activity Group indicator, ++. That way, it is assured that all actions taken on an order will be subject to tolerance limit checks.

---

## Budget Manager Maintenance

When you're maintaining the Action settings for availability control, SAP offers you a choice of whether to return a warning with or without a mail message (see the preceding section, "Availability Control Configuration"). If you chose setting 2 (Warning with Mail), you must establish the proper budget manager settings before the mail process will work.

 **NOTE**   We assume in this section that SAP Office has been properly developed in the system. You will want to clear this with your Basis group before proceeding.

Simply stated, you have to assign a manager ID to an order type and/or object class for the mail to be routed properly. One shortcoming to note is that the assignment is maintained at a high level in the system. There is no opportunity to assign a manager at an order or project level. However, if your solution provides you with unique order types for which responsibility can be properly segregated, the setting is appropriate. Select Controlling ➤ Internal Orders ➤ Budgeting and Availability Control ➤ Maintain Budget Manager to get to the budget manager configuration screen, or use transaction code OK14.

Notice that the entries are controlling area specific. Click the New Entries button to get to the overview entry screen (see Figure 11.26 for the Extreme Sports budget manager settings).

**FIGURE 11.26**  The Budget Manager: Overview of Added Entries settings for Extreme Sports

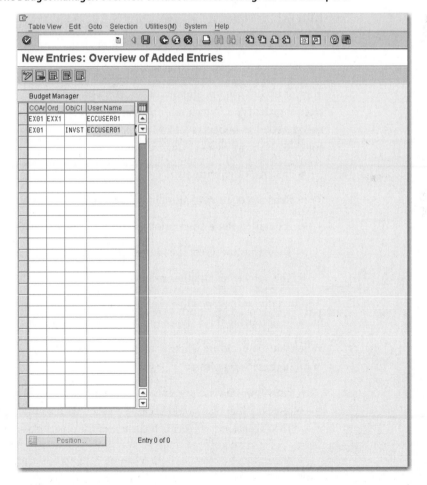

The fields on this screen are as follows:

**COAr (Controlling Area)**   Enter the ID of the controlling area on which these settings will have an impact.

**Order Type (Order)**   If applicable, enter the order type over which the budget manager should be made aware of budget overruns. This field is optional if you will be maintaining the ObjCl field. We recommend that, if possible, you consider only this setting. See the section "Order Type Development" later in this chapter for development details.

**ObjCl (Object Class)**   If applicable, enter the object class over which the budget manager should be made aware of budget overruns. A detailed explanation of object classes is provided in Chapter 9. As with order type, this field is optional if the Order Type field is maintained.

**User Name**   Enter the SAP ID of the assigned budget manager. Check with your Basis group if you have system ID questions.

When you've finished, save the settings.

There is no limit to the number of persons who can be assigned to a given object class or order type. Once users are assigned, every time a properly maintained order has exceeded its budget, a SAP Mail message will be sent to the manager's Office Inbox with the following information:

- ▶ Internal order number

- ▶ Relevant document number, such as an accounting or settlement document

- ▶ A detailed value description of the amount of budget remaining

- ▶ The name and ID of the individual who processed the transaction

- ▶ The name(s) of all other recipients of the message

Additionally, managers will have the ability to run some reporting directly from the message, affording them the chance to quickly analyze the situation.

When you are deciding whether to maintain the order type and/or object class, keep in mind these two points:

- ▶ Only four object classes are available. If assignments are made at this level only, the manager could become deluged with a number of messages daily. The exception to this rule is the use of the object class INVST (Investments).

If your organization has but a few capital managers, it might prove useful to have the assignment at this level.

▶ By maintaining both the order type and the object class, you are stating that you intend to use the same order type with multiple object classes. This should be discouraged from a reporting and analysis view.

The recommended approach is to assign at the order type level first, analyze whether you are receiving the proper level of notification, and then determine if further maintenance is required.

Because there may be opportunities to exclude specific types of costs from the availability control checks, SAP offers the chance to make specified cost elements exempt. You'll find the configuration settings in the next section.

## EXTREME SPORTS BUDGET MANAGER ASSIGNMENT CONFIGURATION ANALYSIS

Within the Extreme Sports order type solution, EXX1 will be used for expense-related corporate projects only. Separate order types will maintain capital only and capital/expense mixed projects. Because of this segregation, a single manager could be assigned to track budget overruns. Extreme Sports likes the flexibility of the SAP Mail system and feels it is a good tool for maintaining awareness. The company centralizes capital management with a few persons, one of which is ECCUSER01. The object class INVST will be used strictly for capital projects and capital investment orders. Both of these will be covered in detail in Chapter 14.

## Exempting Cost Elements from Availability Control

SAP lets you exclude certain types of costs from the tolerance limit checks of availability control by specifying exempt cost elements. Begin by choosing Controlling ➢ Internal Orders ➢ Budgeting and Availability Control ➢ Specify Exempt Cost Elements for Availability Control or using the transaction code is OPTK.

The cost elements exempted from availability control screen appears. Figure 11.27 shows the screen configured for Extreme Sports. Click the New Entries button to get a fresh view.

**FIGURE 11.27** Exempt cost elements for Extreme Sports

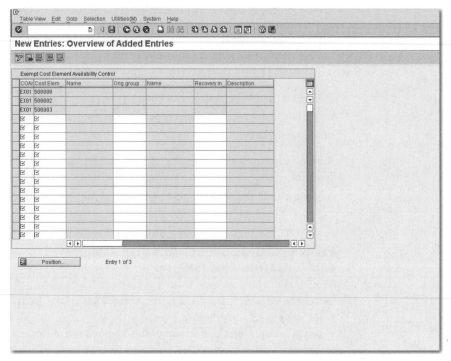

Here are the relevant fields with brief descriptions:

**COAr (Controlling Area)**   Enter the ID of the controlling area on which these settings will have an impact.

**Cost Element**   Enter the ID of the cost element to be excluded from availability control checks. Once the ID is entered, any postings with the cost element will be ignored.

**Name**   This field is automatically populated with the name of the cost element entered in the previous field.

**Orig. Group**   This field is related to product costing. Origin groups allow the system to segregate further material costs. You must create an origin group and costing view maintenance on the material master before you can maintain this field.

**Name**   This field is automatically populated with the description of the origin group.

**Recovery Ind (Indicator)**    This field is related to Joint Venture Accounting. It helps to identify which partners are accountable for which costs. We recommend that you review the SAP notes on the Joint Venture Accounting system before utilizing this field.

**Description**    This field is automatically populated with the description of the recovery indicator.

When you've finished, save the settings. The table can be updated as often as necessary, but changes are not effective in a retroactive manner. The next section will provide a composite of the various number range assignments required for order planning and budgeting.

# Internal Order Planning and Budgeting Number Range Maintenance

Now we will briefly cover the two areas necessary for completing the number range assignments for planning and budgeting:

- ▶ Activity assignments at the controlling area level
- ▶ Number range interval assignments for planning/budgeting

We covered activity assignments in detail in Chapter 8, so the following two sections will be just a review.

## Maintain Number Range Assignment for Planning/Budgeting Transactions

Always remember to review previously established transaction number range assignments when beginning configuration of a new submodule. It is not uncommon to miss needed transactions, and the planning functionality will not work until the assignments are made. The menu path to maintain number range assignments is Controlling ➤ Internal Orders ➤ Planning ➤ Basic Settings ➤ Assign Planning Transactions to Number Ranges, and the transaction code is KANK.

Number range assignments are covered in detail in Chapter 8. Figure 11.28 shows the planning transaction assignments for Extreme Sports's controlling area EX01.

**FIGURE 11.28** Planning transaction assignments for controlling area EX01

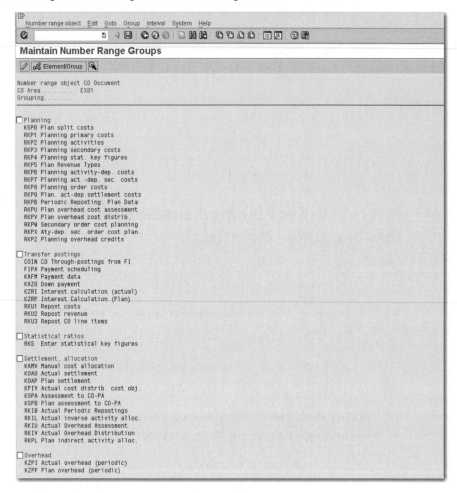

**TIP** When you are in the number range assignment table, it is always prudent to check all transaction assignments.

## Maintain Number Ranges for Planning and Budgeting

SAP links the objects for planning and budgeting under one number range, so maintenance is easy. To get to the number range maintenance screen, select Controlling ➢ Internal Orders ➢ Budgeting and Availability Control ➢ Maintain Number Ranges for Budgeting, or use transaction code OK11.

The number ranges cost planning and budgeting screen appears. This screen is similar to the number range screen for CO document assignment. Number range intervals are used to differentiate between types of postings. The default intervals for planning and budgeting include the following:

**03**    Overall Order Planning

**04**    Order Budgeting

The number range intervals are predefined by SAP and are not subject to change. You do have the ability to determine the range value, so be sure that the ranges are wide enough and that they do not overlap. To maintain the range interval, click the Change Intervals button in the body of the screen. In the resulting screen, you have the ability to create and maintain the planning intervals. Figure 11.29 provides you with a view of the number range intervals for Extreme Sports.

**NOTE**    Be aware that the documents for planning and budgeting do not allow for external numbering. And, as with all number ranges, do not transport them into your production system. Rather, manually create the number range wherever necessary.

**FIGURE 11.29**    The number range intervals for planning and budgeting

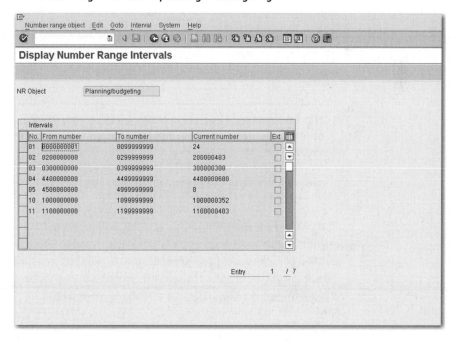

When the number range assignments are complete, planning and budgeting configuration is finished. You are now ready to apply both the planning and budgeting profiles to any order type. The next section is the last in the iterative process of internal order type development. Once it's completed, you will be ready to fully develop an internal order type.

# Internal Order Status Management

Status management is the act of determining and managing what transactions are valid for an order at any given time within its life cycle. The term *life cycle* was coined by SAP to refer to an order's fluid existence, moving from one phase to another until it is closed. The complexity of order accounting is no more visible than the complexity involved with the development of status management.

As with most things in SAP, there are two options to choose from when determining a status management type. Each of these solutions, along with any additional configuration, will be covered in detail:

**General status management**    The most flexible of the two statuses, this approach is recommended because of its ability to be easily applied to multiple order types.

**Order status management**    This strategy is less flexible than general status management in its selection and grouping of transactions. Also, the order status must be coded directly on the order type.

**NOTE**    As of version 6.0 of the R/3 system, the use of order status management has been reduced to being available only for any orders that were in existence prior to this version. Therefore, any additional status management that is being developed should be developed in the general status management approach. We will walk you through the setup of order status management since many companies still have this option available.

You can find the indicator for using either general status management or order status management on the order type master record. Although the configuration method of each varies, there are common threads between them called *phases* or *system statuses*. A phase is the status of an order during its life cycle. Four (standard delivered) phases are available for an order to exist within:

▶ Created

▶ Released

▶ Technically Complete

▶ Closed

As an order moves from one phase to another, the group of allowed business transactions changes. This in turn helps with the ability to control the posting process for each of the IOs that are being used. For example, when an order has the status of Created, FI postings are not allowed but all planning functionality may be available. The concepts that will be covered here may seem complicated or confusing, so please take your time when moving through the material. The first status management type we'll explore is order status management.

# Order Status Management

Order status management is defined for each order type directly on the order type master record. You should understand several key concepts about order status management:

▶ Transaction groups are used to determine what business transactions are allowed for each of the four phases. SAP delivers five groups as defaults. User-defined transaction groups must be developed outside of order status management configuration.

▶ Order status is used to sequence the movement between phases. Transaction groups are maintained at this level. The majority of your up-front strategy time should be spent on this topic. How an order will move between phases is at the core of Internal Order Accounting.

▶ The system status is maintained by SAP as a way of alerting the user that a specific action has been applied to the order. Examples of system statuses include CRTD (Created), REL (Released), and SETC (Settlement Rule Created). In order status management, you have less influence over how the system status updates.

▶ Authorizations can be set at each order status level, meaning that you will have the ability to assign authority to move between statuses.

You begin the development process by entering the order type master record. You can either select Controlling ➢ Internal Orders ➢ Order Master Data ➢ Define Order Types or use transaction code KOT2 (you can also use KOT2_OPA for the same screen).

The maintain order types overview screen appears, offering you many choices. Remember that all order types are controlling area independent, so changes made here will be felt everywhere. If you have previously created an order type, double-click the type to enter the master record. If not, click the New Entries button. (We'll cover new order type development in the "Order Type" section later in this chapter.) For the examples given, order type 0600, which can be seen in Figure 11.30, will be maintained.

**FIGURE 11.30**  The order type master screen for 0600, Extreme Expense Order Type

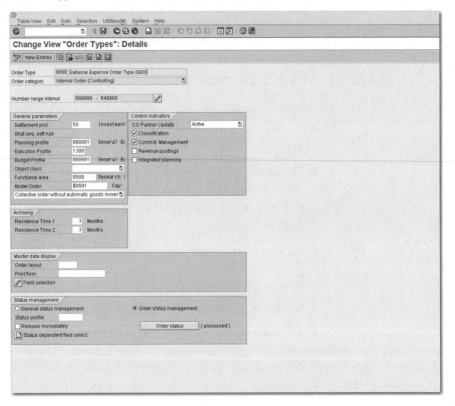

At the change view order types detail screen, select the radio button next to the Order Status Management field. Click the Order Status button and the maintain order types status overview screen appears. The screen will be filled in with the standard order statuses and the standard transaction groups. It is here that you will review the configuration that has been completed and migrated with the older versions of Internal Order Accounting in terms of the order statuses. This information is displayed and is usable in the newer versions of IOs and fully functional, but rather than having an order status process exclusively for IOs, the best business practice is to use the General Order Status approach. (Figure 11.31 shows the completed maintain order types status detail screen.) We'll describe each of the fields, breaking them into three sections: the header, the Phase section, and the Indicator section.

**FIGURE 11.31** The completed Overview of the Order Status detail screen

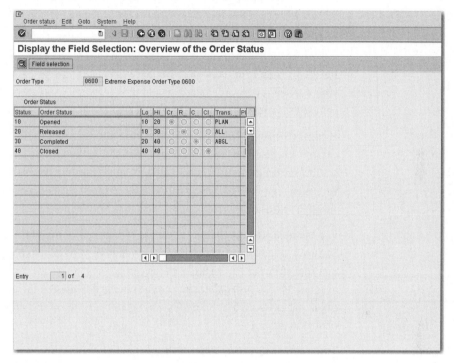

The fields in the header are as follows:

**Order Type**    This field is carried over from the overview screen. It is the ID of the order being maintained.

**Order and Order Status**    Enter a numeric ID and description of the order status in question. If this is your first status, we recommend that you do not start at 1. You may realize later in the order type development that another status is needed below this initial point. Begin at either 5 or 10 to allow for this further development.

An order status strategy might look like the following:

**10**    Opened

**20**    Released

> **30**    Completed
>
> **40**    Technically Complete and Closed

Each of these order statuses would have separate transaction groups assigned, providing a clean differentiation. The naming convention for the order status strategy does not have to mirror the naming convention used for the SAP phases of an order, but in this case and for illustration purposes we have configured it in that manner.

**Lowest Status**    This field represents the lowest order status to which an order can move when it has the order status defined in the Order Status field as its current status. The order status ID does not have to exist in the system to be entered here. If your current lowest order status is 10 but you want to cover potential order statuses below 10 (if you had any), you can enter 01.

**Highest Status**    This field represents the highest order status to which an order can move when it has the order status defined in the Order Status field as its current status. The order status ID does not have to exist in the system to be entered here. If you know that your highest status will be 40 but it has not been entered yet, you can assign it at this time.

For example, assume that order status 10 (Opened) is maintained with a Lowest Status value of 05 and a Highest Status value of 30. When an order of this type has an order status of 10, the order status can go back only as far as 05 and forward only as far as 30. The order status cannot be changed to 40. For the order to be closed, the order status would first have to be changed to a status with a Highest Status setting of at least 40.

**Transaction Group**    Enter the transaction group ID you want to associate with the order status. A transaction group will provide the order with the allowed business transactions that may be initiated. SAP provides five default groups that may be used at any time:

> **ALL**    Contains all transactions an order may initiate.
>
> **ABSL**    Contains all transactions necessary to complete a monthly close for orders.
>
> **NOPL**    Contains all transactions for an order except planning transactions.
>
> **PLAN**    Contains only the order planning transactions.
>
> **RECH**    Contains only transactions that allow primary cost and overhead postings.

You may use any of these groups or create your own (see the section "Transaction Group" later in this chapter). A transaction group must be assigned for you to process any transactions on the order.

A predefined set of business transactions are allowed at each phase. Only these transactions will ever be allowed, regardless of what is contained in the assigned transaction group. To reiterate an earlier example, you will never be able to initiate FI postings to an order if the system status is Create. You can find a complete listing of available business transactions by phase on the order itself. As you change the order status, click the Status button and then the Business Transaction button. This will provide you with a list of allowed and disallowed transactions for that phase.

**TIP**  We recommend that you do not change the delivered transaction groups by adding or deleting business transactions. Rather, create a new group by copying one of the groups were delivered with the system.

Each order status must declare one of the phases in the Phase section. SAP tracks the phases on the order record through a system status. There is a system status with the same name for each of the defined order phases. The phase selected will have an impact on the allowed transactions, so choose carefully. The phases are as follows:

**Created**  This is the initial phase for most order types. Generally, all planning business transactions will be allowed with this phase.

**Released**  This is the most widely used phase. All business transactions are available for use in this phase.

**Completed or Technically Complete**  Generally, all business transactions except planning and budgeting are available for use in this phase.

**Closed**  No business transactions are available for use in this phase.

Finally, here are the fields in the Indicators section:

**Plan Line Items**  Select this field if you would like to document plan line items in this order status.

**Default Status**  Select this field if you want this order status to default upon order creation.

**Deletion Allowed**  Select this field if you want to be able to set the deletion flag on the order when it is in this status.

You can see the previous fields in Figure 11.31 (shown earlier in the chapter) across the top of the Order Status Screen; the headers on the columns are Cr, R, C, and Cl. Repeat the steps as necessary until your entire order status management strategy has been implemented. The next section will take you through the steps of creating the transaction group.

## Transaction Group

To get to the transaction group configuration screen, choose Controlling ➤ Internal Orders ➤ Order Master Data ➤ Status Management ➤ Define Transaction Groups for Status Management or use transaction code KOV2.

The maintain transaction group overview screen appears, showing you the five default groups mentioned earlier. Double-click any one of the groups for an idea of how a maintained transaction group looks. Figure 11.32 shows the transaction group ALL.

**FIGURE 11.32** A detailed view of the transaction group ALL

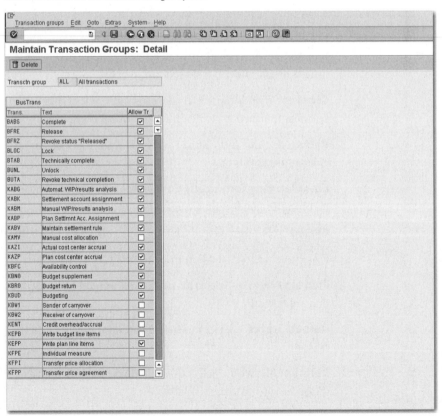

To create your own transaction group, click the New Entries button. The Maintain Transaction Groups New Entry screen will appear. Let's examine the fields:

**Transaction Group**    Enter the ID and description for the new group. The ID can be up to four characters in length.

**Trans (Transactions)**    There are 75 business transactions available for selection. To place one in the group, select the box next to the transaction ID.

When you have finished assigning transaction codes, save the group. You can make changes to these groups at any time, with immediate impact to your order status. Remember the SAP-defined relationship between the phases and allowed business transactions. No harm will come from assigning a transaction group with a disallowed transaction to an order status. The transaction will just not work when the order is in that phase.

For example, suppose you have created a new group called Post that includes the transaction RFBU (FI: Postings). The transaction group is then assigned to an order status with phase Create. The order status will remain valid, with other transactions still functioning. However, when you attempt to make an FI posting to the order with this status active, it will error out.

Transaction groups can be used across controlling areas and order types. Keep this in mind when making any changes to existing groups.

## EXTREME SPORTS ORDER STATUS MANAGEMENT CONFIGURATION ANALYSIS

Extreme Sports has chosen to not use order status management as its tool for controlling its order types. It prefers the flexibility and benefits provided by general status management. These include not having to manually configure the status solution on each of its order types and having greater ability to configure its own status control functions.

# General Status Management

You define the general status management on the order type by assigning a status profile to it. It is this profile that we will configure next. Many of the concepts introduced in order status management, such as order phases and system status, are relevant here. Some items that are not carried over include transaction groups and order statuses. Here are some new key concepts:

► User statuses can be used to provide differentiation from the predefined system statuses. If needed, a user can update the user status on an internal order without affecting the system status, thus giving greater control to the user.

► The order status has been replaced with a new field called Status or Sequence Number. The meanings are similar in that the status number is used to align or sequence the various statuses.

► Allowed transactions are coded directly to each status number. New functionality allows a system status to update automatically when a certain transaction is run. An example would be having the system status automatically set to REL (Released) when the budgeting transaction KBUD is run.

► An Authorization Key field is provided for easy security profile development.

There are three major steps to completing the status profile. They can be completed at the same instance in stages. The steps, in order, are as follows:

1. Define the user status strategy.

2. Assign allowed object types.

3. Define allowed/disallowed transactions per status.

## Defining User Statuses

To access the status profile creation screen, choose Controlling ➢ Internal Orders ➢ Order Master Data ➢ Status Management ➢ Define Status Profile, or use transaction code OK02.

The change status profile overview screen appears. A number of profiles are delivered with your system that you will probably never use. We recommend that you start from scratch when building your new profile because many of the delivered profiles have not been completely maintained. If you have previously created another profile, you can use the copy function during creation. If not, click the New Entry button to open a status profile definition box (see Figure 11.33).

There are three fields to fill out:

**Status Profile**   Enter the status profile ID. The ID can be up to eight alphanumeric characters in length.

**FIGURE 11.33** The New Entry status profile definition box

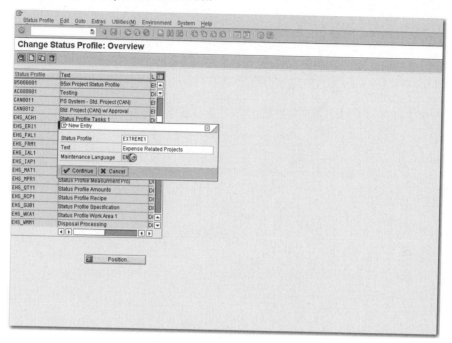

**Text (Description)**   Enter the status profile description. Make the definition clear because it can be used across controlling areas.

**Maintenance Language**   Enter the indicator for the language in which you wish the profile to be maintained. An E represents English.

Click Continue. Notice that your new status profile ID has been placed among the other profiles. You now have a placeholder for your profile. You can save the table and maintain the ID later, or you can continue with the maintenance now. To continue now, select the profile by either double-clicking the profile ID or choosing it on the toolbar. The User Status screen appears (see Figure 11.34).

Here are descriptions of the fields found on the screen:

**Status Number (Sequence or Status Number)**   Enter a two-digit numeric ID. This field defines the order in which the statuses should be processed. It is similar to the Order Status field found in order status management. We recommend that you start the status numbering at 10 or higher. This will allow for new, lower-level statuses to be input later. Also, use consistent gaps between all assigned statuses for the same reason.

**FIGURE 11.34** The User Status screen

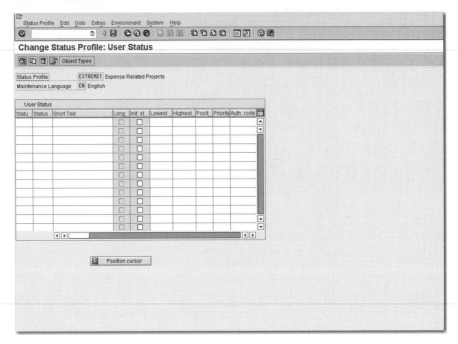

**Status (User Status)**    Enter an ID of up to four alphanumeric characters in length that is representative of the current user status. This status will be visible in the User Status section of the order record.

**Short Text**    Enter a description of the user status. Be clear on what the status represents to make control analysis easier.

**Long Text**    If this field is active, it is a signal to let you know that there is long text available for the status. To enter long text, you first have to be at the default User Status screen. Place the cursor on the status you want to update and choose Goto ➢ Long Text. A text editor window will open for you to enter the information. Save the text and click the green arrow to return to the User Status screen. The LT box will not have a check in it.

**Init. Status (Initial)**    Select this field if the status is to be active upon order creation.

**Lowest (Lowest Status)**    This field represents the lowest status to which an order can move when it has this user status defined as its current status. The user status ID does not have to exist in the system to be entered here. If your current lowest order status is 05 but you want to cover potential order statuses below 05, you can enter 01. See the example in the earlier section "Order Status Management" for additional details.

**Highest (Highest Status)**    This field represents the highest status to which an order can move when it has this user status defined as its current status. The order status ID does not have to exist in the system to be entered here. If you know that your highest status will be 40 but it has not been entered yet, you can assign it at this time. See the example in "Order Status Management" for additional details.

**Position**    On the order record, user and system statuses can be displayed from the Control Data screen by clicking the Status button. The numeric entry in the Position field will determine its location in the status view. SAP will display up to eight statuses at a time. The statuses will default in the order by sequence number.

**Priority**    This field works in conjunction with the Position field setting. If two or more statuses have the same Position setting, the Priority field is used to determine order. A priority 1 takes precedence over a priority 2, and so on.

**Auth. Code (Authority Code)**    This field is used by your security group to define a user's authorization profile. If this field is maintained properly, only users with this authorization key in their security profile will be able to update an order to the defined status. The authorization object used by SAP is B_USERSTAT.

The authorization keys must be defined prior to being added to the status profile. See the section on authorization key configuration for details.

It is helpful to have a control strategy mapped out before beginning the development, but it's not required. You will have the opportunity to change the settings on everything except the position and priority. When you have completed the status definition, save the profile before continuing. Figure 11.35 is an example of a defined user status strategy used by Extreme Sports. The next step will be to define the object types for the status profile.

## Defining Object Types

We first introduced object types in Chapter 9 during reconciliation ledger configuration. As we stated then, only eight object types are available for reconciliation ledger use. However, significantly more exist in other areas of the system, each with its own responsibility. They range from development objects used in ABAP development to production objects used in PP/PC. In status profile configuration, you acknowledge through object type assignment which objects are authorized to use the profile.

**FIGURE 11.35** User status definitions for status profile EXTREME1

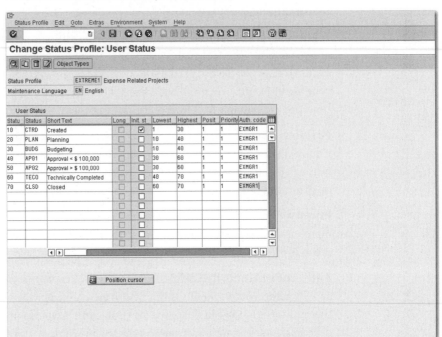

When you configured order status management, you developed directly on the order type. The object type was known immediately. However, in general status management the object type is not recognized until the status profile is assigned. Status profile configuration is being shown as a part of Internal Order Accounting. But because objects outside the module use status profiles as well, you must determine on the profile itself which objects types are authorized.

To assign valid object types, you must be at the User Status screen. In most instances, you will move immediately to this step after completing the status definitions. If not, choose Controlling ➢ Overhead Cost Controlling ➢ Overhead Cost Orders ➢ Order Master Data ➢ Define Status Profile and select the proper profile.

At the User Status screen, click the Object Types button (shown earlier in Figure 11.35). The Change Status Profile: Allowed Object Types window appears, shown in Figure 11.36.

**FIGURE 11.36** The Change Status Profile: Allowed Object Types assignment screen

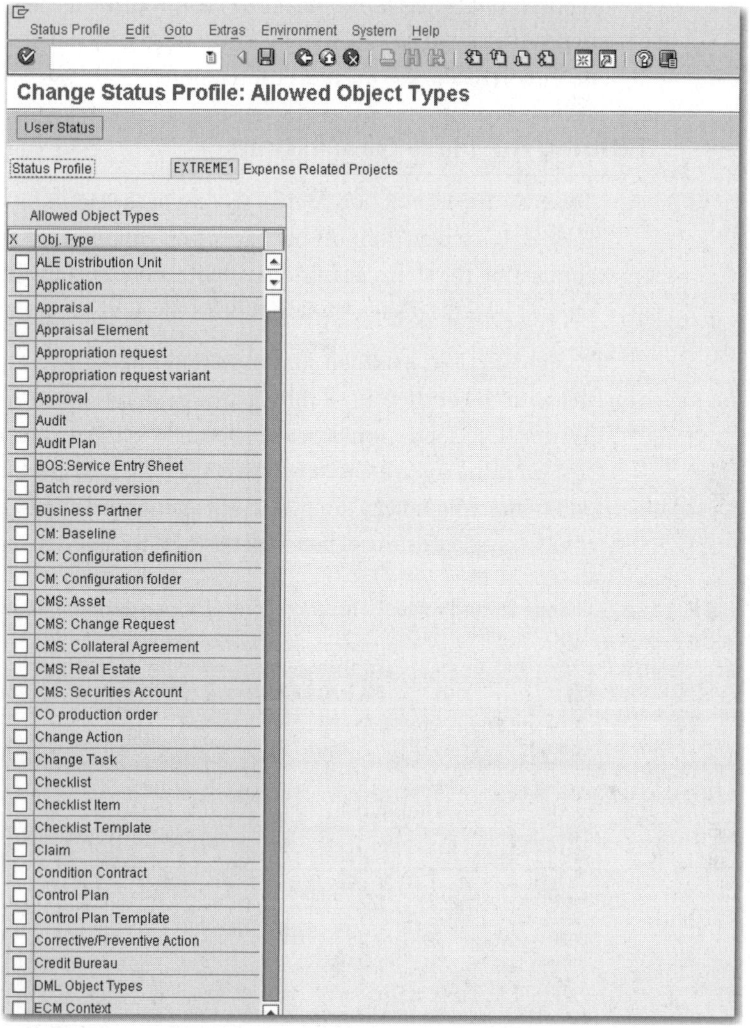

There are too many object types to provide definitions for them all here. Here is a short list of potential objects that can be used in conjunction with Internal Order Accounting:

- ► Internal Order

- ► Capital Investment Program

- ► Maintenance Orders

- ► WBS Element

To authorize an object type, select the box next to the object type name found in the Allowed Object Types section. When you've finished, save the settings. You can update these settings at any time. The last step in status profile development is the definition of allowed business transactions.

## Defining Business Transactions

To access the transaction control section of the status profile, you must be at the User Status screen. In most instances, you will move immediately to this step after completing the status definitions. If not, choose Controlling ➤ Internal Orders ➤ Order Master Data ➤ Define Status Profile, and select the proper profile.

To move to the transaction control section, select a status by either double-clicking the status ID or choosing it through the toolbar (Goto ➤ Transaction Control). A Transaction Control window will appear. When you enter the control window for the first time, the control screen will be empty. To make the first assignments, or to make additional assignments to a previously maintained status, click the New Entries button. A complete listing of potential business transactions appears (see Figure 11.37).

**FIGURE 11.37**  Change Status Profile: Transaction Control screen during transaction control maintenance

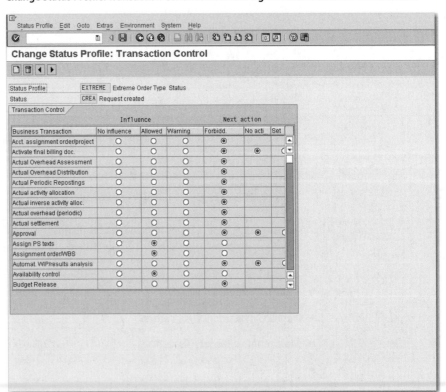

At this point, you begin determining which transactions you want to allow for the status. The window is broken into three main sections: Business Transactions, Influence, and Next Action.

The Business Transactions section contains a listing of the transactions available for selection in the status:

**Transactions**   There are 109 transactions to choose from. Many of the definitions can be found in the SAP Help text.

The Influence section specifies whether the business transaction will be allowed. The fields are as follows:

**No Influence**   This is the default setting. If it's left alone, the business transaction will not appear in the available set viewed here. For the business transaction to receive any reaction, the setting must be changed. The setting does not prohibit the order from using the transaction.

**Allowed (Permitted)**   If this field is set, the business transaction will be allowed for the status being maintained.

**Warning**   If this field is set, the business transaction will be allowed, but a warning will be produced during execution. The user will have the ability to post the transaction.

**Forbidd. (Disallowed)**   If this field is set, the transaction will be disallowed for the status being maintained. This is the opposite of No Influence because you are purposefully eliminating the transaction from the user's authority.

Settings in the Next Action section influence the automatic activation or deletion of a user status:

**No Action**   This is the default setting. If this setting is left on, the execution of the business transaction will have no effect on status activation.

**Set**   If this option is set, execution of the related business transaction will automatically activate the status. For example, your internal order solution calls for an order to be automatically released when the order is budgeted. To accomplish this, the Set status indicator should be set for the Budgeting transaction on the Released user status. The next time an order using this profile is budgeted, the user status will automatically change to REL (Released).

**NOTE**   The Lowest/Highest status settings must work in conjunction with any of the Action settings. If they are not in sync, the action will not take place.

**Delete**    If this is set, execution of the related business transaction will automatically delete the status. This setting is not widely used.

Figure 11.38 offers a view of the transaction control settings employed by Extreme Sports for its expense-related projects. The view shows settings that will automatically set the status to AP01 upon release. Based on the user status settings, the order will have to have moved to a PLAN status before the action will have any effect.

**FIGURE 11.38**  The maintained Transaction Control screen for Status Profile EXTREME1

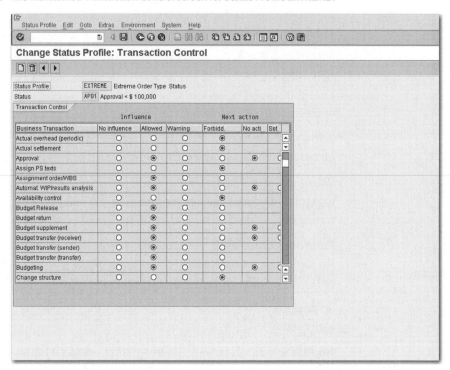

Be sure to properly maintain each user status within the profile. It will be trial and error for a while during the development phase. You will undoubtedly find that certain settings have been misapplied during your configuration. Just be diligent and cover all the bases.

**TIP**  Keep good documentation of the settings as you are developing. This will help immensely when you are ready to configure the solution in the transport client.

The next section is relevant if you are using the authorization keys in the status profile. In it, we will cover the necessary configuration steps for creating a new authorization key.

## Maintaining Authorization Keys

Authorization key creation is a simple one-step process. There is little configuration involved here because all you're doing is setting up an ID. The security group will use this ID and a few authorization objects to establish the proper authorization profile. To access the authorization key window, choose Controlling ➤ Internal Orders ➤ Order Master Data ➤ Status Management ➤ Define Authorization Keys for Status Management or use transaction code BS52.

### EXTREME SPORTS GENERAL STATUS MANAGEMENT CONFIGURATION ANALYSIS

Extreme Sports has chosen to use general status management as its tool for controlling its order types. It plans on using the same status profile on two types of internal orders and a maintenance order type. Updates are easier in this case because a single profile can be maintained as opposed to maintaining three order types separately. Also, the ability to more tightly control the control settings is another plus. In the example provided, status profile EXTREME1 will be used with order type EXX1, which will be configured in the next section.

The authorization key overview screen appears. To define a new key, click the New Entries button. The table will now allow for new authorization keys. Fill in the following two fields:

**Authkey (Authorization Key)**    Enter the ID of the authorization keys. It can consist of up to eight alphanumeric characters. Be sure to make it unique because the ID can be used across controlling areas.

**Text (Description)**    Enter the description of the authorization key.

When you've finished, save the settings. You can enter as many as needed, and the table can be updated at any time.

Status management is now complete. The groundwork has been laid, and you can begin order type development. The next section will cover the configuration steps necessary to build a new order type from scratch.

# Order Type Development

You have now completed the steps to fully develop an order type. At the beginning of this chapter, order type EXX1-Extreme Expense Order Type was shown in its beginning stages (in Figure 11.1). An order type ID can be created and saved as a placeholder with no additional configuration. As stated earlier, and as shown throughout this chapter, order type configuration is an iterative process. Plan, budget, and status profiles must all be created prior to assignment to the order type. Each step has some iterative development as well. All of this needs to be completed prior to the start of setting up the order type. After this we can then finally create an internal order.

## Defining Order Types

Begin the order type configuration process by accessing the order type definition window. Either choose Controlling ➤ Internal Order ➤ Order Master Data ➤ Define Order Types or use transaction code KOT2.

The maintain order types overview screen appears. Remember that all order types are controlling area independent, so changes made here will be felt everywhere. If you have previously created an order type, such as EXX1, double-click the type to enter the master record. If not, click the New Entries button. An order type entry box appears (see Figure 11.39).

Complete the following entry field:

**Order Category**    Enter the category of the order type being developed. There are 13 potential choices. Select 1 for internal orders.

Next, press the Enter key to open the Create Order Type screen. The maintain order types detail screen appears (refer to Figure 11.1 earlier in this chapter). This screen may look familiar because it was accessed during order status management configuration. Notice that the order category was carried over from the entry box and is now not configurable. At this point, if you want to change the order category, you will have to delete the order type and start again. Only the description field is configurable. Begin the process by completing the necessary fields as they are listed:

**Order Type**    Enter the ID for the new order type. The ID can be up to four alphanumeric characters in length. In the text box next to the field, enter a description for the order type.

**FIGURE 11.39**  The order type definition entry screen

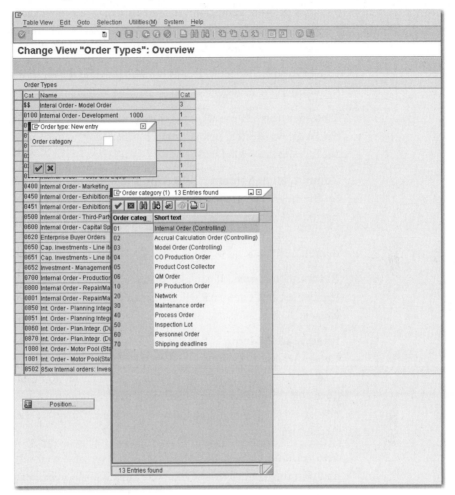

The Control Indicators section determines what areas are active for the order type:

**CO Partner Update**    This field determines how an order will post during CO allocations. This setting will influence the number of data records maintained in order accounting. Three choices are available (Semi-Active is the default setting):

   **Active**    In ranking from highest to lowest with regard to the number of records maintained during allocations, Active ranks number one. A totals record will be maintained for all parties involved.

**Semi-Active**   This is second highest in the number of records posted. During order-to-order allocations, such as settlements, a totals record for both objects will be maintained. For allocations between an order and a cost center, such as repostings, a totals record will not be maintained for the order on the cost center.

**Not Active**   No totals record is maintained on the receiving object regardless of whether it is an order.

**Classification**   If you want to utilize classifications to organize the order type, this field must be selected. Before using classifications, we recommend that you review the literature provided by SAP.

**Commit. Management**   Select this field to activate commitment management for the order type. If it's active, commitments such as purchase requisitions and purchase orders can be tracked on the order type. We recommend that you always select this setting for project-related order types in which procurement is a predominant activity.

**Revenue Postings**   If you plan on tracking revenues on the order type, this flag must be set. If it's not, SAP will return an error when you attempt to post a revenue element.

**Integrated Planning**   This setting relates to the Planning Integration with Cost Center Accounting setting found on the CO version screen. If planning integration is selected here, plan data can be automatically passed to Profit Center Accounting. To enable this setting, the CO Partner Update setting must read Active. You don't need to set this if you do not intend to completely integrate with Profit Center Accounting.

Settings in the General Parameters section determine your settlement, budgeting, and planning controls (these files were all developed in earlier sections):

**Settlement Prof. (Profile)**   Enter the ID of the settlement profile to be used by the order type. The settlement profile controls such things as the settlement and origin structures. We described profile development earlier in the "Settlement Profile" section. For EXX1, settlement profile 90 will be used.

**Planning Profile**   Enter the ID of the planning profile to be used by the order type. The planning profile will determine the levels of planning available on an order type and help define some default planning groups. Complete planning profile development was covered earlier in the "Planning Profile" section. For EXX1, planning profile EXX0 will be used.

**Budget Profile**   Enter the ID of the budget profile to be used. The profile will control, among other things, budgeting views and availability control activation. Complete budget profile and availability control configuration were covered earlier in the sections "Budget Profile" and "Availability Control." For EXX1, budget profile BUDGT1 will be used.

**Object Class**   This will assign the Internal Order to a further group of object classes. There are four groups: Overhead Costs, Investments, Production, and Profit Analysis.

**Functional Area**   If you are using cost of sales accounting, you must assign a functional area to an IO. This is a requirement to create a profit and loss account in Financial Accounting. Some examples of functional areas are Manufacturing, Administration, Sales, and Research and Development.

**Model Order**   If during internal order creation you wish to always copy a specific order, enter the order number here. Then, during order creation SAP will automatically copy the active fields from this reference order into the new order's active fields. You'll have another opportunity to enter a model order during order creation. A Model Order is created in a different transaction code, but all of the same activities that we discussed previously in this chapter still hold. A Model Order starts with a dollar sign ($), which helps you distinguish a Model Order from a Regular Order.

**Collective Order Without/With Automatic Goods Movement**   If you have a collective orders process activated in the IO process, this setting will control whether the link between the Production Orders and Collective Orders will allow automatic goods movement between individual levels of a collective order.

The Archiving section is responsible for deleting and/or archiving the internal order master records. The archiving or deleting of order master records from your database should be a part of your overall archiving strategy. The fields are as follows:

**Residence Time 1**   Enter the number of months that must pass between when the deletion flag was set and when the deletion indicator can be activated on the master record.

**Residence Time 2**    Enter the number of months that must pass between when the deletion indicator was set and when the master record can be archived or deleted.

The combination of the retention periods is the minimal amount of time that the order master record must reside in your database before it can be removed. Keep this in mind when making the setting.

The fields in the Status Management section determine the type of transaction control the order type will use:

**Status Management**    Select this radio button if general status management is to be used. See the "Status Management Configuration" section for details. For EXX1, general status management will be activated. Several settings are available:

> **Status Profile**    If general status management is activated, you must enter a status profile.
>
> **Release Immediately**    If you choose this setting, a new order created with this order type will be released immediately. The setting is effective only when used in conjunction with general status management.
>
> **Status Dependent Field Select. (Selection)**    If this field is used, it will allow the adjustment or changes to the order status and the field selection. Basically allowing the user to identify specific transactions that can be posted to at specific status levels.

Click the change button (paper icon) and this option—Status Dependent Field Selection—will open to another screen where you will be able to change your field selection. Click the Field Selection button to open another screen of field selections. You can identify what fields on each screen the business user would be able to change, required, hide, and so on (see Figure 11.40).

**TIP**   Enter a profile only if general status management is going to be used. Otherwise, the profile setting will be ignored.

**Ord. Status Management (only on specific types of orders)**    Select this radio button if order status management is to be used. See the "Order Status Management" section later in this chapter for details.

**FIGURE 11.40** Change Field Selection: overview of the User Status configuration

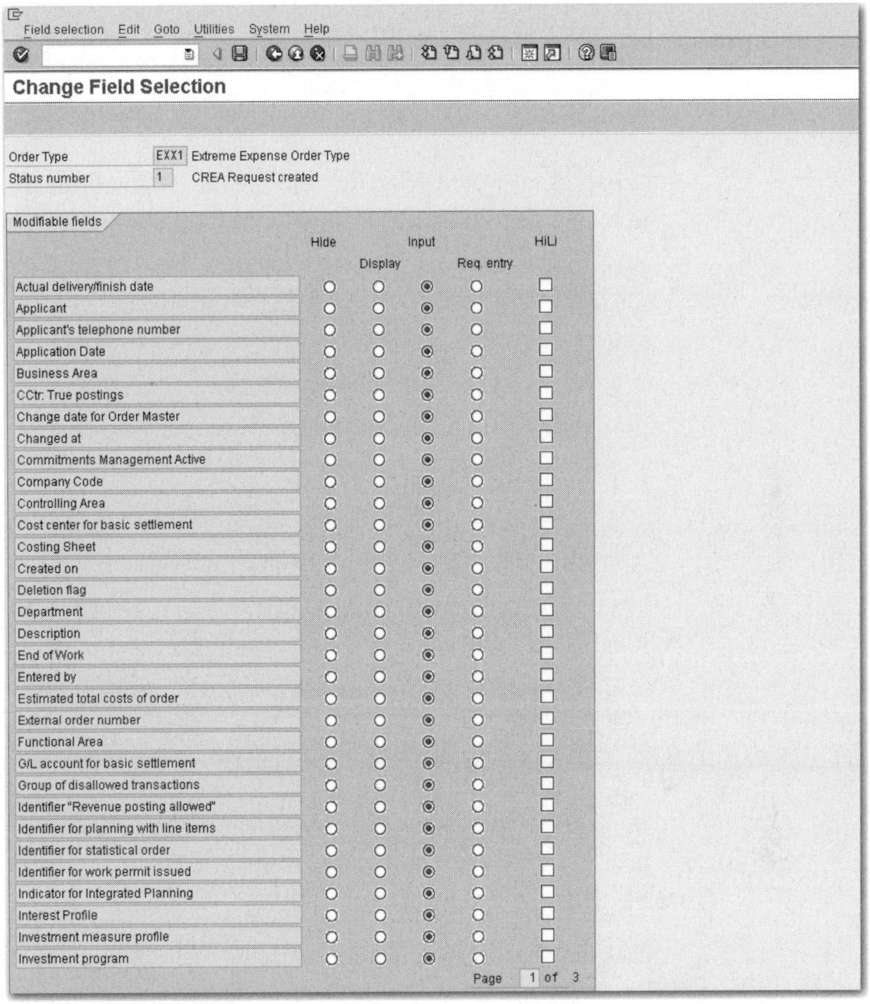

You have gotten as far as you can without saving the order type. There are two sections left: Number Range and Field Selection. Before either of these areas can be configured, the order type must be saved. SAP will display an error message if you forget. If you are happy with the configuration settings so far and want to continue, save the order type (see Figure 11.41). You will remain in the maintain order types detail screen. Continue development with the assignment of the number ranges.

**FIGURE 11.41**  Completed configuration of an order type

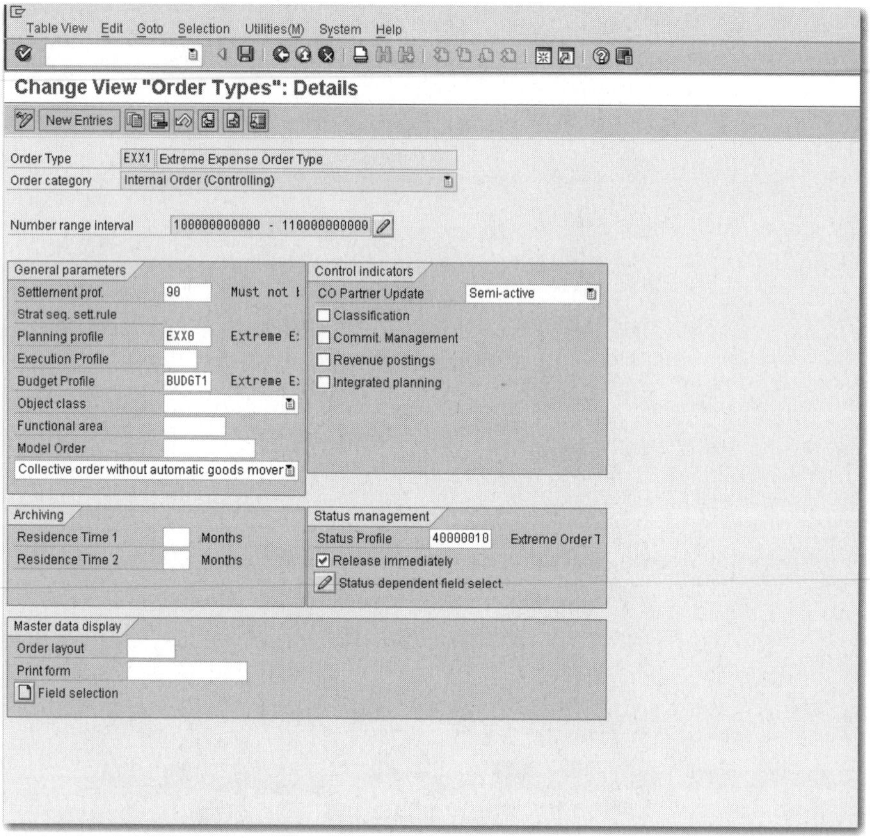

## Number Range Assignment

Click the Number Range button at the top of the change order types detail screen. The Maintain Number Range Groups screen appears. The screen looks similar to the activity assignment screen you saw earlier in this chapter. Each order type within SAP must be assigned to a defined number range group. It is this group assignment from which the new order type will determine its order number.

Scroll the screen and review the default number range groups. If these will not suffice, you can create your own groups. To begin, choose Group ➢ Insert. An Insert Group box appears, asking you to provide a name and number range (see Figure 11.42). For complete interval creation details, see Chapter 7, "New GL Accounting." Save the group when you've finished. The next step is to assign the order type to your new group interval.

**FIGURE 11.42** The Insert Group box completed for expense projects

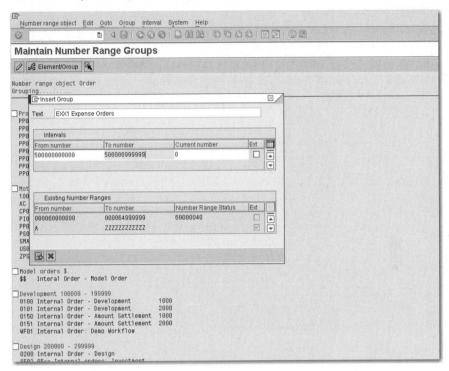

You will find the new order type ID in the Not Assigned section at the bottom of the Maintain Number Range Groups screen. To assign the order type, select the ID by double-clicking it or by using the select element button. Next, place a check mark in the box next to the group to which you want to assign the order type and click the Element/Group button in the header. The order type will move from the Not Assigned category to the proper group interval (see Figure 11.43). Be sure to save the settings when you've finished. Click the green arrow to return to the order type definition screen and we'll continue with the last section of order type configuration.

**TIP** You will know if the Number Range, Order Status, or Field Selection areas have been maintained if the word *processed* appears next to the button on the order type.

**FIGURE 11.43** The EXX1 number range assignment

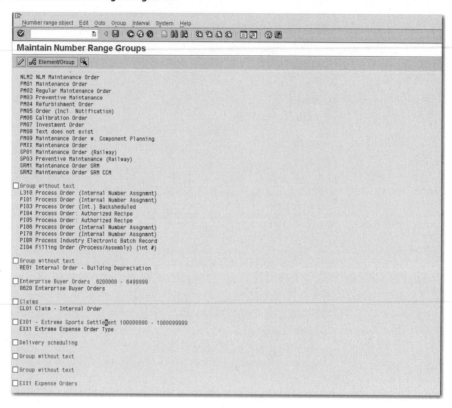

## EXTREME SPORTS NUMBER RANGES CONFIGURATION ANALYSIS

Extreme Sports wanted clean segregation for its expense-related projects, so a new number range interval was created. The order number range of 1000000000–1100000000 was created and the order type EXX1-Extreme Expense Order Type was assigned. For most internal orders, internal number range assignments, like the EXX1 assignment, is the best solution. In those special circumstances in which the order number must tie to another non-SAP ID, external order numbering may be acceptable.

## Field Selection Configuration

For each order type, you must maintain the field selection view before it can be used. The field selection settings offer you control over the order view the user will have during order creation and maintenance. By activating, hiding, or requiring certain fields on the order master record, you can control what information the user maintains. All orders have the same set of fields available to them. To update the field selection, you must be at the maintain order types detail screen.

Click the Field Selection button at the bottom of the screen. When the Change Field Selection screen appears, spend some time familiarizing yourself with all the potential fields before continuing. When you're comfortable, begin the field selection process. Here is an overview of the potential settings:

**Modifiable Fields**    This is a complete listing of each field on the order master record.

**Hide**    If this radio button is selected, the field will not appear on the order master record.

**Display**    If this radio button is selected, the field will appear on the order record, but it will be grayed out, so no changes will be allowed. If you are using a model or reference order to create your order, the Displayed fields will not update with any settings.

**Input**    This is the default setting. If it's left alone, the field will be available for input on the order master record.

**Req. (Required) Entry**    If this radio button is selected, the field will contain a question mark (?) signaling to the user that it is required.

**HiLi (Highlighted)**    If this checkbox is selected, the field setting will be highlighted on the order master record.

It is always a good idea to minimize the number of fields from which the user has to choose on the order master record—and it is a great idea to make required those fields that you absolutely want completed. The settings can be updated at any time, with a retroactive impact to previously created orders. Figure 11.44 gives you a partial view of the field selection maintenance for order type EXX1. Save the settings when you've finished.

**FIGURE 11.44**  Field selection settings for order type EXX1

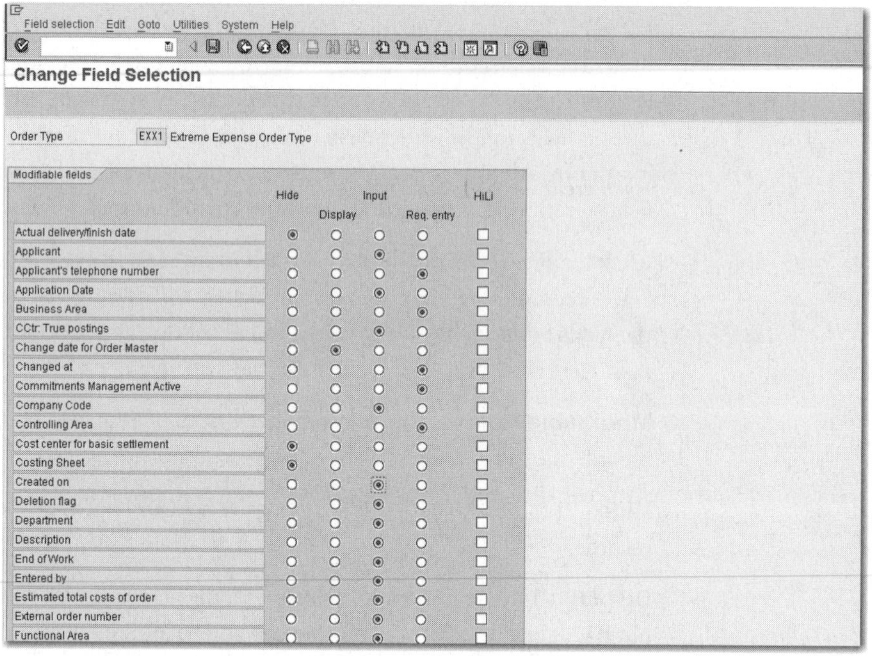

The settings are universally accepted for the order type. But if your solution calls for the use of order status management, you have one more option available to you. This setting is covered in the next section.

## Field Selection for Order Status Management

For those solutions using order status management, a second level of field selection, at the status level, is possible. In addition to the Field Selection button on the maintain order types detail screen, a Field Selection button exists on the status overview screen. If you choose to maintain the order status field selection, we recommend that you do so cautiously.

The settings on the status field selection screen will supercede the settings on the maintain order types detail screen when it comes to making a field required that was previously not required. It will not, however, remove a requirement established by the details field selection view. Also, with the status field selection settings, you have the authority to hide a field that is required by the details field selection views.

Because this is all very confusing, you should proceed with caution. If used properly, the ability to make certain fields required at the various order statuses can be a useful feature. But if you aren't careful, it can also shut down your order processing.

## EXTREME SPORTS FIELD SELECTION CONFIGURATION ANALYSIS

Because order type EXX1 has chosen to use general status management as its control object, all field selection settings will be made from the maintain order types detail screen. Only the fields necessary for entry will be made available to the user during order creation and maintenance.

# Defining an Internal Order

Now that we have worked our way through the entire setup of an order type, we move on to creating an actual internal order. So far we have worked on the objects that must be completed for an internal order, but we haven't created an internal order. This is the one master data item that is required for using Internal Order Accounting. Much of the information required to enter the Internal Order screens has already been defined, but to create an internal order from scratch and close any gaps in the overall process and understanding would be a good way to close this chapter and it will be a good way to finally see the end result.

To start this process from the main menu, choose Accounting ➢ Controlling ➢ Internal Orders ➢ Master Data ➢ Special Functions ➢ Order ➢ Create, or you could use the transaction code KO01 to arrive at this screen. The Create Internal Order: Initial Screen appears. Fill in the appropriate Order Type (see Figure 11.45), and press Enter. In the resulting Master Data screen, start filling in the fields that have not been assigned based on the order type.

**FIGURE 11.45**  Create Internal Order: Initial Screen

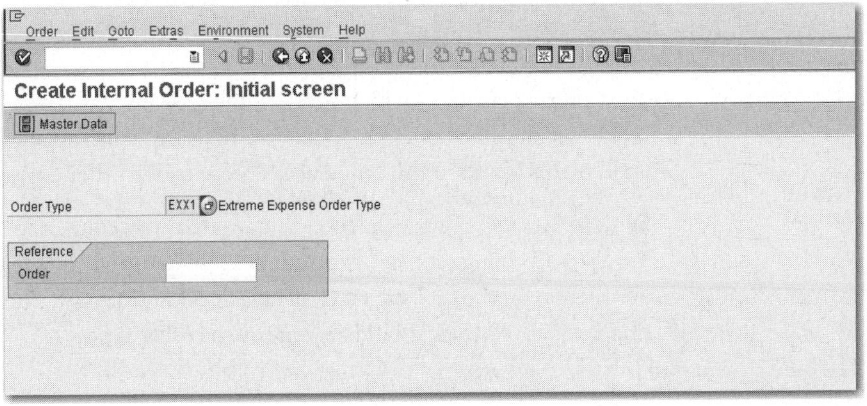

The Assignments section determines what organizational units are needed for the IO to be viable. These assignments are specific to just this one internal order, whereas the configuration that we did for the order type would be reusable in all IOs. Review these settings, and then complete any field that is empty and that will be used for the analysis of the internal order data (as shown in Figure 11.46).

**FIGURE 11.46** The Assignments tab of the Create Internal Order screen

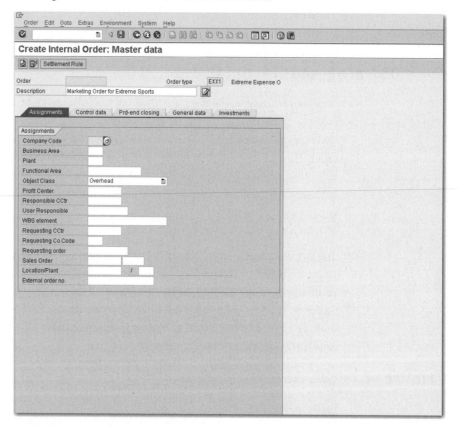

The Control Data tab—which contains the sections Status and Control Data—requires a bit more review and analysis. In terms of information required for creation of this IO, all of this could again be set by the order type (see Figure 11.47):

**System Status** This is the System Status that you configured earlier in this chapter. You can change the status manually from here and change the transactions that are allowed on the IO's status. Generally speaking, most, if not all, of the configuration for these settings should be done by the order type.

**Currency**   This setting would be used if a specific currency is required by this IO.

**Order Category**   The default setting is based on the initial order category you chose.

**Statistical Order**   If this setting is checked, this IO will be assigned postings only statistically, Again, remember that you can create either statistical orders or actual orders—statistical orders are for reporting purposes only to help track information based on statistical postings. No allocations or settlements are required if this type of order is being used.

**Actual Posted CCtr**   If this IO is to be linked directly to a cost center, enter that cost center number here. This field will immediately require that the Statistical Order field be deselected.

**FIGURE 11.47**   The Control Data tab of the Create Internal Order screen

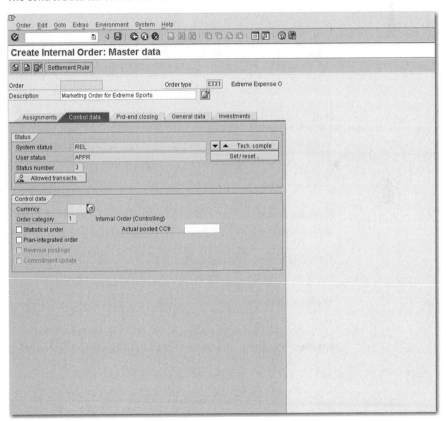

The Prd-End Closing tab also requires a bit more review and analysis. In terms of information required for creation of this IO, all of this could again be set by the order type or be manually entered into each internal order (see Figure 11.48).

**FIGURE 11.48** The Prd-End Closing tab of the Create Internal Order Create screen

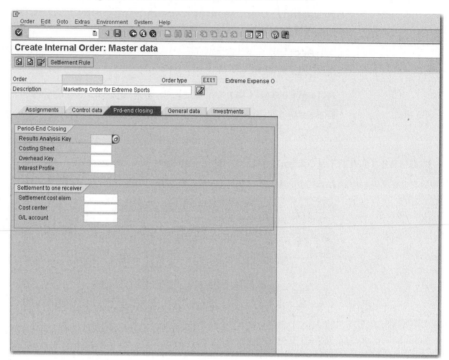

**Results Analysis Key**    This setting determines the valuation of the IO (tracking a sales order, project, or other order with revenue) during period-end closing.

**Costing Sheet**    This setting controls the calculation of overhead assigned to the IO.

**Overhead Key**    This key is used to determine the order-specific or material-related overhead rates that are posted to the IO.

**Interest Profile**    This setting manages the interest calculation for the project order.

**Settlement Cost Elem (Element)**    This is another opportunity for you to assign a settlement cost element. If this is a direct settlement and you only need one cost element, this approach may be useful.

**Cost Center**    In each of these fields—Settlement Cost Elem, Cost Center, and G/L Account—the same scenario applies. If this IO is only posting to one cost center, then use this approach rather than setting up information on an order type.

**G/L Account**    If this setting is enabled, all postings for this internal order go to one G/L account.

You have now completed the configuration of an internal order (see Figure 11.49). You can take this internal order and use it during the posting process. Notice that the IO number—1000000000—is based on the number range that we defined in the configuration.

**FIGURE 11.49**  Completed internal order

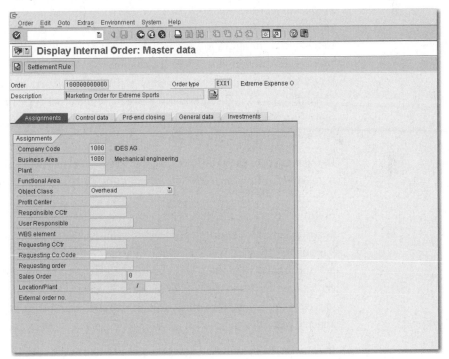

# Summary

The concepts presented in Internal Order Accounting are relatively new and may take some time to incorporate into your current CO environment, but you'll find the process well worth the time and effort. Topics such as settlement structures, settlement cost elements, and order types have not been used in many packaged systems prior to SAP. Because of the depth of many of these topics, we could show only a few examples in this chapter. As with all the chapters, though, we've provided enough detail to lead you to your own conclusions. If you had to pick one area on which to focus the majority of your attention, spend your time with the concepts of settlement. Among all the areas of order configuration, these are the trickiest to master.

When we think about configuring the Internal Order Accounting module in CO, we consider the basic "define, then assign" approach used in most areas within SAP. For example, you have more than five objects to configure correctly before even starting to create an order type. This takes a good bit of planning and analysis prior to the initial configuration and will definitely be worth every minute later in the process of setting up IOs. These critical objects required before setting up the order type are the settlement cost elements, settlement structure, and source structure. Once they are configured, you can move on to the order type and complete its configuration. You can then take the completed order type and assign it to an internal order to create the ID for the IO.

In the process of showing how to set up an IO, we also discussed decisions you have to make regarding the use of IOs for planning and budgeting. The ability to create a ceiling on the budget and set up errors and warnings on certain postings is very useful. Also, the fact that you can have a process to monitor not only the actual postings but the committed postings as well is valuable. Even though the amount has not been posted, you can still include the committed amount into the current posting process. If you set up the commitment correctly, users will receive a hard error once they get to the level of the budget. At this point, a user would then have to receive approvals from other managers to continue to post expenses against the affected cost object.

In some cases, the internal order process—with its unique options for planning and budgeting as well as the ability to track information at a detailed level—makes the IOs more valuable than the cost centers.

# Profitability Analysis

**FEATURING:**

▶ COSTING-BASED VS. ACCOUNT-BASED CO-PA

▶ OPERATING CONCERN DEVELOPMENT

▶ CHARACTERISTIC DERIVATION

▶ ASSIGNING VALUES TO VALUE FIELDS

▶ CO-PA PLANNING

▶ ACTIVATING CO-PA

▶ CO-PA REPORTING

▶ CO-PA TRANSPORTS

The Profitability Analysis submodule within SAP is also known as CO-PA, COPA, and PA. In this chapter, we will refer to it as CO-PA. CO-PA gives you the ability to analyze your profitability on many different segments and characteristics. It acts like an information receptacle that can be analyzed from several angles and viewpoints. CO-PA can combine the elements of gross margin reporting found in the SD module with other relevant expenses that you decide to bring over to CO-PA. That way, you obtain a better view of profitability below gross margin for products, customers, sale organizations, or any other of the many characteristics by which you can report in CO-PA.

We want to be clear about something from the start: CO-PA is a reporting tool and has been developed to do exactly that. This module does not create new records or have anything to do with the overall ERP process. This module allows you to report on many different areas in one spot. If you've configured it correctly, you can combine information from almost all areas—SD, FI, MM, PP, CO, PM, IM, HCM, and so on—and generate a report that will help you analyze your business more carefully and with a much better developed set of information and records. As you can probably guess, this can be one of the most powerful reporting tools in your ECC environment.

In ECC 6.0, the number of combinations that can be reported on is limited only to what you assign and develop within the CO-PA tables. Business users will be able to slice and dice on just about any records that they want, and therefore it may take you a couple of times to be able to successfully set up CO-PA. Many times we've had to go back and redesign the configuration of CO-PA because of changes in the business environment and the focus of the business and in the ECC 6.0 version SAP allows for this type of iterative approach to setting up CO-PA. For example, if you find that your business changes from a customer focus to a product focus, you may not have positioned enough information in your CO-PA tables to do this for you and therefore will have to realign the information and tables. Nicely enough, though, in the newer versions you can accomplish some of this "realignment" with minimal effort.

So, as we go through the process of configuration in CO-PA, focus on the reporting and planning needs of your company, and design the table structures for CO-PA with that in mind.

# Costing-Based vs. Account-Based CO-PA

CO-PA can capture and hold data in two ways—costing based and account based. The operating concern, the central tenet of CO-PA, is the structure that you define to hold data for CO-PA and to use as the basis for reports. An operating concern can use costing-based, account-based, or both forms of CO-PA simultaneously. Both forms use characteristics to store data about the information that is updated in CO-PA. Characteristics include such aspects as customer, sales office, sales group, material number, strategic business unit, company code, profit center, sales employee, controlling area, product hierarchy, and so on. We'll cover these characteristics in more detail in the "Creating Characteristics" section later in this chapter. The main difference in how the two methods store data involves quantities and values. In costing-based CO-PA, values and quantities are stored in value fields. Value fields group together similar values and quantities—a good way to think of value fields is as large groupings of accounts or cost elements. We'll cover value fields in more detail in the "Create Value Fields" section later in this chapter. Account-based CO-PA updates values in accounts—the same accounts (cost elements) that are used in FI and the rest of CO.

Costing based is the original method that was created for CO-PA updates and groupings. Costing-based CO-PA lets you manage information based on when different postings are assigned, such as when sales documents are updated and when data is transferred from FI and other modules. The unique aspect of costing-based CO-PA is that it will allow the analysis of information for marketing, forecasting, what-if analysis, or other approaches to reporting that doesn't necessarily have to reconcile to FI. Normally, the largest amount of data transferred into CO-PA is from SD billing documents. It is important to understand the document flow in SD; the normal document flow is as follows:

1. Sales order creation

2. Delivery (the delivery creates the goods issue, which debits COGS (Cost of Goods Sold) and credits inventory)

3. Billing document (the billing document updates A/R, sales revenue, discounts, freight, and so on)

When costing-based CO-PA is used, CO-PA is updated when the sales order is created and when the billing document is created. In both cases, COGS, revenue, discounts, freight, and so on, are updated all at once. In this example, COGS is updated when the billing document is created because the SD condition type VPRS copies in the COGS from the goods issue. The COGS can also be updated based on an estimate of the COGS posting that will eventually be assigned to FI, but for a specific time frame these postings are based on the timing that we define in CO-PA. Always remember that costing-based CO-PA follows the final updating document, not necessarily when the account was posted.

Account-based CO-PA was created to allow users to reconcile CO-PA data to FI data. It captures values according to the account posted to instead of value fields. Account-based CO-PA is updated at the time the account is posted to or basically when FI is posted. As with costing-based CO-PA, the largest amount of data transferred to CO-PA is normally from billing documents. Using account-based CO-PA, CO-PA is updated during the delivery (goods issue) and the creation of the billing document. The normal SD document flow is as follows:

1. Sales order creation

2. Delivery (the delivery creates the goods issue, which debits COGS and credits Inventory—COGS is updated in CO-PA at this time)

3. Billing document (the billing document updates A/R, sales revenue, discounts, freight, and so on)

As you can see, the difference between this scenario and the costing-based scenario is that in costing based, COGS is not updated at the time of delivery (goods issue); it is updated at the same time revenue, discounts, freight, and so on, are updated—at the time of billing. In account-based CO-PA, COGS is updated in CO-PA at the time of delivery (goods issue); revenue, discounts, and freight are not updated until the time the billing document is created. This can lead to timing differences when analyzing profitability of certain products. COGS can be overstated at any point in time because it is updated before the revenue that is associated with it is updated, which creates time of delivery (goods issue) versus time of billing differences. This also allows for account-based CO-PA to be out of balance with costing-based CO-PA because of update timing differences. An example of this might be when you have a third-party shipment and the invoice is posted prior to the delivery being made.

The other difference between costing based and account based is that it is possible to review and post information at the time the sales order is created in the costing-based CO-PA. This ability is helpful if you have a long-running sales order and you want to do some analysis on the overall profitability of the sales order. Since you can post information into the record at the time the sales order is created and you can also post estimates for other costs such as freight, bonuses, and others, you can immediately identify the profit margins that you will have in the future.

So, which method should you use? It depends on your requirements and how you use CO-PA data. Most companies use costing-based CO-PA because it is more aligned with the true purpose of CO-PA—managing sales profitability information. However, some companies use account-based CO-PA in conjunction with costing-based CO-PA because the accounting department uses SAP to reconcile CO-PA to the general ledger. Because costing-based CO-PA updates based on documents instead of when the currency posts to the G/L, it is a hard battle to fight in terms of making accountants understand that it is not important to reconcile CO-PA to the G/L. Reconciling is not the purpose of CO-PA. Nonetheless, if your users feel compelled to try, it is much easier to do via account-based CO-PA. You can also help mitigate reconciliation fears by making the revenue and sales discount accounts that come off the billing document post automatically only (see Chapter 4, "Accounts Payable," to learn how to set up your G/L accounts to accomplish this task). If you use both methods of CO-PA in your operating concern, the characteristics that you define are valid for both methods. The difference in the two methods is that costing based uses value fields to update currency values and account based stores currency values in their related cost element. The focus of this chapter will be on costing-based CO-PA. Table 12.1 summarizes when elements are updated in the various types of CO-PA.

**TABLE 12.1**    Timing Updates in CO-PA

| Element | Costing Based | Account Based |
| --- | --- | --- |
| Revenue | Billing document or sales order creation | Billing document |
| Sales discount | Billing document or sales order creation | Billing document |
| Freight | Billing document or sales order creation | Billing document |
| COGS | Billing document or sales order creation | Delivery (goods issue) |
| FI expenses | FI posting | FI posting |
| Internal/sales orders | Settlement | Settlement |
| MM variances | FI posting | FI posting |
| PP variances | Settlement | Settlement |

# Operating Concern Development

As we stated earlier, the operating concern is the central tenet of CO-PA. It decides how the data you capture is stored in CO-PA as well as what characteristics are captured for each piece of data. Before you begin developing your operating concern, it is important to map out what type of data you want to capture in addition to the characteristics that are important to your company for CO-PA reporting purposes. It is easy to add characteristics to your operating concern, but it is very difficult to remove them from your operating concern once they have been posted to. Don't think of that state too lightly and think you can, at a moment's notice, add characteristics to your operating concern. Sure, it is reasonable to add characteristics to your operating concern, but you wouldn't want to change a table and add characteristics only to find that you have affected the performance of the reporting process. We will talk about this a bit more later in this chapter.

CO-PA is also somewhat of a system hog in that it stores redundant data, so it is important to store only the information you need for profitability reporting more than once. In CO-PA, you also have a fixed number of characteristics you can use in each operating concern. It is a good idea not to use all of your characteristics in your initial rollout of CO-PA—leave room for your company to grow and to capture new characteristic requirements as your business grows and changes. Remember that we are demonstrating the configuration of costing-based CO-PA in this chapter.

**WARNING**   In all versions of SAP, there are many fixed characteristics that are delivered with each operating concern. In the current version, you can define up to an additional 50 delivered or user-defined characteristics in your operating concern. Don't use up all of your characteristics at once. Also, review the fixed characteristics because there may be some that you can use during reporting. Technical characteristics are available as well, but they are not normally used for reporting purposes.

Once you have your CO-PA design completed, you are ready to define the structure of your operating concern. You will recall that we created the operating concern name (ESOC) in Chapter 8, "Controlling Enterprise Structure," without any of the related structures. To define the structure of your operating concern, select Controlling ➤ Profitability Analysis ➤ Structures ➤ Define Operating Concern ➤ Maintain Operating Concern or use the transaction code KEA0. There is also another transaction code (ORKE) that will quickly get you to a "mini" Implementation Guide (IMG) specifically for CO-PA; we use it all the time.

Once you access this transaction code, you are taken to the Maintain Operating Concern overview screen, shown in Figure 12.1. Extreme Sports's operating concern (ESOC) was selected from the pull-down menu.

**FIGURE 12.1**    The Maintain Operating Concern overview screen

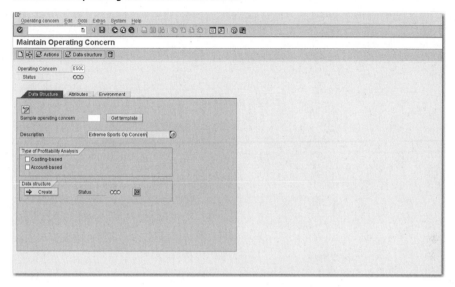

## Operating Concern Attributes

The first step in defining your operating concern structure is to define its attributes. These attributes control the time frame "buckets" and currency valuations in which CO-PA is updated. To create the attributes for your operating concern, you select the Attributes tab, as shown in Figure 12.2, and then choose the appropriate parameters.

Here are explanations of the fields shown in Figure 12.2:

**Currency Types for Costing-Based Profitability Analysis**    Enter the identifier of the currency you want to use as the CO-PA currency. When you use costing-based CO-PA, values are posted in the CO-PA currency and/or into additional currencies that you can identify on this screen. CO-PA stores values in two currencies: either Company Code or Operating Concern. In addition, you can use Profit Center Valuation (a part of Transfer Pricing). You have the ability to use any of the different combinations of currencies and PrCtr Valuations that you would like. Therefore, use one of the following:

- ▶ Operating Concern Currency

- ▶ Company Code Currency

- ▶ OpConcern Crcy, PrCtr Valuation

- ▶ Comp Code Crcy, PrCtr valuation

**FIGURE 12.2**     The Attributes tab of the Maintain Operating Concern configuration screen

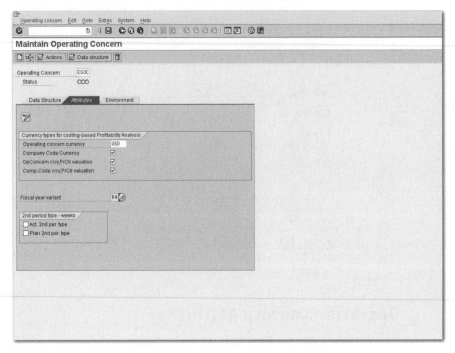

**Fiscal Year Variant**     Enter the identifier of the fiscal year variant you want to use for CO-PA. Your CO-PA fiscal year variant should match your controlling area fiscal year variant. Once you set the fiscal year variant, you cannot change it unless you change it to one that has more posting periods than the original. This is the only parameter that must match the controlling area assignment; the controlling area can then be assigned to the operating concern.

**Act. 2nd Per. (Period) Type**     Select this indicator if you want actual data that is posted into CO-PA to be stored in weekly values as well as in the normal period values (defined from the fiscal year variant). Be careful when deciding whether to use this option and the next. Capturing data in weekly buckets can be a real system drag when it comes to reporting, and you'll need additional database storage for the increased data volume.

**Plan 2nd Per. (Period) Type**    Select this indicator if you want plan data that is posted into CO-PA to be stored in weekly values as well as in the normal period values (defined from the fiscal year variant). Again, be careful when deciding whether to use this option.

Once you have configured your options, click the save icon. Then select the Data Structure tab.

---

### EXTREME SPORTS OPERATING CONCERN ATTRIBUTES CONFIGURATION ANALYSIS

The operating concern of Extreme Sports (ESOC) was assigned attributes in this section. The operating concern currency was set to USD, which is the same as the controlling area currency for Extreme Sports's controlling area EX01. In addition, we turned on the other currency/valuation combinations just in case we decide to activate the PCA/Transfer Pricing process. We set the operating concern fiscal year variant to K4. K4 (Calendar Year plus 4 periods to close) is the fiscal year variant utilized by all of Extreme Sports's company codes. It is also the fiscal year variant for controlling area EX01. Extreme Sports is not required to store profitability data by week. Therefore, we left both the plan and actual indicators for second period type posting periods blank (null).

---

# Creating Characteristics for Your Operating Concern

Now that you have created and saved the attributes of your operating concern, you are ready to create its data structures. The data structure definition controls which characteristics and value fields you will use in your operating concern. Remember, once a characteristic is included in your operating concern and is posted to, it is next to impossible to delete the characteristic. To create the data structures for your operating concern, click the Data Structure Change button, and then click the Create button to open the screen shown in Figure 12.3.

**FIGURE 12.3** Edit Data Structure: Characteristic Screen

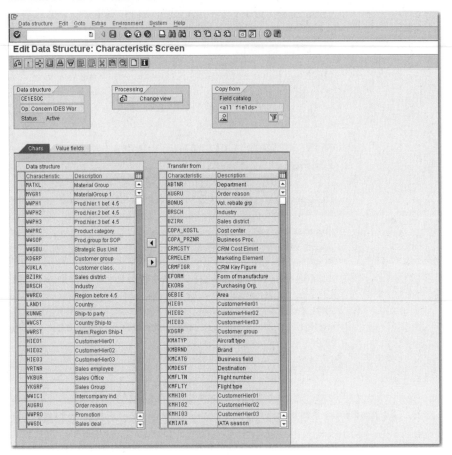

You'll see a message telling you that the changes you are about to make are valid for all clients; this means that changes are client independent. The operating concern structure is client independent, but it must be generated and activated individually in each client in order to receive updates. CO-PA changes are an eclectic mix of client-independent and client-dependent changes. The nature of CO-PA changes will be explained in more detail in the section "CO-PA Transports" later in this chapter. After you close the informational message, you are presented with a pop-up box for the creation of characteristics. Select the Costing Based radio button and then click Continue. You are taken to the create characteristics configuration screen shown in Figure 12.4.

**FIGURE 12.4** The create characteristics configuration screen

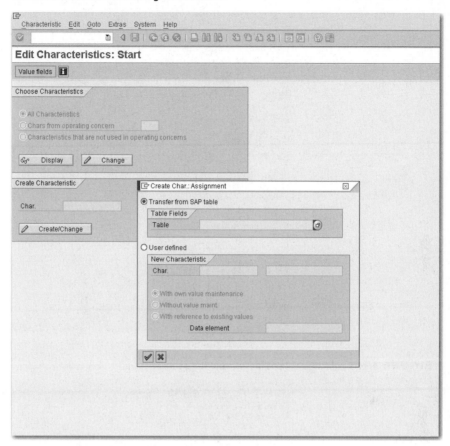

CO-PA comes with many *fixed* characteristics. Fixed characteristics are part of the operating concern and cannot be changed or deleted. To view the fixed characteristics that come with every operating concern, choose Extras ➢ Display Fixed Fields and a dialog box displays listing the fixed characteristics, technical fields, and accounting amounts (for account-based CO-PA), as shown in Figures 12.5, 12.6, and 12.7. Characteristics of type F are fixed characteristics; they are generally available for your use in drill-down reporting. Characteristics of type T are technical characteristics; these characteristics are stored in line items but generally are not available for reporting. Fixed characteristics come delivered with hard-coded *derivations* that determine how the characteristic value is updated and with what. For user-defined and other delivered characteristics, you must create a derivation for the characteristic so that it can be updated with values. Derivations will be covered in detail in the section "Characteristic Derivation."

**FIGURE 12.5** Fixed characteristics for the operating concern

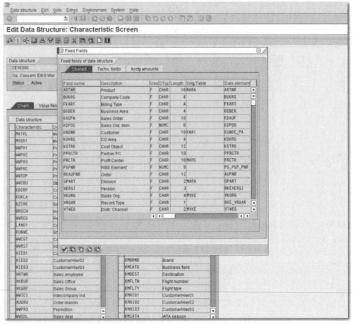

**FIGURE 12.6** Technical fields for the operating concern

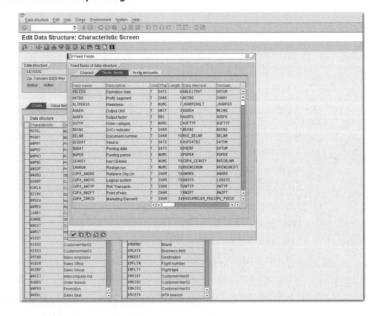

**FIGURE 12.7**    Accounting amounts for the operating concern

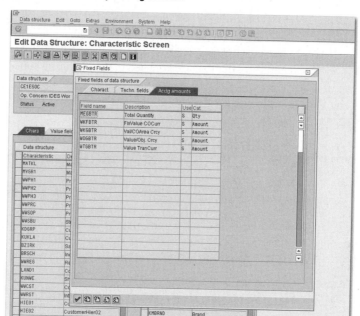

You can add characteristics from already existing characteristics in the field catalog and from reference tables that can be read by CO-PA, or you can add user-defined characteristics. We will add some characteristics of each type to operating concern ESOC. According to SAP's online documentation, you should be able to get all of your profitability reporting needs from an additional 10 to 20 characteristics. Be careful not to use up all of your characteristics in one shot.

The field catalog contains all fixed characteristics and value fields, other delivered characteristics and value fields that can optionally be used in CO-PA, and user-defined characteristics (after they are created in the characteristic catalog). In technical terms, the field catalog is table TKEF. To add a characteristic from the field catalog, click the available characteristic shown earlier in Figure 12.3. If you want to add more than one characteristic at a time, you can select the box next to each characteristic you want to add, or you can choose just a single characteristic. Once you have selected the characteristics, click the arrow button and the system adds them to the list in the create characteristics configuration screen. The characteristics displayed in Figure 12.3 have been selected for Extreme Sports's operating concern. In the "Characteristic Derivation" section later in this chapter, we will show you how to use Derivation to populate these characteristics with characteristic values.

To create characteristics that you need for your operating concern, begin by choosing Controlling ➤ Profitability Analysis ➤ Structures ➤ Define Operating Concern ➤ Maintain Characteristics. You are presented with a screen that lets you view a list of characteristics, characteristics from a specific operating concern, or characteristics that are not used in the operating concern. You can also create a characteristic using this screen (see Figure 12.8).

**FIGURE 12.8**    Edit Characteristics: Start screen

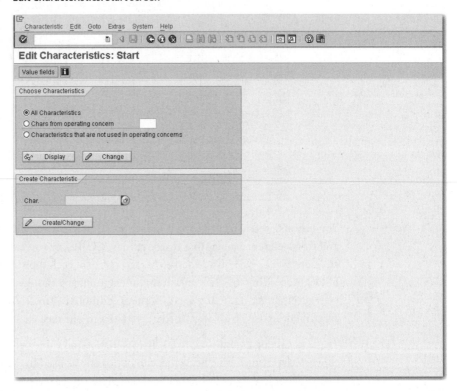

There are several approaches to creating a characteristic, as you can see in the screen that opens when you click the Create/Change button (see Figure 12.9). The first option is to obtain characteristics from a table. To see the specific 18 tables that are available, press F4 to access help (see Figure 12.10). The available tables cover much of the standard information available in the Logistics area, including the Customer Master, Plant information for Material, and Sales documentation, to name a few.

**FIGURE 12.9**   Creating a characteristic assignment

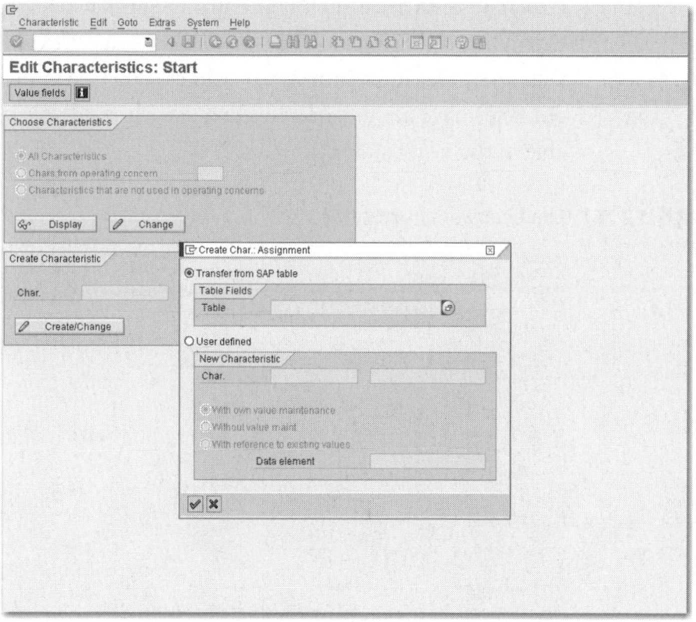

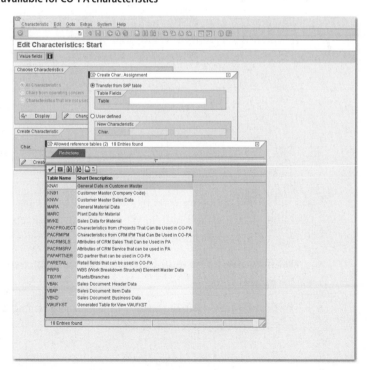

**FIGURE 12.10**   Tables available for CO-PA characteristics

Once you identify the table you want to choose characteristics from, just double-click, and then press the Enter button (Check icon) to access the list of characteristics in this table. Here we have used the KNA1 table and can now choose additional characteristics to include in the field catalog (see Figure 12.11). Notice that grayed-out fields have already been used and are unavailable on this screen (but are available in the field catalog).

**FIGURE 12.11**  Characteristics in the table KNA1

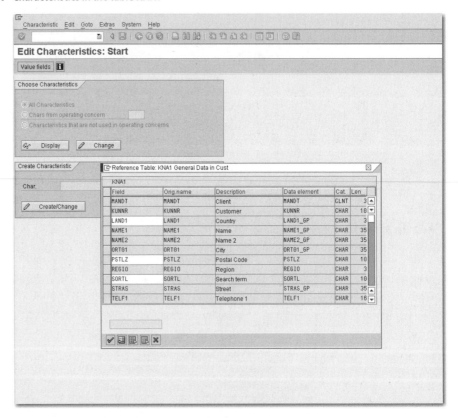

The second option for creating characteristics is to use the User Defined button rather than the Table button. When creating a characteristic using the user defined approach, you can choose among three different options:

**With its own value maintenance**    This characteristic will be created with a table for values.

**Without value maintenance**    This characteristic will not have a table for values but will serve as a placeholder.

**By referring to an existing element**    You can use an existing data element to help populate the values of the user-defined characteristic.

Let's look at a basic example of creating a user-defined characteristic with own value maintenance. You begin by filling in the field for the technical name and description. All user-defined characteristics start with WW<*XXX*>, where <*XXX*> represents three numbers. In our example, we will use WW991 with a description of Freight Items (see Figure 12.12).

**FIGURE 12.12**  A user-defined characteristic

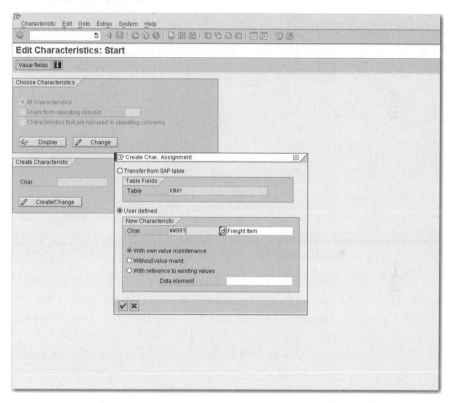

Click the Enter button (Check icon) to move to the next screen. Complete the required descriptions, and then choose whether the data type will allow only numerical or alphanumeric values and specify the length. In our case we are going with CHAR (alphanumeric) and the length of 10. Once you have provided this information, save and activate your characteristic. Notice that this will automatically generate the necessary tables for the check tables. In the case of a user-defined characteristic, the check table will always start with T25* (see Figure 12.13).

**FIGURE 12.13**  The completed characteristic WW991

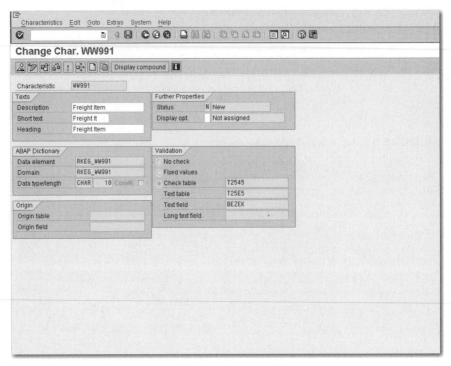

Finally, review the final assignment of this new characteristic to the catalog and its availability to be used in an operating concern (see Figure 12.14).

Extreme Sports would like to make customer planning group a characteristic in its operating concern. You will recall our discussion of customer groups from Chapters 6 and 7. To add Customer Planning Group as a characteristic in the operating concern, we will use reference table KNB1 of the customer master table (company code data). Double-click the table name KNB1 in the Choose Reference Table pop-up screen, and a listing appears of the fields that are available for use as characteristics in CO-PA. We will select field FDGRV (the customer planning group). Adding a field from a table to the characteristic list is the same as adding a field from the field catalog. Once the reference field is added to the characteristic list, you have the option of changing the characteristic field name. You cannot change the data element name, field type, or length. We will leave the field name (FDGRV) the same.

**FIGURE 12.14** The new characteristic in the field catalog

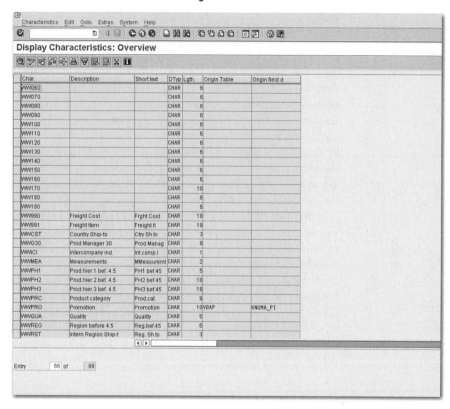

Continue to add more user-defined characteristics to the operating concern. Once the procedure we've outlined is completed for each of your user-defined characteristics, you can choose them from the field catalog and assign them to the ESOC operating concern.

For user-defined characteristics, you can configure two additional fields, which are shown earlier in Figure 12.14. In the area of the ABAP Dictionary is an option for assigning a conversion routine to this characteristic. This will allow you to use a program to manipulate the information assigned to the characteristic. For instance, you can add leading zeroes to the values or right-justify the values. There is also an option to adjust the display of the characteristic for reporting purposes. We tend to leave this option blank and use the reporting functionality to generate the display. Either way is available, and no issues will arise regardless of the approach you use for this field.

## EXTREME SPORTS CHARACTERISTIC CREATION CONFIGURATION ANALYSIS

In this section, you learned that every operating concern comes with fixed characteristics that cannot be deleted or changed. They contain such fields as Company Code, Customer, Controlling Area, and so on. In addition to the fixed characteristics that were delivered with operating concern ESOC, a number of other characteristics were selected for inclusion. The characteristics Country, Product Hierarchy, Sales Office, and Sales Group were some that we selected from the field catalog. These characteristics will help Extreme Sports meet its needs for reporting profitability by sales country and product hierarchy, and will also provide a reporting structure for its sales department by reporting on sales office and sales group. We selected the characteristic Customer Planning Group from the reference table KNB1. (Configuring customer planning groups was covered in Chapters 6 and 7.) Reporting profitability by customer planning group will help Extreme Sports analyze sales by its own customer segmentation strategy and allow it to refine and change customer planning groups as time goes on. We also added the user-defined characteristics Product Group, Product Line, Product Category, and Trade Organization to operating concern ESOC. The Product Group, Product Line, and Product Category characteristics will further help Extreme Sports analyze profitability by its product hierarchy. The characteristic Trade Organization will help Extreme Sports report on sales for different trade organizations, such as NAFTA and the European Union. We'll explore the population of these user-defined characteristics later in this chapter.

# Creating Value Fields for Your Operating Concern

The next step is to create value fields for your operating concern. As we explained earlier, these fields store the values (relating to both currency and quantity) in your operating concern. Value fields take the place of G/L accounts for storing currency data in the costing-based CO-PA. However, creating a one-to-one relationship between G/L account and value fields is not their purpose. A value field should group similar types of currency transactions (such as revenues, sales discounts, and COGS) into one *bucket*. You can also use value fields to store quantities such as sales quantities so you can determine profitability per unit.

To create value fields for your operating concern, choose Profitability Analysis ➤ Structures ➤ Define Operating Concern ➤ Maintain Value Fields, or you can use transaction code KEA6. Remember that this menu path is from the transaction code ORKE (the mini-CO-PA implementation guide). If you are using the general IMG, you would start from Controlling and then use the rest of the menu path. You can also access the screen you need directly from the Create Characteristics screen by clicking the Value Field button on the screen shown earlier in Figure 12.8, or from the Data Structure screen in the Maintain Operating Concern process by selecting the Value Field tab and then clicking the Create button (shown earlier in Figure 12.3).

In either case, you are taken to the Edit Value Fields: Start screen, which lets you create or display a value field (see Figure 12.15).

**FIGURE 12.15** The Edit Value Fields: Start screen

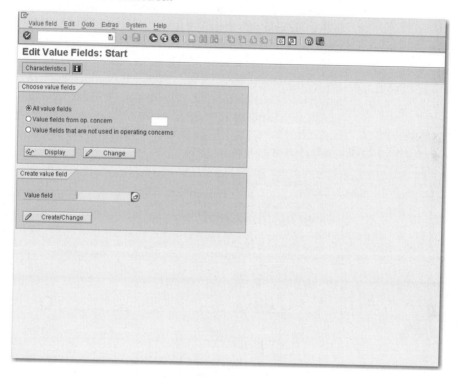

As we mentioned earlier, it is not the purpose of value fields to create a one-to-one relationship between G/L accounts and value fields, although we have seen this approach used so that costing-based CO-PA reconciles to FI. This strategy, of course, eliminates much of the value of costing-based CO-PA in terms of analysis of gross profit margins.

Let's review the options on this screen:

**All Value Fields**    This option displays all value fields available in the value field catalog.

**Value Fields from Op. (Operating) Concern**    This option displays all value fields used in a specific operating concern.

**Value Fields That Are Not Used in Operating Concerns**   This option displays all value fields that have not been used in any operating concern.

**Create Value Field**   This option allows you to create value fields to be stored in the value field catalog.

Unlike with characteristics, no fixed-value fields are activated at the same time you activate your operating concern (unless you consider the fixed accounts used in the account-based CO-PA as fixed-value fields). You must create and then choose each value field you would like to use. But as with characteristics, there are delivered value fields, which are also stored in the field catalog. If you find that the value fields you would like to use are available in the catalog, you can just choose them from the field catalog (remember we are doing this from the screen Edit Data Structure, which is transaction code KEA0) and click the Value Fields tab. The field catalog screen, shown in Figure 12.16, is displayed.

**FIGURE 12.16**   The field catalog screen

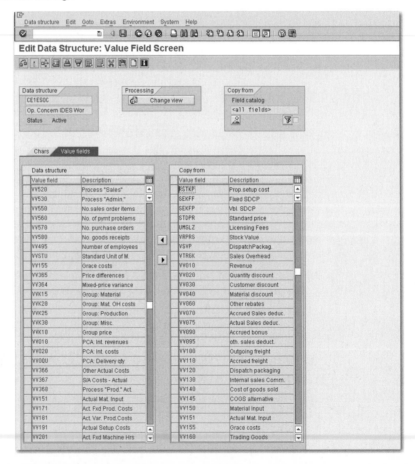

If you make a mistake and create a value field as a quantity and later realize that you would like it to be an amount, don't waste your time trying to change the setting on the actual value field. Just delete that value field and re-create the value field from scratch. The process of switching that one indicator is painful and not worth the trouble.

Figure 12.17 displays the value fields that will be included in operating concern ESOC. The value fields Sales Quantity, Revenue, Stock Value, and Outgoing Freight are just some of the value fields that were selected from the field catalog. In addition, we created some user-defined value fields, including Sales Discounts, Salesmen Salaries, and Promotional Expenses, that are going to be used in the ESOC operating concern, but are not displayed in the list in Figure 12.17. As with user-defined characteristics, a naming strategy should be used for user-defined value fields. Normally, user-defined value field names begin with *VV*. (This naming convention has been used in this book.) In addition to naming the value field, you must add a long description and a short description and select either Qty (quantity) or Curr. (currency).

**FIGURE 12.17**  ESOC value fields

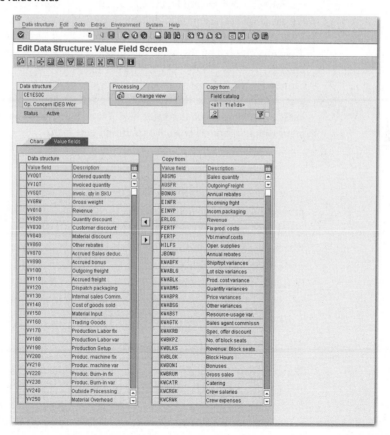

We will show you how to assign values to value fields in the "Mapping SD Condition Types to Value Fields (the SD Interface)" and "PA Settlement Structure" sections later in this chapter.

## EXTREME SPORTS VALUE FIELD CREATION CONFIGURATION ANALYSIS

In this section, value fields were created for operating concern ESOC. Value fields store the quantity and currency values of numbers posted into CO-PA. Used in the costing-based approach to CO-PA, they take the place of G/L accounts and are meant to group similar values together—there normally is not a one-to-one relationship between a value field and a G/L account. The following value fields are some of the fields selected from the field catalog for inclusion in Extreme Sports's operating concern: Sales Quantity, Revenue, Stock Value, and Outgoing Freight. The Sales Quantity value field will capture the quantity (number) of items that are sold and posted into CO-PA. Extreme Sports utilizes several revenue accounts for FI purposes. All revenue postings (regardless of account) will be stored in the Revenue value field. The Stock Value field will store the COGS amount for Extreme Sports's products. The freight that is incurred to ship the product to the customer location will be stored in the Outgoing Freight value field. Some user-defined value fields were included in operating concern ESOC, such as Sales Deductions, Cost of Labor Hours, and Other Expenses. All sales discounts granted on the billing document (regardless of account) will be stored in the Sales Discounts value field. The salaries of Extreme Sports's salespeople will be captured in the Salesmen Salaries value field via a CO-PA cost center assessment. Any promotional expenses, whether incurred on the billing document or FI, will be stored in the Promotional Expenses value field. This value field will be updated via a PA settlement structure from FI or from a condition type in SD.

Now that we have identified the value fields that we will be using, let's review the process of creating a value field and the options within the Create Value Field screen (refer back to Figure 12.15). You start by assigning a value field technical name at this point by filling in the value field area. Once you have included the technical name that begins with VV and has three additional values, click the Create/Change button. You are reminded at this point that this is a client-independent table and you may affect other system processes. Pass by this warning, and you will see to the Change Val. Fld screen (see Figure 12.18).

The fields on this screen are as follows:

**Description**    Assign a description to your value field. It should reflect the purpose of the value field and the amounts or quantities that will be stored.

**Short Text**   Assign a short text to your value field. This could be an additional description that you can use during the reporting process.

**Agg. (Time)**   This is probably the only field on this screen that you will need to review before assigning a value. This setting determines how the values will be displayed in the reports. Normally you will see SUM used in this field since a summarization of the values is the normal typical way to display the data. For those times when you need something a bit different, use one of the other two options. AVG (aggregation average) displays the average of all values stored by this value field. LAS (last) displays the final value that is posted to that value field. Here's an example:

| Period Posting | Stored Values | | Report On | Reported Values: LAS | Reported Values: AVG |
| --- | --- | --- | --- | --- | --- |
| Period | VV001 | VV002 | Period 1 to .. | VV001 | VV002 |
| 1 | 3 | 100 | 1 | 3 | 100 |
| 2 | 3 | 100 | 2 | 3 | 100 |
| 3 | 4 | 120 | 3 | 4 | 106.7 |
| 4 | 2 | 90 | 4 | 2 | 102.5 |

**Value Field Type**   This option specifies whether you are storing an amount or a quantity. Your choice reflects whether you are using a unit of measure (UOM) or a currency.

**FIGURE 12.18**   Change Val. Fld screen

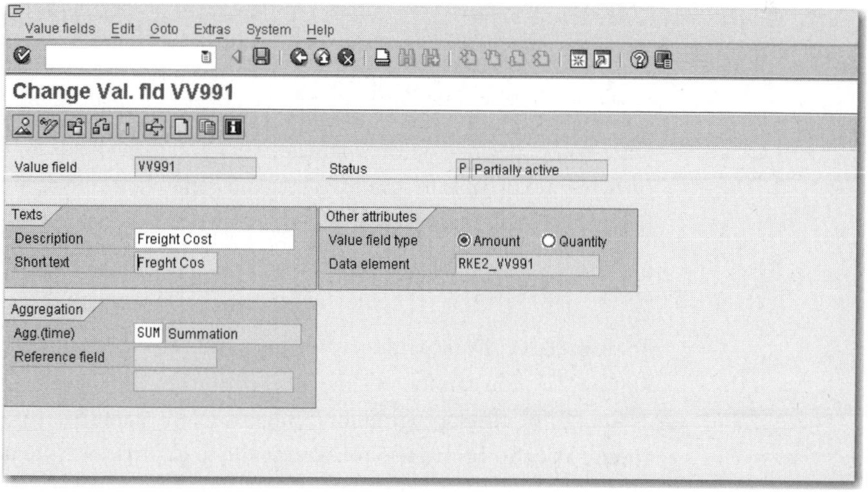

Now that we have defined the value field and all of its attributes, you can save and activate it. This process creates the data element that will be used in the table to store the amounts or quantities. Your new value field will be stored in the value field catalog for your use (see Figure 12.19).

**FIGURE 12.19** The value field catalog

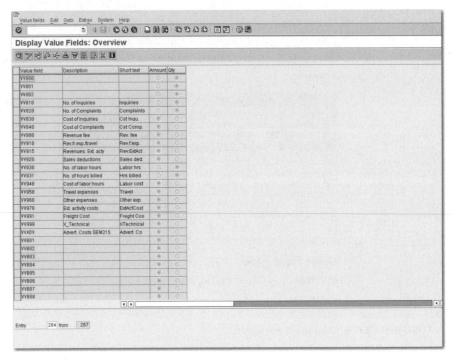

## Save, Activate, and Generate

Once you've decided on the characteristics and value fields for the operating concern, the next step is to save, activate, and generate it. We have added characteristics and value fields to Extreme Sports's operating concern, but they are not saved as part of the operating concern structure yet. Before saving, however, we need to check it for errors.

To do so, select Data Structure ➤ Check from the screen shown earlier in Figure 12.3. You can follow this menu path from the characteristic definition screen as well. If the check program finds no errors, the data structure can be saved. Just choose Data Structure ➤ Save. Saving the structure saves the definition of the selected characteristics and value fields with your operating concern. Choose Data

Structure ➤ Save from one of the operating concern structure screens (characteristic definition or value field definition). The Generate New Check Tables pop-up box that appears informs you that new check tables must be created for some of the characteristics. You can also access this pop-up box if you save and activate your characteristics at the same time you are creating them (see Figure 12.20).

**FIGURE 12.20** The Generate New Check Tables pop-up box

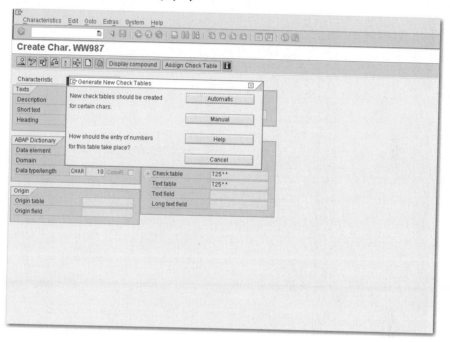

Check tables store the key values for user-defined characteristics that were created in the operating concern. You manually enter the available values for user-defined characteristics in these tables. You can have the system automatically determine the names of the check tables, or you can manually determine them yourself. The names of the check tables are T25xx, where xx is a number. Unless you are using Automatic Link Enabling (ALE), it is normally a good idea to let the system name your check tables automatically. If you use more than one production system that shares information (such as ALE), you'll probably want to name the check tables yourself to avoid naming conflicts with the other distributed system. Extreme Sports will allow the system to automatically determine the names of check tables. Click the save icon to save the operating concern structure. Once the save operation is complete, you'll see the action log for saving and activating the operating concern, as shown in Figure 12.21.

**FIGURE 12.21** The save and activate operating concern action log

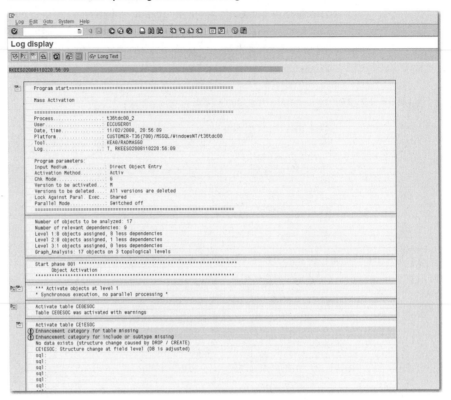

As you can see, domains and data elements were created for the user-defined characteristics and value fields that were included in operating concern ESOC. In addition, check tables and text tables were generated for the user-defined characteristics. (Population of the check and text tables will be covered later in the chapter.) You will also notice that several tables beginning with CE*ESOC were created and saved in the database. All CO-PA tables begin with *CE* followed by a number and then the name of the operating concern (ESOC in our example). We will explain in detail the CO-PA tables that were saved in the next section.

Now that the data structure for operating concern ESOC has been saved, it must be activated. Saving the data structure only creates the tables, domains, and date elements in the database. In order for the tables and other elements to be used, they must be activated. Activation lets the database know that the objects are ready to be used in postings. To activate the data structures, you choose Data Structure ➤ Activate. SAP will generate the appropriate structures in the database and provide you with status information. Once all of the structures have been created and activated in the database, the action log is once again displayed but this time with new messages telling you that each structure was activated in the data dictionary. Once you have reviewed the logs and determined that no additional action is needed, you can click the green arrow until you return to the Maintain Operating Concern screen.

After you dismiss the Maintain Operating Concern screen, SAP displays the Generate Environment pop-up box shown in Figure 12.22. Click Yes to generate the data structures of your operating concern. The generation process may take a few minutes. Once your operating concern has been correctly generated, you should receive the message "Environment of Operating Concern ESOC (your operating concern ID) Has Been Generated Completely." Generating the operating concern creates the internal ABAP programs that are used by CO-PA. Generation is necessary because the table names and structure of the tables are different for each operating concern. After an operating concern is transported, it must be generated in the target client. This will be covered in more detail in the section "CO-PA Transports" later in this chapter.

**FIGURE 12.22** The Generate Environment pop-up box

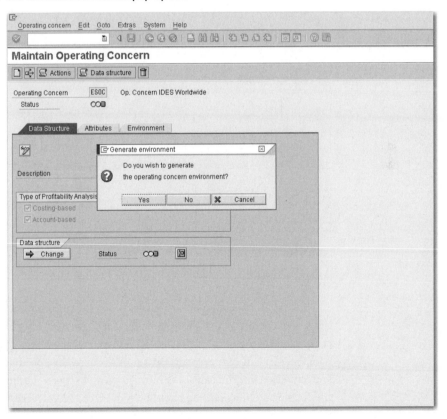

Before leaving this section, let's review some of the information that has been generated by this process. You should do several additional activities before completing your work on the actual operating concern. In the initial screens for the Maintain Operating Concern, review the last tab on this list, Environment (see Figure 12.23). This will tell you whether the operating concern has been successfully generated and activated for use with both cross-client part/portion and also client-specific part/portion. If not, you can execute this process directly from this screen. This will ensure that the operating concern and all of the data structures will be available for multiple clients.

**FIGURE 12.23** The Environment tab of the Maintain Operating Concern screen

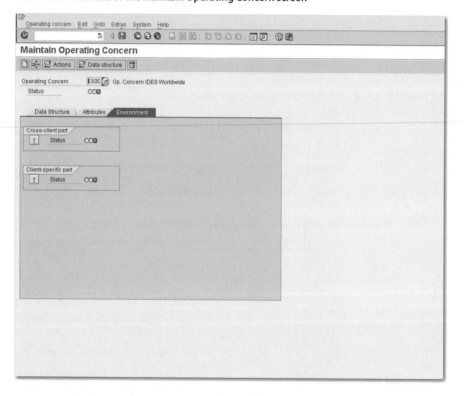

As a follow-up, you can quickly review the overall information about your operating concern with some of the options in the Extras menu (see Figure 12.3). If you choose the Extras option at the top of the screen you will see a context menu list of components. One of the important options is to review the amount of space that you have used up. You can see this by choosing Extras ➤ Technical Limits to open the Technical Limits pop-up box shown in Figure 12.24. Here, you can see that we have used up 39 characteristics of the maximum of 50; 115 value fields of the maximum of 120; and the byte length of our records—1623 of a maximum of 4030—or a maximum of 256 fields in length. This information may not be of too much importance to you, but for the management and maintenance of the system configuration these items are very important.

**FIGURE 12.24** The Technical Limits box

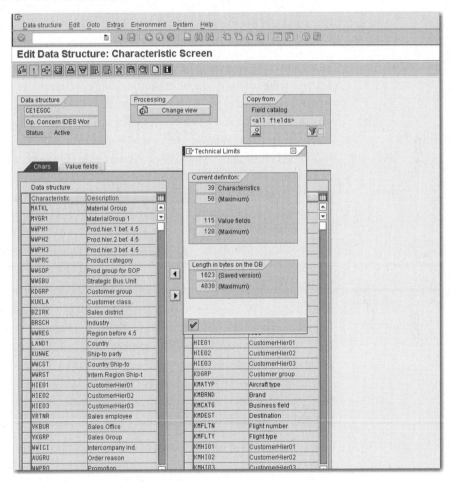

## CO-PA Tables

As you saw in the action log in Figure 12.21, several tables were created from the definition of our operating concern data structure. The most important tables in terms of understanding CO-PA will be explained in this section. You should also consult SAP's online documentation for further detail.

The core tables that form an operating concern are CE1*xxxx*, CE2*xxxx*, CE3*xxxx*, and CE4*xxxx*, where *xxxx* is the ID of your operating concern. We will begin with an explanation of CE4*xxxx* and work our way back to CE1*xxxx*. As you review online SAP documentation and attend SAP training courses, you will notice that CO-PA is often described as a data cube with a picture of a multidimensional cube. This is a good analogy because that is precisely what CO-PA is—a large data cube. You can slice and dice the data cube to use it for reports and to analyze profitability data.

Data is stored in the data cube in *profitability segments*. Profitability segments are unique combinations of characteristics in your operating concern. Not all characteristics are defined at the segment level (such as the technical T-type characteristics in the field catalog). You also have the option to include and exclude some characteristics from the segment level. This can be done from the Change View "Profitability Segment Characteristics" screen (see Figure 12.25). In this process you are deciding what characteristics should be included in your Segment Level table for analysis and reporting purposes. This should be something that you review and set up once. If you decide to make a change after the operating concern has data posted, this will have an impact on the data entries into the table and you may find that reporting performance has been affected. As you can see, you can effectively have one level of granularity for costing based and one for account based and then the list of *not* used.

Table CE4*xxxx* is the profitability segment level table. CE4*xxxx* stores each possible combination of characteristic values (as they are posted) and assigns each combination a system-generated profitability segment number. Profitability segment numbers greatly enhance performance on drill-down reporting. CE4*xxxx* comes with a standard index and a secondary index. SAP will determine which index provides the best performance. You can also create additional secondary index numbers to help with reporting performance.

Table CE3*xxxx* stores data in its first summarized form. Where table CE4*xxxx* stores only combinations of characteristics and creates a profitability segment number, CE3*xxxx* stores the values of value fields along with the profitability segment number. CE3*xxxx* does not store any actual characteristic values (there are no characteristic fields in the database structure of CE3*xxxx*) but instead stores only the profitability segment number. CE3*xxxx* is also utilized by drill-down reporting to enhance performance. Therefore, the CE4xxxx table supplies the pointer to the appropriate values in the CE3xxxx table. This is how the data and characteristic values are stored.

**FIGURE 12.25** The Change View "Profitability Segment Characteristics" screen

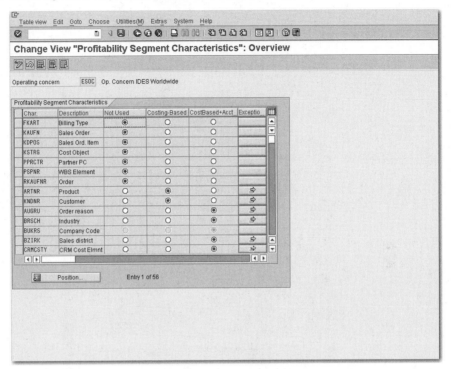

Table CE2*xxxx* stores plan line item data. This table stores all values—characteristic values, value field values, and the profitability segment for all plan postings in CO-PA. All characteristics, including technical T-type characteristics, are included and posted to CE2*xxxx*. So, you can think of this as the line item level table for planned values.

Table CE1*xxxx* stores actual line item data. This table stores all values—characteristic values, value field values, and the profitability segment for all actual postings in CO-PA. As with the actual line items table, all characteristics, including technical T-type characteristics, are included and posted to CE1*xxxx*. You can create drill-down reports from the line item tables (CO-PA drill-down reporting will be covered later in this chapter). You can display line items in CO-PA, but it is a performance-exhaustive and lengthy process. You should access line items only when you absolutely need to view characteristics that are not part of the segment level.

This structure is set up to help with reporting processes. If you can envision the report will initially execute on the CE4xxxx table, find the appropriate indexed values, then go to the CE3xxx table to find the amounts, and then report on that information. If necessary, you might look to develop a drill-down report to compare against the CE1xxxx table (see Figure 12.26).

**FIGURE 12.26** The Status Information box

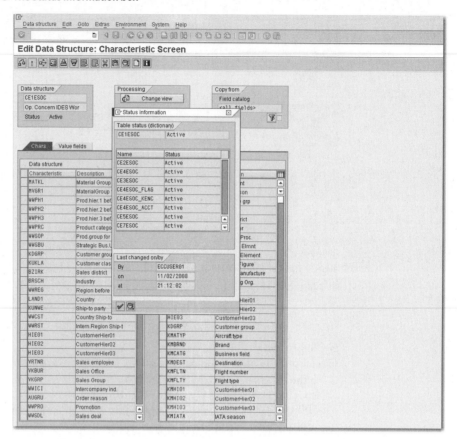

Besides the core tables (CE*xxxx) that we described earlier, you will notice that some additional tables were created. These tables all begin T25xx, where xx equals a number or a letter followed by a number. These tables are user-defined characteristic check tables and text tables, respectively. You will recall from the section "Save, Activate, and Generate" earlier in this chapter that we were given the choice of allowing the system to automatically determine check table numbers or manually assigning them. We chose the automatically create option. The system therefore created tables T2541, T2542, T2543, and T2544. These tables store the valid characteristic values for user-defined characteristics. The tables T25E1, T25E2, T25E3, and T25E4 store the text descriptions of the characteristic values that are defined in check tables T2541, T2542, T2543, and T2544, respectively. We address the population of these tables in the next section.

# Characteristic Derivation

All characteristics are populated based on one of two approaches—either via actual posted values from a record or via derivation. All fixed characteristics that are delivered with your operating concern have a set derivation that is used in ABAP code behind the scenes. Derivation of fixed characteristics cannot be changed. For the other characteristics that are added to an operating concern—from the field catalog, from reference tables, and those that are user-defined—characteristic derivation must be defined. There are three ways to create characteristic derivation: the derivation table lookup, derivation structures and rules, and derivation user-exits.

These approaches will allow additional values to populate the record string upon posting into the operating concern. There are three other approaches to derivation, although they are system processes rather than true create processes. These processes—Move, Clear, and Customer Hierarchy—are very useful and a bit easier to set up than the ones we covered earlier. If you would like to assign a value found in one field to another field, you'd use the Move option. For example, you can move the value in the Customer field to the Sold-To and Ship-To fields. The Clear option clears the field of any values. For example, you could clear the Region value from the characteristic and then with another step insert the appropriate value. The final derivation approach, Customer Hierarchy, is self-explanatory—set this up if you are using the Customer Hierarchy in your operating concern.

Let's review several terms in the derivation process before we move on to the complete setup of the process. As in many areas of SAP, you first define the structure, and then you assign items to that structure. Derivation in CO-PA is no different. First you define a *derivation strategy*, which is nothing but a title or grouping of steps in a derivation process. Then you set up derivation steps and assign them to the derivation strategy. The important thing to remember here is to make sure that you list your steps in the sequence that they should be executed. That way, if you have dependencies between steps you don't have any missed values.

## The Derivation Table

Typically, characteristics added to an operating concern from the field catalog and reference tables automatically generate a derivation in the derivation table. However, you can change the derivations that are created. To view, create, and change derivations in the derivation table, choose Profitability Analysis ➢ Master Data ➢ Define Characteristic Derivation, or use the transaction code KEDR.

Once you access this screen, select View ➤ Display All Steps, and you will see all of the derivation steps included in your operating concern. Figure 12.27 shows the derivation table configuration screen, which is displayed after you complete one of the configuration methods.

**FIGURE 12.27** The derivation table configuration screen

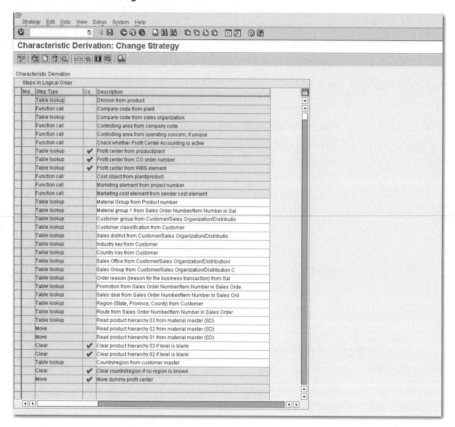

As you can see, the system has already generated entries in the derivation table for the additional characteristics added from the field catalog and from reference tables. These derivation steps have been generated by the system. Do not alter any of the system-generated derivation steps. If you do, you could cause posting problems because the system expects to use the derivation that it created. To better understand these entries, let's take a look under the hood of one of them. By double-clicking the Table Lookup for Read product hierarchy 03 from material master (SD) characteristic, we are taken to the table lookup for derivation entry screen, shown in Figure 12.28.

**FIGURE 12.28** The control table for derivation entry screen

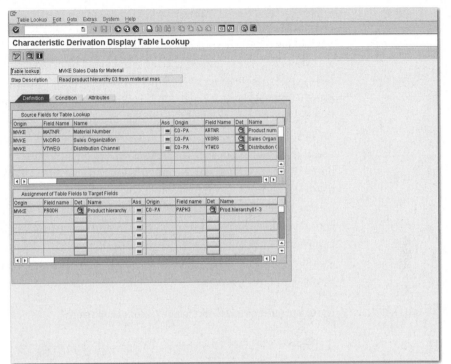

You can see that the characteristic Product Hierarchy is derived from the Material Master. Sales Data table (MVKE; this is listed on the right side of the screen). The field that is used to supply data from MVKE is PRODH. For SAP to use the master data table for derivation, the table's primary key must be able to be formed from characteristics in the CO-PA line item table. The primary key of the table must be entered in the key fields on the top of the screen. In this case, the key field for MVKE is a concatenated key of MATNR, VKORG, and VTWEG.

After reviewing the derivation entry, click the green arrow to return to the derivation table configuration screen. If the record that you are posting includes the values for the material, sales organization, and distribution channel, you will be able to derive the Product Hierarchy and populate the record that is posted with additional values. Not only will the system populate the PRODH field, but it will create a flat version of the product hierarchy as well. When you return to the initial screen, notice the next two derivation steps for Move for Hierarchy 02 and 01. These are the levels 01 and 02 of the hierarchy populating additional information in the posted records.

You will recall from the creation of the operating concern data structure that four user-defined characteristics were created: WWPRG (Product Group), WWPRL (Product Line), WWPRC (Product Category), and WWTRD (Trade Organization). We will now create derivation table entries for characteristics WWPRG, WWPRL, and WWPRC. These three characteristics can all be derived from the single characteristic PRODH (Product Hierarchy). We have already looked at the how the derivation for PRODH is performed. Extreme Sports has defined its product hierarchy so that the first five characters of its product hierarchy represent the product group, the next five characters represent the product line, and the last eight characters represent the product category. To create a derivation table entry, click the Create Step button in the derivation table configuration screen. Choose Table Lookup from the list of steps. Then select the table that you will be using for the Lookup—for example, the Material Master Table, MARA. Once you have accessed the next screen, you can define which field is your ORIGIN and which field will be the TARGET (see Figure 12.29). In this example, we are using the Material number as the initial lookup for the material type. Once the material type is found, it will be assigned to the field Material Group 1.

**FIGURE 12.29** The Characteristic Derivation: Change Table Lookup screen

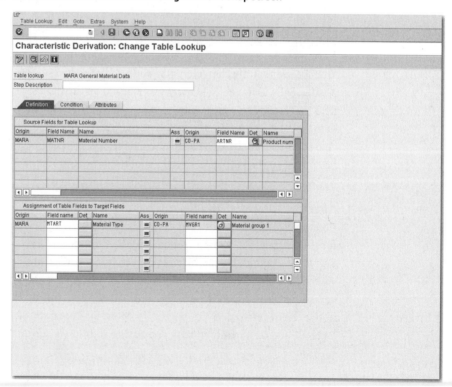

The derivation table entry for Product Category (WWPRC) is shown in Figure 12.30. The existing derivation table lookup was used for this derivation. Characteristic WWPRC uses the same master data table, master data field, and key fields as the characteristic PRODH. The difference is that an offset of 10 characters and a length of 8 characters are assigned to this derivation for WWPRC. The offset is given because Product Category consists of only the last 8 characters of the product hierarchy. The offset ensures that we are picking up the correct characters. The derivation table entries for Product Group (WWPRG) and Product Line (WWPRL) are exactly the same as the derivation for Product Category, with the exception of the offset and field length fields. For Product Group, the offset field is set to 0 and the field length field is 5. For the Product Line characteristic, the offset field is set to 5 and the field length field is also set to 5.

**FIGURE 12.30** The Characteristic Derivation: Change Table Lookup for ESOC operating concern

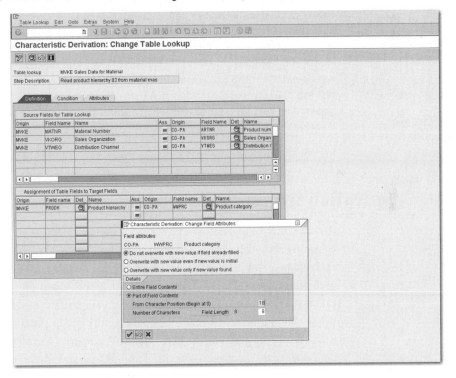

Additional options are available on the derivation process, such as setting a condition on the derivation. So, for example, you may only want to fill a field if the record refers to a specific company. The Condition option can offer you the ability to filter the use of a derivation step. In addition, certain attributes are available, such as requiring the system to issue an error message if no value is found, assigning a validity date to an entry, and assigning a user-defined step ID to each of the derivation steps to manage the sequence.

### EXTREME SPORTS DERIVATION TABLE CONFIGURATION ANALYSIS

In this section, you learned that the system automatically creates entries in the derivation table during operating concern generation for characteristics that were added to the operating concern from the field catalog or from reference tables. We used the derivation table to create a derivation from three of our user-defined characteristics: Product Group, Product Line, and Product Category. The derivation for these characteristics is similar to the derivation for Product Hierarchy because each one of these characteristics is a part of the overall product hierarchy defined for Extreme Sports. The derivation table can be used for characteristics that can be defined by one of the master data tables in the pull-down list inside the table entry and for characteristics in which the primary key of the master data table can be defined by characteristics that occur in the line item table for the operating concern. In addition to these requirements, you can specify an offset to indent the entry and the field length that should be populated for the characteristic. In Extreme Sports's case, Product Group is the first five characters of the product hierarchy, Product Line is the next five characters, and Product Category is the last eight characters. Entries in the derivation table were made for these characteristics.

## Derivation Structures and Rules

Another form of derivation is achieved via derivation structures and rules. Generally, user-defined characteristics are derived this way. Derivation structures and rules use values of characteristics that have already been derived in order to derive the value of characteristics that haven't. In configuration, you define the derivation structure that is to be used by the derivation rule. The derivation structure defines the characteristic that is being derived as well as the characteristic(s) from which it is being derived. The derivation rule is maintained by the user and contains the values of the characteristics that combine to derive the value of the characteristic that is being derived. The best way to understand derivation structures and rules is to just jump in and set a few up to experiment with the process.

To access the configuration screen for derivation structures, select Profitability Analysis ➢ Master Data ➢ Define Characteristic Derivation ➢ Change ➢ Create Step ➢ Choose Derivation Rule, or use the transaction codes KEDR for the Create, Change, and Display of the Derivation Structure.

In this example, we want to create a derivation structure (transaction code KEDR). Click the Create Step button, and you'll see the Create Step pop-up box (see Figure 12.31). Choose the derivation rule option, which opens the rule definition screen.

**FIGURE 12.31** The Create Step pop-up box

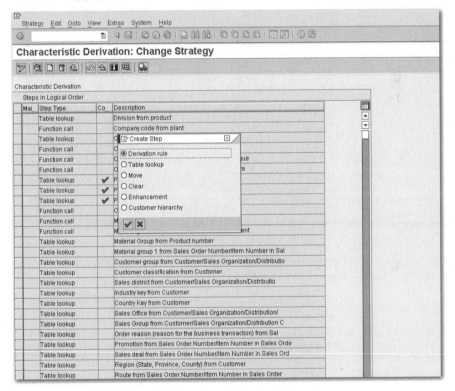

On the rule definition screen, you need to define a textual description (ES Trade Organization in our case). Press Enter, and you are taken to the Characteristic Derivation: Change Structure of Rule Definition configuration screen, shown in Figure 12.32.

**FIGURE 12.32** The Characteristic Derivation: Change Structure of Rule Definition configuration screen

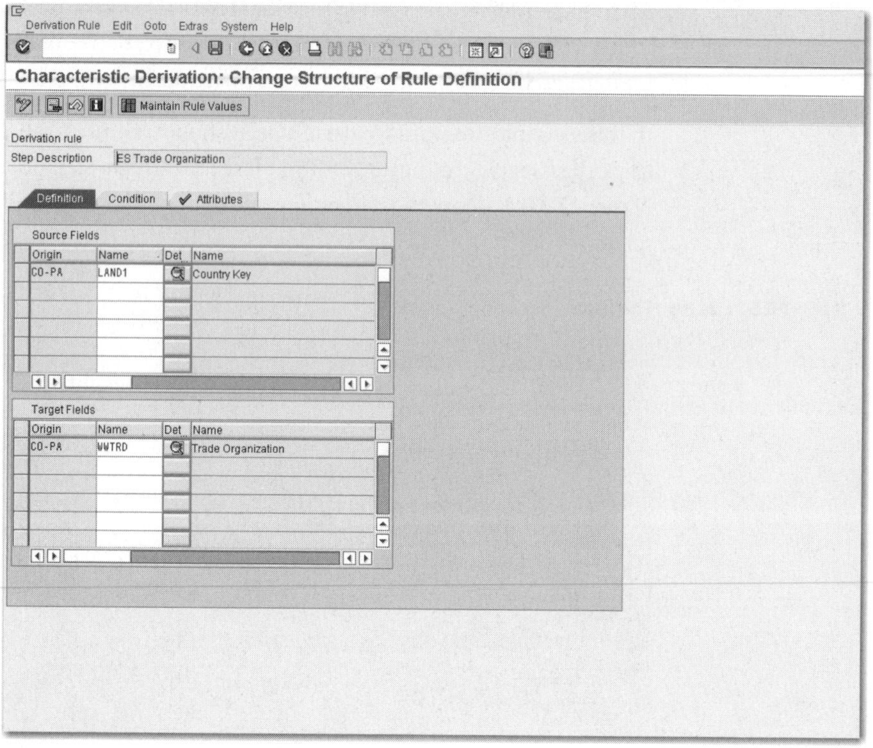

The fields in Figure 12.32 are explained here:

**Step Description**  Enter a description of the derivation step that will be used. Make sure that the description is consistent with the derivation process. For ease of maintenance, it is better to be able to review the descriptions to see what the derivation will be doing.

**Source Fields**  These fields contain the characteristics that you want to use to derive the value of the characteristic. You can define up to seven source characteristics per derivation structure. Remember, the more source characteristics you have, the more difficult it will be to derive the target since all of the source fields must be found.

**Target Fields**  These fields contain the characteristics that you are deriving. You can derive values for up to seven characteristics in one derivation structure. Normally, you will have only one target field.

Once you've entered the information, save the structure by clicking the save icon. Then click the Maintain Rule Values button to access the Maintain Derivation Rules screen shown in Figure 12.32. Once you access the Maintain Derivation Rules screen, you will see a screen that allows the entry of values for the derivation rule (see Figure 12.33).

**FIGURE 12.33** The table for configuring derivation rules

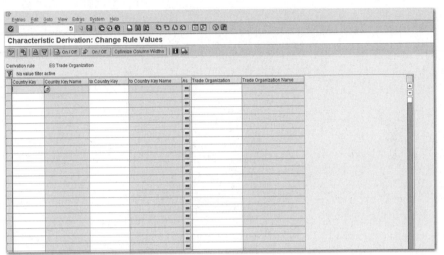

For each derivation structure that is created, a corresponding table is created in the database. The table name is K9xxx, where xxx is a sequential number that is used for naming the tables. You have the option of having the system automatically assign a table name, or you can manually assign it (the xxx numbers only). If you are using ALE, it is a good idea to assign the table numbers manually; otherwise, select the Automatically option. Extreme Sports will allow the system to assign table names automatically.

Before we populate our derivation rule (which is created via our derivation structure), we must maintain characteristic values for the user-defined characteristics that are involved in the derivation structure. You will remember from our discussion on CO-PA tables that the system generated check tables and text tables for each user-defined characteristic in operating concern ESOC. To populate the user-defined characteristic check and text tables, select Accounting ➤ Controlling ➤ Profit. Analysis ➤ Master Data ➤ Charact. Values ➤ Change Characteristic Values ➤ All Charact. On/Off, or you can use the transaction code KES1. Either way, you'll see the Change Characteristics Values selection screen shown in Figure 12.34.

**FIGURE 12.34** The Change Characteristics Values selection screen

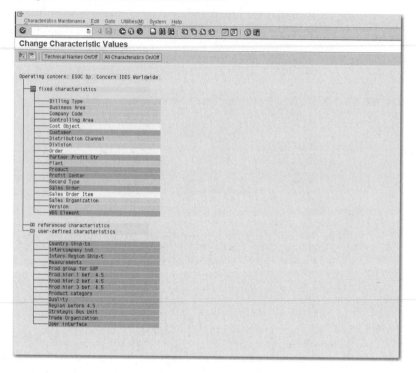

All characteristics, not just those that are user-defined, are available for selection. You have to be careful when maintaining characteristics that were created from the field catalog and reference tables. These characteristics are generated via a check table by the CO-PA system, but they are maintained by the key SAP table. When you create new entries for these characteristics, you are creating entries in the underlying configuration tables. Because these characteristics often deal with data from other parts of the system (not necessarily FI/CO), it is a good idea to not maintain characteristic values for these characteristics in CO-PA; because you create them here, they are available for use in the rest of the system. You should work in conjunction with the developers in charge of the part of the system from which the characteristic is generated to create the entry in the underlying configuration menu. All values currently in the underlying system table are available to CO-PA.

In this example, we will maintain characteristic values for our user-defined characteristic Trade Organization. In order to maintain values for this characteristic, just double-click on the name Trade Organization. After selecting the appropriate characteristic (Trade Organization) and pressing Enter, you are taken to the characteristic values screen.

**TIP** In the Change Characteristic Value screen, the fields are color coded. Choose Utilities ➢ Color Legend to find out which characteristics can be changed. The options include Jump to Transaction, Jump to IMG, and No Jump Possible. You can modify some of the characteristics here, but one like Customer or Product Hierarchy will be unavailable for change unless you are authorized to do so.

We have maintained two values for the user-defined characteristic Trade Organization: NAFTA and EU. These values will be used in our derivation rule. In the technical information on this screen, we see that we are actually maintaining check table T254A and text table T25E4, which were created when we activated our operating concern. You can also use the transaction code SM30 to access a similar screen for entering your characteristic values. In this case you will need to know the T25xx table.

We are now ready to populate our derivation rule. The derivation rule is the front end of the derivation structure that we created earlier. The derivation rule contains the values that make up the logic of the derivation. The derivation rule is typically maintained by the users and is accessed by choosing Accounting ➢ Controlling ➢ Profit. Analysis ➢ Master Data ➢ Maintain Derivation Rules ➢ Create. Alternatively, you can use the transaction code KEDE.

At this point, you are presented with the Characteristic Derivation: Change Rule Values initial screen, shown in Figure 12.35. Here you will fill in the combinations of values that will create the link between, in this case, the Country Key and the Trade Organization. This is the define portion of the derivation rule. We are mapping the values between the regions and the trade organization.

**FIGURE 12.35** The Characteristic Derivation: Change Rule Values initial screen

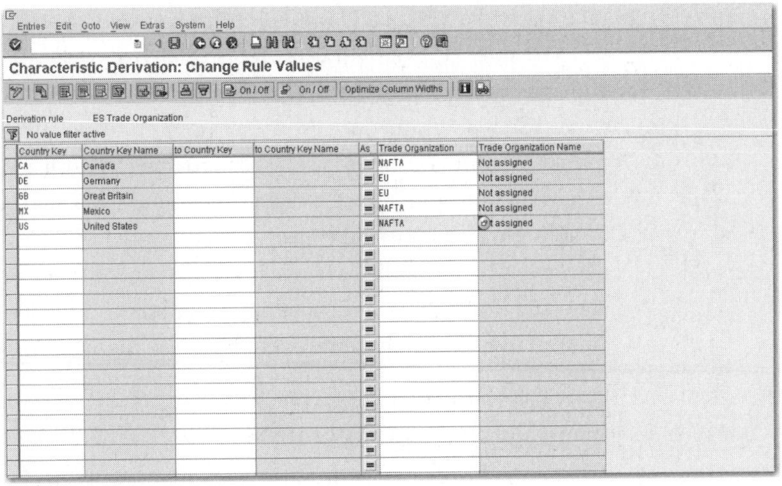

**EXTREME SPORTS DERIVATION STRUCTURES AND RULES CONFIGURATION ANALYSIS**

In this section, a second type of derivation was configured—derivation structure and rules. Derivation structures are simply the configuration behind derivation rules. They define what characteristics you will be using to derive the value of the target (derived) characteristic. Standard delivered (fixed) and additional characteristics from the field catalog and reference tables already have characteristic values maintained for them. User-defined characteristics require that valid values be maintained for them before they can be used in derivation rules and before the proper value name can be displayed in drill-down reporting. The user-defined characteristic Trade Organization had values maintained for it in this section. These values will be used in the derivation rule. The derivation rule (which is based on the derivation structure) was maintained so that different country values derive the trade organization (NAFTA or EU) from values entered in the Trade Organization characteristic value check table.

# User-Exit Characteristic Derivation

If the derivation table or derivation structures do not provide you with enough flexibility to derive all the characteristics you need, there is a third option: user-exit characteristic derivation.

SAP comes with two user-exits for characteristic derivation. The first exit is executed before other types of derivation take place (derivation table and derivation structures/rules). The second exit is executed after other types of derivation take place (derivation table and derivation structures/rules). You'll remember from Chapter 1, "Configuration Tools," that user-exits are delivered programs that you are free to program with your own logic. The user-exit code is called from a main SAP program; once the user-exit has finished processing, it returns to the main SAP program. These user-exits provide you with a lot of flexibility to provide values for complex user-defined characteristics that you might otherwise not be able to use. You should consult with one of your ABAP team members if you decide to use one of the user-exits. You can find out more about the user-exits by choosing Controlling ➢ Profitability Analysis ➢ Tools ➢ SAP Enhancements, or you can use the standard transaction code, CMOD, to view this screen.

Once you've accessed this screen, SAP delivers several standard exits. To find them, choose Utilities ➢ SAP Enhancements on the CMOD screen. In the Exit Name

field, enter the prefix COPA* to find the SAP delivered enhancements. You will
see that you have eight; one is specifically designed for derivations in CO-PA (see
Figure 12.36). This will help you develop your program for derivation.

**FIGURE 12.36** Repository Info System: Exits Find screen for CO-PA

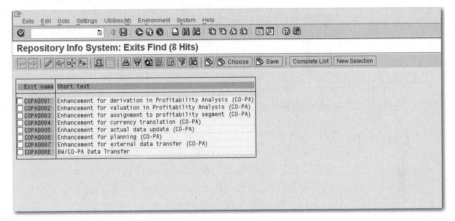

 **TIP**  Be sure to read the online IMG information about the CO-PA user-exits by double-
clicking the task name in the IMG. You will learn that there are user-exits other than just
the exits for characteristic derivation available to CO-PA.

# Assigning Values to Value Fields

You might still be asking yourself, "How do I get currency values into CO-PA if I
don't use cost elements or G/L accounts? What's the deal with these value fields?"
In this section, we explain in detail how you transfer currency and quantity values
to value fields. There are several approaches: mapping SD condition types to value
fields; the PA settlement structure, which maps cost element groups to value fields;
the Costing Sheets method, which uses business logic to derive the values required,
and the Material Cost Estimates method, which offers the ability to use the Material
master cost component structure to populate value fields in CO-PA; and cost center
to CO-PA assessments. Let's look at the most popular approaches to posting information to the value fields for CO-PA.

# Mapping SD Condition Types to Value Fields (the SD Interface)

As you learned earlier in this chapter, the majority of data that is transferred to CO-PA comes from the SD process, including the entire sales order process. One area in SD where we use conditions to represent different activities is in the process of creating a billing document (revenue, discounts, COGS, freight, and so on). The conditions are given values based on the configuration of each condition type (e.g., the Revenue condition type is set to $10/unit). You can also map quantity fields from SD documents to quantity value fields in CO-PA. This is a standard configuration process in CO-PA.

With a basic understanding of what condition types are, you are now ready to map condition types to value fields. This task is the first step in configuring the SD interface. You can open the configuration screen for mapping SD condition types to value fields by choosing Controlling ➤ Profitability Analysis ➤ Flow of Actual Values ➤ Transfer of Billing Documents ➤ Assign Value Fields. The pop-up offers several options, and the one we are looking to review is Maintain Assignment of SD conditions to CO-PA Value Fields. Double-click that option, or you can use the transaction code KE4I.

In the resulting screen, you are prompted to enter the ID of the operating concern that you are configuring. You are then taken to the map condition types to value fields configuration screen, shown in Figure 12.37.

The project team at Extreme Sports has already mapped SD condition types to value fields for operating concern ESOC. To map condition types to value fields, click the New Entries button. After doing so, you can select the correct condition type from the pull-down list (you will need to work in conjunction with your SD team to determine what condition types they are using). You then assign the condition type to a value field that you created earlier. The Transfer +/- field is used selectively in cases where an SD condition type could be either positive or negative; checking this box tells the system to bring those values in without changing the sign. If a condition type isn't mapped, you will get an error during billing document creation, and the accounting documents will not be created or posted.

**FIGURE 12.37** The map condition types to value fields configuration screen

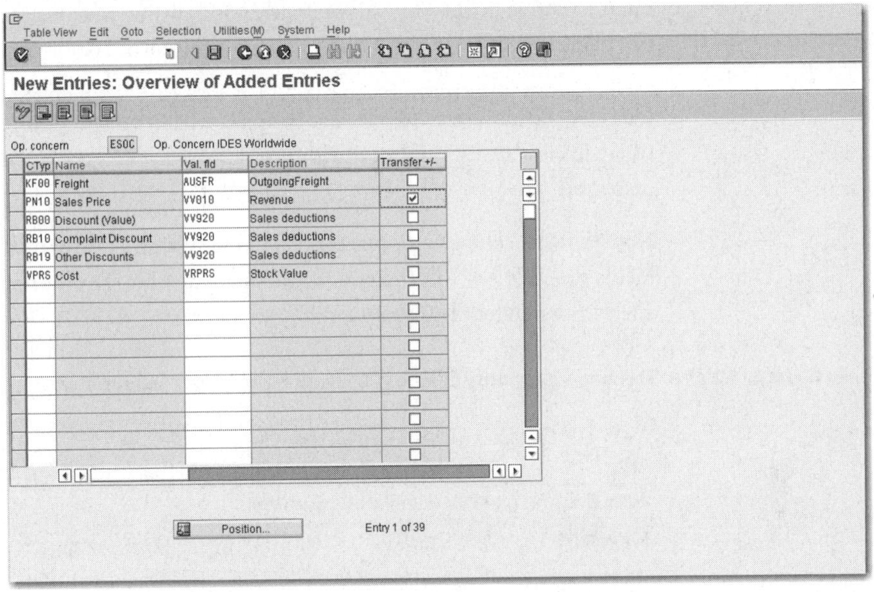

## EXTREME SPORTS MAPPING SD CONDITION TYPES TO VALUE FIELDS CONFIGURATION ANALYSIS

In this section, the SD condition types used by Extreme Sports were mapped to value fields in operating concern ESOC. As you can tell from the configuration, many different condition types can be mapped to one value field. Currently, Extreme Sports is using only standard-delivered condition types for the creation of billing documents. After discussions with the SD team at Extreme Sports, it was determined that the following conditions were being used for the reason specified:

| | |
|---|---|
| KF00 | Outgoing Freight |
| PN10 | Sales Price (Revenue) |
| RB00 | Sales Discounts |
| RB10 | Sales Discounts |
| RB19 | Other Discounts |
| VPRS | Cost (COGS) |

The condition types were mapped to their corresponding value fields in CO-PA. For condition type PN10, which was mapped to value field VV010 or ERLOS (Revenue; this is the standard technical name given to revenue by SAP), the Transfer +/– field was activated so that SD condition types that could have either a positive or negative sign will be transferred in net into CO-PA.

The next step in configuring the SD interface is to map SD quantity fields to CO-PA quantity value fields. You can open the configuration screen for mapping SD quantity fields to CO-PA quantity value fields by choosing Controlling ➢ Profitability Analysis ➢ Flow of Actual Values ➢ Transfer of Billing Documents ➢ Assign Quantity Fields; alternatively, use the transaction code KE4M. The map SD quantity fields to CO-PA quantity fields configuration screen, shown in Figure 12.38, is displayed.

Note that the configuration methods in the Assign SD Quantity Fields to Value Fields shortcut box affect a client-independent table. For more information on client-independent transports, refer to Chapter 1.

**FIGURE 12.38** The map SD quantity fields to CO-PA quantity fields configuration screen

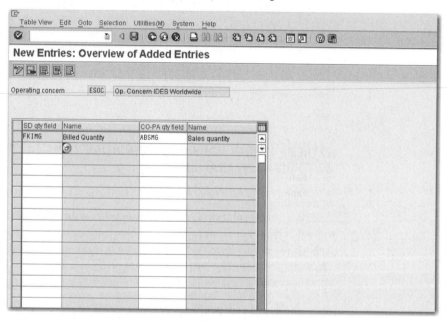

The configuration for this step is similar to the configuration for mapping condition types to value fields. You have the option of assigning the following quantity fields to CO-PA quantity value fields:

**BRGEW**   Gross Weight

**FKIMG**   Invoiced Quantity

**FKLMG**   Billing Quantity in SKU (Stock Keeping Unit)

**KBMENG**   Cumulative Confirmed Quantity

**KLMENG**   Cumulative Confirmed Quantity

**KWMENG**   Order Quantity

**LSMENG**   Required Delivery Quantity

**NTGEW**   Net Weight

**VOLUM**   Volume

The quantity fields that you use depend on your business requirements. The quantity value fields are used in calculations to determine profitability by sales quantity.

## EXTREME SPORTS MAPPING SD QUANTITY FIELDS TO CO-PA QUANTITY VALUE

In this configuration step, SD quantity fields were mapped to CO-PA quantity value fields. Currently, Extreme Sports is using only one quantity value field: (ABSMG) sales quantity. Additional quantity fields may be added at a later time. You do not need to be as judicious with creating value fields as you are when creating characteristics. It was determined that the SD quantity field FKIMG (Invoiced Quantity) best matched the quantity needs of Extreme Sports's profitability reporting requirements. FKIMB was mapped to value field ABSMG.

The final step in configuring the SD interface is to reset value fields. This activity is optional. This functionality is useful if you have certain types of billing documents that you do not want to transfer into CO-PA. A good example might be intercompany sales—you may not want intercompany data skewing your profitability on normal sales. You can access the configuration screen for resetting value fields by choosing Controlling ➢ Profitability Analysis ➢ Flow of Actual Values ➢ Transfer of Billing Documents ➢ Reset Value/Quantity Fields or by using transaction code KE4W.

After following one of the configuration transactions and clicking the New Entries button, you are taken to the reset value fields configuration screen, shown in Figure 12.39.

**FIGURE 12.39** The reset value fields configuration screen

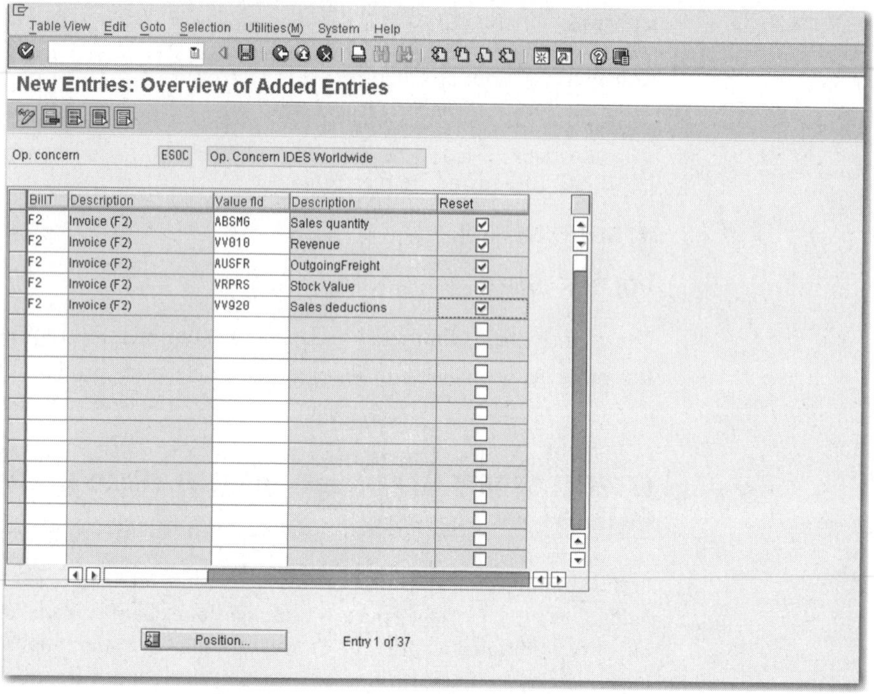

The configuration for resetting value fields is fairly straightforward. Simply select the value fields that are to be reset by billing document type and then click the Reset field. It is important to note that resetting a value field will not stop a CO-PA document from being created. The CO-PA document that SAP creates will contain characteristic values but will not have any values updated in the value fields that are reset. This can be a little confusing when you're reviewing accounting document updates from billing documents because, when you look at the reconciliation ledger, it will look like a CO-PA entry has been created and you'll see that a CO-PA document was created.

## EXTREME SPORTS RESET VALUE FIELDS CONFIGURATION ANALYSIS

Billing document type F2 is used by Extreme Sports to record intercompany sales and is not used for any other purpose. Extreme Sports management does not want to view intercompany sales information in CO-PA—they want the data in CO-PA to reflect profitability to external customers only. Because of this requirement, every value field was reset to 0 for billing document type F2.

# PA Settlement Structure

We covered the concept of CO settlement extensively in Chapter 11, "Internal Order Accounting." In this section, we will focus on the configuration needed for the PA settlement structure. You can use the PA settlement structure to transfer costs from FI and order-related accounting (internal, SD, SM, and PP).

SAP comes with two shell PA settlement structures: FI and SD. The FI settlement structure is the structure that is always used to transfer costs from FI postings to CO-PA. You can use the SD settlement structure or create your own. For order settlement, you assign the PA settlement structure to use in the settlement profile for a specific order type. The configuration of the FI PA settlement structure and other PA settlement structures is exactly the same (again, see Chapter 11 for details on this process). We will focus on the configuration of the FI PA settlement structure in this section. To get to the configuration screen for PA settlement structures, choose Controlling ➣ Profitability Analysis ➣ Flows of Actual Values ➣ Direct Posting from FI/MM from CO or use transaction code KEI2. The PA settlement structure listing screen opens (see Figure 12.40). Despite the menu path alluding to the FI PA settlement structure, as you can see, all PA settlement structures are listed in the PA settlement structure listing screen.

**FIGURE 12.40** The PA settlement structure listing screen

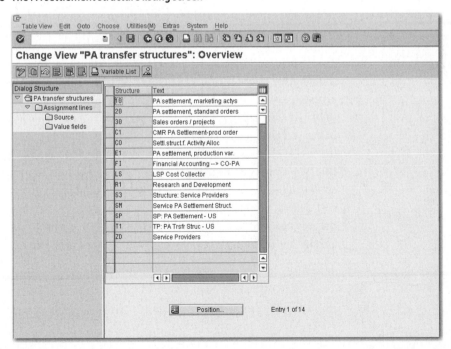

Configure the FI PA settlement structure by choosing FI—Financial Accounting ➢ CO-PA and then click Assignment Lines. You are taken to the PA settlement structure assignment configuration screen, shown in Figure 12.41.

**FIGURE 12.41** The Change View "Assignment Lines": Overview configuration screen

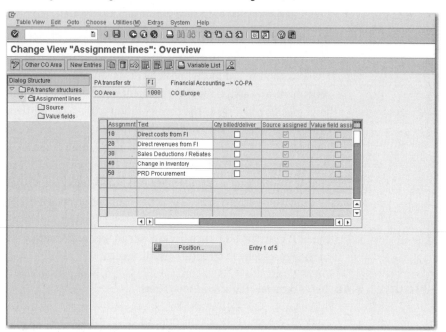

The PA field is for the PA assignment. After clicking the New Entries button, you should place a numerical entry in this field to distinguish this assignment from other PA assignments. Each PA assignment is allocated a cost element group, which in turn is assigned to a CO-PA value field. After deciding on a PA assignment field name, you enter a textual description of the type of values that are being transferred in the cost element group for this assignment. By selecting the Quantity Billed field, you can transfer quantity values from sales orders. After making the required entries in the PA, Description, and Quantity Billed fields, you are ready to assign a cost element group to the entry. To do so, select the PA assignment field by clicking the gray box next to the entry. Then click the Source button. You are taken to the PA Change View "Source": Details configuration screen, shown in Figure 12.42.

**FIGURE 12.42** The Change View "Source": Details configuration screen

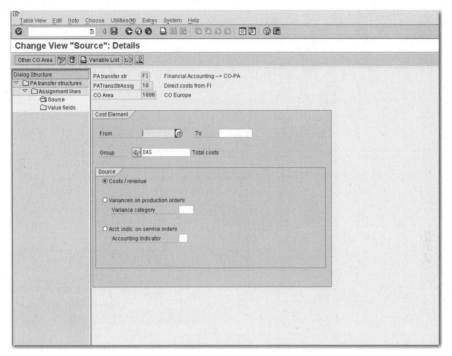

In the Cost Element Group field, use the pull-down box to select the Cost Elem Group entry. This tells the system that a cost element group is being used for the source (costs to settle; see Figure 12.43). In the Set ID field, enter the name of the cost element group that contains the cost elements you want to map in the PA assignment field. A cost element/cost element group can be assigned to only one value field. A value field, however, can have more than one cost element/cost element group assigned to it. The Description field defaults to the description of the cost element group. After entering this information, click the save icon and then click the green arrow to return to the PA settlement structure assignment configuration screen.

You are now ready to assign the cost element group that was assigned to the PA assignment field entry to a CO-PA value field. Begin by clicking the Value Fields option to the left of the screen shown in Figure 12.44. The assign settlement structure line to value fields configuration screen opens.

**FIGURE 12.43**  Display Cost Element Group box

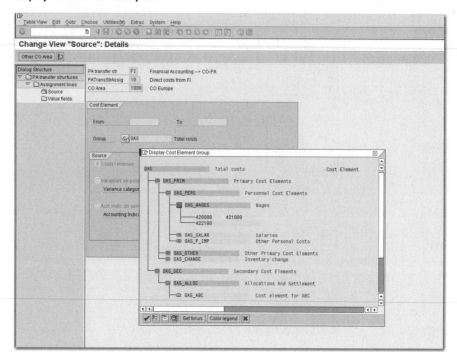

**FIGURE 12.44**  The New Entries: Overview of Added Entries screen

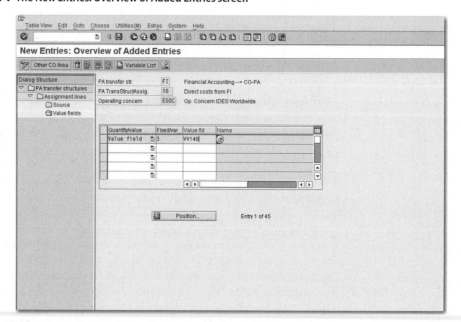

The fields shown in Figure 12.44 are explained here:

**Quantity/Value**   You have the option of selecting either a quantity or a value indicator (a single PA assignment field can be assigned to both a value field and a quantity field [for SD orders] by selecting the Quantity Billed field in the PA settlement structure assignment configuration screen and having a separate line item in this screen for both values and quantities):

1   Value Field

2   Quantity Field

**Fixed/Variable**   In SAP, you have the option of assigning fixed amounts, variable amounts, or the sum of fixed and variable amounts. If you want to be sure to pick up all values, select the Sum of Fixed and Variable Amounts option. The available entries are as follows:

1   Fixed Amounts

2   Variable Amounts

3   Sum of Fixed and Variable Amounts

**Value Fld (Field)**   Select the identifier of the value field in your operating concern to which you want to assign the cost element group. Click the field's pull-down menu to see a listing of available value fields.

Once you have filled out the fields, click the save icon to record all of your value assignments. Once you do, the configuration for the PA settlement structure is complete. You can always go back and add more entries to the structure if needed.

## EXTREME SPORTS PA SETTLEMENT STRUCTURE CONFIGURATION ANALYSIS

In this section, the FI PA settlement structure was configured for Extreme Sports. The only accounts that may receive a direct posting into CO-PA from FI are for promotional expenses. Because of this, PA assignment field 10 was created for promotional expenses. Because these are FI expenses and not revenues from SD orders, we did not select the Quantity Billed field. We mapped the cost element EXPROMO, which contains all of the promotional expense accounts for Extreme Sports, to PA assignment field 10 for promotional expenses. We assigned the cost element group OAS to value field VV140 (Promotional Expenses). These expenses are values, so we selected option 1 in the Quantity/Value field in the assign settlement structure line to value fields configuration screen. Extreme Sports wants all promotional expenses, regardless of whether they are classified as fixed or variable, mapped to CO-PA. Because of this requirement, we selected option 3 for the Fixed/Variable field. As Extreme Sports's business grows over the years, the FI PA settlement structure will be maintained to map additional types of expenses to CO-PA.

## Cost Center to CO-PA Assessments

We covered the concepts and configuration of cost center assessments in great length in Chapter 10, "Cost Center Accounting." In addition to those cost center assessments, you can run cost center assessments into CO-PA. This is a good way to transfer CO expenses that are part of your profitability reporting into CO-PA. Instead of having a receiving cost center, internal order, or cost object, you have a receiving profitability segment (and value field). Some companies choose to transfer all of their P&L (income statement) reporting out of the CO-PA module. The cost center to CO-PA assessment functionality is a necessary tool for this process. We recommend that all costs have a cost center or internal order as the real account assignment object. You should then settle the costs from the internal order or assess the costs from the cost centers into CO-PA. Making CO-PA the real account assignment object for costs and making the cost center or internal order the statistical posting is a messy proposition that has a profound impact on your ability to correct erroneous postings. So, in this scenario your initial posting would be to the cost object—cost center or IO—and then a follow-up allocation or settlement to CO-PA. This process of posting to CO-PA is not *absolutely* necessary, but use this approach if you want to obtain the most complete income statement possible.

The concept of cost center assessments has already been covered, so we will focus on the differences between a normal cost center assessment and a cost center to CO-PA assessment. In this section, the IMG path is the preferred navigation. However, you can also get there through the SAP application menu. To begin customizing cost center to CO-PA assessments, follow the application menu path Controlling ➢ Profitability Analysis ➢ Actual Postings ➢ Period—End Closing ➢ Transfer Cost Center Costs/Process Costs ➢ Assessment (this will take you to the initial screen for executing an assessment cycle; the transaction code for this is KEU5). Once you have accessed this screen, choose Extras ➢ Cycle ➢ Create/Change/Display, or if you want to go directly to Create, use transaction code KEU1. If you are looking to use the Change process, that transaction code is KEU2.

After choosing the Create option you are presented with a screen asking you for the name of the cycle as well as its start date. This screen should be familiar to you from your work in Chapter 10. Enter the cycle name and start date. You will then see the CO-PA Create Actual Assessment Cycle: Header Data screen (Figure 12.45).

**FIGURE 12.45** The CO-PA Create Actual Assessment Cycle: Header Data screen

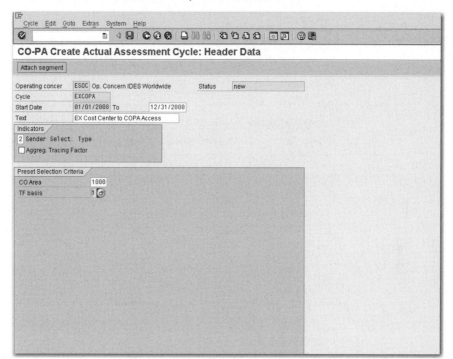

As you can see, the only three fields that are different from the fields on the normal cost center assessment header data screen are the CO (controlling area) field, the sender select type (fixed/var cost split) and the Tracing Factor field. In the CO Area field, enter the identifier of the controlling area to which the operating concern is assigned. In the Tracing Factor field, enter 1 for costing-based CO-PA or 2 for account-based CO-PA. After entering the required header information, clicking the save icon, and then clicking the Attach Segment button, you will see the CO-PA Create Actual Assessment Cycle: Segment screen, shown in Figure 12.46.

This screen should look somewhat familiar to you as well. It is the same as the segment configuration screen for normal cost center assessments, with a few exceptions. We will cover the exceptions here. For a detailed explanation of the rest of the fields, refer to Chapter 10. The Fixed Value Field and Val. Fld Var Cst are required fields. In them, you specify the value field that fixed costs should be posted to and the value field that variable costs should be posted to, respectively. Normally, the value field is the same (but it does not have to be) for both fixed and variable costs. If you have configured a PA Transfer Structure, you can use that object here also. Rather than filling in the two value fields, you can just use the PA Transfer Structure field, fill it in with your structure, and all assignments of value fields will be completed.

**FIGURE 12.46** The CO-PA Create Actual Assessment Cycle: Segment screen

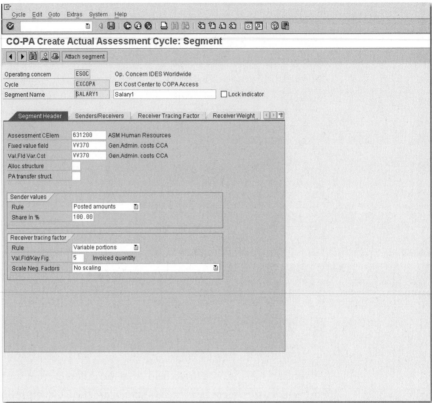

The other difference involves the receiver fields. The only valid receiver for this type of assessment is a profitability segment. You are able to maintain the exact profitability segment that you want to post to. The remaining characteristics for operating concern ESOC appear further down the screen. You are free to define virtually every characteristic except for some of the SAP-delivered characteristics, such as Company Code and Business Area. These characteristics are derived in the normal fashion (through standard delivered CO-PA core ABAP code). This is a perfect scenario to drive home the idea that CO-PA is a reporting tool. In this case, the allocation that is being developed may have a record that could have only 5–8 different characteristics assigned, such as Company Code, Cost Center, and Controlling Area. You can expand this list of characteristics and have a record that can truly help you with your Gross Margin calculations; enhance the granularity of the record by assigning additional characteristics, or better yet, have the system derive additional characteristic links automatically.

**EXTREME SPORTS COST CENTER TO CO-PA CONFIGURATION ANALYSIS**

The configuration of cost center to CO-PA assessments is similar to the configuration of normal cost center assessments. The differences lie mainly in assigning a value field(s) and a profitability segment as your receiver values. Some companies use the cost center to CO-PA assessment functionality to bring overall costs into CO-PA for full P&L reporting. Extreme Sports will use cost center to CO-PA assessments for a limited number of expenses from specific cost centers.

# CO-PA Planning

CO-PA planning provides lots of functionality to allow you to produce the type of planning your company needs. Some of the standard features include:

- ▶ The ability to copy actual values to a plan version

- ▶ The ability to copy values from one plan version to another plan version

- ▶ Top-down distribution to spread a plan to lower characteristic levels based on past history

- ▶ The ability to transfer plan data to Sales and Operation Planning (SOP) or do additional integrated planning

In terms of importance, CO-PA planning is as important as the actual reporting information. If you were to discuss the concepts of planning and budgeting with anyone in a corporation, you would find that it's something that most people realize they need, but since running a business is even more critical, much of the time planning and budgeting is allocated to just one specific time during the year.

CO-PA planning is probably the most integrated and flexible planning solution within ECC. Since you are collecting information from numerous areas within ECC, it only stands to reason that the planning process can be as complex as you want it to be or as detailed as necessary to run your business. As far as required planning goes, CO-PA planning is not required, unlike CCA planning where in some cases it is a required component to create information for activity types which in turn are required by production planning to create standard costs. But if we look at the whole planning process and in terms of the corporate planning process it's the only toolset that will fill the bill for a overall planning component that will pull everything together for planning activities. CO-PA planning can be high level (you can plan the sales information for the year), or it can be detailed (you plan the promotion activities by period for the combination of products, product groups, regions, company codes, and divisions). We could go on and on about the benefits of planning and the toolset that CO-PA offers, but let's just say that you should review your company's needs in this area and see what options are possible in CO-PA.

The standard functionality just described is by and large end-user functionality that requires zero to very little configuration. Most of the configuration steps for planning were shown in Chapter 10. In the following sections, we will address those essential areas that have already been covered, showing the CO-PA menu paths and transactions to achieve the same configuration, as well as some planning configuration unique to CO-PA.

## Planning Versions

We covered planning versions in detail in Chapter 10. You can have several planning versions activated for a controlling area in a single fiscal year. How you use the planning versions depends on the functionality needed by your company (client). CO-PA versions, or the concept of versions, are a bit different than in other areas of CO. In the other areas of CO, version 0 is where actual data is always posted, and planned data is posted to other versions that are created. In CO-PA both actual and planned data are assigned a value in the Indicator characteristic and if you want to assign a version to the planned data you will have to create the new version and assign it to the planned values. To create planning versions for CO-PA, choose Controlling ➢ Profitability Analysis ➢ Planning ➢ Initial Steps ➢ Maintain Versions or use the transaction code OKEQ (remember this transaction code from Chapter 10?). As you'll recall, we discussed these various parameters and covered the requirements for CO-PA planning earlier.

The only other item we'll mention is the actual use of a version. It's interesting to review what a "version" can do for you. Most of the time we think of the version as a placeholder for a slice of information such as current plan or future plan, but the idea of tagging a set of data with a version can be more useful. Versions can be used as a time characteristic, for example, assigning a version to a snapshot of a weekly rolling forecast. Or, the version can also be assigned to a person so that each person can have his or her own different views of the plan. It is not unusual to see a planner having five or more different versions to tag their plan data. Keep this in mind as you review the proposed uses of the versions.

## Planning Revaluation

As with cost center planning revaluation, CO-PA planning revaluation allows you to change plan data without manually rekeying the plan. (We explored this functionality in Chapter 10.) To configure CO-PA planning revaluation, choose Controlling ➢ Profitability Analysis ➢ Planning ➢ Current Settings ➢ Planning Aids ➢ Revaluation Keys ➢ Maintain or use transaction code KEF1 (Create). Once at the revaluation create screen, you assign a revaluation key—a three-digit identifier—to your revaluation and then assign the value fields and the percentage adjustment required. Using revaluation in the planning process will allow you to automatically recalculate a series of value fields. For example, let's say at the beginning of the plan cycle your corporation has defined a specific series of adjustments for all areas; for example, to increase sales by 12% and decrease costs by 5% (see Figure 12.47). If we use this approach, we can automatically assign the appropriate increase/decrease amounts to each of the value fields being planned on.

**FIGURE 12.47**  The Change View "Assign Factors": Overview screen

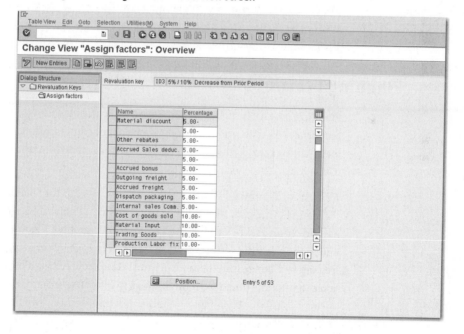

## Planning Layouts

Planning layouts allow the user to enter plan data into the system. The planning layout formulates the screen in which the user enters data. Configuring CO-PA planning layouts is similar to configuring cost center planning layouts, with the exception of the menu path and the table used to create them. One other thing you should know about CO-PA planning layouts is that whatever you define as the profitability segment to be planned becomes the selection screen for the planning layout. All pieces (characteristics) of the profitability segment defined by the planning layout must be entered on the selection screen. This means you may need more than one planning layout if you want to plan at different levels within CO-PA. Some companies do not plan down to the most detailed level; instead, they keep planning at a higher level. They then use CO-PA top-down planning functionality to "drive-down" and spread the plan to lower-level characteristics. To reiterate: To do top-down planning and distribution, you must have all characteristics involved in each level of planning if you want to be able to assign the characteristics required. For example, if you are distributing down from year to month, you will need month in the planning process if you want the posting to be assigned properly.

As we mentioned earlier, the only configuration differences between cost center planning layouts and CO-PA planning layouts is the menu path and the table used to create them. To create CO-PA planning layouts, choose Controlling ➤ Profitability Analysis ➤ Planning ➤ Manual Entry of Planning Data ➤ Define Planning Layout, or you can use transaction code KE14 (Create), KE15 (Change), and KE16 (Display).

## Planning Profiles

Planning profiles tie planning layouts together with the application area to which they relate. As with previous sections, the detail configuration of planning profiles is the same as the configuration covered in Chapter 10 for cost center accounting.

To configure CO-PA planning profiles, choose Controlling ➤ Profitability Analysis ➤ Planning ➤ Planning Framework ➤ Aids for Changeover to the Planning Framework ➤ Display Planner Profiles. You will be asked to either review authorization groups or display CO-PA planner profiles. Choose the latter option, and in the resulting screen adjust the view to change by selecting Table View ➤ Display ➤ Change (or you can use transaction code KP34). From the main menu you can find this under Current Settings in Planning.

## External Data Transfer

Finally...a piece of planning we haven't covered before! CO-PA allows you to use external data transfer functionality to transfer both plan and actual data into CO-PA from files created by external systems. This of section focuses on the external transfer of plan data. Configuring actual external data transfer is exactly the same; only the SAP-delivered upload programs differ.

The first piece of configuration needed for external data transfer is your external data transfer structure. The external data transfer structure is a table that you (or your Basis team) create. The table is used during the upload program to store data and map fields to profitability segments and value fields. You are free to choose what you put into the table—you definitely need all of the characteristics and value fields that you want to plan with. It doesn't hurt to include more, and it probably isn't a bad idea to include all characteristics and value fields while you are creating the table.

In addition to the characteristics and value fields that you are planning on, you must include the version field for planning external data transfer. You are required to enter the proper version on the upload program screen. To create the table, you must have a developer's key. Depending on your project, you may or may not have a developer's key, and your Basis team may or may not want you to create tables. Instead of describing how to create tables, we will focus on looking at the SAP standard delivered external data transfer structure. Although you probably can't use this structure—the characteristics and value fields in your operating concern will more than likely differ from the example table—you can use it as a starting point and possibly make a copy and then tweak that copy. To create an external data transfer structure, choose Controlling ➤ Profitability Analysis ➤ Tools ➤ Data Transfer Between CO-PA and Other Systems ➤ CO-PA External Data Transfer ➤ Define Structure of External Data, or use transaction code KE4D.

You are taken to the create external data transfer structure screen (Figure 12.48), which is the basic ABAP Dictionary: Initial Screen for creating a database table.

**FIGURE 12.48** The create external data transfer structure screen

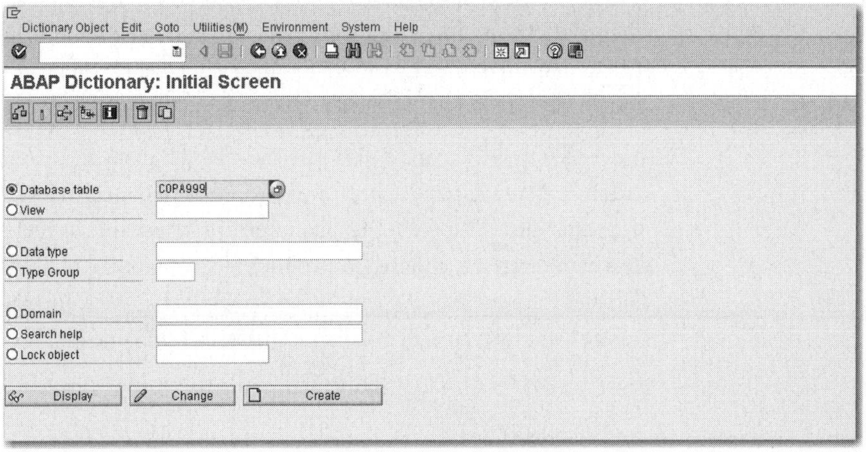

Instead of creating our own external data transfer structure, we will view the sample external data transfer structure. Click the Display button to open the display table/structure data dictionary screen, shown in Figure 12.49.

**FIGURE 12.49** The display table/structure data dictionary screen

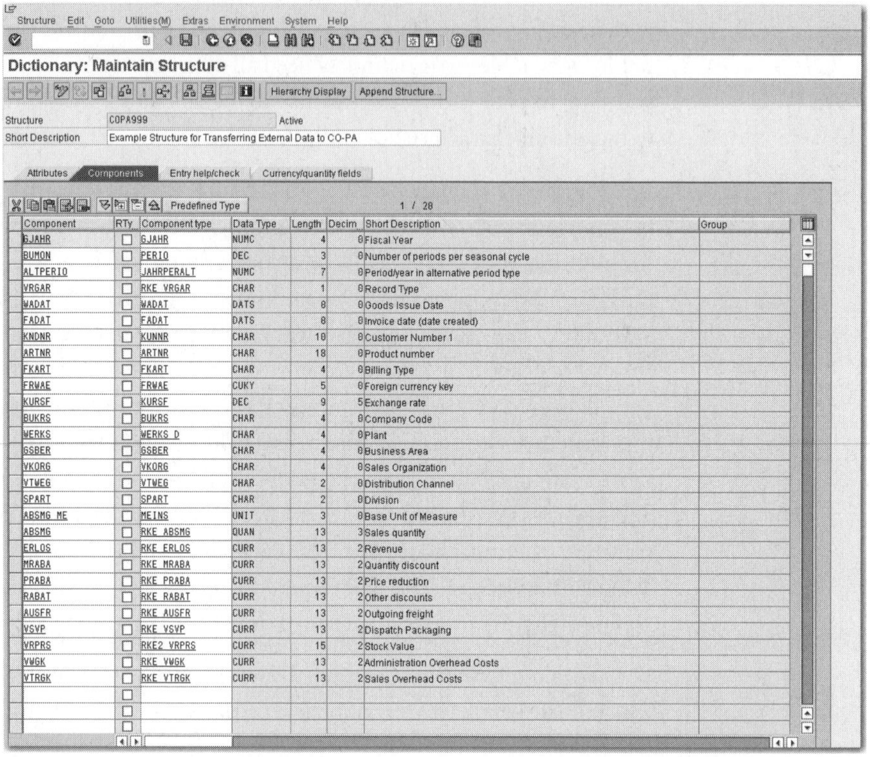


| Component | RTy | Component type | Data Type | Length | Decim | Short Description | Group |
|---|---|---|---|---|---|---|---|
| GJAHR | ☐ | GJAHR | NUMC | 4 | 0 | Fiscal Year | |
| BUMON | ☐ | PERIO | DEC | 3 | 0 | Number of periods per seasonal cycle | |
| ALTPERIO | ☐ | JAHRPERALT | NUMC | 7 | 0 | Period/year in alternative period type | |
| VRGAR | ☐ | RKE_VRGAR | CHAR | 1 | 0 | Record Type | |
| WADAT | ☐ | WADAT | DATS | 8 | 0 | Goods Issue Date | |
| FADAT | ☐ | FADAT | DATS | 8 | 0 | Invoice date (date created) | |
| KNDNR | ☐ | KUNNR | CHAR | 10 | 0 | Customer Number 1 | |
| ARTNR | ☐ | ARTNR | CHAR | 18 | 0 | Product number | |
| FKART | ☐ | FKART | CHAR | 4 | 0 | Billing Type | |
| FRWAE | ☐ | FRWAE | CUKY | 5 | 0 | Foreign currency key | |
| KURSF | ☐ | KURSF | DEC | 9 | 5 | Exchange rate | |
| BUKRS | ☐ | BUKRS | CHAR | 4 | 0 | Company Code | |
| WERKS | ☐ | WERKS_D | CHAR | 4 | 0 | Plant | |
| GSBER | ☐ | GSBER | CHAR | 4 | 0 | Business Area | |
| VKORG | ☐ | VKORG | CHAR | 4 | 0 | Sales Organization | |
| VTWEG | ☐ | VTWEG | CHAR | 2 | 0 | Distribution Channel | |
| SPART | ☐ | SPART | CHAR | 2 | 0 | Division | |
| ABSMG_ME | ☐ | MEINS | UNIT | 3 | 0 | Base Unit of Measure | |
| ABSMG | ☐ | RKE_ABSMG | QUAN | 13 | 3 | Sales quantity | |
| ERLOS | ☐ | RKE_ERLOS | CURR | 13 | 2 | Revenue | |
| MRABA | ☐ | RKE_MRABA | CURR | 13 | 2 | Quantity discount | |
| PRABA | ☐ | RKE_PRABA | CURR | 13 | 2 | Price reduction | |
| RABAT | ☐ | RKE_RABAT | CURR | 13 | 2 | Other discounts | |
| AUSFR | ☐ | RKE_AUSFR | CURR | 13 | 2 | Outgoing freight | |
| VSVP | ☐ | RKE_VSVP | CURR | 13 | 2 | Dispatch Packaging | |
| VRPRS | ☐ | RKE2_VRPRS | CURR | 15 | 2 | Stock Value | |
| VWGK | ☐ | RKE_VWGK | CURR | 13 | 2 | Administration Overhead Costs | |
| VTRGK | ☐ | RKE_VTRGK | CURR | 13 | 2 | Sales Overhead Costs | |

This screen is the same display (Data Dictionary Display) that we discussed in Chapter 1. The required characteristic and value fields are included in the table. Be sure to map all of the characteristics and value fields you need (including the version characteristic) in your table.

The next step is to create a data interface, which maps the external data transfer structure that you just created to your operating concern. When running the upload program, you will specify the data interface instead of the table to be used. To create a data interface, choose Controlling ➢ Profitability Analysis ➢ Tools ➢ Data Transfer Between CO-PA and Other Systems ➢ CO-PA External Data Transfer ➢ Define Data Interface, or you can use transaction code KEFA.

Note that the configuration of a data interface is client independent. After entering the data interface screen you will see the Sender Structure Maintenance CO-PA: Transaction Data screen. This screen shows a standard delivered sender structure that we will review (see Figure 12.50). Choose Sender Structure AC99000 and click the display icon to access the details (see Figure 12.51). Here you can see that this can be set up for either costing-based or account-based CO-PA and either actual or plan data.

**FIGURE 12.50** The Sender Structure Maintenance CO-PA: Transaction Data configuration screen

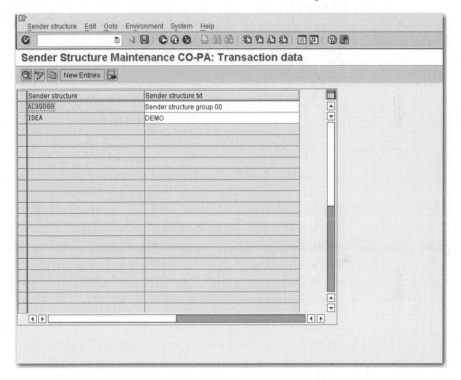

In this screen, if you are going to create another sender structure table, you need to create a one-character identifier and a description for your sender structure. Then use the fields on this screen to tie this sender structure to the external data transfer structure you just created, as well as to your operating concern. So, at this point you have a data dictionary table that you created and have assigned to a sender structure. Now you only have to assign the sender structure to a transfer rule, and in the transfer rule, map the given fields. We outline this process next.

**FIGURE 12.51**  The Sender Structure Maintenance CO-PA: Transaction Data—display of the detail screen

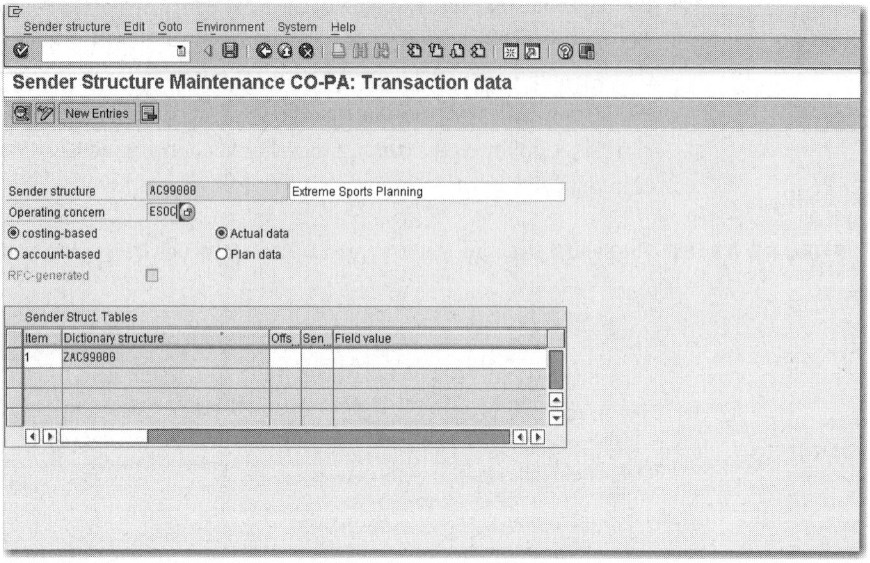

The third and final configuration step for external data transfer is to define your field assignment using a transfer rule. Defining your field assignments simply involves mapping fields from the external data transfer structure (table) to corresponding characteristic and value fields in your operating concern. Doing so allows the upload programs to post data to the correct places in your operating concern. Let's begin by choosing Controlling ➤ Profitability Analysis ➤ Tools ➤ Data Transfer between CO-PA and Other Systems ➤ CO-PA External Data Transfer ➤ Maintain Transfer Rules, or you can use transaction code KEFD.

You are prompted to enter the sender structure that you just created. Enter the sender structure (AC99000 in our example), and you are taken to the maintain field assignments configuration screen, shown in Figure 12.52.

The configuration for this step is fairly simple. Choose the corresponding CO-PA field name (in the Rec. Field column for the characteristic or value field) for each field in the external data transfer structure (in the Sender Fld Val column). You need to map the characteristics and value fields that you are going to use—both your user-defined characteristics and value fields and the standard delivered characteristics. The mapping process holds true only if you use the same data elements in your external data transfer structure that SAP uses in the CO-PA tables.

**FIGURE 12.52** The Maintain Rules configuration screen

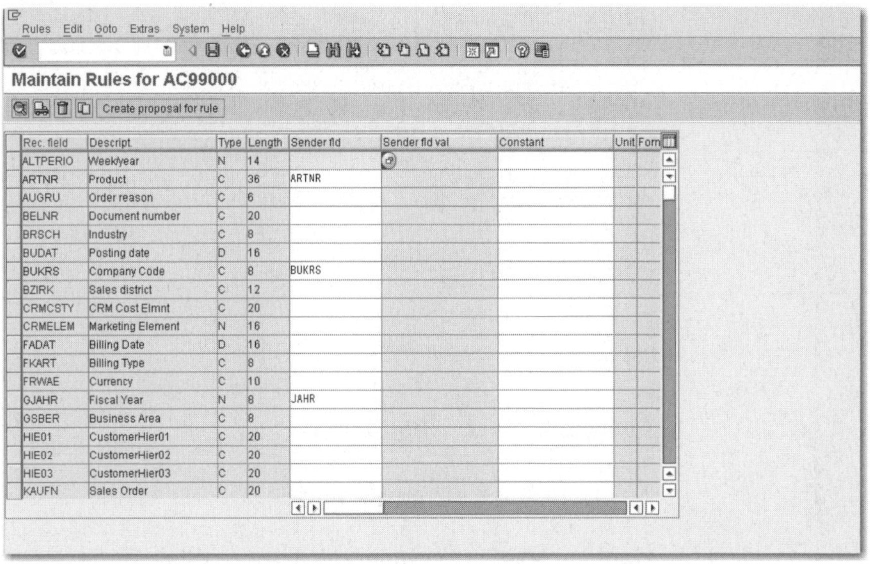

Rules   Edit   Goto   Extras   System   Help

**Maintain Rules for AC99000**

Create proposal for rule

| Rec. field | Descript | Type | Length | Sender fld | Sender fld val | Constant | Unit | Form |
|------------|----------|------|--------|------------|----------------|----------|------|------|
| ALTPERIO | Week/year | N | 14 | | | | | |
| ARTNR | Product | C | 36 | ARTNR | | | | |
| AUGRU | Order reason | C | 6 | | | | | |
| BELNR | Document number | C | 20 | | | | | |
| BRSCH | Industry | C | 8 | | | | | |
| BUDAT | Posting date | D | 16 | | | | | |
| BUKRS | Company Code | C | 8 | BUKRS | | | | |
| BZIRK | Sales district | C | 12 | | | | | |
| CRMCSTY | CRM Cost Elmnt | C | 20 | | | | | |
| CRMELEM | Marketing Element | N | 16 | | | | | |
| FADAT | Billing Date | D | 16 | | | | | |
| FKART | Billing Type | C | 8 | | | | | |
| FRWAE | Currency | C | 10 | | | | | |
| GJAHR | Fiscal Year | N | 8 | JAHR | | | | |
| GSBER | Business Area | C | 8 | | | | | |
| HIE01 | CustomerHier01 | C | 20 | | | | | |
| HIE02 | CustomerHier02 | C | 20 | | | | | |
| HIE03 | CustomerHier03 | C | 20 | | | | | |
| KAUFN | Sales Order | C | 20 | | | | | |

## EXTREME SPORTS EXTERNAL DATA TRANSFER CONFIGURATION ANALYSIS

Extreme Sports will use external data transfer functionality to load plan data into CO-PA. The plan data will be created in other systems and then exported to a sequential file. The sequential file will then be uploaded into CO-PA via the upload program, which will use the external data transfer structure that is created. To configure this functionality, we need an external data transfer structure and an assignment group, and we can then map fields of the external data transfer structure to CO-PA fields (characteristics and value fields).

# The Planning Framework in CO-PA

To complete the setup of planning in CO-PA, let's review the planning framework that CO-PA requires for planning purposes. This framework is different from any of the other areas and gives the planning process in CO-PA a bit more structure and sequence. The planning framework consists of several objects, and we will define each here (see Figure 12.53). We use these objects to manage the planning process and organize the planning activities. Since the technical names of each of the objects are not identified in Figure 12.53, we will reference a specific item in the screen and work through these objects based on that individual grouping.

**FIGURE 12.53** The initial Planning Framework: Overview screen

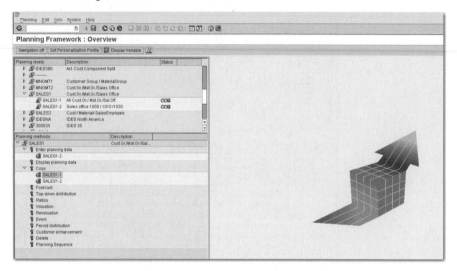

**Planning level** A planning level is something like SALES1 in Figure 12.53 (upper portion of the screen). You use the panning level to determine the granularity level at which planning is to occur. You do this by specifying the characteristics and value fields for planning at this level. You can also identify the characteristic values that you are going to plan on at this level as well as use variables (see Figure 12.54).

**FIGURE 12.54** The Planning Framework: Overview for planning levels

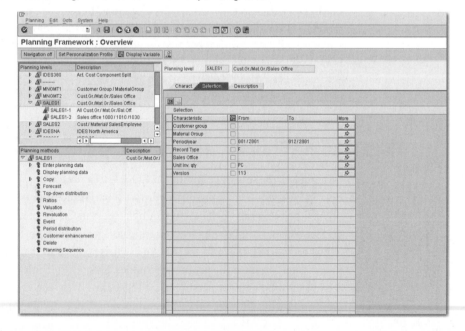

**Planning package**    A planning package is something like SALES1-1 in Figure 12.53 (upper portion of the screen). You can specify characteristic values in a planning package. In this way, you determine the market segment for which planning is to take place for a particular time period. A planning package can be seen as a work package that determines which planning objects are relevant to a specific planner (see Figure 12.55).

**FIGURE 12.55** The Planning Framework: Overview for planning packages

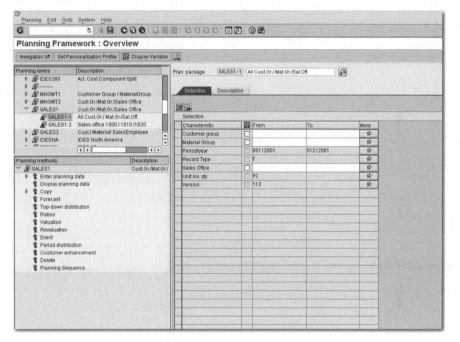

**Planning method**    A planning method is something like Enter Planning Data or Copy in Figure 12.53 (lower section of the screen). Several standard delivered planning methods are available. These are programs that require parameters to be executed—the parameter set. You can see the list of planning methods in Figure 12.56.

**Parameter set**    In Figure 12.53 a parameter set is something like SALES1-2 (found below the Enter Planning Data). The parameter set contains all of the settings necessary for executing a planning method: reference data to be copied, the period shift (if necessary), the specific characteristic values that the data will use for the transfer process, and whether the data will be simply copied or overwritten (see Figure 12.57).

**FIGURE 12.56** The Planning Framework: Overview for planning methods

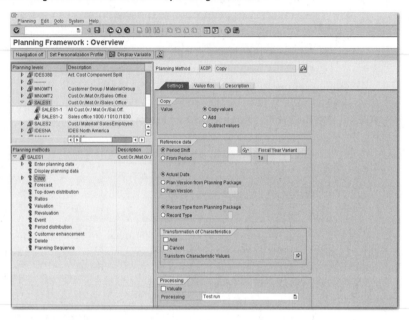

**FIGURE 12.57** The Planning Framework: Overview for a parameter set

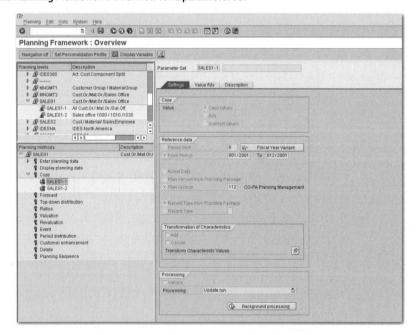

Once this framework is set up, the system is ready for the business user to start the planning process.

# Integrated Planning in CO-PA

Another area where CO-PA offers functionality that we haven't seen in other areas is in the integration of the planned data from CO-PA with all other areas of the ECC system. If we were to consider the position of CO-PA in the planning process, it would basically be at the beginning and end of the planning circle. Initially, CO-PA would deliver high-level information about Sales to SOP (Sales and Operations Planning), which is accomplished with an automatic feed of data into SOP. Once that is done, the start of the entire integrated planning process through Sales and Distribution begins. Next, planned data is fed into Production Planning with Material Requirements Planning (MRP) and Master Production Scheduling (MPS). In these areas, planning is completed on the material and production requirements. Once this is complete, we automatically feed the results into Cost Center Planning for cost analysis. Once we're done in CCA with the planned of activity type values for hourly rates, we take the data and transfer it into the Standard Costing process to complete the standard product cost values. We then take all of that information and roll it up into the CO-PA process to analyze the COGS, comparing standard COGS to what the high-level corporate report requires for gross profit margin. This complete process is beyond the scope of this book, but we will review some of the basics and let you go from there. Begin by choosing Controlling ➢ Profitability Analysis ➢ Planning ➢ Integrated Planning to open the screen shown in Figure 12.58.

**Transfer quantities to SOP**   You can transfer a sales plan from CO-PA into Sales and Operations Planning. Sales quantities can either be transferred by individual products or by product groups. You can use any combination of characteristics and time frames as selection criteria for the transfer. Note that you need to have a unit of measure involved with this transfer process to be successful. You can follow the menu path as described earlier or use the transaction code for this activity (KE1E).

**Transfer plan values to LIS**   The interface between CO-PA and LIS allows for a number of ways to transfer data between these two components. The transfer of information is a two-way highway in this case. Once the planned quantities are available, you can then transfer this information from CO-PA into LIS infostructure tables. Once any additional information is available in the LIS infostructures, you can transfer data back into CO-PA. If you decide to use a combination in the transfer process from CO-PA and SOP to LIS, you can only transfer quantities;

however, going from CO-PA directly to the LIS tables, you can transfer both quantities and amounts. You can use the menu path or the transaction code for this activity (KE1K).

**Transfer plan values to EC-PCA, FI-GL (New), or FI/SL**     You can transfer planning data periodically from CO-PA to these three different components of ECC by assigning the value or quantity fields in CO-PA to the accounts in G/L accounting, Special Ledgers, or Profit Center Accounting. In these transfers, you must use both the Controlling Area and Company Code characteristics since they are critical organizational elements of all these modules. These transfers also require that you set up additional derivation steps to identify the combinations of Controlling Area, Company Code, PCA, and the value field versus the General Ledger (GL) Account. In terms of value fields and GL accounts, if we are going to transfer planning data between CO-PA and FI, we have to map the appropriate value fields to the GL accounts that are going to be receiving the planned data. To review the remaining data transfer options, you can follow the same menu path as above, or you can use the transaction code (for EC-PCA, the code is KE1V; for FI-GL (New), the code is KE1Z; and for FI/SL, the code is KE1Y).

**FIGURE 12.58** Displaying integrated activities from the main menu

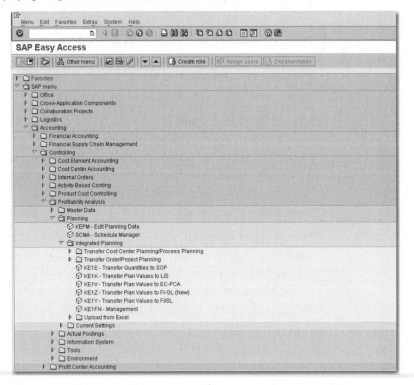

## Planning Number Ranges

As is always the case, don't forget to assign number ranges. We've covered configuring number ranges several times in this book. The unique feature of CO-PA planning number ranges is that you must assign each record type—F (Billing), D (Cost Center Costs), and so on—to an interval. To configure number ranges for CO-PA planning, follow the configuration (IMG) menu path Controlling ➤ Profitability Analysis ➤ Planning ➤ Initial Steps ➤ Define Number Ranges for Planning Data, or you can use transaction code KEN2.

# Activating CO-PA

Costing-based CO-PA was activated for controlling area EX01 in Chapter 8, "Controlling Enterprise Structure." CO-PA must be activated in the controlling area before it will work. You can also activate CO-PA in the controlling area by using the IMG menu path Controlling ➤ Profitability Analysis ➤ Flows of Actual Values ➤ Activate Profitability Analysis or using the transaction code KEKE. Four options are available:

**Blank – Component Not Active**    Neither type of CO-PA will be available on this controlling area.

**2 – Component Active for Costing-Based Profitability Analysis**    Only the costing-based CO-PA is active.

**3 – Component Active for Account-Based Profitability Analysis**    Only the account-based CO-PA is active.

**4 – Component Active for Both Types of Profitability Analysis**    Both types of CO-PA are active.

In addition to activating CO-PA in the controlling area, you must assign the controlling area to an operating concern. A controlling area can be assigned to only one operating concern, but one operating concern can be assigned to several controlling areas. To assign your controlling area to an operating concern, follow the IMG menu path Enterprise Structure ➤ Assignment ➤ Controlling ➤ Assign Controlling Area to Operating Concern or use transaction code KEKK.

The assign controlling area to operating concern configuration screen appears (Figure 12.59).

**FIGURE 12.59** The assign controlling area to operating concern configuration screen

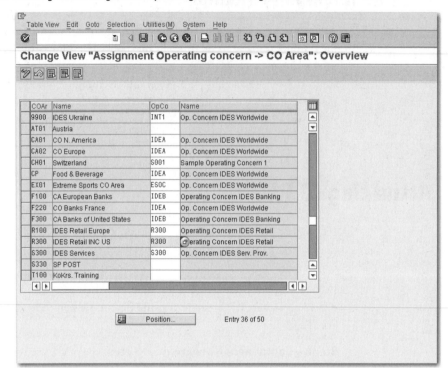

Again, don't forget to assign number ranges. You need to assign number ranges for actual CO-PA postings. To do so, choose Controlling ➤ Profitability Analysis ➤ Flow of Actual Values ➤ Define Number Ranges for Actual Postings or use transaction code KEN1.

# CO-PA Reporting

So, what do we do with all of the profitability data that we're capturing in our CO-PA structures? How can you report off CO-PA data? Very simply, with one of the neatest tools in all of SAP: drill-down reporting. Drill-down reporting affords you the flexibility to slice and dice your CO-PA data any way you want, based on your defined profitability segments, of course. Drill-down reporting can also be used in a few other submodules, such as Investment Management and Treasury (of course, CO-PA data and profitability segments are not used in these submodules).

Drill-down reporting lets you choose the characteristics and value fields that you want to report off. With CO-PA reporting, you can also drill-down on a characteristic to see other characteristic values associated with it (for example, all materials sold to a specific customer).

We'll focus in this section on creating drill-down reporting, not on using the report. Once you build your sample report, be sure to play around with it by running it and trying different drill-downs and features that are delivered in the report. There are numerous approaches to using these reports and the report formats. We have found that as you start to create these reports, you will continue to discover more and more uses and additional functionality that is available. In this section we just get you started with the reporting process.

Generally, there are two different types of CO-PA drill-down reports: basic reports and form reports. *Basic* reports allow you to select a limited number of variables, the characteristics you want, and the value fields you want. Immediately after you do these tasks, your report is ready to be executed. This is a great approach to reviewing your information and allows you to validate the data that was posted. The display of the basic report is generally simpler than that of the form report, and you are more limited in what you can do. *Form* reports allow you to arrange the data and perform calculations in ways that basic reporting does not allow. In this section, we will create a form report. Once you learn how to create a form report, creating a basic report will be a piece of cake. Keep this in mind: whatever you can do in terms of creating form reports or basic reports for your summary information, you can do against the line item level information. Just remember that reporting against line item level information can adversely affect system performance. Therefore, you might develop a strategy (for example, executing line item level reports only during specific times of the day).

## Key Figure Schemes

Using key figure schemes is optional, but we recommend you do. Key figure schemes allow you to create different "buckets" for your value fields. In other words, you can combine and perform calculations on different value fields to come up with a line structure element to use in a report. When creating a report or form, you are allowed to use either value fields or a key figure scheme. Key figure schemes ensure consistency in reporting. For example, suppose you define the element Net Revenue. Whenever you choose to use Net Revenue in a report, you know that the report is performing the same Net Revenue calculation as all other reports that use that element. It can be frustrating when it appears that you are reporting the same information in more than one report and you get different results. By using key figure schemes, you can avoid this situation.

Now that you have a basic understanding of what a key figure scheme is, you are ready to create one. Begin by following the IMG menu path Controlling ➤ Profitability Analysis ➤ Information System ➤ Report Components ➤ Define Key figure schemes or using transaction code KER1.

In the screen that appears, click the New Entries button and you are taken to the key figure scheme overview screen, shown in Figure 12.60.

**FIGURE 12.60** The key figure scheme overview screen

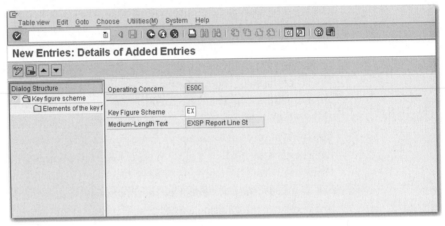

Give your report line structure a two-character identifier in the Key Figure Scheme field and a description in the Medium-Length Text field. Double-click the navigation item on the left called Elements of the Key Figure Scheme. The Change View "Elements of the Key Figure Scheme": overview configuration screen appears (Figure 12.61).

Key figure schemes contain elements, which are formulas that combine value fields. As you can see in Figure 12.60, the key field for each line is key figure scheme (EX in this case) and element (Elmnt). To create a new element, click the New Entries button to access the new line element overview screen, shown in Figure 12.62.

**FIGURE 12.61**  The key figure scheme configuration screen

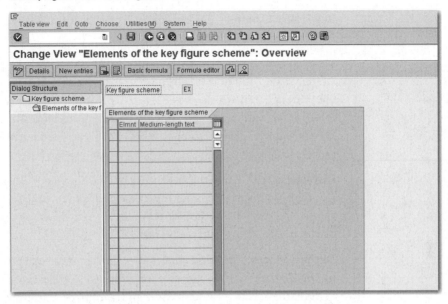

**FIGURE 12.62**  The new line element overview screen

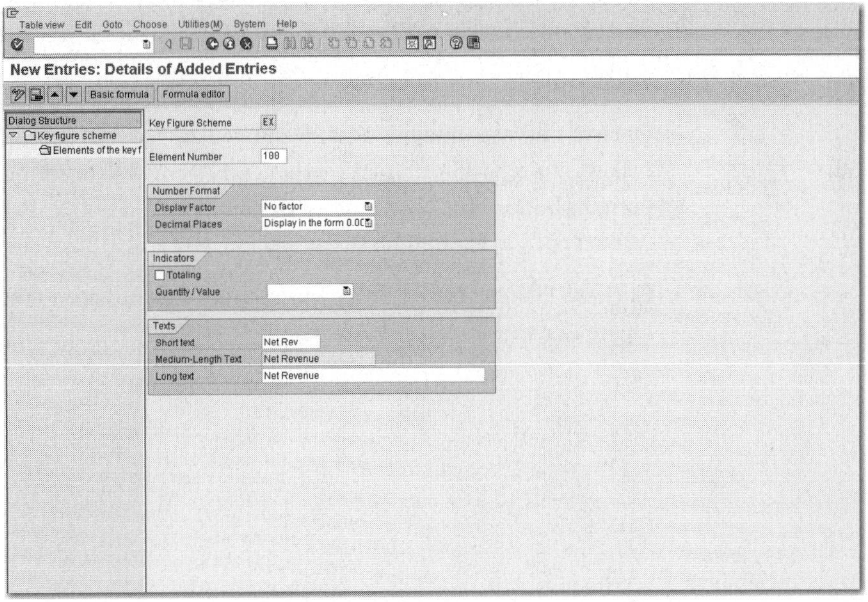

Let's examine the fields shown in Figure 12.62:

**Key Figure Scheme**    The key figure scheme identifier default is based on the key figure scheme you selected for processing.

**Element Number**    This is the identifier that makes the formula unique. CO-PA values are automatically numbered by the system in the number range 9001 through 9999 (this is the final activity that is system generated at the time of saving, activating, or generating the operating concern). This means that you have the number range 1 through 8999 available to you for naming your structure elements.

**Display Factor**    Using this field, you can force the values displayed by this element to default to a display factor for this element. If you leave the field null, the actual value will display. Using the pull-down arrow on this field, you can make the values display in 10s, 100s, 1000s, and so on.

**Decimal Places**    This field controls the number of decimal places displayed for this element. You can choose from 0 through 5. The entry Display Decimals in the Form 0.00 in our example specifies that two decimal places be displayed.

**Indicators**    The fields in the Indicators section—Totaling and Quantity/Value— can be chosen if you are using a user-defined ABAP program to perform formula calculations. You do not need to maintain these fields if you aren't.

**Texts**    In the Texts fields, enter descriptions of what the element is used for.

Once you have maintained these fields, you are ready to define the formula that makes your report line structure element. To create your formula, click the Basic Formula button. The New Entries: Details of Added Entries basic formula overview screen appears (Figure 12.63).

Click the Element field drop-down, and the element selection screen shown in Figure 12.64 appears.

**FIGURE 12.63** The New Entries: Details of Added Entries basic formula overview screen

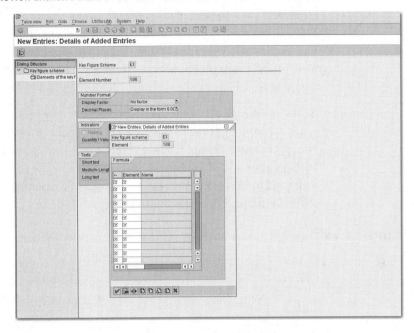

**FIGURE 12.64** The element selection screen

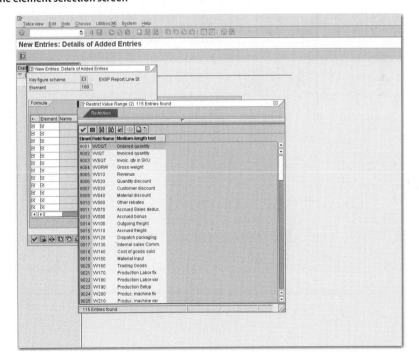

As you can see, all of the value fields in operating concern ESOC have been given an element value between 9001 and 9999. At this point you will select each value field that you want to use in your formula by double-clicking on it. It will default into the New Entries screen, and the values are added to the key figure scheme element basic formula overview screen (Figure 12.63). The updated screen is shown in Figure 12.65.

As you can see, all of the selected value fields are returned to the overview screen. A + sign appears beside each value field, indicating that the values have been added. You can, however, change the sign in this screen to a − sign to subtract values. Multiplication and division can be performed using the Formula Editor option, which will be explained later in this section. The Net Revenue element basic formula screen for Extreme Sports is shown in Figure 12.66.

**FIGURE 12.65** The updated line structure element basic formula overview screen

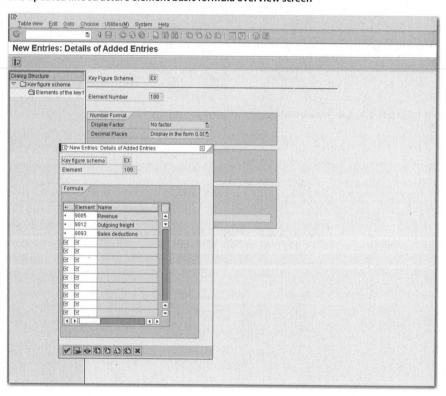

**FIGURE 12.66** The Net Revenue element basic formula screen for Extreme Sports

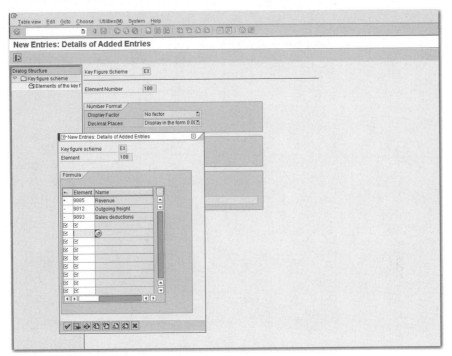

After entering your formula, click the Confirm button (Check icon). You are returned to the new line element overview screen (Figure 12.62). It is now possible to select the element that you just created (in addition to value fields) when you create formulas for new elements.

In the preceding example, we created the formula element by using the basic formula option. You can also use the Formula Editor option to create more complex formulas that use multiplication and division as well as addition and subtraction (which is used in basic formulas). The basic configuration for another element (101, Net Revenue/Unit) has already been created. As its name implies, we need to perform division to create this element. This can be accomplished by using the Formula Editor. The simplest way to do this is to select the elements you want to use via the Basic Formula button. Do not be concerned with the + and – signs at this point. After you use the Basic Formula button to select the proper elements and you return to the new line element overview screen, click the Formula Editor button. You are presented with the line element Formula Editor configuration screen, shown in Figure 12.67.

**FIGURE 12.67** The line element Formula Editor configuration screen

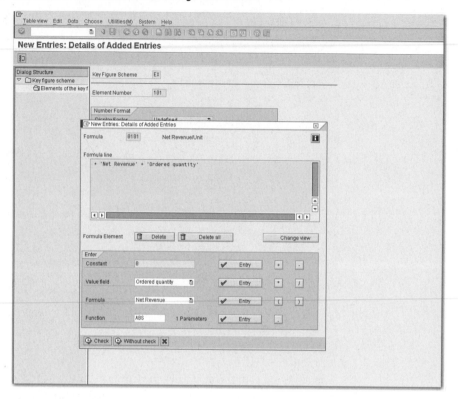

The elements selected—100 (Net Revenue) and 9001 (Order Quantity)—are already in our formula and are being added together. Because it is a formula, a Z is added before each element identifier. This can be seen if you adjust the view by clicking the Change View button on the Formula Editor. From the Formula Editor screen, you can change the + sign to a / sign to divide Net Revenue by Sales Quantity. Do not forget that each formula ends in a semicolon (;). The system defaults to the semicolon, but if you're not careful, it's pretty easy to overwrite it. The edited formula for Net Revenue/Unit is shown in Figure 12.68.

**FIGURE 12.68** The edited formula for Extreme Sports

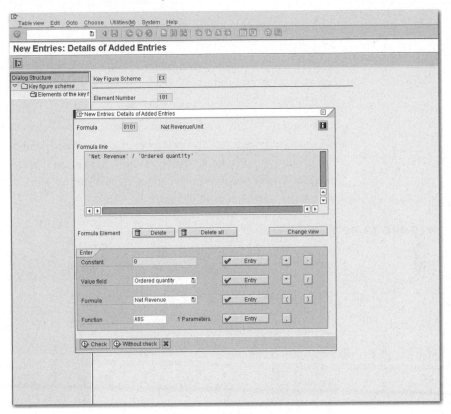

## EXTREME SPORTS REPORT LINE STRUCTURE CONFIGURATION ANALYSIS

Key figure schemes will be in all profitability reports created for Extreme Sports. This approach will ensure consistency in reporting. You learned that you can use both basic formulas and the Formula Editor to combine and perform calculations on different values to create key figure scheme elements. Once you create an element, it can be used in the formula for other elements. Two of the elements of Extreme Sports's key figure scheme structure EX were configured in this section. Additional elements that were not shown were also created to be used later in reporting.

# Forms

Forms allow you to group data and perform calculations in the way that you want on a report. They also define the variables that are used to select data, as well as whether you are bringing plan values, actual values, or both. When you create a report, you reference a form (in our example). Each report can use only one form, but a form can be used by many reports.

Let's jump in. To create a form, choose Controlling ➢ Profitability Analysis ➢ Information System ➢ Report Components ➢ Define Forms ➢ Define Forms for Profitability Reports, or use the transaction code KE34 (Create), KE35 (Change), or KE36 (Display). You are taken to the Report Painter: Create Form configuration screen, shown in Figure 12.69.

**FIGURE 12.69** The Report Painter: Create Form configuration screen

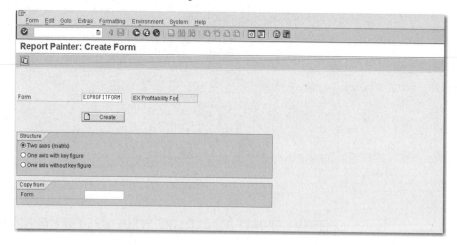

In this screen, you need to define a form identifier (EXPROFITFORM in our example) and enter a description for the form (EX Profitability For in our example). You will also notice that you have the option of creating one of three types of forms:

▶ Two axes (matrix)

▶ One axis with key figure

▶ One axis without key figure

The two-axes form is by far the most flexible of the three types. Using the matrix form (two axes), you are able to define both the row and column structure of your report. In this type of form, you can choose characteristics, value fields, elements of a report line structure, predefined elements, or a formula. As always, you choose the characteristics to be used by the drill-down structure in the report creation itself. We will use a matrix form in our example.

The "one axis with key figure" form allows you to define either the row structure or the column structure. The default screen is to define rows, but you can define columns instead by selecting Goto ➤ Column Display from within the form. In this type of form, you can choose value fields, elements of a report line structure, predefined elements, or a formula.

The "one axis without key figure" form allows you to define either the row structure or the column structure. The default screen is to define columns, but you can define rows instead by choosing Goto ➤ Row Display from within the form. In this type of form, you cannot choose value fields or elements of a report line structure; you can only choose characteristics.

Now let's continue with our example and create our matrix form. From the Report Painter: Create Form configuration screen (Figure 12.69), click Create and you are presented with the Report Painter: Create Form definition configuration screen shown in Figure 12.70, which will help you create the CO-PA form.

**FIGURE 12.70** The Report Painter: Create Form definition configuration screen

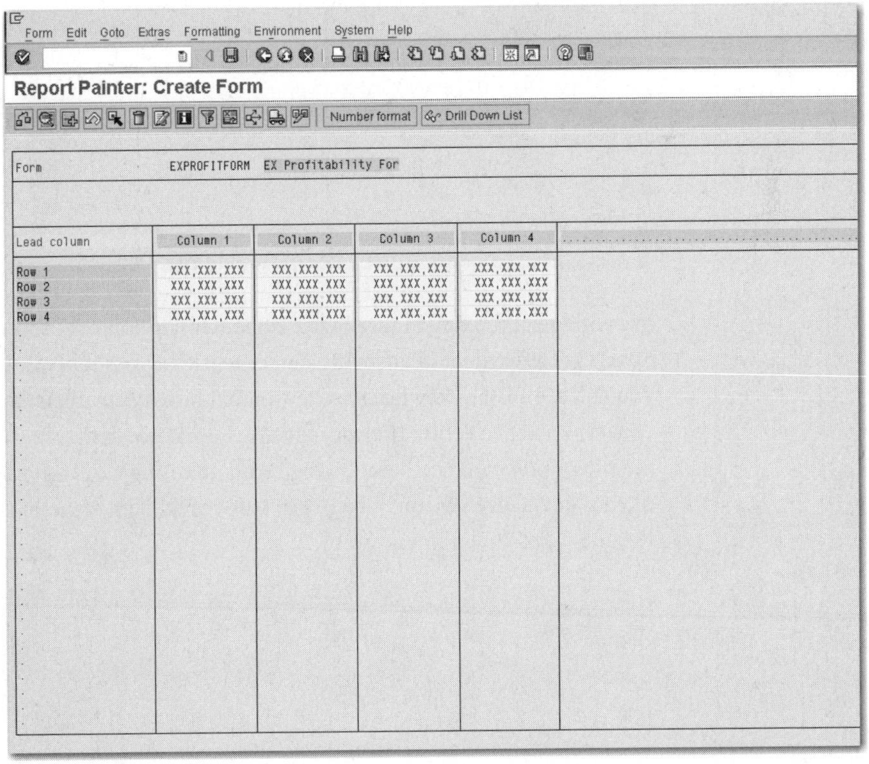

You are free to create both the row and column structures of the report because this is a matrix (two axes) report. When you create your row and column structure, you are creating your detail list. For this form, Extreme Sports would like the detail list to resemble a normal financial statement with different values listed as the rows and Actual, Plan, and Variance Amounts as the columns. Let's begin by defining our rows. Double-click the field that says Row 1. The Select Element Type pop-up box appears, as shown in Figure 12.71.

**FIGURE 12.71** The Select Element Type pop-up box

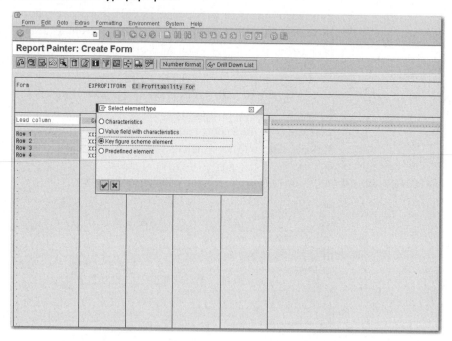

We will select the Key Figure Scheme Element option in accordance with Extreme Sports's requirement of ensuring data integrity across reports. Press Enter, and you will see a list of key figure schemes that have been created for your operating concern. After selecting the appropriate report line structure (EX in our case) and pressing Enter, you will see a dialog box containing a drop-down list of the elements of your key figure scheme. The initial value is the first element that we created—Net Revenue—as shown in Figure 12.72.

**FIGURE 12.72** The listing of elements in the value fields pop-up screen

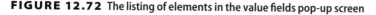
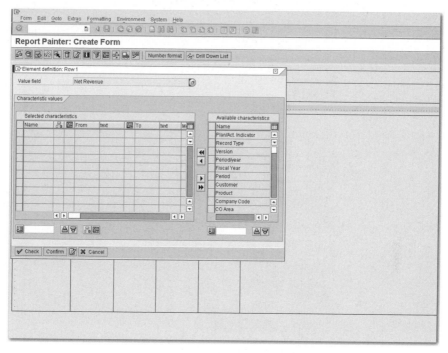

This information should look familiar; these are the same elements (plus a few) that we created for our key figure scheme. In this example, we will select the Net Revenue element radio button. To the right of the Net Revenue field is a list of characteristics from our operating concern. You can use these characteristics to add filters to this row if you desire. For our example, you only need to select characteristics that are unique to the key figure scheme element. You can also select characteristics in the column structure (for plan and actual values in this example), and define characteristics that relate to the entire form in the general data selection of the form (the general data selection will be explained later in this section).

For the purposes of this form, you do not need to select any characteristics with the report line structure elements that are being selected for the row structure. Just click the change text icon (which looks like a pencil and paper) in the element definition window, and you are presented with the Text Maintenance pop-up screen, as shown in Figure 12.73.

**FIGURE 12.73** The Text Maintenance pop-up screen

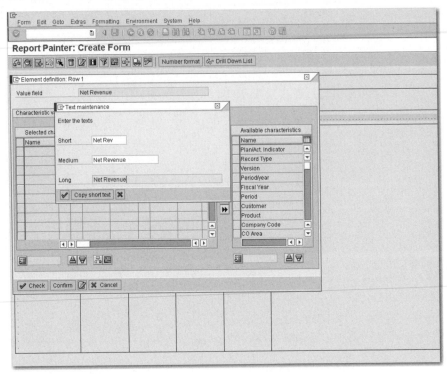

You are free to define the short, medium, and long textual descriptions for your row. After you enter the text values and press Enter, the row is fully defined for your form. We will continue creating the rows that are needed by our form.

We are now ready to define the column structure for our form. To begin creating the column structure, double-click the Column 1 field in the Report Painter: Create Form configuration screen. The Select Element Type pop-up screen appears, except this time you can choose only between characteristics and predefined elements because you used the key figure option (value fields or elements of a report line structure) in our row definition. You cannot mix and match the two within a single row or column structure; it must be one or the other. We will choose the Characteristics radio button and press Enter. The characteristic selection screen (see Figure 12.74) appears. This time, however, we will choose the Plan/Act. Indicator option and other characteristics.

**FIGURE 12.74** The characteristic selection screen

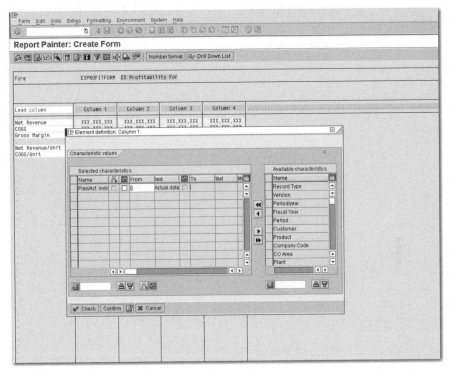

You are allowed to assign a single value to the characteristic value or define the characteristics as a variable. In this example, we have entered a single value, 0, for actual data. You could also specify the value 1 for plan values. However, if you specify plan values, you must also select the characteristic version so you can specify the plan version from which the values should be selected. (Variables will be covered when we discuss general data selections later in this section.) After entering your characteristic values and clicking the change text icon, you are presented with the Enter Text Maintenance pop-up screen. Enter the text for the column and press Enter. The column is defined for your report, and you are returned to the create CO-PA form definition configuration screen. We created the Plan Data column in the same way we did the Actual Data column (except we selected the Version characteristic in addition to the Plan/Act. Indicator characteristic, and in the Characteristic Values screen, we selected 1 for plan data in the Plan/Act. Indicator characteristic and 0 for plan version 0 in the Version characteristic). You are now ready to create the Variance column, which will utilize a formula.

To create the Variance column, double-click the Column 3 field (we already used column 1 for actual data and column 2 for plan data). You are presented with the Select Element Type pop-up box, except this time the choices are characteristics, predefined elements, or formulas (see Figure 12.75). Select the Formula radio button and press Enter. The Enter Formula pop-up box appears (Figure 12.76).

**FIGURE 12.75**  The Select Element Type pop-up box

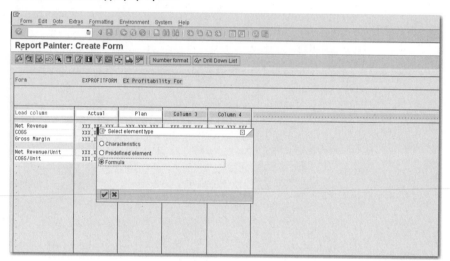

The columns that we have already defined are available for use in the formula, and we can perform addition, subtraction, multiplication, and division in our formulas. In this example, we'll subtract the plan data value from the actual data value to produce the result for our Variance column, which we are currently defining. After entering your formula and pressing Enter, you are presented with the now familiar Enter Texts pop-up screen. Enter your text and press Enter, and you are returned to the create CO-PA form definition configuration screen.

The entire row and column structure for the form is now complete (see Figure 12.77).

**FIGURE 12.76** The Enter Formula pop-up box

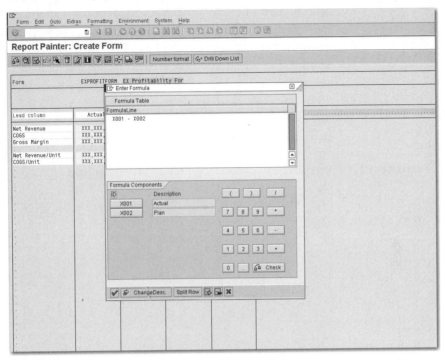

**FIGURE 12.77** The complete row and column structure for form EXPROFITFORM

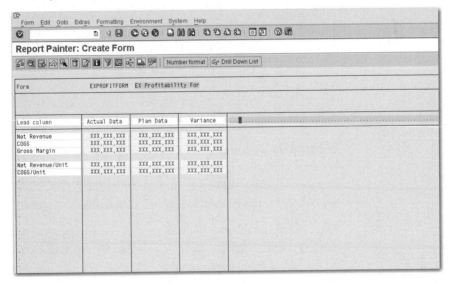

The next piece of configuration that is needed to complete our form is the general data selection. The general data selection defines the information that is needed by the entire form. In the general data selection of the form, you are able to choose various characteristics your form will use. To define your general data selection, choose Edit ➤ General Data Selection ➤ General Data Selection on the form creation screen. When the familiar characteristic selection screen opens, you'll note the only difference is that the characteristics that were selected for the row or column structure are not available for selection in general data selection. Figure 12.78 shows the characteristic values for general data selection screen.

**FIGURE 12.78** The characteristic values for general data selection screen

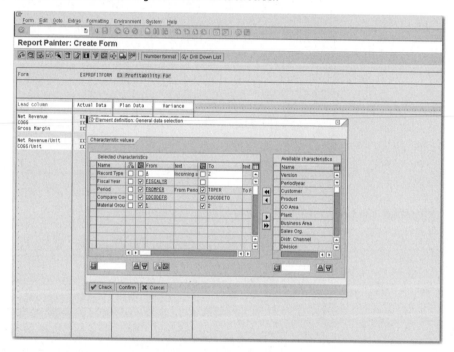

Note that the configuration in the characteristic values for general data selection screen is somewhat different from the configuration in the characteristic values screen that we saw earlier. We have used variables for some characteristic values in this situation. There are two types of variables: local variables and global variables.

Once global variables are defined, they can be used by reporting forms in all operating concerns. Global variables are created for a specific field in a table and can be marked as mandatory, optional, and so on. You can also create global variables for text values, formulas, and many other things. To create global variables, follow choose Controlling ➢ Profitability Analysis ➢ Information System ➢ Report Components ➢ Define Variables for Reports or enter transaction code KE3E. All global variables begin with &. We will not show the configuration of global variables in the book—if you've gotten this far, you can handle it on your own!

Local variables are defined within a form. They can be used only by the form in which they are created. You do not have all of the options you have with global variables when you use local variables. Whether you use global variables or loca variables is up to you. Just know that you have a lot more flexibility to control processing when you use global variables. Local variables begin with $.

To use a variable instead of a fixed value for a characteristic, first select the characteristic value field by single-clicking in it. Next, click the Variable On/Off field, which is the check box beside the field From or To see the bottom of the screen shown in Figure 12.78). The characteristic is now a variable. If you want to use a global variable, select it from the pull-down box in the Characteristic Value field. If you want to use a local variable, enter in the characteristic value field a local variable name beginning with $.

You can also define the drill-down list your report will use. The drill-down list, as explained earlier, includes such things as all materials sold to a certain customer. From within the form, you can specify which value columns are displayed in the drill-down list. Using our form as an example, you might want columns to display actual net revenue, plan net revenue, actual profitability, and plan profitability. To define the columns to be displayed in the drill-down list, choose Extras ➢ Drill-Down Display ➢ Select Row/Columns on the form creation screen. You can then select row/column combinations from the form detail to be combined and used as single columns in the drill-down display. If you do not define your own drill-down structure, the system defaults the drill-down display to groupings of all rows and columns. In this example, the default would be a grouping of net revenue with three columns underneath it for actual data, plan data, and variance, then a grouping of COGS with three columns underneath it for actual data, plan data, and variance— the pattern continues for all of the rows that have been defined in the form. You can view the current structure of your drill-down list by clicking Show Drill-Down List in the Report Painter: Create Form definition configuration screen.

The final configuration step is to check the form for errors. To do so, click the check icon (the button, which is at the far left, looks like a hanging scale made out of monitors) in the create CO-PA form definition configuration screen. After you run the check successfully without errors, you can save the form.

**EXTREME SPORTS CO-PA FORM CREATION CONFIGURATION ANALYSIS**

Extreme Sports wants to provide maximum flexibility in its reporting solution. Therefore, it was determined that form reports and two axes (matrix) forms would be used for this report. Using the matrix form, we were able to define both the row and column structure of the report. In this example, the rows were defined as elements from the report line structure EX—you can also assign characteristics to each element of a key figure scheme or value field, but it was not needed in this case. The column structure of the form used characteristics and formulas to report on actual values, plan values, and the variance between the two. The general data selection of the form allowed us to choose additional characteristics that are used by every piece of the form. We used both global and local variables in defining the general data selection characteristics. There are many more advanced features that can be implemented for specific requirements within the form. The knowledge gained in this section can be applied and will give you a good base to pick up on additional tools you can use as you get more complex reporting requirements.

## Creating the Report

We have now defined all the reporting components needed by our report. The final step is to create the actual report. This is also the simplest step because most of the hard work was done in the other components. At this point, it is important to remember that drill-down reports, like all other reports (with the exception of some ABAP reports), pulls data from summarized information—this means you do not have available to you all the data that is available in the line items that make up the detailed data. CO-PA drill-down reports actually pull data from the CE3*xxxx* table in conjunction with CE4*xxxx*. This is true unless you go to the specific command in the CO-PA menu and create your report directly against the line item table—CE1xxxx. Just choose Controlling ➤ Profitability Analysis ➤ Information System ➤ Define Report ➤ Create Report Based on Line Items, or you can use the transaction code KE91 (Create). You will find that you can use the same form report structures that you just created for the line item reports as well as the reports being executed against the summary tables.

As you learned earlier, you can create two types of reports: basic reports and form reports. We will continue with our example of creating a form report. To create a CO-PA report, choose Controlling ➢ Profitability Analysis ➢ Information System ➢ Define Report ➢ Create Profitability Report, or use the transaction code KE31 (Create), KE32 (Change), or KE33 (Display).

In the first screen, select the Create option, or enter transaction code KE31. You are taken to the Create Profitability Report: Initial Screen, shown in Figure 12.79.

**FIGURE 12.79** The Create Profitability Report: Initial Screen

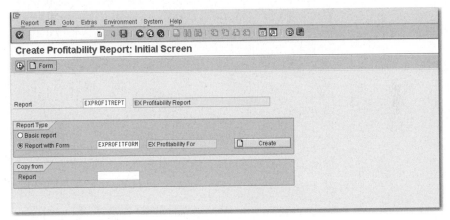

As you can see, you have the option to create basic reports or to create form reports. In this example, we will create a form report using the form we created in the preceding section. Be sure to click the Report with Form radio button and to indicate the form name in the text box. You also need to give the report an identifier as well as a description in the top two fields on the screen. After entering all the required information, click the Create button. You are presented with the Create Profitability Report: Specific Profit. Segment screen, shown in Figure 12.80, where you'll define your report characteristics.

On this screen, you define the characteristics you want to use in the drill-down screen. To drill down (slice and dice) on a characteristic, you must select it in this screen (even if you chose the characteristic in the form definition). If you desire, you also have the option of entering characteristic values to further limit the data pulled for the report. Because we are using a two-axes (matrix) form with key figures, you are not able to define key figures (value fields or elements of a report line structure) within the report. However, when you use basic reports or a one-axis form without key figures, you choose from within the report the key figures to be used.

**FIGURE 12.80** The Create Profitability Report: Specific Profit. Segment screen

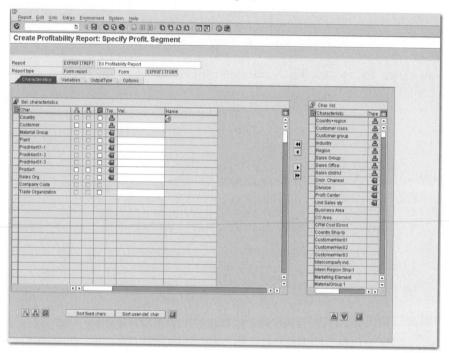

The next tab lets you further define your variables. In this case you can adjust and tweak the variables for this specific report's needs (see Figure 12.81). Here you can define default values for any variable that you have. In our case we have decided to default the company codes 1000 and 2000 in our report. You can also adjust the actual text of the variable to make this a bit more user friendly once the report is executed. (However, the best approach is to take care of this within the actual Form report template.) You can also define whether the variable should be available at the time of report execution, and you can sort the variables by using the sort variable button at the bottom of the page.

**FIGURE 12.81** The Create Profitability Report: Variables screen

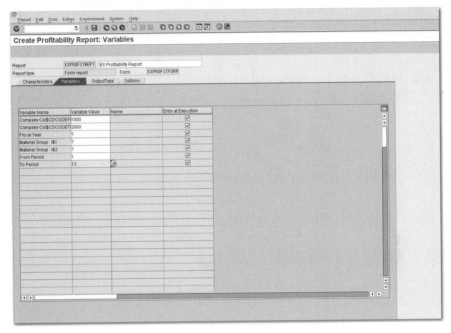

As you get more and more data in the system, and use more characteristics and variables in your report, your reporting performance becomes slower. One way to increase performance is to define in the report the structure from which the data is pulled. You can choose between current data and summarization levels. Current data is by far the slowest method that can be used. Summarization levels are special summary tables that are filled with only specific characteristics that are needed by your report(s). This makes reporting performance much faster. Each report can pull from only one summarization level, but each summarization level can be used by more than one report. You can have more than one summarization level in your operating concern, but make sure that you don't define very many (or more than you need) because summarization merely stores redundant data. You must also take up processing capability within the system to "fill" your summarization levels. The configuration of summarization levels is fairly straightforward (once you understand CO-PA and its data structures, which you know now!). You can configure summarization levels from within the Tools level under CO-PA in the IMG. You can define whether your report should use summarization levels, as well as the reaction of the system if a summarization level is not found. You can accomplish this using the Options tab of the Create Report: Settings screen (see Figure 12.82).

**FIGURE 12.82** The Options tab of the Create Report: Settings screen

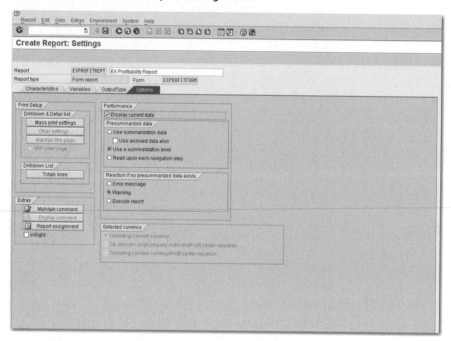

This tab also gives you the options Use Summarization Data, Use a Summarization Level, and Read Upon Each Navigation Step. We are all comfortable with the idea of reading current data, but what is the option Use Summarization Data going to do for us? Summarization data will generate a set of data for a specific report and save that set of data in the cache memory for you to retrieve at the time of report execution. If you set your report to use summarization data, the report will access this set of data, and every time it runs it will update that summarization data with the additional postings that have occurred. You might use this feature on a report that has long runtimes since it will only have to retrieve from the database the delta snapshot of the data. SAP recommends that you use the summarization levels to help with report performance. If is the results are not helpful enough, you can either use the summarization data or check the option to "freeze" your data. You can access the option Frozen Data in the report once it is executed.

If you choose to run the report off a summarization level, you can define whether you get an error, a warning, or no message at all if a summarization level does not exist. If you choose the Error Message option, the report cannot be run until a summarization level has been created (and filled) for it. If you choose the Warning option, the user is presented with a warning saying that a summarization level does not exist for the report. The user then has the option of either canceling the running of the report or running the report off current data. If you choose the No Message option, the report will try to pull data from a summarization level. If no summarization level exists, it will automatically pull the information from current data without any interaction with the report's user.

Output Type, another tab on this screen, lets you define the option types. As you can see in Figure 12.83, this screen lets you define the specific option type for the business user to see. There are five options:

**Graphical Report-Output**　This option lets you define the template that will be used to display the report. Your corporation may have a reporting template that they use and that you can assign here. The other option relates to the output areas and where they show up on the screen. You can adjust the various sections of the report, such as the navigation pane, graphic view, table view, and so on; remove them from the screen; or just change positions on the screen.

**Classic Drilldown**　This option displays the report in a drilldown list. This is the format that has been available since the original CO-PA version and has a number of icons that the end user will need to use during the navigation process. This display is used quite a bit, and once you learn the navigation process in these types of reports, the drilldown process is quite easy.

**Object List (ALV)**　This option displays the information as a list output. It is a convenient report output type and is basically a report in tabular format.

**XXL (Spreadsheet)**　This option displays the information in a Microsoft Excel spreadsheet format. You can access any number of Excel base functions from this screen, including but not limited to the use of a Pivot Table process.

**Available on Selection Screen**　This option will allow the end user to choose any of the previous options when executing the report.

**FIGURE 12.83** Output Type tab

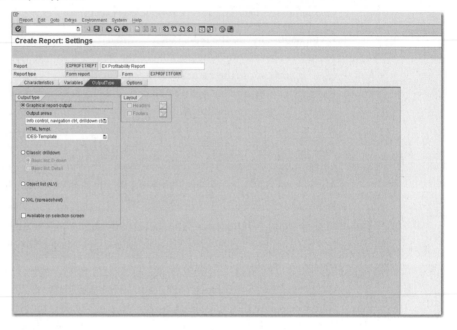

After you have defined all of your characteristic information and how data should be read, click the save icon. The report is now saved, and you can run it.

## EXTREME SPORTS CREATE REPORT CONFIGURATION ANALYSIS

In this section, Extreme Sports completed its reporting configuration by creating the report itself. The report was created as a form report, using the form EXPROFITFORM that we created earlier. From within the report, we configured some of the variables that were defined in the form default values. The report user will be presented with a selection of all the variables and the default values that we entered here. The user has the option to overwrite the default values. We also chose several characteristics to be used in the drill-down functionality of the report. We will be able to group data by each characteristic and drill down to additional data about the characteristic, such as which product groups were sold to customer X. We also set the form to read data from summarization levels instead of current data. If a summarization level is not available for the report, users will receive a warning message that will allow them to cancel the report or to pull the data from current data (the base CO-PA data structures). We were not able to define key figures (value fields or elements from a report line structure) in the report because we defined the report as a form report using a matrix form that already includes the key figures. We are able to define key figures within the report for the basic report type and the single axis without key figures form report type.

# CO-PA Transports

Creating and executing CO-PA transports can be tricky. With a few exceptions, CO-PA transports are not automatically recorded, even when they occur in a client with changes recorded automatically. Because of the technical nature of CO-PA, SAP wants to group specific objects in a transport in the correct order. The transport created by SAP is a combination of both client-independent and client-dependent objects. You learned in Chapter 1 that you should not group client-dependent and client-independent changes in the same transport request. CO-PA is the exception to the rule because SAP creates the transport. To create a CO-PA transport, choose Controlling ➢ Profitability Analysis ➢ Tools ➢ Production Startup ➢ Transport, or you can use the transaction code KE3I. The Choose Transport Objects screen shown in Figure 12.84 opens. Be sure to read the IMG documentation provided with this step to more fully understand the transport creation process.

**FIGURE 12.84** SAP-EIS Transport Tool: Choose Transport Objects screen

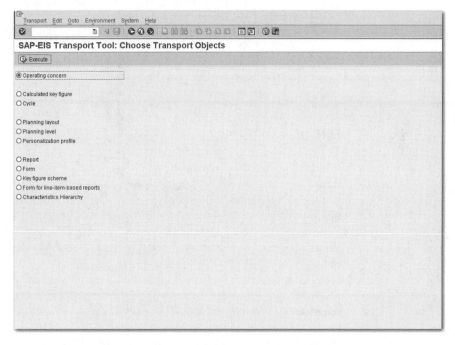

You have several choices of what you can include in your transport. When you select each option, you will be prompted with a list of dependent objects that can be included or excluded. To be safe, it is usually a good idea to include all dependent

objects. When you choose the operating concern option, you *must* choose all dependent objects that are presented (see Figure 12.85). If you do not, you are at risk of corrupting or incompletely defining your operating concern in the source client. After you transport your operating concern, you *must* generate the environment of the operating concern in the source client before the operating concern can be used. You generate the operating concern from the same configuration screens you used to define your data structures and generate the operating concern the first time. In the operating concern configuration screen, click the Generate Environment button that should appear on the toolbar. (If it is not displayed, click the Status button and then the Generate Environment button will appear.) As we explained earlier, you only need to generate the operating concern environment in a single client within a system environment (development, QA, or production). Once you generate the environment in one client, it is generated in all clients within the system environment.

**FIGURE 12.85** Choosing dependent objects

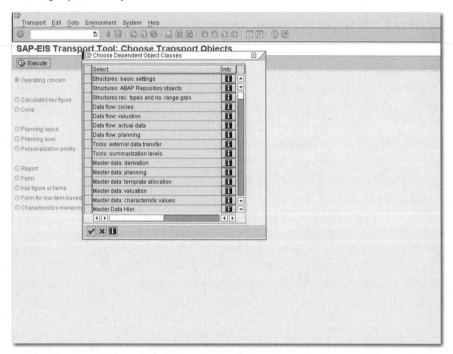

When you run your operating concern transport into a new system environment, it is a good idea to have minimal or (if possible) no activity on the system. You definitely cannot be processing billing transactions or order settlement to CO-PA transactions while the transport is running, and you will get errors in these transactions until the operating concern environment is generated. To minimize this risk, it is a good idea to deactivate CO-PA within your controlling area immediately before the transport is run into the environment and then reactivate CO-PA immediately after the operating concern environment has been successfully generated.

You can transport reports, forms, and planning layouts if you want. Most companies, however, allow these types of reporting transactions to be created directly in production. This is a safe procedure because creating these types of objects is not configuration that affects how the system processes data—they are only structures to pull data for reporting.

# Summary

In this chapter, you learned the concepts and configuration behind the Profitability Analysis (CO-PA) submodule. We discussed the purposes of CO-PA and the various types of CO-PA that can be used: account based and costing based. About 90% of companies that are using CO-PA use the costing-based CO-PA. It's not that account based is not important—it's just that account based has a very specific use: validating the reconciliation of CO-PA to FI.

We then showed you how to create and activate the operating concern data structure and generate the operating concern environment. Next we worked our way through the process of setting up derivation for the characteristics and valuation for some of the additional information we needed from the key figures. Building on the operating concern that we created, we showed you how to configure the rest of the CO-PA functionality needed by Extreme Sports. It is important to keep in mind that CO-PA is a mix of standard configuration and technical table and data structure creation.

We continued our development of CO-PA with the functionality of planning in CO-PA. The use of planning, budgeting, and forecasting in CO-PA is critical to the organization. This is the one place in the ECC system that we need to understand that the ability to plan is available across modules. Therefore, you can plan headcount against FI information, you can plan Units of Production against Customers and Regions, you can plan and budget at a very high level or a very detailed level, and you can take this planned information and automatically transfer it to all the other modules within the ECC system.

Finally, we finished by going through the process of setting up a Profitability Analysis report. Remember that if you are developing reports for account-based CO-PA, you will need to create forms and reports specific to account based and remember to switch your settings for CO-PA to direct you to the account-based CO-PA.

A number of additional functions are available in CO-PA, and this chapter got you started down the road of developing your overall reporting strategy for CO-PA. Please review other ways of getting estimated cost into CO-PA (costing based, of course) such as Valuation using the Cost Component Structure or Costing Sheet options. Review the additional functions available in the Analysis Flow Process area in CO-PA, and these will help with some reconciliation processes in CO-PA. There is also some very good information on using realignment of master data in CO-PA, which can prove valuable if you want to add another characteristic down the road or change a master data combination to your operating concern.

If you remember just one thing from this chapter, it should be this: use characteristics sparingly. Characteristics are limited resources within your operating concern, and as your business changes over the years, you may want to add characteristics. You cannot add characteristics later if you use them all up in the first shot. The fewer characteristics you use, the better your performance will be when reporting in CO-PA.

CO-PA is a powerful tool, and with power comes complexity. Be careful out there. You also need to be aware of the number of key figures that you are using. Don't use up all of your key figures for variances and production order information and later realize you still have additional details you need to collect for discounts or other SD-related information. Good luck and have fun.

# CHAPTER 13

# *Profit Center Accounting*

**FEATURING:**

▶ **INTRODUCTION TO PCA CONFIGURATION**

▶ **BASIC SETTINGS AND MASTER DATA REVIEW**

▶ **ANALYZE AND UPDATE PCA SETTINGS**

▶ **ASSIGNMENTS IN PROFIT CENTER ACCOUNTING**

▶ **ACTUAL POSTING MAINTENANCE**

▶ **PROFIT CENTER ACCOUNTING: PLANNING**

P rofit Center Accounting (PCA) is not an "official" Controlling module component. Instead, it rests in an area of SAP called Enterprise Controlling (EC). EC also contains the applications Executive Information Systems (EC-EIS), Business Planning (EC-BP), and Consolidations (EC-CS). The purpose of PCA is to provide a client with the opportunity to analyze and report internal profitability for its organization using a profit center approach rather than the normal business area or company code. Although PCA resides outside of the CO module, it remains integrated with CO through its controlling area/company code relationships. By its very nature, PCA is a tool that can be manipulated to meet most of your demands. One of the other important responsibilities of PCA is to be the "other" component of EC and CO that will reconcile with FI. In actuality, PCA will reconcile easier to FI than costing-based CO-PA will, and on the same level of accounting-based CO-PA, except that CO-PA has the ability to combine more characteristics with the records.

The chapter will focus on the high-level development needs of most projects. From activating the module within the controlling area to establishing proper planning parameters, the emphasis will be on quickly getting you up and running. Refinements can occur afterward. To begin the process, we'll present an overview of the necessary configuration areas.

## PCA Configuration Overview

Portions of PCA configuration were covered in Chapters 8 and 10 during the setup of the CO Enterprise Structure and Cost Center Accounting. In Chapter 8, "Controlling Enterprise Structure," PCA was activated within the controlling area, and the PCA portion of version 0 was maintained. In Chapter 10, "Cost Center Accounting," the PCA standard hierarchy was defined, and the dummy profit center was created and assigned to the controlling area. This chapter will build upon that configuration.

**NOTE** Review Chapters 8 and 10 before proceeding. Each chapter will provide you with some necessary PCA configuration steps.

In reality there is not much to the configuration of PCA other than the master data linkages. You have the opportunity to maintain version settings and create planning parameters. You will be required to maintain document types, and you can influence the updates during internal goods movements. But the majority of your development time will be spent designing the standard hierarchy and determining profit center assignments. This will be key to fulfilling all reporting and planning requirements. Again, realize that PCA is, generally speaking, a reporting toolset with its own unique approach to setting up tables and processing data.

We're assuming that the reason you are developing PCA is to meet profitability reporting requirements that do not align with your company code structure. At times, areas of responsibility within an organization span existing legal structures and therefore are a matrix-like architecture rather than a linear structure.

A more prevalent scenario is one where the areas of responsibility subdivide a single legal entity, as in a company whose areas of responsibility are geographically based. Each region—potentially North, South, East, and West—is held accountable for profitability targets. The sum of these regions would be equal to a single legal company code. Profit Center Accounting allows an organization to route all profitability—and most balance sheet–related information—to a profit center. Much of this routing is accomplished through the aforementioned PCA assignments. So basically, you are assigning another characteristic, profit centers, to the transactional data to allow for additional reporting purposes; it's only that this reporting is more associated with P&L and balance sheet analysis.

Another module similar in function to Profit Center Accounting is Special Purpose Ledger, or FI-SL. In fact, PCA itself was developed as a preconfigured special ledger solution. FI-SL is SAP's version of the ultimate reporting tool. It allows you to gather, consolidate, and report on information from all other SAP modules and any external source by developing personalized database tables. These tables form what is called a *table group* and are the backbone to FI-SL development. Because PCA is a delivered FI-SL solution, its table group, ledger, and activity assignments are predetermined and not directly configurable without the use of user-exits. However, this in no way limits the functionality or flexibility of PCA's reporting capabilities. Table 13.1 provides you with a breakdown of the PCA table group. These are the primary tables in the PCA area. Now that you understand the configuration of PCA tables a bit more, you can see that all postings to PCA will be statistical in nature. Essentially, it would be that "second" CO/EC posting on a transaction. No real postings are derived from or assigned to PCA.

**TABLE 13.1**     EC-PCA Table Group Contents

| Table | Description |
| --- | --- |
| GLPCO | Object Table for Account Assignment Objects |
| GLPCC | Additional Object Table |
| GLPCA | Actual Line Items Table |
| GLPCP | Plan Line Items Table |
| GLPCT | Summary (Totals) Table, used to facilitate reporting |

The concept of a "ledger," which was mentioned earlier, is worth elaboration. In the FI-SL environment, the ledger is an object related to the table group. It is through the ledger that all fiscal-year variant, company code, and activity assignments are made. The ledger is also key in many of the controls FI-SL establishes to manage transactional updates. With PCA, you get a predefined ledger, called 8A-Profit Center Accounting, that contains all activity assignments necessary for startup. The activity assignments cannot be augmented, but you do have the ability to control SAP's decision-making process during data transfer through a number of user-exits.

As you activate PCA for each of your controlling areas, all assigned company codes are automatically associated with the ledger; thus, no manual maintenance is needed. All controlling areas that exist within any instance use the same table group and ledger.

Because PCA is external to both FI and CO, FI and CO do not have to be in balance at all times within PCA. But usually, as you will see, after a company tries to reconcile CO to FI and this becomes frustrating through costing-based CO-PA, they will turn to PCA for this requirement. In any case, if you use PCA for internal reporting purposes and your intent is not to reconcile to FI, you can include externally generated data through PCA postings without any repercussions. Allowing external postings can become a problem if not carefully monitored. By configuring specific document types, you will have the ability to control whether unbalanced entries are acceptable.

In the next section, you will begin PCA configuration with a review of the basic controlling area and master data settings. As needed, refer to Chapters 8 and 10 for insight into previously configured sections of SAP.

# Basic Settings and Master Data Review

Prior to jumping into the heart of PCA configuration, it is important to spend some time ensuring that you've made the proper basic configuration settings. For PCA, that means reviewing the controlling area for the proper PCA activation, analyzing the specific PCA settings and assignments, and, finally, maintaining the PCA standard hierarchy. The next section will once again take you through the steps necessary to review the controlling area maintenance screens.

## Controlling Area Maintenance

When beginning Profit Center Accounting configuration, the first thing you will want to do is check to see that PCA is activated within the controlling area you are working in and that all the settings are appropriate. The PCA-related controlling area and standard hierarchy settings were maintained in Chapter 10 and are still relevant here. As a refresher, the menu path for getting to the maintenance window and some helpful hints are provided in this section. After setting the controlling area, use the IMG menu path Enterprise Controlling ➤ Profit Center Accounting ➤ Basic Settings ➤ Controlling Area Settings ➤ Maintain Controlling Area Settings or the transaction code 0KE5. It is also possible to use the transaction code ORK2 to access this screen.

Figure 13.1 shows a view of the PCA-relevant controlling area settings. You will recall from Chapter 10 that certain aspects of PCA configuration were completed to maintain the cost center master record. To this end, the PCA-related controlling area settings and dummy profit center were created. Additionally, the PCA standard hierarchy was defined, and profit centers were created to house the newly created cost centers (you'll learn more about this topic in the section "Assignments in Profit Center Accounting" later in this chapter).

Here are some key fields:

**Dummy Profit Center**   The dummy profit center is the default profit center for the entire controlling area. There can be only one dummy profit center per controlling area. We configured EX01_Dummy in Chapter 10.

**Standard Hierarchy**   We created EX01_PCA in Chapter 10. Once you have created and assigned profit centers to the hierarchy, you cannot change the name.

**Elim. of Int. Business Vol.**   Activate this field if you want to eliminate internal activity between two or more account assignment objects that are assigned to the same profit center. This setting can be activated or deactivated even after postings have occurred in the controlling area. However, the effects will not be felt in a retroactive manner. Previous posted amounts will not be picked up or eliminated.

**FIGURE 13.1**     Controlling area settings related to PCA

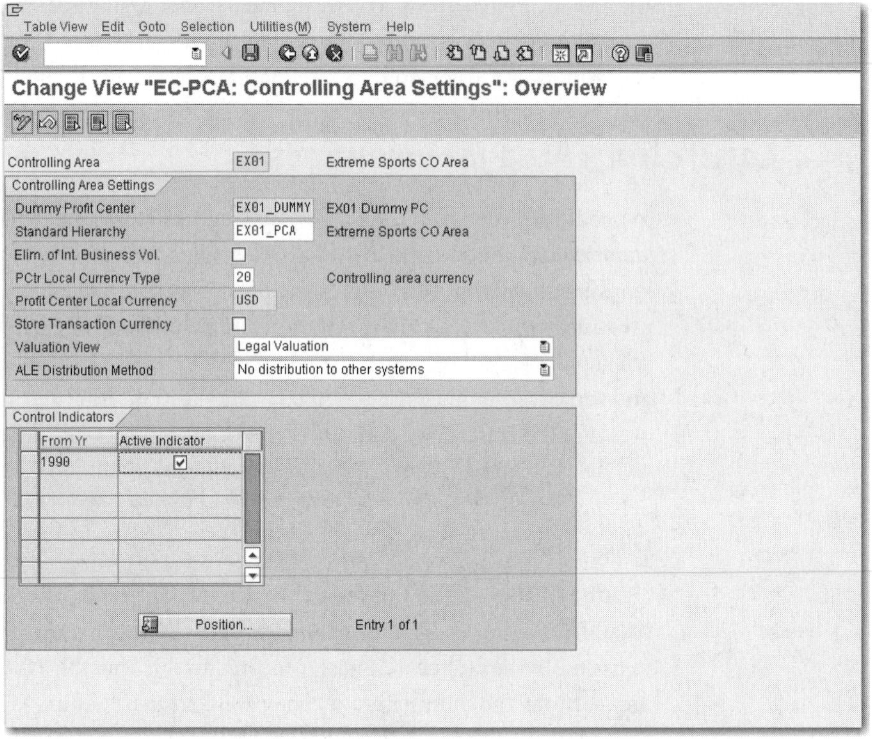

**PCtr Local Currency Type**     This field is for the currency per controlling area. The system updates this currency in the transaction data along with the transaction currency and the local currency. You can have three options: the group currency (30), the controlling area currency (20), and the currency for the Profit Center Accounting (90).

**Profit Center Local Currency**     If you chose the special profit center currency type for a controlling area, you will need to specify that specific currency in this field. These settings are directly related to the fact that PCA can store transactions posted to three different currencies at one time.

**Store Transaction Currency**     If you want the transaction currency stored in PCA, flag this field. Data volumes will increase, but if the transaction currency is different from the controlling area or profit center currency, it may be important for reporting. Like the Elim. of Int. Business Vol. setting, this can be activated or deactivated even after postings have occurred.

**Valuation View**   With the direct link between profit centers and transfer pricing, the use of the Valuation View field has become increasingly important. You use valuation views to show different views of the business transaction in a company. You can define three different views to the data: the Legal view, the Group view, or the Profit Center view. In the Legal view, movements of goods are posted between profit centers at a previously agreed-upon sale price, and in this case, both internal entities generate P&L and balance sheets independently. In the Group view, movements of goods are posted at the group production cost prices and there are no additional surcharges within the group. Finally, in the Profit Center view movements of goods are posted between profit centers at a negotiated transfer pricing amount, which is used for internal profit determination and corporate management. So the important item to be aware of is that the Legal view looks at this as a *sale* and the Profit Center view looks at this as a *transfer* in terms of goods movement.

**ALE Distribution Method**   This setting, whether the Profit Centers will be managed locally or in a distribution approach is exactly the same as with the Cost Centers ALE distribution method described in Chapter 10. Depending on the approach taken with the Profit Centers, whether they are managed centrally or Locally controlled, this parameter will be set. The options here are No Distribution to Other Systems, Centralized Profit Center Accounting, or Profit Center Decentralized or Local.

**Control Indicators**   The system will default the current year as the From fiscal year. All settings are good from this year forward. If you make changes, SAP will identify a new From range. Be certain that Active Indicator is set to Active (checked).

When you have reviewed the settings and are satisfied, save the controlling area and continue to the next section.

# Analyze and Update PCA Settings

Either during the development period or when in production, you have the ability to immediately check the settings for PCA. Because PCA uses the FI-SL tools to update itself with plan and actual data, it must follow the rules that govern that system. These rules and concepts take the form of utilizing customizing specific and internal control tables to monitor and control transaction data updates. At times, such as when customizing transports have an impact on PCA configuration, it is possible that these internal control tables may need regeneration. Through the

Analyze Settings transaction, you will be able to review these control tables to find any resulting inconsistencies. The following is a breakdown of the major sections of the Analyze Settings report:

▶ Fiscal Year Active indicator

▶ Valuation Settings, Currency Types, and currency

▶ PCA settings for the controlling area, which let you know, among other things, the name or the PCA standard hierarchy and dummy profit center

▶ Control parameters for company code assignments attached to the controlling area

▶ Control parameters for both plan and actual postings

▶ General Parameter settings, which provide you with relative currency information

▶ Activity assignments in PCA

▶ Various master data and standard hierarchy checks for profit centers assigned in PCA

The program that is executed by the Analyze Settings screen is helpful in that it provides a concise overview of the PCA environment and can help you quickly track down potential problems.

**NOTE**    Prior to running the program, be sure you have properly set the controlling area. You are not afforded an opportunity during the execution step, and SAP will analyze the settings of the controlling area at that time.

To run the Analyze Settings program, choose Enterprise Controlling ➢ Profit Center Accounting ➢ Basic Settings ➢ Controlling Area Settings ➢ Analyze Settings or use the transaction code 1KE1.

The Display Settings for Profit Center Accounting screen appears, offering an option to run the program with a master data check. If you have any concerns related to PCA in this area, click Master Data, and then execute the program. Figure 13.2 is a partial view of the output from the program. You will have to sort through several pages when reviewing the settings. Unfortunately, if you find errors or inconsistencies or need to make changes, you cannot make them from this screen. You will have to go to each of the affected areas individually to change the settings.

**FIGURE 13.2**    EC-PCA: Display Settings for Profit Center Accounting program

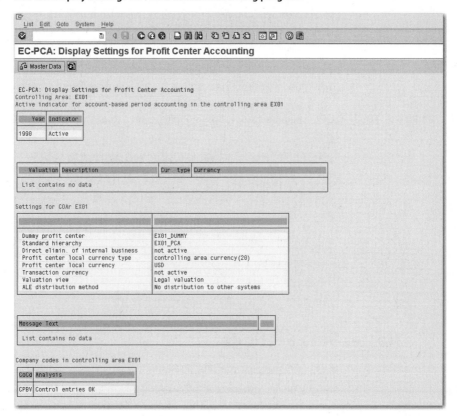

**TIP**    Because the Analyze Settings program consolidates a lot of control information for PCA, it is a great configuration reference guide.

As a result of your analysis, you may realize that inconsistencies exist in one or more of the internal control tables of PCA. These tables control elements such as company code assignment and plan/actual updates. If errors exist, it is probable that a quick regeneration of the environment will solve the problem. The regeneration program is contained in the IMG and can be found using the menu path Enterprise Controlling ➢ Profit Center Accounting ➢ Basic Settings ➢ Controlling Area Settings ➢ Update Basic Settings or the transaction code 0KE4.

You will not see an execution screen because the program is executed immediately. Once it's completed, a results document that segregates the update analysis by controlling area will appear on the screen, or in this case, since all of the settings are correct, you will just get a message at the bottom of your screen. Figure 13.3 shows a view of the results document. Notice that all control information is maintained at the company code level. At this time, you can rerun the Analyze Settings program to ensure that the problem has been resolved. The next section will take you through some of the master data requirements of Profit Center Accounting.

**FIGURE 13.3**    EC-PCA: Regenerate Settings for Profit Center Accounting results for EX01

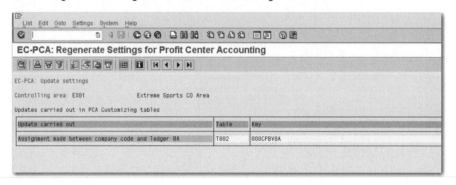

## Master Data Settings

Much of the master data development for PCA, like the standard hierarchy and dummy profit center creation, was covered in Chapter 10, so you should review that chapter before continuing. Here are some of the master data items you should review:

**Maintain the Standard Hierarchy**    If you anticipate that the PCA standard hierarchy will resemble the CCA hierarchy created earlier, you have the option of copying the CCA hierarchy and then augmenting it as you see fit. This must be done prior to any manual creation in PCA. Be sure to create a special node that will contain the dummy profit center.

**TIP**   If a lot of maintenance will be necessary, we do not recommend the CCA copy procedure. It will be less confusing to build the hierarchy from scratch.

**Create the Dummy Profit Center**    In many cases, you should create the dummy before creating the cost center. If you didn't do that, you will need to create the dummy here. Remember that there is only one dummy profit center per controlling area. In all profit centers, reviewing the assignment to the company codes is critical to the posting of transactional data to both the appropriate company code and profit center (see Figure 13.4).

**Create Profit Center Master Records**   After the hierarchy is built, you will need to begin creating the profit centers. As with the standard hierarchy creation process, you have the option of copying the existing cost centers to create your new profit centers. One limitation to the copy process is that each new profit center is created with the same cost center number. Prior to running the copy program, you must create a cost center group containing the set of cost centers to be copied. This set will be entered on the copy execution screen.

**FIGURE 13.4**   Change Profit Center screen: the Dummy Profit Center

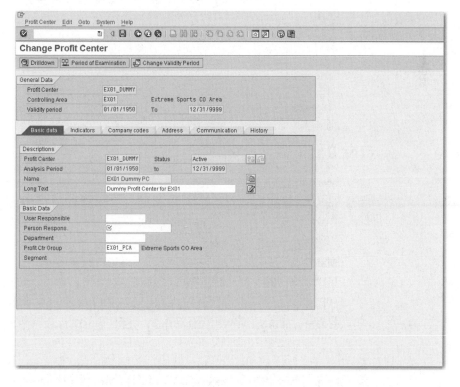

A new area is the maintenance of the time-based fields found on the profit center master record. In CCA, you were limited to what you could influence in this area. In PCA, however, SAP allows you to identify which fields will be time sensitive. To access this window, choose Enterprise Controlling ➢ Profit Center Accounting ➢ Master Data ➢ Profit Center ➢ Specify Time-Based Fields for Profit Centers, or you can use transaction code 0KE7.

The EC-PCA: Time-Based Master Data Fields maintenance screen appears (see Figure 13.5). If it is important to track changes to the master record, each change will need to correspond with a new analysis period. The default analysis period on the master record is the original validity period given to the profit center. New periods can be configured directly on the profit center master record in the manner in which it is configured for the cost center (see Chapter 10 for details). To define a field as time based, check the box next to the field name. When you've finished, save the settings. You can update them as often as you like.

**FIGURE 13.5**     The EC-PCA: Time-Based Master Data Fields screen

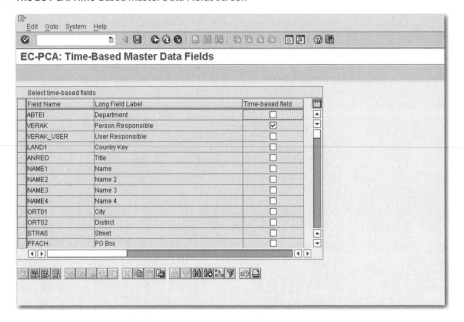

Now that you've established the basic structure of PCA, it is time to begin the assignment process. We'll cover this procedure in the next section.

## EXTREME SPORTS TIME-BASED FIELD MAINTENANCE CONFIGURATION ANALYSIS

Extreme Sports does not have an immediate need to maintain any of the fields at this time. This, of course, may change at a future date.

# Assignments in Profit Center Accounting

Profit Center Accounting is in some sense a parasite. It generates very few transactional postings itself, relying instead on the data being generated by other sources, such as goods movements through production and receiving, billing documents through sales, and other postings that will receive FI accounting treatment. These external transactions update PCA through object assignments. The assignments are an important facet to configuring PCA because, without them, a properly established environment will never include all the data necessary for reporting.

It has already been established in earlier chapters that cost centers and internal orders all require a profit center assignment at creation time when PCA is active. Through this assignment, all updates are passed to PCA and the link to the original object, namely the internal order or cost center, is maintained. You will always know that the PCA posting originated from that object. These types of assignments will not be covered in this section because they are hereditary to the creation process of those master records. Similar to the assignment process of the internal order and cost center is the creation process of the master records of cost objects, projects, maintenance orders, and fixed assets. These are all manually controlled and assigned during creation.

We recommend that you spend your assignment time in one key area: the material master. Through this assignment, the majority of the PCA postings will occur. This section will cover the material assignment concepts and then move into sales order substitutions, which may become necessary based on your material assignment solution.

## Material Master Assignment

With a single assignment on the material master record, you will have identified for SAP the default profit center for all sales orders, production orders, goods movements, material transfers, and physical inventory adjustments. The view to be maintained on the material master record is the Sales: General/Plant data view. The material master view is shown in Figure 13.6 (the lower portion of the screen).

As with all material master maintenance, this setting will have to be maintained for each plant to which the material will be assigned. The Profit Center setting is in the General Plant Parameters field group found at the bottom of the view. Each unique material/plant can have a different profit center assignment. Give the choice of profit center on this master record a lot of thought. Your decision will be partly determined by your company's inventory management philosophy. By this we mean that the decision will be made by the area within your organization that owns the inventory. It could be manufacturing or sales and marketing.

**FIGURE 13.6**    The Sales: General/Plant data material master view

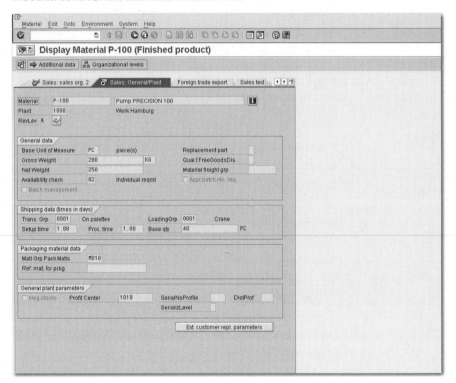

If manufacturing owns the inventory and all the cost responsibility that comes with it, it makes sense to assign the material to a manufacturing profit center. This profit center would then be responsible for all inventory balances and would incur any inventory adjustment charges. If, however, the sales organization is responsible for the inventory, a sales and marketing profit center is appropriate. Your choice here will influence whether the section of this chapter that covers sales order substitution is relevant for your solution.

SAP will route, by default, all revenue and cost of sales data related to the selling of a material to the profit center assigned on the General Plant/Data view of the material master record. Changing the profit center assignment directly on the sales order can supercede the material master assignment. However, doing so may turn out to be impractical; for example, if you have a number of different materials assigned to each sales order, you may decide that each line item of the sales order should go to a different profit center and therefore have to manually maintain the assignment of those profit centers and this can be time consuming. A second method of controlling the profit center assignment is to maintain the sales order substitution, which can be used to route not only the revenue and cost of sales of a sales order but also the accompanying A/R customer balance. In either case, just know that you can reroute this assignment with careful planning.

For a new project, the profit center assignment on the material master is best done during the material master conversion process. Be sure to add the Profit Center field to whatever CATT (Computer-Aided Test Tool) you have built to support the conversion loads. If you are in a maintenance and support mode, it is more likely that you will be adding or changing the profit center assignment on a handful of materials at a time. To assist with these changes, SAP provides you with a tool called fast assignment that will allow you to have an impact on a few materials, an entire product hierarchy, or anywhere in between in a single transaction.

## Fast Assignment

To access the fast assignment screen, choose Enterprise Controlling ➤ Profit Center Accounting ➤ Assignments to Account Assignment Objects to Profit Centers ➤ Material ➤ Perform Fast Assignment or use transaction code MM17

The Mass Maintenance: Materials (Industry) screen appears (see Figure 13.7). Notice that in the initial screen you are looking at the Materials (industry) object type. Usually you would be looking to set up the Mass Maintenance process by assigning the profit center to both the plant and material. Decide what table(s) you will be affecting by choosing one or more, using the parameter to the left side of the screen. For this example, you will use both the Material Descriptions and Plant Data for Material settings to filter the different materials you want to affect. Then select the Fields tab and find the Profit Center Assignment field. Do a search if necessary and use Profit Center (see Figure 13.8)—this is the field that will be affected by the change. You can also see the table that will be affected by this change—in this case, the MARC table. If you were to look at the Material Master, go to the screen Sales: General/Plant, and then highlight the Profit Center field, you would see that the location for the profit center is in the MARC table.

**FIGURE 13.7**    The Mass Maintenance: Materials (Industry) data entry screen

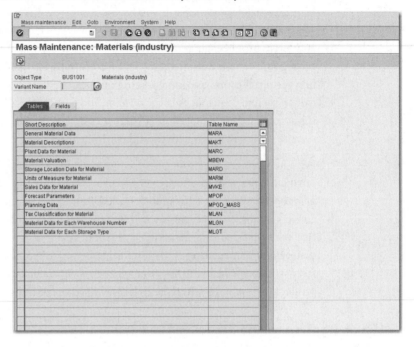

**FIGURE 13.8**    The Mass Maintenance: Materials (Industry) Fields tab

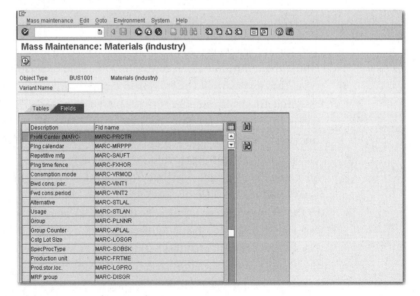

Once you complete these two steps, execute the process. At this time, you will see an additional screen that will require you to provide the material number, language key, and plant before continuing. There are two tabs that you can choose from. Either you will be changing the existing records or you will be creating new records (see Figure 13.9). Begin the process by maintaining each of the relevant fields in the Restrict Data Records to Be changed area. Let's look at each field:

**Material (From/To)**    Enter a material number or a range of material numbers to be updated.

**Language Key**    Since we chose the field Materials Description as an identifier, we need to include the language key that will be effected.

**Plant (From/To)**    Enter the ID of the plant to which the material is assigned. If the material is assigned to more than one plant, use the selection option to fill in the additional plants (arrow to the right of the fields).

**FIGURE 13.9**    The Mass Maintenance: Materials (Industry) screen for the data records to be changed/created

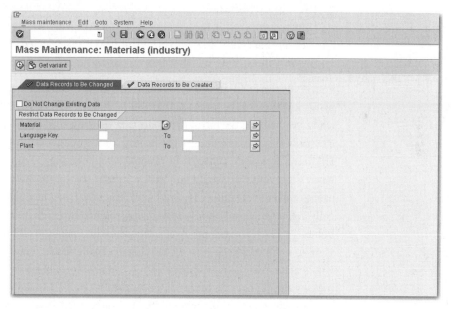

Depending on the initial fields that you decided to use for the filtering process, additional information may be required. Some of the commonly used fields are as follows:

**Material Type**   If applicable, enter the ID for the material type that is to receive the profit center assignment. The material type is maintained at a higher level within the material hierarchy, so the breadth of the change will be great. Examples of a material type include FERT (Finished Goods) and HALB (Semi-Finished Goods). See the SAP Help text for details.

**Material Group**   If applicable, enter the ID for the material group to receive the profit center assignment. The material group is maintained one level down from the material type. See the SAP Help text for details.

**Prod. (Product) Hierarchy**   If applicable, enter the ID of the product hierarchy that is to receive the profit center assignment. You may select the hierarchy at any level, product group, product line, or product category. See the SAP Help text for details.

**Also Assigned Materials**   If this field is selected, SAP will maintain all material numbers that reside in the range, regardless of whether they have previously received a profit center assignment. If this field is not selected, the system will update only those materials that were previously unassigned.

For this example, fill in some information for the materials, language key, and plant, and execute the process. This will take you to an additional display screen where you will see the list of materials that will be affected and the field that will be changed. In our case we chose the profit center, and this is displayed in the screen. Fill in the new profit center to be posted to, and execute the process. If this were a new assignment, you would be seeing a similar screen but there would be no initial profit centers to affect (see Figure 13.10). You now have the opportunity to specifically define which materials are to be maintained by either leaving them highlighted or deselecting them. By clicking the icon that looks like a wrench, you can view an updated screen with all the changes made. If any issues with the changes would arise, this screen would offer you the advantage of reviewing them before making the changes permanent (see Figure 13.11). If all are appropriate, return to the Change screen, click the Select All button, and click Save. The material master records will be updated immediately. This process can also be done via the Material Master using the executable just below the Perform Fast Assignment option.

**FIGURE 13.10** The Mass Maintenance: Material (Industry) screen with the change process

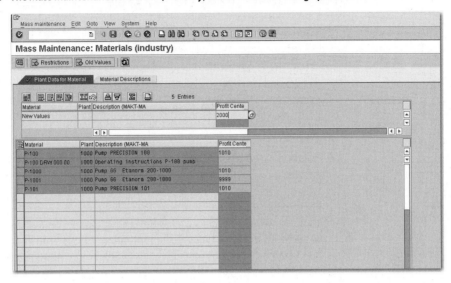

**FIGURE 13.11** The Messages from the Update Task screen

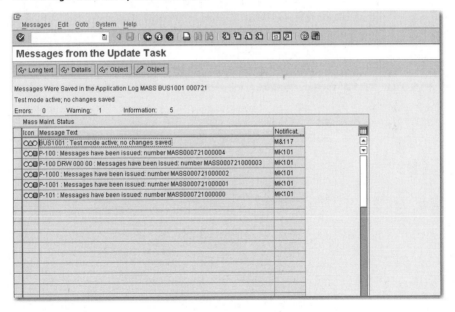

# Sales Order Substitution: Creation

If your solution requires you to assign the material master to a profit center that is different from the one responsible for P&L reporting, you will probably have to maintain the PCA sales order substitution. Like the substitutions that were covered in Chapter 2, "Financial Accounting Enterprise Structure," the sales order substitution uses information from the coding block and reroutes the profit center assignment based on rules that you define. To access the substitution creation screen, choose Enterprise Controlling ➢ Profit Center Accounting ➢ Assignments of Account Assignment Objects to Profit Centers ➢ Sales Orders ➢ Sales Order Substitutions ➢ Define Substitution Rules or use the transaction code 0KEM.

> **TIP**   As we have mentioned a few times now, once the define step is complete, you would assign the substitution to the appropriate process—either at time of billing or at time of order creation and either for other transactions and cross-company or for only cross-company documents.

The substitution creation screen appears (see Figure 13.12). To create a new substitution, choose Substitution ➢ Create or click the Substitution button on the screen. Because we covered substitutions in detail in Chapter 3, we'll provide only the high-level requirements here.

**FIGURE 13.12**   The substitution creation screen

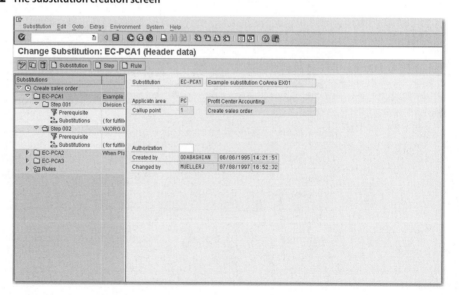

After filling in the substitution identifier and the description, you'll see the following fields on the substitution creation screen:

**Application Area**   The application area is the module or submodule for which you wish to create the substitution. It should always be PC (Profit Center Accounting) for the sales order substitution.

**Callup Point**   The callup point determines when the substitution is run. The callup points that are available depend on the application area selected. For PC (Profit Center Accounting), the only callup point available is 0001 (Create Sales Order).

When you click Enter (Green Check Icon), the Substitutable Fields box appears so that you can insert a substitution rule (see Figure 13.13).

**FIGURE 13.13**   The Substitutable Fields dialog box

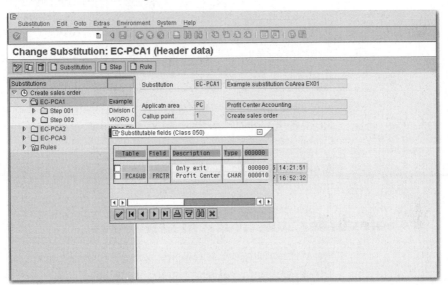

You will be provided with two choices:

**Only Exit**   If you select this field, a constant value selection will not be available for maintenance. The only update path will be through the use of the substitution user-exit explained in Chapter 2.

**Profit Center**   This field gives you the flexibility to substitute through either a constant profit center value assignment or the substitution user-exit. We recommend you choose this field because it does not limit your choices. Figure 13.14 provides you with a view of the sales order substitution EXTREME, used by Extreme Sports.

**FIGURE 13.14**　The substitution rule window for sales order substitution EXTREME

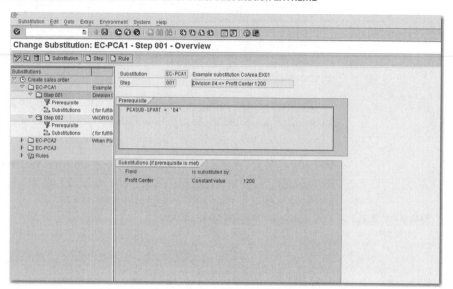

Review Chapter 3, "General Ledger," for a quick update on the concepts of Boolean logic and syntax, which you'll use when you create substitution rules. We have set up a substitution rule so that whenever Division 04 is used in a sales order, Profit Center 1200 will receive the posting.

After you create the sales order substitution, the next step is to determine the activation setting.

## Sales Order Substitution: Activation

When the substitution is complete, you must provide an appropriate activation setting. This setting differs from the one you used in Chapter 2 to activate your functional area substitution. To access the sales order substitution activation screen, choose Enterprise Controlling ➢ Profit Center Accounting ➢ Assignments of Account Assignment Objects to Profit Centers ➢ Sales Orders ➢ Sales Order Substitutions ➢ Assign Substitution Rules or use the transaction code 0KEL.

At the EC-PCA: Substitution for Profit Center in SD screen, click the New Entries button. In the appropriate fields, enter the controlling area and name of the substitution you previously created. In the Active Status column, you are given three activation choices for the substitution:

**0 – Not Active**　Leave the column blank if you do not want substitution activated.

**1 – Other Transactions + Cross-Company (Billing Documents)**    Substitution is used for both cross-company and normal handling. In cross-company handling, substitution is only used for the billing document.

**2 – Only for Cross-Company (Billing Documents)**    Substitution is only used for cross-company handling and only for the billing documents.

**3 – Other Transactions + Cross-Company (Orders + Billing Documents)**
Substitution is used for both cross-company and normal handling. In cross-company handling, substitution is only used for both sales orders and billing document.

**4 – Only for Cross-Company (Sales Orders + Billing Documents)**    Substitution is used only for cross-company handling. In cross-company handling, substitution is used for both sales orders and billing document.

When you've finished, save the activation settings. Figure 13.15 is a view of the activation status for Extreme Sports's sales order substitution EXTREME. This completes the process of material master assignments. It is vital that you communicate this integration point to all appropriate development parties and monitor the posting process to validate that the appropriate profit centers are assigned in the sales process. Even though we worked through this fairly easily, this will be the step that takes the most time. It is critical that you review and validate these settings before posting any transactions to ensure that all postings are getting to the right profit centers. Otherwise, at the end of the period your dummy profit center could be showing hundreds of postings that someone will have to investigate. To help you monitor all PCA assignments, SAP provides you with a tool called the Assignment Monitor.

## EXTREME SPORTS SALES ORDER SUBSTITUTION CONFIGURATION ANALYSIS

In the current and future Extreme Sports organization, the sales and marketing departments are responsible for all finished goods inventory balances as well as all revenue production. Based on this allocation of responsibility, only the responsible marketing profit centers will be placed on the material master record, negating the use of the sales order substitution functionality.

**FIGURE 13.15**  The activation status for sales order substitution EXTREME

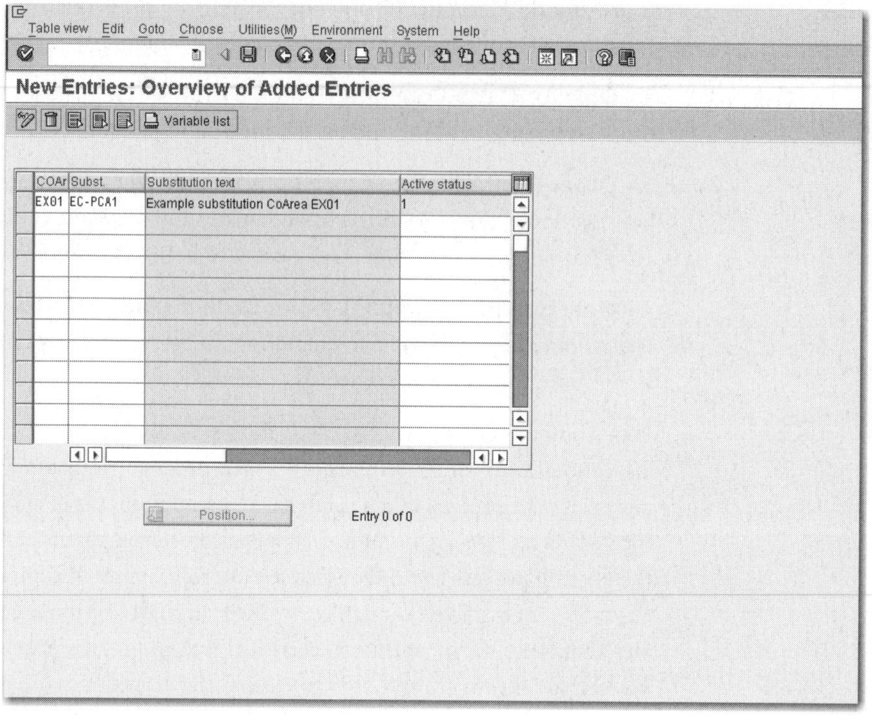

## PCA Assignment Monitor

The PCA Assignment Monitor is a tool that allows you to quickly assign many objects to a profit center or a group of profit centers. Through the monitor you are able to view the following items: materials, cost centers, orders, work breakdown structures, cost objects, and business processes. To access the Assignment Monitor, choose Enterprise Controlling ➢ Profit Center Accounting ➢ Assignments of Account Assignment Objects to Profit Centers ➢ Check Assignments or use the transaction code 1KE4.

The Assignment Monitor window looks much like those you find when accessing the various submodules from the user menu (see Figure 13.16). To review any of the previously mentioned assignment objects, you simply navigate through the user menu and follow the simple selection instructions. Remember that the tool can be as helpful in identifying those things that do not have an assignment as it is for those that do.

**FIGURE 13.16**  The EC-PCA Assignment Monitor main window

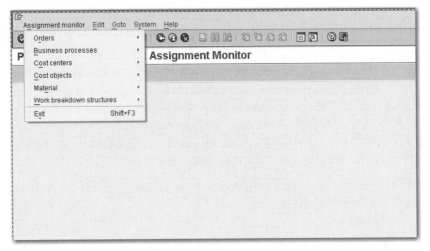

In the next section, we'll begin the process of preparing PCA to accept actual postings.

# Actual Posting Maintenance

Preparing Profit Center Accounting to accept actual postings can be simple or complex, depending on the needs of your company. On the simple side, all that is required is to activate the fiscal-year control parameters, create the proper document types, and define the necessary number ranges. For more complex solutions, additional account assignments may be maintained, and internal goods movements can be defined and segregated to enhance the profitability picture for each profit center. We will touch on the two PCA profitability-reporting philosophies, period accounting and cost of sales accounting, before continuing.

Because both cost of sales and period accounting are supported in the FI, PCA also must allow for either. Period accounting tracks profitability through the use of revenue and cost elements. The principle behind period accounting states that all costs and revenues incurred within a given period—including sales, deductions, cost of sales, costs of production, and all overhead expenses—summed together net the total operating profit. As a delivered system, PCA is set up to support the period accounting approach with the standard reports found in its information system. Cost of sales accounting uses a different strategy.

Cost of sales accounting also tracks revenue, but the revenue is compared to only the cost of sales associated with the quantity sold during the period. Manufacturing costs incurred in the period are held in inventory and not recognized until the time the inventory is sold. Additional selling and marketing and overhead expenses are also recognized in the period, with the net result being the profitability for that period. To facilitate the cost of sales accounting approach, you must first develop and maintain the functional areas and functional area substitution in FI. Chapter 2 covered both of these in detail.

The first step in the configuration process is to maintain the control parameters for actual postings.

### EXTREME SPORTS PROFITABILITY ACCOUNTING APPROACH CONFIGURATION ANALYSIS

Extreme Sports uses the period accounting approach to tracking and reporting profitability. Thus, all configuration demonstrated will support this method of accounting.

## Set Control Parameters

With the control parameters settings, you are defining how postings will update in the PCA environment. Before accessing the window, be sure that the proper controlling area is set—you will not be given an opportunity later. Choose Enterprise Controlling ➤ Profit Center Accounting ➤ Basic Settings ➤ Controlling Area Settings ➤ Activate Direct Postings ➤ Set Control Parameters for Actual Data or use the transaction code 1KEF.

When the overview screen appears, check that the set controlling area is the proper one. Click the New Entries button from the header to open a fresh screen. The settings are maintained by fiscal year. You do not need to make new settings each year; they are good from the year defined forward. Figure 13.17 is a view of the control settings for Extreme Sports's controlling area EX01.

**FIGURE 13.17**  The control parameter settings for controlling area EX01

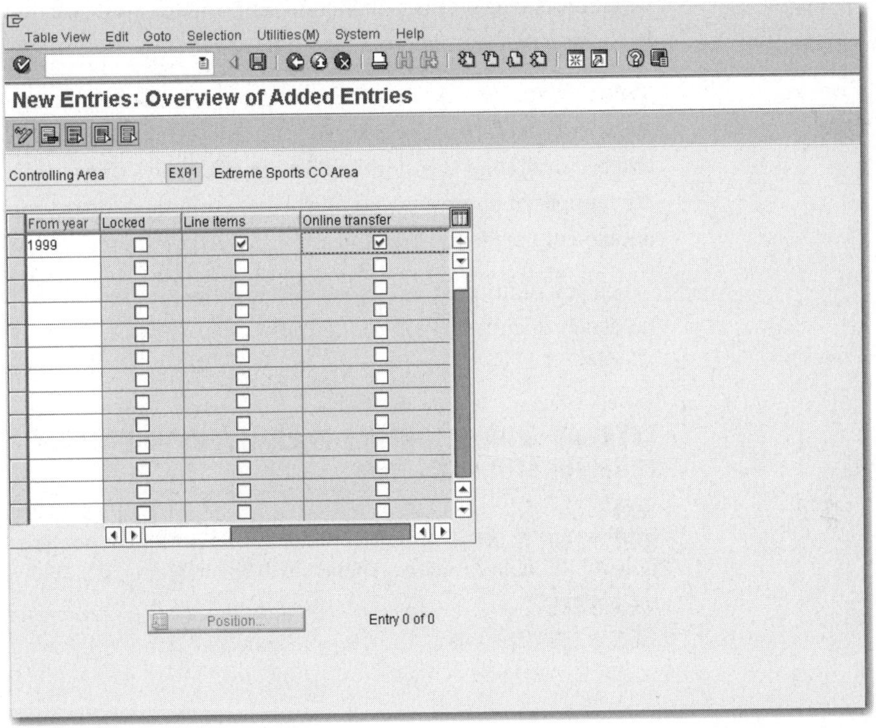

The column names and descriptions are as follows (the control parameters determine how actual postings update in PCA):

**Controlling Area**    The value is inserted automatically and represents the currently set controlling area.

**From Year**    Enter the fiscal year from which the parameter settings should be activated. The settings are good from this fiscal year forward.

**Locked**    Set this indicator if you wish to lock the controlling area from any actual postings for that fiscal-year setting. Set this indicator only if you have configured a new group of fiscal-year settings that begin after the most recent fiscal year identified on the table. For example, fiscal year 1995 is locked only when new settings are available for fiscal year 1997.

**Line Items**    Activate this setting if you want line items transferred to PCA. This will increase the number of documents posted in your system, but in many cases it is a must if you plan to do any detailed analysis.

**Online Transfer**    Activate this setting if you wish SAP to update the PCA ledger automatically during any transaction activity. If this setting is left inactivated, you will be required to transfer the postings manually. This is not recommended due to the number of programs that must be run and the fact that some postings could get double-counted if you are not careful.

When you've finished, save your settings. The next section will take you through the necessary document type configuration steps.

---

### EXTREME SPORTS CONTROL PARAMETERS FOR ACTUAL POSTINGS CONFIGURATION ANALYSIS

Extreme Sports wants as much online transfer activity as possible from its SAP solution. Additionally, line item analysis will be vital, at least initially, to the success of the project.

---

## Define Document Types: Actual

By this time, you have been exposed to the document principle and are familiar with what a document type does in SAP. In FI, the document type lets SAP know, among other things, which transactions are to be posted. In PCA, the document type controls things like what currencies the posting can be maintained in, the document number range, and whether the transaction must be balanced. Earlier in the chapter we stated that PCA exists outside the environments of FI and CO and thus can allow an unbalanced entry to occur. It is through the document type configuration that FI postings are  controlled.

Begin the process by choosing Enterprise Controlling ➤ Profit Center Accounting ➤ Actual Postings ➤ Basic Settings: Actual ➤ Maintain Document Types or use the transaction code GCBX. The valid document types window appears, displaying the default document type A0. You can use this delivered document type or create your own. As with all SAP-delivered objects, we recommend that you create your own. To do so, click the New Entries button, and a fresh screen will appear, featuring these column names:

**Doc. (Document) Type**　Enter a two-character ID that represents the document type.

**TC (Transaction Currency)**　Activate this setting if you want the transaction currency stored at the time of posting. We recommend you enable this setting.

**C2 (Second Currency)**　Activate this setting if you wish to also capture the posting in a second currency (local/company code). We recommend you enable this setting as well.

**C3 (Third Currency)**　Activate this setting if you want to also capture the posting in a third-currency. Again, we recommend you enable this setting.

> **TIP**　It is easiest to select all three currency settings. Updates will occur only for those that exist in the controlling area.

**Bal. (Balance) Check**　Here you are offered the option of allowing unbalanced entries in PCA. You have three options:

**0**　An error is returned if the balance is not zero. This will force all PCA entries to be balanced.

**1**　A warning is returned if the balance is not zero. If you wish to offer the flexibility of unbalanced entries, this is a good setting.

**2**　No balance check is conducted.

**Local/Global**　These columns are grayed out. The settings here represent the number range assignment given to each document type. This will be maintained in the actual number range assignment section.

**Description**　Enter a text description for your document type. Make the description clear because these document types are controlling area independent.

Figure 13.18 shows the settings for document type AX, which will be used by Extreme Sports to post actuals into PCA. You are free to create as many document types as you see fit, without any repercussions. During document entry, the user will be required to enter a document type. If you want to offer different controls for different types of entries, you have that capability.

**FIGURE 13.18** Extreme Sports' document type AX

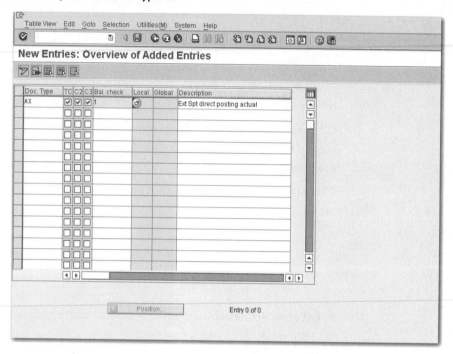

The next section covers the number range assignment for the new document type. You will not be able to make a PCA entry without one.

## EXTREME SPORTS DOCUMENT TYPE FOR ACTUAL POSTINGS CONFIGURATION ANALYSIS

Extreme Sports chose to create its own document type because it wanted to make changes to the settings that were delivered with A0. All three PCA-related currencies will be allowed for actual transactions. The flexibility offered here does not make them required, but rather gives the user the option. As for balance checking, Extreme Sports votes for the flexibility provided by SAP with the assignment of a warning on any unbalanced entries. Although they won't be encouraged, unbalanced entries are an easy way of clearing up an error. Remember, the PCA books are meant for internal reporting only.

# Number Range Assignment: Actual

Like the many number range assignments you have maintained so far, the PCA actuals number range is similar in its configuration steps (see Chapter 10 for additional details). As noted earlier, the document type is used as the number range assignment object and thus must be completed first. To access the number range assignment screen, choose Enterprise Controlling ➤ Profit Center Accounting ➤ Actual Postings ➤ Basic Settings: Actual ➤ Define Number Ranges for Local Documents or use the transaction code GB02.

At the number ranges for local GL documents window, click the Maintain Groups button in the toolbar to open the Maintain Number Range Groups screen (see Figure 13.19). Notice that the Extreme Sports document type AX appears in the Not Assigned area. At this time, you need to check that all relative company code number range intervals have been properly maintained.

**FIGURE 13.19**   The Maintain Number Range Groups screen

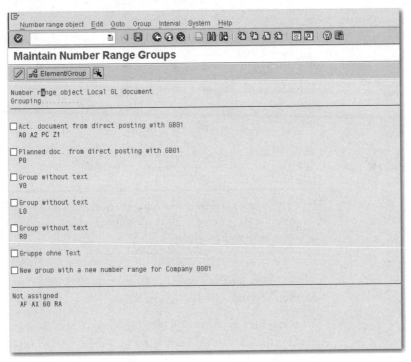

To accomplish this, go back to the initial maintain number range interval screen and select the Change Intervals button in the toolbar. A dialog box appears, asking you to enter a company code. Enter your respective company code ID and press Enter. If the company code number range interval has been properly maintained, a screen similar to the one in Figure 13.20 should appear. If not, click the insert interval icon, and define the number range interval for your company code.

**FIGURE 13.20** The number range interval screen for Extreme Sports's company code 1000

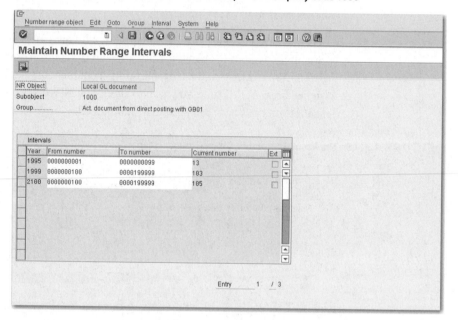

**TIP** Be sure to extend the fiscal year associated with the number range interval far enough into the future. It can be a maintenance nightmare to create new number range intervals for each fiscal year.

When you've finished, save the settings and click the green arrow to return to the Maintain Number Range Groups screen.

To assign the new document type to a range, select the document type by double-clicking the ID directly. Then select the range Act. Document from Direct Posting with GB01 and click the Element/Group button. The selected document type will move to its new assigned range. Save the number range settings.

If you return to the valid document types screen, you should see that the new document type AX now has a number range defined for it under the Local column (see Figure 13.21). You will have to repeat these steps for each new document type created.

**FIGURE 13.21** The number range assignment for document type AX

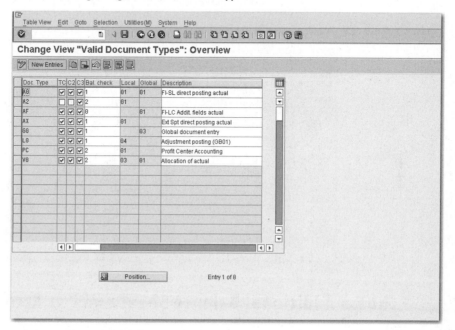

This completes the basic settings necessary for PCA actual postings to occur. The next few sections will take you through some complex settings you'll encounter when completing your PCA solution.

## Assign Revenue Elements to Profit Centers

We covered the default account assignment table TKA3A in detail in Chapter 10. We recommend that you review the section "Maintaining Number Range Assignments" in that chapter before maintaining any additional settings here. In Chapter 10, we established settings to route contract services revenue, revenue element 301000, to the Misc. Sales profit center 140000. The menu path to reach the account assignment table is Enterprise Controlling ➢ Profit Center Accounting ➢ Actual Postings ➢ Maintain Automatic Account Assignment of Revenue Elements to Profit Centers; the transaction code is OKB9.

These settings can be maintained at any time, but the effects are not retroactive. An additional account assignment tool is available to PCA only. This assignment relates a cost/revenue element posting to a single profit. Unique to this table is the ability to assign balance sheet accounts. Remember that balance sheet accounts exist in FI only, meaning you do not have the ability to create cost or revenue elements. PCA allows the assignment of these accounts through this table only (see Figure 13.22).

**FIGURE 13.22** Default account assignment overview

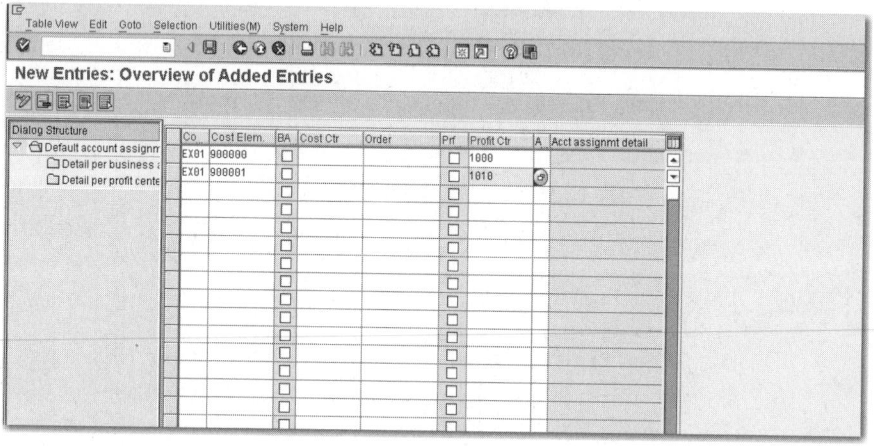

## Choose Additional Balance Sheet and P&L Accounts

In addition to the default account assignment screen covered earlier, you have the choice of assigning additional cost elements or balance sheet accounts to a given profit center. Standard SAP functionality allows you to transfer at period's end the primary balance sheet accounts, including A/P, A/R, assets, material stocks (raw and finished goods), and work-in-process. The balances for the payables, receivables, assets, and material stocks will default to the profit center that is assigned to the relative master record involved: material master for A/P, A/R, and material stock balances; fixed assets for the asset balances. For the work-in-process balance, the profit center assignment on the order or project will be used. To avoid double counting, these accounts should not be maintained in this table.

**WARNING**    SAP will not warn you that you are adding one of these default transfer accounts in the table at the time of entry. The first time you will notice is during your review of the PCA balance sheet.

Use the menu path Enterprise Controlling ≻ Profit Center Accounting ≻ Actual Postings ≻ Choose Additional Balance and P&L Accounts ≻ Choose Accounts to access the additional account assignments screen, or you can use transaction code 3KEH. The settings are controlling area dependent, so be certain that the proper controlling area is set.

At the additional balance sheet and P&L account screen, click the New Entries button to make the new assignments. The configuration settings are simple and require little explanation:

**Acct From/To**   Enter the range of accounts you want to default to a profit center.

**Def. PrCtr (Default Profit Center)**   Enter the ID of the profit center to which the accounts are to be assigned.

When you've finished, save the settings (see Figure 13.23). Remember to avoid overlapping any of the defined transfer balance sheet accounts during maintenance.

**FIGURE 13.23** EX01 additional assignment table

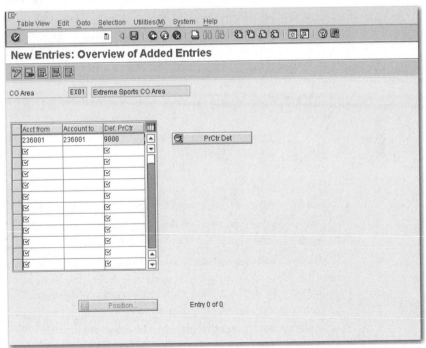

# Balance Carry Forward Indicator Maintenance

If you have maintained any settings on the additional balance sheet and P&L account assignment table, it is necessary to set the balance carry forward indicator for the PCA environment. You will want to properly roll all transferred accounts to the proper retained earnings account. To access the carry forward window, select Enterprise Controlling ➤ Profit Center Accounting ➤ Basic Settings ➤ Balance CarryForward ➤ Allow Balances to Be Carried Forward or use transaction code 2KET.

The overview screen is easy to navigate. Simply select the Balance Carry Forward (Bal. CF) box found in the window (see Figure 13.24). Save the settings when you've finished. The second step in the balance carry forward configuration process is the assignment of the retained earnings account to the chart of accounts. Because this step was completed in the section "Configuring G/L Account Master Records" in Chapter 4, "Accounts Payable," we will not have to configure it here.

**FIGURE 13.24** The balance carried forward activation screen

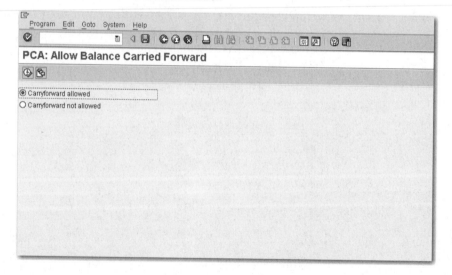

This concludes the section on actual posting configuration. You have now completed enough PCA configuration to ensure that all transactional data flows will update properly and that all direct postings are possible. The next section will take you through the necessary steps to configure basic PCA planning functionality.

**EXTREME SPORTS ADDITIONAL BALANCE SHEET ENTRIES CONFIGURATION ANALYSIS**

Extreme Sports will not be producing full balance sheets out of PCA, so there is no immediate need to maintain this table. The entry shown in configuration was for demonstration purposes only.

# Profit Center Accounting: Planning

You can choose between two standard approaches of Profit Center Accounting planning within SAP: planning the profit center manually and transferring plan data from other CO applications. In many instances, PCA planning is a combination of both types. From a configuration viewpoint, the preparation to use manual planning is a more involved process and is similar to the process we discussed in Chapter 10. The development involved in transferring plan data is centered around CO version maintenance, with some order type configuration sprinkled in. Because the manual approach requires the majority of the configuration effort, most of this section will be dedicated to this approach.

To begin, we'll provide an overview of plan version maintenance, document type creation, and number range assignment for your review. From there, we'll explain PCA's use of planning parameters and the associated configuration. And finally, a brief explanation of the copy plan data transaction will round out the section.

## Plan Version Maintenance

PCA uses and is controlled by the same CO versions, as with all CO applications. Within the version you have the ability to control whether plan data from other applications is updated automatically in PCA or if you have to manually transfer the postings. For automatic updates into PCA, you should expect interaction to come from only Cost Center Accounting and Internal Order Accounting. All other plan data will have to be transferred manually. The valid CO objects available for manual data transfer include the following: cost centers, internal orders, projects, networks, account-based profitability segments, SOP orders (sales/operations-related orders), and MRP orders.

**NOTE** Only account-based CO-PA can transfer plan data to PCA because of the cost element requirement in PCA plan postings. You must have defined both the profit center and controlling area in the CO-PA plan entry.

Plan version maintenance was covered in detail in Chapters 8, 10, and 11, so only a review of some key topics is necessary here. To access the CO version table, choose Enterprise Controlling ➢ Profit Center Accounting ➢ Planning ➢ Basic Settings for Planning ➢ Plan Versions ➢ Maintain Plan Versions or use the transaction code OKEQ.

As you have seen in past maintenance, the CO versions screen appears. As always, SAP allows you to use as many planning versions as you like. Two key screens are related to automating the transfer of plan data:

► The screen with settings for Profit Center Accounting

► The screen with fiscal year settings

## Settings for PCA

Move to the PCA settings window by selecting the version to be maintained and clicking the Settings for Profit Center Accounting button in the Navigation section of the window. The PCA fiscal year–dependent version parameters overview screen appears (Figure 13.25).

**FIGURE 13.25** The PCA fiscal year–dependent version parameters settings

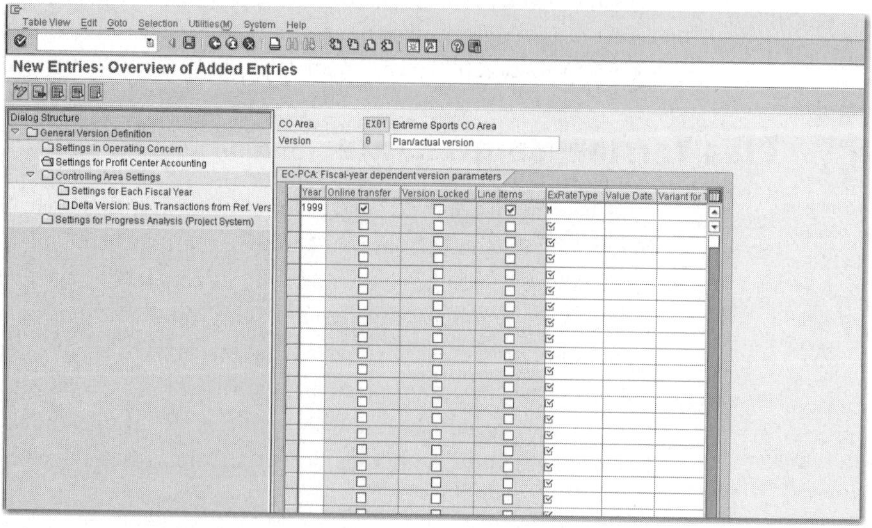

On the PCA fiscal year–dependent version parameters screen, the effects of the following fields are important:

**Online Transfer**    The setting must be activated if you wish to transfer plan postings from CCA and order accounting online. This setting will almost always be activated because of the need to transfer actual in real time.

**Line Items**    This setting must be activated if you want line item changes to be documented. Also, activating this setting will make manual plan transfers easier because you will have the ability to retransfer plan activity. When Line Items is activated, you have the opportunity to retransfer plan items at an individual object (order, cost center) level. If it's not activated, you will have no recourse but to retransfer all the object values for the given type. See Figure 13.26 for a view of the manual transfer screen for PCA plan data.

**FIGURE 13.26**  The EC-PCA: Transfer Plan Data to Profit Center Accounting screen for plan data

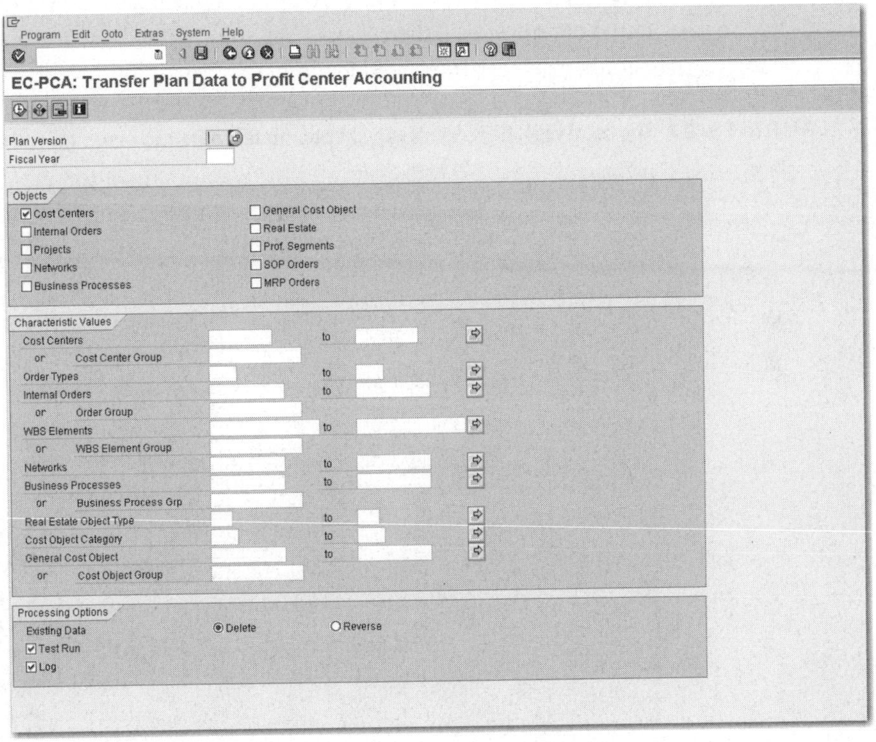

**ExRate (Exchange Rate) Type and Value Date**   Use this field to define the exchange rate type that will be used for the transfer of planned data. You are probably familiar with the exchange rate type M. The Value Date setting is the date that is used for all planning data and the exchange rate type.

**Variant for TP**   This setting is specific to transfer pricing and determines whether actual or plan data is to be valuated. In addition, it determines the order in which the pricing procedures are to be processed to find the transfer price for this specific profit center valuation.

Maintain or review these settings and move to the fiscal year parameters screen.

## Settings for Fiscal Year

Look through the Dialog Structure section of the CO versions maintenance screen to find the Settings for Fiscal Year button and click it. The fiscal year–dependent version parameters detail window appears (see Figure 13.27). Of the many fields found on this screen, there is only one you want to be most concerned with from a PCA perspective: Integrated Planning.

**FIGURE 13.27**   The fiscal year–dependent version parameters detail screen

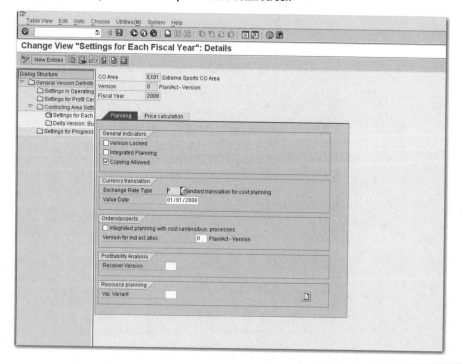

Activate Integrated Planning if you want to transfer plan data from cost centers to Profit Center Accounting automatically online. Although no plan data exists in the version, you can change this setting. If plan data has been posted, the integration indicator can be activated through transaction KP96 (Activate line items and integrated planning). Once it's activated, SAP posts previously planned line items.

To fully automate plan postings into PCA, you have to also maintain each order type to allow planning integration.

## Order Type Maintenance

In the section "Order Type Development" in Chapter 11, you learned that you must maintain the planning integration field to allow plan updates into PCA. Figure 13.28 is a view of the order type EXX1 used by Extreme Sports for expense-related project tracking.

**FIGURE 13.28** The order type master screen for EXX1

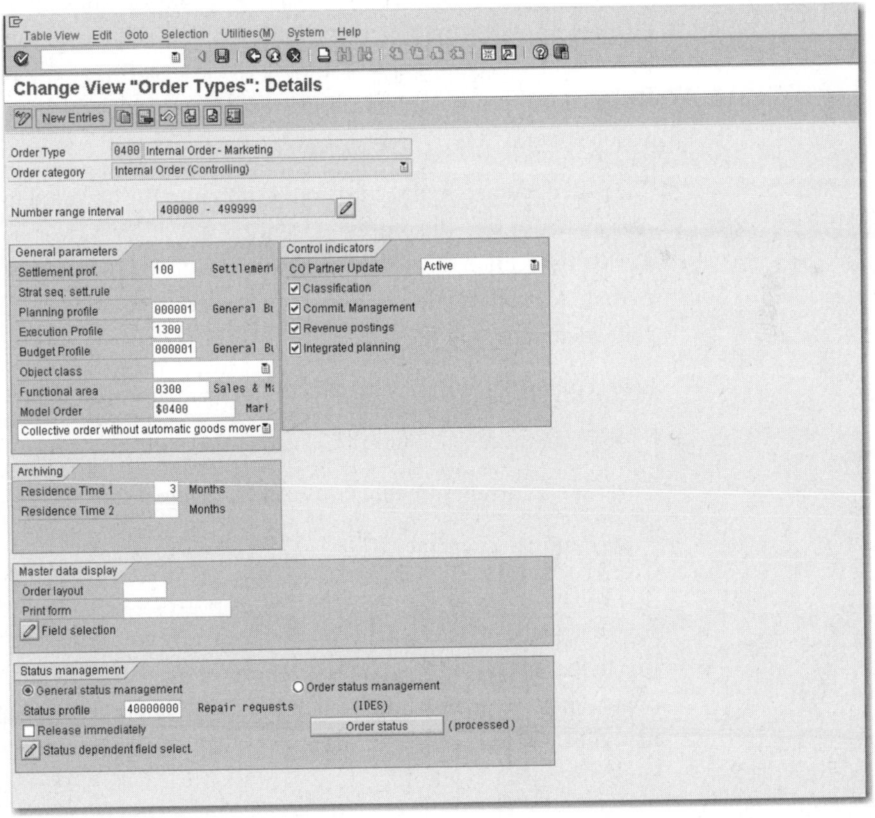

If Integrated Planning is active here, plan data can be automatically passed to Profit Center Accounting. To activate this setting, the CO Partner Update setting must be set to Active. This setting does not need to be activated if you do not intend to completely integrate with Profit Center Accounting.

When maintenance of these three areas is complete, your version is ready to accept automated plan updates from CCA and Order Accounting into PCA. The second task in PCA planning configuration is the development of the planning document type. Similar to the one established to support actual postings, it must be established before any postings can occur.

## Define Document Types: Plan

The plan document type is simple to create. The process is identical to the process for establishing a document type to support actual postings. SAP delivers plan document type PO as the default. You can use this one or create your own. We recommend that you create your own if you anticipate making any changes to the default settings. To access the plan document type screen, choose Enterprise Controlling ➤ Profit Center Accounting ➤ Planning ➤ Basic Settings for Planning ➤ Maintain Document Types ➤ Maintain Document Types for Local Documents or use transaction code GCBA.

The plan document type screen looks similar to the one used to create actual types. As a matter of fact, the process is identical, so we won't re-create the steps here. Review the section on actual document type creation, "Define Document Types: Actual," for detailed descriptions of each of the fields. Figure 13.29 is a view of the plan document type PX, which will be used by Extreme Sports for PCA planning.

Like actual postings, all plan updates can be maintained in three currencies:

- ▶ Transaction currency (TC), held as the primary currency

- ▶ Local currency or company code currency (C2)

- ▶ Reporting currency (C3)

You will also have to maintain these same settings on the planning parameters screen if you want to manually plan in each currency type. You'll learn more about this in the section "PCA Planning Parameters" later in this chapter. You have the opportunity to create as many planning document types as necessary. When you have finished, the last step in the process will be to assign them to a number range.

**FIGURE 13.29** Extreme Sports' document type PX

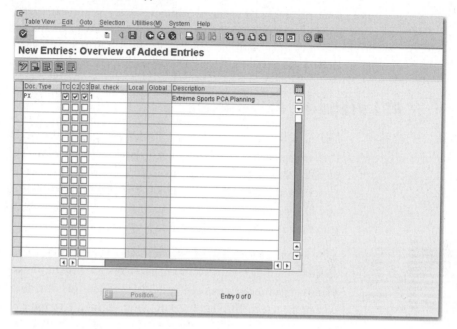

# Number Range Assignment: Plan

The configuration steps to assign number ranges to a plan are identical to the steps to assign number ranges to the PCA actuals. As noted earlier, the document type is used as the number range assignment object and thus must be completed first. To access the number range assignment screen, choose Enterprise Controlling ➤ Profit Center Accounting ➤ Planning ➤ Basic Settings for Planning ➤ Define Number Ranges ➤ Maintain Number Ranges for Local Documents or use the transaction code GB02.

## EXTREME SPORTS DOCUMENT TYPE FOR PLAN POSTINGS CONFIGURATION ANALYSIS

Again, Extreme Sports chose to create its own document type because it wanted to make changes to the settings that were delivered with PO. All three PCA-related currencies will be allowed for plan postings. For balance checking, here again Extreme Sports chose the flexibility SAP offers with the assignment of a warning on any unbalanced entries.

For the exact steps necessary to assign the plan document type and a number range interval, review the section "Number Range Assignment: Actual". The only difference is that you are maintaining the screen for the plan type. Once you've finished, plan document type creation is complete. The next section will take you through the concept of the PCA planning parameters and the accompanying set maintenance.

# PCA Planning Parameters

The manual planning process in PCA follows very closely the process in CCA and the basic use of the planning profiles, planning layouts, and establishment of the default parameters if necessary to execute a planning process. Please refer to the Cost Center Accounting and the Cost Element Accounting discussions, Chapters 9 and 10, for additional details on this approach to planning. This section outlines the use of the Planning Parameters and Sets approach.

Here we will go back another step and work through the process of setting up a specific planning set and planning parameters to help us in the planning process. Planning parameters are used by PCA as the control utility for manual plan entry on a profit center. Through the parameter, you can determine such things as what periods, profit centers, cost elements, and currencies can be planned. During the planning parameter creation steps, you will be asked to provide the parameter with a planning set ID. This is a multidimensional set containing both profit centers and cost elements used in the planning process. To properly maintain the parameter, you must create this set up front.

## Planning Set Creation

SAP delivers with the system four basic planning sets you can use:

**8A-RPRCTR.GLU1**    This planning set allows the use of all profit centers.

**8A-RACCT.GLU1**    This planning set is used as the basic profit center/cost and revenue element planning set.

**8A-SPRCTR.GLU1**    In addition to the objects allowed in 8A-RACCT.GLU1, and 8A-RPRCTR.GLU1, you will be allowed to plan the partner profit center. The partner profit center is the offset profit center on a two-sided transaction.

**8A-BSFAREA-1.GLU1**    This planning set is used when you want to plan the functional area. It is useful only for those companies using the cost of sales approach to report profitability.

Each of these sets contains variables that require the user to enter a profit center group, a cost element group, a partner profit center group, or a functional area during plan data entry. This is fine in most cases because the responsibility lies with the user to determine the proper profit center/cost element mix. If, however, you wish to control the situation more, we recommend that you create your own planning set to be used with your new planning parameter. There is a one-to-one relationship between the planning parameter and the planning set, so choose carefully. It may turn out that multiple sets and parameters will be needed for your solution.

Set creation is table specific; that is, all sets must be assigned to a planning table to be used properly by SAP. For PCA, the table to use is GLU1. You may be thinking that you should use GLPCT, the PCA plan line items table, but GLPCT is used for reporting sets only. If GLU1 is not used, your sets will not be visible in the planning parameter screen.

In addition to the table assignment, there are four different types of sets that can be created to support PCA planning:

**Basic set**    Basic is a set that is used to hold the values, whether individual or within a range of values, of a single type of object like a profit center or cost element. It is used as the building block for more complex single sets and multisets. The basic set can also contain formulas and formula and value variables.

**Single set**    Similar to the basic set, a single set can hold the values of only a single type of object also. However, you can assign a number of basic sets of the same type to easily build a hierarchy or other complex groups.

**Key figure set**    Used mainly in reporting, the data set is used to derive or narrow the values and quantities selected.

**Multiset**    Multiset allows for a complex grouping of two or more objects in a single set using any combination of basic, single, and key figure sets. The one stipulation is that the object type must not be defined more than once within the set. This type of set will be the one you will use predominantly during planning parameter creation.

We covered detailed set creation in Chapter 2, "Financial Accounting Enterprise Structure," so we won't retrace the steps here. You can choose Enterprise Controlling ➤ Profit Center Accounting ➤ Tools ➤ Sets and Variables ➤ Maintain Sets or use transaction code GS01 (Create a Set) or GS02 (Change a Set).

Figure 13.30 shows the resulting screen. You have the ability to copy from an existing set or you can create your own. Spend some time up front planning your set usage. It will be critical that you have all the right objects in place when the user wants to begin plan entry. Figure 13.31 shows the Set Hierarchy for the EXTREME-PCA planning set, and Figure 13.32 shows the subsets for the completed Planning Set for EXTREME-PCA to be used in the planning process.

**WARNING**   Remember to select GLU1 as the table in which to create the planning set.

Once you have completed the set creation, you are ready to create the planning parameter.

**FIGURE 13.30** The Create Set: Initial Screen

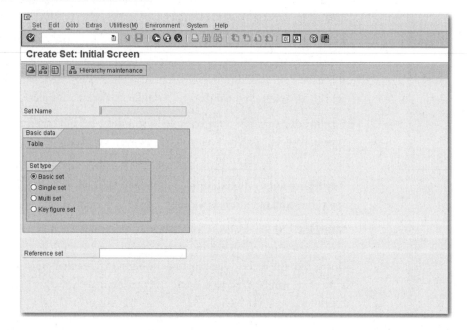

**FIGURE 13.31**  The Change Set Hierarchy: Structure screen for EXTREME-PCA, which will be used by Extreme Sports for PCA plan entry

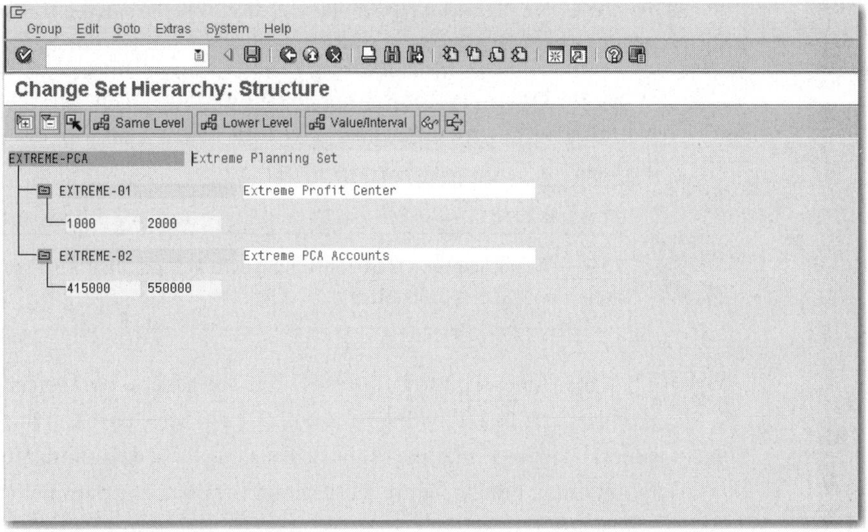

**FIGURE 13.32**  The Change Set: Subordinate Sets screen for EXTREME-PCA (a multiset)

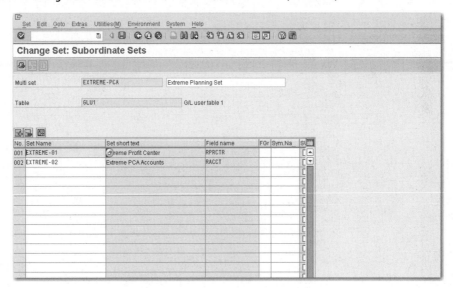

## Planning Parameter Creation

To access the planning parameter creation screen, use the transaction code GP41 to display the create screen.

When the create planning parameters initial screen appears, enter the name of the planning parameter in the field provided. You can copy an existing parameter if you choose.

**TIP**   The parameter will be controlling area independent, so be sure the name you choose is clear and descriptive.

Click the General button or press Enter. The general part screen appears. There are two parts to a planning parameter: the general part and the FI-SL part. On the general part screen, some of the field settings will default in; others you will have to maintain manually. Figure 13.33 shows the planning parameter EX-PCA01, which will be used by Extreme Sports to enter its plan data.

**FIGURE 13.33**   The general part settings planning parameter EX-PCA01

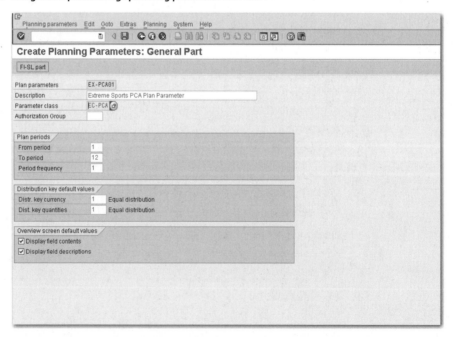

All field settings can be changed except the parameter ID. Review the following fields and their descriptions as you complete your ID:

**Plan Parameters**    The value in this field defaults from the initial screen. The only way to change the ID now is to delete the parameter and start again.

**Description**    Enter enough of a description for your parameter to make it easily recognizable from a selection menu.

**Parameter Class**    Enter **EC-PCA** or **FI-GLX** as the parameter class. This will ensure that the planning parameter is used only in PCA or Special Ledger (FI-SL) planning.

**Authorization Group**    This field is not required. If you are using authorization groups in your security maintenance, this field may be relevant. See your SAP authorizations group for maintenance details.

The fields in the Plan Periods section determine the range of frequency for valid plan periods:

**From/To Period**    Enter the range of periods for which this parameter is valid.

**Period Frequency**    This field relates to the periodicity of plan entry. If you wish to enter plan data on a quarterly basis, the frequency would be 3, or once every three months.

The fields in the Distribution Key Default Values section determine the default distribution for both the currency and quantity amounts. Enter the default distribution key for both types of data. A distribution key is a tool SAP provides that allows you to determine the spread of data across a given period range. With a properly defined distribution key, you could spread annual plan amounts across a 4-4-5 fiscal year or make an even spread by month.

The fields in the Overview Screen Default Values section control the view on the planning screen. They determine whether the objects being planned (profit center/cost element) will be displayed by their ID and/or their description:

**Display Field Contents**    Select this field if you want the ID of the field contents to be displayed. For example, if you want the profit center number to be displayed on the planning screen, select Display Field Contents.

**Display Field Description**    Select this field if you want the description of the field to be displayed. For example, if you want the profit center description to be displayed on the planning screen, select Display Field Description.

It is possible to have both settings on at the same time, and it is often the recommended approach.

This completes the general part of the planning parameter. You must now maintain the FI-SL portion of the parameter to complete the configuration. To migrate to the window, click the FI-SL Part button. As with the general part fields, the FI-SL fields will be described. Figure 13.34 shows the FI-SL portion for planning parameter EX-PCA01.

**FIGURE 13.34** The FI-SL settings for planning parameter EX-PCA01

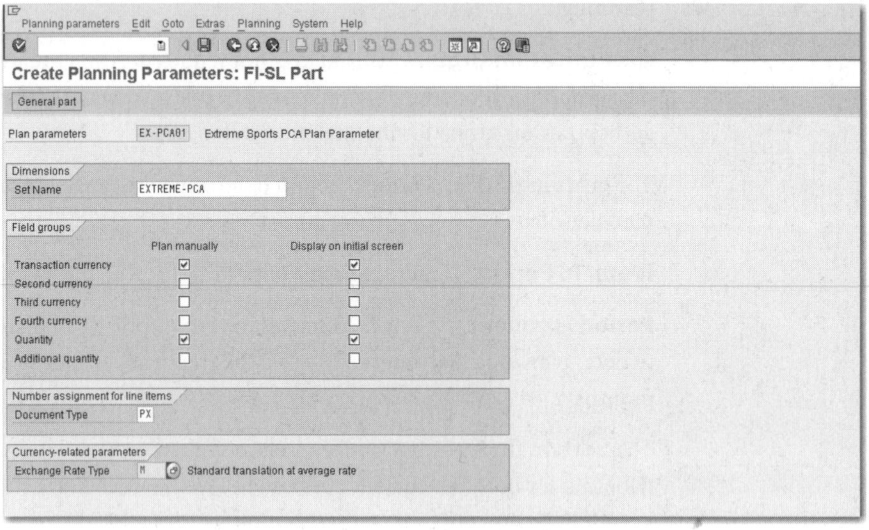

The Dimensions section defines the parameter planning set:

**Set Name**    Enter the ID of the planning set you created earlier. The planning set entry is required. With this setting, you are determining what object values the user will have access to during the planning process. This is a good control mechanism if you want to limit the ability to enter or view plan entries.

The fields in the Field Groups section determine which currency and quantity fields are allowed and/or required during plan entry. The fields are divided into two settings: Plan Manually and Display on Initial Screen. If you want to allow planning in any of these areas, it must be checked in the Plan Manually column. All the Initial Screen setting accomplishes is determining which fields default on the first plan entry screen. The user will have the authority to scroll to the other allowed currencies and quantities. The fields are as follows:

**Transaction/Second/Third Currency**    By activating a currency, you are allowing the user to plan in that currency. Leave these inactive to block any postings.

**Quantity/Additional Quantity**    PCA allows you to maintain two quantity fields. Select one, both, or none.

The Number Assignment for Line Items section assigns a plan document type to your parameters:

**Document Type**    Enter the document type if you are maintaining plan postings at the line item level. If you are, a PCA plan document will need to be created for each plan entry. If not, leave this field blank.

The Currency-Related Parameters setting is necessary when planning in multiple currencies:

**Exchange Rate Type**    Enter the ID of the exchange method relevant to your company's needs. Rate type M, standard translation at an average rate, will default.

When you've finished, be sure to save the planning parameter. This completes the steps necessary for planning parameter creation. You are now at a point in your PCA planning development where you can manually enter plan data. The last section in PCA planning will show you the subtle differences between the copy plan data transaction for PCA and the one found in CCA.

## EXTREME SPORTS PLANNING PARAMETER CREATION CONFIGURATION ANALYSIS

Extreme Sports has decided to take advantage of several of the functionality options offered in the Cash and Liquidity submodule. As Extreme Sports has operations in both Mexico and the United States, they must accurately reflect the results of business activity in both the Mexican Peso and the U.S. Dollar. Extreme Sports has decided to use the functionality that will automatically revalue open items (such as open customer invoices). Extreme Sports considers timely and accurate cash flow and cash forecasts an important tool for effectively managing its business. It is for this reason they are using the cash forecasting tools that help to group cash-related accounts together. The grouping is based on the type of financial activity that takes place in the accounts.

Extreme Sports will be creating a number of planning parameters to support its manual plan entry. It found that the delivered planning sets offered too much breadth. Because each profit center manager will be entering his or her own plan, Extreme Sports would like to narrow the scope of profit centers and accounts to choose from. Additionally, it anticipates one day spent creating new distribution keys to support quarterly plan entries. And the planning parameter is the perfect place to make sure the distribution keys default properly.

## Copy Plan Data

As with Cost Center Accounting, with PCA you have the ability to copy data to various plan versions and actuals to plan. The main difference between the two systems is the parameters that are required to do this copy function process. SAP accomplishes this by extending the source data selections on the PCA side to include the record type. The record type is used to classify the type of data being held in the database and includes four values:

**0**  Actuals

**1**  Plan

**2**  Actual Assessments/Distributions

**3**  Plan Assessments/Distributions

To get a better feel for the concepts, choose Accounting ➢ Enterprise Controlling ➢ Profit Center Accounting ➢ Planning ➢ Copy Data to Plan or use the transaction code 7KEV to view the PCA plan copy window.

**TIP**   If you are looking to use the planning parameters and planning sets that you created in the previous section, you will use the transaction code KE62 to get to the copy function planning screen that will allow the use of these structures.

The PCA Copy to Plan screen appears (Figure 13.35). In the Source Data section, you will see the Record Type setting. By selecting 0 (Actuals), you will be able to copy actual data to a plan version. Additionally, you can see that an entry in the field labeled Plan. Parameters is required. This is SAP's way of limiting the amount of transactional data that will be copied across versions. Everything else should look familiar because it is similar to the CCA copy screen described in Chapter 10.

This brings to an end the PCA planning configuration. You are now ready to begin manually planning and/or transferring your plan data into PCA. It is important that you experiment with the transfer postings to be certain that all the bugs are rung out and that all the users' needs are met. Again, these are just the basic setup steps that will get you moving down the appropriate path to use the PCA planning process. It is important to position PCA planning in the overall planning process along with CO-PA, CCA, and other planning processes.

**FIGURE 13.35** The PCA Copy to Plan screen

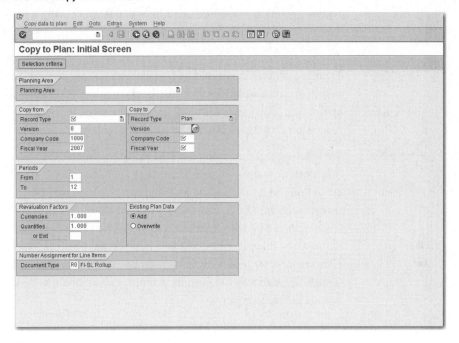

# Summary

Profit Center Accounting development is straightforward in a traditional configuration sense. There is not an infinite number of settings that can be tested to see which ones fit your scenario. Instead, there is a heavy reliance on making the proper object assignments and building an accurate standard hierarchy. Spend some time researching the reporting needs of your client prior to beginning the configuration. The changes become more cumbersome once you begin to have real postings in your environment. And finally, communication with all related modules is critical to success. So, be sure to include the persons from the MM, PP, and SD teams during the design and development phases.

As we mentioned, all postings in the PCA component are statistical in nature and will not create more postings. Therefore, if you have $5,000,000 in revenue moving through the FI module, you should not have more than the same amount showing up in the PCA reports. Since it is statistical in nature, it is a good approach to have reporting against organizational elements that cross company codes and therefore create a matrix approach to reporting. So, if a company is looking for a method of reviewing regional information or lines of business (LOB), a profit center process would work. Again, make sure all master data has been linked correctly to generate the appropriate information.

There is a process in which data transfers to PCA are done at the end of a period or month. In some situations, this may be the method of choice, but posting records on an ongoing basis to PCA is much easier to manage. It also allows you to review your reports on an ongoing basis to see that all data is being posted correctly.

We followed this discussion with the planning process in PCA. Review the planning options that you have in PCA. They are not as robust as in CO-PA, but there are definite uses for planning and analysis. You have the ability to upload Excel spreadsheets into PCA, save these spreadsheets offline, and then upload again similar to what can be accomplished in CO-PA. The planning process in PCA can be a bit more specific in terms of the area that you are planning. You can focus on the planning process in PCA by costs/revenue, balance sheet accounts, or statistical key figures. You can also use formula planning, which could include using calculations against the planning data.

All in all, PCA is a useful component of the EC environment. EC-CS has evolved— now SEM-BCS or BPC (Business Planning and Consolidations) is being used for overall corporate consolidations; the BP (Business Planning) has been upgraded to either BI-IP (Business Intelligence-Integrated Planning) or BPC (Business Planning and Consolidations); and the EIS (Executive Information System) has evolved into BI (Business Intelligence), formerly known as BW (Business Warehouse). PCA is the only portion of this component that is being used on a regular basis.

# Investment Management

**FEATURING:**

▶ **INVESTMENT MANAGEMENT CONFIGURATION**

▶ **PROGRAM TYPES, INVESTMENT MEASURES, AND THE INVESTMENT PROFILE**

▶ **INVESTMENT MANAGEMENT PLANNING AND BUDGETING PROFILES**

nvestment Management (IM) is an example of a SAP module that crosses both FI and CO. Because of the function it provides—namely, capital acquisition management—it purposefully resides in neither. The key integration points involved with either FI or CO are Asset Accounting, General Ledger Accounting, and Internal Order Accounting. Both General Ledger and Internal Order Accounting were covered in detail in previous chapters, so the concepts will be only mentioned here. Asset Accounting is not covered in this book, but its role as it relates to IM will be developed within this chapter.

Another integration point with IM is the SAP module called Project Systems (PS). Through the assignment of Work Breakdown Structures, or WBS elements, spending on PS-related capital projects can be monitored and controlled. Because PS is beyond the scope of this book, WBS development will be mentioned briefly. The focus of configuration will be on the IM module and its relationship to Internal Order Accounting. Let's begin with a brief explanation of IM configuration concepts.

## Investment Management Configuration

Configuring the Investment Management (IM) module is rather simple in that there are not too many working parts to manage. Of the areas necessary to configure to support internal order integration, only the program type and investment profile have not been covered in previous chapters. We've already examined concepts such as order type, user status, and plan and budget profiles. In this chapter, we'll show how they relate to IM configuration.

The configuration in the chapter will be straightforward. We'll show only those parts necessary to get IM up and running in any detail. To this end, we'll only mention asset accounting configuration briefly. Before beginning the project, it is advisable to partner with whomever your asset expert is and let them know what your needs will be regarding asset class development. For demonstration purposes, a preconfigured asset class, 4000R&D (Asset under Construction), will be shown.

Investment Management can be a good analysis tool for monitoring and reporting projects at a high level. Plan/Actual or Budget/Actual comparisons are examples of how IM can be useful. It is not a replacement for Project Systems or Asset Accounting and its task-oriented planning approach.

Before beginning, it is important to understand some of the terminology that will be used in the chapter:

**Investment program**    This is the user-defined capital budget hierarchy used to plan, budget, and monitor all capital spending. The investment program is developed in a hierarchical format. The Investment Programs component provides functions for planning and monitoring of investment budgets encompassing many different measures of an entire corporate group on a cyclical basis. You can benefit from the integration of this component with the Investment Measures and Appropriation Requests components. Measures and appropriation requests can be assigned to investment program positions. By rolling up their plan values in the investment program, you ensure that these measures and appropriation requests are integrated in the comprehensive investment planning process. At the same time, you can budget and oversee the measures using the investment program. Comprehensive investment programs offer the advantage of their direct integration with the individual measures such as orders or WBS elements, in contrast to nonintegrated planning systems. By means of this integration, you are quickly made aware if your comprehensive budget is overrun or within the appropriate tolerances. You can also monitor expenses for external acquisitions as well as internal costs using activity allocation and overhead.

**Program position or investment node**    This refers to a position found on the investment program hierarchy. At the lowest level of a hierarchy, a program position may relate to a capital project or project component. You can make organizational assignments for each program position, such as assignment to a company code, business area, plant, or cost center. When you create new program positions below existing positions in the hierarchy, the system automatically copies the assignments and the general data from the higher-level position to the new lower-level position you are creating. However, if you later change the organizational assignment of a program position that has subordinate positions in the hierarchy, the system does not automatically copy the changes to these subordinate program positions.

**Measure**    This is an internal order, maintenance orders, or a WBS element. The measure, as SAP refers to it, is the cost collector through which spending will be controlled and monitored. It is the key integration object with Investment Management. WBS elements are the collectors associated with Project Systems, whereas internal orders (maintenance orders is a subset of internal orders) are cost collectors found in the CO module. The measure is always assigned to the lowest program position within the investment program.

You begin IM development by creating master data items such as program types, investment profiles, and investment measures.

# Program Types, Investment Measures, and the Investment Profile

Begin your Investment Management configuration by creating the program type, which could be described as the backbone of the investment program. As we've mentioned before, just about 80 percent of all activities within the SAP systems are started and controlled by some sort of type, and this is no exception. The investment program provides an enterprise-wide view of capital spending and budgeting through a hierarchical representation. Two steps are associated with program type development:

1. Create the program type.

2. Assign objects approved for use with the program type.

Within the hierarchy, you'll find the projects that make up your capital investment plan for one or multiple fiscal years, depending on your management style. Figure 14.1 shows a basic example of an investment program hierarchy. To find this hierarchy setup process, select Accounting ➢ Investment Management ➢ Programs ➢ Master Data ➢ Investment Program Structure ➢ Display or use the transaction code IM23. In this example, the program position PROJECT_001 (New Plant Roof) represents a single capital project. The program type is the control mechanism for the investment program; it regulates how planning and budgeting are accomplished through various profile assignments. Additional maintenance, although not required, will allow general status management to be activated through the order type.

**FIGURE 14.1**   Example of an investment program hierarchy

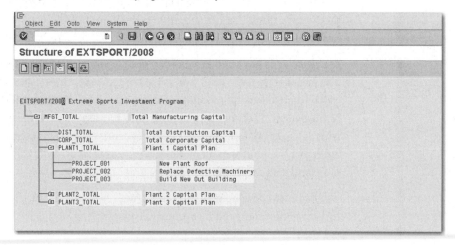

## Creating the Program Type

You can access the program type configuration screen by choosing Investment Management ➢ Investment Programs ➢ Master Data ➢ Define Program Types or by using the transaction code OIT3.

The capital investment program types overview screen appears. As shown in Figure 14.2, SAP will deliver with the system program type 0001.

**FIGURE 14.2**    The Change View "Investment Program Types": Overview screen

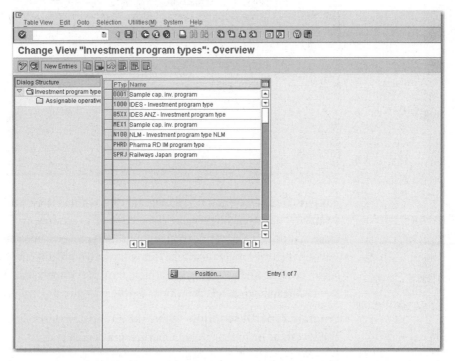

Begin step 1 by clicking the New Entries button to retrieve a detail entry screen. The process for developing a program type is similar to the process for creating an order type because an iterative approach is required. Looking at the screen, you will see fields for a plan profile and a budget profile. Both files will have to be created and assigned prior to attempting any planning or budgeting with the program in a similar way as we explained for Internal Order Types. The same principle applies to the Status Profile field. We examined the status profile development in Chapter 11, "Internal Order Accounting," and the same concepts are at play here (see Figure 14.3).

**FIGURE 14.3** New Entries: Details of Added Entries screen

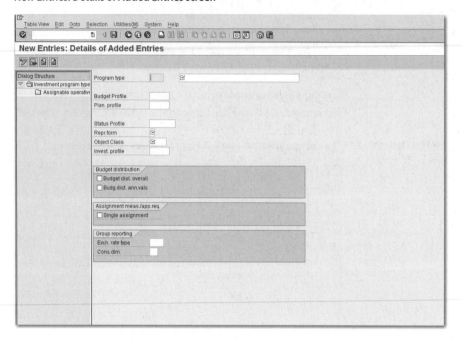

It is possible to create and save a program type without these profiles being assigned. They must, however, be assigned prior to creating an investment program. Once that occurs, the profiles on the program type cannot be altered without first deleting the investment program. This will prove more difficult to do once you have begun creating and assigning investment measures (orders and WBS elements). Review the following field definitions for the program type:

**Program Type/Description** Enter the ID and description of your program type. The ID can be up to four alphanumeric characters in length.

**Budget Profile** The budget profile controls the view for Investment Management budgeting. A budget profile is not required during initial program type creation. We recommend that you create it before developing the capital investment program. The profile is IM specific and thus is different than the one configured for Internal Order Accounting. See the section "Investment Management Planning and Budgeting Profiles" later in this chapter for details.

**Plan. (Planning) Profile** The plan profile is also not required during the initial program type configuration. This profile controls the view for Investment Management planning. It is also IM specific and thus is different than the one configured for Internal Order Accounting. See the section "Investment Management Planning and Budgeting Profiles" later in this chapter for details.

**Status Profile**    This field is not required. Depending on your capital investment planning strategy, you may wish to control investment activity at the program-position level. A program position can be described as a project in the investment program hierarchy (see Figure 14.1). If assigned, the status profile will control the hierarchy node in the same way it controls an order type, by managing business transaction activity. For example, if the status profile is properly configured, you can control when budgeting may occur by determining what the user status on the program position must be set to allow the business transaction. Review the section "Status Profile" in Chapter 10, "Cost Center Accounting," before assigning the profile. The same profile you develop for Internal Order Accounting can be used here in Investment Management.

**Repr. (Representative) Form**    The entry here controls how the program position and the assigned measure are viewed during planning and budgeting. The program position and measure can each be displayed by either its ID, like an internal order number, or its text description. You have four values to choose from:

**1: ID Cap.inv.prog.position/ID Measure**    ID of the capital program position/ ID of the measure (internal order or WBS element)

**2: Text Cap.inv.prog.position/Text Measure**    Text for the capital program position/text for the measure (internal order or WBS element)

**3: ID Cap.inv.prog.posit./Text Measure**    ID of the capital program position/ text for the measure (internal order or WBS element)

**4: Text Cap.inv.prog.posit./ID Measure**    Text for the capital program position/ ID of the measure (internal order or WBS element)

You can change this setting whenever necessary. Because many text descriptions are lengthy, option 1 is a good all-around choice. Many people will easily identify with the order and project ID.

**Object Class**    Enter the object class of the measures that are to be maintained by this program type. With this option, SAP offers the ability to manage investment programs by object class. INVST (Investment) is a proper entry. However, SAP will not force you to use objects of this class type. For example, if INVST is selected here, you will still have the option of using orders with the object class value of OCOST (Overhead Cost).

**Invest. Profile**    The investment profile is responsible for the control functions, including the automatic creation of an asset under construction when you create an internal order or a WBS element, the asset class for the creation of the asset under construction, or the asset class for depreciation simulation.

**Budget Distribution**    This setting determines the budget method for an assigned measure:

**Budget Dist. Overall**    This setting controls the overall budget amount that will be assigned. If this setting is activated, the assigned measure must receive its budget from the node to which it is assigned. In effect, the budget is distributed from the program position. The assigned measure can never receive more overall budget in total than is available on the program position—this is a consistency check.

**Budg. Dist. Ann. Vals**    This setting will control the distribution of the annual budget amount that will be assigned. If this setting is activated, the assigned measure must receive its annual budget from the node to which it is assigned. In effect, the budget is distributed from the program position. The assigned measure can never receive more annual budget in total fiscal year than is available on the program position—this is a consistency check.

**Single Assignment**    This setting specifies that multiple assignments by percentage are not allowed from measures or appropriation requests to different investment program positions. If this indicator is set, then measures and appropriation requests can only be assigned to one program position. This setting determines the budget method for an assigned measure.

**Exch. Rate Type (Group Reporting)**    Defines the exchange rate type that is to be used in planning, budgeting and forecasting against investment management values.

**Cons. Dim. (Group Reporting)**    This setting defines the Dimension in Consolidation for the transfer of group shares from the consolidation process to the investment programs.

For the greatest level of control, you should activate budget distribution for the program type. Otherwise, there is no restriction to exceeding the budget of the program position. If budget distribution is activated, the program type will require a budget profile be assigned.

Figure 14.4 shows the program type ECAP that will be used by Extreme Sports. When you've finished, save the program type. The next step is assigning the approved objects to the new program.

**FIGURE 14.4**    A view of ECAP-Extreme Capital Investment Program Type

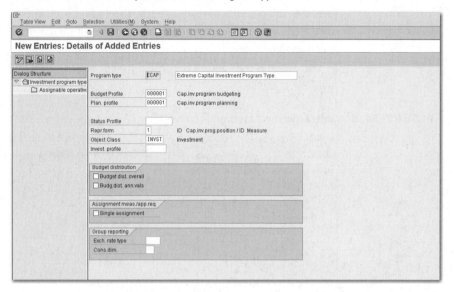

 **TIP**    You cannot delete an investment program from the user menu. You'll find the path in the IMG: Investment Management ➢ Investment Programs ➢ Master Data ➢ Delete Programs. From this window, you will be able to delete any or all investment programs in the system.

## Assigning the Operative Objects or Measures

While creating the investment program, you have to determine which types of measures are allowed for assignment for each position. Remember, measure assignment is the key integration point for Investment Management. If you assign the approved measures to the program type, all investment program positions will default to these settings. The user will not have to manually maintain the Allowed Measures section of the program position.

From the capital investment program types overview screen (shown earlier in Figure 14.2), place the cursor on the new program type, and click the Assignable Operative Objects button. When the resulting assignment screen appears, click the New Entries button to make the necessary assignment. You will have only two choices:

- ▶ OR-Orders
- ▶ PR-WBS Elements

For our example, select Orders (see Figure 14.5), but if you are unsure of whether Project Systems is in scope, select both. There are no detrimental effects from selecting them both. Save the settings when you have finished. Program type configuration is complete, and it can now be used for investment program creation. The next section explores the concept of the investment measure and the development of the investment profile.

**FIGURE 14.5**    Order assignment to program type ECAP

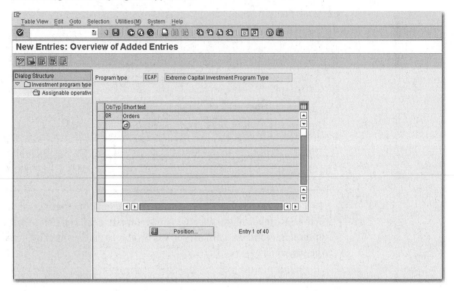

## EXTREME SPORTS PROGRAM TYPE CONFIGURATION ANALYSIS

Extreme Sports will be using Investment Management to help manage its capital-related projects. Because Project Systems is beyond the scope of its project, the configuration is tailored for internal orders rather than WBS elements. Extreme Sports management has no interest in using status management for its investment programs. It feels the control provided by status management on the internal order is sufficient. Budget distribution was activated for the program type. Because it wants the investment program to accurately display and track all capital spending, each order must take its approved budget from the program position.

# Investment Measures

As discussed earlier, two investment measures are available for use with Investment Management: internal orders and WBS elements. With our focus on internal orders, we won't discuss WBS elements. To support Investment Management, you should consider creating a new order type. The IM order type, as it will be referred to in this section, will have to allow for different ways of budgeting and settling costs. This means you'll use order budget profiles different from those created to support expense project tracking.

The concepts for internal order creation covered in Chapter 11 are still relevant here. To help with your development, we've provided the following checklist to outline the key areas when creating the IM order type. The majority of the differences with the order type relate to the integration with Fixed Asset Accounting and the Assets under Construction in particular:

**Settlement structure**   When creating the settlement structure for the IM order type, be certain to make FXA-Asset a valid receiver. Also, keep in mind that you will probably be doing some order-to-order settlements. And for certain amortization projects, it may become necessary to settle to a G/L account.

**Settlement profile**   Again, with the profile, be sure to make a fixed asset a valid receiver. In the Default Object Type field, enter **FXA-Fixed Asset** as the object type. This setting will force the asset as the default receiver on the settlement rule creation screen.

**Source structures**   Depending on how the AuC class, Asset under Construction, will be determined, you may have to create additional structures. You'll learn more in the section "Investment Profile" later in this chapter.

**Object class**   Be certain that the IM order has the object class designation of INVST (Investment). This will make it easier to track within the CO information environment.

**Plan/budget profiles**   You may be able to reuse a plan profile developed for an overhead cost order, but you will almost certainly have to build a new capital-specific budget profile. The main reason for this is related to availability control. Your company probably has different tolerance limits for capital spending than it does for operating expenditures. To build a new capital-specific budget profile, you will have to return to the Overhead Cost Controlling section of the IMG. An additional benefit to creating capital order-specific profiles is the chance to lock your capital order type with a specific investment program type. See Chapter 11 for details.

**TIP**   Using model orders is a good way to ensure that the proper fields are defaulting during order creation.

Your solution may require more than one IM order type, and this is not an issue with Investment Management. Any number of order types can be used in conjunction with a single investment program. We recommend that you review Chapter 11 in detail before proceeding.

## Investment Profile

The investment profile is the link between the internal order and the Asset under Construction. It determines for the user which asset class is to be used for the Asset under Construction and creates the asset. The profile, once created, is assigned directly to the order master record during IM order creation.

### EXTREME SPORTS INVESTMENT ORDER TYPE CONFIGURATION ANALYSIS

Because Extreme Sports segregates its capital spending by real and personal property, it has decided to create two investment order types, one for each property type. The orders will be planned and budgeted; the budget will be distributed from the assigned program position. Settlement configuration will allow for costs to be settled to only fixed assets and other orders. This is to ensure that no operating expenses will be routed through the order and moved to a cost center. Any expenses related to a project will be posted to an expense-related order type.

**WARNING**   You must first create the necessary special Asset under Construction classes to support Investment Management. Consult with your fixed asset consultant before proceeding.

Begin the profile definition by choosing Investment Management ➤ Internal Orders as Investment Measures ➤ Master Data ➤ Define Investment Profiles or by using transaction code OITA.

The investment profile overview screen appears. SAP delivers investment profile 000001 with the system. To create a new profile, click the New Entries button. There is no need to copy the delivered profile because it is simply maintained with a default asset class that you are probably not using. From the new investment profile entries screen, begin building your new profile (see Figure 14.6).

**FIGURE 14.6** New Entries: Details of Added Entries screen

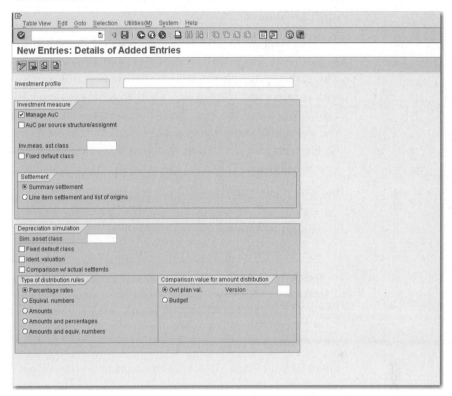

Here is a list of the available fields along with brief descriptions:

**Investment Profile/Description**   Enter the ID and description for the new investment profile. The ID can be up to six alphanumeric characters in length.

The settings in the Investment Measure section determine how the Asset under Construction (AuC) is created and which asset class will be used:

**Manage AuC**   If this field is selected, the system will determine one and only one AuC for each assigned measure. For example, when an investment order is created, the system will automatically create an asset master record that is linked to that order. A settlement rule will be automatically created during the first settlement to the AuC. This setting is recommended for most solutions seeking simplicity in asset management.

**AuC per Source Structure/Assignmt**    If this field is selected, the system will determine which AuC to settle to based on the cost element origin assignment. This solution could potentially involve multiple AuCs per measure. For example, you could create an investment order that segregates real and personal property costs by origin assignment.

After selecting the AuC per Orig. Assignment field, press Enter and a button called Allocate Asset U. Cons. Classes will appear in the body of the window. With the AuC per Orig. Assignment field, you have to manually match each origin group with an asset class. This button is a path to getting to the necessary allocation configuration window. Before clicking the button, save the investment profile. That way, you will be able to maintain the assignments for the profile you are creating. For details, see the section "Define Assignment of AuC Classes per Origin Assignment" later in this chapter.

**Inv. Meas. Ast. Class (Investment Measure Asset Class)**    Enter here the asset class of the AuC you want automatically created. This option is effective only if used in conjunction with the Manage AuC setting.

> **NOTE**    The AuC class must be maintained properly for use with Investment Management. An indicator that is found on the asset class master record and identifies that class for use with IM must be activated. Once it's set, assets of this special class can be posted to only through an investment order settlement.

**Fixed Default Class**    If this field is selected, the user will not have the ability to change the asset class during AuC creation. The investment order will use the asset class defined in the preceding field to build the AuC. If the field is not set, user will have the capability to choose their own asset class. The one limitation with not setting the field is that the order cannot be automatically released during creation; for the investment order, the AuC has to be created before the order's release. In most cases, you will want to activate this field in conjunction with the Manage AuC field setting.

SAP allows for two types of settlement for investment orders. Of these, Summary Settlement is the easier to manage:

**Summary Settlement**    If this option is selected, the order balance is treated as a whole number that can be settled against a single or many receivers. Increased system performance is a key reason for selecting this field, but there is a potential drawback. With summary settlement, you have no audit trail from the asset back to the measure. The costs are settled as a part of the total balance.

**Line Item Settlement and List of Origins**    If this option is selected, each line item on an investment order will be available for separate settlement rule maintenance; that is, each line item can be directed at a different receiver. This solution may provide more control over how costs are allocated but at the price of a potential reduction in productivity. A positive characteristic of line item settlement is the opportunity it provides the user to drill back from the asset to the measure line item. This provides you with a good audit trail. Table 14.1 has examples of both Summary and Line Item settlement.

**TABLE 14.1**    Comparison of Summary and Line Item Settlement

| Summary Settlement: Order 1000 | Actual Posting Settlement Amount |
|---|---|
| Line item 1: Cost Element 600000 | $2,500 |
| Line item 2: Cost Element 610000 | $1,500 |
| Line item 3: Cost Element 620000 | $1,000 |
| Settlement Rule 1 to AuC | $5,000 |
| **Line Item Settlement: Order 1000** | **Actual Posting Settlement Amount** |
| Line item 1: Cost Element 600000 | $2,500 |
| Line item 2: Cost Element 610000 | $1,500 |
| Line item 3: Cost Element 620000 | $1,000 |
| Settlement Rule 1 to AuC1 | $2,500 |
| Settlement Rule 2 to AuC2 | $1,500 |
| Settlement Rule 3 to Order | $1,000 |

SAP gives you the ability to simulate depreciation costs for not only existing assets, but also planned capital expenditures through IM. The settings in the Depreciation Simulation section provide information relating to whether a default asset class should be used for all measures or whether the user should determine the simulation class during measure creation:

**Sim. (Simulated) Asset Class**    Enter the default asset class the system should use during the simulation.

**Fixed Default Class**    If this field is selected, the user will not have the ability to change the asset class investment measure creation. The asset class selection will be taken from the entry in the Sim. Asset Class field. If this field is not set, the user will have the opportunity to enter a depreciation simulation asset class during the investment measure creation.

**Indent. (Indicator for Uniform) Valuation**     SAP allows you to allocate planned depreciation costs derived from the depreciation simulation to the following:

- ▶ Cost centers
- ▶ Asset classes
- ▶ Start-up dates

The costs can be distributed by percentages identified on either the investment order master record or the program position. Figure 14.7 provides you with a view of the distribution rules screen for the program position. The screen is identical to the one found on the order master record. To get to the simulation distribution screen, from the program position, use the menu path Accounting ➤ Investment Management ➤ Programs ➤ Master Data ➤ Investment Program Position Change (see Figure 14.8). Once you have accessed this screen, choose the Depn Simulation Data tab and then select the icon to the far right for additional fields (see Figure 14.9). Once you have accessed this screen, click the Distribution button to access the Dep. Simulation: Distribution screen again.

**FIGURE 14.7**     Dep. Simulation: Distribution simulation fields found on the investment program position

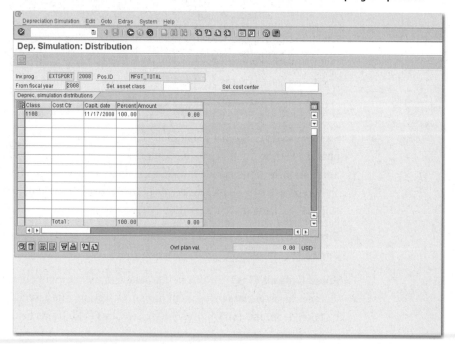

**FIGURE 14.8**    Change Inv. Program Position screen

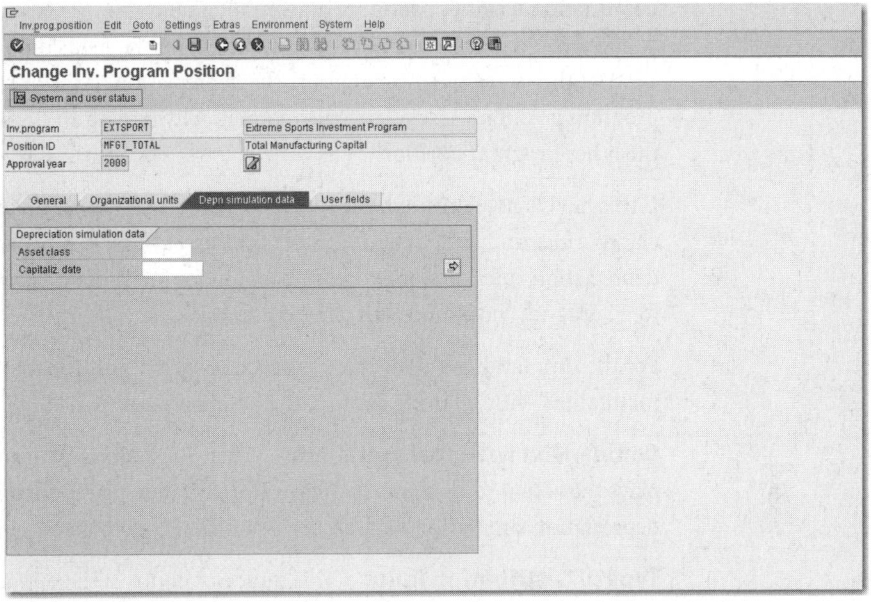

**FIGURE 14.9**    Depr. Simulation Maintain: Overview of Depr. Areas screen

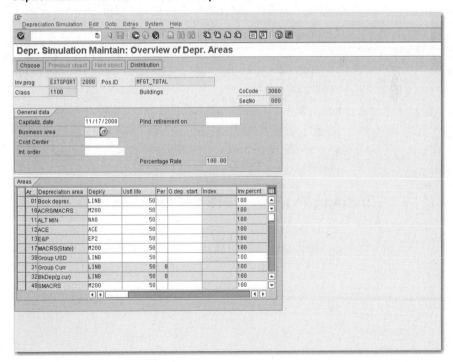

If Indent. Valuation is activated, SAP will keep the distribution start date and the depreciation terms constant for all similar asset classes. This will reduce the amount of effort you will have to undergo to maintain all the fields on the Dep. Simulation: Distribution screen. Any changes to the depreciation terms or start date for one program position's asset class will automatically update all similar asset classes in the other program positions.

If this field is not activated, the system will allow you to manually determine depreciation rules and start dates for each of the asset classes. Any changes made to the depreciation rules on one program position for one asset class will not flow through to all program positions with similar asset classes.

For the simulation to work properly, each program position and/or measure must be maintained with accurate depreciation simulation data.

**Comparison w/ Actual Settlemts**    When you set this indicator, the system displays the actual settlements that have already taken place, during maintenance of depreciation simulation data for orders and WBS elements.

**Type of Distribution Rules**    This indicator controls the options that will be available for settlement processes. You have five options—Percentage Rates, Equival. Numbers, Amounts, Amounts and Percentages, or Amounts and Equiv. Numbers. Identify the appropriate option by checking off the radio button.

**Comparison Value for Amount Distribution**    This setting defines how the depreciation simulation data is checked in the system. Specify if you want the overall plan values to be checked or if you are more interested in the budget values being validated.

When you've finished, save the capital investment profile. Figure 14.10 shows a completed profile. If you selected AuC per Orig. Assignment in the Cap. Inv. Measure section, the upcoming section will be important because it provides the next step in that area of configuration.

## Defining Assignment of AuC Classes per Origin Assignment

If you selected the AuC per Orig. Assignment field during the investment profile configuration, your profile will look similar to the one shown in Figure 14.11.

**FIGURE 14.10**  New Entries: Details of Added Entries for the Investment profile EXCAP

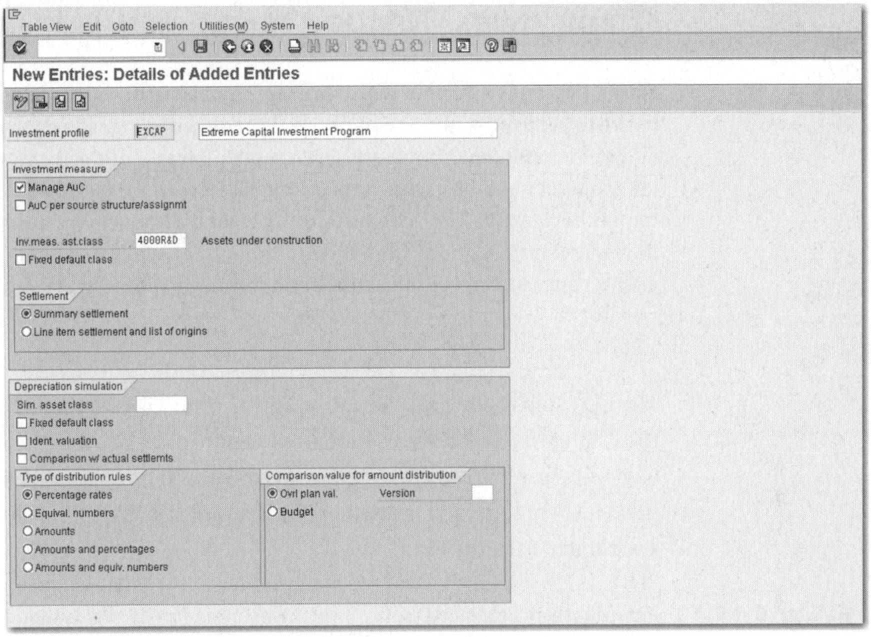

**FIGURE 14.11**  Investment profile EXAMPL using AuC per Origin Assignment

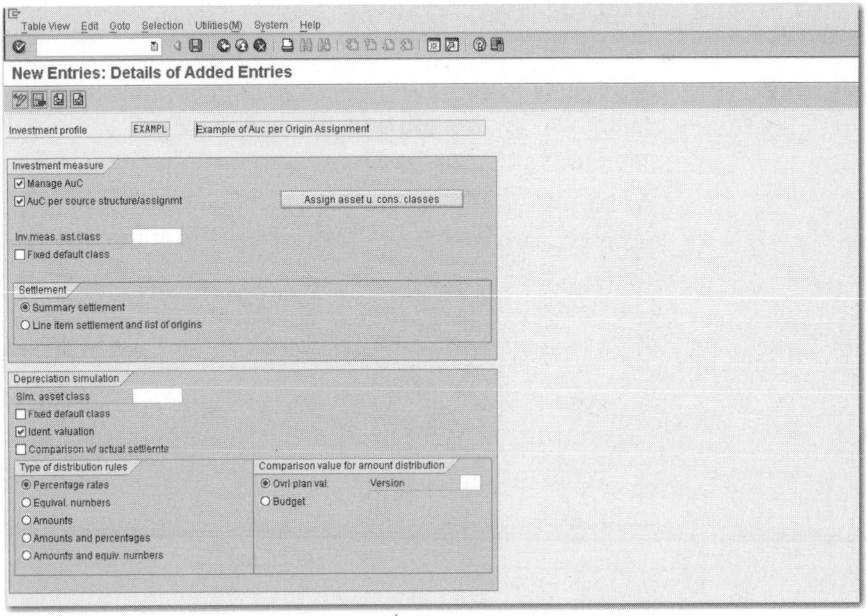

## EXTREME SPORTS INVESTMENT PROFILE CONFIGURATION ANALYSIS

Extreme Sports's investment profile EXCAP is basic in its development. The company's desire to keep order management simple has led it to manage only one AuC per order and to maintain only summary settlements. Because it does not want to allow the user to select another asset class during AuC creation, the Fixed Asset Class indicator has been activated. Extreme Sports's capital management group will be running depreciation simulations from time to time. To ensure some integrity and make the maintenance easier, the indicator for uniform valuation was activated.

The next step in the process is to assign an AuC class to the source structure. From the Change View screen on the investment profile, select the Allocate Asset U. Cons. Classes button. The origin assignment screen appears. Figure 14.12 shows a previously maintained investment profile called EXAMPL; you can see that source assignments already exist.

**FIGURE 14.12**   A previously maintained Display View "Investment Profile – Allocation per Source Structure": O screen for investment profile EXAMPL

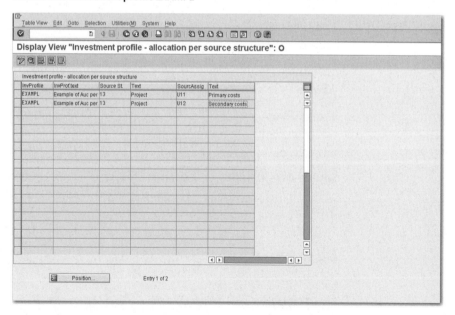

To add new source assignments, click the New Entries button to open a detailed entries screen. Figure 14.13 is a view of a maintained origin assignment.

**FIGURE 14.13**   "Allocation per Source Structure" for investment profile EXAMPL

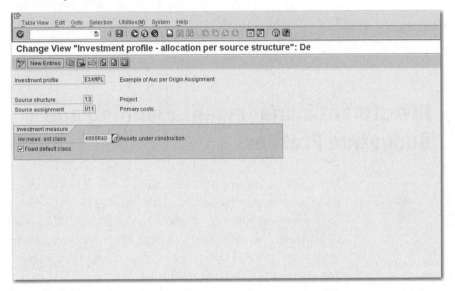

There are only a few fields to maintain, so it should go quickly. Review the list of field definitions here before continuing:

**Investment Profile**   The profile ID will carry over from the preceding screen, so you don't have to enter it here.

**Source Structure**   This field is used to provide differentiation of costs by cost element group. The structure will contain a number of source assignments that define this segregation. We explored source structure development in Chapter 11.

**Source Assignment**   Enter a source assignment found in the source structure defined in the preceding description. In the example provided, there are three source assignments present within the origin structure: U11 (Primary Costs), U12 (Secondary Costs), and U13 (Work in Progress).

**Inv. Meas. Ast. Class**   Enter the default asset class that should be used to create the AuC.

**Fixed Default Class**   If this field is activated, the user will not be able to manually determine the asset class to be used for creation of the AuC.

Save the source assignment when you have finished. Repeat the source assignment step as often as you need to completely cover the entire range of account activity. If an account is posted to an order that is outside of the ranges established here, you won't be able to settle the order.

In the next section, we'll introduce how to develop the necessary planning and budgeting profiles for IM. These profiles are different from those covered in Internal Order Accounting and are necessary to complete the IM program type.

# Investment Management Planning and Budgeting Profiles

Investment management provides numerous solutions for capital planning. You can plan the investment hierarchy directly, entering plan amounts on the lowest investment nodes and allowing the system to roll to a total. The concept is called *bottom-up planning*. Another option is to create as many of your investment measures as you can up front and then plan and assign them to the necessary investment node. You can then run a program that will take the plan from each of the measures and assign it to the investment node. The plan can then be rolled up. In both examples, the plan has to get onto the investment program hierarchy. This is key to the budgeting function and necessary for plan-versus-actual reporting.

Budgeting provides even more options. The process for budgeting is called *top-down*, and as its name implies, budget is distributed from the highest node down until it reaches all the lowest nodes in the hierarchy. If you have activated budget distribution within your program type, the last step for the budget is to distribute it to the assigned measure. Another feature to budgeting is the potential use of budget categories.

Budget categories allow the user to maintain multiple budget types within a single investment program. The most common use of categories is to segregate capital and expense portions of capital-related projects. In this case, both cost components can be planned/budgeted for the investment node and segregated during reporting and analysis. Earlier in this chapter, program type ECAP-Extreme Capital Investment Program Type was created with a plan profile 000001 and budget profile 000001 assigned to it. Each of these profiles will be covered in its respective section. Plan profile configuration will be shown first.

# Investment Management Plan Profile

The plan profile creation process will seem similar to the one you used to create the order profile. To get to the proper configuration screen, select Investment Management ➤ Investment Programs ➤ Planning in Program ➤ Cost Planning ➤ Maintain Planning Profile or use the transaction code OIP1.

The capital investment planning profile screen overview appears. Click the New Entries button and the New Entries: Details of Added Entries screen appears; Figure 14.14 shows the completed investment plan profile 000001, which is used in the investment program ECAP. Click the New Entries button to bring up an empty profile template.

**FIGURE 14.14**  New Entries: Details of Added Entries - View "Planning Profile Investment Program": Details plan profile 1000

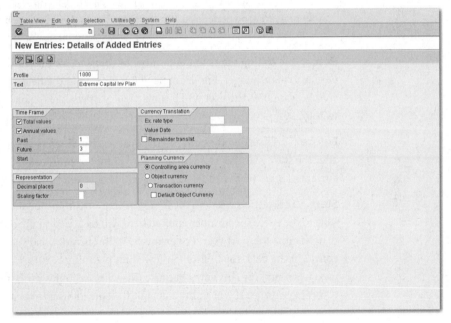

The maintenance is simple, and the necessary fields are described here:

**Profile**   Enter an alphanumeric ID, up to six characters in length, that describes the planning profile.

**Text**   Enter a description for the planning profile. Be clear because the profile is controlling area independent and you do not want its use to be misinterpreted.

The fields in the Time Frame section relate to the planning years available for user input and review:

**Total Values**    Check this field if you want to allow the user to plan for total values on the investment node. At the highest level, an order or project can be planned for total cost regardless of the year it is consumed. For example, if a project has a total planned cost of $500,000, $500,000 would be considered its overall value.

**Annual Values**    Check this field if you want to allow the user to plan annual expenditures for an investment node. For example, suppose a project has a total planned cost of $500,000. This setting would allow the user to plan the cost expenditures across years: $200,000 would be planned for 2000, $200,000 for 2001, and $100,000 for 2002.

**TIP**    Activating the Overall and Annual Values fields does not make them required. If your project has no preference, it is recommended that you activate both.

**Past**    This setting refers to the number of years before the start year the user will be able to plan/budget. For example, if 2 is entered in the field and the current or start year is 2009, the user will be able to view or change the plan or budget back to 2007.

**Future**    This setting is similar to the Past setting. It refers to the number of years after the start year the user will be able to plan. For example, if 3 is entered and the current or start year is 2009, planning will be allowed through 2012.

**Start**    This setting refers to the first year that planning/budgeting will be accessible to the user. The number entered here will be added to the current fiscal year to determine the start year. For example, if the current fiscal year is 2009 and you enter 2 in the field, the first year allowed for planning is 2011. Caution should be used when making this entry because this value becomes the basis for all future planning settings. If you want to default the current fiscal year as the start year, leave this field empty.

**Decimal Places**    Enter the desired number of decimal places in which you want to plan.

**Scaling Factor**    If scaling is important when planning, enter the scaling factor here. For example, if you want to plan in thousands, enter 3 in the Scaling Factor field. As you enter the plan, only the scaled amount will appear. The total amount is entered in the planning table. With a scale of 3, a plan of $1,000,000 is entered as $1,000 on the planning screen.

**Currency Translation**    There are several parameters in this section and they are similar to what we came across in other parameters in Investment Management. Ex. Rate Type is the exchange rate that will be used for currency translation. Value Date is the date that the exchange rate is based on. Remainder Translat. is used for the remainder values after the initial translation is complete. The final amount that is left after currency translation is converted using the parameters in the budget profile.

**Planning Currency**    This indicator defines the currency that planning will occur based on—Controlling Area Currency, Object Currency, Transaction Currency, or Default Object Currency.

When you have completed the profile, be sure to save it. You can now assign the plan profile to your program type as described earlier in the section "Creating the Program Type."

# Investment Management Budget Profile

To create the IM budget profile, you will follow steps similar to those used to create the IM plan profile. To get to the necessary window, select Investment Management ➤ Investment Programs ➤ Budgeting in Program ➤ Define Budget Profile for Investment Programs or use the transaction code OIB1.

The Overview of the "Budget Profile Investment Program" screen appears. To create a new profile, click the New Entries button and a budget profile details screen opens. The field names and descriptions are almost identical to those found on the planning profile screen and described in the preceding section. The one area where the settings differ is with the number of view format choices you have.

When the profile settings are complete, save the profile. Figure 14.15 shows the IM budget profile 2000-Extreme Capital Inv Budget. As you did with the plan profile, you should also assign the budget profile to your program type when it is complete.

## Budget Distribution

Though it has been covered in previous sections, we wanted to take a moment to talk about budget distribution. There are two main steps to developing budget distribution for use within IM:

1. Activate budget distribution within the program type.

2. Assign the program type to the internal order budget profile.

**FIGURE 14.15**  New Entries: Details of Added Entries for IM budget profile 2000-Extreme Capital Inv Budget

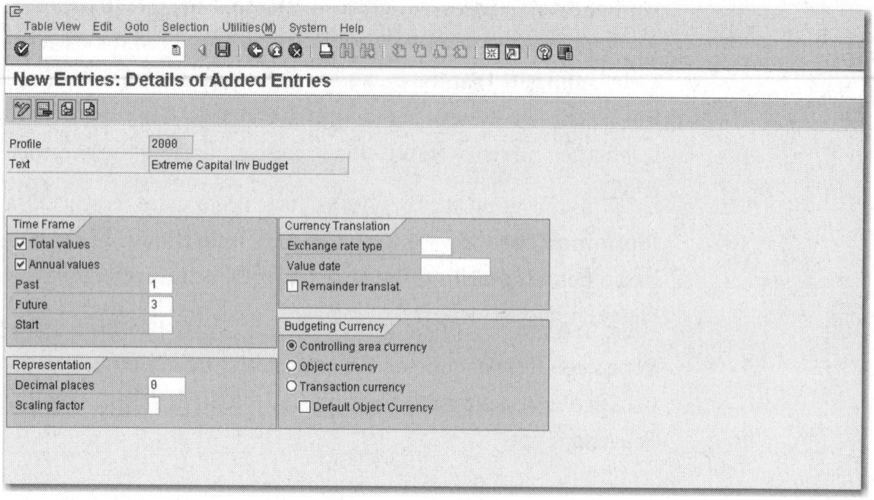

If you have been following along from the beginning of the chapter, you've already accomplished both of these steps by now. If not, you will want to revisit the sections on program type creation and investment measures. Budget categories and their impact on IM budgeting will be covered next.

## Budget Categories

If within your solution the company desires to plan and report on total project costs, including both capital and expense, then budget categories may be right for you. Through the use of categories, both budget and actual costs can be segregated so that they may be analyzed separately from the same investment node. For example, with two budget categories, one called CAPITAL and one called EXPENSE, you will be able to report budgeted capital and expense from the same investment node on your investment program hierarchy.

There are three steps to configuring budget categories:

1. Activate budget categories within the investment program.

2. Create the budget categories.

3. Assign an actual value percentage to each category.

Before proceeding, you need to know about a few of the drawbacks with using budget categories:

▶ You cannot use availability control. SAP does not allow you to distribute budget to the investment measure by category. Each measure must be budgeted manually.

▶ Exact actual costs cannot be sent to each category as they occur. Instead, they are recognized by each category during order settlement through the assignment of a usage indicator. Unfortunately, until the orders are settled, you will not know how much of the on-hand balance represents each category.

▶ Budget categories cannot be planned or budgeted individually. Instead, percentage rates are assigned to each category; the percentage rates correspond to the amount of budget each should receive. As you assign an investment measure to a program position, you will have the opportunity to enter the percentage of the budget each category should receive.

**Step 1: Activate Budget Categories in Investment Program**    To activate budget categories, select the Budg. Catg. field on the investment program master data screen. Figure 14.16 is a view of an investment program for Extreme Sports. Notice the field setting for budget categories. The user begins creating the investment program by choosing Accounting ➢ Investment Management ➢ Programs ➢ Master Data ➢ Investment Program Definition ➢ Create. However, because it is not related to configuration, the creation process will not be covered here.

**FIGURE 14.16**    The master data view of investment program EXTREME

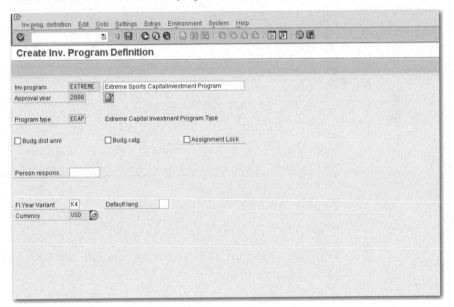

**NOTE**    Review the SAP-provided documentation on investment program creation for details.

**Step 2: Create Budget Categories**    To create your budget categories, select Investment Management ➤ Investment Programs ➤ Budgeting in Program ➤ Budget Categories ➤ Define Budget Categories or use the transaction code OIT8.

When the budget categories per program type screen appears, click the New Entries button to access a creation screen. Figure 14.17 shows a snapshot of the categories defined for program type ECAP.

**FIGURE 14.17**  New Entries: Overview of Added Entries—the change view "budget categories per Program type": Overview definition for program type 0001

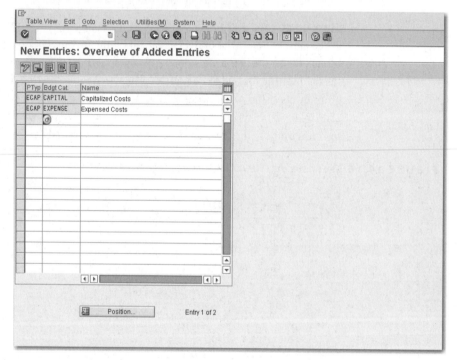

The necessary fields are defined here:

**PTyp**    Enter the program type to which the budget categories belong.

**Bdgt Cat.**    Enter the ID for each budget category. The ID can be up to 10 alphanumeric characters in length.

**Name**    Provide each category with a clear description.

When you've finished, save the categories.

**Step 3: Assign Actual Values by Category**    In this last step, you will define how actual costs will be routed to each of the budget categories. Choose Investment Management ➤ Investment Programs ➤ Budgeting in Program ➤ Budget Categories ➤ Assign Actual Values or use the transaction code OIT5.

At the overview window, click the New Entries button to assign your categories. Figure 14.18 shows the settings for program type ECAP. In this step, you'll assign a usage indicator to each budget type.

**FIGURE 14.18**  Actual values assignment for program type ECAP

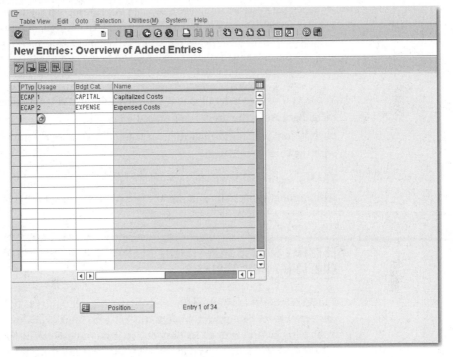

The key fields on this screen are as follows:

**PTyp**    Enter the program type to which the budget categories belong.

**Usage**    This indicator offers three settings (unfortunately, you are offered only three as standard with the system):

**00**    Not assigned; for those costs that cannot be classified as either

**01**    Capitalized to asset; for those costs that should be tracked as they are settled to an asset

**02**    Noncapitalized incidental expenses; for those costs that are settled to an object other than an asset

**Bdgt Cat.**    Enter the ID of each budget category for which you wish to assign actuals. These must be created prior to their assignment here.

**TIP**    SAP offers you the option of creating your own assignments through the maintenance of a user-exit, AAIP0001. Through this exit, you will get the added functionality of assigning actuals by cost element or cost element group. To use this, choose the next item on the menu below the Assign Actual Values. From there go to Utilities ➢ SAP Enhancements and use the user-exit AAIP001 to review the code.

When you've finished, save the assignments. Budget category development is complete. Because of the limitations placed on you, budget categories may not be a viable solution. If it sounds plausible for your situation, we recommend experimenting with the various settings.

The last section within Investment Management planning and budgeting has to do with number range assignments.

## EXTREME SPORTS INVESTMENT PLANNING AND BUDGETING CONFIGURATION ANALYSIS

Budget categories are beyond the scope of the Extreme Sports solution. We provided this example for demonstration only. It is Extreme Sports's intention to fully utilize availability control with all its projects, so it cannot use categories. The company will use bottom-up planning and will enter the plan data directly on the investment program hierarchy. It felt it was too burdensome on its project managers to create a number of capital orders during the iterative planning process. This provides an opportunity to quickly make changes and reassign capital when necessary. Only when a project is going up for review will an order be created and planned. When approved, the order will have the amount of approved capital budget distributed to it.

## Number Ranges for IM Planning/Budgeting Line Items

Investment Management uses the same planning number range assignment table as the one used for internal order planning and budgeting. If the number ranges were previously maintained, you do not have to repeat any steps here. If not, you can use the following menu path to define the necessary number range: Investment Management ➢ Investment Programs ➢ Planning in Program ➢ Define Number Ranges for Planning Line Items, or you can use the transaction code OK11 (see Figure 14.19).

**FIGURE 14.19**  The Number Ranges – Cost Planning and Budgeting screen

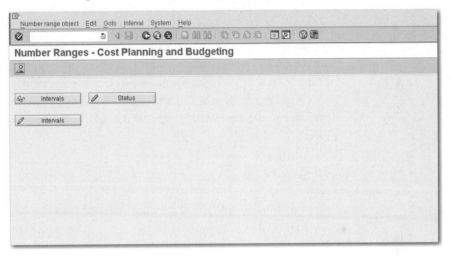

The Number Ranges – Cost Planning and Budgeting screen appears. This screen is similar to the number range screen for CO document assignment. Number range intervals are used to differentiate between types of postings. The default intervals for Investment Management planning and budgeting are as follows:

**10**  Capital investment budgeting

**11**  Capital investment planning

The number range intervals are predefined by SAP and are not subject to change. You do have the ability to determine the range value, so be sure that the ranges are wide enough and that they do not overlap. To maintain the range interval, select the Maintain Interval button (glasses icon) in the body of the screen. From here, you have the ability to create and maintain the planning intervals. Investment

Management plan and budget profile development is complete. You can now safely plan your investment program hierarchy.

# Summary

The information in this chapter focused on getting IM up and running quickly. To write this chapter, we relied on the foundation built in many of the preceding chapters. Concepts such as order type, settlement structure, settlement profile, and user status are as relevant here as they are in Internal Order Accounting. The fact that the majority of IM development here is tied to orders rather than WBS elements is more an issue of scope than of functionality. IM integrates just as well with Project Systems and Asset Accounting as it does with order accounting. Take your time with the chapter and experiment with as many of the settings as possible before settling in on your decision. Again, Investment Management is not built to replace either Asset Accounting or Project Systems, but only to complement these two components with another alternative to manage, track, and control the investment process.

# *FI Closing Cockpit*

## FEATURING

▶ **OVERVIEW OF THE FI CLOSING COCKPIT**

▶ **DEVELOPMENT OF ORGANIZATIONAL HIERARCHIES**

▶ **CREATING CLOSING COCKPIT TEMPLATES**

▶ **CREATING TASKS**

▶ **CREATING THE TASK LIST**

One of the many tasks that you have to complete in the Finance and Controlling areas is the process of *closing* on a periodic, quarterly, and yearly basis. Some companies even have the fun of closing on a daily or even weekly basis. The closing process at any company comes with its own unique challenges, and you want to attempt to close as quickly as possible so that business as usual can continue without a hiccup. You need to pull all the information and data together, validate it, and then tie the balances for all accounts; on top of that, you probably have to do all of this for data that has to be pulled together from multiple systems from multiple countries from numerous company codes, and so on. Needless to say, all of this has its own unique challenges based on the region you're in. If that's not enough to worry about, you have to get this done as soon as possible because of additional regulations based on the Sarbanes-Oxley (SOX) compliance rules. But even without these additional regulations, you still have to organize all of this activity and complete it as quickly as possible since you probably have to submit profit and loss and balance sheet data to your stakeholders. Oh boy, that's a lot to do!

There are many different toolsets you can use to help you complete the closing process effectively and efficiently. Which toolset you choose depends on the process itself and the amount of control and management necessary by the FI closing team. We have also seen many companies managing the financial closing based on an Excel spreadsheet or a project plan and, in a number of cases, relying on the local knowledge of each person in the company since all of the tasks required for the closing process are not organized and stored in one place but are found on personal spreadsheets and notepads.

To alleviate this, SAP has its own components that are available and probably already accessible for you to use (depending on the version you're using). The ECC systems have two options for the closing process: the Schedule Manager and the FI Closing Cockpit. The Schedule Manager has been around since the 4.0 version of R3. It offers the basics for the closing process and works well enough, but if you are looking for additional functionality for management of the processes, error handling, additional user-friendly interfaces, and workflow processes, then the Schedule Manager doesn't have all of the bells and whistles necessary to effectively deliver on those needs. This is where the FI Closing Cockpit comes into play. As you will see, the FI Closing Cockpit has a significant number of additional components that will help in managing and controlling the closing processes for the FI and CO areas. This component can also include the tasks that are required for closing or preclosing activities, which may show up in the areas of Material Management, Sales and Distribution, and Product Costing. Let's just say that if there's something that needs to be accomplished for closing activities, the FI Closing Cockpit can probably accommodate it and offer you enhanced capabilities.

This chapter will show you in detail how to configure the FI Closing Cockpit. As we have done in the previous chapters, we will work through the basics of the configuration and implementation of this product. After you start to use it and work with the overall functionality, you will find that getting started is the hardest part of the whole experience. Since everything that we use here (such as allocations of costs, analysis of the GR/IR accounts, and so on) should already be set up for you, we'll cover how to organize these activities into a component that will give the business user the ability to track and manage all activities from one location.

# Overview of the FI Closing Cockpit

There's a specific order of steps when developing the FI Closing Cockpit. Once you have finished the initial steps and you have worked through a couple of examples, you will be ready to get into your systems and start the process.

The setup process consists of six basic steps, as outlined in Table 15.1.

**TABLE 15.1**    Setting Up the FI Closing Cockpit

| Task | Definition |
| --- | --- |
| Create the organizational hierarchies. | This activity determines the organizational structure that will be used in the closing process. |
| Create templates. | This activity is the process of setting up templates that will work for the entire company for the closing process. |
| Create tasks. | This activity determines the individual items that are all a part of the closing process. Initially, you will spend a lot of your time on this step, but setting this up once will save enormous amounts of time in all future closing activities. |
| Define any dependencies. | This is an optional step, but completing this task will save you additional time in terms of defining dependent steps in the closing process. Once the dependencies are identified and structured, this step can be reexecuted for each of the closing processes. |
| Create the task list. | This activity involves making the overall closing process specific to an individual position's responsibilities. The task list defines unique parameters for each position and the tasks that each person is responsible for executing. |
| Release the task list. | This is the process of moving a task list from the configuration to the application process. Here you can also fine-tune the timing parameters of task execution, and so on. |

Only three transaction codes are required for the configuration and execution of the Closing Cockpit. They can be found in a number of areas in the main menu, and you don't have to go into the IMG for any activities for the setup of the Closing Cockpit. This is not to say that there isn't any system configuration—there is—but for all of the other application setup, you use only the main menu. Anywhere you see a folder that is related to closing, you will find the transaction codes for the Closing Cockpit. We will focus on these directly from the FI main menu. To get to the Closing Cockpit, select Accounting ➤ Financial Accounting ➤ General Ledger ➤ Periodic Processing ➤ Closing ➤ Closing Cockpit, or you can use the transaction code CLOCO for the Closing Cockpit, CLOCOS for the Overview of the Closing Cockpit, and CLOCOC for the Manage Templates and Task Lists view. As you can see by the name, we will use CLOCOC for the configuration and CLOCOC and CLOCOS for the display and execution of the Closing Cockpit.

The final process of executing the Closing Cockpit can be run either from the SAP GUI view or from the SAP Portal. If you want to use the Portal functionality, make sure that you are using the appropriate Enhancement Package for ECC and the appropriate Business Package for the SAP Portal. In addition, with the NetWeaver 7.0 Platform you can also implement the SAP Central Process Scheduler. This will allow you to use the Closing Cockpit across systems and to centrally manage the closing process for any module and across different systems. Therefore, if you have to collect information from another region before you initiate the corporate closing process (as is the normal case), you can manage and execute these external activities directly from the FI Closing Cockpit within the central ECC system.

## Using Variants in the FI Closing Cockpit

The variant tables in the FI Closing Cockpit help centralize the maintenance of the setting for each of the different activities to run. In the Closing Cockpit, you need to fill in a number of items with values at the runtime of the program or other tasks. These values are supplied by the use of the variant tables, specifically, the TVARV table. This table is used to create the variant item and also select the variant values. This process is used in a number of places in the FI/CO environment. For example, in the process of setting up for an audit, you can use this approach to default certain values into a report so that the auditor can execute the report without searching for the values to enter into the variable screens. A basic example is the use of these variant values to help adjust the year entered into a series of reports. You don't even have to enter the reports themselves; just make the adjustments in the TVARV table and SAP will control all of the reports. This allows you to maintain all of these variant values from one central screen, which reduces the amount of redundant changes that you have to make. Use the transaction code SM30 to access the Table Maintenance screen, as shown in Figure 15.1.

**FIGURE 15.1** The Maintain Table Views: Initial Screen

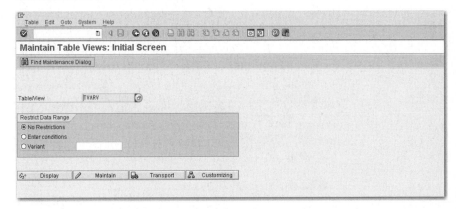

Enter the table name **TVARV** in the Table/View field and click the Maintain button to access the maintenance screen for the variants (see Figure 15.2).

**FIGURE 15.2** The Display Table TVARV: Selection Variables screen

Click the Change button to allow changes to be made in this screen. You will review some of the standard variables that are delivered and review the approach to adjusting the values. The initial screen shows variables that are single parameters, and therefore only one value can be used. We have changed a variable SAP_FAST_CLOSE_BUKRS_P with the value of the company code EX01 for the Extreme Sports Company, as shown in Figure 15.3.

**FIGURE 15.3**    The Maintain Table TVARVC: Selection Variables screen, Parameter tab

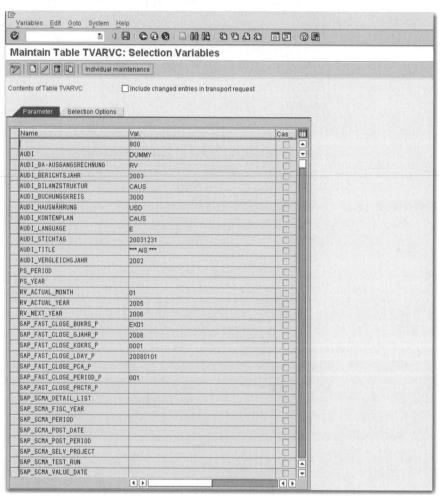

We have also changed another variable on the Selection Options screen: SAP_FAST_ CLOSE_BUKRS_S. It also has the value of the company code EX01. You will see that once you start to set up your tasks in the Closing Cockpit, these will come in handy (see Figure 15.4).

**FIGURE 15.4**    The Maintain Table TVARVC: Selection Variables screen, Selection Options tab

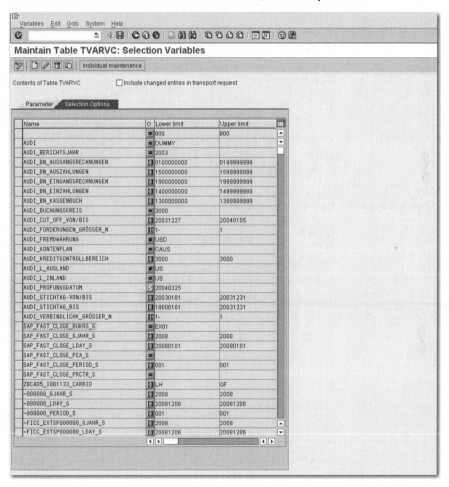

You can create additional variants if necessary for other variables. Once you use this approach, you will find that it's valuable both for managing variables and for use in ABAP programming since these values are now available in a table and can be referenced for other activities both in reporting and in analysis. You can find these variables under the T option once you reach the variant screens.

# Development of Organizational Hierarchies

Organizational hierarchy is the first thing you need to configure in the Closing Cockpit. This feature allows you to organize the closing process according to organizational structures. This means that special features of the individual independent accounting units can be taken into account during closing, for example, at the company code level. This enables you to avoid applying identical process steps to all company codes. During the process of setting up the organizational hierarchy, you will see that you can assign the Extreme Sports controlling area and company code–specific information directly to the organizational hierarchy. The development of the organizational hierarchy is completed in the Closing Cockpit (Manage Templates and Task Lists) transaction. Choose Accounting ➤ Financial Accounting ➤ General Ledger ➤ Periodic Processing ➤ Closing ➤ Closing Cockpit (Manage Templates and Task Lists), or use the transaction code CLOCOC (see Figure 15.5).

**FIGURE 15.5**    Closing Cockpit Display screen

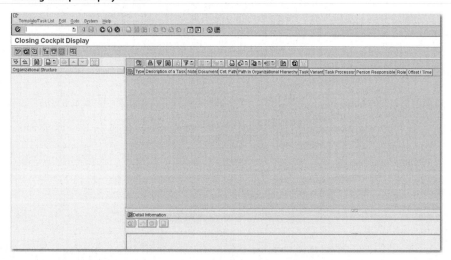

**TIP**   With the Closing Cockpit, we usually see companies take the approach to set up one portion of the closing process at a time and work out all the issues for that set of tasks first, and then add to the closing process. Over a period of approximately four to six months, all of the required tasks for closing can then be found in one place. This is a best business practice when implementing the FI Closing Cockpit.

Switch the screen from Display to Change by clicking the Change icon. You are now ready to start creating your FI Closing Cockpit process. You should review the standard delivered objects before starting from scratch with the complete build since you can copy these templates and then tweak them to satisfy your specific requirements. To review the delivered organizational hierarchies and also to create your own, choose Template/Task List ➤ Organizational Hierarchies. The screen to create, delete, change, and display closing hierarchies opens, as shown in Figure 15.6.

**FIGURE 15.6**    Closing Cockpit Display: Create/Delete/Change/Display Closing Hierarchy dialog box

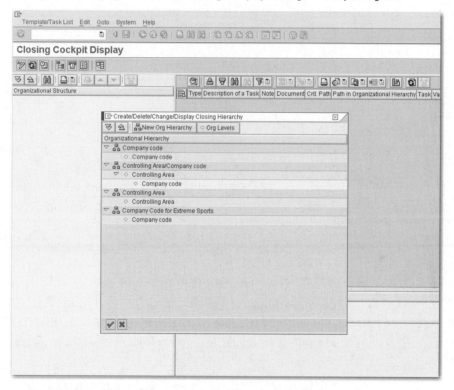

In this dialog box, notice that this is a hierarchy normally based on the different organizational elements that you would be closing against, such as company code, controlling area, and so on. The standards are displayed, but if you need another object to be used, just click the New Org Hierarchy button and fill in some text for the hierarchy. Then click the Org Level button to add organizational elements to your hierarchy. Some other organizational units that you might need are the profit center and the operating concern. Once you click the Org Levels button, you will see the option to use one of the standards or fill in another organizational unit that you need. The example shown in Figure 15.7 is for the Profit Center creation.

**FIGURE 15.7**    Maintain Organizational Levels creation window

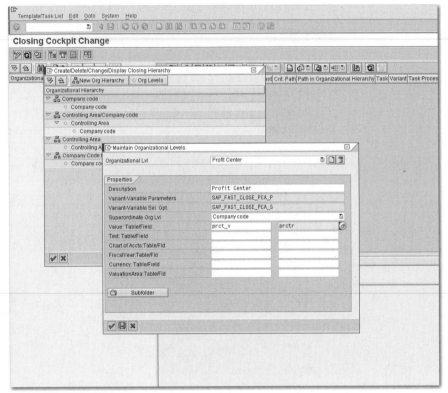

Let's review the options on this screen:

**Organizational Lvl (Level)**    Either use the existing organizational units or create another by using the create icon to the right of the field. This setting will automatically default some of the other fields, such as the two variants for the variable selections.

**Description**    Enter a description of the organizational unit that you are using. This is a text-only field.

**Variant-Variable Parameters**    This setting will automatically default based on the settings in the TVARV table that we discussed earlier. In the case of the profit center, the TVARV table has the link between the PCA table and the variant SAP_FAST_CLOSE_PCA_P.

**Variant-Variable Sel. Opt.**    This setting will automatically default based on the settings in the TVARV table that we discussed earlier. In the case of the profit center, the TVARV table has the link between the PCA table and the variant SAP_FAST_CLOSE_PCA_S.

**Superordinate Org Lvl**    This setting defaults to one of the organizational units that have been defined based on the configuration of your systems. In this case, Superordinate Org Lvl would be set to Company Code.

**Value: Table/Field**    You must fill in either this parameter or the Text parameter for all Organizational Lvl objects. In the case of the profit center, the table where the Profit Center master is located is PRCT_V and the field that stores the Profit Center Number is PRCTR. You will need to know these parameters from the system before completing any or all of these entries.

**Text: Table/Field**    You must fill in either this parameter or the Value parameter for all Organizational Lvl objects. In the case of the profit center, we filled in the Table value and therefore don't need to complete this field. Otherwise, this field entry would be the text table for the profit center and the field that holds the actual text.

**Chart of Accts: Table/Fld**    You must fill in this field for those organizational units that require a COA to be available. Organizational units like company code are elements that require this entry. You would obtain this setting from the table that stores the organizational unit and the field that holds the specific values.

**FiscalYear: Table/Fld**    You must fill in this field for those organizational units that require a fiscal year to be available. Organizational units like company code and controlling area are elements that require this entry. You would obtain this setting from the table that stores the organizational unit and the field that holds the specific values.

**Currency: Table/Field**    You must fill in this field for those organizational units that require a currency to be available. Organizational units like company code and controlling area are elements that require this entry. You would obtain this setting from the table that stores the organizational unit and the field that holds the specific values.

**ValuationArea: Table/Fld**    You must fill in this field for those organizational units that require a Valuation Area to be available. Organizational units like company code are elements that require this entry. You would obtain this setting from the table that stores the organizational unit and the field that holds the specific values.

Once you complete the initial folder, you can continue to create additional sub-folders or same-level folders by either clicking the Subfolder button at the bottom of the screen or accessing the Org Level screen again and continuing the process. Remember, this is the structure for the organizational levels and not the organizational levels themselves. A nice thing about the Closing Cockpit is that once the actual template is generated with this basic structure, it automatically creates a set of folders for each controlling area or company code. Therefore, you need to create the basic structure only, and the system will take care of the rest.

### EXTREME SPORTS CLOSING PROCESS

In the Extreme Sports case, we will look at using one of the standard delivered organizational hierarchies for controlling area and company code. This will satisfy the needs of our closing process, and we will alter the template to give us the exact process that we need.

# Creating Closing Cockpit Templates

You are now ready to create or copy the Closing Cockpit template. This template is used to structure the individual steps of a process. In this interface, all users involved in the closing process can either access the relevant activities or review what is happening to the tasks running in the background. The template should be reviewed and discussed in depth before completion. Each and every task involved in the FI Closing process must be identified and then assigned to the template. If steps are not included, then you have defeated the purpose for this process. The creation of templates removes all dependency on local knowledge. All companies have some basic structure of the closing process stored somewhere. Take that information and use it as a starting point for building the template. Once this is complete, your closing process will not be as stressful as it is now. We've known situations where one person is so critical to the closing process that they have to work 80 hours a week during the last week of the month and the first two weeks of the next month. They have just enough time to recover before having to start all over again. You can avoid this situation once the FI Closing Cockpit is completed.

To access the create screen for the template, stay in the Closing Cockpit Change screen, and choose Template/Task List ➤ Create Template; the Create New Template dialog box appears, as shown in Figure 15.8.

**FIGURE 15.8** Create New Template dialog box

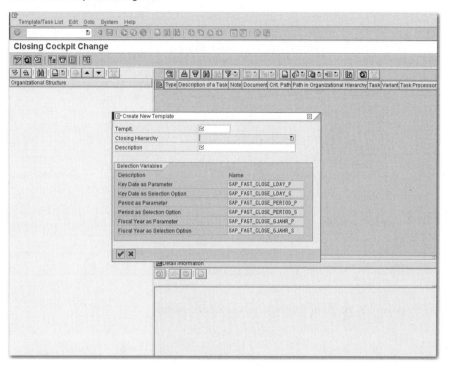

As you can see, most of the fields are defaulted with variants from the TVARV table. This allows you to manage much of the information that is general to the Closing Cockpit from the central screen of the TVARV table. Enter a technical name and assign the organizational hierarchy that you either just created or will use from the standards and then fill in a description. In this case, you will start from scratch building all of your folders, tasks, flow definitions, and so on. We would rather start with something that we can tweak. But it's still a good idea to review the standard templates that are delivered with the system and see whether you want to copy something for your own use. Let's go back and use the Copy option. If you choose Template/Task List ➤ Other Template/Task List, you will see that you have two standard templates, which you can just copy (see Figure 15.9).

In this case, you will choose the template 1-FC-MONTH to copy and then personalize the copied object. Double-click the object and it is displayed on the screen. Then from the top toolbar choose Template/Task List ➤ Save As, and you will be presented with a screen that is very similar to the create screen. Complete the same information, and then click Transfer and Close (the check mark), as shown in Figure 15.10.

**FIGURE 15.9**    Closing Cockpit Display: Select Template or Task List window

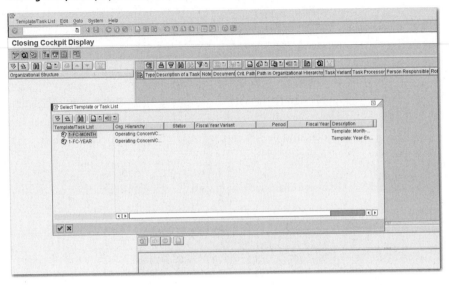

**FIGURE 15.10**    Basic Data from Template Save window

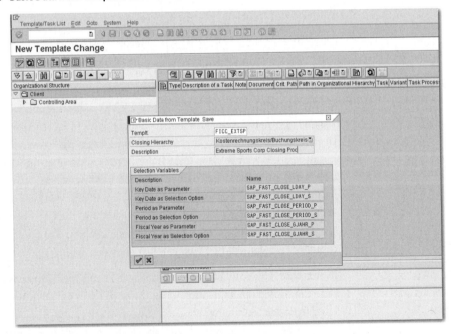

Once this is complete, you will see your technical name on the top portion of the screen. Now, right-click the Controlling Area folder and select the Change Values option in the context menu to access the controlling areas. Then from this screen click the Change button to find your controlling area—as we did to find EX01 for Extreme Sports. Once you fill in the technical name of your controlling area, execute the task by hitting Enter, and you will see that your controlling area has the plus sign to the left. This allows the Closing Cockpit template to use the attributes of the controlling area in the process (see Figure 15.11); do the same for the company code, and your company code attributes will be used by the Closing Cockpit (see Figure 15.12).

**FIGURE 15.11** Change Characteristic Values for Controlling Area window

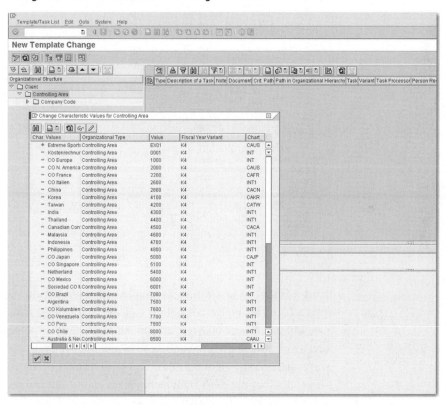

**FIGURE 15.12**   Use this screen to change characteristic values for your company code.

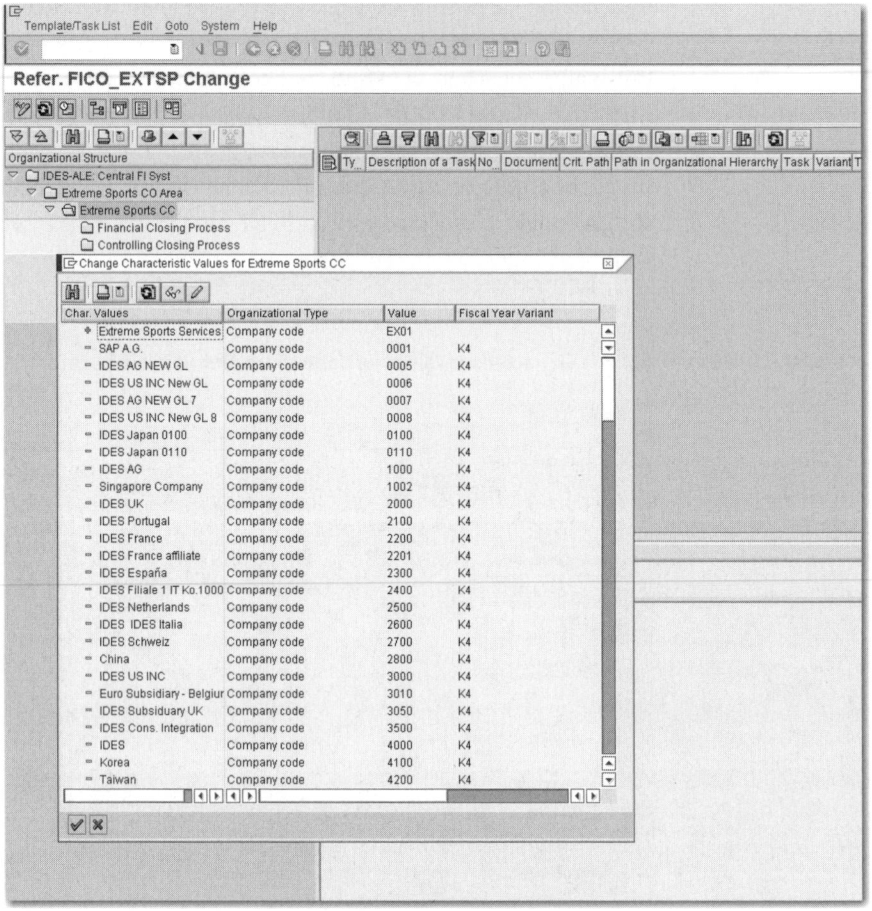

Using this process or creating the template from scratch after you choose either approach and assign the two objects together, you will see that the system will generate a hierarchy and take into account all organizational objects. Therefore, your hierarchy may end up being quite a bit bigger than you initially thought. Not to worry—just choose all of the nodes that represent either controlling areas or company codes that you don't want to use. Then, right-click and select Delete for all the nodes you don't want. We deleted about 30 additional company codes that we didn't want to include in the Extreme Sport closing process.

Now that you have copied over a standard template with the assigned organizational hierarchy, let's see what you have already available for you to work with in the hierarchy structure. If you look at the information available in Figure 15.13, you can see that with the copy of the standard available Closing Cockpit we have copied over multiple folders and information involving Preparatory Closing Tasks, Actual Closing Tasks at Period-End, and subsequent Closing Tasks. The good part about this is all you need to do to fine-tune this is to delete what you don't need or want as a part of the initial Closing Cockpit configuration. At this point, we'll leave everything as is since this is just the initial step, and if everything works out well, we should be able to accomplish the entire closing process for all areas of the company within the FI Closing Cockpit.

**FIGURE 15.13**  Refer. FICC_EXTSP Change screen for the FI Closing Cockpit

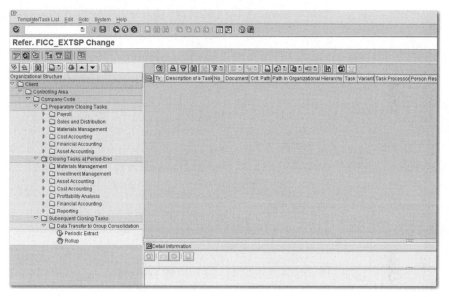

Because of the sheer number of them, we can't go through all of the different folders and review each and every one of the tasks that have been already assigned; we stopped counting once we got to approximately 100 different tasks and activities that are included in this initial Closing Cockpit template. We are getting ahead of ourselves in terms of the configuration, but once we go over the actual configuration process, you will be able to come back to all of these objects to identify any sorts of enhancements or parameters that would be necessary to complete the implementation.

Let's take a look at a couple of other items. If you double-click the Company Code folder, you will see that this generates a list of activities that are found under all of the folders in that specific area. Figure 15.14 shows a long list of activities, and there are now additional icons that are specific to the Closing Cockpit and the Schedule Manager. These icons refer to the various types of tasks that you can create in this area. We will review this in the next section. I just wanted to show you all of the processes that are already defined (generic as they may be) for you to reduce the amount of ramp-up time for the Closing Cockpit.

**FIGURE 15.14**  Refer. FICC_EXTSP Change screen displaying the different tasks available via standard delivered content

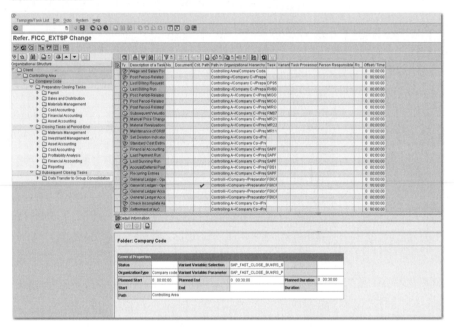

As we walk through the configuration of each task, we will review the different attributes and information necessary to complete this process. We will refer directly to the columns that you see in Figure 15.14. Also notice at the bottom of the screen the information based on the variant variables and planned start and ending dates. As you double-click any of the objects in this screen, the same sort of information will appear at the bottom as a summary of configuration values that you've defined. If you look at one additional view of this information, you can double-click the Financial Accounting folder and see that the tasks defined directly under this folder are displayed. Using this approach, you can review all tasks in a list that you've defined as part of the closing process for FI (see Figure 15.15).

**FIGURE 15.15**  A display of the tasks defined under the Financial Accounting folder of preparatory closing tasks

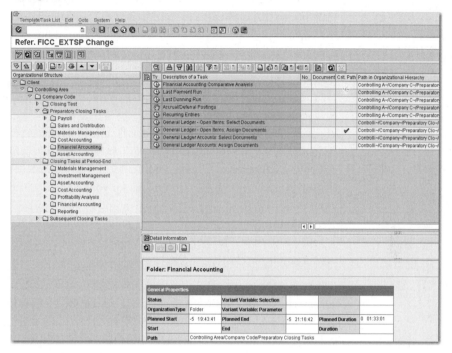

Once you have created a template, you have defined all of the basic parameters for an organizational process. Therefore, you can use a particular template for different organizational hierarchies. This strategy helps reduce the amount of work required for completion of the FI Closing Cockpit.

Before we close on this topic, let's look at two additional options under the Template/Task List context menu. The first is Import Template from Closing Cockpit. This allows you to import a Closing Cockpit template from another system that you are linked to via the RFC link. If you decide to do this, once you choose this option you have to fill in an RFC to another system and the Closing Cockpit template that you want to import. This is also the case for the second option, Import Schedule Manager Task List. As we mentioned, the Schedule Manager has been around for quite some time and may have been developed in some way or shape by someone else in your company. Therefore, your company may have already developed its template of tasks, activities, and flows. If so, you can import that structure from the Schedule Manager into the Closing Cockpit and use the additional functionality available. Once you choose this, you will need to fill in an RFC link; if you want to use the Schedule Manager configuration in the current system, you can leave the RFC connection blank. Identify the task list and also assign a closing hierarchy at this time so that during the import process the two are linked.

## Creating a Folder or Subfolder

The process for creating a folder or a subfolder is the same; it just depends on the level that you have identified the folder. Any folder that is directly assigned to the lowest level of the organizational hierarchy is listed as a folder. Any folder that is created at a lower level, under the folder, is called a subfolder. As you can see, the designation is only semantics in nature. You can assign the same items to either a folder or a subfolder. In creating another folder you are expanding the defaulted organizational hierarchy to customize it for your company. These folders have the same options as the folders for the controlling area and company code, but most are not used since there is no link between a folder like Cost Accounting and an organizational element. The folders and subfolders are text nodes to assign specific tasks and organize the closing process.

The process of creating these folders and subfolders is straightforward. Just click an existing folder, such as Company Code, and using the context menu choose create a subfolder (see Figure 15.16). Once you do this, you will be required to fill in a description and identify the hierarchy level—either a folder or at the level of the organizational elements, which in this case is either at the level of the controlling area or company code (see Figure 15.17).

**FIGURE 15.16** Choosing Create Subfolder from the context menu for the Company Code folder

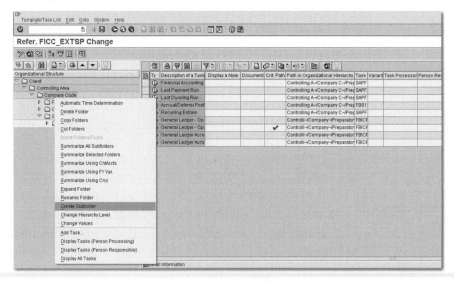

**FIGURE 15.17**  Specify Hierarchy Level and Description window

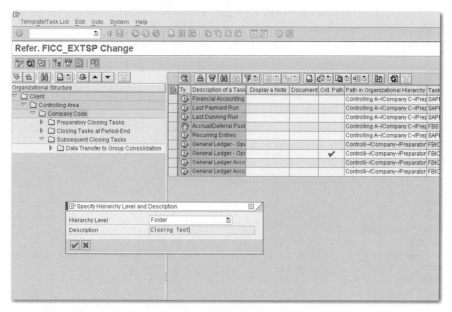

You are now ready to take the template and the associated organizational hierarchy and assign additional tasks to the hierarchy.

# Creating Tasks

The next most time-consuming process after creating the template (that is, if you create the template from scratch) is creating and linking the tasks. Tasks are activities that you create that do the actual activity or process. These tasks are assigned to different folders or subfolders in the hierarchy depending on the executable that is being included in the Closing Cockpit. Tasks are individual activities that are to be performed as part of the overall process in the task list. Four different tasks are possible in the Closing Cockpit: a transaction, a program, a note, and a flow definition.

**NOTE**  These are the same four tasks that you can create in the Schedule Manager.

Since these tasks are assigned directly to the specific folder, the business user in the Closing Cockpit application can navigate directly to the required transaction or background processing for programs and flow definitions from the central Closing

Cockpit interface. Figure 15.18 shows the four different tasks included in the Closing Cockpit: Display/Create/Change Task window.

**FIGURE 15.18**  Closing Cockpit: Display/Create/Change Task window

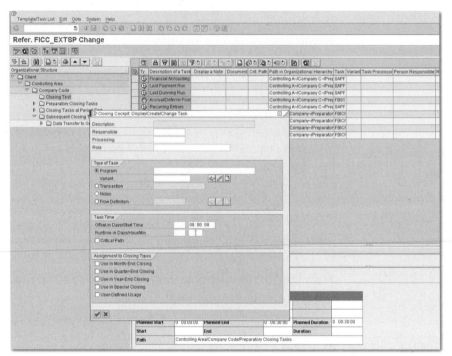

The easiest of the four is the note. A note is used primarily as a reminder or milestone identifier. The note can't be executed or processed, but it does allow nonstructured information to be captured by the Closing Cockpit so that comments can be managed and forwarded to the appropriate people. As you know, a large part of the closing process involves validation steps and confirmation points. The note can help you with these steps.

The transaction task has the ability to display a transaction in the system and allows the user to execute this transaction manually from the task list and go directly from the Closing Cockpit to the relevant application transaction. The transaction process is important to the overall processing in a closing activity. You must review numerous reports, postings, tables, and other items or structures during the closing process. Transactions or transaction codes are your access to these items. This will give the user the ability to cover all informational requirements and not only be able to execute all programs for closing activities, but give the business user direct access to the reports or transactions that are necessary to fulfill the process. If you only use the Closing Cockpit for some basic activities, you should try it for collecting and executing transaction codes.

In the next two tasks you up the ante. You now start to look at using programs in the Closing Cockpit process. The programs are similar to those you might run and execute manually during the closing process. They can include in the FI area things such as dunning processes, depreciation runs, GR/IR activities, comparative analysis, recurring entries, currency translation, among others. In the CO area they can include allocations, settlements of internal orders, distribution processes, reconciliation of FI and CO, CO-PA activities, and many others. Go through your closing process in your head and think about the numerous programs that you have to run to close out the books. There are two options when you use programs: running a program with a variant and running a program without a variant. The big difference between the two is with a variant you can run the program in the background; if you don't use a variant, you will have to manually fill in the values, and then execute the program online. At this point, if you wanted to stop, you would have taken care of nearly all of the processes and activities that you complete in closing FI or CO. But if you want to go a bit further with your configuration, you can set up a flow definition.

A *flow definition* is a combination of multiple programs with variants that are to be processed automatically and in sequence. Such programs are combined to form a logical flow chain with unique predecessor and successor relationships. When a flow definition is executed (either in the background or online), all of the related programs are processes in a specific sequence; then the results are made available for analysis under Detailed Information in the monitor screen. A flow definition also has a number of extras that will help with the overall flow of the closing process. For example, a flow definition can use a *worklist*, which is a group of items (such as Internal Orders) that will be accessed by the program before the initial step is executed. A worklist helps with the speed of the flow definition. Rather than the program accessing the database every time it runs, it only has to access the worklist to get the next internal order or other cost object. Worklists are only available for Orders (Sales Orders, Production Orders, Internal Orders, Project System Orders, and so on) and are not available for cost centers or other cost objects. The flow definition also allows the execution of the steps in sequence; the next step does not start until the prior step is completed.

Now let's review the configuration of each task in detail.

# Notes

As we mentioned, *notes* are used basically as a reminder or milestone identifier. Notes can be used to simplify complex processes. You can use a note, for example, to refer to necessary organizational preliminary activities that cannot be portrayed in the system, or to communicate instructions to users regarding the parameters to use in the transactions. Once included in the task list, notes cannot be subsequently changed manually because they are linked to neither a transaction nor a program. Notes solely serve as reminders. To configure a note in the template, first position your cursor on the folder that you will assign the note to, right-click, and choose Add Task from the context menu. You will then see a screen similar to Figure 15.18. At this point, let's take care of most of the fields on this screen. Then we will move through the four tasks.

**Description**    Enter a description of the task specific to the actual task

**Responsible**    Enter the person who is listed as responsible for this task. Therefore, if there is anything wrong with the task, this person will be called to fix the issue.

**Processing**    Enter the person who is listed as being in charge of executing the task. This person is responsible for the initial execution of the task.

**Role**    If no specific person is responsible for or assigned to a process, then you assign the process to a role. The person who is assigned the role is either responsible for or available to process the task.

In the Task Time section, you'll see the following fields:

**Offset in Days/Start Time**    Specify the date when the task is to be performed in relation to a key date valid for a template or task list. The offset specifies how many days before or after the key date the task should be performed. If the task is to be performed on the same date as the key date, the value is zero.

**Runtime in Days/Hours/Min**    Enter an estimate of the total runtime for the activity. This setting allows the user to estimate if the closing process is behind or ahead of the planned timing to execute the close.

**Critical Path**    If this parameter is checked, the task is a critical path task and you can't execute anything after this task unless this task has been executed successfully or based on the outcome that the user expects.

In the Assignment to Closing Types section, you'll see the following fields:

**Use in Month-End Closing/Quarter-End Closing/Year-End Closing/Special Close**    This setting defines the closing process assigned to the task. The activity can be assigned to more than one closing time frame. Therefore, it would not be unusual to see something that is included in both the month-end and quarter-end processes. A special close might be a short year close; for instance, a corporation may have merged with another company and they need to do a short year close to allow consistency going into the next year's activities.

**User-Defined Usage**    This is a unique closing type that is user customized. The task can be assigned to a different timing for the closing or linked to a specific organizational element.

Now that you have learned about the various parameters on the initial screen, let's focus on the note itself. Click the Notes radio button and enter the description, the responsible person, and the closing process it is assigned: month, quarter, and so on. Notice that you can assign a processing user since you can't process a note (see Figure 15.19). Once that you have filled in all the information, use the Enter icon (check mark) to create the note.

**FIGURE 15.19**  Closing Cockpit Display/Create/Change Task window for a note

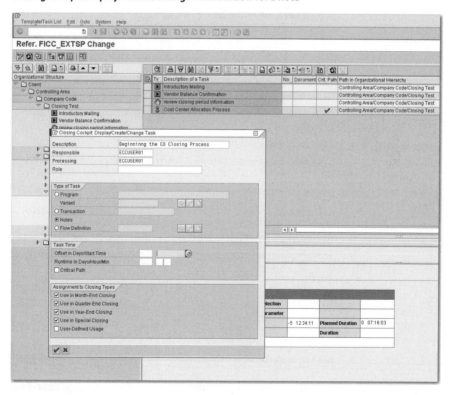

Once the note is created, use the Display a Note field to enter the information that you want to communicate to users. You are given several options, including Office Document and Note. If you choose Note, you a dialog box displays where you'll enter your note information (see Figure 15.20).

**FIGURE 15.20** The Note dialog box for entering information for a note

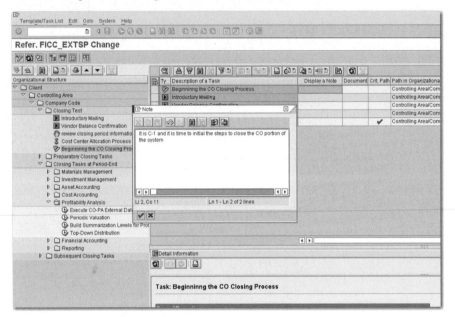

The final view of the note is displayed in Figure 15.21. As you can see, the note is displayed as an icon. You can read it, or you can email it to other members.

**FIGURE 15.21** Note in the Closing Cockpit Task List screen

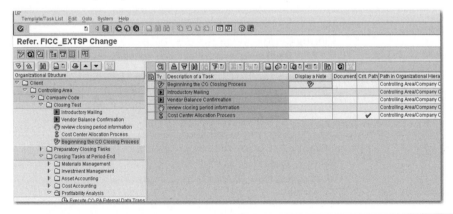

**NOTE** In the web application of Closing Cockpit, you also have an option to store *comments* and information about *messages sent*. You can use comments to take notes, which you can view even after the closing in the details of a task in the task list on the *Comments* tab. On the *Messages Sent* tab, after the closing you also can check whether messages were sent for a task and see their subject lines.

## Transactions

Since we have reviewed all of the other parameters in the Create Task screen (Figure 15.18), we can now focus on the specific task in this case. Let's review the configuration of a transaction as a task. With the transaction task, you can include individual activities that are to be performed during a process as transactions in the task list template. In this way, the transactions can subsequently be executed manually from within the task list. Users can then navigate from the Closing Cockpit application directly to the required transaction from the *Closing Cockpit: Display/ Create/Change Tasks screen*. To store a transaction in the task list template within a task folder for periodic processing, choose *Transaction*. Enter the transaction code in the corresponding field, and change the description of the transaction accordingly. We are going to review transaction code OB52, which is the screen that displays the Open/Closed Periods (see Figure 15.22).

**NOTE** If you are using a transaction code and you get a message that it is not available to be used in the Closing Cockpit, use the maintenance process with transaction code SM30 and add that transaction code to the table SCMATRANSACT.

Once this activity is complete, use the Enter icon (check mark) to complete the process. The transaction task appears below the Closing Test folder; the icon looks like a waving hand. These tasks (transactions) will be manually executed from the Closing Cockpit monitor.

## Programs

With the Program task, you can run an executable from the Closing Cockpit rather than just a transaction or note. Standard programs are generally available for processing activities in the background. If these programs are included in the task list template with corresponding parameters, you can later start background processing directly from the Closing Cockpit. If you would like to execute a program without a variant, the report can be started and processed online in the task list of the Closing Cockpit application. Subsequently, you can check the start, end, log, and spool list for background processing directly in the detailed information as well as in the list display in the Closing Cockpit (transaction CLOCO) application. From the detailed information, you can analyze and repair background jobs containing errors.

**FIGURE 15.22** Closing Cockpit: Display/Create/Change Task dialog box

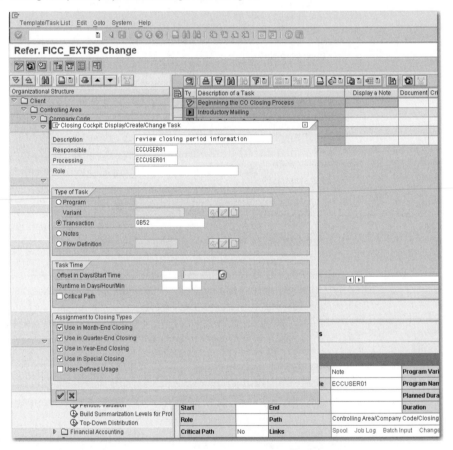

To store a program in the task list template within a task folder for periodic processing, choose *Program.* Enter the program that you want to make available in the task list for background processing, changing the program description if required. When editing tasks, you can create a variant for the selected program or assign an existing variant. To create a variant for the program, choose *Create.* You can store the parameters Period From, Period To, and Fiscal Year as variables in the attributes of the variant so that, if changes are made during processing, adjustments do not need to be made in all program variants used in the Closing Cockpit.

To enter parameters as variables, choose *Attributes*. At this point you can lock the parameters against changes. To ensure that the valid values for the variables can later be determined automatically from the header information of the derived task list and updated in the table TVARV, you could assign for the program variants those variables in the table TVARV that are used in the header information of the task list template or the organizational levels.

Period:      SAP_FAST_CLOSE_PERIOD_P

Fiscal year: SAP_FAST_CLOSE_GJAHR_P

Once completed, save your entries.

**NOTE**   If you are using a transaction code and you get a message that it is not available, use the maintenance process and add that transaction code to the table SCMAPROGRAMS.

In our example we start with a program for sending an email once the closing process starts, as shown in Figure 15.23.

**FIGURE 15.23**  Closing Cockpit Display/Create/Change Task for a Program Task window

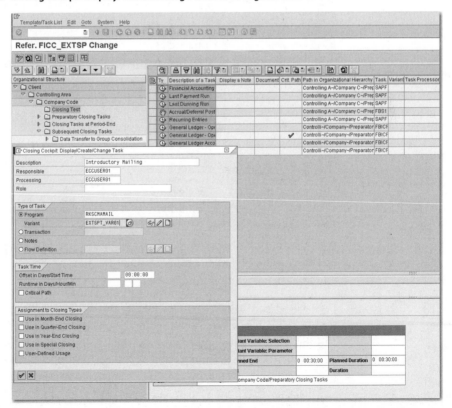

In this process, we are using the program RKSCMAMAIL. There are thousands of programs in the ECC environment. You will have to review the available programs within your areas and then populate the field with the program name. We'll now go through the process of setting up the variant. The variant technical name is EXTSPT_VAR01, as shown in Figure 15.23. Click the Enter icon (check mark) to access the Variants: Change Screen Assignment dialog box. Choose the For All Selection Screens option (see Figure 15.24).

**FIGURE 15.24** Variants: Change Screen Assignment dialog box

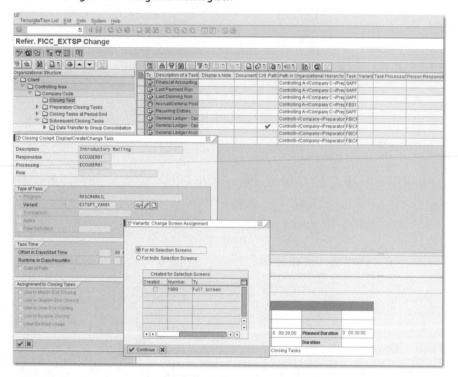

Click the Enter icon (check mark) to open the Maintain Variant screen. Here you type the information that will be displayed in the email text and specify the users you want to receive the email notice. As you can see in Figure 15.25, you can choose SAP User Name, Distribution List, or Internet Address. You can also link this system to Microsoft Outlook and Lotus Notes.

Next, click the Attributes button, and you are presented with the Variant Attributes screen. This is where you can configure the variant to read from different locations within the ECC system. It is also one of the screens that even though the fields are grayed out you can still fill them in. You just need to use the F4 help to pick the entry. As you can see, a series of fields become available that you can assign as parameters. All of these fields are used in the program, so depending on the program that you use, the fields will vary. In this case we will not change anything included in the variant (see Figure 15.26).

**FIGURE 15.25** Maintain Variant screen

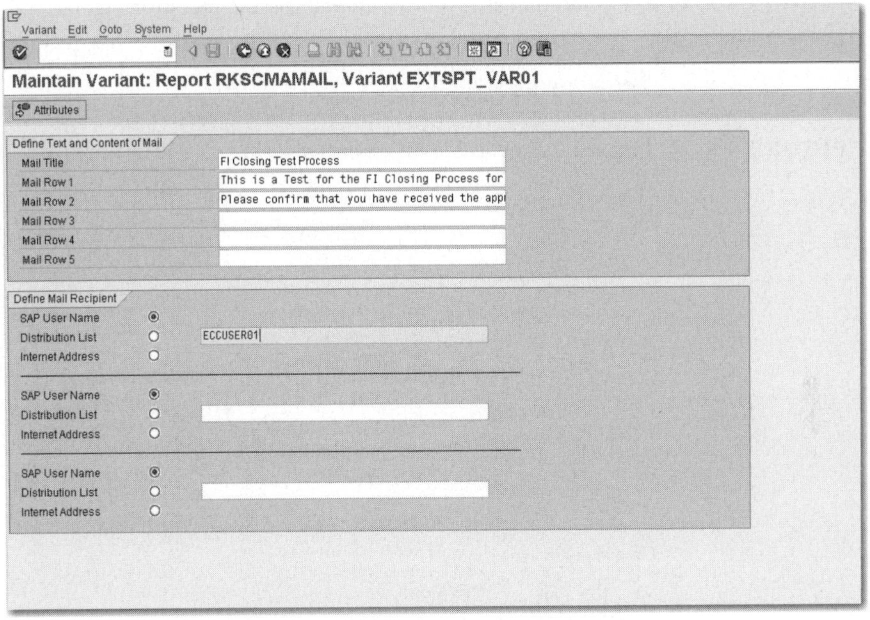

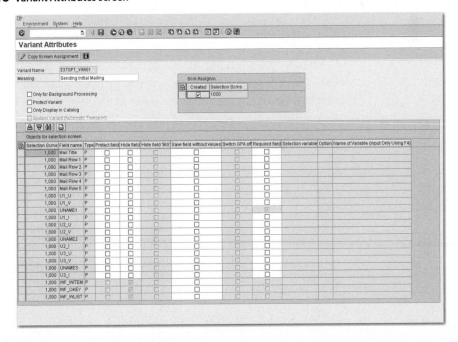

**FIGURE 15.26** Variant Attributes screen

In another program that we are using in this process, the Vendor Balance Confirmation or SAPF130K (see Figure 15.27), we will be modifying the attributes of the variant. Let's review this portion of the setup.

**FIGURE 15.27** Using the Program task in the Closing Cockpit: Task screen

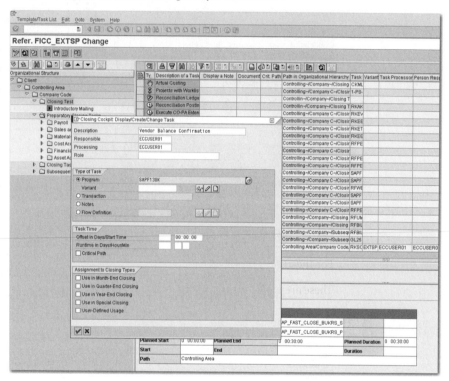

If you move directly to the Variant Attributes screen, you'll see that the various fields you can modify, and as we mentioned earlier, these fields are being generated by the program. In this case, we would like to modify the Company Code, Reconciliation Key Date, Date of Issue, and Date for Reply fields. In Figure 15.28, we have assigned the variant to the selection variable T for the TVARV table and the name of the variable is SAP_FAST_CLOSE_BUKRS_S (look familiar?). We have been working with this variable for some time. This is the one that we assigned the company code EX01 in the TVARV table. Therefore, during the execution process, this program will only affect the vendor balance in the company code EX01. Notice the next variant: the selection variable is D for Dynamic and the name of the variable is Last Day of the Current Month. This is found by the system based on the system parameter using the company calendar to insert the last day of the current month.

**FIGURE 15.28** Variant Attributes screen with Company Code assigned to selection variable T

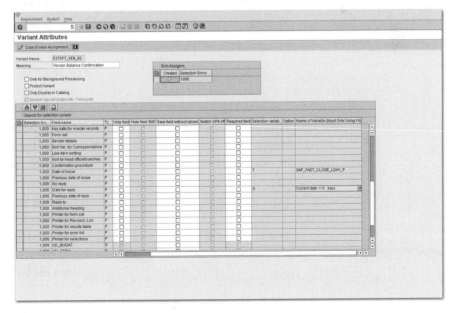

For the other two parameters, we used both variables as well (see Figure 15.29).

These are examples of two different programs to be used in the Closing Cockpit.

**FIGURE 15.29** Variant Attributes for Date of Issue and Date for Reply screen

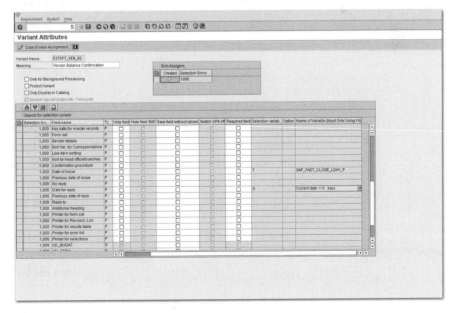

# Flow Definitions

A *flow definition* is a combination of different programs, both standard and customized. Flow definitions are used for multiple programs with variants that are to be processed automatically. Such programs are combined to form a logical flow chain with unique predecessor and successor relationships. When a flow definition is executed or scheduled to be executed, all of the related programs are processed in the specified sequence. The results are then made available for analysis under the Detailed Information section. In the flow definition, you group tasks that are to be executed in a particular order. You use the standard workflow within the Closing Cockpit to control these flow definitions. You can structure subflows and include them in a flow definition. You can insert user decisions for testing purposes.

Numerous programs and hundreds of flow definitions can be used. I suggest that you review one flow definition that is familiar to you either in the FI or CO area and work with that one first. Make sure that you are comfortable with the process and know how to manage the execution of these flow definitions before attempting to realign the configuration to set up flow definitions. Again, this is a case where starting from scratch in building a flow definition is not the best business practice. If you think about this, we are using many of the standard programs during our closing process. Why not create a link between programs that have to be run in sequence? They will then lend themselves nicely to the flow definition you set up.

Let's start with using a program from the Cost Accounting area. In our example we will configure the use of the flow definition for cost center allocations. In Figure 15.30 we start the creation process by completing the description of the flow definition.

Click the Enter icon (check mark), which takes you to a dialog box that requires you to choose one of the applications available. You can choose among approximately 40 applications. In this case, the applications will generate a flow definition that has been standard delivered, and you can customize it however you need (see Figure 15.31).

**FIGURE 15.30**  Initial step to configure a flow definition in the Closing Cockpit

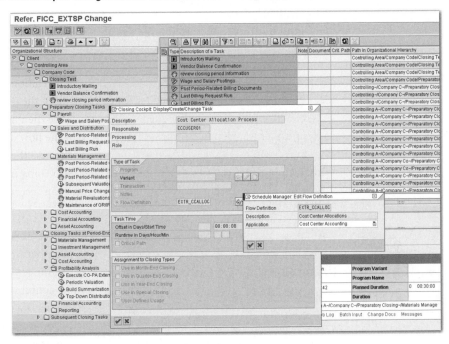

**FIGURE 15.31**  Schedule Manager: Edit Flow Definition screen

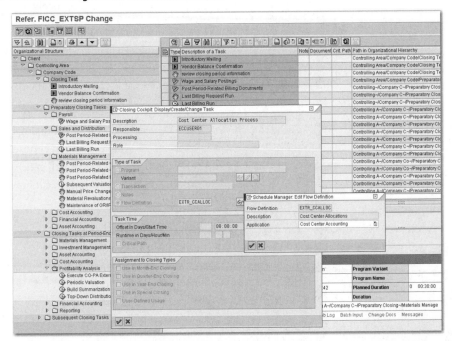

Dismiss this screen by clicking the Enter icon (check mark) and the system generates the full list of programs for the execution of the cost center allocation process (see Figure 15.32). You may or may not use all of these activities. Notice something about the icons? They are the program icons—thus reinforcing the idea that a flow definition is a grouping of programs to be run. Several icons are available, including the following:

With the quick info text Workflow: Start/End Workflow

With the quick info text Program: Assign Program with Variant

With the quick info text Flow Definition: Assign Flow Definition

With the quick info text User Decision: Assign User Decision

With the quick info text Fork: Assign Parallel Processing

**FIGURE 15.32** Closing Cockpit: Display/Create/Change Task screen

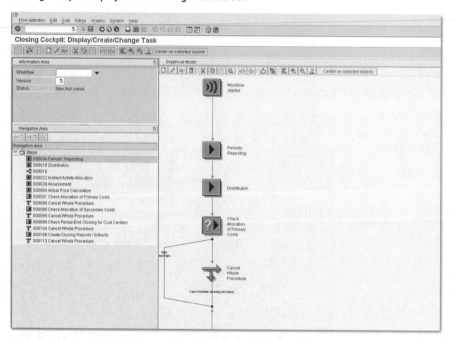

Each has unique responsibilities. Workflow is the standard workflow delivered with the system. This feature helps with processing of information and communication via the use of ABAP programs. Assign Flow Definition lets you assign a flow

definition to another flow definition. User Decision lets you assign a task to a user who needs some sort of user intervention, such as signing off report results. The Fork item offers a way to do parallel processing within the flow definition.

If you double-click one of the programs in this flow definition, you can observe the details of the process (see Figure 15.33). If you look at the Distribution program, you see the setup information. Since a number of these fields are similar for many of the steps, you can review them from this screen. If you were to create a step in the flow definition from scratch, you would use the same screen but you'd have to fill in each field with the necessary information:

**FIGURE 15.33** Flow Definition: Task Details screen

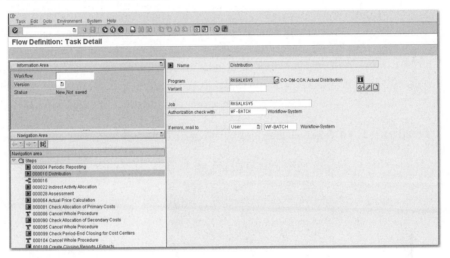

**Name**    Enter the name of the program here.

**Program**    This field contains the defaulted ABAP program that will execute the distribution process. If you are in the process of creating a program from scratch, you can do a search on all programs available. Once you have found a program that is similar to what you need, you can then copy it and enhance the program where necessary. You can narrow your search by choosing the application, such as CCA or COPA.

**Variant**    This field contains the same variant variables that we have been working with in the Programs area.

**Job**    This field specifies the background job technical name. The field allows the user to predefine the parameters of execution. It also lets you manage the program execution. Reviewing the job status will show you how the program is running.

**Authorization Check With**    This field generates an authorization check to confirm that the person running the flow definition and the Closing Cockpit is authorized to do so. In most cases the field is assigned to the workflow system. This means that a specific workflow process is used to monitor the authorization check.

**If Errors, Mail To**    This field identifies the person who will be notified if there is an error in program execution. Again, this is often assigned to the workflow process. In this case, the person(s) responsible are listed in a table and the workflow uses the table as a lookup for the email address(es) to execute this activity.

Another example is the Indirect Activity Allocation program. As you can see in this case, the variant has been defined and included in the flow definition. Therefore, in the previous case, some manual intervention may be needed since there was no variant, while in this case, the program gets the necessary parameters from the variant entries and then executes the program (see Figure 15.34).

**FIGURE 15.34** Flow Definition: Task Detail screen for the Indirect Activity Allocation program

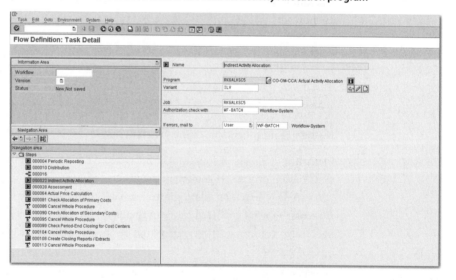

Finally, let's look at inserting another program or flow definition in the current flow definition. As shown in Figure 15.35, you right-click the line between any of the different programs and choose the Create option. This generates a screen similar to the previous two, but all of the fields are blank for you to fill in.

**FIGURE 15.35** Create/Display/Change screen for a flow definition

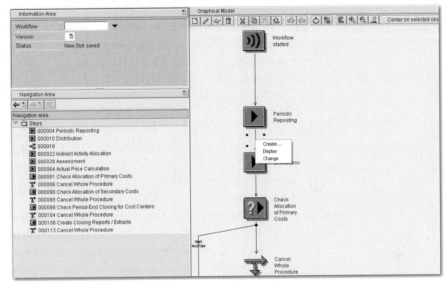

Figure 15.36 shows the completed view of the flow definition via the Closing Cockpit task screen. We have identified this flow definition as critical to the process, as shown by the green check box in the row.

**FIGURE 15.36** Refer. FICC_EXTSP screen with the flow definition assigned

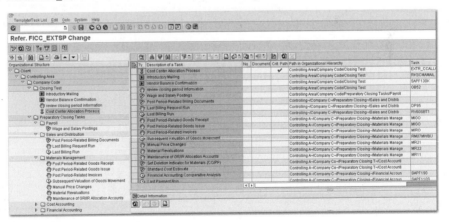

## Dependencies

One of the many improvements with the Schedule Manager and the Closing Cockpit is the use of dependencies between tasks. Programs and transactions that have been included in the task list template using chronological process steps as part of an organizational structure frequently involve business-related or system-related dependencies that need to be portrayed for the process flow to be processed smoothly. In the configuration of the Closing Cockpit, you can display these predecessor relationships under dependencies. When you enter a relationship between programs and transactions here, this relationship is checked during subsequent processing in the application.

To define dependencies, choose Dependencies at the bottom of the screen (see Figure 15.37). Select the task for which you want to define one or more (hierarchical) predecessor relationships. The combination of relationships is managed from the standpoint of the successor. In this way, an activity can have more than one predecessor. If the selected task in the *Dependencies* detail screen appears, you can use drag and drop to assign to this activity any same-level or hierarchical predecessor from the task list template. By creating dependencies in the *Closing Cockpit* application, you have ensured that programs and transactions can only be scheduled or executed once the predecessor activities have been processed successfully (without errors).

This dependency process can be configured in the Closing Cockpit change screen using a drag-and-drop process for the items for which you want to create a dependency (see Figure 15.37). The dependency link is found at the bottom of the screen.

**FIGURE 15.37** Dependencies portion of the Refer. FICC_EXTSP screen

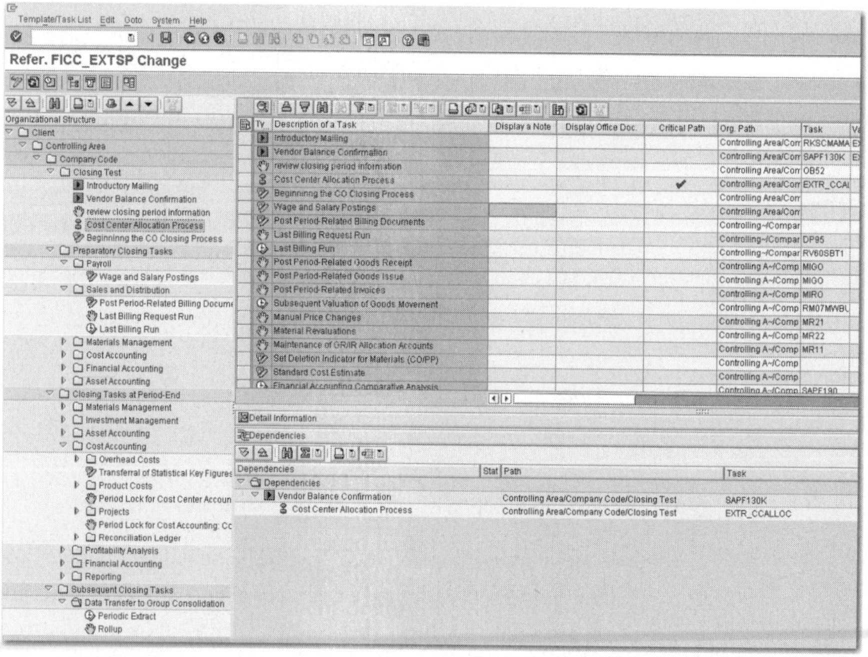

# Creating the Task List

The final activity for using the Closing Cockpit is to create a task list for the template. The task list is used to present and execute the template tasks. To perform programs included in a task list, you specify variant values. With the separation of the task template from the task list, you can define the structured process flow as a generic template and then make a task list available for processing with specific parameter values. The task list generated from the template automatically updates the time-related program parameters of the selection variants when you enter corresponding header information in the task list.

To complete this step from the Change screen for the Closing Cockpit, choose Template/Task List ≻ Create Task List (see Figure 15.38). From the current task list template, the system creates a task list of the same name. You enter values for the *Key Date*, *Fiscal Year*, and *Posting Period* parameters for this task list. On the basis of the closing type selected in the task list, the system transfers from the task list template to the task list only those activities that are permitted in the task definition for that particular closing type. So, depending on whether you are creating a task list for month end, quarter end, or year end, these tasks are assigned automatically to the task list. You can make last-minute adjustments to data items of a task in the list prior to the release, such as *Person Responsible*, *Planned Duration*, or *Planned Start*.

**FIGURE 15.38** Create New Task Plan Using Template FICC_EXTSP window

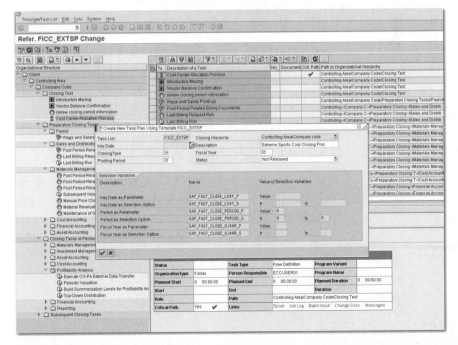

After filling in the necessary parameters, we are looking at a task list for the Monthly process (Closing Type = M) for the year 2008 (fiscal year = 2008) and the first period (Posting period = 1). Therefore, if you review the variable variants in Figure 15.39, you will see that the values have been inherited by the variables. If you are satisfied with the settings, make sure you release the task list before leaving the screen by using the context menu off of the Template/Task List option on the toolbar. You can always come back in and release later, but you will not be able to assign any tasks for execution unless the task list is released.

**FIGURE 15.39** Create New Task Plan Using Template FICC_EXTSP—released

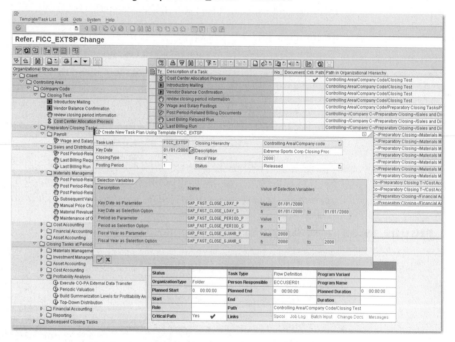

Once this is completed, if you go back and review the actual template that was just assigned to the task list, you will see that the status has been updated to Release (green flag). Figure 15.40 shows the screen view.

Now that you have assigned the task template to the task list and released the list, you can review the combination of these two objects and manually process one of the tasks. In Figure 15.41, you can see that we are able to schedule the selected tasks.

**FIGURE 15.40** Select Template or Task List—released version

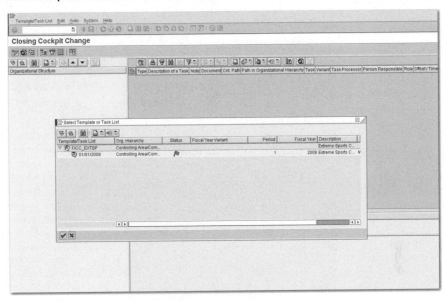

**FIGURE 15.41** Task list from the template FICC_EXTSP ready to be executed

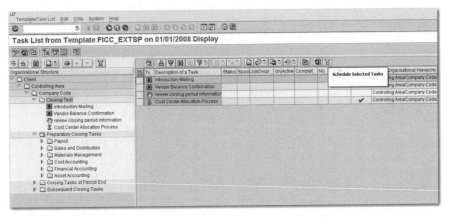

Taking the initial executable—Introductory Mailing—and executing this task, you can see that once you run this task you get a message that the task has been scheduled successfully. Since this is a program and you set it up to execute immediately upon scheduling, you should see some results fairly quickly (see Figure 15.42).

In this case, once you close this system message, you get another SAP Office Express message that there's something in your inbox for you to read. With the appropriate workflow settings, you're able to click the Inbox button on this message to access the inbox information (see Figure 15.43).

**FIGURE 15.42** Closing Cockpit messages

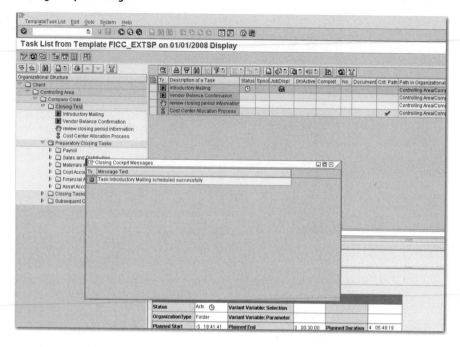

**FIGURE 15.43** SAP Office Express message

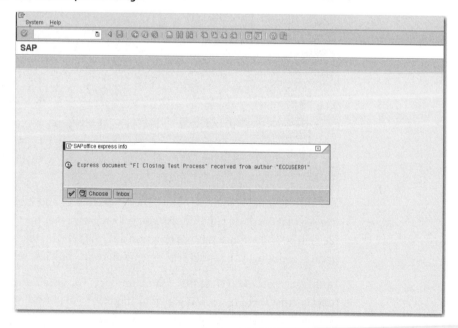

Review the Inbox message, which includes information about the FI Closing Test Process. This is what we expected from the Closing Cockpit (see Figure 15.44).

**FIGURE 15.44** Business Workplace of SAP user—Inbox messages

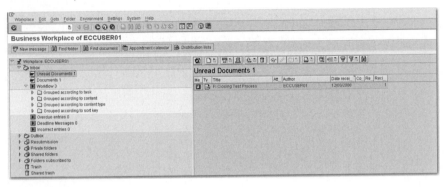

Go back to the Closing Cockpit to review the results of the execution of the task. You can see that we have an updated status on this task and it has generated a series of messages to inform you of the task's process. If the status is Green, a spool job is available to review the process. There's also a job log for this specific task (see Figure 15.45).

**FIGURE 15.45** Task list from Template FICC_EXTSP with updated results for the initial task

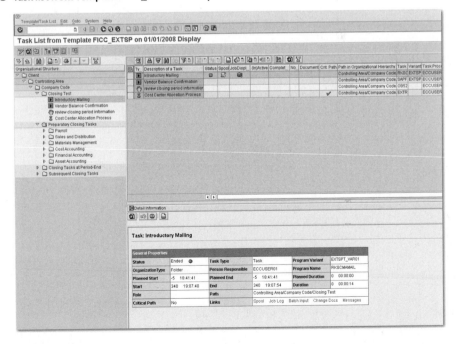

Also notice the series of executable links at the bottom of the screen for the Spool, Job Log, Batch Input, Change Docs, and messages. If you click a link, you see that you have updated information on the task. In our example, you are looking at the job output to validate that the message was delivered (see Figure 15.46).

**FIGURE 15.46** Job Log Entries for RKSCMAMAIL/EXTSPT_VAR01

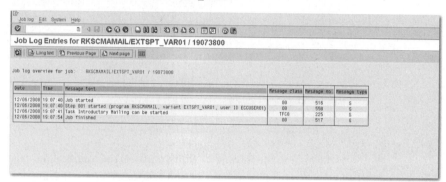

Now that you know the process works (at least for one task), you can import this task list into the Closing Cockpit monitor for the user and use the monitor to execute the Closing Cockpit. To do this, select Accounting ➤ Financial Accounting ➤ General Ledger ➤ Periodic Processing ➤ Closing ➤ Closing Cockpit (Overview) or use the transaction code CLOCOS. Click the Change button, and then from the Template/Task List choose ➤ Import Template from Closing Cockpit. Choose your Closing Cockpit task list (see Figure 15.47) and import the list.

Next, you will see all the tasks that you created in a graphical view. You can modify the timing and management of the tasks but you can't do anything dealing with the true configuration process. Therefore, if you just drag one of the task boxes in the graphic view, you will see that the time expands in the properties box in the lower portion of the screen (see Figure 15.48).

In each of the boxes or diamonds is the first one or two initials of the task. If you expand the box or diamond, you can see more of the task's title. At this point you are ready to start scheduling and executing the tasks assigned to the FI Closing Cockpit.

**FIGURE 15.47**  Import Template from Another System window

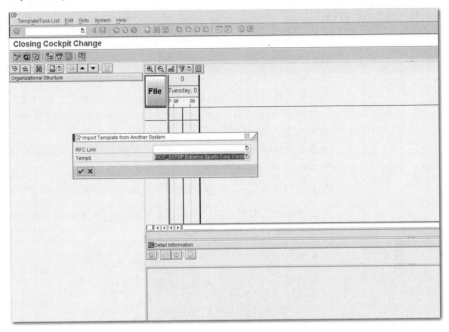

**FIGURE 15.48**  Task List from Template FICC_EXTSP in the Closing Cockpit monitor

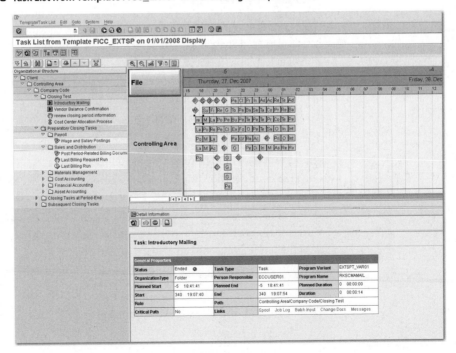

# Summary

The FI Closing Cockpit is one of the newest components in the ECC environment. It provides good capabilities to help with the closing process and you will experience an immediate improvement and efficiency during your closing process. In this chapter, we outlined the initial setup and basic configuration of the Closing Cockpit. You can probably see why this feature is intended not only for FI and CO but also for any of the other components in the SAP systems that need to be managed at period end. In many of the figures, you saw the folders for the MM, PP, and SD areas. As you work your way through the setup process, you will learn that there are more than 400 programs and flow definitions available for closing activities.

Just remember that you can use the Closing Cockpit in many situations, including but not limited to the following:

► When an activity is recurring

► If more than one person is involved in the process

► If the activity can be organized into a series of executable steps

► If the activity needs to be documented

► If the activity needs to be managed throughout its process and therefore the status of the activity must be updated

There are numerous benefits to implementing the Closing Cockpit, such as automation of activities associated with the close and the ability to pass the starting parameters for the relevant tasks to each of the jobs. The Closing Cockpit eliminates most of the bottlenecks and dependencies in the closing process and makes them transparent to the user. Most importantly, it creates a central repository for all documents, logs, and comments related to the close.

It is important to define the organizational hierarchy correctly before working through the configuration. Making a copy of some of the SAP-delivered Closing Cockpit templates is probably the best way to initially review the functionality. Once you get your feet wet on the functionality and setup process, you will see how easy this process is. If most portions of your closing process are standard, then quite a few of the flow definitions can be used directly out of the box and the other may require only minor changes for users, variants, and email addresses.

We suggest setting up the Portal view of the Closing Cockpit because of the additional functionality and the user experience it provides. Please review the information online at `http://help.sap.com` that is necessary to set up the Closing Cockpit in the portal since additional business content must be activated. You'll also benefit from some research into the use of the distributed capability of the Closing Cockpit using the Central Process Scheduler in conjunction with the Redwood Software add-on. You can find information about the add-on in a number of places, including the help files at `http://help.sap.com`.

# Useful Transaction Codes, Tables, and Programs

n this appendix, we will present the configuration transaction codes relevant to the topics discussed in this book. We'll also list transaction codes not covered as well as useful programs and tables. The tables are arranged via subject content that, in most cases, corresponds to the chapters of the book.

**TABLE A.1**    **General and Cross-Module Configuration Transaction Codes**

| Transaction Code | Description |
|---|---|
| SE10 | Customizing Organizer |
| SPRO | Enter the IMG |
| SM30 | Table maintenance |
| SM31 | Extended Table Maintenance |
| SE11 | Data Dictionary change and display |
| SE12 | Data dictionary display |
| SE16 | The Data Browser |
| SU53 | Authorization object request |
| SE38 | Run/change/display a program |
| SA38 | Run a program |
| SM35 | Batch input session overview |
| SE01 | View transport logs |
| GGB0 | Create/change validation |
| GGB1 | Create/change substitutions |
| GGB4 | Activate validations and substitutions |
| SNRO | Maintain number range objects |

**TABLE A.2**    **General and Cross-Module Configuration Tables**

| Table(s) | Description |
|---|---|
| E071 and E071K | Transport tables; displays all transports affecting a given object |
| V_GB01C | Customizing table for Boolean fields in substitutions and validations |
| GB01 | SAP-delivered table that lists all fields that can be used in substitutions and validations |
| SADR | Address data (which doesn't transport well) |

**TABLE A.3**  General and Cross-Module Configuration Program

| Program | Description |
| --- | --- |
| RGUGBR00 | Program to regenerate sets, validations, and substitutions |

**TABLE A.4**  FI Enterprise Structure Transaction Codes

| Transaction Code | Description |
| --- | --- |
| OBY7 | Copy chart of accounts |
| OB29 | Fiscal year variant |
| OBBO | Posting period variant |
| OX02 | Company Codes—create, check, and delete |
| OBY6 | Company Code global data |
| EC01 | Copy Company Code |
| OY01 | Country definitions |
| OB22 | Additional parallel currencies |
| OX03 | Business Areas |
| OKBD | Functional Areas |
| OBBG | Assign country to tax calculation procedure |
| OBCO | Specify structure for tax jurisdiction codes |
| OBCP | Define tax jurisdiction codes |
| FTXP | Maintain tax rates |
| OBCL | Set tax codes for non-taxable transactions |

**TABLE A.5**  General Ledger/Chart of Accounts Transaction Codes

| Transaction Code | Description |
| --- | --- |
| OBD4 and OT37 | Account groups |
| OB53 | Retained earnings variant |
| OB15 | Sample account rule types |
| FSK2 | Sample account data transfer rules |
| OB67 | Allocate a Company Code to a sample account rule type |
| OBY9 | Transport chart of accounts |
| OBY2 | Copy G/L accounts from the chart to the Company Code |
| OBC4 | Field status variants |

**TABLE A.5**    General Ledger/Chart of Accounts Transaction Codes *(continued)*

| Transaction Code | Description |
|---|---|
| OB41 | Posting keys |
| FBKP | Automatic account assignments |
| OB40 | Define tax accounts |
| OBYA | Cross-Company Code automatic account assignment |
| OBYC | MM automatic account assignment |
| OB58 | Financial statement versions |
| O7Z3 | Line item layouts |
| OBVU | Special fields |
| O7S7 | Sort variants |
| O7R1 | Totals variants |
| OBA4 | Tolerance groups |
| OB57 | Allocate users to tolerance groups |
| FBN1 | G/L number ranges |
| OBA7 | Document types |
| OBU1 | Assign default posting keys to document types |
| O7E6 | Fast entry screens |
| OBL1 | Automatic postings documentation |
| OB32 | Maintain document change rules |

**TABLE A.6**    General Ledger/Chart of Accounts Programs

| Program | Description |
|---|---|
| RFBISA10 | Copy Multiple G/L accounts from Company to Company or from Client to Client |
| RFBISA20 | Import G/L accounts Created by RFBISA10 (copying from client to client) |
| RFTAXIMP | Import tax codes/tax jurisdiction codes |

**TABLE A.7**    General Ledger/Chart of Accounts Tables

| Table | Description |
|---|---|
| BSEG | G/L document line item table |
| TTXD | Tax jurisdiction code structure table |
| T030 | Automatic account assignments table |
| TZUN | G/L account sort key (Allocation field) table |

**TABLE A.8**   Accounts Payable Transaction Codes

| Transaction Code | Description |
|---|---|
| FI12 | House banks |
| FCHI | Check lots |
| FCHV | Void reason codes |
| FBZP | Payment program |
| OBD3 | Vendor groups |
| XKN1 | Create number ranges for vendor groups |
| OBAS | Assign number ranges to vendor account groups |
| FK15 | Copy vendor master records creation program |
| FK16 | Copy vendor master records upload program |

**TABLE A.9**   Accounts Receivable and Credit Management Transaction Codes

| Transaction Code | Description |
|---|---|
| OBB8 | Terms of payment A/R and A/P |
| OB46 | Interest indicator |
| OB82 | Make interest indicator available to the interest calculation program (arrears) |
| OBAC | Reference interest rates |
| OB81 | Assign reference interest rates to interest indicators |
| OBV1 | Interest calculation automatic account assignment |
| OBBE | Reason codes |
| OBCR | Reason code conversion version |
| OBCS | Map external reason codes to internal reason codes |
| OBXL | Assign G/L accounts to reason codes |
| OBXI | Cash discount amount |
| OBA3 | Customer tolerance groups |
| OB45 | Credit control areas |
| OB01 | Credit risk categories |
| OB02 | Credit representative groups |
| OB51 | Assign employees to credit representative groups |
| OB39 | Days in arrears calculation |
| OBD2 | Customer groups |

**TABLE A.10**   Treasury Transaction Codes

| Transaction Code | Description |
| --- | --- |
| OB10 | Create lockbox accounts |
| OBAY | Define lockbox control parameters |
| OBAX | Lockbox posting data |
| OT05 | Source symbols |
| OT14 | Planning levels |
| OT13 | Planning groups |
| OT47 | Assign logistics transactions to planning levels |
| OT17 | Treasury groupings |
| OT18 | Treasury grouping headers |
| OT16 | Cash management account names |
| OT29 | Activate company code treasury updates |
| OBBY | Electronic bank statement transaction types |
| OT55 | Assign transaction types to house hanks |
| OT57 | Electronic bank statement posting rules |
| OT51 | Map external transactions to posting rules |
| OT59 | Posting rules automatic account assignment |
| GCRF | Currency translation ratios |

**TABLE A.11**   NEW General Ledger Accounting Transaction Codes

| Transaction Code | Description |
| --- | --- |
| FAGL_ACTIVATION | Activate the New General Ledger Accounting |
| FAGL_SCENARIO | Scenario Maintenance in New G/L |
| FAGL_SCENARIO_ASS | Scenario Assignment in New G/L |
| GSP_RD | Define Document Splitting Rules |
| OC08 | Maintain Transaction Types for Consolidation |
| OBA7 | Define Document Types for Entry View |
| GLN1 | Flexible G/L: Actual Document Types |
| OK17 | Define Account Determination for Real-Time Integration |
| FGI0 | New Drilldown Reports for the NEW GL |

**TABLE A.11** NEW General Ledger Accounting Transaction Codes *(continued)*

| Transaction Code | Description |
|---|---|
| FBL1N | Line Item Display Reports for Vendor |
| GLPINST | Install Totals Table for Planning in the NEW GL |
| GLPV | Define Planning Versions for the NEW GL |
| FAGLGA11 | General Ledger: Create Actual Assessment Cycle |
| FAGLGA27 | General Ledger: Create Plan Assessment Cycle |
| FAGLGA31 | General Ledger: Create Actual Distribution Cycle |
| FAGLGA47 | General Ledger: Create Plan Distribution Cycle |
| FAGLSL25 | Execute General Ledger Rollup |
| KDF | Prepare Automatic Postings for Foreign Currency Valuation |
| FB01L | General Posting for Ledger Group: Header Data |
| FB50L | GL Account document for Ledger Group: By Company Code |
| OADB_WZ | Setup of Parallel Valuation for the New G/L |

**TABLE A.12** CO Enterprise Structure Transaction Codes

| Transaction Code | Description |
|---|---|
| OX06 | Controlling Areas |
| OKKP | Activate CO Components for Controlling Areas, Basic Data, and Assignment of Company Codes to Controlling Area |
| KANK | CO Document Number Ranges |
| KEP8 | Operating Concern Definition |
| ORKE | COPA Implementation Guide |
| OKEQ | Planning Versions |

**TABLE A.13** Cost Element Accounting Transaction Codes

| Transaction Code | Description |
|---|---|
| OKB2 | Automatic Cost Element Creation |
| OKB3 | Create Batch Input Session for Automatic Cost Element Creation |
| KA06 | Create Secondary Cost Elements |
| KA01 | Create Primary Cost Elements |
| KA02 | Change Primary Cost Elements |

**TABLE A.13**      Cost Element Accounting Transaction Codes *(continued)*

| Transaction Code | Description |
|---|---|
| KA04 | Delete Primary Cost Elements |
| KA23 | Display Cost Element Collective Processing |
| KAH1 | Create Cost Element Groups |
| KAH2 | Change Cost Element Groups |
| KB11N | Enter Manual Reposting of Costs |
| KB41N | Enter Manual Reposting of Revenues |
| KB61 | Enter Repost Line Items |
| KB21N | Actual Postings – Activity Allocation for Cost Elements |
| KSAZ | Overhead Costing Sheet |
| KALA | Activate Reconciliation Ledger |
| OBYB | Maintain Automatic Account Assignments for the Reconciliation Ledger |
| OK13 | Number Ranges for Reconciliation Ledger Activity |
| OKP1 | Change Period Lock |
| SM35 | Automatic Creation of Primary and Secondary Cost Elements using the Batch Input Process |
| OKA6 | Change view "Cost Element Attributes" Overview |
| OKEK | Change: Time-Based Fields (Cost Elements) |
| S_ALR_870135* and 36* | All Standard Delivered Cost Element Reports in the Information System |

**TABLE A.14**      Cost Center Accounting Transaction Codes

| Transaction Code | Description |
|---|---|
| KSH2 | Cost Center Standard Hierarchy |
| OKEON | Change Cost Center Standard Hierarchy |
| OKENN | Display Cost Center Standard Hierarchy |
| OKE5 | Profit Center Accounting Settings for the Controlling Area |
| KCH1 | Profit Center Standard Hierarchy – Create |
| KCH2 | Profit Center Standard Hierarchy – Change |
| KE59 | Create Dummy Profit Center |
| OKA2 | Cost Center Categories |
| OKEG | Cost Center Time Dependency Fields |
| KS01 | Create Cost Center |

**TABLE A.14**     Cost Center Accounting Transaction Codes *(continued)*

| Transaction Code | Description |
| --- | --- |
| KS02 | Change Cost Center |
| KS03 | Delete Cost Center |
| KS12 | Change Cost Center Collective Processing |
| KS13 | Display Cost Center Collective Processing |
| KS14 | Delete Cost Center Collective Processing |
| KSH1 | Create Cost Center Group |
| KSH2 | Change Cost Center Group |
| KSH3 | Display Cost Center Group |
| KK01 | Create Statistical Key Figures |
| KK02 | Change Statistical Key Figures |
| KK03 | Display Statistical Key Figures |
| KK03DEL | Delete Statistical Key Figures |
| KAK2 | Change Statistical Key Figures Collective Processing |
| KBH1 | Create Statistical Key Figure Group |
| KBH2 | Change Statistical Key Figure Group |
| OKE1 | Activity Types Time Dependency Fields |
| KL01 | Create Activity Types |
| KL02 | Change Activity Types |
| KL03 | Display Activity Types |
| KL04 | Delete Activity Types |
| KL13 | Display Activity Types Collective Processing |
| KL14 | Delete Activity Types Collective Processing |
| KLH1 | Create Activity Type Group |
| KLH2 | Change Activity Type Group |
| KLH3 | Display Activity Type Group |
| KPR2 | Create/Change Resources |
| KPR3 | Display Resources |
| KB11N | Enter Manual Reposting of Costs |
| KB13N | Display Manual Reposting of Costs |
| KB14N | Reverse Manual Reposting of Costs |
| KB41N | Enter Manual Reposting of Revenues |

**TABLE A.14**     Cost Center Accounting Transaction Codes *(continued)*

| Transaction Code | Description |
|---|---|
| KB61 | Enter Repost Line Items |
| KB63 | Display Repost Line Items |
| KB64 | Reverse Repost Line Items |
| KB21N | Enter Activity Allocation |
| KB65 | Enter Activity Allocation Reposting |
| KB51N | Enter Sender Activities |
| KB15N | Enter Manual Cost Allocation |
| KB31N | Enter Statistical Key Figures |
| BATCHMAN | Transfer of External Data to CO |
| KCAU | Assessment Receiver Types |
| KSW1 | Periodic Repostings |
| KSW5 | Execute Actual Periodic Repostings |
| KSA3 | Actual Accrual Calculation for Cost Centers |
| KSAJ | Maintain CO-OM Accrual Calculation: Target = Actual Credit Overview |
| KSV1 | Create Actual Distribution Cycle |
| KSU1 | Create Actual Assessment Cycle |
| KSES | Change/Create View "Allocation Structures": Overview |
| KSC1 | Create Actual Indirect Activity Allocation Cycle: Initial Screen |
| CPT1 | Create Template for Activity Allocation |
| OKES | Change/Create View "Splitting Structures": Overview |
| KP04 | Set Planner Profile |
| KP97 | Copy Plan to Plan Data |
| KP98 | Copy Actual to Plan Data |
| KSPU | Revaluate Plan Costs |
| KSP4 | Planning Overhead Allocation |
| KSVB | Planning Distribution |
| KSUB | Planning Assessment |
| KPU1 | Planning Revaluation |
| KP65 | Cost Planning Layout |
| KP34 | Planning Profiles |
| OKB9 | Cost Element Automatic Account Assignment |
| S_ALR_870136* | All Standard Delivered Cost Center Reports in the Information System |

**TABLE A.15** Internal Orders Transaction Codes

| Transaction Code | Description |
|---|---|
| KO04 | Order Manager |
| KO01 | Create Internal Order |
| KO02 | Change Internal Order |
| KO03 | Display Internal Order |
| KOK2 | Manual Collective Processing of Orders |
| KOK4 | Automatic Collective Processing of Orders |
| KOH1 | Create Order Group |
| KOH2 | Change Order Group |
| KOH3 | Display Order Group |
| OKO6 | Settlement Structure |
| KO88 | Individual Processing of Settlement for Period-End Closing |
| KONK | Maintain Number Ranges for Orders |
| OKEU | Change/Create Source Structure |
| OKO7 | Settlement Profile |
| SNUM | Settlement Document Number Ranges |
| OKOS | Internal Order Planning Profile |
| OKOB | Budget Profile |
| OKOC | Availability Control |
| OK14 | Budget Manager Maintenance |
| OPTK | Exempt Cost Elements for Availability Control |
| KANK | Planning Number Ranges |
| OK11 | Maintain Number Ranges for Planning and Budgeting Objects |
| KOT2 | Order Status Management |
| KOV2 | Transaction Groups |
| OK02 | Status Profile |
| BS52 | Authorization Keys for Status Management |
| KOT2_OPA | Create/Change Order Types |
| S_ALR_870129* and 30* | Internal Order Reports in the standard Information System Report Tree |

**TABLE A.16**    Profitability Analysis Transaction Codes

| Transaction Code | Description |
| --- | --- |
| KEA0 | Operating Concern Maintenance |
| KETE | Operating Concern Templates: Overview |
| KECP | Copy/Import Operating Concern |
| KEA5 | Edit Characteristics |
| KES1 | Change Characteristic Values |
| KES3 | Define Characteristics Hierarchy |
| KEA6 | Edit Value Fields |
| KEDE | Maintain Derivation Rules |
| KEND | Maintain Realignments |
| KEQ3 | Set CO-PA Segment Characteristics |
| KEDR | Define Characteristic Derivation Strategy |
| KE4K | Derivation Table |
| KE04 | Create Derivation Structures |
| KE05 | Change Derivation Structures |
| KE07 | Create Derivation Rules |
| KE08 | Change Derivation Rules |
| KE4A | Define Condition Tables |
| 8KEV | Create Condition Types and Costing Sheets |
| KE45 | Assign Value Fields to Conditions Types |
| KE4I | Assign Condition Types to Value Fields |
| KE42 | Change Condition Types to Value Fields |
| KE4M | Map SD Quantity Fields to CO-PA Quantity Value Fields |
| KE4W | Reset (zero out) Value Fields |
| KEI1 | CO-PA Settlement Structure |
| OKB9 | Automatic Account Assignment of CO-PA segment to Posting |
| KEU1 | Create Cost Center to CO-PA Assessment |
| KE21N | Create Line Items |
| KE4H | Assign Costing Keys to Products |
| KE4J | Assign Costing Keys to Material Types |
| KEPC | Assign Costing Keys to Any Characteristics |

**TABLE A.16**    Profitability Analysis Transaction Codes *(continued)*

| Transaction Code | Description |
|---|---|
| KE4R | Assign Value Fields to Cost Component Structure |
| KP34 | Planning Profiles |
| KE4D | External Data Transfer Data Structures |
| KE4Z | External Data Transfer Assignment Groups |
| KE4E | Map External Data Transfer Fields to Characteristic and Value Fields |
| KE4U | Define and Assign Valuation Strategy |
| KEN2 | CO-PA Planning Number Ranges |
| KEKK | Assign Controlling Area to Operating Concern |
| KEN1 | CO-PA Actual Data Number Ranges |
| KER1 | Report Line Structures |
| KE34 | Create Forms |
| KE31 | Create Report |
| KE3I | Create Transports |
| KEC3 | Define Currency Translation Keys |
| KE21S | Simulate Valuation |
| KEAT | Check Value Flow in Billing Document Transfer |
| KEAW | Check Value Flow From order/Project Settlement |
| KE4ST | Simulate Billing Document Transfer |
| KE4TS | Simulate Sales Order Transfer |
| KEDU | Create/Refresh Summarization Levels |
| KELR | Execute Data Transfer from BW to CO-PA |

**TABLE A.17**    Profit Center Accounting Transaction Codes

| Transaction Code | Description |
|---|---|
| ORK2 | PCA Configuration |
| 1KE1 | Analyze Basic Settings |
| 0KE4 | Update Settings |
| KE51 | Create Profit Center Individual Processing |
| KE52 | Change Profit Center Individual Processing |
| KE55 | Change Profit Center Collective Processing |

**TABLE A.17** Profit Center Accounting Transaction Codes *(continued)*

| Transaction Code | Description |
| --- | --- |
| KCH4 | Change Standard Hierarchy |
| KCH5N | Change Standard Hierarchy |
| KCH1 | Create Standard Hierarchy or Profit Center Group |
| KCH2 | Change Profit Center Group |
| ORK1 | Profit Center Time-Based Fields |
| GCBX | Maintain Document Types for Actual Postings |
| MM17 | Mass Maintenance for Materials |
| OKEM | Sales Order Substitution |
| OKEL | Activate Sales Order Substitution |
| 1KE4 | Assignment Monitor |
| 1KEF | Control Parameters for Actual Data Transfer |
| GCBX | Actual Document Types |
| GB02 | Number Range Assignments |
| OKB9 | Assign Revenue Elements |
| 3KEH | Assign Additional Balance Sheet and P&L Accounts to PCA |
| 3KE5 | Period-End Closing Assessment |
| 4KE5 | Period-End Closing Distribution |
| 1KEK | Period-End Closing Transferring Payables/Receivables |
| 2KES | Period-End Closing Balance Carryforward |
| 2KET | Activate Balance Carry Forward for PCA |
| OKEQ | Maintain Versions |
| GCBA | Plan Document Types |
| GP41 | Plan Parameters |
| S_ALR_870097* and S_ALR_870133* | Standard reports for Profit Center Information System |

**TABLE A.18** Investment Management Transaction Codes

| Transaction Code | Description |
| --- | --- |
| IMA11 | Individual Processing of Appropriation Requests |
| IMAM | Mass Change Processing of Appropriation Requests |

**TABLE A.18** Investment Management Transaction Codes *(continued)*

| Transaction Code | Description |
| --- | --- |
| IM22 | Change Investment Program Structure |
| IM23 | Display Investment Program Structure |
| IMEO2 | Change Enterprise Organization – Programs |
| IMEO3 | Display Enterprise Organization – Programs |
| IM01 | Create Investment Program Definition |
| IM11 | Create top Position Investment Program Position |
| IM12 | Change Investment Program Position |
| IM35 | Edit Program Planning |
| IM32 | Edit Original Budgeting |
| IM33 | Display Original Budgeting |
| OITA | Investment Profile |
| OIP1 | IM Plan Profile |
| OIB1 | Budget Profile |
| OIT8 | Budget Categories |
| OIT5 | Assign Actual Values to Budget Categories |
| OK11 | Number Ranges |
| S_ALR_870127*, 28*, and 29* | Reports for Investment Management (found in the standard report information system) |

**TABLE A.19** FI Closing Cockpit Transaction Codes

| Transaction Code | Description |
| --- | --- |
| CLOCO | Closing Cockpit |
| CLOCOS | Closing Cockpit (Overview) |
| CLOCOC | Closing Cockpit (Manage Templates and Task Lists) |

# INDEX

**Note to the reader:** Throughout this index **boldfaced** page numbers indicate primary discussions of a topic. *Italicized* page numbers indicate illustrations.